FROMMER'S

COMPREHENSIVE TRAVEL GUIDE

BRAZIL

3RD EDITION

by Michael Uhl

PRENTICE HALL TRAVEL

NEW YORK • LONDON • TORONTO • SYDNEY • TOKYO • SINGAPORE

FROMMER BOOKS

Published by Prentice Hall General Reference
A division of Simon & Schuster Inc.
15 Columbus Circle
New York, NY 10023

ISBN 0-671-84673-6
ISSN 0899-2827

Design by Robert Bull Design
Maps by Geografix Inc.

FROMMER'S BRAZIL, 3RD EDITION

Editor-in-Chief: Marilyn Wood
Senior Editors: Alice Fellows, Lisa Renaud
Editors: Charlotte Allstrom, Thomas F. Hirsch, Peter Katucki, Sara Hinsey Raveret, Theodore Stavrou
Assistant Editors: Margaret Bowen, Lee Gray, Ian Wilker
Editorial Assistant: Gretchen Henderson
Managing Editor: Leanne Coupe

Special Sales

Bulk purchases of Frommer's Travel Guides are available at special discounts. The publishers are happy to custom-make publications for corporate clients who wish to use them as premiums or sales promotions. We can excerpt the contents, provide covers with corporate imprints, or create books to meet specific needs. For more information write to Special Sales, Prentice Hall Travel, Paramount Communications Building, 15 Columbus Circle, New York, NY 10023

Manufactured in the United States of America

CONTENTS

LIST OF MAPS

INVITATION TO THE READERS

In researching this book, I have come across many wonderful establishments, the best of which I have included here. I am sure that many of you will also come across appealing hotels, inns, restaurants, guesthouses, shops, and attractions. Please don't keep them to yourself. Share your experiences, especially if you want to comment on places that have been included in this edition that have changed for the worse. You can address your letters to:

Michael Uhl
Frommer's Brazil
c/o Prentice Hall Travel
15 Columbus Circle
New York, NY 10023

A DISCLAIMER

Readers are advised that prices fluctuate in the course of time and travel information changes under the impact of the varied and volatile factors that affect the travel industry. Neither the authors nor the publisher can be held responsible for the experiences of readers while traveling. Readers are invited to write to the publisher with ideas, comments, and suggestions for future editions.

SAFETY ADVISORY

Whenever you're traveling in an unfamiliar city or country, stay alert. Be aware of your immediate surroundings. Wear a moneybelt and keep a close eye on your possessions. Be particularly careful with cameras, purses, and wallets, all favorite targets of thieves and pickpockets.

CHAPTER 1

GETTING TO KNOW BRAZIL

Vast, mysterious Brazil—beyond the confines of Rio de Janeiro and its famous beaches—is a continent-sized nation that is virtually terra incognita to most North Americans, even those who routinely travel to distant and exotic corners of the world. Yet despite its seeming remoteness, Brazil is actually a viable destination for a broad spectrum of today's North American tourists, including vacationers, retirees, and part-time adventurers. Whether or not Brazil is right for you is one of the questions this guide will attempt to help you answer. It may just turn out that a well-planned Brazilian vacation could be one of the high points of your world traveling experiences.

If you were to ask most North Americans what kinds of facts and notions Brazil conjures up in their minds, you would be likely to get the same half-dozen responses from one and all. To us Brazil is Third World poverty; the shrinking rain forest; the $120 billion foreign debt; Pele, the soccer phenomenon; ultramodern Brasília, the capital; movie goddess Sônia Braga; and of course, Rio de Janeiro—especially Rio at Carnival time.

The list seldom extends beyond these well-honed media images. We tend not even to know that Brazilians speak Portuguese, not Spanish. It's strange that we North Americans, during the course of our history, have expressed so little curiosity about South America in general. But our lack of interest in Brazil is especially intriguing, because like the United States, Brazil is immense and potentially powerful—and is, as we are, a patchwork of distinct cultures, captivating geographies, and fascinating regional characteristics.

Only a dribble of North Americans have really explored Brazil and know something of its vastness, its history, and the place it occupies in the modern world. There are those Brazil aficionados who have been aptly nicknamed "Brazil Nuts." Having discovered Brazil's charms, they keep returning year after year, disdaining all other world destinations for the opportunity of getting to know this single colossus better and better on each successive visit.

The Brazil Nuts have discovered that the object of their infatuation may indeed be a Third World country with all the widespread poverty and social problems that unhappy status entails. But beyond the shroud of misery, they have also seen other realities—the emerging and already mammoth industrialized country with world-class cities, and a country of such uncommon natural beauty and fecundity that, among all nations, it best exemplifies the ideal of the tropical paradise on earth. A favorable exchange rate for those with U.S. dollars or other "hard" currencies makes accessible many pleasures—like eating in the finest restaurants and staying in the most luxurious accommodations—that at home are the prerogatives of only the most affluent.

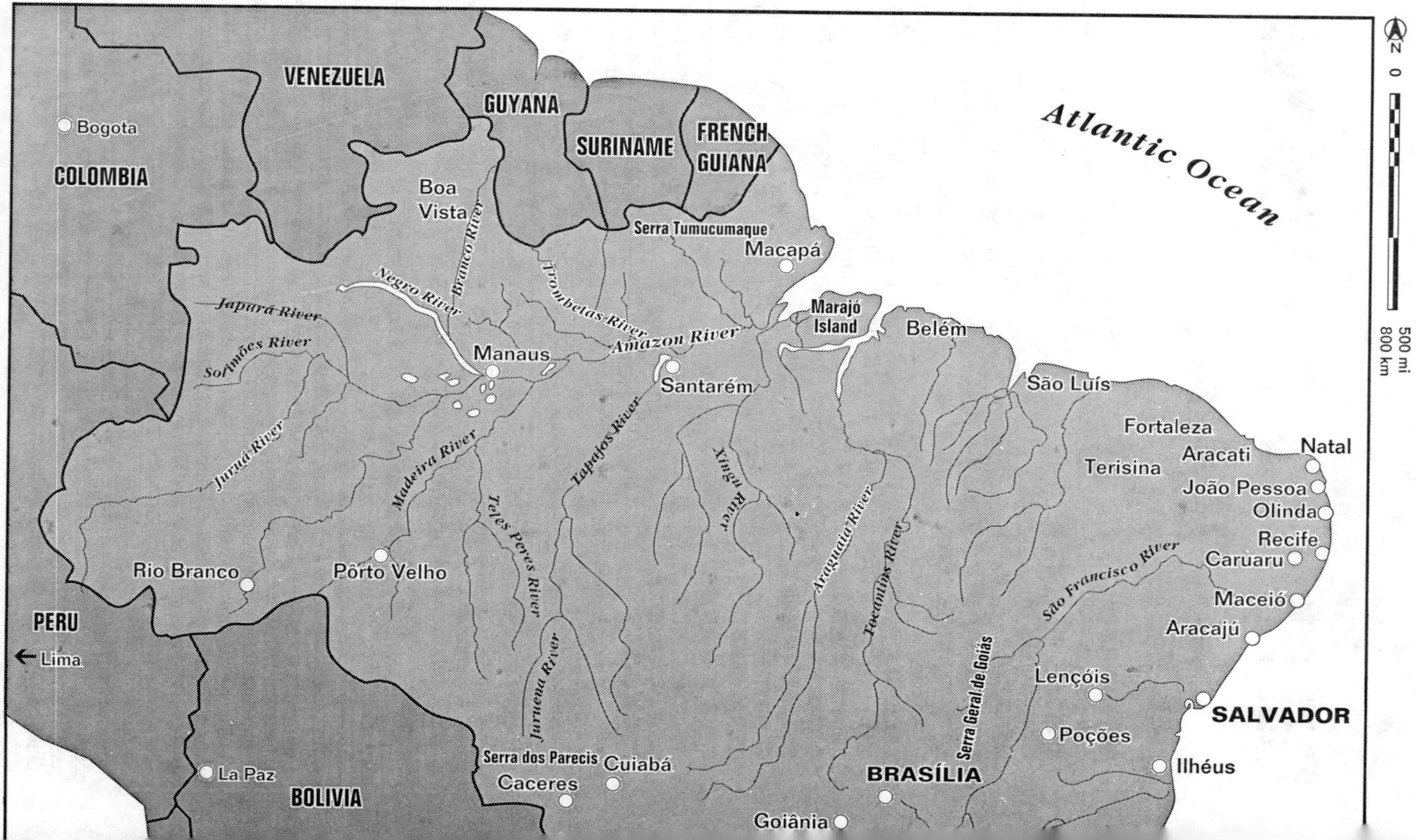

N
0
500 mi
800 km
Atlantic Ocean
VENEZUELA
GUYANA
SURINAME
FRENCH GUIANA
COLOMBIA
Bogota
PERU
Lima
BOLIVIA
La Paz
Boa Vista
Serra Tumucumaque
Macapá
Marajó Island
Belém
São Luís
Fortaleza
Natal
Aracati
Terisina
João Pessoa
Olinda
Recife
Caruaru
Maceió
Aracajú
SALVADOR
Lençóis
Poções
Ilhéus
BRASÍLIA
Goiânia
Serra Geral de Goiás
Serra dos Parecis
Cuiabá
Caceres
Manaus
Santarém
Pôrto Velho
Rio Branco
Negro River
Branco River
Trombetas River
Amazon River
Japurá River
Solimões River
Juruá River
Madeira River
Teles Peres River
Juruena River
Tapajós River
Xingu River
Araguaia River
Tocantins River
São Francisco River

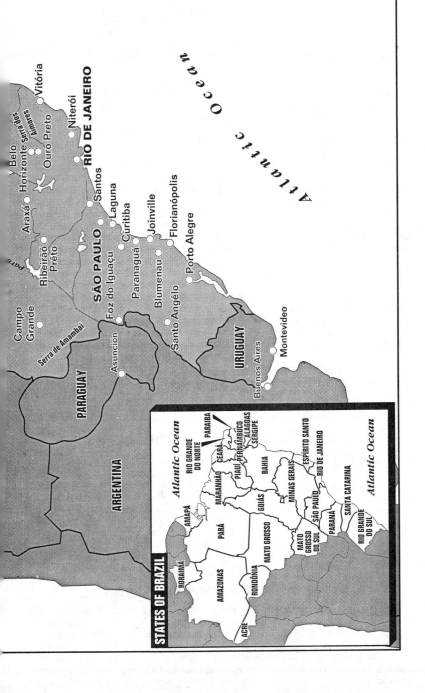

BRAZIL

Atlantic Ocean

Vitória
Niterói
RIO DE JANEIRO
Belo Horizonte
Serra dos Aimores
Ouro Preto
Araxá
Santos
Ribeirão Preto
SÃO PAULO
Laguna
Curitiba
Joinville
Paranaguá
Florianópolis
Blumenau
Porto Alegre
Campo Grande
Foz do Iguaçu
Serra de Amambai
Santo Angêlo
URUGUAY
PARAGUAY
Asunción
Montevideo
Buenos Aires
ARGENTINA
PARANÁ

STATES OF BRAZIL

Atlantic Ocean

RORAIMA
AMAPÁ
AMAZONAS
PARÁ
MARANHÃO
CEARÁ
RIO GRANDE DO NORTE
PARAIBA
PERNAMBUCO
PIAUI
ALAGOAS
SERGIPE
ACRE
RONDÔNIA
MATO GROSSO
GOIÁS
BAHIA
MINAS GERAIS
ESPÍRITO SANTO
MATO GROSSO DO SUL
SÃO PAULO
RIO DE JANEIRO
PARANÁ
SANTA CATARINA
RIO GRANDE DO SUL
Atlantic Ocean

❓ DID YOU KNOW . . . ?

- Brazil was named for *pau brasil*, a tree which provided Europeans of the 16th century with a popular, vermilion-colored dye.
- Brazil's landmass is larger than that of the continental United States, not counting Alaska.
- Early chroniclers of Spanish expeditions in the Brazilian rain forest either imagined or saw female warriors there. These *Amazons* provided the name that has stuck to the region ever since.
- Driven from his throne by Napoléon in 1808, King John VI of Portugal settled in Rio de Janeiro, making Brazil the only New World colony from which a European monarch ruled his empire.
- Brazilians were governed by emperors under a monarchy that endured until 1889.
- Many Brazilians believe that it was their countryman, Alberto Santos Dumont, who invented the airplane.
- Brazil's most famous international performer, Carmen Miranda, a Hollywood star and Las Vegas headliner during the thirties and forties, was actually born in Portugal.
- In his day, soccer phenomenon Pele was the highest-paid athlete in the world.
- Brazil during the 20th century has produced one international music craze after another, including samba, bossa nova, lambada—and currently the percussion rhythms typical of bands like Olodum.
- While Brazil has 26 states covering a vast territory, one state, São Paulo, in the southeast, is home to over 20% of the country's population, and produces more than 30% of its wealth.

The allusion to "tropical paradise" may sound like so much promotional hype. Yet what other nation on earth can claim a beachfront of nearly 5,000 miles where the sun shines virtually all year round? Life along coastal Brazil is spent outdoors much of the time in lush tropical surroundings. And every population center—whether big city or fishing hamlet—has its *movimento*, its *action*, its outdoor scene which the visitor can experience. There are market stalls and craft bargains everywhere, beach culture, promenades at dusk along splendid boulevards, and café society with excellent food and drink found at bargain prices, no matter where you go, down to the smallest main square in the simplest village. Brazil is also a land saturated with the pulsating rhythms of samba: as a musical people, Brazilians have few rivals on this planet.

The Brazilians are as difficult a group to sum up or stereotype as any among the peoples of the world. I can almost guarantee, however, that whatever the differences—the most formidable of which is the language barrier—if you make the slightest effort in Brazil, you will penetrate the somewhat set patterns of the tourist experience and get as much authentic people-to-people contact as you can handle.

1. GEOGRAPHY, HISTORY, POLITICS & THE ECONOMY

GEOGRAPHY

Brazil is divided into five distinct regions: north, northeast, central-west, southeast, and south. The country is the world's fifth largest—larger than the continental United States, but smaller than Canada, China, and the former U.S.S.R. Brazil borders all the nations of South America with the exceptions of Chile and Ecuador. Its 3,319,666 square miles, or 8,511,965 square kilometers, cover almost half the continent. Over 70% of Brazil's 146 million inhabitants are under 30 years of age.

THE REGIONS IN BRIEF

Regionalism is the essential reality of modern Brazil. And many of the country's cultural distinctions are based on accidents of geography as much as any other factor. The great rain forests covering much of what is known as Amazônia have proven impossible to conquer along any conventional models of development. Northeastern Brazil is subject to long periods of drought, alternating with less frequent, but equally destructive flooding. The northeastern *sertão* is a parched wilderness of scrub growth, ribbed with rocky ridges and bare mountains, barely hospitable to the rugged millions who make it their home. And yet the region, as with all desert landscapes, has its peculiar fascination and beauty. The coastal lowlands are a narrow strip of land running the length of the coast, once site of the great Atlantic forest, and for centuries the focal point of agriculture, commerce, and industry. Not far inland (often a mile or less) from the coastal strip rise the great plains and high plateaus that characterize much of southern, southeastern, and central Brazil. Here are the most fertile lands, producing much of the world's coffee and cocoa, and vast harvests of citrus fruit and soybeans as well. Much of interior Brazil—where the land is good—continues to be laid out in vast private holdings, or *latifundia,* which may or may not be in productive use, and are the source of much of the power—and powerlessness—in Brazil to this very day.

For most travelers to Brazil—Americans very much included—beach life is the beginning and the end of their Brazilian adventure. But the Brazil of the interior is where the real adventure begins. These vast internal regions with all their hidden secrets and attractions are only just now becoming hospitable to international tourists, meeting the minimum standards of comfort and ease of transportation that are generally demanded. Brazilians themselves have only recently grasped the potential of their country as a tourist destination to ultimately rival not only the great sunshine spas of the Caribbean and the Mediterranean, but also the remote and romantic backwaters of Asia and Africa—which attract that segment of the world traveling population who want to see "what it's really like" before "it" disappears.

Amazônia and Minas Gerais What is this other Brazil beyond the beaches and the shoreline? It's the region known as Amazônia, still very sparsely inhabited, and covering literally half the country with wetlands, river systems, and rain forests. In contrast, it is São Paulo, only one of the country's 26 states, yet an industrial powerhouse producing an amazing 35% of the nation's GNP, and boasting as its capital the world's third-largest city. It is Minas Gerais, where the record of Brazil's gold and mineral boom has been preserved in several historic towns that have been declared "treasures of the world."

Central Brazil Central Brazil seems like the American West of the last century, with the modern world present as only a thin overlay in the form of the airplane, the automobile, and the electrification of its cities and municipalities. Set among this rural antiquity is the space age capital, Brasília—space age because it was conceived and constructed in the manner one imagines the first planetary colonies will be built—transported section by section from the civilized world to the empty wastelands of the cosmos.

The South Southern Brazil, a corner bordering Argentina, Uruguay, and Paraguay, is actually somewhat temperate in climate. This region was settled largely by European and Asian immigrants, who today produce the great cash crops of coffee and soybeans, raise the meat cattle, and make the country's beer and wines.

The Northeast The Northeast is the cradle of Brazilian culture at its oldest. Here the original Portuguese colonials and their African slaves merged with the pre-Columbian natives and formed the *caboclo,* the core stock of the Brazilian race, blending as well the traditions, spiritual values, customs, legends, music, cuisine— even the languages—of three continents into a unified people who have endured the harsh desertlike conditions of the sertão for almost five centuries. Bahia, a large state, stands alone at midcoast. Gateway to the northeast, with its capital at Salvador, Bahia was the center of power and wealth of the South Atlantic during the first three centuries of Brazil's history, and is today a region uniquely influenced by both the aristocratic traditions of the original Portuguese planters and by the popular customs of the descendants of the captive and far more numerous Africans.

Rio de Janeiro Finally there is Rio—the city that is itself synonymous for many world travelers with the very idea of Brazil. Rio has long, and justifiably, been an obligatory stop for any sophisticated traveler whose ambition it is to visit and enjoy all the truly great cities of the world.

THE PEOPLE

Ethnically and racially Brazil is as diverse a nation as any on the globe. Today only approximately 100,000 pure Native Americans survive from the millions (estimates range from two to five million) who, in a great variety of subcultures and tribal groups,

IMPRESSIONS

We progress at night while the politicians sleep.
—BRAZILIAN SAYING, QUOTED BY JOHN GUNTHER, *INSIDE SOUTH AMERICA*, 1967

You cannot disillusion a Brazilian.
—PETER FLEMING, *BRAZILIAN ADVENTURE*, 1933

---

inhabited the land when the Portuguese arrived in 1500. The mark of these indigenous cultures is visible on the features and in the customs and values of many contemporary Brazilians, who trace some portion of their ancestry from the original inhabitants. After slavery was introduced in the early 16th century, the descendants of Africans soon outnumbered their white overlords. The blending of these two races has produced the sizable mulatto segment of Brazil's population. Western European immigrants—Italians, Germans, Spaniards, for the main part—and the Portuguese (who never stopped coming) came in waves during the 19th and early 20th centuries. They were joined by equally large numbers of Japanese, who began to arrive in Brazil after the turn of the current century.

THE ECONOMY

One reason Brazil manages to feed most of its population is because the country is really a vast greenhouse. Nature provides endless varieties of fruit and seafood, and crop returns are generally very high. It may surprise some to learn, therefore, that, in addition to being a great agrarian producer, Brazil has the eighth-largest industrial output of the world's nations as well. The south and southeast regions account for virtually all the heavy industry, producing everything from cars and consumer goods to aircraft, weapons, and machinery. No country can boast of greater mineral and gem deposits, much of which, it is believed, has yet to be discovered, much less mined.

For all of its wealth—real and potential—Brazil has always had an economy oriented toward exports, based often on the rising and falling cycles of a single commodity. Even today with its mighty industrial base, much of what Brazil produces must be sold abroad to pay off the astronomical $120 billion foreign debt, which represents loans once believed to offer the miraculous means to affect the country's rapid development. Instead, Brazil today remains trapped in debt, assuring for the foreseeable future its traditional position as the great country of the future with the perennial economy of a banana republic.

A "sleeping giant" was how Brazil's romantic poet, Castro Alves, once described his country. All the realities, the expectations, even the stereotypes of the great nation are contained in that simple observation. The Brazilian identity has adapted itself to the image of the "sleeping giant," and so Brazilians never cease to wonder, "When will the giant awaken?"

Since Brazil—because of its size, its parallel New World heritage, its wealth and potential—is inevitably compared with the United States, many Brazilians have come to believe that Brazil ought to "be" like the U.S. Trying to understand why Brazil is *not* like the U.S., and more positively, what grand role the country is destined to play in world events, is one of the great preoccupations of both popular and intellectual Brazilian culture.

One might be tempted to respond, "Brazil is fine just the way it is." From the vantage point of the casual visitor, this is certainly a valid perspective. All categories of international travelers to Brazil—sun worshipers and other hedonists, groups and individuals with special interests, freewheeling adventurers, and businesspeople—can discover and appreciate during even the briefest of stays a distinct and indefinable "Brazilian-ness," those qualities and graces peculiar to any nation that do not demand explanation or require justification. Not surprisingly, even Brazilians are not always conscious of their true uniqueness, nor of the almost mystic appeal their country has for so many visitors, who, on arriving home, proclaim rapturously to their friends that "Brazil is the ultimate destination!"

Brazilians, by and large, cannot be so sanguine. They live the reality of an underdeveloped—or at least unevenly developed—country. A portion of the country is modernized on the scale of anything you would find in the most developed of nations; another portion sustains a mass of people under primitive circumstances, and often in misery; and a third portion is virtual wilderness, uninhabited, and perhaps uninhabitable. The most severe consequences of this uneven development in Brazil, both economic and geographical, is the inability of the nation to provide employment and the necessities of life for a large segment of its population. This does not mean that the visitor will be assaulted with an endless panorama of wretchedness and oozing sores. The visual reality, owing perhaps to the luxuriant tropical setting, is seldom harsh even to the most delicate observers. But all will undeniably perceive the tenuous coexistence of two distinct worlds throughout Brazil: a consumer society embracing an elite 30% of the population; and a subsistence society—healthy in many respects, but at the fringes accounting for some of the planet's highest rates of infant mortality and child malnutrition, and a life expectancy far lower than that in the industrialized nations.

It is from this torpor of underdevelopment that seemingly grips their country in endless cycles of economic and political chaos that Brazilians would like their "sleeping giant" to be awakened. How Brazil arrived at this impasse is a complex and intriguing question, for which no simple interpretation exists. As with other nations, however, some insights can perhaps be gleaned from an understanding of the past. Only the thinnest sketch of Brazilian history will be presented here. This is, after all, a guidebook, not a history text. But the outline is here, as are the titles of some suggested reading for those—avid prevacation researchers and armchair travelers alike—who wish to deepen their knowledge of Brazil, and read more widely from the story of its almost 500 years of existence.

HISTORY

The history of Brazil begins largely as an account of the land's colonization by a single dominant culture, the Portuguese, who first came to the eastern coast of South America as commercial explorers in the year 1500. The Portuguese had been pioneering the unknown navigational routes around Africa to India for some years before the expedition under Pedro Alvares Cabral departed from Lisbon. He was bound for India when he sighted the coast of Brazil in April of that year and claimed the "great island" of Vera Cruz for the crown of Portugal. The first landfall was made in the harbor of Porto Seguro, today a small city to the south of Salvador in the state of Bahia.

The explorers found friendly Tupis, but little in the way of precious wealth. Only a cargo of *pau brasil,* a dyewood much prized in Europe by cloth makers for its reddish hues, could return a profit against the costs of expeditions to Brazil by the early merchant adventurers. Such was the intensity of the trade in brazilwood that the land derived its name from that commercial tree. By the 1530s Portugal had settled on a plan to colonize its new territory, at least to the extent of creating large plantations of sugarcane. European tastes for this new spice and stimulant had been developing for some time. Supply was the main problem. But the establishment of the plantation system on the vast unfarmed tracts of the New World provided the solution not only to the supply of sugar, but to that of tobacco, and ultimately, coffee and cocoa as well.

THE COLONIAL PERIOD Administratively, Brazil was divided by the Portuguese crown into 17 *capitânias,* or captaincies. For 100 years each captaincy functioned as a

DATELINE

- **1500** On April 22, the fleet commanded by Portuguese explorer Pedro Alvares Cabral records the first documented sighting of Brazil by Europeans.
- **1533** The Portuguese establish their first permanent colony in Brazil at São Vicente, near current-day Santos, the port city of São Paulo.
- **1567** Troops under Brazil's governor, Mem de Sá, expel a colony of French Protestants from Rio de Janeiro.
- **1630** The Dutch, based in Pernambuco under Calvinist soldier and intellectual Johan Maurits, begin their
(continues)

virtually separate colony, governed by a nobleman (often from afar), but ultimately subordinated to the king of Portugal. The most successful of the early colonies were Pernambuco and São Vicente (the coast of São Paulo state). Native Americans were enslaved to work the sugar fields, and when they proved unadaptable, or simply scarce, the practice of importing Africans—who unlike the natives could not simply disappear back into the forests from which they came—began in earnest. The early planters were more adventurers than colonists; they were the venture capitalists of their day. They came to the New World to rough it for a few years (though not with their own hands, to be sure) and make their fortunes, delaying or resuming family life until their return to Europe. So typical was this experience that it was even a subject of early English fiction. Robinson Crusoe, hero of the novel by Daniel Defoe, begins the fatal voyage that will leave him stranded on an uninhabited island for decades, from the port of Salvador (Bahia), where he had been living as a successful tobacco planter in the early 1600s.

From the union of these European adventurers with the native and slave women, a new, uniquely Brazilian race was forming—bred in the New World and tied to it by blood, but taking its organizational and political cues from the dominant Portuguese culture of the male overlords. In time many of the planters could see no reason for returning home, and the crown itself had shifted its policy to one of genuine colonization, sending out families to accompany their mercantile and military expeditions. Society in Brazil rapidly developed into a hierarchy of three classes: slaves, freemen of mixed race (a kind of soldier and pioneer class), and the local Portuguese who governed, though not without the predictable tensions between their interests and those of the distant crown.

During the first two centuries of modern Brazil's history, the plantation system gradually spread along much of the fertile coastal area, as great landed estates came to replace the once-dense Atlantic forest. At the same time military expeditions patrolled the offshore waters, and continually added new territories resulting from conquest of the native inhabitants and victories over European rivals who, at various points along the coast, had attempted to establish colonies of their own. The French, for example, occupied an island off what is today Rio de Janeiro but where, at the time, the Portuguese had yet to settle. They were finally defeated by the Portuguese and driven from the southern region after a 12-year occupation. The French later founded the city of São Luís, capital of Maranhão, in the north, but their stay in that region was of even shorter duration. Only the Dutch managed to invade—and hold for 24 years—a significant section of Brazilian territory.

Owing to a legitimate right of succession, the Portuguese crown in 1580 had passed to the heir to the Spanish throne. For 60 years, until the restoration of its independent monarchy, Portugal—and Brazil—were to be dominions of Spain. In a war with Holland, Spain had denied the Dutch access to Brazilian ports, endangering what had been the preeminent position of the Dutch commercial fleet in the world trade and distribution of sugar. In retaliation, the Dutch invaded the northeastern coast of Brazil and occupied considerable territory in Pernambuco, Bahia, and other regions to the north. By the time Holland was expelled in 1654, both the Dutch and the English had established sugar plantations throughout the Caribbean, and the favored Brazilian position in the world sugar market was ended. Ironically, the legitimate Spanish claim to much of what is modern Brazil was eroded during the period of Spain's dominion over Portugal. By the Treaty of Tordesillas (1494) papal authority had divided the New World between Spain and Portugal. Portugal's share of South America was actually only the great bulge of Brazil, stretching in a line from Belém, at the mouth of the Amazon, to just west of São Paulo. Internal politics during the late 1500s and early 1600s kept the Spaniards from contesting the expansion into Spanish territory by the explorers and authorities in Brazil, who were, after all, claiming all their conquests in the name of the House of Castile.

THE BANDEIRANTES Expansion into the vast interior of Brazil was carried on primarily by two groups: missionaries, especially Jesuits; and pioneers, who were called *bandeirantes*, or standard-bearers. The missionaries had accompanied the earliest voyages to Brazil, and were ever after caught between the shifting policies of the crown, now favoring the peaceful conversion, now the conquest of the "heathen" natives. Most churchmen favored the former policy and opposed the enslavement and maltreatment of the natives. Nonetheless the pacification of the Native Americans by the missionaries, and their concentration into mission settlements, made the natives easy targets for the bandeirantes, who, at least initially, were nothing but glorified slave hunters.

The bandeirantes were merely the instrument of the oppression and virtual extermination of the Native Americans. The demand for cheap labor by the gentry (that is, the planter class) not only sanctioned the enslavement of Native Americans, but provided a solution for another socioeconomic problem as well. For the bandeirantes were largely that class of racially mixed Brazilians who were neither fish nor fowl. They were not of the ruling European group, nor were they slaves. The *mamelucos, mulatos,* and *mestiços* (as the various mixtures were called) had to fend for themselves. In great numbers they banded together under the flag of a single leader, to whom they pledged complete fealty, and then penetrated deep into the unexplored interior of the continent, seeking captives, and later mineral riches, but leaving one settlement after another in their paths. They fought the Jesuits, the colonial authorities, and each other, but in the end it was the bandeirantes who discovered the El Dorado that the original explorers had sought in Brazil 200 years earlier.

THE GOLD CYCLE In 1693 gold was discovered in the hills of Minas Gerais. Soon thereafter came the discovery of rich diamond deposits in the same province. Until the beginning of the 18th century Salvador had been the jewel of Brazilian colonial cities, the center of power, commerce, and culture in the South Atlantic of the early Americas. And while Salvador would continue to shine in the course

DATELINE

clares Brazil independent of Portugal.

• **1840** A 14-year-old Dom Pedro II is crowned emperor of Brazil.

• **1870** Allied Brazilian and Argentine forces secure victory over Paraguay in a war that began in 1864. Paraguay's great military genius and patriot, Marshal Francisco Solano López, is killed during the final engagement at Cerro Cora on March 1.

• **1888** Slavery is abolished in Brazil.

• **1889** A military coup d'état overthrows the Brazilian monarchy. Pedro II, who had ruled for almost 50 years, is exiled to Paris.

• **1897** After four bloody military campaigns, the millenarian village of Canudos in the interior of Bahia is finally destroyed by the Brazilian army.

• **1930** Following years of unrest, and a failed communist-inspired rebellion under the leadership of Luís Carlos Prestes, Getúlio Vargas seizes power, bringing to an end Brazil's old republic.

• **1942** Brazil enters World War II on the side of the Allies, authorizing the establishment

(continues)

DATELINE

of a U.S. air and naval base in Natal.

• **1945** A bloodless military coup forces Vargas from power. But the former dictator is constitutionally elected to the presidency in 1950. In 1954 he commits suicide.

• **1960** On April 21, Pres. Juscelino Kubitschek inaugurates the new capital of Brasília, located some 600 miles from the Atlantic coast in the country's sparsely populated interior.

• **1964** A military coup overthrows Pres. João Goulart, with the aid and encouragement of the U.S. government, ushering in repressive military dictatorship that would last for over 20 years.

• **1989** For the first time in 29 years, Brazilians select a president, Fernando Collor de Mello, in direct elections.

• **1992** Eco-92, a UN-sponsored conference on world ecology and development attended by the heads of states of most major nations, is convened in Rio de Janeiro. Collor de Mello is impeached when corruption in his administration is exposed.

of Brazil's history, a new pole of power was to arise in the booming goldfields of the interior, and events and tastes for the next hundred years, called the Gold Cycle, would be strongly influenced by Vila Rica, known today as Ouro Preto.

Such was the wealth flowing from Brazilian gold and diamond mines during many decades that the coffers of states and the vaults of bankers throughout Europe were filled to overflowing. Here was capital enough to finance an Industrial Revolution, and a world mercantile economy! But much glitter was to be scattered over the varied landscapes of Brazil as well. Architecturally and artistically the flowering of baroque forms in towns and villas throughout Brazil during the course of the 1700s reflected a genuine Belle Epoque. Many were the instant fortunes, and the opportunities for displays of pseudo-aristocratic ostentation. Carriages of gold, costumes of golden thread, and gold nuggets cast at the feet of visiting performers were among the gestures of great extravagance that defined the style of the era. Craftsmanship in building and decor was highly prized, and boatloads of artists and artisans migrated from Portugal to the colonies in response to this rare and bountiful patronage.

Politics in the mining region became inflamed by the ideas of revolutionary republicanism that were then sweeping the world. But whereas the events of 1776 in the United States and of 1789 in France caused in those countries the overthrow of monarchic governments, the republican rebels in Brazil failed. The Inconfidência Mineira, the Minas Uprising of 1789, with its headquarters in Vila Rica, was crushed by the Brazilian aristocracy, ever loyal to the crown, with the help of resident Portuguese troops. One principal rebel leader, Tiradentes, whose low social position left him without sympathetic influence in high places, was executed. Other leaders were more fortunate. Tiradentes was hanged, his body quartered and transported by cart as a grotesque warning to republicans in the four corners of the settled land; his head was set on a pike in the main square of Vila Rica, which today bears his name.

THE EMPIRE Much republican ferment stirred within Brazil from the late 1700s and throughout most of the 1800s as well. Rebellions were frequent but always unsuccessful. A single happenstance effecting the fortunes of the Portuguese crown all but ensured that the establishment of a republic in Brazil was to be forestalled for some time. The sudden arrival of the royal family from Portugal in 1808, fleeing in advance of Napoléon's occupation of Lisbon, brought to Brazil not only the power of the throne, but thousands of the empire's aristocrats of highest rank. This solid aristocratic block gave new tenor to the economic grip of the great land barons, which is where the real power traditionally lay in Brazil, and in many ways still does to the current day. The exiled Portuguese monarchy ruled its overseas empire from Rio de Janeiro—till then a relatively sleepy harbor compared with Salvador—for the brief span of a dozen years. In 1820 Dom João VI resumed the throne his mother had been forced to abandon in Portugal, leaving behind a royal seed, his son Pedro, to serve as regent in a land now viewed as being equal in importance with Portugal.

Weakly, the Portuguese parliament tried to reassert its control over the government and finances of the now-powerful colony. But the Brazilian aristocracy was jealous of its own power, and soon influenced Pedro to declare independence, crowning the young prince as Brazil's first emperor. After 10 years, Pedro I abdicated and returned to Portugal, but he, in turn, left his young son, also named Pedro, to continue the royal line. Pedro II, following a decade of corruption under a government of regents and general popular unrest, was declared Brazil's second emperor in 1840, at the age of 14. Pedro II, a somewhat modern man with many liberal and progressive ideas, managed to reign fairly peacefully for the next 50 years, when he was suddenly deposed in 1889, and the republic was finally installed by military men, who have since created their own tradition of rule in the country. The emperor had a great interest in the political and literary works originating in the United States of his day, and was particularly fond of Hawthorne and the New England transcendentalists, like Emerson and Bronson Alcott. His majesty, visiting the U.S. in his later years, made a pilgrimage to the Concord burial ground where many of the bards he admired were laid to rest.

As the flow of gold and diamonds began to diminish, other natural and agricultural products rose in importance in both regional and national terms. Coffee was first introduced from French Guiana in 1727, and became a crop that ultimately spurred the expansion of plantations beyond the current state of Rio de Janeiro, deep into São Paulo and other southern and central territories. Coffee wealth was the basis on which the current industrial and agricultural power of São Paulo was built. The rubber cycle began in the mid-19th century. Brazil had a virtual monopoly on rubber—the tree was found in great numbers only in the Amazon. But the rubber trees occurring in nature were spread out some distance one from another. Large numbers of individual tappers were needed to gather the latex, which was collected by boat, and thus the banks of the great river for many leagues were tamed and settled. Out of the rubber wealth grew the cities of Manaus and Belém, which also saw their periods of grandeur.

The production of all Brazilian wealth depended largely on slave labor until that institution was finally abolished in 1888, an act that was one principal cause of Pedro II's downfall. Both the longevity of the slave system, and the utter failure of the early Brazilian republic to integrate the blacks into the productive economy thereafter, can account for the disparity in wealth and class privilege that still characterizes modern Brazil. The republic engaged for years thereafter in the extension of its administrative power throughout the country, but suffered from a chronic lack of the necessary reforming zeal that would have gradually transformed Brazil from a semifeudal to a modern agrarian/industrial state. In many ways the very feudal mentality of most rural Brazilians—including the peons attached to the vast estates of the north and northeast regions—made even the extension of central republican rule a task of considerable difficulty.

THE REPUBLIC Driven somewhat mad by years of marginal existence, ignorance, and neglect, many rural inhabitants viewed the new state as a virtual anti-Christ. One of the most bizarre episodes of Brazilian history occurred when masses of religious zealots from all over the northeast fled to Canudos, an abandoned ghost town in the barren interior of Bahia, under the influence of the fanatic Antônio Conselheiro, to avoid the sacrilege of civil matrimony and other abominations that the new federal government was imposing on the populace. It took three increasingly major military expeditions to destroy the millenarian village, and but for a handful of survivors, all of its inhabitants.

The task of consolidating federal power in Brazil occupied the first 30 years of this century. But the process of orderly transition through democratic means from one government to another was never firmly established. Presidents were elected or appointed and deposed in revolving succession, depending on the course of various regional political crises and revolts. One of the great romantic rebellions occurred when military reformers under Carlos Prestes formed an armed column that crisscrossed the interior of Brazil and the frontiers of neighboring South American countries for several years. The Prestes column failed to rally their phlegmatic countrymen to revolutionary fervor, and so it disbanded. Prestes himself later came to head the Brazilian Communist Party, at first allied to the Soviets and later to the Chinese.

THE VARGAS ERA   A military strongman with fascist leanings, Getúlio Vargas seized power in a 1930 coup following a decade of continuous rebellion. Vargas's rise was a classic reflection of the confrontation between left and right that was taking place throughout Europe in those years and which culminated in the Spanish civil war. Under Vargas, Brazil would later enter World War II on the Allied side, participating in the Italian campaign. During the war an American base was established near the city of Natal as a resupply depot for the North African campaign (Africa is relatively close to Brazil from that point on the northeastern coast). To one degree or another, Vargas maintained his control of the government until his suicide in 1954, when a new era, for better and for worse, was inaugurated in Brazilian politics.

With the election of Juscelino Kubitschek de Oliveira, a medical doctor from Minas Gerais, in 1956, it seemed that a new spirit of democracy was dawning in Brazil. The political conditions of the succeeding 30 years, however, proved as volatile and unpredictable as they had been at any other time since the departure of Dom Pedro II. Juscelino (in recent years, Brazilian presidents and politicians of benign visage are referred to by their first names; heavies, particularly generals, whose image is always that of a stern father, are spoken of by their last names) played Augustus to the Caesar of Getúlio Vargas. Leaving untouched the essential social and economic deficiencies affecting the Brazilian majority, Juscelino launched an awesome program of development at the top. In one bold stroke he built the moonscape capital of Brasília, shifting the locus of governmental power from its traditional east-coast moorings to the sparsely inhabited interior. The new road to Brasília then continued northward through a swath cut from the jungle on to Belém, the delta city of the Amazon River. Foreign investments multiplied, as did borrowed capital, for Juscelino was determined to give particular impetus to the country's industrial development. Juscelino's was a vision of grandeur, mixed with a childlike insistence on instant gratification. Leaving the government in disastrous financial straits, Juscelino had, with his impulsive changes, accomplished much. His legacy of financial instability has also had far-reaching consequences.

Succeeding Juscelino in 1961 was the eccentric nationalist Jánio Quadros, who had gained a reputation for being a cost-cutter as mayor and then governor of São Paulo. Brazilians of all political stripes still shake their heads in disbelief when recalling the bizarre, short-lived presidency of this strange politician, who arose again recently from virtual obscurity and was once again elected mayor of São Paulo. Jánio, it was rumored, spent hours watching Hollywood westerns in the basement of the Presidential Palace. He found the Federal Congress intractable, and could not adapt his tone of autocratic righteousness to the horse-trading idiom of the legislature. Jánio's fierce pride in Brazil translated into a foreign policy of nonalignment, a popular stance until he offended the right by praising the Cuban revolution and presenting Ché Guevara with a medal in Brasília. After slightly more than six months, Jánio resigned, hoping, it was said, that congress would beg him to resume his post. It did not.

THE MILITARY IN POWER   The man in succession, Vice President João Goulart, was feared. He was a protégé of Getúlio Vargas, charismatic, and given, perhaps, to a left-leaning brand of populism. After some struggle, the succession was allowed, as the congress showed an uncharacteristic faith in the viability of democratic institutions to right themselves during crises. Goulart's presidency had the same impact on the military in Brazil during the early 1960s as did that of socialist Salvador Allende on the Chilean army 10 years later. It was enough to imagine that Goulart would disturb rural feudalism with his modest proposals for land reform, or concede certain powers to labor unions, or limit the power of foreign investors, to send shock waves through the circles of power. On April 1, 1964, a bloodless military coup d'état took place—encouraged avidly by the American government—and for the next 20 years Brazilians would be ruled by the "generals" who subjected both their opponents and the populace at large to varying degrees of repression and cruelty.

Brazil during this extended period of military dictatorship was a saddened country. Despite its historical tale of woe, Brazilians had always managed to feel good about where they lived, and to squeeze much joy from the sensual pleasures of their climate and from a bountiful nature. They had also become accustomed to speaking their minds on political matters. During the military dictatorship, newspapers were censored and political debate ceased, both in public meetings and as heated café conversation, for no one could be sure whom they could trust. The military leaders ruled by intimidation, but for a while at least, they really did make the economy hum. Economic growth was so high that Brazil was widely noted by advocates of Western-style development as a success story among developing countries. The oil crisis of 1973 sharply stemmed Brazil's forward economic motion. The resultant and sudden jolt to the mobility of a growing middle class—including many technical and industrial workers—ultimately created broad popular pressure for a return to democracy. The relaxing of tensions was gradual, but by 1979 a general amnesty was declared and a series of open local and state elections occurred in quick succession.

BRAZIL TODAY On December 15, 1989, Brazilians, in a direct presidential election for the first time in 29 years, chose conservative Fernando Collor de Mello over socialist union leader Luis Ignacio Lula da Silva, following a closely fought campaign. Owing to the current age of voter enfranchisement—16—most of the Brazilian electorate wasn't even born the last time Brazilians selected their national leader through a direct democratic election. The Brazilian population was exceedingly demoralized as outgoing Pres. José Sarney left office in early 1990, bequeathing his fellow citizens an overheated economy suffering from a rate of inflation nearly 1,000% per year. Voters were further dismayed when Collor's presidency ended in disgrace in 1992; he was impeached when corruption of an astounding magnitude in his administration was exposed, sparking widespread outrage.

Should the current leaders succeed where their many predecessors failed in stemming Brazil's chronic inflationary ills, the country may be a very different place to visit in the years to come. So far, as we move toward the mid-1990s and Brazil tries to put the trauma of Collor's impeachment behind, this success has been elusive.

2. FAMOUS BRAZILIANS

Jorge Amado (1912–   ) World-renowned novelist whose tales are set primarily in the Brazilian northeast. Some of the better known English translations of his novels are *Dona Flor and Her Two Husbands, Gabriela, Clove and Cinnamon,* and *The Violent Lands.*

Sônia Braga Brazil's latest export to Hollywood, who has starred in several critically acclaimed films, including *Dona Flor and Her Two Husbands* and *Kiss of the Spider Woman.*

Antônio Carlos Jobim (1932–   ) Innovative musician and composer, whose many contributions to bossa nova and samba, like "The Girl from Ipanema," have become standards of both Brazilian and international music.

Carmen Miranda (1913–55) Hollywood superstar and Las Vegas headliner during the thirties and forties. Miranda was known for her elaborate headdresses adorned with models of tropical fruits. Though born in Portugal, she grew up in Rio de Janeiro.

Pele (Edson Arantes do Nacimento; 1940–   ) Voted the athlete of the century in 1980, Pele led Brazil's national soccer teams to three world cups, and permanent possession of the trophy. Pele last played for the New York Cosmos during the 1970s.

Alberto Santos Dumont (1873–1932) Born in Minas Gerais, and educated in France, Santos Dumont was one of the great pioneers of aviation. His famous flying machine, the *Grasshopper* (1909), is considered the forerunner of the modern light plane. Santos Dumont committed suicide, apparently having become depressed by the use of aircraft in warfare.

Heitor de Villa-Lobos (1887–1959) Villa Lobos is considered the foremost Latin American composer of the 20th century. He drew much of his inspiration from the Brazilian folk and Afro musical traditions. His best-known composition is *Bachianas brasileiras*.

3. ART, ARCHITECTURE & LITERATURE

ART There is, to be sure, some very exciting work being done in both painting and carving, but you have to really search it out. The artistic face presented to the tourist in attractions like street fairs, and in many of the most visible galleries, is superficial—and often just plain tacky. This vision of Brazilian art is somewhat disappointing. Much of the work is technically dull, meant strictly to decorate, not illuminate or startle. Even the primitives tend to be very derivative, as if their creators, too, had already seen the unself-conscious oils depicting the dramas of daily life that flowed from places like Haiti 20 years ago, and decided to copy rather than elaborate a style suitable to their own realities. Wood carving is quite popular in Brazil, but the results are often clunky, lacking any gracefulness in design, as if the value in the work were in the species and volume of the wood itself.

Nor are there great public collections of modern or classical world art in Brazil compared with the museums of Europe or the United States. There are, however, a number of unique smaller exhibits, the Chácara do Céu in Rio and the Fundação Maria Luiza e Oscar Americano in São Paulo for example, both of which are the former homes of wealthy art patrons whose private collections are on display. The one great event of the Brazilian art world of international significance is the Bienal—the biannual art exhibition that takes place in São Paulo during odd-numbered years, which attracts not only the best of Brazilian art, but wide participation as well from artists throughout the world.

Before the modern era, Brazilian artisans and artists produced mostly sacred art, works reflecting themes of strictly religious significance. The vast quantity of sacred art throughout the country, whether found in its original church setting or housed in one of many national or regional museums devoted to the genre, is generally of much greater interest to the visitor than the contemporary art scene. The baroque period in particular, which lasted throughout the 18th century, was the great epoch of Brazilian art and architecture which, given the spirit of the times, took the form of elaborately carved altars and images, great allegorical panels painted on church ceilings and walls, finely wrought silver and gold ceremonial accoutrements, and of course, the elegant structures of the churches and dwellings themselves. Of special note are the sculptures of Antônio Francisco Lisboa, known as Aleijadinho, scattered among the historical cities of Minas Gerais, though concentrated primarily in Congonhas do Campo. The museums of sacred art in São Paulo and Salvador are first rate. Among my personal favorites is the tiny church museum lovingly maintained by a single curator in the interior city of Goiás Velho.

ARCHITECTURE The Brazilian architectural patrimony from the colonial and baroque periods is unique in all the Americas for its stunning simplicity and elegance, as well as for the sheer numbers of structures and neighborhoods that have been preserved and restored throughout the country. The historical cities of Olinda (five miles from Recife) and Ouro Preto are considered to be "world treasures" by UNESCO, as is the Pelourinho section of Salvador. Virtually every city in Brazil, however, has its historical architectural relics, some even more pristine than those mentioned above, like Goiás Velho, Paraty, Belém, and João Pessoa, because they have yet to be commercially exploited and promoted as major tourist attractions. Indeed virtually everywhere curious visitors wander throughout this immense country, they are bound to discover some sampling of antique churches, homes, or buildings, dating from at least the 18th century. Some of the old structures, moreover, were built a hundred years before the Pilgrims settled in North America. Special-interest travelers, lovers of history as seen through its preserved buildings, will be particularly rewarded by their travel in Brazil beyond the beaches of Rio.

LITERATURE   Until the middle of the 19th century Brazilian writers told their stories in the manner of their mentors, in that florid, biteless style then fashionable in the belles lettres of Portugal. A more unified Brazilian identity began to emerge during the reign of Dom Pedro II in the last century, and from that time Brazilian literature began to reflect reality in a style of its own, more direct and representational. Every generation since then has produced remarkable fiction. The great book of Brazil, however, remains a work of nonfiction, *Os Sertões,* or *Rebellion in the Backlands,* by Euclides da Cunha, a stunning account of the downfall of millenarian Antônio Conselheiro and his followers, and their destruction by the new republican government in the interior town of Canudos.

Readers of novels have long accompanied the boom in Latin American fiction that began with the successful translation of Colombian Gabriel García Marquez's *One Hundred Years of Solitude,* and opened the American book market to other greats of Latin American literature, including many Brazilians. From the earlier fiction came new translations of Machado de Assis, who captured with considerable grace the ennui of bourgeois life in Rio during the latter part of the last century. Brazilian fiction written during the first half of this century is vastly underrepresented among republished translations, however. Some essential names from this period are Raquel de Queiroz, Graciliano Ramos, José Lins do Rego, Vianna Moog, and Eric Veríssimo, all of whom mined the modernist vein, transforming material from life and folklore into vivid, realist prose.

In a category by himself, today a veritable institution in Brazil, is the novelist Jorge Amado. Avon has published a great many of Amado's novels in recent years, including *Gabriela, Clove and Cinnamon, The Violent Lands,* and *Dona Flor and Her Two Husbands.* Within Brazilian society, Amado has received all honors, and despite his long-standing ties to the world Communist movement, political bigotry does not tarnish his stature as Brazil's literary laureate and cultural hero, even among the most stolid conservatives. Reading a few good Amado novels before visiting Salvador in Bahia is a painless way to get your cultural introduction to this region of Brazil, and at the minimum provide some kind of background against which to compare your own impressions.

Avon also publishes the zany, pointed social satires of Márcio Souza, a Brazilian "new left" activist during the days of the military dictatorship and now a successful novelist and playwright. *The Emperor of the Amazon* got Souza banned in his native Amazônia by the very governor his novel satirized. *Order of the Day* is a novel parodying the Brazilian penchant for joining mystical sects, and is written in the format of a sci-fi thriller. As yet untranslated is the *Flying Brazilian,* Souza's touching fictionalized life of Brazilian aviator Alberto Santos Dumont. Two other Avon paperbacks that give a flavor of Brazil's contemporary fiction are Ivan Angelo's *The Celebration,* a scathing portrait of decadence in a middle class that made great social gains during the recent dictatorship, and *Sergeant Getúlio,* by João Ubaldo Ribeiro, a novel of brilliant malevolence which has gained high critical praise internationally, and makes Stephen King's *The Shining* seem like a Mother Goose tale. This introduction to Brazilian literature merely scratches the surface, but these books have the advantage of being available from American publishers, and are therefore likely to be in library systems as well.

4. CULTURAL & SOCIAL LIFE

The story of Brazilian culture is considerably brighter than that of the country's political and economic history. This is, of course, good news to those tourists who are going not to live there, but for a brief escape from their own pressing realities. Tourists need only sample the very best of Brazil and its captivating popular culture: beach and café life, music and dance, tropical ambience and wildlife, crafts, and above all, food.

BEACH CULTURE The good life throughout much of Brazil is associated with the sun, the beach, and good beer at a reasonable price. The one great leveler of all economic distinction in Brazil, in fact, is a sunny day at the beach. On weekends in Rio—and in the other coastal cities as well—everyone flocks to the beach when the weather is right. And the weather is seldom wrong. Half the crowd on the beach will be moving at a furious pace, consumed in some variety of sporting activity: pickup soccer games, body and board surfing, volleyball, jogging, exercise, and *fréscobol,* a paddleball game played by two people. The other half will be completely at rest, surrendering to the totally passive act of getting a perfect tan.

Vendors stroll up and down the strands all day, offering delights to eat and drink. There are small boys selling *picolés,* popsicles of tropical fruit flavors. Strong shirtless men carry pineapples or coconuts, which they open or slice on demand with the razor-sharp machetes they carry slung at their sides. Others hawk cold beer and soda from Styrofoam coolers, or sell hats and tanning lotion to shield the sun, mats to lie on, or cotton kites to fly.

✪ The Brazilian bikini is somewhat akin to the emperor's new clothes in the Hans Christian Andersen tale.

Never far from the beach—and frequently right there on the sand with you—will be a food stand where snacks are sold, or a restaurant under some rustic covering with tables and chairs, selling *frutos do mar* (seafood) typical of the area you are visiting. These are the outdoor parlors of Brazilian beach culture, where friends and family entertain themselves and each other in convivial bliss, with food and drink and conversation, watching the panorama of sky, sea, and virtual human nudity that surrounds them—the Brazilian bikini being somewhat akin to the emperor's new clothes in the Hans Christian Andersen tale.

CAFÉ SOCIETY The other great source of leisure activity in Brazil that is relatively accessible to all is the outdoor café. Throughout Brazil every neighborhood, every town square, every beachfront avenue will offer some popular spot for indulging the incomparable pleasure of communing with surrounding society from the vantage point of a chair in an outdoor café. There are outdoor cafés to fit every pocketbook and every mood in the large cities. And in the smaller towns, often a single establishment in a village square, illuminated by a few strings of naked lightbulbs, will serve as a meeting place for all the town's inhabitants. *"Da um chopp"* ("Bring me a draft") is the perpetual cry of thirsty patrons who demand an endless flow of cold beer to lubricate the animated café chatter. Side dishes (*porções*) stream in continuous succession from the kitchen, with plates of french fries, bits of roasted meat, or *salgadinhos*—uniquely Brazilian appetizers of meat, shrimp, chicken, cheese, or eggs, all encased in a crust or batter. On the weekends, and in the evenings beginning with Thursday night, the cafés often stay jammed until the wee hours. There is probably no better way to experience the raw energy of Brazilian culture than from within the ambience of an outdoor café.

LANGUAGE The language of Brazil is Portuguese, an Indo-European language of the Romance group, all members of which derive more or less directly from Latin. When spoken slowly, Brazilian Portuguese can be moderately intelligible to speakers of Spanish or Italian, its closest relatives in the Romance group. Nonetheless there are many distinctions in syntax and pronunciation between Portuguese and those two, and all the other languages to which it is more or less closely related, including English. I will give one relatively technical example on pronunciation.

As with French, Portuguese uses many nasalized vowel sounds. These particular sounds are not found so prominently in most Western languages, and so they present obstacles for many wishing to learn spoken Portuguese. To complicate matters, sometimes these nasal vowels occur in combination, forming so-called nasal diphthongs. Take the Portuguese word for bread, *pão* (the tilde accent over the *a* indicates the nasal element). A reasonable facsimile for this sound in English occurs in words like *found*. The *ou* in this word represents a pairing of two English vowels, a diphthong in linguistic jargon. And the air which produces this sound is expelled through the mouth. When nasalized, the same sound in Portuguese is expelled through the nose. In other words, the mechanical trick is to train the muscles of your inner mouth to route certain sounds through the nasal passages rather than out the mouth.

There are many other distinct elements which impart to Brazilian Portuguese its exotic sound. Some of these are covered briefly in the Appendix. Many other resources are available for anyone who wants to study Portuguese before traveling. In addition to phrase books and taped lessons which can be bought or ordered through bookstores, there are often classes at local colleges or language institutes. Practically speaking, a few hours invested in learning some Portuguese before traveling to Brazil—especially for those traveling beyond the main tourist routes—can make your trip a lot smoother, if only because you could understand something quite simple being told to you by a bus driver or waiter. A reading knowledge of Portuguese is easily achieved by anyone who knows Spanish, and useful for gaining access to the country's lively and intelligent newspapers and magazines.

RELIGION Brazil is primarily a Catholic country—the most populous in the world, in fact—and every brand of Catholicism flourishes here from the most traditional to the most radical. Protestantism has made its inroads over the years, and most denominations are present in the larger cities. There are small but religiously active Jewish communities in most big cities as well. The other main religious movement in Brazil is the spiritism brought by the Africans, blended with the practices and beliefs of the original natives, and today widely practiced by Brazilians of all backgrounds and races. These religions—known as macumba, candomblé, and umbanda—have also become something of a tourist attraction in recent years, in much the way Santería and voodoo, two related cults, have been in countries like Cuba and Haiti.

5. PERFORMING ARTS & EVENING ENTERTAINMENT

Brazilian music has had wide influence throughout the world in recent decades. From the classical compositions (especially for the guitar) by Heitor Villa-Lobos, to the suave and lyrical bossa nova of Tom Jobim and João Gilberto, to the intoxicating rhythms of the *batucada* (played by the Afro-Brazilian drum-and-percussion bands, or *baterias*) that give the samba its universal trademark, Brazilian music has finally gotten the global attention it deserves. Brazilian vocalists like Milton Nascimento and Gal Costa today routinely give concerts in major venues like Carnegie Hall or Lincoln Center in New York City, and it is hardly a rare occurrence to find a Brazilian percussionist working in many jazz and Latin bands both in the U.S. and around the world.

In Brazil itself, music is everywhere. There are piano bars with accomplished musicians in the many hotels and restaurants. Discos offer the best of international and Brazilian hits and standards. *Gafieiras* (traditional dance halls) have recently revived in popularity among lovers of the Big Band sound in nightclub settings. Intimate clubs offer the best in Brazilian folk and country music, with its clear ties to the melancholy ballads of the Iberian Peninsula, filtered through regional Brazilian life and times. Chamber music and recitals are frequent occurrences in salons and theaters. Many poolside and luncheon restaurants hire trios to serenade their guests with traditional Brazilian favorites. It's not infrequent in these places for an individual or couple to suddenly spring to their feet and begin to dance in the wild and pulsating steps of the samba. Music has a way in Brazil of continually drawing people from smaller circles into larger and larger groups, showering feelings of goodwill in every direction. Street bands of percussionists are also not uncommon, and few events can match the excitement of a public rehearsal of a bona fide Carnival band preparing for that yearly pre-Lenten extravaganza when all of Brazil becomes an outdoor dance hall for at least five days.

6. SPORTS & RECREATION

Many Brazilians have become quite exercise-conscious in recent years. Most mornings along the coast, before the beginning of the workday, the beaches are already crowded with joggers or other fitness enthusiasts working out individually or in groups.

The best hotels all have health clubs, open to guests for a minimal fee. Exercise academies offering classes in aerobics also proliferate, and can be found in even the smallest cities of the interior. These can be located by looking in local phone directories or periodicals.

BEACH RENTALS Along the beaches of the northeast—in particular, Natal, Maceió, Recife, and Fortaleza—a variety of water-sport equipment is readily available for rent, including kayaks, sailboats, jet skis, and windsurfing equipment. The rental of horses is also fairly common, particularly on beaches located on the outskirts of these and other cities.

CAMPING Camping is not terribly popular in Brazil. But a number of options are available in major cities or resort areas. Where campsites exist, these will be listed in the appropriate places throughout the book. In general, unless specifically forbidden, no one will hassle you if you set up a tent on some remote beach. Just make sure by checking with someone familiar with the area that the place you choose is safe. A number of tour operators specializing in so-called eco-tourism offer excursions that involve camping out in the Amazon rain forest. For a list of these operators, see Chapter 2.

DIVING & SNORKELING For information on how to rent equipment, or on specific organized programs that might be available, contact the information sources listed in each chapter, particularly those in Salvador, Rio, Natal, Maceió, Florianópolis, and Manaus.

GOLF Golf courses are rare. Guests at five-star hotels in Rio can often gain admittance to the Gávea Golf Course, and São Paulo has several courses. One or two other hotels or resorts, like the Quatro Rodas in Salvador, have their own nine-hole facilities.

HIKING Increasingly, certain tour operators specializing in nature or outdoor activities offer an interesting range of hiking or trekking excursions. See especially the appropriate headings in the sections on Rio, Manaus, and Natal.

SPECTATOR SPORTS The major spectator sport in Brazil is soccer. Every city has a stadium, and seats are always available. Formula One racetracks exist in both Rio and São Paulo (see these chapters for more exact information). Horse racing is also available in both Rio and São Paulo.

TENNIS Many major hotels and most resorts offer tennis facilities. There are few public courts in Brazil, São Paulo being the single exception I am aware of.

7. FOOD & DRINK

FOOD

It's not easy to get a bad meal in a Brazilian restaurant. Culinary skills and food quality seem consistently high in public eating establishments of varying price ranges throughout the country. To be sure, cooking styles and basic ingredients change, sometimes very radically, from region to region. If tastiness and absence of indigestion are two reasonable criteria on which to judge restaurant food, Brazilians in this field rate extremely high. Not that the food is fancy, and certainly it's often far from delicate. But it is virtually always well prepared, served in generous portions—platters or stew pots groaning with succulent meats or brimming over with a dozen varieties of fin- and shellfish—and always accompanied by numerous delightful side dishes.

MEALS & DINING CUSTOMS When dining in Brazil, you'll need to pace yourself. The breakfasts served by most tourist-quality hotels (included in the price of your room) can be lavish, so tempting to many that any idea of a formal, sit-down lunch at midday is quickly abandoned. The two-meal diet—breakfast and dinner—is a common response among international tourists to the abundance of food in the meals put before them. Another useful strategy to consider is the single-meal-for-two option. Say, two or three people go to an average-priced restaurant for lunch. The ambience is comfortable, tables covered in white starched linen, and the waiters, while not formal, are pros in their own right, well trained and helpful. You order one serving of breast of chicken, sautéed in some sauce of the cook's invention. The platter arrives with enough meat, rice pilaf, mashed potatoes—usually two starchy foods, good news to carbohydrate fans—and everyone fills their plate. You order separately a large hearts-of-palm salad and whatever side dishes you might want, plus beer or freshly squeezed fruit juice, and finally coffee, and the bill comes to about $4.50 apiece.

The **couvert** is a common feature of most restaurant meals. It means cover, and usually includes bread and butter, a little pâté, and some hard-boiled quails' eggs. The couvert, which generally costs a dollar or two at moderately priced restaurants, is optional and may be refused.

THE CUISINE Haute cuisine is not the forte of the Brazilian kitchen. But the point is not to seek in Brazil food you could only find in New York or France. Instead turn your imagination in the direction of the best in home-cooking. Then imagine eating this fare twice a day in a great variety of seafoods, pastas, poultry, or meat, with side dishes of rice, beans, potatoes, and greens, not to mention a whole lot of delicious foods you've never heard of. That's Brazilian cooking, with its emphasis on heartiness and taste, and it's likely to keep your palate in a state close to ecstasy during your stay in Brazil.

Meals fall roughly into two categories: traditional dishes and international dishes. One traditional dish, **feijoada**—a pork and black-bean stew—is routinely eaten every Saturday throughout the country by rich and poor alike. Thus two styles of feijoada have emerged, a fancy buffet style with all the ingredients (including prime cuts of beef and pork) served separately, popular with hotels, and the more funky home-style feijoada served stewlike from a single caldron preferred by the more traditional restaurants. The traditional accompaniments of feijoada are white rice, **feijão** (black beans), **couve** (shredded kale), orange slices, and **farinha** (manioc flour). International dishes are those bearing familiar names, like veal milanese or beef Stroganoff, made especially appetizing because they are prepared by some typically competent Brazilian cook, and because any number of side dishes from rice and beans to *farofa* or *pirão* can add the inimitable ingredients that make any Brazilian meal truly Brazilian.

Farofa is totally unique to Brazil. Flour ground from the manioc root is fried in oil. Bits and pieces of many things, from egg to tortoise meat, may be added to the pan, and the dish arrives at the table looking like a sawdust pilaf. Its taste is positively addictive, especially when used to soak up juice from black beans or to thicken pirão. A dictionary defines **pirão** (found in Bahia and throughout the northeast) as "manioc mush." Doesn't sound appetizing? It is. Mixing pirão with rice and farofa, all accompanying a seafood stew and a well-chilled beer, is eating pleasure at its tropical best.

Food is definitely a drawing card for Salvador, capital of Bahia state. *Vatapá, xim xim de galinha,* and *moquecas* are the centerpieces of Bahian cooking. **Vatapá** is also a kind of mush, made from bread dough, cashew nuts, and dried shrimp, while **xim xim** (pronounced approximately "shing shing," the final letter, however, being a nasal vowel, not a consonant) is a chicken dish prepared with native herbs.

Moquecas are fish stews, and all three dishes are spicy, and cooked in the strongly flavored **dendê,** or palm oil.

"Comida mineira" is how the food of Minas Gerais is known, one of two regional cuisines of any complexity that can rival the uniqueness of the Bahian fare. The food in most other regions and cities, including Rio and São Paulo, is often called international, and would be more accurately described as "general Brazilian." In both Rio and São Paulo, traditional Brazilian food has become just one more specialty like Italian or Japanese food. But there is little room for complaint about the eating in either of these culinary capitals. Southern Brazil is cattle country, and justly prides itself on its **churrascaria**—steak and mixed-grill houses. The **rodízio,** or round-robin way of serving all the beef, chicken, turkey, and pork you can eat carved right at your table, is the southern culinary tradition that evolved from this prosperous animal husbandry. Exotic river fish and even game are commonly eaten throughout Amazônia. Beyond these distinctions, there is always some dish, snack, or dessert unique to each place that is routinely offered to visitors for their satisfaction and approbation, and these items will be mentioned in turn according to their proper place in the narrative.

No discussion of typical Brazilian food would be complete without mention of **canja,** an excellent chicken soup, as hearty and healthful as any you will ever taste.

One can say, without exaggeration, that there are a hundred varieties of edible fruits that are either native to Brazil or were adapted to its fertile soil. Buffet breakfasts at the top hotels offer a fresh selection daily, minimally including **pineapple,** several types of **melon** and **bananas,** and **mango.** The more exotic fruits, like **caju** (each of which bears a single cashew nut), **tamarind,** and **breadfruit,** along with dozens of new varieties to discover, can be purchased from vendors and at open markets on the streets. If you express enough curiosity at any given stand, the vendor is very likely to offer a slice for you to taste. Practically any bar, lunch counter, or restaurant you stop at will include freshly squeezed orange juice on its menu. A dozen other varieties of fruit juices, pure or in combination, can be had at the juice bars popular throughout the country.

The bounty in fruit throughout Brazil is only matched by the abundant catches from the seas of **frutos do mar**—shellfish, fin fish, shrimp, crab, lobster, and octopus—a steady harvest seemingly without end, from the omnipresent ocean along the coast and from the many river systems inland. One island city—Florianópolis, capital of Santa Catarina state—has a large inland lake where restaurants serve a round-robin of dishes called a *sequência*—all shrimp prepared in a variety of ways.

BRAZILIAN BEVERAGES

In addition to the **fruit juices** already mentioned, Brazil produces a popular soft drink, **guaraná,** made from a berry of the same name. Other international soft drinks like Pepsi, Coke, Fanta, and so forth are widely available. **Mineral water,** plain or carbonated, is a common sight at Brazilian meals, as tap water tends to be avoided for direct consumption. Ask for *agua mineral,* either *sem* or *com gaz* (with or without fizz).

The most popular alcoholic beverages are **beer** for most occasions, wine at meals, and a cocktail called a *caipirinha,* made from **cachaça** (a potent sugarcane brandy), crushed fresh limes, and sugar over ice. Brazilian brewers can hold their own with any of the great beer makers worldwide. Brand names like Antarctica and Brahma are most popular, and cast American beer in a poor light when compared for body and taste. A .75-liter (18-oz.) bottle of Brazilian beer costs between 75¢ and $1 in most bars and cafés. Brazil also has a flourishing **wine** industry, which, like the breweries, is located in the south, heavily populated by descendants of German and Italian settlers. An excursion in the wine-growing areas, with obligatory stops for tasting along the way, is an ideal way to visit Rio Grande do Sul, Brazil's southernmost state, bordering Uruguay and Argentina. In restaurants, Brazilian domestic wines are comparable in price to their California equivalents purchased retail. Imported wines, French in particular, are steeply priced, as are imported whiskies—some brands of scotch fetch almost $10 per drink. A good Brazilian wine can be had in most restaurants for $6 . . . or less.

The better grades of cachaça can also be drunk pure, like cognac. Sippers of whisky might find this inexpensive drink an adequate substitute, though pinga, as the drink is also called, which can be quite smooth, has none of whisky's smoky taste. Northeasterners from the countryside refer to cachaça as honey, or *mel.* The welcoming drink for those on package tours will most certainly be a **caipirinha.** Once they've discovered it, many drinkers will ask for nothing else for cocktails or when café-hopping.

Caipirinhas are also de rigueur—only for those who enjoy alcoholic beverages, of course—when eating the Brazilian national dish, feijoada. That is, until the end of the meal, when the other national drink, coffee, is served.

Brazil is, and has been for some time, a major world producer of **coffee** beans. Brazilians drink their *cafezinhos* (little coffees) frequently throughout the day, served in demitasse cups and usually made quite sweet. For those who like black unsweetened coffee, ask for *café sem açúcar* (the *em* in *sem* is a nasal vowel, but if you say "sang," you will be understood; the *ç* in *açúcar* is pronounced like an *s*). Coffee with milk can be hard to come by after breakfast, when Brazilians drink their own version of café au lait, *café com leite (leite* is pronounced *lay-*chee).

Great boxes of Brazilian coffee can be purchased in the airport duty-free shops before returning home, as can bottles of cachaça.

8. RECOMMENDED BOOKS, FILMS & RECORDINGS

BOOKS   Eggheads and armchair travelers (the original couch potatoes) may find useful the following book list: Alexander von Humboldt's *Personal narrative of travels to the equinoctial regions of the New Continent during the years 1799–1804* (published between 1814 and 1829); William H. Edward's *A Voyage up the River Amazon* (1847), Alfred Russell Wallace's *A Narrative of Travels on the Amazon and Rio Negro* (1853), Henry Walter Bates's *The Naturalist on the River Amazons* (1863), and Richard Spruce's *Notes of a Botanist on the Amazon and Andes* (1908).

For additional titles, see Section 3 of this chapter.

FILMS   The great *auteur* of the Brazilian film industry was Glauber Rocha. Typically, his films used the myths and legends of northeastern Brazil to explore the depths of human perfidy and passion. *Deus e O Diabo Na Terra do Sol* is considered his masterpiece.

Perhaps the best-known Brazilian film is *Black Orpheus,* which won an Academy Award as the Best Foreign Film of 1959, and introduced millions of viewers to the sights and sounds of Carnival.

Today the Brazilian film industry turns out a few films a year, mostly lightweight comedies for domestic consumption. Some major Brazilian talents, like actress Sônia Braga, have been absorbed by Hollywood into the idiom of international filmmaking. Brazil itself, as far as the dramatic arts are concerned, has become a major exporter of television soap opera series, primarily to Europe.

RECORDINGS   Music is Brazil's middle name. Any representative selection of Brazilian recordings might include *TXAI* (Milton Nascimento), *Circulador* (Caetano Veloso), *Meu Bom, Meu Mal* (Gal Costa), *Ao Vivo em Montreaux, Falso Brilhado* (Elis Regina), *Feijoada Completa* (Chico Buarque), *Extra* (Gilberto Gil), *P'ra Ouvir e Dançar* (Orquestra Tabajara), plus any number of albums by Tom Jobim, João Gilberto, Cazuza (especially those recorded with Barão Vermelho), Olodum (the percussion band that recorded with Paul Simon), and many other artists too numerous to mention. Other general categories of music include carnival samba selections, and such Brazilian folk traditions as *choro* and *forró.*

CHAPTER 2

PLANNING A TRIP TO BRAZIL

Most travelers from the northern hemisphere reach Brazil for the first time by flying down to Rio. Flights to Brazil take between 5 and 12 hours, depending on where you leave from in North America and where you land in Brazil. Steamship travel, of course, has long vanished from the globe. In its place are the cruise ships that call at half a dozen ports in the course of their two- or three-week sojourns in South America. Rio is a popular one- to two-day stop on many such cruises. Intrepid land travelers with time on their hands have been known to drive to Brazil along the sometimes desolate Pan American Highway. I wouldn't deign to advise such seasoned travelers on so brave an undertaking. They certainly have my admiration. However, most of us must adapt ourselves in our travels to the great cattle cars of the sky. To their credit, the major airlines that provide air service to Brazil have managed to make what could be a long and tedious flight into a diverting and reasonably pleasant experience.

Finding the right flight to Brazil is not particularly complicated. But first you do have to make several decisions. Do you want to visit Brazil during the peak season, or the low season—or perhaps during Carnival? How long will you want to stay? Do you want to stay only in Rio, or will you travel a bit around the country? Do you want to go with an individual ticket and book all your own land arrangements, or will you want to choose from a wide range of tour packages, which include hotel accommodations, airport transfers, and even some sightseeing excursions? And finally, will you want to go on a regularly scheduled flight, or take advantage of group rates by flying with a charter?

1. INFORMATION, ENTRY REQUIREMENTS & MONEY

SOURCES OF INFORMATION

First of all, get as much information as you can before you actually travel. In purchasing this book you have made a good start. Back issues of travel magazines at the library are also recommended.

Your local travel agent, or any of the tour operators specializing in Brazil listed in Sections 6 and 7 of this chapter, are good potential sources of information, as is **FUNTUR,** the Brazilian Tourism Office located at 551 Fifth Ave., Suite 519, New York, NY 10176 (tel. 212/286-9600; fax 212/490-9294).

An additional source of information before you depart is the **Brazilian consulate,** located in eight major U.S. cities. Contact the one nearest you: **Chicago**—20 N. Wacker Dr., Suite 1010, Chicago, IL 60606 (tel. 312/372-2179); **Dallas**—2050 Stemmons Fwy. #174, Dallas, TX 75258 (tel. 214/651-1855); **Houston**—1333 W. Loop South, Suite 1450, Houston, TX 77027 (tel. 713/961-3065); **Los Angeles**—8484 Wilshire Blvd., Suite 711, Beverly Hills, CA 90211 (tel. 213/651-2664); **Miami**—2601 S. Bayshore Dr., Suite 800, Miami, FL 33133 (tel. 305/285-6200); **New Orleans**—650 Poydras St., Suite 2504, New Orleans, LA 70130 (tel. 504/588-9187); **New York**—630 Fifth Ave., 27th floor, New York, NY 10111 (tel. 212/757-3080); and **San Francisco**—300 Montgomery St., Suite 1160, San Francisco, CA 94104 (tel. 415/981-8170). There's also a consulate in **Toronto,** located at 77 Bloor St. W. #1109, Toronto, ON M5S 1M2 (tel. 416/922-2503).

Most airports, including Rio's (which is likely to be your point of entry), have excellent to fair tourist information centers. The one in Rio is excellent at this writing. But if the state government changes—in Rio or in any state—the tourist information apparatus is also subject to change, sometimes for the better, sometimes not. In this regard, however, Brazil is stabilizing somewhat, since the country is really promoting tourism and a consensus about the importance of facilitating the way for foreign tourists is growing.

Where they exist, I have included useful telephone numbers and addresses of information centers and booking agencies throughout this guide.

ENTRY REQUIREMENTS

DOCUMENTS A passport, valid for at least six months from the intended date of arrival and bearing a visa for Brazil, is required for all citizens of the U.S., Canada, Australia, and New Zealand. British and Irish citizens require only a valid passport to visit Brazil. Tourist or transit visas, generally processed within one working day, are obtained from the nearest Brazilian consulate in the U.S. (or, in the case of the other nationalities referred to above, their respective country of origin). One passport-size photograph, along with your round-trip ticket and a duly completed and signed application form, are required for the free visa, valid for 90 days (for tourists) or 10 days (transit).

Specialized Visa & Travel Consultants, 33 E. 33rd St., New York, NY 10016 (tel. 212/725-6153; fax 212/725-6242), will secure your Brazilian visa for a fee of $50 (plus an additional $10 payable to the Brazilian consulate). Contact them initially for a visa application and to verify any changes in fee structure or procedures. Then complete and return the application to SVTC by express mail along with your valid passport plus all necessary fees and photographs. Your passport containing the valid visa will then be returned to you promptly, also by express mail (included in the price of the service). I have used this service on several occasions and have found it both convenient and reliable.

CUSTOMS Besides clothing and personal belongings, tourists entering Brazil may bring one of each of the following items: a radio, a tape deck, a camcorder, a typewriter, film, and a camera. You are further allowed to bring to Brazil items totaling $500 as gifts, including any liquor or cigarettes you purchase at the duty-free shop, and to return with $600 worth of Brazilian merchandise, not including certain craft items that are duty-free.

MONEY

Brazilian inflation is among the worst in the world. Brazilians joke that you can walk into a supermarket and see a product marked at a certain price, and by the time you reach the checkout counter, the price has already risen. The American dollar is somewhat inflation-proof in the Brazilian economy, because the dollar is always strong in relation to the cruzeiro. So depending on whether the dollar is strong or weak on the world market, you will find prices in Brazil either incredibly cheap or only reasonably so. On the other hand, prices the world over tend to go up faster than personal income. Therefore you may find that costs in Brazil are higher in absolute terms than those listed as of this writing. It is unlikely, however, that in the foreseeable future Brazil will cease to be a bargain destination for American tourists, especially those who travel with group or package promotional airfares.

CASH/CURRENCY The Brazilian **cruzeiro** is one of the most inflationary currencies in the world. Hyperinflation plagues the nation's economy. Some years back, the Brazilian government took measures to artificially control the cruzeiro's official rate of exchange on the world economic market. This led to the creation of a quasi-legal black market rate that functions domestically in Brazil, and generally benefits those with sufficient means to speculate in the volatile fluctuations of the cruzeiro against the dollar.

Currently there are three rates of exchange in Brazil: an official exchange rate, the *câmbio oficial;* a tourist exchange rate, *o dólar turismo;* and the "black-market rate," *o paralelo* (the parallel money market). All three rates are published daily in the economic sections (and sometimes on the front pages) of the major Brazilian newspapers, which dispels the notion that trading in the black market will involve you in some risky or nefarious dealings.

The official exchange rate is increasingly limited to the practices of international trade, involving central banking services and the securing of letters of credit. The tourism rate was recently created by the Brazilian government to gain control over the free-trading parallel market, and for the past few years, the *paralelo* and the *turismo* have functioned at or near parity.

Assuming you know the current parallel or tourism rate of exchange before arriving in Brazil (having glanced at the Brazilian daily during your incoming flight), you may still expect to exchange at three to four points below the rate listed in the paper. Why? Well, changing money is a sideline for many people in the service sector of the tourist business. In general, these small-scale money traders are not dealing with huge sums of money. They therefore attempt to negotiate the lowest possible rate in order to maximize their profit margin. You may be able to haggle for a point or two. The key to these negotiations, however, is knowing what the parallel or tourism rates actually are when you go to change money.

Since the creation of the tourism rate, foreign visitors no longer need to engage in romantic back alley dealings to achieve a favorable rate of exchange. You may now trade your dollars (or pounds) at a reasonable rate in the comfort of your hotel, or in any branch office of the Banco do Brasil. Storefront **câmbios**—often affiliated with travel agencies—are also widely in evidence, and may offer you a slightly higher rate on the parallel market. Given the volatility of the cruzeiro, it generally doesn't make sense to exchange more than $100 or $200 at a time. The parallel rate seldom drops, and you can do some serious sightseeing on that limited amount of money. The more money you exchange, however, the better rate you ought to find.

Please note: Under normal circumstances, the tourism and parallel rates are valued anywhere from 25% to 100% higher than the official rate of exchange. On one recent visit to Brazil, however, everything in the currency market was topsy-turvy. For the first time ever, the official cruzeiro was trading at a higher rate than its counterparts on the parallel or tourism markets. The general feeling was that the government intervention causing this unnatural state of affairs could not long continue. But in Brazil—especially where the cruzeiro is concerned—you never know!

The abbreviation for the cruzeiro is **$CR.** In the Brazilian reckoning of money, commas and periods are employed exactly *opposite* from North American usage. One thousand six hundred cruzeiros is written, $CR 1.600, while 10 cruzeiros and 50 centavos appears as $CR 10,50.

CREDIT CARDS & TRAVELER'S CHECKS American Express, Diners Club, MasterCard, and VISA are most in evidence. Remember that you will charge your purchase in cruzeiros but you will pay in dollars, which, until recently, were computed at the official rate of exchange. Today, credit-card purchases are computed at the *turismo* rate as it appears in the financial section of the daily newspapers on the day of your purchase.

Traveler's checks, incidentally, trade at a point or two lower than cash, though no one can argue with the good sense of traveling with as little cash as possible, unless you are ranging deep into the interior where traveler's checks and credit cards are virtually useless. Whenever exchanging traveler's checks, you will be required to present your passport.

WHAT THINGS COST IN RIO

	U.S. $
Taxi from the international airport to the Zona Sul (Copacabana or Ipanema) in a comfortable car with a safe driver	27.00
Air-conditioned bus (Greyhound-style) from airport to downtown Rio	3.50
Local phone call (using token called a *ficha*, one per every 3–5 minutes)	.05
Double at Copacabana Palace (deluxe)	190.00
Double at Praia Ipanema (moderate)	110.00
Double at Novo Mundo (budget)	48.00
Lunch for one at Forno e Fogão (moderate) *	12.00
Lunch for one at Boca da Panela (budget) *	6.00
Dinner for one Ouro Verde (deluxe) *	23.00
Dinner for one at Casa da Feijoada (moderate) *	15.00
Dinner for one at Gula, Gula (budget) *	8.50
Bottle of beer (600ml) in café	1.00
Bottle of Coke in café	.35
Roll of ASA 100 color film, 36 exposures	10.00
Museum admittance	.75
Movie ticket	3.00
Tourist show, with dinner (Scala)	50.00

*Includes 10% service charge (tip), and one nonalcoholic beverage or beer; there is no sales tax.

WHAT THINGS COST IN NATAL

	U.S. $
Taxi from airport	10.00
Local phone call (per 3–5 minutes)	.05
Double at Hotel Vila do Mar (deluxe)	140.00
Double at Hotel Genipabu (moderate)	50.00
Double at Pousada Mar Azul	15.00
Lunch for one at Carne do Sol (moderate) *	10.00
Lunch for one at O Crustacio (budget) *	6.50
Dinner for one at Augusta Restaurant (deluxe) *	18.00
Dinner for one at Moqueca Capixaba (moderate) *	11.00
Dinner for one at Coco Beach (budget) *	7.00
Bottle of beer (600ml) in a café	.75

*Includes 10% service charge (tip), and one nonalcoholic beverage or beer; there is no sales tax.

2. WHEN TO GO—CLIMATE, HOLIDAYS & EVENTS

CLIMATE Most of Brazil lies immediately south of the equator. What seasonal variation exists can be found in the temperate south, where temperatures can hover around the freezing mark at night and early in the morning—but only in the deep winter months of July and August. Winter afternoons in the south will often be sunny and warm, even beach weather. Generally the climate runs from comfortably tropical along the coast to unbearably humid and sticky in parts of the interior and the Amazon. Along the tourist coast—from Santos (São Paulo) in the south to Fortaleza (Ceará) in the north—the mercury ranges from a low of 65°F to a high of 95°F. Strong ocean breezes on the northern beaches often mitigate the heat, if not the burning power, of the tropical sun.

HOLIDAYS Principal holidays and festivals with their dates are as follows:

January 1: New Year's Day—and the feast day of Iemanjá, goddess of the sea, accompanied by much public celebration.

February: Carnival, the extended Mardi Gras celebration that brings Brazil to a standstill for at least five days before Ash Wednesday each year.

March/April: Good Friday and Easter Sunday.

April 21: Tiradentes Day, in honor of the Brazilian republican martyr.

May 1: May Day.

June: Corpus Christi.

June/July: The Festas Juninas, important winter holidays on the feast days of saints John, Peter, and Anthony.

September 7: Independence Day.

October 12: Our Lady of the Apparition.

November 2: All Souls' Day.

November 15: Proclamation (of the Republic) Day.

December 25: Christmas.

Like North Americans in recent years, Brazilians have the habit of celebrating certain holidays not on the official dates, but on the Monday that falls closest to the official date. The *feriadão* (feh-ree-ah-*downg*), or long holiday weekend, is the result, meaning that you may find stores and banks unexpectedly closed if you have only consulted the "official" calendar.

BRAZIL CALENDAR OF EVENTS

JANUARY

☐ **Festa de Iemanjá.** Rio's feast of Iemanjá turns New Year's Eve into a genuine pagan celebration, a homage to the goddess of the sea whose worship was introduced to New World culture by its African inhabitants. White-garbed celebrants begin to arrive on the beaches—especially Copacabana and Ipanema—during the day to mount their endless circles of candles and the altars of offerings—from flowers to cosmetics—that will be cast upon the waves at midnight in the hope that they will be acceptable in the sight of Iemanjá, the mother of all. A memorable experience.

☐ **Celebrations in Salvador.** New Year's Day in Salvador, Bahia, is commemorated by a popular boat procession called the **Festa do Nosso Senhor do Bom Jesus dos Navigantes.** January 6th in Salvador honors the **Feast of the Magi** with a street festival. And the third Sunday of the month is reserved for what many Salvadorans consider their most traditional festival, the Festa do Nosso Senhor do Bomfim. (See Chapter 12 on Salvador.)

FEBRUARY/MARCH

☐ **Carnival.** On February 2, the city of festivals, Salvador, stages it own homage to the goddess Iemanjá. But the main event of the month, Carnival, is celebrated all over Brazil toward the end of February during the week which precedes Ash Wednesday. Rio, Salvador, and Recife—in that order—host the country's three most important Carnival extravaganzas. (See chapters on these cities for more detailed information.)

MARCH

☐ **São Paulo Grand Prix.** Brazil's world-class Formula One drivers rev up for the annual São Paulo Grand Prix.

APRIL

☐ **Holy Week.** Holy Week normally falls sometime between late March and mid-April. Two of Brazil's most beautiful historical towns, Paraty in Rio de Janeiro state, and Ouro Preto in Minas Gerais organize traditional religious processions known for their pageantry and fervor.

JUNE

☐ **Festas Juninas.** June is the month that Catholic Brazil celebrates the feast days of its favorite saints, Anthony (June 13), John (June 24), and Peter (June 29). Parties are held primarily in private clubs and at home. The predominant theme is a recognition of Brazil's peasant culture and the rural experience in general. Children dress up in their versions of country costumes, and barbecues and bonfires are also typical elements of these celebrations. If you're in town during these times, you can try to have your hotel arrange an invitation for you to a private club. The low-key parties are typical of Brazilian home comfort and hospitality, and are a very pleasant way to get closer to the culture.

JULY

☐ **July School Holiday.** All schools in Brazil close during the month of July, when the country's "winter" month turns into a great holiday season to rival that of the summertime. July is considered part of the high season, and prices, hotels in particular, rise accordingly.

AUGUST

☐ **Horse Racing.** The sport of kings has its day at the track in Rio, the annual sweepstakes at the Jocqui Club.

SEPTEMBER

☐ **The Bienal.** The grand art exposition of South America, the Bienal, which takes place during odd-numbered years only, opens its doors in São Paulo to a star-studded cast of internationally known artists.

OCTOBER

☐ **Oktoberfest.** Descendants of German immigrants in southern Brazil, particularly in Blumenau, Santa Catarina, break out the tubas and tubs of beer for the fall rites of the Oktoberfest.

DECEMBER/JANUARY/FEBRUARY

☐ **Summer Holiday.** For most Brazilians, summer begins around December 15. Classes are let out, the busy Christmas and New Year season are on the horizon, and most of the population tries to spend as much time at the beach as possible. Summer really doesn't come to an end until after Carnival.

3. HEALTH, INSURANCE & SAFETY

HEALTH

SHOTS While not required, the Brazilian government recommends that visitors to the Amazon region get yellow fever and malaria vaccinations. In 1991, cholera broke out in the Andes, principally in Bolivia. The disease crossed into Brazil along the frontier, but was generally contained in the most remote regions of the Amazon basin, where hygiene and sanitary conditions are primitive. The Brazilian public health service mounted a massive, and thus far successful, campaign to combat the disease and prevent it from developing into epidemic proportions, as was the case in several of its neighboring countries throughout the Andes.

THE SUN Chances are, at least one of the reasons you're going to Brazil is because of the country's perennial surf and sun. I have found that the sun's burning rays are particularly powerful in the Amazon, especially while traveling by riverboat. But, in truth, the sun can be dangerous all over Brazil most months of the year. Sunscreen is a must for northern palefaces (black and white) who travel to Brazil from nonsunny regions, or during nonsunny times of years. Hats and good glare-screening sunglasses are also necessary additions to your kit. A word of advice: Buy your sunscreen before you arrive in Brazil. The cost of a good sunblock is at least double what you'd pay in the U.S., and that probably holds true for the other English-speaking countries as well.

THE WATER The conventional wisdom says that you don't drink the tap water. Most Brazilians drink bottled water in restaurants, and filtered water at home.

INSECTS Bring lots of insect repellent if you're planning to spend any time in the Atlantic or Amazon rain forests. Unfortunately, the right stuff is probably almost as lethal to human health as it is to the bugs. But while toxic chemicals may kill you in the long run, mosquitoes will drive you mad in the here and now. Also it's not a bad idea to bring a top-of-the-line mosquito net with you, if you're planning any serious forest trekking or camping.

INSURANCE

Before traveling, review your own insurance policy's health and accident coverage. If you feel the coverage is inadequate, or if you wish to add supplementary medical protection, or guard against the possibility of trip cancellation or lost luggage, a number of short-term options are available.

HealthCare Abroad (MEDEX), 107 W. Federal St., P.O. Box 480, Middleburg, VA 22117-0480 (tel. 703/687-3166, or toll free 800/237-6615; fax 703/687-3172). This company offers a policy good for from 10 to 120 days, at a cost of $3 a day, which includes $100,000 worth of accident and sickness coverage. Trip-cancellation insurance is also available for prepaid, nonrefundable tickets and packages only. The premium costs 5% of the trip purchase price. Lost-luggage insurance is priced at $1 per day.

Travel Insurance Pak, Travelers Insurance Co., 1 Tower Sq., 15 NB, Hartford, CT 06183 (tel. 203/277-2318, or toll free 800/243-3174), can provide you with 6 to 10 days of accident and illness insurance for $10. For $20 you can purchase $500 worth of coverage for damaged or lost baggage for 6 to 10 days. Trip-cancellation insurance is also available at a cost of $5.50.

Access America, 6600 W. Broad St., Richmond, VA 23230 (tel. 804/285-3300, or toll free 800/424-3391; fax 804/673-1491), offers $10,000 of medical coverage for 9 to 15 days at $49. Trip-cancellation insurance added to the medical package runs $89, and a more comprehensive policy to include the above coverage plus $50,000 of death benefits, costs $111. The company staffs a 24-hour hotline for emergencies.

Many tour operators and travel agencies also offer a variety of travel-related insurance policies. And major credit-card companies will often provide free accident insurance when you purchase your ticket using their card.

Travel Guard International, 1145 Clark St., Stevens Point, WI 54481 (tel. toll free 800/826-1300 outside Wisconsin, 800/634-0644 in Wisconsin), can provide you with a comprehensive, seven-day package for $59 that includes accidental death, emergency assistance, medical coverage abroad, trip cancellation, and lost luggage.

IS BRAZIL SAFE?

Brazil has garnered in recent years an undeserved reputation for being a criminally infested country, and therefore a place best to be avoided by the tourist, who is by nature already somewhat vulnerable in any foreign land.

There is indeed crime—far too much crime—in the large Brazilian cities. It is crime based on the eternal clash between the haves and the have-nots. Residents of big cities throughout the world live with the ever-present possibility of being mugged, much as residents of Los Angeles adapt to the inevitability of earthquakes. Rio, São Paulo, Salvador, and Manaus are no exceptions to this global rule.

Luck and circumstance protect most of us from crime, even in cities where street crime is common. But more important than luck is how one chooses to behave under conditions that are unfamiliar and potentially hazardous. If you are not an urban dweller, and therefore unfamiliar with the rules of being street savvy (or even if you are, and you happen to forget yourself when traveling abroad), here are a few tips that should go a long way toward protecting you from the typical street crime, which is a crime of opportunity:

- Do not tempt a thief with dangling gold chains or expensive gems or watches.
- Carry your photographic equipment in a bag—but never bring anything you aren't willing to part with to the beach. The street urchins of Rio, for example, while rarely dangerous to your person, can operate very swiftly—and are difficult to detect, much less capture once the deed is done.
- If you like to walk the streets at night, do so only where you see throngs of Brazilians taking their nocturnal constitutionals. And even then, you look different than they do, so out of common courtesy—as well as self-protection—don't go out of the way to call attention to yourself.
- Don't ride the public buses unless you have really gotten to know the city and speak some Portuguese. You could be an easier target in a contained space. Also, buses are sometimes, though rarely, held up in broad daylight, like stagecoaches and trains of yore.
- At night, travel to and from your hotel by taxi. Someone at the restaurant or nightclub you've gone to will be happy to call you a cab, if there is not already a line of hacks in the vicinity. I give this advice somewhat halfheartedly, since you are much more likely to be ripped off—at least in Rio—by the hordes of dishonest cab drivers than by the street people. Still, even if you end up paying three times what you should, you will at least be assured of getting home safely.
- Spend some time figuring out the unfamiliar money values before you hit the street. And never flash large wads of cash in public. Do what Brazilians do when at the beach. Tuck the equivalent of a few dollars into your swimsuit. Wet money will buy you a fresh pineapple or a soft drink as readily as dry money.
- On a positive note, you are in South America and thus are very unlikely to be a

target of terrorism in a large department store or at the airport—conditions which travelers to Europe must sometimes confront.

- If you are unlucky enough to get mugged, don't resist! Give the thief what he wants with as much dispatch as possible. Because what he really wants is to get away from you—with the goods—quickly and with no complications.
- To be on the safe side, leave everything you don't need with you on a given excursion—including money and documents—in your hotel, preferably under lock and key in your room's individual safe (if there is one), or with the concierge at the desk. Personally, while I have never been robbed, I always carry "thief money" when traveling in any big city (except to the beach). This is the equivalent of $15 to $20 loose in a pocket, to cough up on demand if the occasion ever arises.
- You will be happy to learn that outside of the four large Brazilian cities mentioned above, crime in Brazil is not a great problem. You can walk virtually anywhere, day or night, within the cities of the interior or in the smaller cities of the northeast like Aracajú, Maceió, João Pessoa, and Natal—where even the beaches at night are not out of bounds. I base my evaluation of this on both personal experience and on the say-so of local officials wherever I have traveled. Nevertheless, you, dear reader, must satisfy yourself as to whether or not a particular place feels secure and comfortable. Local orientation in every case is a must.

4. WHAT TO PACK

When it comes to clothes, Brazil practices an informality that is fully suitable to its tropical climate. Here's an opportunity to show off your sportswear wardrobe by day as well as night. Bring along plenty of shorts and T-shirts. Cotton is your best bet for comfort in hot and sticky climates. Jackets and ties are not required for men at dinner in even the best of Brazil's five-star restaurants, but women, in such situations, will likely feel most comfortable in a lightweight dress. (Brazilian women are extremely elegant in their informality!)

It's always a good idea to bring along at least one sweater or shawl, especially in the winter (July, August), or when traveling to cities in the higher elevations (Ouro Preto, Campos do Jordão, Gramado). Or sometimes you'll just want a light wrap when the air conditioning is a bit higher than you might like.

A bottle of Woolite, or some similar cold-water wash, is very useful for washing out underwear, socks, and most other items of apparel as well. Clothes will dry quickly, even in your hotel room bathroom; anything still wet on a day you plan to travel can be wrapped in one of those plastic laundry bags provided by most hotels.

A good pair of walking shoes or sneakers is a must in Brazil, and some kind of beach footwear as well.

5. TIPS FOR THE DISABLED, SENIORS, SINGLES, FAMILIES & STUDENTS

For all intents and purposes, Brazil functions as a Third World country. Little surplus has been generated by the country's economy to date to create special facilities or services for the disabled, much less for seniors, students, or singles. The best bet for seniors and disabled persons who are considering a trip to Brazil would be to find a tour that provides them with the necessary planning and support. To do so, you may contact one of the organizations listed below.

FOR THE DISABLED The **Federation of the Handicapped,** 211 E. 14th St., New York N.Y. 10011, is a membership organization (dues $4 annually) offering summer tours to its membership.

The **Society for the Advancement of Travel for the Handicapped,** 347 Fifth Ave., New York, NY 10016 (tel. 212/447-7284; fax 212/725-8253), will provide members with a list of tour operators specializing in tours for the disabled. Send them a self-addressed, stamped envelope. Yearly membership is $40, $25 for students and seniors.

The **American Foundation for the Blind,** 15 W. 16th St., New York, NY 10011 (tel. 212/620-2000, or toll free 800/232-5463), issues identity cards for the legally blind for $10, and provides much useful information to the sightless, though unfortunately very little that is travel related.

FOR SENIORS The U.S. government prints a pamphlet, *Travel Tips for Senior Citizens* (publication no. 8970, available for $1 through the U.S. Government Printing Office, Washington, DC 20402 (tel. 202/783-5238). For a free copy of *101 Tips for Mature Travelers,* write or phone Grand Circle Travel, 347 Congress St., Boston, MA 02116 (tel. 617/350-7500, or toll free 800/343-0273).

The **American Association of Retired Persons,** 1909 K St. NW, Washington, DC 20049 (tel. 202/872-7737), has become a powerful voice on behalf of seniors in the U.S. Members are eligible for discounts on hotels, airfares, and car rentals. The association has an affiliated travel agency, AARP Travel Service, 100 N. Sepulveda Blvd., Suite 1020, El Segundo, CA 90024 (tel. toll free 800/227-7737), which specializes in tours for seniors.

The **National Council of Senior Citizens,** 925 15th St. NW, Washington, DC 20005 (tel. 202/347-8800), a nonprofit organization, also provides seniors with information on travel. Your $12 membership fee ($16 for couples) entitles you to a monthly newsletter, which includes tips on travel.

SAGA International Holidays, 120 Bolyston St., Boston, MA 02116 (tel. toll free 800/343-0273), caters to the travel needs of clients who are 60 or older. Their all-inclusive tours include travel insurance.

FOR SINGLE TRAVELERS **Grand Circle Travel** (see above) also specializes in tours for single seniors.

Singleworld, 401 Theodore Fremd Ave., Rye, NY 10580 (tel. 914/967-3334, or toll free 800/223-6490), gears itself to singles traveling solo as well as singles who wish to travel in the company of other singles. Their specialties are both tours and cruises, matched by age and sex for up to quadruple occupancy. Singleworld charges a $25 membership fee, good for one year beginning the date of departure, which entitles clients to a quarterly newsletter and a free T-shirt.

FOR FAMILIES My advice to anyone traveling to Brazil with small children is to choose the most comfortable resort you can find in the locale you've chosen to visit, and not try to move around too much. Babysitting service is available throughout the country, but in most cases, language is going to be a barrier, though not as much as you might imagine. True kid lovers—and there are plenty of them in Brazil—find a way to communicate across cultures. For older kids, who are still more or less under the parental wing, and who are good travel companions, the ecological or adventure tours in the Amazon would probably have a particular appeal.

FOR STUDENTS Students, especially those on tight budgets, will find that airport and bus station tourism counters are their best sources for information on the availability of safe, inexpensive accommodations in a given area. Youth hostels, called *albergues* in Portuguese, do exist in most of Brazil's large cities. A number of these establishments are listed throughout the text. No special membership to the

International Youth Hostel movement is required for young people to stay in a Brazilian albergue.

6. ALTERNATIVE/ADVENTURE TRAVEL

Most people who visit Brazil book their tickets and package tours through their local travel agents. The services they receive are, in general, quite adequate, since the majority of North Americans going to Brazil do not venture much beyond the beaches of Rio de Janeiro. For those who wish to travel more extensively in Brazil, however, there are a number of organizations and agencies that cater to a range of special interests, including adventure, urban culture, study and nature tours, and much more. In addition to these specialists, and a description of what they offer, I have also listed the major charter companies and travel clubs that provide some of the most economical flights to Brazil under "Package Tours" in Section 7, "Getting There."

URBAN & ECOLOGICAL ADVENTURES One American travel company specializing almost exclusively in Brazil has shown steady growth in this difficult market for some very basic reasons. Adam Carter of **Brazil Nuts,** 1150 Post Rd., Fairfield, CT 06430 (tel. 203/259-7900, or toll free 800/553-9959; fax 203/259-3177), and his associates truly love Brazil and know the country well. And through their special bookings and escorted tours, they really know how to show visitors to Brazil a good time. An eight-day/seven-night escorted tour of Rio, for example, covers all the obligatory sights and threads its way through the city's nightlife, visiting a "nontouristy" music club every night. Another 13-day package takes in Rio, Búzios, and Salvador, and the yearly escorted Carnival tour to Rio is one of Brazil Nuts' most popular packages.

Now for the first time, those traveling to Rio independently can partake of Brazil Nut's "Rio Like a Native" tours on a day-by-day basis. The company has recently opened offices in Rio, and is offering regularly scheduled day and evening excursions that promise to show the visitors aspects of the *cidade maravilhosa* they would be unlikely to discover on their own. Day excursions run about $25 per person, and evening outings (with all meals, drinks, club entrances, and transport), cost $40 to $45 per person. All groups are led by a Brazil Nuts guide who is well versed in the history, music, and popular culture of Brazil. For details you may contact Brazil Nuts at the toll-free number listed above, or upon arrival in Rio de Janeiro at 021/511-3636.

Brazil Nuts has also become very active in the areas of adventure and nature travel in Brazil, working closely with a dynamic new Brazilian company called **Blumar,** Rua Visconde de Pirajá 580, subsolo 108/109, Ipanema, in Rio (tel. 021/511-3636), which makes all necessary ground arrangements and provides some specialty services of its own. Blumar promotes a number of outdoor sporting events and activities, from the Rio Marathon to Grand Prix Formula One Motor Racing, to special packages for diving and scuba enthusiasts. Blumar can also tailor special tours to a full range of professional and corporate needs.

JEWISH HERITAGE TOURS **Grand Prix Journeys,** 425 Madison Ave., New York, NY 10017 (tel. 212/319-8600, or toll free 800/242-7749; fax 212/486-0783), offers a 13-day Jewish heritage tour of South America, visiting Buenos Aires, São Paulo, and Rio de Janeiro. The main tour combines visits to centers of Jewish history, culture, public service, and religion, with opportunities to observe the life of Jewish communities. A day at Iguaçu Falls on the Brazil–Argentina border is also included. The land portion of the tour runs from $1,429 to $1,744 per person, double occupancy. A rigorously kosher meal plan can be substituted for an additional fee. In support of the program, VARIG Brazilian Airlines has produced a 22-minute videotape presentation and a 24-page Jewish travelers' guide to South America.

EDUCATIONAL/STUDY TRAVEL **International Study Tours Ltd.,** 225 W. 34th St., Suite 913, New York, NY 10122 (tel. 212/563-1202, or toll free 800/833-3804), specializes in "educational travel for those who seek knowledge and understanding of a foreign culture beyond the scope of the usual sightseeing tour." The tour programs are created in conjunction with Brazilian universities and research centers, and include lectures and field trips, plus the presentation of certificates to participants. Participating universities are in Rio, Salvador, São Paulo, Ouro Preto, Brasília, Niterói, Belém, Recife, and Porto Alegre. Study tours are also organized for the Pantanal, and in Manaus (the Amazon capital) may include a study cruise or a sojourn at a jungle lodge.

Some U.S. universities and cultural institutions that offer educational tours to Brazil are:

The **New York University School of Continuing Education,** 331 Shimkin Hall, Washington Square, New York, NY 10003 (tel. 212/998-7133), occasionally offers a two-week cultural program called "Brazil: Carnival and Beyond," to Bahia, Belo Horizonte, Brasília, and Rio—with seats for the Carnival parade.

The **American Museum of Natural History Discovery Tours,** Central Park West at 79th Street, New York, NY 10024 (tel. 212/769-5700), sometimes offers an Amazon Wildlife Adventure tour.

The **National Trust for Historic Preservation,** 1785 Massachusetts Ave. NW, Washington, DC 20036 (tel. 202/673-4138), offered a tour entitled "Brazil: New World in the Tropics," with a focus on colonial and modern architecture in a three-week swing through six Brazilian cities. While this tour is not scheduled for 1992 or 1993, interested parties might still inquire.

ADVENTURE/WILDERNESS   A quick visit to Rio's botanical gardens and zoo may be as close as most visitors will be able to get to the flora and fauna of Brazil. But even this cursory exposure is recommended and will convey some sense of the country's unique animal and plant life. True nature aficionados will want to construct a more demanding itinerary for exploring sections of the Amazon or the Pantanal, a great wildlife reserve in the country's south-central region. Special tour operators can fashion excursions to the needs of the most adventurous nature travelers, taking you far from the beaten tourist paths to remote and untrammeled areas for field study and exploration. Special-interest tours for birdwatchers and flower enthusiasts, including orchid lovers, are also available.

In the early 1980s **Focus Tours,** 14821 Hillside Lane, Burnsville, MN 55337 (tel. 612/892-7830), or Rua Alagoas 1460, Suite 503, Belo Horizonte, Minas Gerais 30330 (tel. 031/223-0358; telex 39-1976 FOCSBR), inaugurated the concept of "conservation tourism" in Brazil. Founder Douglas Trent, a Michigander, is himself a trained ecologist. The majority of the company's tours are custom designed, and concentrate on taking groups or individuals to various "natural destinations." Among these are the Amazon, the Pantanal, the Atlantic forest regions, the *cerrado* of central Brazil, and the *sertão* of the northeast. Focus Tours donates a portion of tour proceeds to a number of private Brazilian conservation organizations, parks and reserves, a campaign that is endorsed by the National Audubon Society.

The **Nature Conservancy,** 1815 N. Lynn St., Arlington, VA 22209 (tel. 703/841-5300), writes: "We are currently working in three biologically important regions in partnership with local conservation organizations. In the grasslands of central Brazil, the Pro-Nature Foundation (FUNATURA) is developing a long-term protection and management plan for the Grande Sertão Veredes National Park with Conservancy support. In the Atlantic rain forest of southern São Paulo and Paraná, we are supporting the work of the Society of Wildlife Researchers (SPVS). The Pantanal, the world's largest wetland, is the focus of our collaboration with the Foundation for the Conservation of Nature (FBCN). Each of these areas is subject to threats on its species and their habitats from outside and from within the region, and each harbors a great array of biological diversity." For a closer view of the Nature Conservancy at work, you may join the organization, and participate in one of its many international trips "to the world's most spectacular natural areas." For information on the calendar of scheduled trips—all of which are escorted by naturalist guides—contact the conservancy.

BRAZIL REALITY TOURS   An organization called **Project Abraco,** c/o Resource Center for Nonviolence, 515 Broadway, Santa Cruz, CA 95060 (tel.

408/423-1626), invites you to "explore the Brazil of the poor who make up 80% of the population." The escorted trip runs around $2,100, and includes guides, round-trip airfare from Miami, meals, and lodging.

SPECIAL-INTEREST TOURS   Those with specialized interests should consider **Brazilian Views,** 201 E. 66th St., Suite 21G, New York, NY 10021 (tel. 212/472-9539), the brainchild of Suzanne Kincaid Barner, who lived in Brazil for 35 years. Her company offers expertly guided customized tours for those whose interest is in fiber arts/crafts, with workshops in needlework and weaving; horticulture; wild orchids in a private reserve; birdwatching; and fishing. A nature safari tour focuses on the rare maned wolf and the endangered golden lion tamarin and muriqui (woolly spider) monkey, in a retreat amid tall mountains in the lush Atlantic rain forest.

7. GETTING THERE

BY PLANE

A booklet called *Air Travelers' Fly Rights* is published by the U.S. government. It is available for $2.75 per copy from the Superintendent of Documents, U.S. Government Printing Office, Washington, DC 20402. Order stock no. 003-006-00106-5.

THE MAJOR AIRLINES   Many travelers get their first taste of Brazil the moment they embark on a **VARIG Airlines** widebody bound for Rio or São Paulo. Not only is VARIG Brazil's flag carrier for all international flights to Brazil from abroad, including the United States and Canada, but the airline is also the country's principal, and according to a poll taken by the prestigious *Folha de São Paulo* newspaper, its most popular domestic carrier as well. The other major domestic airlines are **Transbrasil** (tel. toll free 800/272-7458) and **VASP** (tel. toll free 800/732-8277), both of which also offer a limited number of flights from the U.S. to Brazil.

VARIG (tel. toll free 800/GO-VARIG) offers more flights from the U.S. and Canada to more cities in Brazil than any other airline, including flights from New York, Chicago, Los Angeles, Miami, San Francisco, and Toronto to Rio and on to São Paulo, as well as flights from Miami to Belém and Manaus. From these Brazilian gateways, VARIG can make connections to other cities in Brazil.

Varig's principal competition in the American market, Pan American, went belly-up at the end of 1991, and two other U.S. carriers, **American Airlines** (tel. toll free 800/433-7300) and **United Airlines** (tel. toll free 800/538-2929), have assumed the Brazilian routes once serviced by the former giant and pioneer of world aviation.

American has inaugurated a daily nonstop flight from Miami to Rio, as has United. Whereas United has a daily nonstop flight to Rio from New York, the destination of American's nonstop flight from New York is São Paulo. Since both these airlines are just beginning to position themselves in the Brazilian market, you may find them offering some unbeatable promotional fares in the short run.

REGULAR FARES   Currently your cheapest option (apart from one-of-a-kind promotional fares) with all regularly scheduled airlines flying to either Rio or São Paulo in Brazil are the bulk and LLIT21 airfares.

On VARIG, **bulk tickets** are valid for a 6- to 15-day stay with no stopovers. **LLIT21 fares** allow a 7- to 21-day stay and two stopovers. Since VARIG divides its year into high, middle, and low season, the actual price you pay depends on when you schedule your visit. Currently, the cheapest bulk rate from the U.S. to Rio ($675, embarking from Miami) is offered during the low season—April 1 to June 20 and September 15 to December 9. The 21-day ticket for the same period from Miami is $996 round-trip, and $1,140 from New York. The middle season covers January 11 to March 31 and August 8 to September 14. During this period, a round-trip bulk fare from Los Angeles to Rio would cost $825. The high season runs from June 21 to

FROMMER'S SMART TRAVELER: AIRFARES

1. Shop all the airlines flying to your destination.
2. Ask for the lowest-priced fare available—not only the discount rates.
3. The availability of inexpensive airfares changes from day to day, so keep checking with your travel agent or calling the airlines. Since airlines hate to fly with empty seats, cheaper seats may become available as you near the departure date.
4. Fly during the off-season, if possible—spring, summer, or fall when traveling to Brazil.
5. Make sure to check out the APEX (Advance Purchase Excursion) fares.
6. If it's cheaper, you may want to fly Monday to Thursday rather than over the weekend.
7. Check out the "Other Good-Value Choices" (see below).

August 7 and from December 10 to January 10. The round-trip bulk fare from New York at this time is $825 and the LHIT21 rate, $1,290. During **Carnival,** there is a surcharge of $60.

Note that certain restrictions apply to these airfares. Reservations, ticketing, and payment must be completed 14 days prior to departure, and a penalty may be assessed for cancellation or for any itinerary changes.

The next cheapest individual rates for VARIG are the 30-day **APEX fares.** With this kind of ticket you must stay a minimum of seven days and a maximum of one month. These fares, too, are divided into peak- and low-season tariffs, but your return reservations may be left open. The low-season economy fare from New York to Rio in early 1992 was $1,396 while the high-season ticket cost $200 more or $1,596, which was also the price for an excursion ticket during Carnival. Normal economy tickets good for one day to one year cost $1,752, or $876 one-way. All ticket prices include an $18 airport and exit tax.

OTHER GOOD-VALUE CHOICES **Group and charter flights** generally offer the cheapest airfares of all. For the names and telephone numbers of ticket wholesalers, see also "Package Tours," below; or contact the tours desks of any of the major airlines that fly to Brazil.

The **BACC (Brazilian American Cultural Center),** 20 W. 46th St., New York, NY 10036 (tel. 212/242-7837, or toll free 800/222-2746 outside New York City), offers inexpensive charter fares to Rio from Miami, New York, and Los Angeles.

BY SHIP

Many cruise ships making the South America run call at Brazilian port cities. The itineraries of these cruises change from year to year. For an up-to-date listing of ships with Brazilian ports-of-call, contact the **Brazilian Tourism Office** in New York City (tel. 212/286-9600). Some examples of cruises calling in Brazil are:

Fantasy Cruises (tel. toll free 800/437-3111). Fantasy's yearly 52-day South America cruise leaves Miami in September, and, in Brazil, calls at Rio, Salvador, Recife, and São Luís. Fares begin at $5,995, plus $228 in port charges, and does not include airfare to and from Miami.

Royal Viking (tel. toll free 800/346-8000). Royal Viking's ship, the *Sun,* circles South America in 50 days, on one cruise yearly that departs from Ft. Lauderdale. In Brazil, the ship calls at Rio and Recife. Inside cabins cost $14,985, outside cabins are $17,485, plus $370 in port fees; a partial credit for airfare is included.

Princess Cruises (tel. toll free 800/421-0522). The *Island Princess* will be cruising the Amazon in 1993–94, calling first at Santos (São Paulo), Rio, and Recife before descending the river for Santarém and Manaus. The 14-day cruise is priced at $3,990, plus $145 in port charges.

PACKAGE TOURS

In cooperation with VARIG Airlines, along with most of the other carriers flying to Brazil, **Grand Prix Journeys,** 425 Madison Ave., New York, NY 10017 (tel. 212/319-8600, or toll free 800/242-7749), offers dozens of different package tours to destinations throughout Brazil.

The following international companies offer special vacation packages to Brazil—primarily to Rio de Janeiro—and may be booked through your travel agent: American Express, Council Charter, and Abreu Tours.

The major tour operators or vendors who operate exclusively, or significantly, in the Brazilian market, in addition to those already mentioned above in the section on "Alternative/Adventure Travel," are:

Ecotour Expeditions, P.O. Box 1066, Cambridge, MA 02238 (tel. 617/876-5817, or toll free 800/688-1822). For more detail on Ecotour's programs, see Chapter 14, on the Amazon.

Questers Worldwide Nature Tours, 257 Park Ave. South, New York, NY 10010 (tel. toll free 800/468-8668). For more information on Quester's nature tours to the Amazon and the Pantanal, see Chapter 14.

HOTUR Inc., 20 E. 53rd St., New York, NY 10022 (tel. 212/371-8885).

Marnella Tours, Inc., 33 Walt Whitman Rd., Suite 239, Huntington Station, NY 11746 (tel. 516/271-6969).

Portuguese Tours, Inc., 321 Rahway Ave., Elizabeth, NJ 07202 (tel. 201/352-6112).

South American Vacations, 5777 W. Century Blvd., Suite 1160, Los Angeles, CA 90045 (tel. 213/670-8441).

Tourlite International, Inc., 1 E. 42nd St., New York, NY 10017 (tel. 212/599-3355).

South American Fiesta, 31 Madeline Rd., Ridge, NY 11961 (tel. 516/924-6200, or toll free 800/334-3782).

8. GETTING AROUND

BY PLANE

The best option for North Americans who want to travel around Brazil by air is the **VARIG Air Pass.** It must be purchased outside Brazil before you depart, and is available in two versions, both add-ons to your international flight to Brazil on VARIG. For $440 you may add four cities in Brazil (or five, if you include Santarém) for travel within a 21-day period. You can buy extra passes under this system for $100 apiece, which can gain you huge savings. The time limit does not begin until you use the air pass for your first domestic flight.

BY TRAIN

There is little travel by train in Brazil, although what exists is fairly inexpensive and reasonably comfortable. There is a weekly train running between São Paulo and Brasília, but travel by train to other cities is sparse. For example, there are only two trains each week between Rio and Belo Horizonte, and the trip takes 13 hours. You'd generally do better by bus.

BY BUS

Beyond flying, Brazilians who don't own a car—the vast majority, that is—do their traveling by bus. Every major city has its *rodoviária,* usually a major terminal with direct or indirect bus connections to every corner of the country. Bus travel is slow and inexpensive. The most comfortable buses are called *leitos,* and have reclining seats and tend to make fewer stops than the common bus, the *coletivo* or *comum*. For those who have the time and the inclination to rough it, bus travel through Brazil is highly recommended. There is no better way to see the country, or to gain exposure to the widest possible range of the day-to-day Brazilian reality.

BY CAR

There are car-rental agencies in most airports and in all major cities. Car rental is not recommended for most short-term visitors to Brazil: There are just too many rules to learn in too short a time to make the experience worthwhile. For example, how do you find fuel on Sunday when most filling stations are closed? You'd be better off renting a car with a driver if you want to do any serious touring. The cost isn't much more than a standard car rental, and you can leave the responsibility of driving to a professional. Note that **gas prices** are roughly double the U.S. rate per gallon, with the state-subsidized alcohol fuel slightly less than double.

If you do insist on renting a car, make your arrangements with a major rental agency, like Avis, Hertz, National, or Budget *before* you travel. You will thus pay the international rates, which are much lower than those charged in Brazil.

DRIVING RULES   The rules of the road in Brazil are roughly equivalent to those in the U.S. There are certain material and cultural factors, however, which make driving a very different experience in Brazil than it is in the States. First of all, there are very few four-lane roads, and many roads—especially between cities—are poorly surfaced. Brazilians drive like Europeans; they cluster like race-car drivers and seldom obey the speed limits. Fortunately, they tend to be very good drivers for the most part; but one senses that many of the auto accidents that occur in Brazil could have been avoided by driving more defensively. Brazilians will pass under almost any circumstances, so if you are a slow-lane driver, stay alert and try to give way whenever possible.

ROAD MAPS   The best road maps are produced by Quatro Rodas, the Brazilian equivalent of Rand McNally. They're available at all newsstands and bookstores.

BREAKDOWNS & ASSISTANCE   Since Brazilians say they pay more for their automobiles than do people anywhere else in the world, their mechanics tend to be first-rate at keeping cars on the road as long as possible, using every trick in the book to avoid the high cost of replacement parts. The Brazilian word for a car repair garage is *oficina*. If your car-rental company lets you down in the event of a breakdown, it won't be difficult to find a reasonably priced mechanic.

DISTANCES FROM RIO

	Miles		Miles
Belém	2,013	Maceió	1,405
Belo Horizonte	275	Manaus	2,740
Brasília	701	Natal	1,707
Cuiabá	1,315	Porto Alegre	963
Curitiba	520	Recife	1,528
Florianópolis	693	Salvador	1,068
Fortaleza	1,770	São Luís	1,862
Goiânia	813	São Paulo	266
João Pessoa	1,598	Vitória	319

SUGGESTED ITINERARIES

Why go to Brazil? Traditionally among Brazil travelers the words *Rio de Janeiro* have always provided sufficient justification for their visit. Today, alas, Rio suffers from a not entirely deserved reputation as a city of widespread violence. In my view, it is a city of great violence, not widespread, but much contained within the worlds of poverty and drug trafficking—hardly the milieu of a typical tourist itinerary. When violence finds the occasional tourist, usually the cause is poor judgment—being somewhere you shouldn't be—or just the plain bad luck of being in the right place at the wrong time. Personally, I wouldn't let Rio's poor press keep me from getting back there each year for a week or so anymore than I'd refuse to visit my congressperson in Washington just because that city reportedly is statistically the most homicidal in the nation.

A new generation of Brazil fanciers could care less about Rio's traditional allure, yet seems bent on visiting the Amazon regions, sometimes spending long periods of time hopping from one river town to the next. It's still rough going in the Amazon (the Tropical Hotel in Manaus duly excepted), so if you can take the delays, the bugs, and the heat (or rain), the uniqueness of the forest and river life make this a one-of-a-kind experience.

Some people "do" all of Brazil, others just "do" the main attractions. As you read on, you will find many more answers to the question of why one might visit Brazil, including—ideally—some answers to questions of your own.

The must-see cities or destinations in Brazil, in descending order of importance (from the author's point of view), are Rio de Janeiro, Salvador, Natal, Belo Horizonte (including Ouro Preto and the other historical cities), Florianópolis, Iguaçu, Maceió, Recife, and São Paulo. Gateway cities for the Amazon and Pantanal are Manaus, Belém, and Santarém for the former, and Cuiabá and Campo Grande for the latter. The best jumping-off points from which to explore the Atlantic rain forest are Iguaçu, Curitiba, Rio, Belo Horizonte, and São Paulo.

IF YOU HAVE ONE WEEK

My suggestion for a one-week Brazilian vacation is to pick one city, and stay put. If you're not opting for an adventure tour to the Pantanal or the Amazon, treat Brazil as a laid-back and sensual beach, music, and culinary experience. The less you have to travel around, the more likely you are to get the most out of what Brazil has to offer. Any of the tour operators listed above can provide you with the necessary ground arrangements for a given Brazilian destination, including hotel reservations, airport transfers, escorted day and night excursions, and so on.

My first choice would be Ipanema beach in Rio de Janeiro, with a two-day side trip to either the Costa Verde (say Ilha Grande), or the Costa do Sol (say Búzios). Staying in Ipanema puts you near some of the city's best restaurants and nightspots in nearby Leblon and the Lagoa.

My second choice would probably be Salvador, and I'd stay at the Hotel Tropical if I wanted a more city-based, cultural experience, or at the Sofitel Quatro Rodas, if the beach was my priority. The nearby island of Itaparica, or the Praia do Forte up the northern coast, especially the former, are obligatory side trips.

My third choice would be Natal or Florianópolis for a beach experience, or Belo Horizonte/Ouro Preto for a grand culinary and historical tour. See listings on these respective destinations for more detail.

IF YOU HAVE TWO WEEKS

Day 1: Fly into Rio; embark same day for Iguaçu. Stay at the Hotel das Cataratas, the only hotel with a view of the falls. Or, if the urban scene appeals more, and you want to be closer to the restaurant and nightlife scenes, choose a hotel in the town of Foz do Iguaçu.

Day 2: Visit the Brazilian side of the falls in the morning, and the Argentinean side in the afternoon. Eat dinner in either Argentina or Paraguay.

Day 3: Take the Macuco Safari river tour in the morning, and depart for Belo Horizonte in the afternoon.

Day 4: Spend the night at a hotel in the Savassi neighborhood, and choose from any number of good restaurants for dinner that night. Depart by car or bus early the next morning for Ouro Preto. Tour the historical treasures, and stay over night at the Pousada Mondego.

Day 5: Return early to Belo Horizonte and fly to Salvador. Spend what remains of the day on the beach. Eat a good meal that night, preferably Bahian food, and attend a show.

Day 6: Tour the city's churches, markets, and historical sites. Go to a club at night for some good, Afro-based music.

Day 7: Take an all-day tour, either to Cachoeira or Itaparica, and travel that night to Rio.

Day 8: Spend the remaining week in Rio. Rest up after your whirlwind tour by spending the first day on the beach.

Day 9: Spend the morning touring downtown Rio, and the afternoon/early evening going to Corcovado and Pão de Açúcar.

Day 10: Mix the day between beach time, and hanging out in Ipanema or Copacabana, shopping, walking, or café-hopping. Try the Casa da Feijoada or Gula, Gula for lunch, and one of the city's fancier restaurants for dinner.

Day 11: Leave early for a tour of Rio's suburban beaches to the north; stopping for lunch at 476 in Pedra de Guaratiba. Go on to Mangaratiba for the private boat awaiting to take you to Ilha Grande. Stay at one of the local *pousadas* (Expeditours in Rio—call 021/287-9697—can take you there and make all necessary arrangements).

Day 12: Spend the day hiking around Ilha Grande, and beach hopping. Return that evening to your hotel in Rio.

Day 13: Another open day to enjoy the beaches, restaurants, and shops of Rio. Depending on season, and day of the week, go to a gafieira or samba school rehearsal, and do what the Cariocas do—stay up all night.

Day 14: Sleep late, spend the day working on your tan. Enjoy one last great dinner in Rio before leaving for the airport.

IF YOU HAVE THREE WEEKS

Days 1–7: See above. For the second week, I would recommend one of several options, a tour of the northeastern beaches, a week in and around the Amazon rain forest, or a week in Pantanal. Let's say you choose the Amazon; here's a suggested itinerary.

Day 8: You have flown on to Belém, where you have spent the night in a hotel. This morning, you will tour Ver-O-Peso market, and then fly to the delta island of Marajó in the afternoon. Stay at the Pousada dos Guaras (arrangements for transport and accommodations can be made through CIATUR in Belém 091/228-0011).

Day 9: Visit Araruana beach.

Day 10: Return to Belém early, and fly directly to Manaus. If your budget allows, treat yourself to a day and night at the Tropical Hotel. That night, especially if it's Thursday, Friday or Saturday, check out the action at the huge, beachside Papagaio Club, right outside the entrance to the grounds of the Tropical Hotel.

Days 11–12: Leave early for a two-night stay in one of the jungle lodges; see Chapter 14 for more information.

Day 13: Return to Manaus, and tour the city; don't forget the Museu de Ciências Naturais, a little gem of a museum on the outskirts of town.

Day 14: Relax in the morning, and travel on to Rio in the afternoon.

Days 15–21: See the suggested Rio itinerary above.

9. WHERE TO STAY

First- and tourist-class hotels in Brazil are classified by the government, receiving from one to five stars depending on quality and facilities. Most travel agencies and tour operators who "sell" Brazil place their clients in four- and five-star hotels, but don't be put off by the room rates for these properties that appear in this guide. These prices are "rack rates," the high-season rates someone might pay if they walked into the hotel right off the street. Travel agencies and tour operators acquire these rooms much more cheaply, and therefore, when offering you a land package, can charge a price considerably below the official rack rate.

So, unless you are going off to Brazil with a true adventurer's spirit, bent on making all your own arrangements, prepared to take pot luck—not at all a bad idea if you've got the time and inclination—the most economical option for securing accommodations in Brazil that meet international standards is through the assistance of a travel specialist.

Where alternatives exist—condos, apart-hotels, house rentals—for those seeking long-term accommodations, I have included these listings in each chapter.

10. WHERE TO DINE

Where you will eat your breakfast is a foregone conclusion. In all Brazilian hotels, breakfast is provided in the price of the room. Five-star hotels offer the most extravagant breakfast buffets, including sometimes as many as a dozen hot dishes, along with a spectrum of tropical fruits, cold cuts, breads, rolls, pastries, and more. The simpler the hotel, the simpler the breakfast, which can be pared down to a very satisfying café au lait, bread, butter, and bananas.

A few tips about Brazilian restaurants, repeated in several places throughout the text, are in order. A 10% service charge is always included in the bill, and Brazilians treat this as the gratuity, perhaps leaving a bit more in a better restaurant where food is served up with a flourish. The *couvert*—usually bread, butter, olives, hard-boiled quails' eggs, and some kind of pâté—is optional in most restaurants, and may be refused. Portions tend to be very generous, and it is not unusual for Brazilians to order one serving for two people, at least in an ordinary, day-to-day kind of establishment. Steakhouses, called *churrascarias,* often employ the all-you-can-eat system called *rodízio,* where a dozen types of skewered meats endlessly circulate round-robin style.

Portions are not only generous, but meals are generally much cheaper in Brazil than in the U.S. São Paulo and Rio tend to have the priciest restaurants, but only in comparison with the inexpensive eateries you will routinely discover in the hinterlands throughout the rest of the country. And even in those two great metropolises, there are culinary bargains galore.

Drinking is also a bargain in Brazil, especially if you choose a nontrendy bar or outdoor café. Beer is seldom more than $1 a bottle, and local drinks, like *caipirinhas,* are roughly the same price.

11. WHAT TO BUY

Crafts in Brazil are a mixed bag. As with the art scene, you often have to ignore the "official" displays—the weekly "hippie" fairs and artisan centers—in favor of popular markets and roadside stands, where the less touristy items can be found. Much is made, for example, of Brazilian leather and needle crafts, but an amateur's eye can often easily see that the craftsmanship in assembly and design just isn't there. The biggest collections of schlock goods are usually found at the state- or city-subsidized centers, like the Mercado Modelo in Salvador or the Sunday Hippie Fair in Rio's Ipanema neighborhood.

Not all the official crafts centers are tourist traps, however. Some notable exceptions are the state-sponsored craft shop in Cuiabá, Mato Grosso (which is close to a steady supply of well-made baskets and pots by the state's large Native American population), the attractive artisan galleries in the tourist office in Aracajú, and the Asian Fair in the Liberdade section of São Paulo. The soapstone containers and figures found throughout Minas Gerais, particularly at the craft center in Belo Horizonte, are quite attractive, but very brittle and even when well packed tend to travel badly. Municipal markets, like those in Aracajú, Natal, and São Luís, are better bets for finding truly unique and often useful craft items—hammocks, rugs, rustic cutting boards, and handmade tools. The Ver-O-Peso market in Belém (and its counterpart in Manaus) is a veritable bazaar, fascinating as much for its general active waterfront ambience as for the hundreds of fetish objects and potions on sale there.

The general shopping scene for clothes, shoes, and gemstones of excellent quality—with modest price tags by North American standards—is a popular source of activity among international visitors.

FAST FACTS: BRAZIL

American Express Where available, listings of American Express offices or representatives are included in their appropriate place in the text.

Babysitters The very best hotels offer babysitting services. You can expect to pay around $5 per hour, perhaps even more. Remember, you are hiring a bilingual babysitter, not a neighbor's teenage daughter or son. Otherwise, you must pretty much resolve to have the kids with you, unless they're old enough to go to the pool or game room by themselves. For this reason, if you're planning to travel with children, you'd be best off selecting a self-contained resort where there are likely to be both programs for children and babysitting when required. Fortunately, there are many such resorts throughout Brazil, and families may travel to even the large cities like Rio, São Paulo, and Salvador and find such accommodations no farther away than the municipal outskirts.

Business Hours White-collar business hours are normally from 9am to 6pm Monday through Friday, with an hour for lunch. Office lunch-hour periods are usually staggered from noon till 3pm. Longer hours and obligatory work on Saturday are the rule for most service and nonunion blue-collar jobs.

The shops in Brazil are open from 9am to 6:30pm Monday through Friday, and from 9am to 1pm on Saturday. Shops close as late as 10pm during the month of December. Banks are open from 10am to 4:30pm Monday through Friday. If the city you are visiting has a shopping center, chances are it will be open six to seven days a week from around 10am till as late as midnight.

Camera and Film Photographic film for most modern cameras is widely available throughout Brazil, as is tape for video cameras, especially in the larger cities. Film, however, is not one of the bargain items in Brazil, and can be priced at double the U.S. amount. Many photo bugs bring all the film they will need, and store it in their hotel refrigerators to keep it fresh. Unless you are on an extended vacation, it's probably best to delay processing until you get home. Very rarely will you be restricted in the use of your camera, and then, generally only in museums and churches. If you are with a tour group, your guide will inform you where restrictions are in effect.

Cigarettes American cigarettes were once fashionable in Brazil, but have all but disappeared from most counters where tobacco products are sold. Shops in all the better hotels sell American cigarettes, as do the top restaurants. Brazilian cigarettes appear to be of comparable quality, however, and are priced at around 50¢ a pack. There is little antismoking consciousness in Brazil, so nonsmokers should prepare themselves for the assault. It would be most surprising, however, if some Brazilian smoker in your company should refuse to extinguish his cigarette when asked to do so politely. A total stranger will probably be less accommodating.

Climate See "When to Go," earlier in this chapter.

Crime See Section 3, "Health, Insurance & Safety," earlier in this chapter.

Currency See "Information, Entry Requirements & Money," earlier in this chapter.

Customs See "Information, Entry Requirements & Money," earlier in this chapter.

Documents Required See "Information, Entry Requirements & Money," earlier in this chapter.

Driving Rules See "Getting Around," earlier in this chapter.

Drug Laws Recreational drug use is widespread in large Brazilian cities, and drugs like marijuana and cocaine are dirt cheap by American standards. But woe be it to the foreigner who falls into the hands of the Brazilian police as the result of a drug bust. They will make your life miserable for you, and you may even have to do some time.

Drugstores In the large cities, drugstores called *farmácias de plantão* are open 24 hours a day. Your hotel staff or a friendly cab driver will know the address of an all-night drugstore if one is required. Prescription drugs are not as tightly regulated in Brazil as they are in the U.S. For a fee of, say, $5—supposedly to pay a doctor for the necessary paperwork after the fact—you can often get those antibiotics or sleeping tablets you neglected to bring with you. Brazilian medications are manufactured by the familiar multinational pharmaceutical companies, so the brand names will be recognizable.

Electricity What we refer to as "house current"—110 volts AC—is rare in Brazil. Rio is said to be wired with 110, but my impression nonetheless is that there are a considerable number of 220-volt lines throughout the major hotels as well. Bathrooms in these hotels usually provide an alternate house current receptacle suitable for electric shavers, but not hairdryers. The top hotels often provide "hard-wired" hairdryers as an extra bathroom feature. Bring the necessary 220-volt converter if you have any equipment you wish to run (slide projector, hairdryer, tape player, etc.), and always check with the hotel staff before plugging in anything. Some hotels provide these transformers or adapters for guests. Adding to the confusion is the widespread use of 127-volt current in cities like Salvador, Manaus, and Curitiba. Be particularly careful where there is no central hot water and showers are equipped with visible electric hot-water heaters. People have been known to get electrical shocks in such showers if the heaters are inadequately grounded.

Embassies and Consulates All foreign embassies are of course located in the capital, Brasília, in the interior. Since most foreign travelers make Rio their headquarters in Brazil, many governments have established consulates there to service the needs of their citizens. See the Rio and Brasília chapters for specific addresses.

Emergencies Luxury and first-class hotels generally have physicians on call. For any emergency care, dental or medical, it would be wise to consult with a member of the diplomatic mission of your country of origin.

Etiquette Generalizing about etiquette is a somewhat meaningless exercise. One could fairly suggest, though, that Brazilians are—or can be—more formal and more ceremonial than Americans. The Portuguese language itself retains both the formal mode of address (*o senhor, a senhora*) as well as the familiar form (*você* or *tu*, depending on the region). American brashness and straight talking can at times grate on Brazilians. The culture gap is based to some degree on Brazilian hypersensitivity to gradations of social class in their country, which have no functional counterpart in largely middle-class America. Needless to say, it is up to the individual traveler to unravel in a given situation the mysteries of cross-cultural differences.

Gasoline See "Getting Around," earlier in this chapter.

Hitchhiking While not illegal in Brazil, nobody does it.

Holidays See "When to Go," earlier in this chapter.

Information See "Information, Entry Requirements & Money," earlier in this chapter.

Language Brazilians speak Portuguese, the linguistic legacy of the country's original Portuguese colonizers. The Brazilian accent differs from that of Portugal, much in the same way that American and British English differ. A useful vocabulary list and pronunciation key can be found in the Appendix of this guide. English is spoken by designated staff at the major hotels, specialized tour guides, and at airport information centers. Otherwise it would be fair to say that English—other than pidgin—is not widely spoken throughout Brazil, particularly as you travel any distance from the large urban centers. Spanish can be a reasonable lingua franca in Brazil, but you may still find it difficult to understand the responses in Portuguese. A simple phrase book, available at or through your local bookstore, ought to provide some help in this regard.

Laundry Hotels have normal two-day service and a special express service, which costs about 50% more. Hotel laundry service, while convenient, is nonetheless expensive. Travelers with a container of Woolite (in powder form, if available, in the event it opens in your suitcase), or some equivalent cold-water soap, and a summer wardrobe of wash-and-wear clothes will be able to avoid high-priced hotel laundry fees. The other option is to find the nearest *tinturaria* (dry cleaner) or *lavandaria* (laundry).

Liquor Laws No doubt they exist. I have never seen them applied. Brazilians are big beer drinkers, and you will often see teens drinking beer in the cafés. Kids routinely buy beer and liquor for their folks at the local stores and markets.

Lost Property   Lost or misplaced items are not necessarily gone forever in Brazil. Chances are, if you go back to the place where you last remember having the item in your possession—bars and restaurants in particular—it will be there waiting for you. Losses in cabs are more problematical, but you can have your hotel make inquiries at the local *delegacia* (police precinct) or central branch of the post office. Report all lost traveler's checks and credit cards to the appropriate organization immediately.

Mail   The most convenient way to handle your outgoing mail is to purchase stamps from the reception desk in your hotel, and to have the staff mail your letters and postcards for you. The post office, *correio* (co-*hay*-yu), is open from 8am to 6pm weekdays, and until noon on Saturday. The cost of international postage has skyrocketed in recent years; it's more expensive to send a first-class letter from Brazil to the U.S. than vice versa.

Map   Quatro Rodas maps are the best available in Brazil; you can purchase them at newsstands and bookstores.

Newspapers and Magazines   The top newspapers are the *Folha de São Paulo, Jornal do Brasil,* and *O Globo.* The *Latin American Daily Post* is an English-language rag published out of São Paulo four days a week, with a Rio edition; it's good for entertainment, real estate, and business news. The very expensive *International Herald Tribune* is available generally only in Rio, São Paulo, and Salvador, as are the *Wall Street Journal, New York Times,* and *Miami Herald,* as well as *Time* and *Newsweek.*

Passports   See "Information, Entry Requirements & Money," earlier in this chapter.

Police   Brazil has a tradition of military rule, under which the police have considerably more power than in the U.S. The presence of the PMs (military police) on the street—depending on how they are behaving—can be as ugly as it is reassuring. If you have a problem on the street, it is the local citizen who is more likely to come to your aid than the police. While cops on the beat will seldom hassle tourists, they are still best avoided.

Radio and TV   Most hotel rooms have music piped in from a handful of local radio stations, with the Brazilian equivalent of elevator music. With your own radio, you ought to be able to pick up some of the best of Brazilian popular and country-style music no matter where you are. Some—but not all—luxury and first-class hotels have satellite dishes that pick up CNN newscasts throughout the day, and generally that big game or prizefight you thought you were going to miss is carried by Canal Bandeirante (channel varies from city to city). Brazilian TV is definitely worth tuning in on: The prime-time soaps and miniseries are a major export to Western European countries. Discreet female and male nudity often appears in both commercials and shows.

Restrooms   Brazilians have yet to become overly proprietary about their bathrooms. Restaurants you are not eating in and hotels where you are not staying will nonetheless cheerfully allow you to use the facilities when necessary. There are otherwise few public toilets, and they are best to be avoided anyway, since they tend to be filthy.

Safety   See Section 3, "Health, Insurance & Safety," earlier in this chapter.

Taxes   There is no sales tax. What you see on the sticker—if there is one—is what you pay. Otherwise one bargains, and that of course is a science that some shoppers thrive on and others find a nuisance. Most hotels charge an across-the-board 10% service tax. So if the rate is $70 a night, it's really $77. Please take note that every item appearing on your final hotel bill—long-distance phone calls, room service, laundry—is subject to this 10% tax. Restaurants also add 10%, but in this case it's the whole tip. Depending on the nature of your airline ticket, you may have to pay a token airport tax between internal destinations, and an $18 exit tax when returning home. Taxes and tariffs on items like U.S. cigarettes, imported liquor, and gasoline—at any given time about double what we pay—are all high.

Telephone, Telex, and Fax   The telephone system in Brazil is generally reliable, but not without its glitches. Dial tones will sometimes be elusive, transmissions weak, broken connections not infrequent—the system is about 80% there. If you can avoid making long-distance phone calls from your hotel room, your billing rates will be roughly 50% lower. Like room-service food, telephone calls and every other service you purchase within the hotel will be priced at a premium. Most hotels will not charge for local calls, however. Wherever you call from, however, you may now dial direct, both within Brazil and internationally. Phone service is good overall, though pay phones (*orelhoes*—which you could translate as "Dumbo ears") are a minor nightmare. The main problem is that you must use tokens, and inevitably there is no place nearby to buy them. Newsstands at airports—and supposedly elsewhere—sell these phone tokens, called *fichas* (*fee*-shas). They come in a five-pack, and are inexpensive. If you're lucky, someone near the phone you want to use will know the nearest place to buy fichas. Or better yet, stick to your hotel phone—it's a lot easier. Telephone company offices, called EMBRATEL, located in airports and at other locations, facilitate phoning from a public space. There are attendants to place the calls for you.

Your hotel will send your telex or fax messages; if they receive either of these forms of communication, you will be notified immediately. Fax machines are now widespread throughout Brazil.

Time   There are three time zones in Brazil. Eastern and parts of central Brazil are three hours behind Greenwich mean time, which is two hours ahead of U.S. eastern standard time. West-central Brazil and most of the Amazon basin are four hours behind GMT, while far-western Brazil, primarily the state of Acre, is five hours behind GMT, therefore occupying the same time zone as New York. Daylight saving has been introduced throughout most of Brazil during the South American summer months of December through February. Not all cities (Belém, for example) participate in this time change. Be aware of this potential confusion when making flight reservations during periods of daylight saving in either hemisphere. VARIG agents in New York once listed my flight time erroneously from Belém to Santarém; both cities are located in the Amazon River state of Pará, but they set their clocks differently during Brazilian summer.

Tipping   As with bargaining, there is no mechanical answer to how much or how little you should tip a person rendering a service, be it in an institutional setting like a hotel or restaurant or in some individual context. Brazilians are on the whole light tippers. In a sense there is no such thing as spare change in a country with Brazil's yearly rates of inflation—except for the super-rich. Tourists, of course, are held to a higher standard, and generous tips are always appreciated, especially by those who really earn them, like tour guides.

Tourist Offices   See "Information, Entry Requirements & Money" in this chapter, and also specific city chapters.

Visas   See "Information, Entry Requirements & Money," earlier in this chapter.

Water   See "Health, Insurance & Safety," earlier in this chapter.

Yellow Pages   These exist in some cities, though they are as yet not terribly widespread.

INTRODUCING RIO

Rio has long been a mecca for sun worshipers and escapists of every stripe. The city has enjoyed this status for over 50 years. Initially, however, Rio was primarily an exotic destination for South American sophisticates and international jet-setters. Most North Americans' first view of Rio was as a playground for swells, the perennial image of the city as depicted in a handful of Hollywood movies, where the plot involved some faction of the Cole Porter set in the act of "putting on the ritz." But the era when only the super-chic in their first-class steamship cabins, or at the other end of the travel spectrum, foot-loose adventurers who wandered the world in tramp freighters, dared dream of visiting Rio are long gone. Group travel and package flights have brought dreamy, steamy, and somewhat distant Rio within the reach of today's typical globetrotter whose ambitions are to "see the world," or at least its principal cities. And Rio, distinguished for its physical beauty, its sublime beach culture and café society, and its unique brand of urbane sensuality, must certainly be counted among them.

A BIT OF HISTORY   Before there were *bairros* (*bye*-whos, Rio's many unique neighborhoods), the region surrounding Guanabara Bay was a great forest inhabited by indigenous tribes. On January 1, 1502, a fleet under Portuguese command sent to survey the territorial discoveries of Alvares Cabral, and thought to have been navigated by the Italian explorer and enigmatic historical figure Amerigo Vespucci, entered the mouth of Guanabara Bay. A halfhearted attempt to set up a permanent camp failed, and for years thereafter subsequent Portuguese explorers—including Magellan—used the harbor for safe anchorage during their various expeditions.

The French knowingly poached on Portuguese New World territory in search of a colonial empire of their own, in what was already by the early 1500s a rapidly shrinking world. The Huguenot admiral Villegaignon landed a formidable troop of soldiers in 1555—and subsequently large numbers of colonists—on several islands near the mainland in Guanabara Bay. A settlement here was christened Coligny. In 1567 the tenacious French were forcibly removed from their beachhead, part of which today is the downtown Santos Dumont Airport, by troops under Brazil's governor-general, Mem de Sá, who from the city of Salvador in the northeast supervised Portugal's strategic dominance over production for a new and growing world sugar market. During the bloody siege pressed by Mem de Sá against the French interlopers, a fort was established on high ground in what is now downtown Rio, and this stronghold evolved into Rio's first Portuguese colony, São Sebastião do Rio de Janeiro.

Rio has rewarded handsomely the hard-fought victory of the Portuguese, having been at the center of important historical events in Brazil since the city's rise to national dominance in the mid-1700s. Although the French returned and sacked the town in 1711, Rio had already become the principal port for Europe-bound shipments of gold from nearby Minas Gerais. Having finally eclipsed Salvador in importance, Rio became the colony's capital in 1763. Most of what remains from the layout of that city can be found close to the waterfront, notably several old churches and monasteries, the Praça XV (square) of colonial administrative buildings, and the Passeio Público, Rio's first public park.

Rio was suddenly thrust into world prominence after the Portuguese monarchs, fleeing the Napoleonic Wars, settled there in 1808 and ruled their empire from the city

WHAT'S SPECIAL ABOUT RIO

Beaches

☐ Leme, Copacabana, Ipanema, Leblon, Pepino, Barra da Tijuca, Recreio dos Bandeirantes, Prainha, and Grumari: some of the most stunning urban and suburban ocean beaches in the world. They're packed to the max almost any sunny weekend of the year.

Ace Attractions

☐ Corcovado and Pão de Açúcar, two mountain prospects from which to view and feast upon the natural beauty of Rio de Janeiro. The two must-see sights in Rio.

Excursions

☐ Búzios, two hours to the south, has been Rio's elite weekend watering hole for over a decade.

☐ Paraty, some three-and-a-half hours to the north, is one of Brazil's most charming and authentic historical cities.

The Atlantic Forest

☐ The vast in-town Tijuca Park, with dozens of options for birdwatching, hiking, and climbing.

☐ Petrópolis, Teresópolis, and Nova Friburgo, nearby mountain retreats surrounded by parklands.

☐ Itatiaia, a great park preserve about 100 miles inland from Rio, with excellent facilities for camping and trekking.

☐ Ilha Grande, another option for experiencing what remains of Rio's Atlantic forest.

Rio's Lifestyle

☐ The best of Rio is Rio itself—a taste of its beaches, unhurried moments of strolling its streets, or lounging in its cafés, and grazing within its great variety of spectacular restaurants.

---

for a span of 13 years. That historic accident implanted the only post-Columbian monarchy to actually take root and flourish in the New World, forestalling the establishment of a republic in Brazil until nearly the 20th century. The royal presence, however, led to the creation of many basic institutions—including printing, till then suppressed in the colony—which had the effect of modernizing Rio and other Brazilian cities to the European standards of the time.

Brazil's relatively enlightened monarch, Pedro II, who ruled during much of the 19th century, made Rio his home, and nearby Petrópolis in the mountains, the site of his summer palace. The residences of Dom Pedro and his family, along with other collections of royal memorabilia, are open to the public. Rio experienced tremendous growth during Dom Pedro's reign, but nothing compared with what has occurred in this century. Even until well into the 20th century, bairros like Copacabana and Ipanema were fishing villages and summer hideaways. The spread of the city always seemed to outdistance the development of its basic services, from paved roads to sanitation. And such remains the case today in the outlying areas, and even in the inner-city shantytowns, the *favelas,* most of which, however, were removed in recent years from the fashionable neighborhoods.

1. ORIENTATION

Rio de Janeiro is capital of a state with the same name, located roughly midway down the eastern coast of Brazil. We forget sometimes how much farther to the east South America is than our own continent (and how close to Africa!). Looking at a world map, and drawing a line longitudinally north, Rio de Janeiro would be positioned in the Atlantic somewhat equal with Cape Farewell in Greenland. So much for longitude. The city's latitude, however, places it foursquare in the Tropic of Capricorn, with emphasis here on the word "tropic."

Two thirds of the way down the somewhat elongated coastal state, the relatively unbroken shoreline jogs radically inland. So strong was the water's current at this great indentation that the first Portuguese explorers believed they had sailed into the mouth of a great river estuary. Since their discovery was made on New Year's Day, they called the place "January River," or Rio de Janeiro. Later explorers would discover that what was initially thought to be a river was really a vast bay, which the natives called Guanabara.

It is along the western shore of Guanabara Bay, and along the sandy regions of the open sea to the south, that the city of Rio de Janeiro was planted and has since grown into a sprawling metropolis of 10 million inhabitants. Since the coastal mountain range comes virtually to the edge of the sea in this region, the city's growth in many areas has been limited to narrow strips of alluvial lands, earth and sand deposited along the base of the mountain range by beating waves and tidal action over the centuries. It is this juxtaposition of mountains—some lush with tropical vegetation, others barren and volcanic—with an endless and majestic seascape that accounts for Rio's reputation as a city of extraordinary natural beauty.

ARRIVING

If your package or ticket does not include **airport transfers**—where a tour-company van or hotel car is there to meet you—you have several options for getting to your hotel. The **luxury car service** of two airport companies, **Cootramo** and **Transcopass,** is the most costly, and the most hassle-free. You pay a fixed rate, calculated according to neighborhood zones: figure $20 to $25 to get to Copacabana or Ipanema. With **metered taxis,** you will have to negotiate a price, which will probably be less expensive. The modern and comfortable cars of the luxury services, plus the professional mien of their drivers, make this the recommended option.

A Greyhound-style **bus,** called the *frescão* (because it's air-conditioned), leaves for the Zona Sul about every half hour. While the bus costs only about $3 and stops near all the major hotels, you may not care to drag your suitcases that extra block or two when you've just arrived. The route taken by the frescão will skirt closer to downtown than your private cab, and the ride can be an interesting first orientation to the city. The **public bus**—actually a series of buses—from the airport to the city or beach areas is even more of an adventure, which only the most intrepid will need to experience.

TOURIST INFORMATION

This guide is an indispensable reference to the life and attractions of Rio de Janeiro, and much that is of interest in the city's environs as well. After reading it, accompanied by consultations with knowledgeable friends and travel professionals (agents and tour guides, that is), you should know pretty much what there is to see and do before you get to Rio. These sources cannot tell you, however, who will be appearing at a particular jazz or samba club during your stay, nor what the hottest or newest discos, bars, and restaurants are at precisely that moment. Here are some useful suggestions on where to get that information.

The state and the city promotional arms are named TurisRio and Riotur respectively. TurisRio maintains an **information center** with a highly animated and competent staff at Rio's international airport (Sector C, 1st floor; tel. 398-4073), on Ilha do Governador (Governor's Island), a 30- to 45-minute drive from most areas in the Zona Sul. If you don't have a hotel reservation, they can help you. They can also give you basic transportation information: where to catch the airport bus, how to get to Petrópolis, Búzios, Paraty, or other destinations, popular or personal, within the state of Rio, or Estado do Rio, as most Brazilians call it. These are the first people to take your questions to when you land. The information center is open daily from 5am to 11pm.

Both **TurisRio** (tel. 021/221-8422) and **Riotur** (tel. 021/297-7117) maintain offices downtown at Rua da Assembléia 10. And they both distribute printed materials on a variety of excursion options. Riotur also maintains branches in much-frequented locations like Pão de Açúcar (Sugar Loaf Mountain), Av. Pasteur 520, in Praia Vermelha, near the entrance to the cable car (open from 8am to 7pm); at the overlook on Corcovado Mountain (open from 8am to 7pm); in the downtown bus station, Terminal Rodoviário Novo Rio, at Av. Francisco Bicalho 1 (tel. 291-5151, *ramal,* or extension, 143), located in São Cristóvão, slightly to the north of the downtown area (open from 6am till midnight); and at the Carnival Museum, Praça da Apoteose, downtown (tel. 293-7122), open from 10am to 5pm. English and other major Western languages are spoken at these locations. Alô Riotur (tel. 242-8000) has tourist information in English Monday to Friday 9am to 6pm.

The city of Rio de Janeiro has installed a direct tourist-assistance telephone line. Dial 1516 in any of the following situations:

• If you are lost in the city.
• In case of personal injury or accident.
• If documents or personal belongings are lost or stolen.
• If you need to get in touch with your consulate.

Remember, if you are calling from a public phone, you will need a token called a *ficha* (see "Telephones" in the "Fast Facts" section of Chapter 2). On the other hand, many hotels, restaurants, bars, and shops in Rio will allow you the use of their phone for local calls.

The principal sources of information for most tourists, once settled in the city, are the desk staff at their various hotels. The hotel *portaria* is where you will deposit and retrieve your room key, pick up messages, and find out about local hot spots and tours. Just remember that while the portaria staff can really be a most immediate and valuable source of information, and their services will cost you nothing, chances are your informant will receive a commission if you accept his recommendation. And while their recommendations are generally quite sound, porters have been known to steer people away from certain choices in favor of others to guarantee their fees. The porters, by the way, will also be a key source for finding out where to change money on the "parallel" market, though most hotels now offer an exchange at the nearly comparable "turismo" rate.

There are a number of **publications** that can be consulted for current cultural listings. Rio's daily newspapers all have entertainment sections, the best of which can be found in the *Jornal do Brasil* and *O Globo.* While they are obviously written in Portuguese, it isn't too hard to retrieve basic information like movie titles, locations, and times, and who may be appearing in what club or concert. Hotels also often provide guests with English-language publications, like *Rio This Month* in *TV Guide* format, or the *Daily Post,* which appears four times weekly.

CITY LAYOUT

Modern Rio, internally, is divided into a southern and a northern zone—**Zona Sul** and **Zona Norte.** Separating the two zonas is a downtown area called the Centro. The area of interest to international visitors is the Zona Sul, where the best beaches, nightspots, sights, lodgings, restaurants, and shops are found. The Centro is also of interest, particularly for its historic buildings, but also for some fine and traditional restaurants, many cultural activities, like theater, concerts, film, and bistros, and for its block upon block of popular retail stores. There is nothing wrong with the Zona Norte. It is, for example, what Brooklyn and the Bronx are to Manhattan in New York City, a vast blue-collar community with many fine neighborhoods, and with many pockets of poverty as well, and these, in the case of Rio, are on a scale of a developing, not a developed, country. In years to come, guidebooks will no doubt begin to reveal the attractions and mysteries of the Zona Norte, for there are popular nightspots, bars, and restaurants that only the cognoscenti frequent. Some tourists approach the fringes of the Zona Norte these days when going to Maracanã Stadium for a soccer match, or penetrate more deeply to visit the rehearsal sites of the great working-class samba clubs, which provide the mass spectacles around which Rio's unrivaled Carnival is organized. But the Zona Sul is still where 90% of the action is. Plus it possesses something the bay-bordered and interior northern zone will never have—some of the finest ocean beaches in the world.

MAIN ARTERIES & STREETS   In Ipanema, the avenues of principal interest are the oceanfront Avenida Vieira Souto, which turns into Avenida Delfim Moreira on the Leblon end of the beach. Ipanema's main shopping thoroughfare is Avenida Visconde de Pirajá, two blocks from the beach, along which are located some of the most fashionable boutiques, gemstone emporiums, and shoe stores in the city. Avenida Ataulfo de Paiva is the main commercial street in Leblon, lined with the more day-to-day kinds of shops and services. Running along the Ipanema side of the overflow canal and a narrow green space called Allah's Garden (Jardim de Alah) is Avenida Epitácio Pessoa, which then winds around the right bank of the Lagoa. On the Leblon side of this boundary between the neighborhoods is Avenida Borges de Medeiros, encircling for its part the Lagoa's opposite shore.

Copacabana's famous oceanfront boulevard is called the Avenida Atlântica, a four-lane, divided road that accompanies the seven-mile-long beach from one end to the other. The dividing line between Copacabana and Leme beaches is the Avenida Princesa Isabel, which begins at the Avenida Atlântica, runs through the tunnel into Botafogo, and connects with roads leading downtown.

The principal downtown streets are the wide Avenida Presidente Vargas, and the Avenida Rio Branco, which cross each other on the near side of the city, close to the water.

The nine-mile-long Avenida Sernambetiba runs the length of the Barra da Tijuca beachfront.

NEIGHBORHOODS IN BRIEF   The *bairros* (*bye*-whos) are Rio's many neighborhoods. From the point of view of the transient visitor, the two most important bairros in Rio are **Copacabana,** with its justly famous strand and the city's highest concentration of fine hotels, and **Ipanema,** with Rio's best restaurants and boutiques, and its own beach of world renown. **Leme,** an extension of Copacabana, and **Leblon,** connected to Ipanema, are two other bairros close to the center of tourist activities. Slightly more remote are the oceanfront neighborhoods of **Vidigal** and **São Conrado,** where two of the city's most elegant resort hotels are located.

Farther out along the ocean coast is the bairro of **Barra da Tijuca,** a nine-mile (15 km) stretch of beach developing rapidly into a site of residential condominiums and sprawling shopping malls. Beyond Barra is Rio's only remaining stretch of pristine, still somewhat sparsely populated ocean beach, **Recreio dos Bandeirantes,** where shantytowns and weekend homes of the well-to-do stand side by side—a perfect place to escape the city's other swollen weekend beaches.

Other bairros of Rio that readers of this guide will become familiar with in the course of the narrative are **Botafogo** and **Flamengo,** the once-fashionable bayfront neighborhoods, still the center of yachting in Rio, and home to some exceptionally good gourmet and seafood restaurants. **Laranjeiras, Glória, Catete,** and **Lapa** are neighborhoods that all have their individual charms and attractions, and are closer in to the Centro, Rio's modern and active commercial and cultural downtown hub. **Cosme Velho,** jumping-off point for the ascent to **Corcovado**—affording from its summit one of the most extraordinary views you will ever get of any city—and **Santa Teresa** are two vest-pocket neighborhoods, off the beaten track, where many houses of Rio's past eras are preserved. The **Parque Nacional da Tijuca** is Rio's great inner-city national park, set among the slopes of various connected hills and mountains. **Gávea** offers golf and shopping, and **Urca** is a quietly elegant neighborhood at the foot of Sugar Loaf Mountain, the other spectacular promontory offering for its part a view of Rio from the edge of the sea.

STREET MAPS   Maps are available, for a fee, at most of the above-mentioned information centers, or they can be purchased at local bookstores and newsstands, including those at the airport and bus station. For car travel, buy a copy of the *Quatro Rodas,* a Brazilian road guide complete with a country map.

2. GETTING AROUND

Public transportation in Rio—mostly a network of buses—is quite extensive. Most tourists, though, are likely to get around the city by cab or on transportation provided by a tour company for a particular excursion.

BY SUBWAY   The subway goes no farther into the Zona Sul than its terminal station in Botafogo, but this is the best means of public transportation for getting around in downtown Rio. To take advantage of this thoroughly clean and modern system, you must first get to the Botafogo station by either cab or bus. From there the many stops within the city will bring you within close range of your downtown destination. Change from *linha* 1 (line 1) to *linha* 2 (line 2) at the Estácio station for the bus terminal in São Cristóvão or Maracanã Stadium. Another important line 1 stop in the Centro is Cinelândia, for the Teatro Municipal and the Sala Cecília Meirelles. This is also the closest stop to the in-town Santos Dumont Airport, where you get the air shuttle to São Paulo or any number of air-taxi services to resorts like Búzios.

BY BUS   For most tourists, riding the public buses, even the *frescãos,* is not recommended. The public buses—which are virtually free from the standpoint of a tourist's purse—are crowded, driven maniacally, and too often (since they have been, on occasion, targets for roving bandits), dangerous. That said, the odds of a safe bus ride are still overwhelmingly in your favor. And if you've got the desire, buses can take you to virtually every corner of the city for next to nothing. Some of the best routes are those that follow the seaside avenues. Bus stops are indicated by signs with the word "Ônibus," but buses must be flagged, since there are no automatic stops except at the beginning and the end of the lines. You enter the rear of the bus and get off from the front. Travel with a lot of small change, since fare takers will not accept large bills, and often don't even have change for smaller ones. Buses marked "Metro" go to the subway station in Botafogo, while those indicating "Castelo" go downtown. It is generally possible to ride the bus hassle-free along the beachfront, say, from one end of Ipanema beach to the other end of Leblon. The open-sided buses called *jardineiras* exist for this purpose.

The downtown terminal for the air-conditioned special buses is **Menezes Cortes,** Rua São José (tel. 224-7577). Here you can not only board a frescão back to the Zona Sul after a day in the Centro, but also catch buses to Petrópolis, Teresópolis, and other side-trip destinations within the state.

BY STREETCAR & PASSENGER TRAIN   The Carioca subway stop places you near the terminal point of Rio's only remaining streetcar line, the **bonde,** which makes the dramatic ride over the *arcos,* the arched structure of an 18th-century aqueduct, to the historical hillside neighborhood of Santa Teresa. The bonde, which is ridden by thousands of commuters daily, is by reputation the most dangerous of all Rio's public transports. Despite the presence of special police, the open-sided trolleys are vulnerable to hit-and-run assaults by roving street urchins.

Few **passenger trains** leave Rio for out-of-state destinations. But there is still a train running to the relatively nearby city of Belo Horizonte. The Dom Pedro II train station is located in the Centro off Praça Cristiano Ottoni (tel. 233-1494) while the Estação Barão de Mauá is on Avenida Francisco Bicalho, also downtown (tel. 296-1244).

BY TAXI   There are three varieties of cabs in Rio. Most plentiful are the **common**

RIO ORIENTATION

SANTO CRISTO

Av. Marechal Floriano
Av. Presidente Vargas
Buenos Aires
Campo de Santana
CENTRO
Nilo Peçanha
República
Dantas
do Chile
Av. Rio Branco
Av. Mem de Sá
Av. Kubitschek
Pres.
Av. G. Justo

LAPA
Praça Mahatma Gandhi

TUNNEL
GLÓRIA
CATETE
Av. Augusto Severo
Av. Beira Mar
Av. Infante don Henrique
Praia do Flamengo

Guanabara Bay

FLAMENGO

TUNNEL
① **Praia de Botafogo**
Av. João-Luiz-Alves
URCA PÃO DE AÇÚCAR

✝
CORCOVADO MTN.
Jardim Botânico
Av. Pasteur
Av. Portugal
②
Praia Vermelha

BOTAFOGO
Nações Unidas
LEME

Rodrigo de Freitas Lake
Praia do Leme

COPACABANA
Praia de Copacabana
Av. Atlântica

Ocean

IPANEMA
Praça General Osório
Av. Vieira Souto
Praia de Ipanema

Atlantic

Information ⊘

Church ■✝

American Express ①
Cable Car ②
Santos Dumont Airport ③

metered cabs, small cars painted yellow, which are hailed from the street or from official taxi queues throughout the city. The meter has two flag settings, labeled 1 and 2. The no. 2 setting adds 20% to the fare and is used after 11pm, on Sundays and holidays, when outside the old city limits, or when climbing particularly steep inclines, like the access road to Corcovado. Meters are seldom calibrated to keep up with Brazil's inflation. The meter reading, instead, is used as a base, and the true price is calculated by reference to the *tabela,* an official table of updated equivalents that should be posted on the vehicle's rear window. Brazilians usually quote the meter figure aloud, and look closely over the driver's shoulder while he consults his own copy of the tabela. Thus do Cariocas themselves try to keep from being overcharged by Rio's notorious meter hacks, who have become particularly devious as a result of runaway inflation and the high cost of fuel.

The second type of cab is the **radio taxi** (general number 260-2022), which can be hailed on the street or called for by phone. One reliable company is **Coopatur** (tel. 290-1009). The fare of a radio taxi seems to be roughly twice that of a metered cab when both are playing by the official rules. Radio-cab drivers will often try to sign on with you for your entire stay, which, if the price and the driver are agreeable, can be a beneficial relationship to both parties.

Finally, there are the **luxury cabs.** Most first-class hotels have a fleet of these cars and the fare is generally four times what a metered cab ought to cost. The exorbitant price of the private cars makes the inevitable hassles with metered-cab drivers all the more frustrating, since on occasion you can feel stranded between options, all of which are unacceptable.

BY CAR   In terms of car rentals, you are probably best off limiting your patronage to **Hertz, Avis,** or **Budget.** Then, if something goes wrong—as not infrequently occurs in the case of cars rented throughout South America—there will be someone nearby to whom you can forward your complaints. Hertz (tel. 398-3162) and Avis (tel. 398-3093) have locations at the international airport, and all three companies have outlets in Copacabana: Hertz, Av. Princesa Isabel 334 (tel. 275-4996, or toll free in Brazil 011/800-8900); Avis, Av. Princesa Isabel 150 (tel. 542-4249, or toll free in Brazil 011/800-8787); and Budget, Av. Princesa Isabel 254 (tel. 275-3244). The Avenida Princesa Isabel is a principal access route in Copacabana between the Centro and the northeastern shore in one direction and the city's southern beaches and southwestern shore in the other.

FAST FACTS   RIO

American Express   There's an office at Praia de Botafogo 228, bloco A, 5th floor, sala 514 (tel. 552-7299), that's open Monday through Friday from 9am to 6pm.

Area Code   The area code for Rio is 021.

Babysitters   Consult the concierge in your hotel.

Bookstores   The most interesting bookstore in Rio may be Kosmos, located downtown at Rua do Rosário 155, a shop specializing in hardcover books, as well as old prints and engravings. If you're looking for a paperback classic, try the Leblon bookshop Argumento, Rua Dias Ferreira 199 (tel. 239-5294).

Car Rentals   See "Getting Around," earlier in this chapter.

Climate   See "When to Go," in Chapter 2.

Crime   See "Safety," below.

Currency Exchange   If you enter Cambitur, Rua Visconde de Pirajá 414 (tel. 287-2244), and wish to change money, the rather formidable-looking guard will admit you to the "bank room" in the back of the store, and there you will be able to trade dollars or traveler's check for cruzeiros at near the daily parallel rate. Cambitur is open Monday through Friday from 9am to 6pm. *Warning:* One block down and across the street is another cambio, the Casa Piano, which I do not recommend. These days, what with the innumerable monetary reforms constantly in progress, you can often do just as well changing money at the Banco do Brasil, or in your hotel.

Dentist   In the event you require a dentist for emergency treatment and you are unable to obtain a reference from your hotel or consulate, try the Policlínica, Rua Barata Ribeiro s/n (tel. 275-4697), or Dentário Rollin, Rua Cupertino Durão 81, Leblon (tel. 259-2647).

Doctor   The Rio Health Collective, Av. Ataulfo de Paiva 135, Suite 1415 (tel. 325-9300 or 511-0949), refers travelers to English-speaking doctors in every area of medicine.

Drugstores   There are 24-hour-a-day drugstores (*farmácias de plantão*) operating in neighborhoods throughout Rio. Again, check for the most convenient location through your hotel staff. In Copacabana, try the Piaui, Av. Barata Ribeiro 646 (tel. 255-3959); in Leme, the Leme, Av. Prado Júnior 237A (tel. 275-3847).

Embassies and Consulates   Embassies are located in the nation's capital, Brasília. Some consulates in Rio are: United States, downtown (Centro) at Av. Presidente Wilson 147 (tel. 292-7117); Canada, also in the Centro section at Rua Dom Gerado 35 (tel. 233-9286); the U.K., in Flamengo at Praia do Flamengo 284, on the second floor (tel. 552-1422); and Australia, in Botafogo at Rua Voluntários da Pátria 45, on the second floor (tel. 286-7922).

Emergencies   The first place to turn for help is your hotel staff, if at all possible under the circumstances. Many hotels have physicians on duty or on call. During regular business hours, your consulate is also a reasonable place to turn for advice on medical care, and for doctor or dentist referrals. (See "Hospitals," below, for additional information).

Eyeglasses   If suddenly you find yourself in need of a new pair of glasses, your best bet would be one of the major eyeglass chains, Ótica Brasil or Ótica do Povo, with affiliated branches in all the city's major shopping centers (see "Savvy Shopping" in Chapter 6). There's a branch of Ótica Brasil at Rua Visconde de Pirajá 282 (tel. 287-2776); a branch of Ótica do Povo is nearby at Rua Visconde de Pirajá 121.

Hairdressers and Barbers   All luxury and first-class hotels have their own—sometimes unisex—hairdressers. Most American travelers in Brazil will therefore not have to leave their hotels when seeking a shampoo, a haircut, or styling. These facilities at the top hotels, like restaurants and bars, are generally open to the public. Standard barbershops seem to be well concealed in Brazil, although your hotel staff will be able to direct men who want to treat themselves to the luxury of a cheap and close shave done the old-fashioned way. Prices for beauty and barbershop services vary from hotel to hotel, but are generally 30% to 50% cheaper than in the U.S.

Holidays   See "When to Go" in Chapter 2.

Hospitals   Among the hospitals offering emergency care in Rio 24 hours a day are the Hospital Miguel Couto, Rua Mario Ribeiro 117, Gávea (tel. 274-6050), and the Hospital Souza Aguiar, Praça da República 111, Centro (tel. 296-4114). Telephone operators at these hospitals are not likely to speak English, however. Private clinics will more probably have staff and doctors who do speak English and other languages. One conveniently located clinic is the Centro Médico Ipanema, Rua Anibal Mendonça 135, in Ipanema (tel. 239-4647); you can also try the Clínica São Vincente, Rua João Borges 204, Gávea (tel. 529-4422).

Private ambulance services include the Clinic Savior (tel. 227-6187 or 227-5099) and Pullman (tel. 236-1011 or 257-4132). You can also dial 193 for a central ambulance referral service.

Information   See "Tourist Information," earlier in this chapter.

Laundry and Dry Cleaning   If you don't want to take advantage of your hotel's quick, convenient laundry and dry cleaning services, try Laundromat, Rua Miguel Lemos 56, Copacabana.

Libraries   The Biblioteca Nacional, Av. Rio Branco 219, Centro (tel. 240-8929), open Monday to Friday from 9am to 8pm, and Saturday from 9am to 3pm; the Biblioteca Pública do Estado do Rio de Janeiro, Av. Presidente Vargas 1216 (tel. 224-6184), open Monday to Friday from 9am to 8pm.

Lost Property   Try the central branch of the post office, downtown, Av. Presidente Vargas 3077 (tel. 273-8222), open Monday to Friday from 8am to 6pm, and on Saturday till noon. The tourist office suggests that you call 159 to report lost property.

Luggage Storage and Lockers There are a minimum number of lockers available at the international airport, at the in-town Santo Dumont airport, and at the main downtown bus station, Rodoviária Novo Rio, Av. Francisco Bicalho 1 (tel. 291-5151). For short-term storage—after checking out, and before traveling—most hotels are willing to cooperate.

Newspapers and Magazines The two major daily papers in Rio are the *Jornal do Brasil*, and O *Globo*. There are 24-hour-a-day newsstands in Ipanema on Praça General do Osório and Praça N. S. da Paz, and downtown on the Praça XV.

Police The police emergency number is 190, which may be dialed from any pay phone without a token.

Post Office There are numerous branches of the post office in the Zona Sul. Avenida Nossa Senhora de Copacabana, which runs parallel to the oceanside Avenida Atlântica the length of Copacabana beach, has two postal branches, at nos. 540 and 1298. In Ipanema there is a branch in the principal square, Praça General Osório. Post office hours tend to be from 8am to 5pm weekdays, on Saturday till noon. The post office at the international airport is open 24 hours a day. Postcards and letters can also be mailed through the porter's desk of your hotel.

Radio Rádio Jornal do Brasil, 940 AM, specializes in Brazilian pop music and newscasts. Rádio Globo, 92.5 FM, features a range of Brazilian and international musical selections; Rádio 105 FM is the youth culture, rock station.

Religious Services The Mosteiro São Bento, Rua Dom Gerado 68, Centro (tel. 291-7122), offers a 10am mass on Sunday with Gregorian chanting by the monks; for Jewish services on Friday at 6:30pm and Saturday at 9:30am, there is the Associação Religiosa Israelita, Rua Gen. Severiano 170, Botafogo (tel. 295-6444); the Lutheran church, Rua Carlos Sampaio 251, Centro (tel. 323-8548), has Sunday services in German; there is a Methodist church on Rua Jardim Botânico 648, in Jardim Botânico (tel. 294-9179), with services on Sunday at 6pm; the Anglican Igreja do Cristo, Rua Real Grandeza 99, Botafogo (tel. 226-2978), has a Sunday mass at 8am; and the Catedral Presbiteriana, Rua Silva Jardim, Centro (tel. 262-2330), has a service on Sunday at 10am.

Restrooms Public restrooms can be found in most hotel lobbies; in a pinch, head for the best restaurant in your vicinity, where you are will likely meet no objection to using the facilities.

Safety For a general orientation to safety, see Chapter 2, Section 3. In Rio, follow the crowds; there is safety in numbers. Stay off the beaches at night, and travel by cab when going any distance to and from your hotel after dark.

Taxes See "Fast Facts: Brazil" in Chapter 2, under the entry "Taxes."

Taxis See "Getting Around," earlier in this chapter.

Telegrams and Telex You can send your telegrams through International Cables by Telephone (tel. 000222). If you are a guest at a first-class hotel, send telex or fax transmissions through the front desk.

Telephones Telephone centers—quieter and more comfortable than street pay phones—are in locations throughout the city. There are centers open 24 hours a day in Copacabana at Av. Nossa Senhora de Copacabana 462, in the Centro at Praça Tiradentes 41, in the Novo Rio bus terminal, and at the international airport. Other centers with fixed schedules are in Ipanema at Rua Visconde de Pirajá 111 (open from 6:30am to 11pm), in the Santos Dumont Airport (open from 6am to 11:30pm), in the downtown Menezes Cortes bus terminal (open on weekdays from 6:30am to 10:30pm), and at Barra Shopping, in Barra da Tijuca (open from 10am to 10pm Monday through Saturday).

Pay phones require *fichas*, slotted slugs which can sometimes be hard to come by, even if the public apparatus itself is in functioning order. Try to find a newsstand or a tobacconist who may sell the tokens, or if you plan to use the pay-phone system a lot, stock up at a telephone center.

Transit Information There is no central number; the desk clerk at your hotel should be able to provide this information.

3. NETWORKS & RESOURCES

Most of the networks and resources you will find in large cities like New York, London, and Los Angeles are simply not available throughout Brazil, including Rio. There is, for example, no rape crisis center and no counseling for gay men or lesbians. The special services or discount prices you might expect to find in the U.S. for students and seniors also do not exist here.

Some of the important resources that do exist are:

- **The Centro Valorizacão da Vida** The Center for the Valorization of Life operates various suicide hotlines (tel. 254-9191, 254-9393, and 256-6738).
- **Alcoólicos Anónimos** Alcoholics Anonymous has several telephone numbers: 233-4813, 253-9965, 235-3086, and 240-6738.
- The **NEDAD** drug addiction center (tel. 284-8322).

RIO ACCOMMODATIONS

Rio, in case you've missed the point, is a beach town. The best hotels, a good portion of the entertainment and shopping scenes, and the preponderance of popular eating spots are all located in the beach neighborhoods of the Zona Sul, particularly in Copacabana, Leme, Ipanema, and Leblon. Slightly more remote, but compensatingly luxurious and self-contained, are two resort hotels in the beachside neighborhoods of Vidigal and São Conrado. It makes no sense to stay in one of the many hotels located downtown, the Centro. There is virtually no residential life downtown, and so the streets tend to be empty after dark, except in the immediate vicinity of the Teatro Municipal or other nightspots. You may want to play downtown some nights, but all except the most confirmed inner-city buffs and students engaged in their rites of passage with budget to match will want to wake up to the smell of salt water and the sound of the surf. The best crash-pad lodgings for backpackers, students, and other budget tourists can probably be found in Flamengo, where the back streets are appropriately threadbare and the location is advantageous, close to both the Centro and Copacabana.

It is *not* wise to arrive in Rio without a hotel reservation. Since most visitors apparently wish to stay on the beach in Copacabana or Ipanema, and since there are few potential construction sites in these neighborhoods for new seaside hotels, the number of available rooms is limited. During the peak season—in the summertime from Christmas until after Carnival, and in the winter during the July school holiday, and on holiday or special-event weekends throughout the year—Rio's hotels easily fill to capacity. Even during the so-called off-season in Rio, if you arrive without a reservation, you are unlikely to secure a satisfactory room in a prime location with a view of the beach. You may have to settle for a perfectly nice room several blocks from the strand. This may not be the end of the world, but if your expectation of a Rio vacation includes a view of Copacabana's magnificent sweeping curve, you may be disappointed.

Most hotels add a 10% service surcharge to their bills, which will apply to package clients only when they purchase extras like midnight room service, poolside drinks, restaurant meals, and so forth. A characteristic attraction of Rio's hotels is that you can stay in the best room in town for much less than what a room of comparable quality would cost in New York, London, or Paris. With the package-rate reductions further cutting the price quoted at the reception desk by up to an additional 30%, Rio delivers a lot of comfort in its lodgings at wholesale prices.

There is certain standard equipment in most of Rio's tourist hotel rooms. Bathrooms generally have bidets, a reminder of the continental influence in Brazil. The minibar was almost certainly American-inspired, and it is not one of our most admirable cultural contributions. Even the most underrated rooms contain these little refrigerators now, stocked with overpriced beverages and snacks. It's easy to beat the minibar monopoly, however. Do a little shopping at the food store in your hotel's neighborhood and stock the refrigerator with your favorite items—which will cost you a quarter of what the hotel wants to charge you. Your room may also contain a small private strongbox called a *cofre*. There is generally a daily fee for its use at most hotels, and the key may be obtained at the reception desk.

APARTMENT RENTAL SERVICES   Those who wish the option of renting a fully equipped apartment in Rio should contact one of the following services.

Fantastic Rio, Av. Atlântica 974, Apt. 501, Leme (tel. 021/541-0615, fax 021/237-4774, telex 21/23602), can offer you one of 25 luxury beach apartments, ranging in price from $30 a day for a one-bedroom flat, to $140 a day for a four-bedroom apartment right on the Avenida Atlântica.

Yvonne Reimann, Av. Atlântica 4066, Apt. 605, Copacabana (tel. 021/227-0281), has a chain of 20 first-class apartments, fully equipped, which she rents to tourists vacationing in Rio. Her prices, based on a minimum stay of one week, begin at $30 a night for a two-room flat, accommodating up to three persons.

1. COPACABANA & LEME

Copacabana and Leme are the names given to a 7km- (4¼-mile)-long, cove-shaped beach just south of the entrance to Guanabara Bay and to the residential neighborhoods that embrace it. Three quarters of the beach belongs to the Copacabana end, one of the world's most densely populated neighborhoods, according to the local claim. Leme beach, at the opposite end of the mushroom-cap curve, is a tiny, quiet neighborhood, one of Rio's most charming. The beach is an unobstructed wide stretch of white sand and rugged, pounding surf. The boundary line of the two neighboring bairros is the wide Avenida Princesa Isabel, which tunnels under a mountainous spine and goes on toward Botafogo and the Centro. Watching the sun go down over Copacabana from some perch high above the ground, and seeing the electric lights begin to sparkle in the dark of a clear southern sky and streak along the empty strand and up and down the neighboring mountains, few will avoid surrender to a subversive reflection on the infinite value of pure idleness.

VERY EXPENSIVE

COPACABANA PALACE HOTEL, Av. Atlântica 1702, Rio de Janeiro. Tel. 021/255-7070. Fax 021/235-7330. Telex 21/21482. 122 rms, 103 suites. A/C MINIBAR TV TEL

$ Rates: $130–$195 single; $145–$220 double; $295–$420 suite. AE, DC, MC, V.

Before the era of the high-rise five-star hotels, this was the best address in Rio, and many travelers still hold to that opinion. Thanks to recent multimillion-dollar renovations, the Riviera-style grand hotel is guaranteed a bright place in Rio's pantheon of hotels for years to come. The Copacabana Palace doesn't market to package tours, but the hotel does a brisk business with individuals, groups, and conventions. The well-heeled tend to favor this palazzo over the less formal atmosphere of the newer fine hotels. And who is to gainsay their choice? A suite at the Copacabana Palace is still a way to treat yourself royally when staying in Rio.

Like a fancy centerpiece, the Copacabana Palace stands near the midpoint of the beach. Today the seven-story building of carved stone has been combined with a more modern 10-story annex. A circular drive leads past several elegant shops (jewelers, florist, bookstore) into a lobby which conveys a European-style reserve, almost a clublike atmosphere.

Those rooms and suites along the front of the building are smallish but bright, furnished in mahogany. Armchairs and sofas are newly upholstered in fine floral-patterned fabrics, and baths are tiled, though small. The pricier rooms face the sea.

Suites are sizable and luxuriously appointed, with a separate sitting room. Baths in the suites are mostly large and old-fashioned in white porcelain and tiles, with a pedestal sink and freestanding tub. All units have high ceilings although most are without balconies.

Dining/Entertainment: To one side of the hotel is the glassed-in and casual Pergula restaurant, behind which spreads one of Rio's largest swimming pools, with outdoor tables, chairs, and waiter service. The Bife de Ouro restaurant is one of Rio's finest without the pyrotechnic flashiness of French service, and prices are very reasonable (about $21 to $38 per person for dinner). There's also a 500-seat theater hosting numerous productions, starring many well-known Brazilian and international artists.

Services: The Copacabana Palace offers numerous amenities, such as parking, room service, and an in-house beauty salon.

Facilities: Swimming pool, 14 different function rooms with a total capacity of 2,500 persons.

INTERNATIONAL RIO, Av. Atlântica 1500, Rio de Janeiro. Tel. 021/ 295-2323. Fax 021/542-5443. Telex 21/39614. 177 rms, 13 suites. A/C MINIBAR TV TEL
$ Rates: $123–$146 single; $134–$165 double. AE, DC, MC, V.
A relatively new hotel along the Copacabana strand is located not far from the Hotel Ouro Verde and approaching the Leme end of the beach. The International Rio offers rooms in a first-class tourist-hotel setting. Among its amenities are two bars, a restaurant, 24-hour room service, valet parking, a rooftop pool, and a meeting/ convention room with a capacity of 25 to 250 participants.

MERIDIEN, Av. Atlântica 1020, Rio de Janeiro. Tel. 021/275-9922. Fax 021/541-6447. Telex 21/23183. 500 rms. A/C MINIBAR TV TEL
$ Rates: $160–$200 single; $180–$220 double. AE, DC, MC, V.
The posh Meridien occupies one corner of the intersection where Avenida Princesa Isabel leads to downtown Rio, at the boundary between Copacabana's red-light district and the staid, family neighborhood of Leme beach. The Meridien is Leme's only luxury hotel, and is a favorite of European tourists. With its 37 floors of glass and steel, the Meridien is a portent of the architectural change bound one day to transform the skyline of this famous strand. The lobby is all business, designed not for lingering but to funnel guests and visitors efficiently to various facilities.

Modern in every way, the rooms are decorated in bright pastel shades, with ultramodern furnishings. There are no balconies. The ample windows are sealed and equipped with blackout draperies. All rooms offer safe-deposit boxes.

One of the Meridien's best assets is its location in Leme. This section of the beach is pleasantly quiet, especially on weekdays. Both on Avenida Atlântica and the parallel Avenida Gustavo Sampaio, a block from the ocean, are several attractive hangouts and some excellent restaurants. All the necessary neighborhood stores and services can be found among Leme's few back streets: a pharmacy, newsstand, stand-up corner bar, laundry, and more.

Dining/Entertainment: The hotel has two fine restaurants: on the ground floor, the Café de la Paix; and on the roof, the St. Honoré, with its reputation for gourmet dishes and one of the city's great panoramic views. There is a popular disco, Rio Jazz Club, open only to guests and private members, and a bar.

Services: 24-hour room service, parking, and beach service (providing towels and umbrellas).

Facilities: Facilities include a shopping arcade, a small movie theater, computerized conference rooms, a pool, and barber and beauty shops.

RIO ATLÂNTICA SUITE HOTEL, Av. Atlântica, 2964, Rio de Janeiro. Tel. 021/255-6332. Telex 21/36893. 228 rms and suites. A/C MINIBAR TV TEL
$ Rates: $100 single, $130–$140 single suite; $110 double, $140–$150 double suite; $200 Oceanic Suite. AE, DC, MC, V.
Copacabana's newest choice hotel, the Rio Atlântica Suite Hotel, is the first deluxe

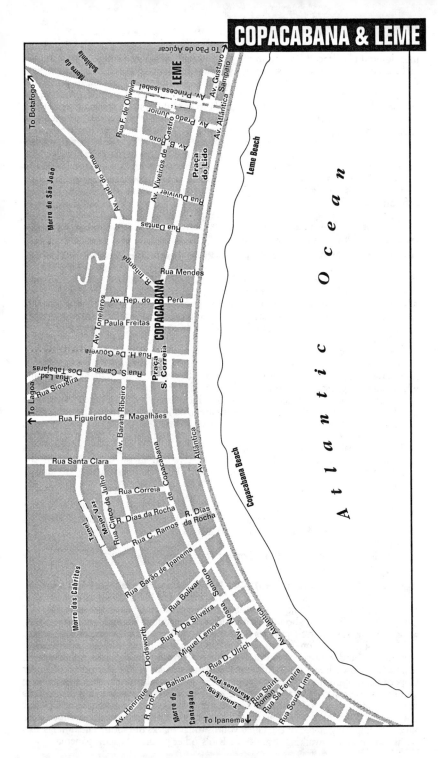

COPACABANA & LEME

establishment to open along the beachfront in many years. Spread over 18 floors, the marble- and glass-faced Rio Atlântica would seem to squeeze snugly into a market niche all its own on Rio's most famous strand—being half the size of its two elegant five-star competitors, the Rio Palace and the Meridien, and therefore providing, presumably, more intimate service and surroundings. As for the accommodations, the emphasis here is on suites, the hotel's attempt to appeal to business executives in town on moderately extended stays. The spaciousness of the lobby and the presence of a rooftop pool suggest that, despite its apartment-building scale, the hotel possesses some of the self-contained ambience of a genuine, full-service resort that characterizes Rio's most luxurious establishments. Depending on how quickly the hotel catches on, the Atlântica Suite could offer quality digs at bargain prices for a year or two. The sea-fronting Oceanic Suite also promises to be an eye-catcher.

Dining/Entertainment: There's a Swiss-style restaurant, the Helvetica, and a café-brasserie, the Ao Ponto.

Services: Massage, parking.

Facilities: No-smoking floors, rooms for the handicapped, rooftop pool, Nautilus machines, and an auditorium.

RIO OTHON PALACE, Av. Atlântica 3264, Rio de Janeiro. Tel. 021/255-8812. Fax 021/263-4564. Telex 21/22655. 606 rms. A/C MINIBAR TV TEL

$ Rates: From $135 single; from $162 double. AE, DC, MC, V.

The Rio Othon Palace, located toward the southern end of Copacabana beach, is a 30-story brown-glass tower that is spaced between its neighbors in such a way that every one of its rooms offers at least a partial water view. Call the Othon semideluxe. It has all the five-star amenities, and caters heavily to package-tour operators. Many Americans spend their stays very enjoyably at the Othon Palace.

The atmosphere is one of constant motion, and the public areas—the tiny pool, the rooftop bar—have a worn-out look in places. Unlike the other large beachfront hotels, the Othon Palace lacks transitional space between the sidewalk and the lobby, which subjects guests to a gauntlet of hustlers right up to the entrance.

All the rooms have balconies, and they have been recently redecorated with tasteful streamlined furnishings. Bathrooms are lined in marble, and accommodations provide in-house video and multilingual TV channels.

Dining/Entertainment: The Estância Restaurant on the third floor serves *churrasco* (steaks and grilled meats, Brazilian style) and is worth a try for its panoramic view of the beach. Breakfast is served in lavish buffet style in the Samambaia coffee shop, also on the third floor. Other facilities include an "underground" disco in the basement.

The rooftop Skylab bar opens to a sun deck with a small open-air pool. The Skylab is one of the hotel's most popular drawing cards, attracting a steady flow of local residents as well as guests. Small wonder, as the bar is aptly named. This is the best close-up view of the hills behind Copacabana.

Services: Parking, massage.

Facilities: There is a small pool on the roof, as well as an exercise club, a beauty salon, and a business center.

RIO PALACE, Av. Atlântica 4240, Rio de Janeiro. Tel. 021/521-3232. Fax 021/227-1454. Telex 21/21803. 418 rms. A/C MINIBAR TV TEL

$ Rates: $160–$190 single; $180–$210 double. AE, DC, MC, V.

The Rio Palace is about the number-one choice for visiting North Americans, and the staff actively pursues the American tourist market. Independent of this possible attraction for some, the Rio Palace is above all one of the most comfortable and best-situated hotels in all of Rio de Janeiro. Two tall U-shaped towers in brown-hued tones of stone and glass occupy the farthest corner of Copacabana, opposite the beach's end which borders a historical site, a diminutive and still-active military fort. (Out of the old barracks, a group of young lieutenants marched in open rebellion one morning in 1922 and confronted a superior government force about halfway up the beach, where several of their number were killed; an imposing statue of the fallen youths today marks the spot.) The hotel is also within five minutes' walking distance of Rio's other premier beach, Ipanema.

All rooms at the Rio Palace have sheltered balconies, half of which face an interior court and overlook a swimming pool; the other half give some eye-filling views of the surrounding sea. The terrace at poolside is probably one of the most popular spots in Rio to languish in the noonday heat, or to soak up evening cocktails and pay tribute to the setting sun. As you look out beyond the terrace wall, you'll see the madcap scene of Rio's early-morning exercise mania unfolding on the beach below, as walkers, joggers, and bike riders share the wide, beach-long sidewalk with its famous mosaic pattern of undulating black lines against a sea of white.

The rooms are large and offer every comfort in tasteful furnishings. The hotel features a CNN satellite channel and regularly scheduled English-language movies.

Dining/Entertainment: Le Pré Catelan is the hotel's principal restaurant, contributing to the Rio version of haute cuisine. Excellent food is served in the Atlantis restaurant, off the pool. And here in the morning a groaning breakfast buffet is set up with pastries, fruits, juices, meats, and cheeses, along with chafing dishes of bacon and eggs. Coffee and milk are served piping hot directly at your table.

A favorite congregating place, day or night, is the lobby bar, near the hotel's entrance. The Horse's Neck Bar and the Palace Club, a private nightclub, are perennial nightlife favorites for visitors and residents alike. Shows in the hotel's auditorium feature international talent—including Frank Sinatra on one occasion.

Facilities: Swimming pool, indoor parking, health club with sauna and massage, beauty salon, conference rooms, and an auditorium.

EXPENSIVE

CASTRO ALVES, Av. Nossa Senhora de Copacabana 552, Rio de Janeiro. Tel. 021/255-8815. Fax 021/263-4564. Telex 21/38184. 74 rms. A/C MINIBAR TV TEL
$ Rates: $50 single; $55 double. AE, DC, MC, V.

Facing the Praça Serzedelo Correira, this small Othon hotel bears the name of Brazil's most beloved poet. Public plazas are rare in Copacabana, making this small park a welcome patch of green along this street of shops, apartments, and eating spots, one block from the water. Hotel patrons also eat their buffet-style breakfast on the pleasant La Mole premises. Other than room service, there are few other amenities provided by the hotel.

The poet Castro Alves, for whom the hotel is named, was Brazil's answer to Lord Byron, a "compleat" romantic given to the self-destructive melancholia and bohemian lifestyle made popular by the English poet of that early 19th-century age. His passion for life was unrepressed in his verse, though he was cut down prematurely by consumption when only 24 years old. Alves was a great lover of his country's natural beauty, a confirmed republican, and one of the most committed voices of his time against slavery.

COPACABANA PRAIA, Rua Francisco Otaviano 30, Rio de Janeiro. Tel. 021/521-2727. Fax 021/287-3344. Telex 21/31734. 55 rms. A/C MINIBAR TV TEL
$ Rates: From $106 single; from $118 double. AE, DC, MC, V.

The Copacabana Praia is located right behind the Rio Palace, a short walking distance from both Copacabana and Ipanema beaches. All of the rooms at this very small hotel face the front and have balconies. The staff is friendly and caters with equal grace to individual clients and small groups, many of whom are from the States. Rooms are

---

IMPRESSIONS

Delay in Brazil is a climate. You live in it. You can't get away from it. It should, I think, be a source of pride to the Brazilians that they possess a national characteristic which is absolutely impossible to ignore.
—PETER FLEMING, *BRAZILIAN ADVENTURE*, 1933

fully equipped with the normal amenities and contain individual thermostats. The Pícollo restaurant/bar serves international and local food. There is a small dip pool and sun deck on the roof, and a sauna as well.

DEBRET, Rua Almirante Gonçalvez 5, Rio de Janeiro. Tel. 021/521-3332. Fax 021/521-0899. Telex 21/30483. 104 rms. A/C MINIBAR TV TEL
$ Rates: $59–$91 single; $65–$100 double. AE, DC, MC, V.

The Debret is obviously named for the romantic and naturalistic French painter Jean-Baptiste Debret, whose paintings and graphics provide a rich visual chronicle of early-19th-century life in Brazil. The hotel is a converted apartment building with newly renovated guest rooms. It actually sits on Avenida Atlântica but has its entrance on this side street. The hotel's intimate lobby, adorned with sculpture and paintings, invites lingering. The rooms in the Debret are really a cut above those in Rio's other three-star hotels in comfort and in the quality of furnishings, fixtures, and decor, which is formal colonial. The front rooms (actually in this case, the side rooms) view the ocean. A brand-new restaurant has been added to the 12th floor. Room service is available 24 hours.

HOTEL CALIFORNIA, Av. Atlântica 2612, Rio de Janeiro. Tel. 021/257-1900. 117 rms. A/C MINIBAR TV TEL
$ Rates: $85–$110 single; $95–$120 double. AE, DC, MC, V.

This hotel with the felicitous name will remind some people of the popular song with the same title. A further distinguishing mark of the 12-story Mediterranean-style building is its location smack-dab at the midpoint of the lengthy concave avenue. The closest the hotel comes to reflecting a West Coast image, however, is the bright sidewalk bar you pass at the lobby entrance, with its striped slatted chairs and tables, and multicolored umbrellas. Otherwise, the hotel has a somewhat European atmosphere, and caters to a repeat clientele of vacationers and businesspeople alike.

The rooms are very pleasant, with homey furnishings and balconies. A few deluxe rooms facing the ocean feature huge verandas with two entrances. Accommodations have large tile baths with pedestal sinks and enormous tubs. All rooms are air-conditioned, but those in beachfront accommodations may get the same effect more naturally—especially on the upper floors—by trapping the cool breezes off the ocean through an open balcony door. Some single rooms are quite small, and if they don't face the street, a bit dark as well. In addition to the marble-lined lobby, the other public spaces include a lounge, meeting rooms, and a pub with cigarbox-style paneling. Le Colonial restaurant specializes in both Brazilian and international meals. The hotel, one of the Othon group, provides guests with umbrellas and towels for the beach.

LANCASTER, Av. Atlântica 1470, Rio de Janeiro. Tel. 021/541-1887. Fax 021/263-4564. Telex 21/37858. 70 rms. A/C MINIBAR TV TEL
$ Rates: $66 interior single; $73 interior double; $90–$100 deluxe front room. Children under 8 stay free in parents' room. AE, DC, MC, V.

The Lancaster, an Othon hotel, occupies one of those smart deco buildings (this one is a converted apartment house) that grace this famous ocean avenue. Narrow and small, the building's white facade sports a rack of curved balconies. Near the Ouro Verde and Copacabana Palace, the Lancaster offers a suite-size room as its standard accommodation. Enter the lobby past a sunken sidewalk bar. Off the lobby a small game room houses a first-class table-soccer game. The Lancaster restaurant is quite small, almost family-scale, perfectly suitable for breakfast and for light meals.

The Lancaster's rooms are divided by partitions into a sitting area with TV, couch, table, and chairs, and a sleeping area with a modern bath. Only the front rooms have balconies. Rooms elsewhere overlook an interior court, and seem a bit dreary for lack of light; they also have sleeping areas that are slightly smaller than those on the avenue. Special services include a car-rental agency, babysitting, and free use of beach towels and umbrellas.

LEME OTHON PALACE, Av. Atlântica 656, Rio de Janeiro. Tel. 021/275-8080. Telex 21/23265. 166 rms, 28 suites. A/C MINIBAR TV TEL

$ Rates: $90 single; $100 double. AE, DC, MC, V.

The Leme Othon Palace is one of 10 Rio hotels in the Othon group—nine of these are located in Copacabana, and six are on the beach. It is midway into Leme, the quiet beach, and therefore probably has the best objective location of any hotel along the 7km (4¼-mile) strip. Approximately a third of the rooms in this large rectangular block offer ocean views. Rooms are adequately furnished, but otherwise nondescript. They do have covered balconies, however.

Entrance to the lobby is on a side street. The Leme Palace has the experience and capacity to handle large groups reliably.

Dining/Entertainment: A second-floor restaurant is reliable for lunch, or as a fallback for the odd evening a guest might prefer to stay close to home. The Leme Pub offers live music, and a ground-floor coffee shop recalls a saloon in Portugal with its typical blue-and-white tiles.

Services: Valet parking.

Facilities: Beauty salon.

LUXOR CONTINENTAL, Rua Gustavo Sampaio 320, Rio de Janeiro. Tel. 021/275-5252. Fax 021/541-1946. Telex 21/21469. 123 rms. A/C MINIBAR TV TEL

$ Rates: $66–$96 single; $73–$105 double. AE, DC, MC, V.

The Luxor chain has four hotels in Rio, three of which are in Copacabana or Leme. The Continental is not on the beach, but it occupies a prized location. This principal back street of Leme is a genuine neighborhood, complete with colorful street life, shops, and restaurants. The beach is only a block away. Recently redecorated, the 19-story Continental has adopted the color scheme of the other Luxor properties, making free use of vibrant and fiery shades of orange, red, and yellow.

The rooms are smaller than average, and half the baths lack tubs, but all have bidets and some have phone extensions. Only the corner rooms offer narrow views of the beach through spaces in between neighboring buildings. Otherwise the hotel looks out onto back streets and nearby hills.

Dining/Entertainment: The 320 Restaurant and Poty Bar are available for dining and drinks, to the accompaniment of live piano music. The Carmelo coffee shop occupies the mezzanine, and has its own entrance.

LUXOR COPACABANA, Av. Atlântica 2554, Rio de Janeiro. Tel. 021/257-1940. Fax 021/255-1858. Telex 21/23971. 123 rms. A/C MINIBAR TV TEL

$ Rates: $85 single, $100 superior single, $110 deluxe single; $95 double, $105 superior double, $115 deluxe double. AE, DC, MC, V.

The Luxor Copacabana is centrally located along Copacabana's sweeping curve. This early version of the glass-and-steel structure is unusually thin, and offers the unique feature of balconies with its side rooms and excellent views of the ocean. The reason for this architectural option is that the building next door sits back on the sidewalk considerably farther than the hotel, creating a welcome jog in the straight line of the long sidewalk promenade.

A predominance of natural woods—particularly *jacarandá,* or Brazilian rosewood—in the furnishings, headboards, and trims give the rooms a very masculine look. Natural plank floors stand out sharply against the bright primary colors of the decor, giving the rooms a feeling of both warmth and vitality. Lamps, ashtrays, and wall decorations are of modern design, as are the bathroom fixtures. Not all baths have tubs, but all have showers and bidets, as well as wall-phone extensions.

Front rooms have glassed-in balconies, and breakfast nooks complete with table and chairs. Corner suites that face the ocean are quite large and have spacious verandas filled with potted plants. There is excellent shopping in the boutiques on nearby side streets, and behind the hotel on Avenida Nossa Senhora de Copacabana. The hotel's terrace is home to the Fogareiro bar and restaurant. The Luxor Copacabana's rooms are divided into three categories—standard, superior, and deluxe—depending on size, location, and decorative appointments.

LUXOR REGENTE, Av. Atlântica 3716, Rio de Janeiro. Tel. 021/287-4212. Fax 021/267-7693. Telex 21/23887. 250 rms. A/C MINIBAR TV TEL

$ Rates: $84 single; $93 double. AE, DC, MC, V.

The Luxor Regente is the largest of the Luxor hotels in Rio, and is close to the Ipanema end of Copacabana beach. Not only is the Regente favorably located, it is also a very versatile hotel, since it can appeal to and accommodate individual travelers and—given its size—groups as well. During a recent stay at the Regente, my first three days were serene; then a group of vacationing Uruguayan teenagers arrived and suddenly the place felt like Fort Lauderdale at Easter. The "kids" were full of energy and enthusiasm, and—while they strained the resources a bit, especially at breakfast time—they also added a welcome carnival-style atmosphere. Groups are always coming and going at the Regente, but not every day, so that a nice balance in the public spaces is maintained between the waves of animation and peace and quiet.

Because of its labyrinthine interior—rooms are distributed among several towers and annexes—the intrinsic environment at the Regente is varied as well. I have stayed in both the older but attractive beachfront rooms with their old-fashioned verandas, and the more modern internal rooms tucked deep within the hotel and accessible by a separate bank of elevators. I prefer the former for the off-season, when the Regente is less crowded, and the latter for the high season, for the opposite reason.

The small lobby seating area makes a very comfortable cocktail lounge, with a view of beach and street life that is both intimate and removed. Service at the hotel is superb—friendly and attentive—while facilities of note include the excellent Forno e Fogão restaurant (see separate review in Chapter 5) and a large branch of the H. Stern jewelry store, staffed by salespeople who seem as intent on educating potential buyers about gemstones as they are on selling them.

MIRAMAR PALACE HOTEL, Av. Atlântica 668, Rio de Janeiro. Tel. 021/247-6070. Fax 021/521-3294. Telex 21/21508. 150 rms. A/C MINIBAR TV TEL

$ Rates: $90–$115 single; $100–$125 double. Beachfront rooms about 25% more. Off-season (Apr–Sept) $70 single; $80 double. AE, DC, MC, V.

The Miramar Palace Hotel is a near neighbor of the Rio Palace, on the southern end of the beach. Here where the fort sits, a point jutting into the sea forms a slight protective pocket from the relentless beating of the South Atlantic. A half-dozen fishing boats are still hauled to the sand at this spot, an appealing anachronism in the otherwise seamless urbanity of Copacabana. The Miramar has surveyed this prospect for some time, and has a venerable reputation.

The lobby, reached through an entrance on a side street, is strictly functional, and the two smallish elevators are slow. A stylish staircase leads to a mezzanine and a restaurant with a wide-angle window view of the beach scene across the avenue. The rooms are quite comfortable, almost homey, not at all fancy in their decor. Still, one gets the feeling of a Copacabana from a bygone age, one not too distant perhaps, but past nonetheless. Even the service is somewhat premodern, as the staff exhibits a kind of good-natured friendliness that can't be taught in hotel training seminars.

Dining/Entertainment: The large glassed-in café and bar at the edge of the sidewalk has long been a favorite place to hang out for some refreshment along the avenue. Other amenities include the Conves, a tearoom (taking afternoon tea is fashionable in Rio), the rooftop Ponto do Comando bar with an open-air deck, and a third-floor coffee shop above the restaurant, which is visible from the lobby through a central atrium. The Âncoradouro is a better-than-average dining spot, where dinner will cost $9 to $12 per person.

OLINDA, Av. Atlântica 2230, Rio de Janeiro. Tel. 021/257-1890. Fax 021/263-4564. Telex 21/38185. 96 rms. A/C MINIBAR TV TEL

$ Rates: $75–$100 single; $85–$110 double. AE, DC, MC, V.

Café-style tables and chairs occupy the sidewalk at this hotel's entrance, and are surrounded by potted plants and hedges for privacy. The Olinda also has a small but old-fashioned lobby complete with overstuffed armchairs and table lamps. A three-star hotel fronting the sea at this central location along the Copacabana beach, the Olinda is somewhat a bargain. The hotel also has a restaurant and a beauty parlor. Rooms are airy, comfortable, and cheerfully undistinguished in decor. Rooms facing the beach begin to be competitive in price with the better hotels in the area. Babysitting service is available on request.

OURO VERDE, Av. Atlântica 1456, Rio de Janeiro. Tel. 021/542-1887.
Fax 021/542-4597. Telex 21/23848. 66 rms. A/C MINIBAR TV TEL
$ Rates: $60–$65 back room; $81 front single; $100 front double. AE, DC, MC, V.

The Ouro Verde is refined and efficient, a perennial favorite of corporate travelers, journalists, and aesthetically demanding clients in general. Lacking a pool and other required amenities like hairdressers and saunas that would qualify the four-star hotel for official deluxe status, the Swiss-run Ouro Verde nonetheless has few peers in the city for quality of service and the general tastefulness of its rooms and public spaces.

Rooms are all uniquely furnished, with fine wooden pieces. Graceful watercolors decorate the walls. Embroidered towels embellish the modern combination baths. Rooms with covered verandas face the ocean. A reservation well in advance is an absolute necessity.

The Ouro Verde is located beyond the Copacabana Palace toward Leme, but still close to the central stretch of the beach. The small lobby stands at the bottom of an atrium which rises all the way to the roof. The architectural details are rich in marble and highly polished hardwood moldings and trim. An enclosed miniature garden at the rear of the lobby is the picture of a Portuguese *quintal*, an old-fashioned backyard. Off the lobby are formal sitting and reading rooms with club furnishings and tapestries. The clientele is all word-of-mouth; the hotel does not advertise, and does not accept groups.

Dining/Entertainment: The Ouro Verde Restaurant, on the mezzanine overlooking the beach, is one of Rio's most popular, serving finely turned meals on linen-covered tables made elegant by silver candlesticks, china, and crystal. A barrier of plants separates a street-level bar from the distractions of the street.

Services: Valet parking, room service.

PLAZA COPACABANA, Av. Princesa Isabel 263, Rio de Janeiro. Tel. 021/275-7722. Telex 21/31198. 165 rms. A/C MINIBAR TV TEL
$ Rates: $61 single; $68 double. AE, DC, MC, V.

The Plaza Copacabana, located on the Copacabana side of the furiously busy eight-lane access road, is an 18-story four-star hotel about two blocks from the beach. Behind the lobby is a multilevel lounge with a restaurant overlooking an atrium which rises to an unusual domed ceiling. The high-ceilinged rooms are comfortably furnished. This would be a convenient hotel for those whose interests or business took them frequently to the Centro while in Rio, since the Botafogo Metro station is just a short cab or bus ride away. Perhaps because of its location, so near the tunnel and on the fringes of the Copacabana red-light district, the Plaza is not as expensive as the typical four-star hotel. Conference facilities are available.

REAL PALACE, Rua Duvivier 70, Rio de Janeiro. Tel. 021/541-4387. Fax 021/542-2398. Telex 21/34218. 60 rms and suites. A/C MINIBAR TV TEL
$ Rates: $65–$70 single; $75–$80 double; $125 suite. AE, DC, MC, V.

The Real Palace was built in 1984 on this side street two blocks from the beach. If the rooms are compared with, say, the Lancaster's, they are much smaller, half as attractive, and almost twice the price. Suites are the hotel's best bet. They are much more elegant, and offer three times the space of the standard rooms. Suites have private saunas, shower with water massage, and two rooms—one with two large double beds and the other with leather armchairs and a couch, and a glass-topped table with four comfortable chairs. There is a small rooftop dip pool and a restaurant serving Spanish food.

TROCADERO, Av. Atlântica 2064, Rio de Janeiro. Tel. 021/257-1834.
Fax 021/263-4564. Telex 21/37856. 116 rms. A/C MINIBAR TV TEL
$ Rates: From $66 single; from $75–$100 double. AE, DC, MC, V.

The Trocadero is located at the corner of Rua Paula Freitas, two thirds of the way down the Copacabana strip. Part of the Othon group, the Trocadero has been a favorite among traditional beach hotels for many years. While not cramped, the rooms aren't terribly spacious. Standard rooms facing the hotel's interior are actually larger than the deluxe front accommodations, which have good sea views but no balconies. All rooms have old-fashioned baths with porcelain fixtures, plus writing desks.

Redecorating is overdue throughout the entire hotel, as the public spaces are beginning to look a bit shabby. Yet one senses that the clientele might prefer this old-slipper ambience over the sometimes polyester slickness of more modern second-class hotels. Standards of service remain high at the Trocadero, which is similar to the Miramar in its personalized touch.

Dining/Entertainment: Next to the lobby entrance is a sidewalk café, behind a partition of shrubs, with access to an inside bar through a separate door. The Moenda restaurant is one of the few eateries left in Copacabana where real Brazilian food is served, including the funky moqueca fish stews of Bahia.

MODERATE

ACAPULCO, Rua Gustavo Sampaio 854, Rio de Janeiro. Tel. 021/275-0022. Fax 021/275-3396. Telex 21/37854. 123 rms. A/C MINIBAR TV TEL
$ Rates (including breakfast): $39–$41 single; $44–$46 double. AE, DC, MC, V.

The Acapulco is a moderately priced alternative to the Meridien or the Leme Palace for those wishing to stay in Leme, and who want to experience the vest-pocket atmosphere of a back-street neighborhood and still be only a block from the beach. The deluxe double-occupancy rooms are large, with smallish beds, and have balconies facing the street, where the rear of the towering Meridien dominates but does not darken the skyline. Even the smaller rooms off the front have a comfortable appearance. Other features in this hostelry are parking facilities, a restaurant, and a coffee shop. The Acapulco does not charge 10% for service, which adds to its genuine bargain status.

BANDEIRANTES OTHON, Rua Barata Ribeiro 548, Rio de Janeiro. Tel. 021/255-6252. Fax 021/263-4564. Telex 21/37854. 96 rms. A/C MINIBAR TV TEL
$ Rates: $50–$65 single; $55–$70 double. AE, DC, MC, V.

The Bandeirantes Othon is a relatively small hotel built more for commercial travelers than for tourists. This stretch of Rua Barata Ribeiro has less charm than the area around Rua Santa Clara, farther to the north. The rooms are comfortable, however, and the hotel's location three blocks from Copacabana beach makes it a fair choice for budget-conscious travelers who like modern surroundings. The hotel has a coffee shop and bar, and offers limited parking as well as 24-hour room service.

COPACABANA HOTEL RESIDÊNCIA, Rua Barata Ribeiro 222, Rio de Janeiro. Tel. 021/255-7212. Fax 021/255-8872. Telex 21/39102. 100 rms. A/C MINIBAR TV TEL
$ Rates: $50 single; $60 double. AE, DC, MC, V.

Travelers of the American highways have long been familiar with motels offering "efficiency" accommodations, which always include a refrigerator and stove, along with some pots, plates, and eating utensils. The idea was that you could stop in an area of interest for several days and—especially when traveling with children—you could economize on food by preparing your own meals.

The term for such units in Brazil is "apart-hotel," generally two-room suites with bath and kitchenette. This one, the Copacabana Hotel Residência, is well located in a nice side-street quarter, and is far more modern than the old roadside cabins reminiscent of family travel in the U.S. A sitting room with attached kitchenette and a separate bedroom add spacious comfort to normal single-room hotel accommodations. There is even a separate laundry sink for washing out clothes and bathing suits. In addition to parking facilities, the hotel has a small pool, an exercise room, a sauna, and a restaurant in which the average meal will run about $12 per person. The price could make the hotel's location, three blocks from the beach, an acceptable sacrifice.

COPACABANA SOL, Rua Santa Clara 141, Rio de Janeiro. Tel. 021/257-1840. Fax 021/255-0744. Telex 21/33907. 70 rms. A/C MINIBAR TV TEL
$ Rates: $57 single; $55 double; $65 suite. AE, DC, MC, V.

While beyond Rua Barata Ribeiro, the third major avenue in from the seaside Avenida

Atlântica, this hotel is still only a 5- to 10-minute walk from the beach, and for the price, you may find the stroll worth the savings. The surrounding neighborhood is filled with good, inexpensive restaurants, and the street life is relatively quiet, yet colorful, with open-air markets and many sidewalk vendors.

The hotel is new and quite attractive in appearance, and offers features not usually required of a three-star hotel, including restaurant, bar, parking, and room service. The rooms are large and well furnished.

EXCELSIOR, Av. Atlântica 1800, Rio de Janeiro. Tel. 021/257-1950. Fax 021/256-2087. Telex 21/21076. 184 rms. A/C MINIBAR TV TEL

$ Rates: $52–$71 single; $58–$79 double. AE, DC, MC, V.

The Excelsior is a large beachfront hotel on the same block as the Copacabana Palace. Once undoubtedly a fashionable hotel, this Horsa group property is well broken in, but not without its charms. You enter from a side street into a spacious lobby where on one end a pleasant bar overlooks the ocean. A stairway leads to the mezzanine restaurant, also with a wraparound view of the beach scene, where a business buffet lunch is served daily.

The location and size of the Excelsior make the hotel popular for groups in the budget range. Rooms are larger than those in hotels constructed in more recent years. Furnishings are plain, but comfortable, and decorative prints brighten the walls. Tiled baths have large porcelain tubs. The good service and discount rates compensate for the somewhat dreary wood-paneled corridors.

PRAIA LIDO, Av. Nossa Senhora de Copacabana 202, Rio de Janeiro. Tel. 021/541-1347. 43 rms, 2 suites. A/C MINIBAR TV TEL

$ Rates: $50 single or double; $60 suite. AE, DC, MC, V.

The small Praia Lido near the Rua Duvivier cross street, is another option for the budget-minded, or to be kept in mind as an alternative for beach-area lodgings when the better hotels are booked. The lobby to the hotel is found up a flight of stairs. Suites contain private saunas.

RIO COPA, Av. Princesa Isabel 370, Rio de Janeiro. Tel. 021/275-6644. Fax 021/275-5545. Telex 21/23988. 110 rms. A/C MINIBAR TV TEL

$ Rates: From $60 single; from $70 double; $85 deluxe room. AE, DC, MC, V.

The Rio Copa is only a stone's throw from the tunnel leading to the center of the city, and three blocks from the beach. The hotel is relatively new, with double-glazed windows that effectively soundproof the rooms from the traffic below. Accommodations are spacious, with Scandinavian furnishings and baths with showers. The view above the muted din of the street is of Copacabana's rooftops, and is wide and appealing. Luxury doubles offer half again as much space as the standard rooms, but the L-shaped design and narrow dimensions of the sitting area make the space impractical. Other hotel features include executive meeting rooms, Le Baron restaurant, La Princesse bar, and a coffee shop open 24 hours a day.

Right before the tunnel on the Leme side are two private alleyways worth a quick peek if you find yourself near this stretch of the avenue. If you identify yourself at the security gate as a curious tourist, you may enter under the arch at the Edifício Winston (Av. Princesa Isabel 254), walk past the row of charming houses to the end of the alley, and climb the stone stairs. You will be climbing the leeward slope of a hill on whose opposite face is the infamous Favela de Babilônia, a shantytown of folkloric stature once memorialized in a poem by Elizabeth Bishop. The stairs rise several flights. The view from the top is confined to rooftops, but you will also suddenly be in close contact with the dense green vegetation that covers the hill, much the way it must have been long before the New World was colonized.

RISHON, Rua Francisco Sá 17, Rio de Janeiro. Tel. 021/247-6044. A/C MINIBAR TV TEL

$ Rates: $40–$45 single; $45–$50 double. AE, DC, MC, V.

The Rishon is located on a side street very close to Copacabana beach. This small hotel has large and comfortable rooms. On the roof is a small dip pool and an ample sun deck. The hotel provides room service, and houses a restaurant/bar as well, where food prices are considerably less than those charged at beachfront hotels only half a block away.

RIVIERA, Av. Atlântica 4122, Rio de Janeiro. Tel. 021/247-6060. Telex 21/23851. 108 rms. A/C MINIBAR TV
$ Rates: $59 single; $64–$90 double. AE, DC, MC, V.

The Riviera is half a block from the Rio Palace and its large neighboring arcade of chic boutiques, and the Cassino Atlântico. The nicest rooms in the Riviera face the beach. The excellent location at this tranquil end of the strand compensates somewhat for the generally worn appearance of the lobby and other public spaces, and the sparseness of the room furnishings. The hotel is in the process of a piecemeal renovation. The most expensive doubles are deluxe and include a sea view. The hotel has room service, a restaurant, and a sidewalk bar.

BUDGET

The budget hotels in Copacabana tend to be simple back-street affairs with a limited number of rooms, quite happy to maintain their status of informality in the shadow of the neighborhood's more elegant establishments. Always clean, they are the best bet for that small minority of North American travelers who come to Rio each year without prepackaged accommodations. You pay less at these hotels, and while you will not experience the inner life of a resort with its many luxuries, large and small, you will likely get a step or two closer to the average Brazilian reality.

ANGRENSE, Travessa Angrense 25, Rio de Janeiro. Tel. 021/255-0509. 36 rms. TV
$ Rates: $15 single; $25 double. AE, DC, MC, V.

The Angrense is located at the far end of a dead-end lane that's entered from Avenida Nossa Senhora de Copacabana, about 100 feet in from Rua Santa Clara. This stripped-down boardinghouse is a suitable choice for unbearded youths and superannuated bohemians alike. Many of the rooms have no air conditioning.

APA, Rua República de Perú 305, Rio de Janeiro. Tel. 021/255-8112. Fax 021/256-3628. Telex 21/30394. 54 rms. A/C MINIBAR TV TEL
$ Rates: $36 single; $45 double. AE, DC, MC, V.

Another choice in a quiet corner of the neighborhood, the Apa is a three-star hotel with two-star rates. And while the rooms are furnished in early Salvation Army, the beds are full-size twins, a rare offering for a hotel in the bargain range. Services include parking, a coffee shop, and round-the-clock room service. The Apa is about a five-minute walk from the Trocadero section of the beach.

BIARRITZ, Rua Aires Saldanha 54, Rio de Janeiro. Tel. 021/521-6552. Fax 021/287-7640. Telex 21/30366. 40 rms. A/C MINIBAR TV TEL
$ Rates: $32 single; $35 double. AE, DC, MC, V.

The Biarritz is on a narrow avenue that runs for around 10 blocks between and parallel to Avenida Atlântica and Nossa Senhora de Copacabana. The Biarritz sits a short block from the beach, right behind the Othon Palace. The marble entrance and stately awning suggest more elegance than you will find inside. Beware also of the small beds. Otherwise, there are modest but acceptable rooms, and a public TV salon. Room service is also provided.

GRANDE HOTEL CANADÁ, Av. Nossa Senhora de Copacabana 687, Rio de Janeiro. Tel. 021/257-1864. Telex 21/39371. 72 rms. A/C MINIBAR TV TEL
$ Rates: From $25 single; $27–$45 double. AE, DC, MC, V.

The Grande Hotel Canadá, located near the busy Rua Santa Clara intersection, is a two-star hotel. The rooms have been recently redecorated, and are agreeably nondescript. The hotel also has an American bar (a euphemism for a smallish alcove equipped with a traditional bar and stools). There is also a public TV room and room service.

HOTEL DIPLOMATA, Praça Demétrio Ribeiro 103, Rio de Janeiro. Tel. 021/521-4443. Telex 21/40347. 30 rms. A/C MINIBAR TV TEL

$ Rates: $32 single or double. Discounts (sometimes up to 30%) available fc paying in cash. AE, DC, MC, V.

The Hotel Diplomata is on the Praça Demétrio Ribeiro, set in from Avenida Princesa Isabel, across the street from the Suppentopf Restaurant. This is another very informal, small hotel with a good location for anyone who wants to be at the beach, but who needs quick access to downtown. Like other hotels in this area, it is but a short cab ride to the Metro stop in Botafogo. The rooms are plain and simple, with no frills.

MARTINIQUE, Rua Sá Ferreira 30, Rio de Janeiro. Tel. 021/521-4552.
Fax 021/287-7640. Telex 21/30366. 60 rms. A/C MINIBAR TV TEL
$ Rates: $32 mini-single; $35 double. AE, DC, MC, V.

 The Martinique, half a block from Copacabana beach, is every bit as comfortable as many more highly rated hotels, at half the price. The hotel is also located in the same desirable environs as the Rio Palace and the Miramar hotels, accessible by foot to both Ipanema and Copacabana. The beds are smaller than those I usually like in hotels and tend to prefer in my own home. For a large person, a small bed can be a big factor in choosing a hotel room. The hotel has a nice little lobby and a bar. Room service is also provided.

TOLEDO, Rua Domingos Ferreira 71, Rio de Janeiro. Tel. 021/257-1990. Fax 021/287-7640. Telex 21/30366. 112 rms. A/C MINIBAR TV TEL
$ Rates: $32 single; $35 double. AE, DC, MC, V.

Among Rio's two-star beach hotels, the Toledo is a cut above the average. The quiet street on which it is located is half a block from Avenida Atlântica, which it parallels. Some accommodations are unusually large. The hotel has a coffee shop and bar.

Ⓕ FROMMER'S SMART TRAVELER: HOTELS

VALUE-CONSCIOUS TRAVELERS SHOULD CONSIDER THE FOLLOWING:

1. Purchase your hotel accommodations through a travel agency or tour operator; the price will be lower than the hotel's "rack rate"—the rate you would pay right off the street.
2. If possible, travel in the off-season, mid-March to late June, and August to mid-December. Hotel rates are at their lowest during these periods, sometimes 50% lower than the high-season rate.
3. Take advantage of the breakfast that's probably included in the price of your hotel room.
4. Where hotels offer a half pension (either lunch or dinner included), it is usually cheaper for you to dine on this plan than to order meals in the hotel restaurant à la carte.
5. If your travel plans in Brazil are open-ended, or your budget does not include a stay in a first-class hotel, check at the airport tourism information counter for the location of a clean, inexpensive, and safe hotel.
6. Make your arrangements with a tour operator who knows the Brazilian market well; they may know of special hotel promotions for groups or individuals.

QUESTIONS TO ASK, ESPECIALLY IF YOU'RE ON A TIGHT BUDGET:

1. Is there a surcharge for long-distance calls? Often there is, especially in the luxury hotels.
2. Is the hotel service fee of 10% included in the quoted price of your land package?

2. IPANEMA & LEBLON

Rounding the Apoador Point and at a right angle to Copacabana are the even-longer ocean beaches of Ipanema and Leblon. At the point itself is the sizable spit of sand actually called Apoador beach, long a favorite of surfers. Ipanema then stretches on until the overflow canal of a nearby lagoon makes a natural separation between it and the continuing beach, from here designated Leblon until the abrupt end of the cove at the base of two mountain peaks called Os Dois Irmãos (The Two Brothers).

Unlike Copacabana, which is bounded on three sides by mountains, Ipanema and Leblon occupy an isthmus between the ocean and the immense inland lagoon called the Lagoa Rodrigo de Freitas, but known to all as simply Lagoa. Both neighborhoods are more modern than Copacabana, having really come into their own over the past 30 years. Ipanema and Leblon are the neighborhoods of Rio's elite, with its trendiest boutiques, most *in* restaurants, and hottest discotheques.

The chart-busting pop song "The Girl from Ipanema," by the late poet Vinícius de Morais and the very much alive musician Antônio Carlos Jobim, probably did as much to promote tourism in these neighborhoods as any other single factor. And still there are relatively few hotels in Ipanema and fewer still in Leblon, both of which retain their primary characteristic as residential neighborhoods. As a result, hotel room prices here have skyrocketed in recent years.

VERY EXPENSIVE

CAESAR PARK, Av. Vieira Souto 460, Rio de Janeiro. Tel. 021/287-3122. Fax 021/247-7975. Telex 21/21204. 220 rms. A/C MINIBAR TV TEL
$ Rates: $168–$225 single; $182–$244 double. AE, DC, MC, V.

The Caesar Park is not only the best hotel along fashionable Ipanema beach, but one of the top deluxe establishments in the entire city. Service at the Caesar Park combines the cool efficiency one associates with European hotels with the easygoing informality so typical of Brazilians. Seen from the outside, the concrete, rectilinear structure is not terribly impressive as an architectural object. But inside, attention to detail is the Caesar Park trademark. Everywhere, from the well-polished wood-paneled elevators to the walls in all public areas, are touches of decorative finish—prints, watercolors, posters—contemporary pieces that are both pretty and beguiling to the eye.

This pampering carries over to the accommodations, which are light, spacious, filled with well-stuffed furniture, and finished with the best of paints and fabrics in subtle tones reminiscent of an autumn marshland. The elegant baths are equipped with such extras as terry-cloth bathrobes, scales, hairdryers, bathing lotions, and even aftershave for men. Such thoughtful items—which are provided only in Rio's finest hotels—add an element of home comfort.

The public spaces are even more attractive than the rooms. A rooftop pool, where breakfast is served daily, offers the best view of any hotel in Rio, a 360° panorama taking in Corcovado and the Lagoa basin, the beaches of Ipanema and Leblon, and the mist-shrouded Dois Irmãos (Two Brothers) and Pedra da Gávea (Lookout Rock) mountains. This latter peak is a launching pad for hang gliders, which on occasion land on the sand near the hotel, a jolting experience if you don't see the flyer's approach and the two of you are suddenly sharing the same beach towel.

If your group or package offers the Caesar Park as an option, pay the premium and grab it. It will still be cheaper than paying the normal rates.

Dining/Entertainment: One floor below the rooftop terrace is the justly respected Petronius restaurant, specializing in fine seafood dishes. Along the corridor leading to Petronius are a series of giant tanks displaying tropical fish and crustaceans gathered from local waters. The Mariko Sushi Bar is also located on this floor.

Services: Massage, lifeguards on beach.

Facilities: Beauty shop, boutiques and newsstand, H. Stern and Amsterdam Sauer jewelry shops, sauna, banquet room, and small conference center seating up to 250 persons.

MARINA PALACE, Av. Delfim Moreira 630, Rio de Janeiro. Tel. 021/ 259-5212. Fax 021/259-0941. Telex 21/30224. 163 rms. A/C MINIBAR TV TEL
$ Rates: $128–$154 single, $142–$172 double. AE, DC, MC, V.

The Marina Palace is the best hotel on the Leblon end of the beach. Leblon is even more residential than Ipanema, but among its numerous avenues and side streets are scattered many attractions in the form of shops, restaurants, clubs, and bars.

The Marina Palace also seems strikingly close to the mountain peaks of Gávea as they are seen from the rooftop pool area, which is spread with lounging chairs for sunbathing and also has a bar. The hotel's bedrooms are adequate in every way, but lack the sparkle of other five-star hotels, and the large windows in the rooms are inexplicably sealed.

Dining/Entertainment: The second-floor restaurant, Gula, Gula, is quietly gaining in reputation among locals as a fine eating spot. The ocean view from the window seats is especially dramatic.

Facilities: Hotel facilities include meeting and banquet facilities, indoor parking, a coffee shop, a sauna, and a beauty shop.

EXPENSIVE

EVEREST RIO, Rua Prudente de Morais 1117, Rio de Janeiro. Tel. 021/287-8282. Fax 021/521-3198. Telex 21/22254. 169 rms. A/C MINIBAR TV TEL
$ Rates: $120–$145 single; $140–$170 double. AE, DC, MC, V.

The Everest Rio is on a tree-lined avenue one block from the water, directly behind the Caesar Park. While given a deluxe rating by the Brazilian tourist board, the Everest does not invite comparison with the city's finest hotels. The hotel's general appearance is streamlined and modern, but not luxurious. Rooms are very light, sporting floor-to-ceiling windows and functional Scandinavian-style furnishings.

The Everest offers special rates to business travelers who are in the city for more or less prolonged stays, and so there are often many longtime residents among the hotel's guests. The hotel does offer many first-class amenities, including a rooftop terrace 23 stories high with a stunning view from Corcovado to the sea. Other special features include a reasonably priced restaurant serving international fare, three bars located throughout the hotel, executive meeting rooms and convention facilities, a sauna, and a beauty parlor.

LEBLON PALACE, Av. Ataulfo de Paiva 204, Rio de Janeiro. Tel. 021/ 511-2000. Fax 021/274-5741. Telex 21/40498. 72 rms, 13 suites. A/C MINIBAR TV TEL
$ Rates: $70 single; $81 double. AE, DC, MC, V.

It's not on the beach, but Leblon finally has a new first-class hotel that can absorb some of the increased demand by international tourists who wish to be housed comfortably in the popular neighborhood. Rooms have plush carpets, and uncluttered, modern lines characterize the furnishings; queen-size beds are standard in many rooms.

The hotel is something of a bargain, with many facilities and services included in its modest rate, like an in-house drugstore, and an elegant lobby bar. La Cage restaurant, serving lunch and dinner menus of international cuisine, doubles up as the morning breakfast room. And the Leblon Palace hopes to attract business travelers with such features as its fully equipped meeting rooms, a business center with fax, copier, and computer, plus secretarial services.

MARINA RIO, Av. Delfim Moreira 696, Rio de Janeiro. Tel. 021/239-8844. Fax 021/259-0941. Telex 21/30224. 70 rms. A/C MINIBAR TV TEL

$ Rates: $128–$145 single; $142–$160 double. AE, DC, MC, V.

The Marina Rio is a smaller and less expensive version of the Marina Palace, and is located a block farther down the beach. Both hotels are under the same management, and guests at the Marina Rio may, for no extra charge, use all the facilities of its larger companion hotel. The accommodations of the Marina Rio are functional and roomy, also with sealed windows and without balconies. There is a second-floor restaurant and piano bar.

PRAIA IPANEMA, Av. Vieira Souto 706, Rio de Janeiro. Tel. 021/239-9932. Fax 021/239-6889. Telex 21/31280. 105 rms. A/C MINIBAR TV TEL

$ Rates: $95–$120 single; $110–$135 double. AE, DC, MC, V.

The Praia Ipanema is under the same management as the Sol Ipanema. The guest rooms are more slickly decorated than at the companion hotel, with bold designer colors for walls and fabrics. Most rooms have token balconies, which are too small for comfortable sitting. But they do add to the room's ocean view, and allow the option of natural ventilation by leaving open the balcony door.

Dining/Entertainment: La Mouette restaurant occupies the hotel's mezzanine with its own ground-level view of the local beach surroundings. A lobby bar is an additional feature.

Services: In-house hairdressing salon.

Facilities: Sun deck and a dip pool suitable for children.

SOL IPANEMA, Av. Vieira Souto 320, Rio de Janeiro. Tel. 021/267-0095. Fax 021/247-1685. Telex 21/21979. 90 rms. A/C MINIBAR TV TEL

$ Rates: $100 single; $115 double. AE, DC, MC, V.

The Sol Ipanema is located near the cross street Vinícius de Morais, named for the poet and lyricist who wrote "The Girl from Ipanema." The Garota de Ipanema pub and café, which the poet frequented, is a popular daytime hangout, one block from the hotel. Rio's most fashionable shops are also nearby.

The Sol Ipanema has rooms on 15 floors, decorated in Brazilian earth tones with a generous use of rosewood throughout. Bahian tapestries add texture and folkloric themes to the general ambience. As for the small dip pool and sun deck found on the roof, a bellhop was heard to comment that "No one comes up here." When asked why, he simply pointed to the gorgeous Ipanema beach down below and right across the street. Other features include a restaurant and bar, as well as parking facilities.

MODERATE

APOADOR INN, Rua Francisco Otaviano 177, Rio de Janeiro. Tel. 021/247-6090. Telex 21/22833. 50 rms. MINIBAR TV TEL

$ Rates: $27–$36 single; $30–$40 double, $60 oceanview double. AE, DC, MC, V.

The Apoador Inn is one of only two hotels in Rio where access to the beach does not involve crossing a heavily trafficked avenue. Located on a promenade overlooking Apoador beach, this hotel has become a particular favorite among repeat visitors to Rio. The ocean-fronting rooms are especially desirable accommodations.

While by no means fancy—many rooms in fact provide only cot-sized beds—there is a cozy familiarity about this hotel that justifies use of the term "inn" in its name. Many guests hang out, day and night, at the small coffee shop restaurant on the premises, with its unusually close-up view of the beach and the sea. The Apoador offers special discounts to "firms, diplomats, and airline personnel." Advance reservations are an absolute necessity for oceanview rooms.

ATLANTIS COPACABANA, Rua Bulhões de Cavalho 61, Rio de Janeiro. Tel. 021/521-1142. Telex 21/35392. 87 rms. A/C MINIBAR TV TEL

$ Rates: $51 single; $55 double. AE, DC, MC, V.

The Atlantis Copacabana, its name notwithstanding, is closer to Ipanema than to Copacabana, in a very attractive building on a quiet street. Given a three-star rating, the hotel is really closer to a first-class establishment, considering its general

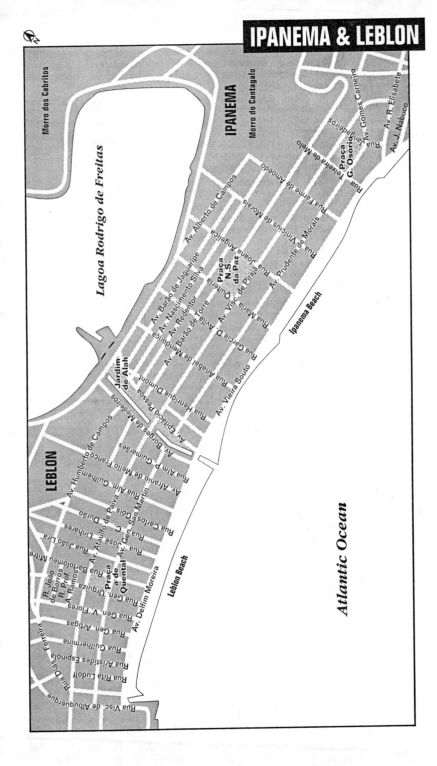

IPANEMA & LEBLON

IPANEMA

Morro do Cantagalo

Morro das Cabritos

Lagoa Rodrigo de Freitas

Av. Gomes Carneiro

Rua Teixeira de Melo

Praça
G. Osório

Rua Vendadores

Av. R. Elisabete

Av. J. Nabuco

Av. Alberto de Campos

Rua Farme de Amoedo

Rua Vinícius de Morais

Rua Prudente de Morais

Av. Barão de Jaguaripe

Av. Nascimento Silva

Rua Joana Angélica

Rua Maria Quitéria

Av. Redentor

Praça
N.S.
da Paz

Av. Visc. de Piraja

Av. Barão de Torre

Av. Henrique Dumont

Rua Garcia D'Avila

Rua Anibal de Teviâo

Jardim
de Alah

Av. Epitácio Pessoa

Av. Vieira Souto

Av. Borges de Medeiros

Rua Alm. P Guimarães

Ipanema Beach

LEBLON

Av. Humberto de Campos

Av. Afranio de Mello Franco

Rua Alm. Franco

Rua Carlos Góis

Av. Guilherme

Av. Ataulfo de Paiva

Rua José Linhares

C. Dias

Av. Gen. San Martin

Rua João Lira

Av. Bartolomeu Mitre

Praça
a de
Quental

Rua Gen. Urquiza

Av. Delfim Moreira

R. Prof.
A. Ramos

R. João
de Barros

Rua Dias Ferreira

Rua Rita Ludolf

Rua Aristides Espinola

Rua Guilhermina

Rua Gen. Artigas

Rua Gen. V. Flores

Rua Visc. de Albuquerque

Leblon Beach

Atlantic Ocean

appearance and many facilities. The room dimensions are average, but well appointed with all the comforts. There is a rooftop sun deck with pool, and two bars, one an appealing spot off the lobby, and another a piano bar called the Gaivota (Seagull), where light meals are also served.

HOTEL RITZ, Av. Ataulfo de Paiva 1280, Rio de Janeiro. Tel. 021/239-2232. Fax 021/294-1890. Telex 21/32911. 32 apts. A/C MINIBAR TV TEL
$ Rates: $70–$77 single; $76–$82 double. AE, DC, MC, V.

Repeat visitors to Rio who want to be near the active beach life yet also spend some time in a quiet part of town are encouraged to look into this residential hotel in Baixo Leblon, one of Rio's most appealing neighborhoods and only minutes from Ipanema. Baixo—or Lower—Leblon is packed with some of Rio's best restaurants and nightspots, not to mention a slew of more informal sidewalk cafés and many shops, both plain and fancy.

The Ritz offers deluxe apartments, each equipped with a large bedroom and spacious living room, plus a commodious veranda that stretches between both rooms and is accessible from either. A kitchenette, full bathroom, and a marble-topped dining table serving four and set apart from the seating area, round out the living space. The decor and furnishings are very modern but livable, and there isn't a hokey touch in the whole place. Facilities include a house restaurant and a small pool area that is almost conspiratorially intimate.

MAR IPANEMA, Rua Visconde de Pirajá 539, Rio de Janeiro. Tel. 021/274-9922. Fax 021/275-5545. Telex 21/36994. 81 rms. A/C MINIBAR TV TEL
$ Rates: $62 single; $74 double. AE, DC, MC, V.

Ipanema's newest hotel is two blocks off the beach on busy, fancy Rua Visconde de Pirajá, where many of Rio's best shops are located. The smart 14-story high-rise fronts the Praça General Osório, where the Hippie Craft Fair takes place each Sunday, and maintains acoustical isolation from its potentially noisy environs with double-plated windows. Rooms are comfortably furnished, spacious, and pleasantly decorated, and the hotel's mezzanine-level restaurant has a homey feel about it.

RIO-IPANEMA HOTEL RESIDÊNCIA, Rua Visconde de Pirajá 66, Rio de Janeiro. Tel. 021/267-4015. Fax 021/259-2191. Telex 21/37140. 117 rms and suites. A/C MINIBAR TV TEL
$ Rates: $65 double; $85 suite. 35% extra for one extra person. AE, DC, MC, V.

Rio-Ipanema Hotel Residência is an apart-hotel option for Ipanema, facing the neighborhood's principal square, the Praça General Osório. On these spacious grounds the Hippie Fair (or Feirarte, as it is officially called) is mounted every Sunday. The daily street life around the plaza is one of Rio's most colorful scenes. In addition to many stands of familiar and unfamiliar fruits and vegetables, there are multitudes of sidewalk vendors selling everything from household knickknacks to toiletry items. Among the most interesting displays are the strange assortment of roots, barks, and dried plants spread on wide patches of the sidewalk, and used for flavoring foods and for a host of medicinal teas and home remedies.

The ultramodern residence hotel overlooking this appealing hurly-burly scene offers two-room apartments with large verandas that front on the plaza as well as two-bedroom suites.

BUDGET

CARLTON, Rua João Lira 68, Rio de Janeiro. Tel. 021/259-1932. Telex 21/23833. 50 rms. A/C MINIBAR TV TEL
$ Rates: From $45 single; from $50 double. AE, DC, MC, V.

The Carlton is located on a tree-lined back street in Leblon. The atmosphere in Leblon is very sedate, and this mood is reflected in the Carlton, a beacon of shabby gentility in a sea of affluence. The accommodations are roomy and comfortable, each with a private bath. The hotel also has a coffee shop restaurant, and a bar.

IPANEMA INN, Rua Maria Quitéria 27, Rio de Janeiro. Tel. 021/287-6092. Telex 21/22833. 56 rms. MINIBAR TV TEL

$ Rates: $27–$32 single; $30–$42 double. AE, DC, MC, V.
This hotel is located around the corner from the Caesar Park and is owned by the same group as the Apoador Inn several blocks away. The Ipanema Inn's front rooms offer an oblique view of the sea. Given its side-street location, the higher the floor, the better the view. Like the Apoador, the rooms are simple in the tradition of a real beach hotel. The hotel is definitely a reasonable option for anyone who is beach- and budget-minded at the same time. Television sets in the rooms are optional. There are also a small bar and a souvenir shop in the hotel. The souvenirs include fossil-fish amulets, lacquered piranhas, and Brazilian tarot cards.

VERMONT, Rua Visconde de Pirajá 254, Rio de Janeiro. Tel. 021/521-0057. 54 rms. A/C MINIBAR TV TEL
$ Rates: $45 single or double. AE, DC, MC, V.
The Vermont is several doors in from the corner of Rua Vinícius de Morais. This hotel is central to Ipanema's most fashionable shopping area, and still only two blocks from the beach. The atmosphere is spartan, but all the basics are there, including private baths in all the rooms. The hotel also has a bar and offers room service.

3. VIDIGAL & SÃO CONRADO

These two areas are further stretches of Rio's Atlantic Ocean beachfront. Vidigal was once a shantytown that has been transformed into a chic cliffside and canyon neighborhood of the well-to-do. São Conrado in the early 1960s was still a remote, even primitive beach. Today high-rises and condominiums dominate the skyline, but the beach is still among the most popular in the city.

INTER-CONTINENTAL, Av. Prefeito Mendes de Morais 222, Rio de Janeiro. Tel. 021/322-2200. Fax 021/322-2758. Telex 21/21790. 500 rms. A/C MINIBAR TV TEL
$ Rates: $180 single; $200 double. AE, DC, MC, V.
This just might be Rio's most luxurious hotel, but it suffers from some of the same disadvantages as the Sheraton. The Inter (as it is called) occupies a place in the moonscape of condominiums that is São Conrado. The spirit of orderly architectural harmony that guided the growth of Copacabana and Ipanema seemed to have vanished as development spread along the shore to São Conrado and Barra da Tijuca. Both beaches lack in their surroundings any of the intimate scale that we associate with neighborhoods. The buildings glitter, but the streets are cold. The background, of course, is the unceasing natural beauty of the Rio mountains and seascapes.
The inner environment is everything in high-rise heaven, and the Inter does not disappoint. The lobby is elegant, lined with stylish shops. But the real hotel life centers around a geometrical arrangement of pools, lounging chairs, and outside eating areas. This is the most insulated and sensuous poolside in Rio. On those many days when weather permits, the skies over the Inter are filled with the soaring antics of hang-glider enthusiasts, who launch themselves from Lookout Rock, cheek-by-jowl with the hotel. Across the road is the lovely São Conrado beach, somewhat abandoned on weekdays, and destitute of such services as roadside food stands and vendors, except on the weekends when it's a very popular and animated spot.
Accommodations in the hotel are among the best in Rio: spacious, with comfortable sitting areas, and balconies that let you get closer to the natural surroundings. The decor is cool and stylish, with well-designed and original Brazilian furnishings, and the walls are covered with textured paper. The baths are in stone and marble, fully equipped with robes and lotions, while the rooms all have individually controlled air conditioning.
The Inter is extremely popular with American travel groups, and is often included as an option in the most expensive packages.
Dining/Entertainment: Liberally distributed throughout the hotel are numer-

ous lounges, bars, and restaurants, including the Monseigneur, with French cooking and service, where dinner is likely to run from $18 to $30 per person. Fresh pasta dishes are the specialty at Alfredo di Roma, where a typical evening meal might cost $12 to $18. The Papillon discotheque is a favorite nightspot for the younger set, especially on weekends. A bar off the lobby has a satellite TV and features major U.S. sporting events.

Services: Complimentary shuttle bus to Ipanema and Copacabana; laundry and valet service; 24-hour room service.

Facilities: Beauty shop; gallery of boutiques and gift shops; sauna; tennis courts; nearby golf course; 12 meeting rooms; and ballroom/banquet hall seating 1,300 people.

NACIONAL, Av. Niemeyer 769, Rio de Janeiro. Tel. 021/322-1000. Fax 021/322-0058. Telex 21/23615. 520 rms. A/C MINIBAR TV TEL
$ Rates: $100–$115 single; $110–$130 double. AE, DC, MC, V.

The Nacional, part of the Horsa group with hotels throughout Brazil, is a 26-story glass-and-steel cylindrical tower designed by Oscar Niemeyer, principal architect for the country's ultramodern capital, Brasília. The hotel has pretensions to luxury, but the poor upkeep makes it more suitable for the convention trade, which the Nacional pursues over the conventional tourist down on a package and looking for splashy digs in a five-star resort. Major renovations, however, are now being undertaken to upgrade this hotel.

The most striking feature of the pie-shaped rooms is the view. Niemeyer's design democratically distributes a dramatic slice of the natural surroundings to virtually all rooms. Accommodations are brightly decorated, but not up to the quality of other five-star hotels. The hotel has several restaurants and bars. There is a ground-level pool area which is large and appealing. A private tunnel leads under the roadway to São Conrado beach.

RIO SHERATON, Av. Niemeyer 121, Rio de Janeiro. Tel. 021/274-1122. Fax 021/239-5643. Telex 21/21206. 617 rms. A/C MINIBAR TV TEL
$ Rates: $140–$160 single; $160–$180 double. AE, DC, MC, V.

The Rio Sheraton is Rio's only genuine resort hotel, set on an outcropping of rocks behind a small, private beach in Vidigal. This is the city's other hotel where you can take a dip in the ocean without crossing a street. A sprawling complex, the hotel's public areas stretch from roadside to shoreline six stories down.

There are advantages and disadvantages involved in staying at the Sheraton. Unlike what you'll find in the other beach neighborhoods already described, there is no street life here among the hills and cliffs of Vidigal. You are dependent on transportation to get from here to anywhere else in the city. The advantages are that once you are at the Sheraton, you don't necessarily have to go anywhere else—a boon to those travelers who crave the womblike atmosphere of a truly self-contained resort.

Millions were spent in recent years to repair what had been a reputation for shoddiness. The hotel now sparkles, and the rooms are warm and well decorated. The lobby is of cathedral proportions, but rectilinear and modern, sheathed in brown-tinted glass. Full of movement, the lobby seems like a busy crossroads, with people coming to and from the arcade of shops, the One Twenty-One bar, or one of the service desks.

Room at the Sheraton are trimmed out in fine hardwood and appointed with attractive rugs and wall hangings. The use of brass lamps and huge TVs recessed in bookshelves adds to the comfortable denlike atmosphere. All rooms have tile combination baths and balconies with dramatic ocean views. The units in the five-story wings are much larger than those in the 26-floor main tower.

Dining/Entertainment: In all, there are seven restaurants and bars within the Sheraton complex, including Valentino's, where fine Italian cuisine is served. The Casa da Cachaça is a bar specializing in cocktails made with Brazil's native sugarcane brandy, cachaça.

Services: Tour desk.

Facilities: Three flood-lit tennis courts and an equal number of freshwater pools are distributed on several levels of the spacious grounds. Also for the fitness-minded are a health club, a sauna, and a Nautilus and massage center. A beauty salon and lobby shops round out the offerings.

SÃO CONRADO PALACE, Av. Niemeyer 776, Rio de Janeiro. Tel. 021/ 322-0911. Telex 21/23611. 160 rms. A/C MINIBAR TV TEL
$ Rates: $40–$50 single; $45–$55 double. AE, DC, MC, V.

This hotel will begin to figure more and more in the future for medium-priced tour packages. The hotel's location is at the foot of Rio's largest working-class hill town, which has little to do with the São Conrado's appeal or comforts. The population of the Rocinha favela is said to number some 600,000. But while Rocinha may be no place to walk around unaccompanied, it is a bona fide neighborhood, albeit mostly of the urban poor—not a den of thieves and desperadoes. Such elements may be there, but their presence is just as disturbing to the majority of the favela's residents as it is to outsiders.

The São Conrado Palace occupies a hollow among several clusters of lowland high-rises close to the shore. Still, guests must ride a hotel shuttle bus the short distance to the São Conrado beach. The shuttle, which also makes runs to Copacabana and Ipanema, is furnished free of charge and operates on a regular schedule. Inside, the hotel is of genuine four-star quality, brand new and generously spacious in both its rooms and its public areas, and service is particularly attentive. Accommodations are large and furnished with good, simple taste, similar to first-class staterooms on cruise ships. Understated but well-chosen prints personalize the units, which are equipped with balconies and baths with lots of elbow room. Beyond the large, somewhat institutional lobby is a ground-level pool area that rivals those at most of the best hotels. Potted trees and umbrellas give the veranda a secluded air. Other features include a bar and a restaurant.

4. BARRA DA TIJUCA

Only 25 years ago Barra da Tijuca, an extension even farther southward of Rio's magnificent shoreline, was virgin beach, surrounded by summer homes and squatters' shacks. Since the late 1970s, however, Barra has been the site of rapid development all along the 15km- (9-mile) long beach. Today the strands are lined with mammoth high-rise buildings, mostly condos, built on the reclaimed swamplands that edged the sea. A long shallow lake separates the development along the shore from that inland, where in addition to more residential complexes are some of the largest supermarkets and shopping centers in South America, and quite probably the world. Surrounding the lake are the remaining marshlands, which serve as a habitat for wildlife. In the

---

 FROMMER'S COOL FOR KIDS: HOTELS

Rio Sheraton *(see p. 76)* The Sheraton's location right on the beach makes it the hotel of choice for anyone traveling with youngsters. Three spacious pools and lots of room to run around will add to the kids' sense of freedom.

Inter-Continental *(see p. 75)* You have to cross the road to get to São Conrado's Pepino Beach, right across from this resort hotel, but there is a tunnel for doing so. The Inter—as it is known for short—also has a very elaborate network of pools surrounded by a spacious patio. And furthermore, there's a close-up view of the hang gliding from the neighboring peak called the Pedra da Gávea.

morning sky it is common to see large birds spread their wings and soar high above the protected marsh.

Barra tends to be popular with tourists from the southern cone of South America—Argentines, Uruguayans, Chileans—who come to sun in Rio during their winter or to shop for bargains all year round. Barra's hotels fill to capacity on at least two occasions during the year, Carnival and the Grand Prix Formula One race held in the spring at the nearby auto track.

Perhaps the visitors from the southern cone are quite happy staying out in Barra because they are not anywhere near as hampered by the language barrier, and are thus able to get around town with a fair amount of ease. Most first-time North American visitors are not usually content to be in Barra. It's just too far from the action of Ipanema and Copacabana, a good half-hour cab ride away. Some tour packages offer very good deals, however, if you stay in Barra, where hotels are new but still relatively inexpensive. For those who already know Rio somewhat, Barra could be a very tempting base, especially if you have a car.

Also prominent on the lodging landscape in Barra are the many **motels.** At least in Rio, motels rent by the hour (and overnight), and are used strictly by lovers for their assignations. Some are truly outlandish in the opulence of their decor, worthy of a visit as cultural artifacts if for no other reason. The most famous of these pleasure palaces, **VIP's,** is located in Vidigal, set among the chic villas that are nestled in the folds of the mountains.

RIO HOTEL RESIDÊNCIA, Av. Sernambetiba 6250, Rio de Janeiro. Tel. 021/385-5000. Telex 21/39756. 270 apts. A/C MINIBAR TV TEL
$ Rates: $88 side apt; $100 rear apt; $118 front apt. No credit cards.
Somewhat typical of the apart-hotels in Barra, the Rio Hotel Residência caters to vacationing families and corporate people on extended stays. The two-bedroom apartments include a sitting room and large balcony/terrace, plus full kitchen and bath. Sports facilities include two squash courts, tennis and volleyball courts, and a large swimming pool. The hotel is further distinguished by the presence of La Petit Paris French-style restaurant, a nice addition to this somewhat suburban zone with its still-considerable allotment of wide-open spaces.

TROPICAL BARRA, Av. Sernambetiba 500, Rio de Janeiro. Tel. 021/399-0660. Fax 021/287-7640. Telex 21/30366. 140 rms. A/C MINIBAR TV TEL
$ Rates: From $32 single; from $35 double. AE, DC, MC, V.
The Tropical Barra, an attractive three-star hotel, is frequently offered as a choice in the least expensive package tours to Rio. The hotel sits across the boulevard from the beach and its accommodations are modern and comfortable. The Tropical Barra also offers such amenities as its own restaurant and bar.

5. GLÓRIA & FLAMENGO

These are two contiguous neighborhoods along the entrance to Guanabara Bay on the Rio side. The beaches at the mouth of the bay are polluted and no longer suitable for swimming, a singular example of our relentless fouling of our own nests. The island-filled bay and its environs are still beautiful to look at and definitely worth a day-trip on one of the many excursion boats. But the environment of the bay's marine life has been all but obliterated by the dumping of human and industrial waste.

Both Glória and Flamengo are close in to the city, and serviced by subway. Some 30 years ago these were still fashionable neighborhoods. Hollywood stars and heads of state all stayed at the Hotel Glória, and Flamengo, with its enormous apartments, was the residential preference among many of the city's most affluent citizens. Fickle fashion has moved the center of action farther down the beach, but both neighborhoods are bearing up well. In fact, the grand old apartments are once more in great demand because of the shortage of good housing in the city's highly speculative real estate market.

As alluded to elsewhere, there are numerous hotels of the simplest variety throughout the back streets of Flamengo. If you're on the lookout for rock-bottom prices, it's preferable to stay in this section rather than downtown, because you will be in a residential area, as opposed to in the city, which tends to empty after business hours.

EXPENSIVE

GLÓRIA, Praia do Russel 632, Rio de Janeiro. Tel. 021/205-7272. Fax 021/245-1660. Telex 21/23623. 630 rms. A/C MINIBAR TV TEL
$ Rates: $70–$100 single; $87–$125 double. Discounts available for groups. AE, DC, MC, V.

The Glória, Brazil's largest hotel, is very popular with the tour operators who package the least expensive trips to Rio. In the past the Hotel Glória was on a par with the Copacabana Palace, attracting a jet-set clientele from all over the world. Today, with most tourists to the city wanting beachfront accommodations, the Glória has accepted its role as a mass-market alternative for those who want the scale of a full-size hotel and all its services, but at discount prices.

Set close to the sidewalk, the massive white stone building in the grand style overlooks—approximately a quarter of a mile across a wide park—a section of Flamengo beach and the harbor. From here the historic downtown square, Praça XV, is about a 20-minute walk, though this is not recommended. The most direct route hugs the main thoroughfare, and there are no sidewalks in places. Subway access is rapid and direct, on the other hand. Rooms at the Glória are comfortable, but with no pretensions to luxury. The hotel's buildings curve around small but well-landscaped grounds, including a rock garden and an attractive pool area with surrounding patio. A second pool has been added, and the hotel's two restaurants have recently been reorganized and redecorated. There are several bar environments, a breakfast room, and a sauna, among other facilities.

MODERATE

NOVO MUNDO, Praia do Flamengo 20, Rio de Janeiro. Tel. 021/205-3355. Fax 021/265-2369. Telex 21/33282. 191 rms. A/C MINIBAR TV TEL
$ Rates: $42–$48 single; from $47–$50 double. AE, DC, MC, V.

This very large, 40-year-old hotel, facing Flamengo beach, is something of an institution in Rio. This was once a fashionable address, and the hotel has maintained high standards of service and maintenance. Rooms, all with private bath, are large, comfortably furnished, and spick-and-span. The hotel has a restaurant, parking facilities, a barbershop, and an American bar.

BUDGET

In addition to the listings below, there are other simple, cheap hotels of acceptable quality near the Glória Metro stop, like the **Hotel Turístico,** Ladeira da Glória 30 (tel. 021/225-9388). Rooms here have small balconies and are priced in the $9 to $12 range. The nearby **Monte Castelo,** Rua Cândido Mendes 201 (tel. 021/222-1733), is even cheaper, with rooms costing from $7 to $9.

HOTEL FLÓRIDA, Rua Ferreira Viana 69, Rio de Janeiro. Tel. 021/245-8160. Fax 021/225-7360. Telex 21/33400. 230 rms. A/C MINIBAR TV TEL
$ Rates: From $25 single; from $28 double. DC, MC, V.

In Flamengo is the ever-popular Hotel Flórida, which has gained a quiet reputation over the years as one of Rio's most steadfast hotels in the bargain range. Rooms with glossy parquet floors recall the neighborhood's more elegant days, and contain good private bathrooms with traditional porcelain fixtures. Hotel facilities include an unpretentious but reliable restaurant, and a swimming pool was added in 1992. The Flórida is one block from Flamengo beach, and right next to the Metro station.

HOTEL PAYSANDU, Rua Paisandu 23, Flamengo, Rio de Janeiro. Tel. 021/225-7270. 68 rms. A/C MINIBAR TV TEL
$ Rates: From $22 single; from $25 double. No credit cards.

This seven-story hotel is right off the Praia de Flamengo. The Paysandu's reasonably large rooms have painted walls and carpeted floors, and are equipped with either one double or two twin beds. Windows have wooden shutters to keep the sun out.

HOTEL VENEZUELA, Rua Paisandu 34, Rio de Janeiro. Tel. 021/205-2098. 29 rms. A/C TV TEL

$ Rates: $10 single; $13.50 double. No credit cards.

This is one among many of the backpacker specials that proliferate on the back streets of Flamengo and Glória. Rooms are clean, if spartan, and each is equipped with a bed, a small writing table, and an armoire in lieu of a closet.

RIO DINING

Compared with the rest of Brazil, Rio is one of the country's most expensive cities. Yet restaurant food in the *cidade maravilhosa* is still a bargain for most North American visitors. Eating *bom e barato* (well and cheap) is, after all, a national Brazilian pastime that few visiting travelers will disdain. Most main courses in the vast majority of restaurants—the exception is almost inevitably a fancy lobster or shrimp dish—seldom go higher than $10, and many a good deal less. A typical meal at a good restaurant, including domestic beer or wine, dessert, and service, will rarely exceed $20. The service charge of 10% is always included with the bill. You can also leave a few small bills on the table to sweeten the tip, but this is completely discretionary.

FANCY FOOD, LOCAL DRINKS Rio also has its share of fancy and expensive restaurants. These tend to offer French-style cooking and service, and to be located in the best hotels. But even if your taste runs to gourmet meals, or you just want to splurge, the bill will seem modest when compared with a similar eatery in other major world cities. The trick to dining economically in Brazil, even in the chicest places, is to stay away from imported beverages, which can cost you two to three times more than you're used to paying at even the most expensive bars and restaurants back home.

SKIP LUNCH With the generous breakfasts included in the price of your room at virtually all the hotels mentioned in this guide, many travelers will feel the need for only a light snack at lunchtime. Rio abounds in small cafés, fast-food emporiums (both of the homegrown and multinational variety), juice bars, and traditional lunch counters. You can eat very well in Brazil at these simple establishments. Many of these snack bars will be described in more detail at the end of this section.

SURF & TURF Brazilians are big meat and seafood eaters, as the country and coastal waters are supplied with an abundance of both commodities. Most restaurants I will mention offer extensive meat and seafood menus. "Extensive" is perhaps too weak a word to describe menus that not infrequently offer a choice of 30 to 50 items. Even specialty restaurants like churrascarias outdo themselves in the variety of their dishes. The phrase "all you can eat" takes on new meaning in a churrascaria that serves its food *rodízio* style. Rodízio means that the various cuts of meat are served on skewers in an endless round right at your table. As for fish, fin and shell varieties alike, seafood lovers will find in the Brazilian selection of *frutos do mar* an unprecedented cornucopia of delights. Even where seafood is not featured, at least several varieties of fish filet and a number of shrimp dishes will most likely be included on the menu. Brazilians retain the European dining option of having both fish and meat courses in a single meal. The steaming fish stews, served in general only at seafood restaurants, are firmly in the tradition of the brimming and succulent *mariscadas* found throughout Spain and Portugal. As for fin fish, each region can boast a fresh catch of several species that are the favorite of local palates, prepared in a variety of ways, familiar and unique.

1. COPACABANA & LEME

There are restaurants of every category densely packed inside the borders of this great district. Dress is never formal, even where the service is ceremonial. Neither jacket nor tie is required for men dining in Rio, except in one or two business restaurants downtown. The Copacabana area is particularly informal, as people constantly drop into the many restaurants on the way to or from the beach.

EXPENSIVE

LE BEC FIN, Av. Nossa Senhora de Copacabana 178. Tel. 542-4079.
   Cuisine: FRENCH. **Reservations:** Required.
$ Prices: Appetizers $5–$13; main courses $9–$19. No credit cards.
   Open: Dinner daily 8pm–2am.
For over 40 years, Le Bec Fin has been one of Rio's shining culinary institutions. While not cramped, seating with only nine tables is intimate, in subdued and comfortable surroundings, while service is civilized and deliberately slow. As in all good French restaurants, emphasis is on the food. Lobster and duck are particular specialties, with many traditional plates from steak au poivre to steak Diane always available as well.

LE PRE CATELAN, in the Rio Palace Hotel, Av. Atlântica 4240. Tel. 521-3232.
   Cuisine: FRENCH. **Reservations:** Required.
$ Prices: Appetizers $12–$20; main courses $18–$27; fixed-price lunch $15. AE, DC, MC, V.
   Open: Lunch Mon–Fri noon–3pm; dinner Mon–Fri 7:30pm–midnight.
Le Pré Catelan is a fine French restaurant serving nouvelle cuisine for lunch and dinner. Though it's ensconced discreetly on the premises of the Rio Palace Hotel, you need not enter the hotel to get to the restaurant, which is serviced by a separate elevator right before the main entrance to the lobby. Elegant decor, imaginative cuisine, and service with a flourish combine to maintain the restaurant's reputation as one of Rio's best. Supervision of the fare is in the hands of a highly regarded French chef, who maintains very consistent standards of quality in the preparation of many complex and subtle dishes.

   The cushioned banquettes and large tables encourage an abundant meal, consumed at a civilized pace. Part of the enjoyment involves allowing ample time to take in the surrounding scene among your animated fellow diners and to observe the staff in its perpetual state of formal attentiveness. Periodically, at the signal from a captain, in unison waiters lift the silver covers from the principal dishes when they arrive at a given table.

   For dinner you may order from a *menu confiance,* which includes appetizer, main course, and dessert, for around $25, or choose from a wide selection of à la carte suggestions. For a first course, you might have duck or rabbit, each in its own delicate sauce, followed by an even more elaborate and succulent main course of lobster, large shrimp, or a prime cut of lamb or beef. A soufflé or a plate of mixed pastries and a strong cup of aromatic Brazilian coffee will round out the meal—in all, a memorable culinary experience. Two people can dine and fully indulge their culinary passions, eating several courses, drinking both cocktails and wine, and still escape for only slightly more than $100 between them.

OURO VERDE, in the Ouro Verde Hotel, Av. Atlântica 1456. Tel. 542-1887.
   Cuisine: FRENCH. **Reservations:** Required on Sun and holidays.
$ Prices: Appetizers $4–$8 (escargots $19); main courses $7–$15; lunch buffet $10. AE, DC, MC, V.
   Open: Daily noon–1am.

   Spoken of in Rio with a praise bordering on reverence, the Ouro Verde has no trouble living up to its exhalted reputation as one of Rio's finest traditional French restaurants. Climb the stairs from the lobby of the Ouro Verde Hotel to the mezzanine. The relatively small room displays elegantly set tables, each with silver candlestick, silver salt shaker, and pewter pepper mill to complement the starched-linen covers and the fine settings of crystal and china. A select few of these tables line the front wall beside large windows that admit welcome ocean breezes along with a wide view of the beach.

   The food and impeccably professional service soon direct your attention away from the seating arrangements and the view. Daily at lunch there is a cold buffet with a choice of some dozen platters, including salade niçoise, various pâtés, smoked meats and cold cuts, vegetables, and greens. Typical specialties served at both lunch and dinner are shrimp sautéed in whisky, shredded veal in cream sauce with hash browns, and rolled beefsteak, filled with diced, sautéed onions and sweet pickle, smothered in a deep brown gravy. For dessert there is diplomatic pudding—a concoction of bread, raisins, and liquor and, of course, crêpes Suzette.

MODERATE

The price range for meals in this category is fairly broad, starting as low as $6 for simple fish dishes and going no higher than $20 for the most expensive plates.

ATLANTIS, in the Rio Palace Hotel, Av. Atlântica 4240. Tel. 521-3232.
   Cuisine: INTERNATIONAL. **Reservations:** Not needed.
$ Prices: Appetizers $3–$8; main courses $6–$15. AE, DC, MC, V.
   Open: Daily 6am–1am.
Adjacent to the pool on the terrace of the Rio Palace Hotel, the Atlantis functions as an all-purpose quality restaurant for both lunch and dinner. Guests of the hotel also use the Atlantis as a breakfast room in the morning. With a wide-ranging menu, the restaurant can serve practically anything from sandwiches to full-sized meals: inside the restaurant itself, on the terrace overlooking Copacabana beach, or at poolside tables. On Saturday the Atlantis features a formal feijoada, and on Sunday, a brunch.

BIFE DE OURO, in the Copacabana Palace, Av. Atlântica 1702. Tel. 255-7070.
   Cuisine: INTERNATIONAL. **Reservations:** Recommended.
$ Prices: Appetizers $4–$12 ($18–$25 for shrimp and lobster); main courses $12–$25. AE, DC, MC, V.
   Open: Lunch daily noon–4pm; dinner daily 7pm–midnight.

   Overlooking the street through gauzy curtains and narrow blinds at ground level in the Copacabana Palace is an unheralded but excellent steakhouse, the Bife de Ouro. There are curved banquettes and large potted plants to screen the views from table to table. On the walls are the large canvases of artist Jorge Guinle Filho, explosions of powerful colors that are true to their tropical inspiration.

   This unusually pleasant interior does not overshadow the good food, however, which is very reasonably priced—no beef or steak dish is more than $12. Appetizers include creamed soups and smoked fish. Figs flambé over ice cream and coffee brewed at your table add the final touches to an epicurean meal. The service at the Bife de Ouro is just right, attentive but not solicitous. The lunch and dinner menus are the same.

   The other restaurant at the Copacabana Palace is the **Pergula,** a more informal day-room environment for lunch and light meals, overlooking both the street and the hotel's magnificent pool area.

CAFE DE LA PAIX, in the Meridien Hotel, Av. Atlântica 1020. Tel. 275-9922.
  Cuisine: FRENCH. **Reservations:** Accepted.
$ **Prices:** Appetizers $4–$10; main courses $8–$15. AE, DC, MC, V.
  Open: Daily 6am–midnight.
The Café de la Paix is the Meridien Hotel's everyday restaurant. Since this is also the Meridien's breakfast room, the early morning crowd is generally made up of the hotel's guests, though the café is a favorite choice for power breakfasts among local businesspeople as well. The street entrance opens directly onto Avenida Atlântica, opposite Leme beach, and the café's brasserie ambience makes a pleasant and suitable setting for casual meals at any time of day. Reasonably priced casseroles suggesting French country fare are the house specialty and include a seafood stew at $13, coq au vin at $10, pot au feu at $7.75, and a lamb stew at $10.95.

ENOTRIA, Rua Constante Ramos 115. Tel. 237-6705.
  Cuisine: ITALIAN. **Reservations:** Recommended.
$ **Prices:** Fixed-price menu $30. No credit cards.
  Open: Dinner Mon–Sat noon–1am.
Enotria is located several blocks in from the beach, near the corner of Avenida Barata Ribeiro. This tiny, and newly renovated, two-story restaurant serves some of the best Italian food in Rio. Love seats and armchairs add a touch of the salon to the Enotria's atmosphere. All pastas and breads are prepared daily in the Enotria's own kitchen. At the gourmet shop next door, which is under the same management as the restaurant, you can buy take-out for those midnight snacks back in the hotel. The Enotria offers daily specials from a fixed-price handwritten menu as well as à la carte selections. Some dishes include *tortelli di porri* (cheese-filled tortellini), *giamberoni ai pinoli* (shrimp in cognac with pinoli nuts), and for dessert, *pera alla Cardinali* (chilled stewed pears, with ice cream and strawberry mousse).

FIORENTINA, Av. Atlântica 454. Tel. 541-2441.
  Cuisine: ITALIAN. **Reservations:** Not needed.
$ **Prices:** Appetizers $3–$6.25; main courses $4–$9 (shellfish dishes up to $14). AE, DC, MC, V.
  Open: Mon–Fri 11:30am–2am, Sat–Sun 11:30am–6am.
The Fiorentina is an inexpensive Italian café-restaurant near Máriu's that has long been a favorite watering hole for Rio's artistic and theatrical community. In fact, my own introduction to the place was in the company of several Amazonian actors, based in Rio and active in experimental theater. What is so special about the Fiorentina is that it is probably the only remaining beachfront café in Copacabana/Leme that my companions could afford to eat in. The joint is a hot spot on many weeknights, but especially on weekends.

FORNO E FOGÃO, in the Hotel Luxor Regente, Av. Atlântica 3716. Tel. 287-4212.
  Cuisine: INTERNATIONAL. **Reservations:** Not needed.
$ **Prices:** Appetizers $1.50–$6 (shrimp up to $10.50); main courses $5–$10 (shrimp dishes $20–$23). AE, DC, MC, V.
  Open: Daily noon–midnight.
The Forno e Fogão is recommended for its very tasty, yet moderately priced, dishes. Often when a hotel like the Regente caters not only to tourists but to a sizable number of business travelers, there is a strong motivation to keep up the standards of its kitchen. I recently ate two business lunches at the Forno e Fogão and both were excellent. If I were staying near the Regente in Copacabana for five or six days, I would seriously consider taking at least one meal here. The supremo de frango, a generous portion of breaded chicken in a cheese-and-tomato sauce, was particularly good, as was the cultured trout.

MÁRIU'S, Av. Atlântica 290. Tel. 542-2393.
  Cuisine: BARBECUE. **Reservations:** Not needed.
$ **Prices:** Fixed-price rodízio meal $13, dessert and beverage not included. AE, DC, MC, V.
  Open: Daily 11:45am–3am.

Well into Leme is Máriu's, the only churrascaria along this oceanside avenue. The restaurant occupies the first two floors of a modern building, and overlooks the beach through a facade of plate glass. Inside, Máriu's serves its barbecued fare round-robin or *rodízio* style, the cuts including, sirloin, lamb, loin of pork, sausages, and smoked ham. You can eat as much as you want, but leave some room for the many side dishes of salads, french fries, farofa, cold asparagus, and hearts of palm. Its beachfront location makes Máriu's a more expensive choice than the average churrascaria, but for $13 a person, depending on your bar bill, meat eaters can eat and drink divinely.

A MARISQUEIRA, Rua Barata Ribeiro 232. Tel. 237-3920.

Cuisine: SEAFOOD. **Reservations:** Not needed.
$ Prices: Appetizers $4–$9.25; main courses $4.75–$15. AE, DC, MC, V.
Open: Daily 10am–midnight.

Offering over two dozen fish dishes, this Portuguese-style seafood restaurant is in one of Copacabana's most genial back-street environments. If you want something really light, try the caldo verde, that wonderful and traditional Portuguese soup made from purée of potato and filled with crispy kale and slices of country sausage. The best bets (and best bargains) are the fish filets, mostly in the $5 to $8 range.

There is a branch of A Marisqueira in Ipanema as well, at Rua Gomes Carneiro 90 (tel. 267-9944).

POMME D'OR, Rua Sá Ferreira 22. Tel. 521-2548.

Cuisine: FRENCH. **Reservations:** Recommended Fri–Sat.
$ Prices: Appetizers $5–$6.50; main courses $8.50–$11. AE, DC, MC, V.
Open: Daily noon–2am.

The Pomme d'Or, located near the venerable Miramar, is also a perennial favorite among local residents who are fond of French cooking at reasonable prices. The restaurant occupies a large, attractive space and offers a list of daily specials.

SHIRLEY'S, Rua Gustavo Sampaio 610. Tel. 275-1398.

Cuisine: SEAFOOD. **Reservations:** Not needed.
$ Prices: Appetizers $5–$7; main courses $7–$15.50. No credit cards.
Open: Daily noon–1am.

Shirley's is the epitome of a neighborhood restaurant. Tucked into the space of a small storefront, the restaurant only has a dozen tables. And the perpetual line for seating underscores the popularity of this primarily Spanish-style establishment. A typical fish plate costs between $7 and $10, while lobster dishes run about $15.50.

BUDGET

AROSA, Rua Santa Clara. Tel. 262-7638.

Cuisine: BRAZILIAN/INTERNATIONAL. **Reservations:** Not needed.
$ Prices: Appetizers $1.75–$3.75; main courses $5.50–$10.50. AE, DC, MC, V.
Open: Daily 11am–midnight.

The Arosa is a clean, well-lighted place that was once one of an abundant species of restaurant throughout Copacabana, a species that now is sadly all but extinct. So thank your stars for the Arosa. It's the kind of place you could dine at regularly, in between those weekly binges at pricier restaurants. The interior is paneled in light-toned woodwork, and the spacing among the tables is very generous. The menu features meat, chicken, and seafood dishes. There is a delicious pan-fried filet of fish with a pilaf of white rice.

BONINOS, Av. Nossa Senhora de Copacabana at Rua Bolívar. Tel. 262-7638.

Cuisine: INTERNATIONAL. **Reservations:** Not needed.
$ Prices: Appetizers $2–$5; main courses $2–$12. No credit cards.
Open: Daily noon–midnight.

Boninos is an old-fashioned tearoom and restaurant. The back room is a pleasant air-conditioned salon, ideal for a quick afternoon pick-me-up. In front is a lunch counter, serving ice-cream sundaes as well as coffee, tea, and diverse snacks and pastries. Most items on the menu are priced between $2 and $3, while shrimp platters run up to $10.

NOGUEIRA, Rua Ministro Viveiros de Castro 15. Tel. 275-9848.
Cuisine: BRAZILIAN. **Reservations:** Not needed.
$ Prices: Appetizers $1.50–$3; main courses $4–$12.50; daily specials $4. No credit cards.
Open: Daily 11am–4am.

The Nogueira Restaurante cooks *tudo na brasa,* everything on the grill, making this corner café at the intersection of busy Avenida Princesa Isabel (on the Copacabana side) the Brazilian equivalent of an American "bar & grill." "Neighborhood tavern" is another term that comes to mind—but again, Brazilian-style, with the requisite complement of outdoor tables on the sidewalk. Late-nighters love this place. I am told that most nights (mornings?) it's hard to find an empty table around 3am. The menu features about 70 dishes—mostly seafood, meat, and fowl—with most dishes big enough for two.

PASTELARIA MIGUEL DE LEMOS, Rua Miguel de Lemos 18E. Tel. 521-0295.
Cuisine: LIGHT FARE. **Reservations:** Not needed.
$ Prices: All items 50¢–$3. No credit cards.
Open: Daily 8am–midnight.

When the munchies struck one afternoon, I leaned against the counter at the Pastelaria Miguel de Lemos, and ordered a fresh-squeezed orange juice and a *coxinha de galinha,* also fresh—from the oven. The coxinha is a chewy pastry filled with a kind of spicy ratatouille of chicken, and I don't think the whole snack cost much more than a buck.

2. IPANEMA & LEBLON

This is *the* restaurant district of Rio de Janeiro, where people go to see and be seen, or where gourmands maintain their perpetual vigil for the latest in new wave culinary artistry.

Today, Leblon—especially Lower or Baixo Leblon—refers to a place of unprecise boundaries at the far end of the neighborhood beneath the mountain peaks that block Leblon's expansion westward. This little cul-de-sac community has several zones: the end of Leblon beach, the triangle where its two principal thoroughfares (Ataulfo de Paiva and Dias Ferreira) meet, and the quiet streets around the Praça Atahualpa. The following restaurants described below are located in lower or Baixo Leblon: Café Look, Luna Bar, La Mole, Arataca, Bozó, Buffalo Grill, Antiquárius, Piccadilly Pub, Real Astoria, and Tatsumi.

EXPENSIVE

ANTIQUÁRIUS, Rua Aristides Espinola 19. Tel. 294-1496.
Cuisine: PORTUGUESE. **Reservations:** Required.
$ Prices: Appetizers $3–$10; main courses $7–$24. No credit cards.
Open: Daily noon–2am.

Popular, tiny, and crowded, the Antiquárius is perhaps the best Portuguese restaurant in Rio. It specializes in *bacalhau* (codfish), that denizen of northern Atlantic waters with its grotesque visage and flaky, delicate meat. No country today upholds the tradition of codfish cookery more than Portugal. But the fish must be imported to Brazil, and so its cost is always twice the price of steak, and sometimes priced higher than shrimp and lobster. Maine lobstermen, who often discard this unwanted interloper from their traps, would be surprised to learn how much a good codfish will fetch in Brazil. The Antiquárius offers many codfish dishes, including the standard Portuguese concoction, many times more appetizing than its basic ingredients of bacalhau, scrambled eggs and potatoes, would imply. The cost is about $19. Other daily specials, primarily seafood, are listed at $8, $10, and $15.

BUFFALO GRILL, Rua Rita Lufolf 47. Tel. 274-4848.
Cuisine: STEAK. **Reservations:** Not needed.
$ Prices: Appetizers $4–$7; main courses $8–$15. AE, DC.
Open: Daily noon–2am.

One of Rio's most unique and charming steakhouses is the Buffalo Grill, where an elfish maître d' named Garrincha pampers a select clientele with the tenderest cuts of meat, prepared to perfection using skills and years of accumulated experience that have made him a semilegendary figure in the world of Rio's churrascarias. The restaurant is also the only one in Rio to serve genuine buffalo steaks, not our North American bison, but the Asian species. Now, this may not sound like much of a distinction—is buffalo that different from beef, you might legitimately wonder? Well, to my taste it is, somewhat sweeter, agreeably gamy, and very tender. I recommend the *picanha* cut over the filet, as it is served with a strip of tasty fat that blends well with the meat. I found the filet a bit too rich. An order of picanha for two costs $22, including a variety of trimmings. Other types of grilled meats are also offered, like beef, lamb, and chicken. And filet mignon dishes head the list with nearly a dozen different preparations, all around $10, from steak au poivre to Filet Tom—named for frequent patron composer Tom Jobim, who prefers his steak smothered in béarnaise sauce and accompanied by new potatoes with tiny onions.

The Buffalo Grill, incidentally, occupies both floors of a corner building, with a separate piano bar downstairs, and the restaurant upstairs, an elegant space where tables on the windows face both streets. The bar, with its own menu of canapés and appetizers, stays open slightly later than the restaurant on weekends.

ESPLANADA GRILL, Rua Barão da Torre 600. Tel. 239-6028.
Cuisine: STEAK. **Reservations:** Required on weekends.
$ Prices: Appetizers $3–$6; main courses $8–$15. AE, DC, MC, V.
Open: Lunch Mon–Fri noon–4pm; dinner Mon–Wed 7pm–2am; Fri–Sun noon–2am.

The Esplanada Grill is currently one of Rio's most fashionable dining spots. On Friday afternoons, when the downtown executives break early for the weekend, the Esplanada is crammed with beautiful people from lunchtime till late into the night. The restaurant's decor is itself a subtle event, a mixture of high-tech and traditional, and by no means flashy or obvious. You must look closely to see the innovations: For instance, the highly stylized concrete wall columns are inlaid with fine polished hardwood, and this and other effects suggests an architectural vision of some freshness.

But the Esplanada is essentially a steakhouse, and the quality of food is what brings people back again and again, once the vicarious thrill of rubbing elbows with the in-crowd wears thin. The meats are indeed superb, combining buttery tenderness with rare taste. According to Cardoso, the Esplanada's manager, the owners raise their own beef cattle on the flat plains of the South American pampas; they don't serve the "*boi de Minas*," Cardoso explained with a touch of irony, that is, cattle bred in the nearby hilly state of Minas Gerais. "There is no musculature on this meat," he explained. Whatever its pedigree, the *picanha bordon*, at $15—about the most expensive cut on the menu—was one of the best pieces of meat I'd ever eaten. Twenty-five other cuts and combinations of meat are priced from $8 to $15, and the Esplanada's menu also features a half-dozen elaborate salads ($3 to $6) for noncarnivores.

MARIKO SUSHI BAR, in the Caesar Park Hotel, Av. Vieira Souto 460. Tel. 287-3122.
Cuisine: JAPANESE. **Reservations:** Recommended.
$ Prices: Appetizers $3.50–$11; main courses $9.75–$30. AE, DC, MC, V.
Open: Lunch daily noon–3pm; dinner daily 7pm–midnight.

The Mariko Sushi Bar is the top-of-the-line sushi bar at the Caesar Park Hotel, expensive and elegant. Prices on the higher end of the spectrum are for elaborate complete meals, featuring a great variety of plates (including sushi) that are served in traditional style.

PETRONIUS, in the Caesar Park Hotel, Av. Vieira Souto 460. Tel. 287-3122.
   Cuisine: SEAFOOD. **Reservations:** Recommended.
$ **Prices:** Appetizers $4–$13; main courses $8–$24. AE, DC, MC, V.
   Open: Dinner daily 6pm–1am.

This restaurant is the pride of the Caesar Park Hotel. The Petronius is a picture of swank in its decor and of romance in its mood—banquettes divided by etched panels of glass, and a grand piano on a raised platform between an alcove bar and the dining area, the formal air and attire of the staff, and the starlit Ipanema night seen through windows high above the beach.

The Petronius specializes in seafood served in a manner that only French cuisine could inspire. The fish in pastry or the soufflé of codfish (unbelievably good) are samples of the imaginative presentations that emerge from the kitchen. The Petronius may have the further distinction of being the only restaurant in Rio that serves its martinis with pimiento-stuffed green olives. As for dessert, the little goblets of chocolate filled with liqueur and topped with whipped cream require no additional commentary. An excellent and expensive restaurant. Expect to spend $40 to $50 per person for a no-holds-barred bout of feasting.

MODERATE

ALBÉRICO'S, Av. Vieira Souto 236. Tel. 267-3793.
   Cuisine: SEAFOOD. **Reservations:** Not needed.
$ **Prices:** Appetizers $3–$4; main courses $8–$17. AE, DC, MC, V.
   Open: Daily 11am–2am.

Albérico's is Ipanema's most animated beachfront café. On any given night of the year when the weather is hot and a cool breeze blows off the Atlantic, hordes of young people gather at the Albérico's sidewalk tables, sometimes in parties of 20 or more. Albérico's is also a restaurant with a more private second-story dining area, where silhouetted diners sit framed by open windows at twilight. Full seafood dinners are available, but most of the celebrants are satisfied with snacks, light meals, and the free flow of *chopp*—draft beer.

ARATACA, Rua Dias Ferriera 135. Tel. 274-1444.
   Cuisine: AMAZONIAN. **Reservations:** Not needed.
$ **Prices:** Appetizers $2.50–$4.75; main courses $4.75–$10 (shellfish dishes around $15). AE, DC, MC, V.
   Open: Daily 11am–2am.

Immediately next door to La Mole is the Arataca, a restaurant featuring exotic regional dishes from the Amazon. *Tucunaré, pirarucu,* and *surubim* are among the Amazon river fish on the menu, along with the signature dish of Pará state, a spicy duck dish of Indian origin, called *pato no tucupi* ($8). The house cocktail is the *batida de cupuaçu* ($1.30), a blend of vodka or *cachaça* with one of the Amazon region's tastiest fruits. Arataca also has a second branch, in Copacabana.

BANANA CAFE, Rua Barão da Torre 368. Tel. 521-1460.
   Cuisine: SANDWICHES/PIZZA. **Reservations:** Not accepted.
$ **Prices:** Appetizers $3–$5; main courses $8–$15. No credit cards.
   Open: Daily noon–4am.

The hottest in-spot for the teenybopper to young adult set in Rio for the past two summers. It could be ice cold by the time you get there, but for the moment, the place is packed most nights, especially from Thursday through Sunday. There's always a line. It's not a place you go to for the food, but to encounter your compatible opposite.

BOCA DE PANELA, Rua Dias Ferreira 247. Tel. 274-2277.
   Cuisine: BRAZILIAN. **Reservations:** Not needed.
$ **Prices:** Appetizers $2.50–$4; main courses $5–$13. No credit cards.
   Open: Tues–Sat 11:30am–midnight, Sun 11am–10pm.

This hole-in-the-wall on the mezzanine level of an old building in Baixo Leblon is what Brazilians would call a *boa dica*—a good tip. The words "bargain" and "authentic" apply to both the food here, and the blue-collar ambience. Daily specials include such standards as *bobó de camarão,* a Bahian shrimp stew ($5), and *carne seca a mineira,* jerked beef, Minas-style ($5). The baked rabbit ($11) is served on Sunday only, while the house special, available anytime, is *maminha de alcatra a campanha,* a country-style eye round ($13 for two).

BOZÓ, Rua Dias Ferreira 50. Tel. 294-1260.
   Cuisine: BRAZILIAN/SPANISH. **Reservations:** Not needed.
$ Prices: Appetizers $3–$5; main courses $4–$9 (shrimp and shellfish stews up to $18). AE, DC, MC.
   Open: Daily 10am–4am.

In contrast to the bright and open-air style of its rivals, the Bozó has a cavelike atmosphere. Behind an entrance facade that mixes wood paneling with a large display window filled with liquor bottles lies a quiet and orderly interior, invisible from the street, that suggests the dining room of a modest private club. On the menu is *comida típica*—typical Brazilian fare, favorite dishes from Minas and Bahia like *lombinho tropeiro,* pork loin with beans and farofa ($6) and *moqueca de badejo,* a sea bass stew ($8).

The Bozó delivers carry-out meals as well. Bozó's Spanish owner, Manuel Fernandez, also features many seafood casseroles—like Spanish-style octopus ($8). The Bozó is known locally for its excellent *pastels*—especially the *pastel catupiri*—a made-to-order pastry filled with melted Brazilian ricotta cheese (about 50¢ each).

CANECO 70, Av. Delfim Morais 1026. Tel. 249-1180.
   Cuisine: BRAZILIAN/INTERNATIONAL. **Reservations:** Not needed.
$ Prices: Appetizers $3–$5; main courses $5–$8. No credit cards.
   Open: Daily 10am–4am.

On the Leblon stretch of the beach at the corner of Rua Rainha Guilhermina, the Caneco 70 offers the advantages of being both an outdoor café and a popular restaurant. A large open space, it is an ideal lunch and beverage spot in between sessions in the sun. Or for a genuinely funky feijoada, come here on Saturday. Sundays, another national dish, cozido is also served, a beef-and-vegetable stew originating in the northeast. Both dishes cost about $8, and as the waiter explains, "Um da pra dois" ("One serving is enough for two"). For a more quiet meal, the second-floor terrace is suggested.

CASA DA FEIJOADA, Rua Prudente de Morais 10. Tel. 267-4994.
   Cuisine: BRAZILIAN. **Reservations:** Not needed.
$ Prices: Appetizers $2–$5; main courses $6–$10. AE, DC, MC, V.
   Open: Mon–Fri noon–midnight, Sat–Sun noon–1am.

Finally, someone has opened a restaurant where one may eat the Brazilian national dish, feijoada, any day of the week, not just at the traditional Saturday lunch. Just at the very beginning of Ipanema, and somewhat obscured from the street by a newspaper stand, is the Casa da Feijoada. Owner Leonardo Braga, who spent three years in California and speaks English quite well, decided that the time was overdue for the black bean, a former staple of the local diet, to make its comeback in Rio. The full-blown feijoada feast includes soup (*caldo verde* or black bean), salad, *batida* cocktail and the usual array of pork and beef cuts served with white rice, fried manioc, *couve* greens, orange slices, and *farofa*—all for $10. Those who fancy other regional Brazilian foods will probably find the taste they have in mind on the house menu as well; everything from *tutu a mineira* to *caldeirada de pescador,* the latter a mariscada to rival the finest. The restaurant will also deliver meals within its general vicinity (which may include some of the hotels at the *posto* 6 end of Copacabana). The Casa da Feijoada is a must stop for anyone visiting Rio who wants to sample an authentic home-style feijoada.

GROTTAMMARE, Rua Gomes Carneiro 132. Tel. 287-1596.
   Cuisine: ITALIAN SEAFOOD. **Reservations:** Accepted only for parties of more than six.
$ Prices: Appetizers $3–$10; main courses $8–$30. AE, DC, MC.

Open: Lunch Sat–Sun noon–2am; dinner daily 7pm until the last customer leaves. Guests staying in hotels at the Rio Palace end of Copacabana can easily walk the several blocks to the Grottammare, a popular Italian seafood restaurant. Simply head down Rua Francisco Sá, which after several blocks turns into Rua Gomes Carneiro after you have crossed the Avenida Bulhões de Cavalho. The restaurant specializes in salads, pasta dishes, and grilled fish—whatever species turn up daily in the nets of the fishermen who supply the Grottammare. Pastas and salads generally run $5 to $8.

GULA, GULA, in the Marina Palace Hotel, Av. Delfim Moreira 630. Tel. 259-5212.

Cuisine: NEW WAVE/INTERNATIONAL. **Reservations:** Not needed.

$ Prices: Appetizers $3–$5; main courses $7–$12; all-you-can-eat buffet $7.50. AE, DC.

Open: Tues–Sun noon–midnight.

A hotel restaurant in Leblon with possibilities is the Gula, Gula. Attractively perched on the mezzanine floor, and looking out over the beachfront through a wall of windows, the tables are covered in tea-service pink and the daily specials, including steak, shrimp, and fish platters, are affordably priced.

GULA, GULA, Anibal de Mendonça 132. Tel. 259-3084.

Cuisine: SALADS. **Reservations:** Not needed.

$ Prices: Salads $2.75–$4; main courses $6. No credit cards.

Open: Tues–Thurs and Sun noon–midnight; Fri–Sat noon–1am.

This establishment is somehow related, but very distinct in atmosphere and culinary mission from the main branch of the Gula, Gula chain located off the beach in Leblon's Marina Palace Hotel. This Gula, Gula occupies a two-floor storefront on an Ipanema side street, and is much frequented by local office workers during lunch hours, and by neighborhood denizens looking for a light, tasty, and inexpensive dinner at night. My lunch there—though I could not hear a word my companions spoke from across the table for the din—was superb. We sampled a variety of spicy salads, combining chicken with veggies, rice, potatoes, and what have you. With mineral water to drink and two desserts between us, I don't think the bill exceeded $15 for the lot.

LORD JIM, Rua Paul Redfern 63. Tel. 259-3047.

Cuisine: ENGLISH. **Reservations:** Accepted.

$ Prices: Appetizers $3–$8; main courses $6–$15. No credit cards.

Open: Tues–Sat 4pm–1am, Sun 11am–1am.

From Lord Jim's, on the last street in Ipanema before crossing into Leblon, the British lion holds forth in this genuine public house re-created in the tropics. Boisterous and rowdy in a good-natured way, the weekend crowds exercise their Anglo-Saxon nostalgia for pub life to the tune of endless rounds of good English bitters, kidney pie, and a rousing game of darts. 'Ey what? Lord Jim's is the crossroads and meeting ground for Rio's English colony and therefore a favorite attraction for many visitors to Rio from the diverse countries of the English-speaking world. In addition to the traditional English fare—roast beef, Yorkshire pudding, fish-and-chips—tea is served daily from 4 until 6:30pm.

MEDITERRÂNEO, Rua Prudente de Morais 1810. Tel. 259-4121.

Cuisine: SEAFOOD/PASTA. **Reservations:** Not needed.

$ Prices: Appetizers $5–$12; main courses $6–$15. AE, DC, MC.

Open: Daily noon–2am.

This festive-looking eatery with a definite flavor of the Mediterranean shore occupies the first and second floors of a corner house. Divided rooms and balconies provide separate areas for intimate dining amid nautical bric-a-brac and polished woodwork. It's generally crowded, so reservation or not, you will probably have to wait a few minutes for a table. For a filling and satisfactory meal, try the spaghetti Mediterrâneo ($13), a concoction of pasta and fresh seafood, including giant shrimp, mussels, fish, and squid. With a couple of draft beers to wash it all down, the meal will cost you about $16, including service. Mussel and fish dishes run between $7 and $12, while lobster can cost as much as $20.

PICCADILLY PUB, Av. General San Martín 1241. Tel. 259-7605.
Cuisine: INTERNATIONAL. **Reservations:** Recommended on weekends.
$ Prices: Appetizers $3.50–$5; main courses $8–$10. AE, DC, MC.
Open: Daily 7:30pm–1am.
This is Leblon's answer to Ipanema's Lord Jim. The Piccadilly, with its bar downstairs and restaurant on the second floor where nouvelle cuisine is served, keeps pub-type hours.

PORTO DI MARE, Rua Maria Quitéria 46. Tel. 247-9506.
Cuisine: ITALIAN. **Reservations:** Recommended.
$ Prices: Appetizers $5.50–$6.25; main courses $9.50–$23. AE.
Open: Daily 11:30am–2am.
Porto di Mare, a short walk from the Caesar Park Hotel, is an attractive Italian restaurant with traditional checkered tablecloths. If candles in empty straw-wrapped bottles of Chianti were added to the table settings, the ambience would resemble those intimate Italian restaurants of New York's Greenwich Village in the 1960s. Pasta dishes average $4.50, while fish plates are $9 and up.

REAL ASTORIA, Av. Ataulfo de Paiva 1235. Tel. 294-0047.
Cuisine: SPANISH. **Reservations:** Not needed.
$ Prices: Appetizers $5–$15; main courses $9–$20. AE, DC, V.
Open: Daily 11:30am–4am.
The third large avenue in from the beach is Avenida Ataulfo de Paiva, recommended for its street life, a variety of shops and services, and a number of snack shops and restaurants, like the Real Astoria, an attractive place offering Spanish specialties.

LE STREGHE, Rua Prudente de Morais 129, on Praça Gen. Osório. Tel. 287-1369.
Cuisine: ITALIAN. **Reservations:** Recommended.
$ Prices: Appetizers $3–$10; main courses $6–$20. AE, DC, MC, V.
Open: Dinner daily 7:30pm–2am.
The name means "witch" in Italian, an allusion to the artful brewing up of new-wave cuisine Italian style, the trademark of Le Streghe. To satisfy himself that a given dish embodies a particular taste from Italy, the owner will sometimes amuse Customs officials with suitcases filled with cheese or herbs on his return from visits to his old homeland. Le Streghe is one in a trio of nightspots under the same roof, a former private house across from Ipanema's main square, the Praça General Osório. In addition to the restaurant there is a popular piano bar, and the Calígola discotheque.
    The food is very good, as the kitchen turns out some delicious variations using familiar basics like veal and pasta. Noshing before the meal can mean sampling the prosciutto or eating delicate breaded crab legs. Prices are quite reasonable given the quality of the meals: Veal dishes run about $8 to $10, pastas are between $4 and $5, and the shellfish dishes are priced somewhat higher, as high as $20 for the green pasta with seafood sauce.

TATSUMI, Rua Dias Ferreira 256. Tel. 274-1342.
Cuisine: JAPANESE. **Reservations:** Recommended.
$ Prices: Appetizers $1–$2.50; main courses $8.50–$18.50. V.
Open: Daily 7pm–midnight.
Tatsumi, on a back street in Leblon, is great for sushi, sashimi, and saké. For $12 you can fill yourself to blissful satisfaction, if raw fish and tempura are to your taste. And that includes dessert, plus a few rounds of flavorful Japanese beer.

UN, DEUX, TROIS, Av. Bartolomeo Mitre 123. Tel. 239-0198.
Cuisine: BRAZILIAN. **Reservations:** Required.
$ Prices: Appetizers $4.75–$9; main courses $7.75–$25. No credit cards.
Open: Lunch Sat–Sun noon–3pm; dinner daily 7pm–2am.
Un, Deux, Trois, another Leblon favorite, is a good choice for both dinner and dancing. The restaurant, however, is separate from the nightclub, and separate reservations are required for both establishments. Fare is standard Brazilian often labeled "international" in restaurants throughout the city. The nightclub features dance-band music and a supper-club environment. There is a reasonably priced

feijoada served every Saturday. The nightclub remains open till the wee hours on the weekends.

VIA FARME, Rua Farme de Amoedo 47. Tel. 227-0743.
  Cuisine: ITALIAN. **Reservations:** Recommended.
  $ Prices: Appetizers $4.75–$6.75; main courses $11.50–$21.50. No credit cards.
  Open: Daily noon–2am.
A block or so from both the beach and the popular Garota de Ipanema bar is this restaurant which emblazons its menu with the slogan: "La Vera Cucina Italiana— Genuine Italian Cooking." The Via Farme's popularity since opening five years ago attests to the veracity of that claim. Diners may choose from a varied menu that includes traditional meat, fish, and pasta dishes as well as pizza.

READERS RECOMMEND

Restaurante Ming, Rua Visconde de Pirajá 112. Tel. 267-5820. "I was able to find an excellent Chinese restaurant in Ipanema, the Restaurante Ming, where dinner for two cost approximately $20."—Donella Novak. [*Author's note:* Restaurante Ming is open daily from noon to 2am. Appetizers run $2.25 to $2.75, and main courses are priced from $5.25 to $12.75. No credit cards are accepted.]

BUDGET

Typical of the excellent lunch counters found throughout the city are the **Chaika** and the **Padaria Ipanema,** both at Rua Visconde de Pirajá 325 (tel. 227-6900), near the Praça da Paz square. You may just want to pick up one of those delicious loaves of bread you've been eating at breakfast in your hotel for a picnic on the beach. Or you may want to take a quick lunch break from a shopping spree in the nearby boutiques. In that case, either at the counter or in a booth, the perfect snack to satisfy both your palate and your schedule is a plateful of tasty, inexpensive salgadinhos. These little pies and pastries are filled with cheese, chicken, minced meat, egg, or shrimp, and cost between 25¢ and 50¢ each.

CAFE LOOK, Av. Ataulfo de Paiva 900. Tel. 259-0594.
  Cuisine: INTERNATIONAL. **Reservations:** Not needed.
  $ Prices: Appetizers $2–$5; main courses $3–$10. No credit cards.
  Open: Daily noon–4am.
Featured at the Café Look, which sits just opposite the Praça Antero Quintal, are many blue-plate specials, with meat dishes averaging $5; fish, $5.50; and pasta, $3.
  Similar in style, appearance, and menu is the **Luna Bar,** just up the block.

GAROTA DE IPANEMA, Rua Prudente de Morais, at the corner of Rua Vinícius de Morais. No phone.
  Cuisine: LIGHT FARE. **Reservations:** Not needed.
  $ Prices: Appetizers $2–$5; main courses $4–$12. No credit cards.
  Open: Daily 8am–late.
This outdoor café on Rua Vinícius de Morais is a very popular daytime hangout for enjoying a cooling, freshly squeezed cup of orange juice, or a well-chilled glass of draft beer. The steak sandwich, smothered with a fried egg, is the perfect lunch or between-meal snack.

GAROTA DO LEBLON, Rua Aristides Espinola 44. Tel. 239-3249.
  Cuisine: INTERNATIONAL. **Reservations:** Not needed.
  $ Prices: Appetizers $2–$5; main courses $5–$13. DC, MC.
  Open: Daily noon–4am.
This is Baixo Leblon's answer to the Garota de Ipanema, though more of a combination bar/restaurant than its rival up the beach. Pizza, with a wide variety of toppings, seems to dominate the menu. Deliveries are made throughout the neighborhood.

LA MOLE, Rua Dias Ferreira 147. Tel. 294-0699.
  Cuisine: ITALIAN. **Reservations:** Not needed.

$ Prices: Appetizers $3.50–$4; main courses $3.50–$9. No credit cards.
Open: Daily 11am–2am.

Turning the corner on Ataulfo de Paiva where Rua Dias Ferreira comes in on an angle, you will encounter another cluster of oft-frequented neighborhood restaurants in Baixo Leblon, like La Mole. La Mole calls itself *o lugar da gente*—the "people's choice," and one correspondent of a large circulation U.S. daily newspaper who lives in the neighborhood swears by the place. One Saturday afternoon when I walked by, the cars were parked two and three deep on the street out front, complete with a uniformed attendant, whose clients were lunching at several restaurants on the block, including the very animated La Mole, which has branches in four other locations throughout the city.

3. VIDIGAL & SÃO CONRADO

There are a number of fine restaurants that make a spin out to São Conrado worth the effort. For those staying at one of the São Conrado hotels, these restaurants are the perfect option for evenings when you don't feel like hopping a cab to Ipanema or Copacabana.

EXPENSIVE

MONSEIGNEUR, in the Hotel Inter-Continental, Av. Prefeito Mendes de Morais 222. Tel. 322-2200.
   Cuisine: FRENCH. **Reservations:** Accepted.
   $ Prices: Appetizers $5–$15; main courses $12–$30. AE, DC, MC, V.
   Open: Daily 7pm–1am.

Monseigneur is an upper-bracket French restaurant. While it may not be strictly required, men might feel more comfortable in a jacket and tie as a complement to the formality of the decor and service. The seating is warm and posh, and tables richly set. For the originality and quality of its food the Monseigneur has few rivals among the city's fine French restaurants. The duck and veal are prepared very well in rich, tasty sauces. The desserts—like warm chocolate bonbons filled with ice cream—are equally excellent. For a moderate binge you will spend about $40 per person, including beverage. Women, by the way, are presented with a long-stemmed rose on leaving the establishment.

FROMMER'S SMART TRAVELER: RESTAURANTS

1. Most restaurants offer daily specials, which are considerably less expensive than à la carte items.
2. A 10% service charge is included in all restaurant tabs throughout Brazil, which pretty much covers the tip.
3. The *couvert* is optional in most restaurants, and may be refused even after it has been brought to the table.
4. Consider having a light lunch or skipping lunch all together. The Brazilian buffet breakfast—especially the feast served at the first-class hotels—ought to easily tide you over if you plan to dine early. Otherwise, pick up a snack on the beach or at one of the *salgadinho* counters.
5. Fixed-priced menus are generally not as economical as à la carte selections, though the value per quantity of food is probably greater.
6. The cost of alcohol will not cause your tab to skyrocket in Brazil, unless you insist on drinking imported whisky or wine.

MODERATE

ALFREDO DI ROMA, in the Hotel Inter-Continental, Av. Prefeito Mendes de Morais 222. Tel. 322-2200.
  Cuisine: ITALIAN. **Reservations:** Not needed.
$ **Prices:** Appetizers $4–$9; main courses $8–$21; full meal $15–$20. AE, DC, MC, V.
  Open: Lunch daily noon–3pm; dinner daily 7:30–11:30pm.
Alfredo di Roma is a classy pasta house with its roots in Italy at the original Alfredo's, where the fettuccine dish by the same name was said to have been created. Naturally, all the pasta is made fresh on the premises. The restaurant is bright and overlooks the hotel's pool terrace and the peaks of the Pedra da Gávea mountain. Pasta dishes of numerous varieties predominate on the menu, which offers a selection of chicken, veal, and seafood choices as well.

EL PESCADOR, Praça São Conrado 20. Tel. 322-0851.
  Cuisine: SEAFOOD. **Reservations:** Accepted.
$ **Prices:** Appetizers $6.15–$7.75; main courses $12.50–$15.50. AE, DC, MC.
  Open: Daily noon–midnight.
El Pescador is another eating option for guests staying at the hotels in São Conrado. The restaurant's dining terrace is recommended, weather permitting. *Frutos do mar* (fruits of the sea) from local waters are served in a great variety of ways, but you can also dine on typical Spanish dishes and mixed barbecue grill. Portions at El Pescador are especially generous. This restaurant is located in the same complex as the popular discotheque, Zoom.

GUIMAS II, Estrada da Gávea 899. Tel. 322-5791.
  Cuisine: INTERNATIONAL/CONTEMPORARY. **Reservations:** Recommended.
$ **Prices:** Appetizers $1–$5; main courses $5–$14. No credit cards.
  Open: Daily noon–2am.
Guimas II is the clone of a very popular, artsy dive located in Gávea not far from the Jockey Club racetrack. The "new" Guimas, however, is no true carbon copy; the name and menu are the same, but the setting—among the swank boutiques of the São Conrado Fashion Mall—is super chic, while the original has overtones of a bohemian café. What happened was that the original Guimas was extremely popular—lines formed each evening by 8:30 to secure a table in the relatively small eatery where no reservations were accepted. So along comes Guimas II, and no one can blame the owners or backers for trying to cash in on the phenomenon. Despite the exact duplication of the menu, though, these two establishments ought to be thought of as completely different restaurants, so radically different are they in ambience and style. Guimas II is a fair size, fancy, and suitable for a power lunch—or a tourist luncheon tied into a swing through the fashion mall. Guimas I is quirky, informal, and remote but still possesses a *je ne sais quoi* characteristic of a really "in" spot. A dish I would recommend at either place is the *pato da fazenda*—braised duck—or the trout in garlic sauce.

OASIS, Praça de São Conrado. Tel. 322-3144.
  Cuisine: STEAK. **Reservations:** Not needed.
$ **Prices:** Rodízio $13, not including beverage and dessert. AE, DC, MC.
  Open: Daily 11am–midnight.
Oasis is not far from the Inter-Continental Hotel on the road that goes to Barra da Tijuca. You won't find a better *churrascaria* (barbecue house) in Rio than the Oasis, where the meat is served *rodízio* style. Proof of this statement is the fact that the Oasis is a favorite of the Cariocas themselves. Like most churrascarias, the restaurant is large, plain, and simple—the white tableclothes are the one concession to decor.
  To begin the rodízio ritual at the Oasis, the tables are covered with side dishes: fried bananas, potato salad, hearts of palm, tomatoes, lettuce, chips, fried manioc, farofa, and various condiments and sauces. The meat starts arriving immediately, carried on skewers by waiters who are moving constantly from table to table. The agility of the waiters is their trade as they carve the juicy slices with unerring dexterity

directly onto your plate. Try to convince the waiters (against the tide of their generous impulses) that you really *do* want tiny slices on the first round. That way you can try everything that interests you and select more carefully from the endless offerings that follow, until you say "uncle" and call for your bill. Among the alcoholic beverages, good Brazilian beer is the proper accompaniment, with perhaps a shot of cachaça as an apéritif. Mineral water—both with and without carbonation—aids the digestion, say Brazilians, who always have a bottle or two open on their tables. For about $10 a person, you can have as good a *churrasco* blowout at the Oasis as anywhere in Rio.

There is another Oasis located downtown at Rua Gonçalves Dias 56 (tel. 252-5521). Their hours are weekdays only, from 11am till 4am.

4. BARRA DA TIJUCA & BEYOND

The segment of Barra beach closest to São Conrado is the most developed. After the first 6km (3½ miles) or so, the remainder of the 20km (12-mile) beach becomes more and more sparsely settled—an undeniably short-term state of affairs given the pace at which all of Rio's remaining virgin coast is being developed for tourism and luxury apartments. This first stretch of Barra, however, is a landscape of high-rise complexes, usually centered on a fair chunk of real estate, and often separated by an equally generous space from its neighboring structures. Across Avenida Sernambetiba is the beach. On the edge of the sand, many trailers and stands cater to weekend bathers with an ample selection of food and beverages, but there is no sidewalk life. It is the land of shopping malls—some of the largest in the world—magical commercial hamlets offering entertainment as well as access to hundreds of shops.

BARRA

There is still something of an urban-frontier look about Barra. Scattered among these condo fortresses are a handful of very good restaurants, to the relief of both beachside residents and the seasonal tourists as well, who have the option to dine well locally.

LOKAU, Av. Sernambetiba 13500. Tel. 433-1368.
    Cuisine: SEAFOOD. **Reservations:** Accepted.
$ Prices: Appetizers $5–$25; main courses $9–$30 (beef dishes $9–$10, seafood dishes $15–$30). No credit cards.
    Open: Mon–Sat noon–3am, Sun noon–7:30pm.

 FROMMER'S COOL FOR KIDS: RESTAURANTS

Fast Food Ask your hotel desk staff where the closest **Bob's** or **Gordon's** is; these are the most popular Brazilian fast-food chains. There is also a McDonald's on Avenida N. S. de Copacabana, in Copacabana, where the kids can experience what they like best back home, adapted to the Brazilian reality.

Pizza Always a good bet with kids, pizza is very popular in Rio. Try **Bella Blu,** Rua Siqueira Campos 107 in Copacabana, or Rua Gen. Urquiza 102 in Leblon.

La Mole This is another chain of popular pizza/pasta restaurants that the kids ought to like. The La Mole restaurant in Baixo Leblon (see p. 92) should prove to be a hit.

The Lokau sits informally by the side of the road, deep in Barra, under an unassuming open-air structure with a thatched roof. Don't be misled by appearances into thinking this is a *barraca*, a simple beach bar; it's actually one of Rio's hottest, most expensive seafood eateries. An added touch of the rustic is the use of oil lanterns for illumination, since there's no electricity. Nor does public transportation come this far along the beachfront; you're pretty much confined to coming and going by cab, rented car, or a local friend who provides the ride. It may be a hassle to get here, but both the scene and the food repay the effort.

MERIDIANO, Av. Sernambetiba 6250. Tel. 385-5771.
   Cuisine: EASTERN EUROPEAN/INTERNATIONAL. **Reservations:** Recommended.
$ Prices: Appetizers $2–$7; main courses $7–$20. AE.
   Open: Tues–Sun noon–midnight.

Installed in the space formerly occupied by Le Petit Paris, and attached to the Rio Hotel Residência, the Meridiano offers an enticing sampler of East European dishes. For starters, there's a choice of salads—Ukrainian with herring, potato, beet, and carrot, or Muscovite with smoked turkey, deviled eggs, and mushrooms. Stuffed cabbage called *golubtsi* is one of several hot first-course selections. Main dishes range from the Russian beef-filled blintzes to the traditional goulash. And if these delicacies from countries behind what was once quaintly called the Iron Curtain don't appeal, the Meridiano has a separate, and extensive, menu of international platters for your perusal.

PETIT LIEU, Estrada da Barra da Tijuca 1636, loja 210. Tel. 399-7798.
   Cuisine: FRENCH. **Reservations:** Accepted.
$ Prices: Appetizers $2.50–$8.50 (escargots $15); main courses $6–$18. AE.
   Open: Lunch Tues–Sun noon–3pm; dinner Tues–Sun 7:30pm–midnight.

Les poissons, les fruits de mer, les viandes, les volailles: they're all here, all the classic French recipes that have brought satisfaction to diners for generations. The sauces are the familiar ones, the tried and true: suprême, au poivre, vin rouge, champagne, beurre noir, provençale, and many more. For dessert, try the crêpes Suzette ($7), made from the ground up at your table, or the banana flambé ($6.50).

AROUND BARRA

Beyond Barra is yet another string of beaches continuing down the so-called Costa Verde (Green Coast) for a dozen miles or so until reaching Rio's suburban city limits. First comes **Recreio dos Bandeirantes,** a favorite retreat for weekenders, those with vacation homes, and day-trippers too, who come out to enjoy the unblemished beach. The lone restaurant across from the 6km (3½-mile) beach is the **Âncora,** open daily from 9am till midnight. **Prainha** comes next, refuge of the middle class, as well as a favorite spot for surfers. Finally there is **Grumari,** end of the line, virtually deserted on weekdays, and home to the rustic beach bar, the **Vista Alegre,** a roadside favorite with a great view down the coast, if you happen to find yourself in the vicinity.

VARGEM GRANDE

QUINTA, Rua Luciano Gallet 150. Tel. 437-8395.
   Cuisine: BRAZILIAN. **Reservations:** Required.
$ Prices: Fixed-price menu $22.
   Open: Irregular hours; call ahead.

You'll never find this place on your own. So you'll need to call Luís Correa de Araujo—owner, chef, and chief resident—on two counts, first to see if and when he is having a seating, and second, to have your designated driver get exact directions. The Quinta is actually landscape-artist Luís's beautiful suburban home, a walled-in complex where greenhouses, potting sheds, and formal tropical gardens await the approbation of the botanically minded who come to visit or to eat.

The neighborhood, incidentally, is called Vargem Grande, somewhere just beyond the borders of Barra, and inland within the vast borough called Jacarepaqua.

The story behind the restaurant is an oft-told tale: Luís's friends held him in such high regard as a cook that they suggested he go public. Quinta, which means "country place," is the result of their nudging. The home's covered patio is rigged to hold as many as 50 diners, who will be served "the best that I have to offer on that day," says Luís. A typical menu will begin with a cocktail and some pâté maison with fresh-baked French bread, followed by pasta with a spicy tuna sauce, crayfish, and, for the main course, baked snook, accompanied by mashed carrots and mashed breadfruit. For dessert, there will be an array of homemade sweets.

PEDRA DE GUARATIBA

About an hour's drive from Rio's Zona Sul, some 50km (31 miles), is the Pedra de Guaratiba beach, well beyond Barra da Tijuca toward Angra dos Reis. Two restaurants in this region have become famous in recent years, attracting a steady stream of weekend gourmets.

CÂNDIDO'S, Rua Barros de Alarcão 352. Tel. 395-1630.
   Cuisine: SEAFOOD. **Reservations:** Not needed.
$ **Prices:** Appetizers $3–$9; main courses $7–$15. AE.
   Open: Sun–Fri noon–9pm, Sat noon–11pm.
Simple in appearance, Cândido's has retained for a decade a reputation as one of the finest seafood restaurants in or around Rio. The *santolas,* a variety of crab imported from Chile that are considered a great delicacy, are priced at about $40 per kilo (2.2 lb.). The lobster stew, a Bahian-style moqueca, costs $15, while the crab version of the moqueca is $5. Also available are a variety of shrimp and fish dishes in the $8 to $15 range.

QUATRO SETE MEIA, Rua Barros de Alarcão 476. Tel. 395-2716.
   Cuisine: SEAFOOD. **Reservations:** Required.
$ **Prices:** Appetizers $2–$8; main courses $8.50–$13. No credit cards.
   Open: Tues–Thurs 11am–5pm, Fri–Sun 11am–10pm.
The reputation of the 476 had long preceded it before I finally had a chance to eat there. Few of the fantasies postponed in this life are as worth the wait as the meal Bartolomeu Morais, the homegrown half of this Canadian-Brazilian coproduction, put before my friends and me. Clearly, though Bartolomeu has been at this demanding enterprise for over 17 years, the creative fires within him have not been dampened by stress or repetition.

The key to Bartolomeu's culinary genius is the simplicity of his creations, and their faithfulness to the kitchens of his native Alagoas in Brazil's northeast. Our meal began with several rounds of strong *cajuroskas*—cocktails of crushed caju fruit and vodka—and a homemade fruit chutney, scooped to the mouth with slices of hot bread. A generous order of large shrimp, bathed in garlic oil and grilled in their shells, followed. But the crowning point of the meal was the fish-and-shrimp moqueca, seasoned with the flesh and juices of fresh mangoes, the best I have ever tasted. Much smaller and more informal than its nearby rival, Cândido's, the 476 is filled with bric-a-brac accumulated from the owners' world travels, which add a quirky, intimate charm. And the open-air terrace offers a fine view of a coast very active with fishing craft. Expect to pay between $20 and $25 per person at this rustic gourmet haven by the sea.

TIA PALMIRA, Caminho do Souza 18. Tel. 310-1169.
   Cuisine: SEAFOOD. **Reservations:** Not needed.
$ **Prices:** Appetizers $4–$7; main courses $6–$13; fixed-price meal $10 for adults, $5 for children 8 and under. No credit cards.
   Open: Daily noon–midnight.
Perhaps the most popular of the many seafood restaurants in Barra de Guaratiba is Tia Palmira, sitting at the top of an incline with a private parking lot. A typical meal might include, for beginners, fried shrimp, *pastel de camarão* (small shrimp turnovers), and mussels. Main courses could be fried filet of fish and a baked dish of marinated fish, plus *bobó de camarão* (a shrimp paste), vatapá, pirão, rice, and octopus farofa. For

dessert, a cavalcade of fresh fruits along with varied sweets of coconut, melon, banana, and jackfruit (*jaca*).

READERS RECOMMEND

Taba do Guará, *Rua Belchoir da Fonseca 399, Pedra de Guaratiba. Tel. 395-0842. "Opened in June 1989 by its owner and head chef, José Ricardo de Oliveira, a native of the village, Taba do Guará specializes in moquecas and other typical Brazilian seafood dishes, and also features excellent massa (pasta) and carne (beef) plates. Some guests claim that it is now the best restaurant in the village, where prices, however, continue to be more modest than those of its rivals. The restaurant is open on Friday, Saturday, and Sunday from noon to midnight; closed May through August.*

The town of Pedra de Guaratiba can be reached from the beach avenues of Copacabana and Ipanema by a beautiful drive along a spectacular highway through São Conrado and Barra da Tijuca, up and over a little mountain and into the quiet countryside beyond. The Santa Cruz bus from Castelo (downtown) also runs on the same beach avenues. It is easy to understand why so many people visit Pedra for a relaxing change from Copacabana and Ipanema."—James W. Partridge, Berkeley, Calif.

---

5. THE LAGOA & JARDIM BOTÂNICO

An immense lagoon, the Lagoa Rodrigo de Freitas occupies much of the center ground between the bairros of Copacabana and Ipanema. On the margins of the Lagoa, as the district is always referred to in conversation, are some of Rio's most exclusive houses and apartment buildings—and a number of its better bars and restaurants as well. Jardim Botânico designates a neighborhood as well as a vast public garden.

EXPENSIVE

ANTONINO, Av. Epitácio Pessoa 1244. Tel. 267-6791.
   Cuisine: FRENCH/INTERNATIONAL. **Reservations:** Accepted.
$ Prices: Appetizers $5–$12; main courses $10–$25; full meal $40. AE, DC, MC, V.
   Open: Daily noon–2am.
Antonino is quiet elegance by the shaded banks of a lagoon. At night the glass facade at Antonino's always seems bathed in shimmering sepia tones, adding to the experience of dining there. Even the solemn formality of the waiters seems an anachronism, albeit a pleasant one. From the font of this genteel sensibility, Antonino's has managed to maintain the consistently high standards of its kitchen. Here you will eat the familiar dishes, including spring lamb or *badejo* (sea bass), cooked to perfection.

CASTELO DA LAGOA, Av. Epitácio Pessoa 1560. Tel. 287-3514.
   Cuisine: INTERNATIONAL. **Reservations:** Accepted.
$ Prices: Appetizers $4–$9; main courses $8.50–$18; full meal $20–$25. AE, DC, MC, V.
   Open: Daily 11am–5am.
The back room at the Castelo da Lagoa is a clubhouse for one of Rio's best-known society journalists and his circle, primarily actors and actresses. The restaurant's decor is even a little flashy in a Hollywood sense, but the prices are reasonable and the food reliable. The vichyssoise, followed by grilled *langostino* (a kind of saltwater crayfish), makes for a tasty lunch, especially if you have time to linger in the tranquil atmosphere of a table in the outdoor patio. At dinner the restaurant tends to fill up, and the movement of customers is constant between the restaurant and the attached Chiko's Bar, where there is always a solid jazz group to entertain in what is one of the most popular bars for singles and couples in Rio.

TROISGROS, Rua Custodio Serrão 62. Tel. 226-4542.

Cuisine: FRENCH. **Reservations:** Accepted.
$ Prices: Appetizers $5–$15; main courses $12–$27; full meal $35. AE, DC, MC, V.
Open: Dinner Mon–Sat 7:30pm–midnight.

Troisgros, on the Jardim Botânico end of the Lagoa, near Botafogo, is operated by a French chef who was formerly with Le Pré Catelan at the Rio Palace Hotel. The chef personally supervises the creation of all meals, and so his menu is limited and includes a set plate from appetizer to dessert, which changes from day to day.

MODERATE

GUIMAS, Rua José Roberto Macedo Soares 05. Tel. 259-7996.
Cuisine: NOUVELLE. **Reservations:** Not needed.
$ Prices: Appetizers $1–$5; main courses $5–$14; full meal $15. No credit cards.
Open: Daily noon–2am.

Guimas is one of the hottest small restaurants in Rio, with only a dozen or so tables. It's almost impossible to get a seat without waiting for an hour. The ambience is bistro style, with contemporary graphics and posters announcing art exhibitions or plays filling the walls. Each table is set with a cup of crayons, for doodling on the paper table cover. Typical dishes are the linguine with smoked whitefish, and the spicy scalloped chicken served with beets. Guimas, despite its popularity, is not a household word among Rio's cab drivers. It's not far from the Jardim Botânico end of the Lagoa. Ask your driver to call ahead for directions, if possible (he can call from the porter's desk if you're leaving for the restaurant from your hotel). The cab ride from Copacabana ought to be in the $3 to $4 range.

BUDGET

COUVE FLOR, Rua Pacheco Leão 724. Tel. 239-2191.
Cuisine: BRAZILIAN. **Reservations:** Not needed.
$ Prices: Appetizers 75¢–$3; main courses $1–$5. No credit cards.
Open: Daily 11:30am–11pm.

The Jardim Botânico is a quiet, residential neighborhood nestled against the hilly interior of the Zona Sul, and not necessarily a center of gastronomy. One little, family-style eatery there, though, is worth attention. At the Couve Flor you pay by the serving, selecting from a variety of hot dishes—the lasagne seems very popular—and cold salad platters displayed in a deli case. First you find an empty table, then order what you want at the counter, and the waitress brings your meal when it's ready. It's a great place to mix and match tastes; for example, I combined traditional black beans and rice with a fancy pasta and tuna fish salad, and then had a big dish of strawberry ice milk for dessert. With a fresh orange juice, my bill came to about $4. To get to the Couve Flor, go to the street just beyond the Botanical Gardens—assuming you are coming from Copacabana or Ipanema/Leblon. That street is Pacheco Leão; turn left, then continue for about a quarter of a mile.

6. GLÓRIA, FLAMENGO & BOTAFOGO

Flamengo and Botafogo were the fashionable beachfront neighborhoods during the early 20th century until the 1950s. As desirable residential areas, they have undergone a revival in recent years as well, because of the high rents demanded for much smaller apartments in other districts. There are a fair number of fine restaurants to be found in both these bairros, especially tucked away on the back streets, but also overlooking the Baia da Guanabara. The nearby beaches have long been replaced by the ocean beaches from Leme onward as desired swimming and tanning spots.

EXPENSIVE

BARRACUDA, Marina da Glória. Tel. 265-3997.

Cuisine: SEAFOOD. **Reservations:** Not needed for lunch; recommended for dinner.
$ Prices: Appetizers $3–$8; main courses $7.50–$23. AE, DC, MC, V.
Open: Mon–Sat noon–midnight, Sun noon–11pm.

The Barracuda is nestled dockside among the moorings of pleasure cruisers and yachts bordering the neighborhoods of Flamengo and Glória. You actually have to drive onto the wharf through a guarded gate to get to the restaurant. Dining is inside and there is no particular view of any note, but the decor is appropriately nautical. The Barracuda is one of the few seafood restaurants in town where you can order a mixed-seafood barbecue served on a skewer. The apple salad is also an unusual and welcome accompaniment. A seafood lunch for two, including appetizers and a couple of caipirinhas to wash it all down, will cost perhaps $40 in all. The restaurant's proximity to downtown makes it a favorite spot for business luncheons.

CLUBE GOURMET, Rua General Polidoro 186. Tel. 295-3494.
Cuisine: FRENCH. **Reservations:** Accepted.
$ Prices: Fixed-price meal $40. No credit cards.
Open: Lunch Sun–Fri noon–3pm; dinner daily 8:30pm–1am.

Clube Gourmet is another chef-owned upper-bracket eatery. It has an unimposing exterior on a narrow back street in Botafogo across from an old cemetery. Inside, the converted town house is smartly decorated and informal. Typical of the dishes is the veal Margherita, flavored with tomato and cheese, and leg of lamb, delicately spiced and cooked in white wine. A soufflé of *maracujá* (a mangolike fruit) is popular for dessert.

LAURENT, Rua Dona Mariana 209. Tel. 266-3131.
Cuisine: FRENCH. **Reservations:** Recommended on weekends.
$ Prices: Appetizers $6–$15; main courses $12–$31; full meal $40–$50. AE, DC, MC, V.
Open: Dinner Mon–Sat 8pm–midnight.

Formerly the head chef at the St. Honoré, the owner opened his own fine restaurant in 1986 here in the heart of Botafogo. Once a large and lovely private house, the many rooms add intrigue and intimacy to the dining experience. The food is superb, and special attention is given to soups and salads. A menu dégustation, consisting of five courses, is priced at $50 per person.

SOL E MAR, Av. Repórter Néstor Moreira 11. Tel. 295-1947.
Cuisine: SPANISH/SEAFOOD. **Reservations:** Not accepted.
$ Prices: Appetizers $4–$11; main courses $7–$17. AE, DC, MC, V.
Open: Daily 11am–3am.

The Sol e Mar can be found on the same dock where the Bâteau Mouche excursion boats used to board; the cruises were discontinued after one craft sank with a boatload of tourists. The Sol e Mar (Sun and Sea) is a very expensive Spanish-style seafood restaurant. A large deck sticks out over the bay, and from it you can appreciate one of the best close-up views of Pão de Açúcar from sea level in Rio. This is a most peaceful spot to enjoy a drink or a light meal either before or after a night on the town.

MODERATE

AMAZÔNIA, Rua do Catete 234D. Tel. 225-4622.
Cuisine: PORTUGUESE. **Reservations:** Not needed.
$ Prices: Appetizers $3.75–$6; main courses $6–$9 (shrimp dishes up to $18). No credit cards.
Open: Daily 11am–midnight.

The Amazônia occupies an unassuming spot on Flamengo's main commercial strip, about a kilometer from the beach front. Tucked above the traffic and spread over a large second-story space, the restaurant has a decidedly European flavor. You won't find many tourists in here, but a Rio banker of my acquaintance swears by the place.

CAFE BRASIL, Rua Capitão Salamão 35. Tel. 266-6483.

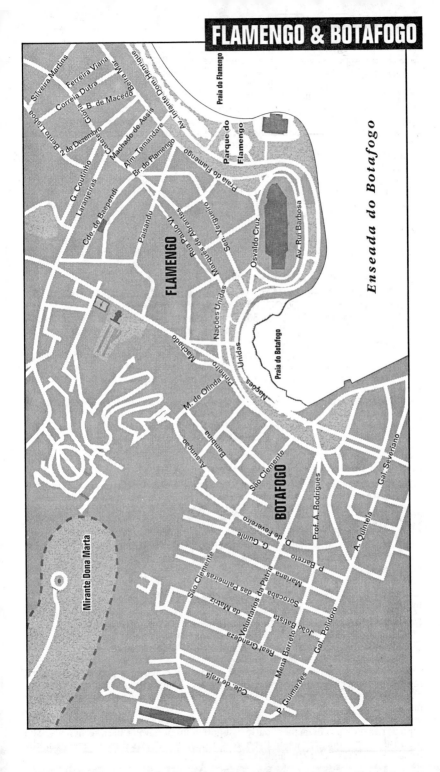

Cuisine: BRAZILIAN. **Reservations:** Recommended for dinner on weekends.
$ **Prices:** Appetizers $1.50–$5; main courses $5–$12. AE, DC, MC.
Open: Sun–Thurs 11am–1 or 2am, Fri–Sat 11am–4am.

This was probably the great restaurant find I made in Rio during the update of the guide's current edition. It would be hard to sound a critical note about my culinary experience at the Café Brasil, a new restaurant occupying a beautifully restored colonial house in Humaita, Botafogo's compact nightlife district. When you are in good company, as I was for that evening meal among a very animated group of Brazilian friends, the food has to be really special to rise above the human performances. By the end of the meal, the food had captured the spotlight.

Our crowd inclined toward "comida mineira" that night, dishes typical in their preparation and accompaniments of the cooking from Minas Gerais state. But we began the meal with the generous *couvert* of *pão de queijo*—cheese bread, *queijo mineiro*—Minas-style white cheese soaked in olive oil and oregano, and, for appetizers, the ubiquitous *pastel*—cheese-and-meat pastries fresh from the deep fryer (50¢). Our main courses, however, were the meal's star attractions, a perfectly broiled *picanha* steak, with *feijão tropeiro*—black beans and farofa on the side ($8), *peixe na telha*—river fish served on the clay tile in which it was cooked ($7), and *tutu a mineira*—a mixture of pork loin and a black-bean purée ($6).

CHURRASCARIA MAJÓRICA, Rua Sen. Vergueiro. Tel. 245-8947.
Cuisine: STEAK/SEAFOOD. **Reservations:** Not needed.
$ **Prices:** Appetizers $1.25–$3.50; main courses $6–$8 for meat dishes, $9.50–$18 for fish and shellfish dishes. No credit cards.
Open: Daily noon–10pm.

A Carioca friend who knows Rio's restaurant scene intimately says that this Flamengo churrascaria is the best in the city. All the meats and fish are on display in a huge glass-faced cooler; you select the cut of meat or fish filet that appeals, and the chef puts it right on the grill in front of you. Speaking as a confirmed carnivore, the meat did look mouth-watering. The Majórica also has a branch in Petrópolis (Avenida 15 de Novembro; tel. 42-2498).

BUDGET

Around the corner from the Café Brasil are two hot night spots that cater primarily to singles, the **Boutequim Bar & Restaurant** and **Linziom.**

BOUTEQUIM BAR & RESTAURANT, Rua Visconde Caravelas 184. Tel. 266-0407.
Cuisine: BRAZILIAN/INTERNATIONAL. **Reservations:** Not needed.
$ **Prices:** Appetizers $2–$5.50; main courses $5.50–$9.25. No credit cards.
Open: Mon–Fri 11:30am–1:30am, Sat–Sun 11:30am–2:30am.

The Boutequim is a veritable hive of inner and outer environments, housed in an antique colonial dwelling. The extensive menu offers the simple, homespun, and inexpensive selections that appeal to office workers on their lunch break, and to the hordes of young people who frequent the bar by night. The outside tables are for the drinking, snacking crowd, while inside, a dining room is segregated from the barroom by a wall of windows.

CAFE LAMAS, Rua Marquês de Abrantes 18. Tel. 205-0799.
Cuisine: INTERNATIONAL. **Reservations:** Not needed.
$ **Prices:** Appetizers $3–$6; main courses $5–$12. No credit cards.
Open: Daily 6:30am–4am.

Café Lamas, located on a back street in Flamengo, is one of Rio's oldest restaurants, though no longer at its original site. The interior is reminiscent of the popular Lisbon cafés, which no doubt served as model and prototype for a style of public eatery now disappearing from the scene in Rio. The Lamas keeps café hours, making it a convenient choice for afternoon lingering or early-morning meals—breakfast or supper, depending on whether you've just gotten up or haven't been to bed yet. The food is standard quality fare and very reasonable, with a varied menu, including the usual snacks, meat, chicken, and fish dishes.

LINZIOM, Rua Visconde Caravelas 180. Tel. 286-5635.
 Cuisine: INTERNATIONAL. **Reservations:** Not needed.
$ **Prices:** Appetizers $3.50–$5.75; main courses $6.50–$7.25. No credit cards.
 Open: Sun–Thurs 5pm–1:30am, Fri–Sat 3pm–4am. Happy hour daily 5:30–7:30pm.
The Linziom has an artsy, publike ambience, and appeals to a professional and cosmopolitan clientele. The multileveled inner space is open and attractive; original artworks decorate the walls. Food is straightforward—filet, for example, or grilled chicken; you pick your own side dishes.

RESTAURANTE RIO GALICIA, Rua do Catete 265. Tel. 265-6149.
 Cuisine: BRAZILIAN/INTERNATIONAL. **Reservations:** Not needed.
$ **Prices:** Appetizers $1–$5; main courses $5.50–$11. AE, DC, MC, V.
 Open: Daily 8am–midnight.
This reliable eatery belongs to the Portuguese/Spanish genre of the type that has all but disappeared from Copacabana, but which seem to flourish still in Flamengo. The menu is extensive, featuring dozens of beef, chicken, and fish platters. The *mariscada carioca,* the fish stew, looks to be a bargain at $9.

7. CENTRO

The restaurant scene downtown, from the tourist's point of view, is actually somewhat of a novelty. The whole Centro is packed with places to eat, catering primarily to the lunchtime needs of the thousands who work there. The variety runs the gamut from simple *galetos* (barbecued chicken stands) to some fine clubs and restaurants, including the few places in Rio where men are required to wear jackets and ties. Many downtown restaurants don't even serve dinner, and are closed for the weekends. Those places that remain open at night and on Saturday and Sunday usually provide other attractions, in most cases their location or some historical significance. They are not just tourist attractions, however, because you are just as likely to find residents as well as nonresidents in them.

EXPENSIVE

ENGLISH BAR, Rua do Comércio 11. Tel. 224-2539.
 Cuisine: INTERNATIONAL. **Reservations:** Accepted.
$ **Prices:** Appetizers $4–$12; main courses $11–$23. AE, DC, MC, V.
 Open: Lunch Mon–Fri noon–4pm; cocktails served Mon–Fri noon–8pm.
The English Bar is a popular choice among business types who work downtown and who want to eat well without traveling to the more fashionable areas. Prime rib of roast beef is a favorite meal here, but the menu is fully international, offering French, Spanish, and Portuguese specialties as well.

MODERATE

ALBA MAR, Praça Marechal Âncora 184. Tel. 240-8428.
 Cuisine: SEAFOOD. **Reservations:** Not needed.
$ **Prices:** Appetizers $2.50–$5.75; main courses $5–$15. DC, MC.
 Open: Mon–Sat 11:30am–10pm.
At one point some years back, when the Alba Mar was about to be closed, a dozen waiters decided to pool their resources and buy the place, forming a partnership that still endures. The restaurant has been operating since 1933 in the last remaining cast-iron and leaded-glass building—an octagonal tower—of what was once the dockside municipal market. It's a short walk from Praça XV, and should be considered as a lunchtime option during a visit to this historic square. Be careful on the walk: There are few sidewalks once you get close to the water's edge, and the traffic is relentless. Eating at the Alba Mar will not necessarily be the culinary high

point of your stay in Rio. But the view of the waterfront and the bay from the third-floor windows will more than compensate for the simple fare.

BAR LUÍS, Rua da Carioca 39. Tel. 262-6900.
Cuisine: GERMAN. **Reservations:** Not needed.
$ Prices: Appetizers $2.75–$6.50; main courses $5–$13. DC.
Open: Mon–Sat 11am–midnight.

The Bar Luís is another traditional and informal lunch spot, a favorite of the journalists and editors who work in the nearby offices of book publishers and periodicals. Founded in 1887, it is even more venerable than the Colombo, though the atmosphere is more saloonlike than continental. The Rua da Carioca is also one of Rio's oldest, where an annual costume festival takes place in the second week of August every year. The Bar Luís offers good solid German eats—veal Holstein, wurst and kraut, kasseler, and other delights—at reasonable prices.

CAFE DO TEATRO, in the Teatro Municipal, Av. Rio Branco. Tel. 262-4164.
Cuisine: INTERNATIONAL. **Reservations:** Not accepted.
$ Prices: Prix-fixe menu $15. AE, DC, MC, V.
Open: Lunch Mon–Fri 11am–4pm.

The Café do Teatro is located in Rio's grand old opera house. The restaurant's Doric columns and walls of mosaic tiles make you wonder if perhaps you haven't stumbled onto the stage setting for one of the classical productions. The food is also classically international, as the Café do Teatro is under the stewardship of the same group that owns and operates Antonino's on the Lagoa.

COLOMBO, Rua Gonçalves Dias 32. Tel. 232-2300.
Cuisine: CONTINENTAL. **Reservations:** Not needed.
$ Prices: Appetizers $3–$7; main courses $6–$16. No credit cards.
Open: Mon–Fri 11am–6pm.

The Colombo is a genuine fin-de-siècle café, opened in 1894 and an unchanging Carioca landmark in a city that has shed its skin a dozen times since this café was built. It's a favorite spot for munching *salgadinhos* or pastries with a steaming cup of *cafezinho* or an ideal setting for an afternoon spot of tea. Fortunately the art nouveau decor is made of stone and crystal or you might be tempted to eat that, too. The second-story gallery encircles an oval opening above the café's ground floor, and is an ideal setting for a downtown luncheon. The Colombo's prices are only slightly higher than other typical café's, which means it remains an economical choice.

REAL MERCANTIL, Av. Alfredo Agache 3A. Tel. 224-1891.
Cuisine: SEAFOOD. **Reservations:** Not needed.
$ Prices: Appetizers $2–$4; most main courses $6–$10, shrimp and cod dishes about $12–$20. No credit cards.
Open: Daily 11am–10pm.

Under the same family ownership since 1870, the Real refers to itself as the *"rei das peixsadas"*—Rio's seafood king. Needless to say, given its downtown location and its reputation for reliability, this is a favorite lunch spot for business executives, especially those who work at the nearby stock exchange. For a lunch on the lighter side, there's a choice of fish filets in the $7 to $9 range; less expensive, but very filling and palatable is the *sopa de leão* ($6.50), a pipping hot stew brimming over with innumerable species culled from the local seas.

8. SANTA TERESA

BAR DO ARNAUDO, Rua Almirante Alexandrino 316. Tel. 252-7246.
Cuisine: NORTHEAST BRAZILIAN. **Reservations:** Not needed.
$ Prices: Appetizers $2–$5; main courses $3–$6. No credit cards.

Open: Wed–Sun noon–10pm.

⭐ ⓢ One very special restaurant in the neighborhood called Santa Teresa, which sits in the hills overlooking the Centro, is the Bar do Arnaudo. An excursion to Santa Teresa is described in the next chapter, and the best choice for lunch for anyone taking this excursion is this delightful and slightly bohemian hangout specializing in food from the northeast. *Carne seca, carne de sol* (sun-dried jerky), and *sarapatel* (minced sweetbreads) are the typical dishes. But the way to try everything, including dessert and plenty of beer—for less than $10—is to order the large-portion appetizers called *pratos diversos* on the menu.

9. SPECIALTY DINING

DINING WITH A VIEW

LE SAINT HONORE, in the Hotel Meridien, Av. Atlântica 1020. Tel. 275-9922.
   Cuisine: FRENCH. **Reservations:** Recommended.
$ Prices: Appetizers $7–$18; main courses $15–$27. AE, DC, MC, V.
   Open: Lunch daily noon–3pm; dinner daily 8pm–midnight.
Wrapped in windows, Le Saint Honoré occupies the top floor of its hotel, 37 floors high. By day the restaurant is bathed in natural light, and at night the grand panorama of curvaceous Copacabana beach and its surrounding mountains is projected on the glass.
   Delicate seafood dishes are a specialty of the St. Honoré's kitchen. But whatever you sample in this fine restaurant—from the delectable hors d'oeuvres served before the meal to something suitably rich from the dessert tray—you will be satisfied with both the quality and the value.

TIBERIUS, at the Caesar Park Hotel, Av. Vieira Souto 460. Tel. 287-2122.
   Cuisine: INTERNATIONAL. **Reservations:** Recommended on weekends.
$ Prices: Appetizers $5–$11; main courses $9–$16. AE, DC, MC, V.
   Open: Daily 7am–11:30pm.
As Shecky Green might comment, "With a view like that, how bad can the food be?" There's not only Rio's best rooftop view, but good standard Brazilian fare from appetizer to main course. Lunch will cost somewhere in the $10 to $15 range.

LIGHT, CASUAL & FAST FOOD

Botequims, juice bars, pizza parlors, and fast-food establishments abound among the side streets of Copacabana. A **botequim** is usually a bar with a small counter where patrons stand for a quick nip of pinga (cachaça), a beer or soft drink, or a cup of cafezinho. Depending on its size, the botequim may also have a grill for turning out a *mixto* sandwich (grilled cheese and ham) or some similar eat-on-the-run specialty.
   The **juice bars** are less common than botequims but never more than a few blocks from any given point in the neighborhood. Having a *vitamina* (an instant dose of vitamins) in the form of a squeezed or blended fruit drink is an old Carioca tradition—especially the morning after a binge on the town without the benefit of much sleep. A great variety of fruits is usually in season at all times of year.
   Several chains of **pizzerias** (really simple Italian restaurants) are located throughout the city. A branch of **Bella Blu** is at Rua Siqueira Campos 107. **Pizza Pino's** is at Rua Constante Ramos 32, and the **Bella Roma** can be found at Av. Atlântica 928. Pizza, spaghetti and meatballs, lasagne, and so forth. Generally open from 10am to midnight, or later on weekends.
   For fast food, a **Bob's** or a **Gordon's**—and now a **McDonald's**—is always somewhere in the vicinity. There is some novelty in Brazilian junk food, for those who may be curious. But I was also intrigued by the very "idea" of a McDonald's in Brazil—the tastes and food preparations of our two cultures being so different. Could the McDonald's "taste" that is so thoroughly standardized throughout the United

States be duplicated in a country whose palate might not recognize, or even automatically reject, the "junk food" flavor and reproduce an unacceptable hybrid. In the Copacabana McDonald's I ordered my usual, cheeseburger, small fries, and Coke. I was impressed; inside my mouth, I might have been in Peoria.

Last—and probably best—are the **galetos,** the barbecued-chicken counters that also usually offer a variety of grilled meats as well.

A popular daytime hangout for the Leme beach and neighborhood crowd is located on the opposite side of Avenida Princesa Isabel, on the corner of Avenida N. S. de Copacabana, called the **Taberna do Leme.** The Taberna is really just a bar, with the usual fast-food salgadinhos, so the clientele spills out onto the sidewalk, some women but mostly bare-chested men, each with a draft beer in hand, clustered in affinity groups, chatting away. There is something appealing about this informal scene that makes you want to glue yourself right into the picture.

LUNCH COUNTERS & PÉS SUJOS   There are innumerable galetos, *leitarias* (luncheonettes), and pés sujos scattered throughout the labyrinth of downtown streets. *Pé sujo* is a slang name for those lovable greasy spoons that even the most discerning gourmets love to eat in from time to time, usually for the bar life as well as some snack food that is unavailable elsewhere.

For Bahian-style food, try the **Oxalá,** a lunch counter in the Cinelândia section at Rua Francisco Serrador 2 (tel. 220-3035). The counter is Loja 1 (Store 1) inside a gallery of shops. All the Bahian specialties, from moqueca seafood stews to vatapá and *xim xim de galinha,* are served up in simple and large portions. Open during business hours, Monday through Saturday. Meals range between $4 and $8.

Among the most popular *pés sujos* (literal translation is "dirty feet") to be found downtown are: **Arco do Telles,** Travessa do Comércio 2, open till 8pm weekdays only. The specialty here is calf's foot, for $1. The **Ocidental,** on Rua Miguel Couto 124C at the corner of Marechal Floriano, is open Monday through Saturday till 11:30pm, and the treat here is fried sardines, about 75¢ a dozen. The **Farão,** at Rua do Lavradio 192, open till 11pm Monday through Saturday, serves a mean *cabeça de galo* (rooster head) soup, made with kale, manioc flour, and two eggs. The **Tangara,** Rua Alvaro Alvim 35, is the place for *batidas*—blended drinks made with cachaça and tropical fruits—for less than 50¢, including one made from *jilo,* an edible variety of deadly nightshade or belladonna. **Bar Monteiro,** Rua da Quitanda 83 (tel. 231-2274), open daily from 10am till 9pm, is a favorite *pé sujo* among stockbrokers and bohemians alike. A friend and I drank six drafts between us, and snacked on a platter of codfish balls (a house specialty), and the tab came to a total of $6.50.

BREAKFAST/BRUNCH

Unless you are traveling through Brazil dressed in sackcloth and living on park benches, your breakfast (and/or brunch if you're a late riser) will be consumed at your hotel. The usual hours for the morning feast are between 6 and 10am.

LATE NIGHT/24-HOUR

Most of the beachfront cafés stay open every night until the wee hours. Some good bets for a predawn supper are **Café Lamas** (Botafogo), **Caneco 70** (Leblon), **Nogueira** (Copacabana), **Café Garota de Ipanema** (Ipanema), and **Bozó** (Baixo Leblon). The big nightclubs often stay open till 5 or 6am on weekends, and usually keep their kitchen staff on standby. Some of the beachfront *barraquinhas* stay open round the clock, but the most reliable 24-hour option I know of is offered by room service in most hotels.

PICNIC FARE & WHERE TO EAT IT

Near the Praça N. S. da Paz in Ipanema is a deli/bakery called the **Padaria Ipanema,** Rua Visconde de Pirajá 325 (tel. 227-6900). Sometimes when I'm in Rio and I feel like hanging around my hotel, especially if my room has a balcony, I'll pick up about a dollar's worth of bread (two loaves), and a few dollar's worth of cold cuts and cheese (enough for three to four persons). I store the leftovers in my minibar fridge for midnight snacking when the in-house video movie comes on.

A slightly fancier selection of imported cheeses and wines, plus all manner of domestic delights, can be purchased in Leblon at **Mango Especiarias,** Rua General Artigas 470 (tel. 259-3439), open from 10am till 8pm daily. A good Brazilian claret runs about $5 a bottle here, and most credit cards (AE, DC, MC) are accepted. If you don't want to picnic in your room, take your feast to the beach or into the Botanical Gardens.

CHAPTER 6

WHAT TO SEE & DO IN RIO

While Rio is primarily a city to be enjoyed as a spa by day and as a feast or party by night, it's also a great shopping center and a city of numerous environmental and cultural attractions. Rio can further lay claim to hosting what even P. T. Barnum would have had to acknowledge is the real "greatest show on earth," the annual street Carnival with its cast of tens of thousands. Droves of international visitors are lured to Rio each year specifically to take part in this extraordinary week-long celebration.

There are at least two attractions that most people, regardless of their differences, are guaranteed to enjoy. Such is their fame that even 150 years ago, in the 1830s, Charles Darwin could write in his journal during the voyage of the *Beagle:* "Everyone has heard of the beauty of the scenery near Botafogo." He was referring to Corcovado and Pão de Açúcar. From these two heights—especially Corcovado—Rio can be seen for miles around in all directions. The views reveal the city's general layout, the contours of its 90-km (56-mile) shoreline, along with all its principal created and topographical features. Of the latter, Darwin humbly noted that "every form, every shade so completely surpasses in magnificence all that the European has beheld in his own country, that he knows not how to express his feelings."

The vistas and scenery praised by Darwin are still there for you to see today. No matter how much Rio develops, nothing seems to diminish or obscure the beauty of its natural setting. But the Rio of today is also a vastly different place from the sleepy South Atlantic town visited by the great naturalist in the 1830s, one that provides all the urban distractions that we would expect to find in one of the truly great cities of our own day. And depending on one's particular interests, each place described here—whether historical site or formal garden, inner-city forest or bayscape, art museum or jewelry exhibition—has its special recommendations.

SUGGESTED ITINERARIES

IF YOU HAVE ONE DAY   Have a leisurely breakfast at your hotel. Then spend the remainder of the morning at the nearest ocean beach. Go to a Brazilian restaurant like Casa da Feijoada (in Ipanema) or Máriu's Churrascaria (in Leme or Copacabana) for lunch. Visit either Corcovado or Pão de Açúcar in the afternoon (if you choose the latter, make sure to be there around sundown when you can have a cocktail and enjoy the view as lights come on all over the city). Dine at a seafood restaurant around 9pm, then go to a club for some live music, or hang out in a sidewalk café, quaffing chopp (draft beer) until you are ready to retire.

IF YOU HAVE TWO DAYS   Spend Day 1 as recommended above. If you're feeling energetic, and didn't go to sleep too terribly late, get up early on your second day and join the Cariocas on the beachfront for some morning exercise. Eat breakfast back at your hotel, and then head for the beach. Choose one of the poolside restaurants in a major hotel for lunch. In the afternoon, go to either Corcovado or Pão de Açúcar, whichever of the two you missed the day before. Dine well in a fine restaurant and join the fun downtown at a *gafieira* dance hall (Thursday through Sunday) or at a samba school rehearsal (held on Saturday). On the slower nights of the week, go to a piano bar in one of the major hotels.

IF YOU HAVE THREE DAYS Spend Days 1 and 2 as recommended above. Hang out and relax at the beach or poolside all day on your third full day in Rio. Break for lunch at the Garota de Ipanema bar or the Gula, Gula. Spend the late afternoon strolling the commercial streets of Copacabana, or Ipanema and Leblon, to get a taste of the street life, or do some shopping. Go for dinner in Baixo Leblon (Bozó, the Buffalo Grill, Arataca, or Antiquários are good choices) or Gávea (perhaps at Guimas). Afterward, catch some live music in the bars around the Lagoa.

IF YOU HAVE FIVE DAYS OR MORE See above for suggestions on how to organize your first three days. On Day 4, organize a day-trip to Pedra de Guaratiba, visiting the suburban beaches coming and going. Eat lunch at 476 or Cândido's. After a morning in the sun on Day 5, and a picnic on the beach for lunch, head downtown and take the walking tour outlined later in this chapter. Afterwards, relax in one of the many pés sujos, noshing on whatever exotic tidbits the house has to offer. If you still want something to eat when you return to the hotel, sample the room service, and check out Brazilian television. If you have more time after Day 5, take a day-trip, or spend a weekend along either the Costa Verde or the Costa do Sol.

1. ATTRACTIONS

THE BEACHES

Beaches in Rio are as basic an ingredient of daily life as food and shelter. And on the weekend the beaches are life itself. Rio's coast is 130km (80 miles) long, and dozens of beaches dot the shoreline from one end of the city to the other. There are 23 beaches on Governor's Island alone, the island in the Zona Norte where the international airport is located. There are no bad beaches in Rio, only beaches that keep getting better the farther you go from the center of town. There are bay beaches and ocean beaches, but—in the Zona Sul, at least—only the latter are good for swimming. The Cariocas have gone and gummed up this part of the bay and now it's too polluted for bathing. I suggest you take your dips in the ocean.

   Flamengo: This is the first beach of the Zona Sul, and closest to downtown Rio. You might check it out if you're at the Hotel Glória or the Novo Mundo. Swimming is not advised, but it's fine for sunbathing. The surroundings are pleasant, and you have all of Flamengo Park behind you to explore. The kids might like the tractor-pulled train that tours the park, and the large playground.

   Botafogo: Botafogo beach is next along the shore, a tanning spot primarily for local residents of this still-charming neighborhood, Rio's most fashionable through-out much of the 19th century.

   Praia Vermelha: Near the Pão de Açúcar cable-car station is the football field–length Praia Vermelha, a somewhat protected ocean beach said to be popular with swimmers. A morning here could be tied in with a stroll around Urca, the nearby vest-pocket neighborhood, and maybe a day-trip to Sugar Loaf for lunch or a drink.

   Leme and Copacabana: These are the first real pearls in the chain. Wide, sandy ocean beaches at their best, they are remarkably clean—considering the use they get—and the South Atlantic here always seems to provide a moderately frothy sea.

Apoador, Ipanema, and Leblon: These beaches form the next stretch of shoreline going down the coast, brimming over with its variety of scenes, from teenyboppers to tourists. Neighborhood residents still predominate along this strand, with each family or group occupying its own piece of the turf. Ipanema, in particular, is always an exciting beach, an endless swirl of activity, of which the bold preening of young beauties in the scantiest of bikinis lends more than a thread of legitimacy to the "Girl from Ipanema" story.

São Conrado: São Conrado (or Pepino, the beach's traditional name) can teem with activity on the weekends, yet be virtually deserted Monday through Friday. Close to the deluxe Inter-Continental resort hotel, the beach is the official landing strip for hang-glider enthusiasts, who sweep down from the surrounding mountains. The Gávea golf course runs along much of São Conrado beach. Interested golfers who wish to play the course may make arrangements through their hotel, but for weekdays only.

Barra da Tijuca: After São Conrado, the suburban and more remote beaches begin with a great sand reef some 20km (12½ miles) long known as Barra da Tijuca. Barra is definitely a weekend beach, one of the most frequented in the city. If you're ever looking for a condo along a beach that is serene enough during the week and wildly active on the weekends, Barra is the place. The beginning of Barra, the "PP," is Rio's current "in" beach.

Recreio dos Banderantes: Recreio, as locals refer to this beach, is a community of summer and weekend houses, one of the last that remains in Rio proper, right on the ocean. Some blocks in Recreio are fully developed with houses—villas really, with gardens and swimming pools—occupying every lot. Other blocks contain only a single dwelling or two. The many empty house lots are the flattened remains of white sandy dunes, alive with beach vegetation. There are also large empty expanses of this sandy scrubland still undeveloped, especially the land nearest the hilly parts of the neighborhood. In an hour's walk through these sandy fields you can reap two dozen varieties of wildflowers, thistles, and exotic seedpods, the delicate products of an ocean-bounded ecosystem. A good deal of the land in Recreio is still occupied by the poor, whose colorful shantytowns manage to seem so appealing from the outside and at the same time so forbidding. One does not enter the *favela* world easily in Brazil.

Prainha: Beyond the high rock formations at the end of Recreio beach is the small strip of sand known as Prainha—Little Beach. You have to drive over those rocks to get to Prainha, a beachhead for the middle class against the tide of the masses they fear is about to sweep over them from the city's remote and crowded slums.

Grumari: The last beach, Grumari, approaches the city line, and is the most undeveloped stretch of ocean beach that Rio still possesses. From here you can move on to explore the southern shores of the state, along the lovely Costa Verde (Green Coast), which is described in Chapter 7.

GENERAL INFORMATION   The ocean surf is often very powerful in Rio, and the **undertow** can be treacherous. Be careful not to overextend yourself, especially if you're unfamiliar with or out of practice playing in heavy waves. Experienced ocean bathers will find the bodysurfing rugged and exciting, while swimmers must look for the most protected coves or await calm seas in order to practice their crawls. Where the waves are high, you will usually find surfboarders. They're fun to watch and they keep to well-defined areas, but it's best to be alert when flying surfboards are in the air.

During the week, especially in Copacabana and Ipanema, the beach attracts a fair crowd of fitness buffs from the time the sun comes up till it's time to go off to work. Then for the remainder of the day—at least during the **off-season** (April through June and August through October)—the beaches remain sparsely peopled. Even Copacabana and Ipanema are quiet during these months, but for a few nannies with preschoolers, and the usual crowd of bon vivants. Tourists may also be found weekdays on the major beaches, gathered in small pockets on the sand in front of their respective hotels. Thus you can always tell the Rio Palace crowd from that of the Othon, the Copacabana Palace, or the Meridien, but only during those months when the daytime crowd is light and the scene subdued. There are always a few vendors on

Copacabana as long as there's someone to sell to, and many of the trailer cantinas on the beach side of Avenida Atlântica also remain open throughout the year.

The **high season** for tourism in Rio coincides with those months when Cariocas themselves are on vacation or holiday. The summer school holiday extends from Christmas through February (and into early March for Carnival when Ash Wednesday falls late on the calendar). July is the month-long winter school holiday. And while November, December, and March are not holiday months in Brazil, the tourist business remains strong in Rio at those times as well. Rio's beach life is at its richest and most intense on a daily basis during this high season.

On **weekends,** regardless of the season, as long as the sun is shining in Rio's obliging climate, capacity crowds will flock to the beaches from all over the city, providing a rare common ground for the mingling of Brazil's two vastly separate economic realities. And when it's crowded, no matter what beach you go to or where you sit, at least three minor sporting events will be taking place near your umbrella (supplied by your hotel, or rented from a beach vendor). The game might involve a dozen men—of all ages—playing pickup soccer. Or it may be a hard-fought game of volleyball, one of the best-loved sports in Brazil. Almost certainly you will see the fast-paced *fréscobol,* where two friends use large wooden paddles to smash a rubber ball back and forth in the air. Despite the apparent chaos and the blanket-to-blanket crowds, a convivial atmosphere reigns, and only rarely do the energies of one activity spill over into those of its neighbors.

Stepping gingerly among the reclining bodies are the scores of **vendors,** who will offer you food and drink, souvenirs or beach mats, sun hats, and sunscreen. Sometimes the vendors sing or use noisemakers, less to entertain than to penetrate the somnolent state of the sunbathers they hope to attract as clients. Cries of *"sorvete"* ("ice cream"), *"agua de coco"* ("coconut water"), *"amendoins"* ("peanuts"), and *"cerveja bem gelada"* ("well-chilled beer") can be heard from one end of the strand to the other as long as the sun is shining.

All of Rio's beaches are public, and none contains bathhouses or changing rooms, much less reliable restrooms. (When the need arises, cross the avenue to the nearest restaurant.) Rio by day is strictly a come-as-you-are town. In the beach neighborhoods, people parade around everywhere in **bathing suits** all day. Women often use sarongs to cover their swimsuits when going to or from the beach, but you're just as likely to see men and women traveling about in just their bikinis.

Only the principal beaches have **lifeguards,** and none too many at that. There is also a very discreet police presence on those beaches, like Copacabana, most frequented by tourists, usually a pair of patrolling young officers dressed in mufti (tank top, shorts, and baseball cap) who only stand out when you suddenly realize that the object hanging from their waists is a revolver. The cops are there primarily to intimidate the urchins. Many of the children are said to be homeless, and they likewise patrol the beaches for targets of opportunity in their hit-and-run banditry. If they don't see a camera or wallet, they'll run off with your sneakers. There are also street children on the sidewalks, hanging out at the outdoor cafés, usually selling peanuts or chewing gum or candies. The best way to deal with them when they surround your table is to smile and buy something from one of them, or just make a small donation.

OTHER TOP ATTRACTIONS

CORCOVADO, with trains to the summit leaving from Cosme Velho station.
A giant statue of Christ the Redeemer stands with outstretched arms on the summit of Corcovado, or Hunchback Mountain, 2,400 feet above sea level, and dominates the landscape in Rio. During the day, but particularly at night when the statue is bathed in floodlights, the landmark can be seen clearly from many points in the city, from Ipanema to the Centro and beyond. Photographs of the statue overlooking Rio have become almost synonymous with the city itself. But Corcovado was a beloved landmark in Rio, as Darwin's remarks demonstrate, long before the monumental statue was constructed.

Initial access to the peak was along a road that followed the ridgeline from the Alto da Boa Vista, an ascent that required more leisure time than most of Rio's citizens could afford. To democratize the experience of the renowned view, Dom Pedro II ordered the construction of a passenger train, completed in 1885, that could carry a group of sightseers to the summit and back in a short time. Initially a steam engine, and later Brazil's first electric train, the railroad has been modernized many times in the last century, and the climb today can be accomplished in only 20 minutes.

The imposing statue of **Christ the Redeemer** was conceived as a fitting monument to mark the centennial of Brazilian independence in 1921. The project was underwritten by thousands of donations collected in churches throughout the country. Finally, in 1931 the statue was completed. Constructed of reinforced concrete and coated with soapstone, the massive figure with the welcoming arms rises 120 feet above a spacious observation platform, and weighs over 1,000 tons.

The view from this observation deck is truly unforgettable. Make sure you have a map along to help you identify what you are seeing. Trace the shoreline from deep within the bay all the way to Leblon. In a single glance embrace all of Lagoa and the Jardim Botânico. From the summit of Corcovado, all of Rio's disjointed parts fall into place, and the city suddenly becomes knowable in a way that could not be imagined before.

The best time to make the ascent is in the afternoon around 4 or 5pm, when the sun is already low on the horizon and the light is evenly distributed above the landscape. Try to organize your visit to Corcovado on the clearest possible day as well. But even if you are forced to make your visit when the weather is overcast, don't fail to make the ascent on that account. The sensation of being above the clouds can be very powerful in and of itself, even if the panorama is somewhat obscured by the ocean mists.

Many tours stop at the **Mirante Dona Marta** before climbing all the way to the top. From this vantage point 1,200 feet above the ground, both Corcovado and Pão de Açúcar can be seen, and you get a closer view of the surrounding neighborhoods. Some tours, especially the smaller groups traveling by van, will also make a quick detour near the train station to a nearby cobblestone courtyard called the **Largo do Boticário** to view the facades and setting of some lovely old town houses with wooden balconies and pantile fronts. The courtyard is a graceful residential cul-de-sac, entered through a metal archway, where gas lamps, a central fountain, shady trees, and its own babbling brook add to the charm.

Directions: If you want to go by yourself, take a public bus or cab to the Cosme Velho train station. Bus no. 583 leaves from Copacabana, and a number of buses leave from the downtown Menezes Cortes bus terminal. The train—which climbs sometimes at a 30° angle and has a tractor system similar to that of a roller coaster—leaves every 20 to 30 minutes from 8:30am to 6:30pm and costs approximately $2.25 round-trip. The last returning train from the summit leaves at 7pm. The train ride is a worthwhile excursion in its own right, as it crosses deep ravines with dramatic views, and cuts intimately through the dense tropical vegetation on the surrounding slopes. There are a number of stops along the route to the top where residents who live on the hillside get on and off, so you get to see something of local life along the way as well.

You may also choose to go by **cab or private car** all the way to the top along the paved road that zigzags up the slopes. This is the most expensive option, but also the most convenient, especially if time is a factor. The arrangement you make with your

---

IMPRESSIONS

He thought Rio Janeiro the best place in the world for a great capital city.
—R. W. EMERSON, QUOTING WILLIAM WORDSWORTH IN CONVERSATION, *ENGLISH TRAITS*, 1856

It is hard for man to make any city worthy of such surroundings as Nature has given to Rio.
—JAMES BRYCE, *SOUTH AMERICA*, 1912

driver usually includes his waiting for the return trip. Tour lines offer organized bus tours, some of which go directly to the top while others take you to and from the Cosme Velho train station. These bus tours leave from your hotel and operate on fixed schedules, generally costing around $20. The buses are accompanied by a tour guide who points out the sights, usually in four or five different languages, and answers your questions.

PÃO DE AÇÚCAR [SUGAR LOAF MOUNTAIN], with cable cars to the summit leaving from Praia Vermelha station, Av. Pasteur. Tel. 541-3737 or 295-2397 for information about shows, climbing excursions, or other activities and special events.

Sugar Loaf Mountain is the eternal counterpoint to Corcovado. While the Hunchback Mountain occupies an inland setting and is covered with lush vegetation, Pão de Açúcar stands virtually naked, a huge cone-shaped hunk of metamorphic rock composed primarily of granite, quartz, and feldspar that clings to the very shoreline of the great bay. Whether you are observing Pão de Açúcar from Corcovado or vice versa, the visual pleasures are equally stunning.

No roads lead to the summit of Sugar Loaf. Either you ride the cable cars or you climb—and most visitors choose the way of least resistance. The sleek gondolas, made from hardened aluminum and wrapped in acrylic windows, can carry more than 1,000 passengers an hour on their two-stage ascent. The first ride takes you to the top of the Morro da Urca (Urca Hill), the neighboring peak, and a second car completes the journey to Sugar Loaf itself. During both legs of the climb you are suspended in midair for approximately three minutes. It is reassuring to note that there has never been an accident.

The name *pão de açúcar* is of uncertain origin. Some say the mountain was named by the Portuguese, who compared its shape with that of the ingots or "loaves" of raw sugar that were shipped to market from the refineries. A more esoteric—and probably romantic—theory holds that the name derives from the Tupi Indian phrase *pau-hn-acugua*, meaning a remote hill that is high and pointed. Yet it is undoubtedly true that the hill was made less remote when the first cable-car system was installed in 1912, a simple affair of wooden carriages that remained in service until the more high-tech system in current use was inaugurated in 1972.

The first recorded ascent by a climber was that of an Englishwoman in 1817. Many more followed, until all faces of the mountain were conquered. Today, climbing the Pão de Açúcar is a weekly event, as the safety lines of enthusiasts can be seen dangling from the rocks on any clear day. A more gentle ascent—but still a vigorous hike—can also be arranged, chaperoned by the organization that runs all the concessions on the mountain. As with Corcovado, however, the main reason for visiting Pão de Açúcar is for its unique view of bay and city. A sundown excursion is particularly exciting, for there is no better place to see the illuminated city after dark.

While Pão de Açúcar's altitude is only 1,300 feet (roughly the same height as New York's World Trade Center), the unique location of the huge rock gives it a virtually unobstructed view of much of the city. As is also the case when visiting Corcovado, it is extremely useful to have a map along to help you distinguish one feature or area from another. Of special note is the close-up view of Botafogo harbor, and the full visual sweep of the 15km- (9-mile) long bridge that connects Rio with its companion city, Niterói, on the opposite shore of the bay. Just south of Niteroi begins another unbroken shoreline that includes the pristine beaches of Piratininga, Itaipú, Itacoatiara, and Itaipuaçu. Both the mouth of the bay and the coast beyond Niterói can best be viewed from the garden walk on the far side of the hill.

In addition to its function as an overlook, the Pão de Açúcar complex is also home to various entertainment programs, several bars, and even a restaurant, most of which are actually located on the Morro da Urca. Every Monday night from about 10pm till midnight the samba school **Beija Flor** presents a cabaret version of Carnival with colorful costumes, music, and dance in a covered amphitheater. The show costs $12 a ticket. Live performances of top singers and musicians are also staged in the amphitheater, known as the **Concha Verde** (Green Shell) on Thursday through Saturday nights.

While in the area, walk or ride through the neighborhood of **Urca,** nestled at the foot of the hill of the same name. Urca is just a handful of streets seemingly unattached to the rest of the city, not particularly elegant, but with private houses and a shady, small-town feeling. Residents there must feel themselves among the most privileged in all of Rio, being so close to the principal zones of the city yet in so private and tranquil a setting overlooking both ocean and harbor.

Directions: Take bus no. 511 from Copacabana or bus no. 107 from downtown to the Praia Vermelha station, Av. Pasteur. Or take a cab, which from Copacabana ought to cost no more than $3 or $4. Then just climb the stairs to the ticket office, pay the $2 round-trip fee, and ride to the top. The cable cars run from 8am till 10pm continuously if the demand is heavy, or at 30-minute intervals when traffic is light. Cars also function later to accommodate those attending special events. There is a gift shop in the boarding station for film or souvenirs, and a tourist information center, open during business hours only.

PARQUE NACIONAL DA TIJUCA, on the slopes of Serra da Carioca.

The Tijuca National Park must be one of the largest—if not *the* largest—inner-city parks in the world. The park is an immense forest growing on the slopes of the Serra da Carioca (Sierra Carioca) that cuts across the center of metropolitan Rio, dividing the Zona Norte from the Zona Sul. Stretching at one end from the Mirante Dona Marta, which overlooks the neighborhoods of Laranjeiras and Botafogo, to the Alto da Boa Vista and the Floresta da Tijuca at the other extreme, the park is a voluminous natural preserve of vegetation typical of the Atlantic forests that once lined the eastern coast of Brazil. Most (but not all) of the vegetation is second growth. The park was once the neighboring estates of early aristocrats and planters. These same slopes a hundred years and more ago were mostly cleared and covered with plantation crops of coffee and sugarcane.

The park is etched with several major arteries, many smaller roads, and numerous paths and trails. A pleasant half-day, or even an all-day, excursion can be made in the park. A typical itinerary might be a long orientation drive, lunch at one of the two isolated restaurants, and at least one stop to cool off in the cascades of water that fall from the rocky walls at various locales along the sides of the roads. Make sure you bring suitable dress and a towel so you can take to the water.

There are entrances to the park at the most extreme points throughout the city. So when you're traveling from one neighborhood to another, you can trade the urban backdrop for a tranquil green space by routing your drive through the park, if you don't mind taking the extra time. If you were downtown, for example, you would drive through Santa Teresa, and then continue up the mountain chain into the park via Cosme Velho and Corcovado. From there, you could drive the whole length and breadth of the park, and emerge through the gate in the Jardim Botânico, on the far shore of the Lagoa district. On this drive you would pass two of the park's most famous overlooks. The first is the **Vista Chinesa,** with its Chinese Pavilion, a poignant memorial to immigrants from China of the last century who were settled in the vicinity on what were at that time tea plantations. Up the road, the **Mesa do Imperador** (Emperor's Table) was once a favored picnic spot for the family and court of Dom Pedro I. From both heights you will have an unparalleled view of the city's southern sectors. The park is so vast that there are even entrances to it from as far away as São Conrado and Barra da Tijuca.

From Copacabana or Ipanema, the most direct route to the **Floresta da Tijuca** (Tijuca Forest), a separate entity within the national park with many points of interest, is to enter the park in São Conrado and follow signs to the **Alto da Boa Vista,** where there is a formal common, the Praça Afonso Vizéu and an English tavern called the Robin Hood. The entrance gate to the floresta is off this plaza. Heading straight on, you pass the Cascatinha de Taunay, a small waterfall named for the baron whose estate once occupied these lands. Farther on is the tiny **Capela Mayrink,** a delightful sample of an old rural chapel in pastel pink and white with a reproduction of the original altar panels painted by Portinari (the originals were added to the depleted collection of the Modern Art Museum). The chapel is popular for society weddings, but has been closed to the public of late.

Past the chapel, the road divides and forms a series of loops through the remainder

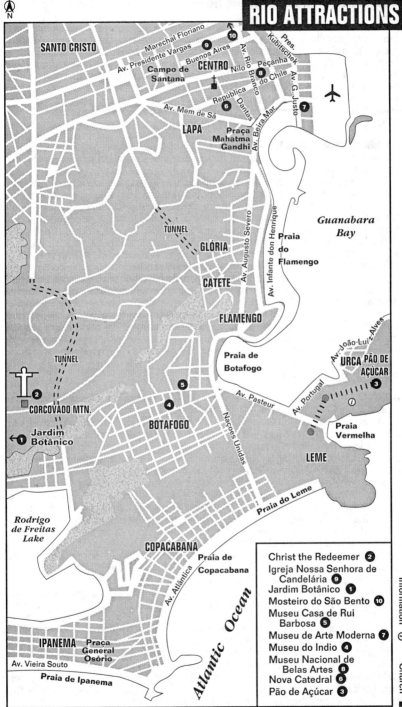

RIO ATTRACTIONS

SANTO CRISTO

Marechal Floriano
Av. Presidente Vargas
Buenos Aires
CENTRO
Campo de Santana
Nilo Peçanha
Av. do Chile
Av. Rio Branco
Pres. Kubitschek
Av. G. Justo

República
Dantas
Av. Mem de Sá
Av. Beira Mar

LAPA
Praça
Mahatma
Gandhi

TUNNEL
Av. Augusto Severo
GLÓRIA
Av. Infante don Henrique

CATETE
Praia
do
Flamengo

*Guanabara
Bay*

FLAMENGO

TUNNEL
Praia de
Botafogo
Av. João-Luiz-Alves
URCA PÃO DE
AÇÚCAR

CORCOVADO MTN.
Av. Pasteur
Av. Portugal

Jardim
Botânico
Nações Unidas
BOTAFOGO
Praia
Vermelha

LEME

*Rodrigo
de Freitas
Lake*

Praia do Leme

COPACABANA
Práia de
Copacabana

Av. Atlântica

Atlantic Ocean

IPANEMA
Praça
General
Osório
Av. Vieira Souto
Praia de Ipanema

Christe the Redeemer ❷
Igreja Nossa Senhora de
Candelária ❾
Jardim Botânico ❶
Mosteiro do São Bento ❿
Museu Casa de Rui
Barbosa ❺
Museu de Arte Moderna ❼
Museu do Indio ❹
Museu Nacional de
Belas Artes ❻
Nova Catedral ❻
Pão de Açúcar ❸

Information ⓘ

Church ∎✝

of the grounds. The two park restaurants are to be found beyond this point. If you fancy international food like curried shrimp or chicken Maryland, turn off to the left for **Os Esquilos** (The Squirrels; tel. 258-0237), open for lunch only, from 11am to 7pm Tuesday through Sunday. To the right is a more rustic Brazilian restaurant called **A Floresta** (tel. 258-7802), where hummingbirds flit among the rafters, open from noon to 8pm. Both restaurants are favorite luncheon spots for locals when they want a respite from the swelter and motion of the city. Beyond the A Floresta restaurant the road continues to **Bom Retiro,** where it ends and a trail leads to the **Pico da Tijuca** (Tijuca Peak), at an altitude of over 3,000 feet.

GUANABARA BAY AND PAQUETÁ.

For those who wish to be not just *in* the water, but also *on* it, there are several boat excursions available.

Paquetá has been a popular weekend and tourist destination for many years. No motor vehicles are allowed on the island, but you may hire a horse and carriage for about $5 an hour, or for $1 an hour there are bicycles for rent. Since Paquetá is quite small, these modes of transportation are completely adequate for getting around. The island has several beaches and hotels and is crowded on the weekends, but quiet during the week. Once a pristine fishing village, Paquetá has lost some of its allure since its heyday as a summer colony 30 years in the past. But it is an island in a beautiful bay, and accessible by inexpensive ferry service.

A variety of craft, from windsurfing boards to cabin cruisers, may be rented through private agencies and owners. For more information, visit or call the **Marina da Glória** (tel. 285-3749).

Ferry: Ferry for Paquetá leaves from Praça XV downtown, and costs 50¢ each way for the 1½-hour trip. Regularly scheduled ferries leave every 2 to 3 hours Monday to Saturday between 5:30am and 11pm, Sunday 7am to 11pm. **Hovercraft:** Hovercraft service leaves every hour on the hour from 8am to 5pm from same dock, making the trip in a third of the time, for $1 each way during the week, $3 on weekends. Call 224-0001 for information.

JARDIM BOTÂNICO, bordering Av. Jardim Botânico where it becomes Av. São Clemente. Tel. 274-8246.

A visit to the Botanical Garden must certainly rank high on the list of activities for nature lovers and birdwatchers. The gardens were the pet project of Dom João VI, who ordered the initial plantings soon after arriving from Portugal in 1808. This was the age that inspired the greatest naturalists who ever lived, including Baron von Humboldt, and subsequently, Darwin. Dom João was clearly caught up in the naturalist vision of his day, which combined mercantile practicality with a dreamy romanticism. The garden was created as both a nursery for the adaptation of commercially desirable plants and as a great temple to nature, suitable for private walks and meditations. One has only to study the famous painting that depicts Humboldt and his native guides deep in the Amazon forest of the late 18th century to grasp the power of that melancholy vision.

The conscious motivation for Dom João VI no doubt had more to do with the challenges of growing spices and fruits introduced from the East Indies—nutmeg and cinnamon, breadfruit and avocado. From the West Indies came many species of palm trees that were not indigenous to Brazil. No one driving by the great wall of the Jardim Botânico in Rio can fail to be moved and impressed by the 100-foot-high royal palms that stand at the periphery of the garden like sentinels and line the avenue at the main entrance. Along with these, the garden is filled with thousands of equally archetypal trees and plants, its 340 acres divided between "natural" stands and more cultivated groves. The native plants are particularly fascinating, like the Régia Victória, a water lily native to the Amazon with a giant pad up to 20 feet in diameter, and the orchids, with their intoxicating aromas that saturate the air. As for birds, there have been some 140 sightings, including occasional flocks of toucans, a creature that must have the most beautiful eyes of any on the planet.

Admission: 75¢.

Open: Daily 8am–6pm. **Bus:** Getting there by bus is relatively easy. The Botanical Gardens border the Av. Jardim Botânico, a principal thoroughfare from

FROMMER'S FAVORITE RIO EXPERIENCES

Café Society   The essence of Rio is best experienced from the vantage point of a café table, preferably on the beachfront by day, but practically anywhere after the sun goes down.

Walking Rio's Back Streets   Exploring various neighborhoods— Copacabana, Leme, Ipanema, Leblon, Botafogo, Flamengo, or the Centro— reveals crowds, vendors, and open-air fruit and vegetable fairs.

Dining in Baixo Leblon   You'll enjoy an excellent meal at any number of the excellent restaurants hereabouts—perhaps *pasteis de queijo* at the Bozó or a late-night nip at the Academia da Cachaça.

A Night Out in Baixo Gávea   Near the Guimas I restaurant are several cafés where the Carioca live-and-let-live spirit reigns supreme most evenings, especially on the weekends. A great place to spend a night out with friends.

Discovering Rio's Cuisine   Practically anywhere you dine, you'll find that the more real the Brazilian food, the better. Soup lovers shouldn't forget the caldo verde, while seafood fans shouldn't miss an outing to Pedra de Guaratiba.

An Excursion into Rio's Environs   The Ilha Grande boasts great beaches and a chance to do some hiking in the Atlantic forest, while a 3½-hour drive from Rio will bring you to Paraty, one of Brazil's most charming historical cities.

Gávea to Botafogo, where it becomes the Av. São Clemente. Many buses travel this route, like those marked "via Jocqui" or "Jardim Botânico."

THE MUSEUMS OF FLAMENGO & BOTAFOGO

CARMEN MIRANDA MUSEUM, Aterro do Flamengo, across from Av. Rui Barbosa at the southern end of Flamengo Park. Tel. 551-2597.
The Portuguese-born chanteuse and one-time Las Vegas headliner Carmen Miranda helped put Brazil on the map for many Americans in the 1930s and 1940s with her Latin rhythms and outrageous hats of dangling fruit and full-skirted *baiana* costumes, many of which are on display in this small, tidy collection.
   Admission: 10¢ Tues–Sat, free Sun.
   Open: Tues–Fri 11am–5pm, Sat–Sun and holidays 1–5pm. **Subway:** Flamengo station.

MUSEU CASA DE RUI BARBOSA, Rua São Clemente 134. Tel. 286-1297, ext. 45.
The house of this remarkable statesman and jurist has been open to the public since 1930. Author of Brazil's first constitution after the founding of the republic, Rui Barbosa was also a lifelong abolitionist. In his zeal to obliterate the memory of the cruel institution, Barbosa ordered all official records and documents relating to slavery destroyed following emancipation. This action was strangely out of place from a man who could read in seven languages and who devoted his life to scholarship. Barbosa's library of more than 30,000 volumes is open to the public, as are the many rooms of this rambling pink mansion.
   Admission: 25¢.
   Open: Wed and Fri noon–4pm. **Subway:** Botafogo station.

MUSEU DO INDIO [NATIVE AMERICAN MUSEUM], Rua das Palmeiras 55, Botafogo. Tel. 286-8899.

This exhibition of Native American artifacts is small but intelligently displayed. After an hour's study of the photographs and cultural objects, you'll have a fairly good idea of the diversity of Brazil's tribes and the manner in which they lived. Particularly beautiful are the items of dress and adornment that were expertly crafted from the raw material of nature—feathers, bones, shells, and noble hardwoods—into headdresses, jewelry, and various practical utensils for eating or storing food. Tapes of native language and music are also available, and there is an inventory of films that document the contemporary lives and struggles of Brazil's remaining natives.

Admission: Free.
Open: Tues–Fri 9am–6pm.

MORE ATTRACTIONS

Rio has a small but animated amusement park, the **Tívoli,** along the shores of the Lagoa, open on Thursday and Friday from 2 to 8pm, on Saturday from 3 to 11pm, and on Sunday from 10am to 10pm.

Next door is the city's only open-air drive-in theater, and across the street is the racetrack called the **Jockey Club** (see Section 4, "Sports & Recreation," below).

Rio also has a **Planetarium,** Rua Padre Leonel Franca 240 (tel. 274-0046), located in Gávea, for those who are interested in a formal presentation of the Rio starscape. Astronomy shows take place on Saturday and Sunday at 5:30 and 6:30pm.

MUSEU DO PALÁCIO DO ITAMARATI [ITAMARATI DIPLOMATIC MUSEUM], Av. Marechal Floriano 196, Centro. Tel. 291-4411.

Itamarati is the name still used when Brazilians refer to their Foreign Service, once housed in this palace when Rio was the country's capital. Initially a private residence, the palace was built in 1854 and later served as official home for Brazil's presidents from 1889 to 1897. The museum's collection consists of tapestries, old furnishings, and other historical artifacts, some of which relate to the life of Brazil's most distinguished foreign minister, the Barão do Rio Branco, who was a major force in South American diplomacy during the 19th century.

Admission: 25¢.
Open: Tues–Fri 11:30am–4:30pm.

MUSEU DA CIDADE [CITY MUSEUM], Estrada de Santa Marinha, s/n Parque da Cidade, Gávea. Tel. 322-1328.

This museum is located on the grounds of what was formerly a private estate and is now a well-tended public park. The City Museum documents both the development of Rio and the central role the city has played in the history of Brazil. The displays are laid out chronologically by century, and there is a special room devoted to a collection of pharmaceutical objects.

Admission: 25¢.
Open: Tues–Fri 1–5pm.

MUSEU DE FOCLORE EDSON CARNEIRO [MUSEUM OF FOLKLORE], Rua do Catete 181, Catete. Tel. 285-0441.

The Museu de Foclore Edson Carneiro is a separate collection of craft goods, musical instruments, and items from everyday life, located at the Museum of the Republic.

Admission: 50¢.
Open: Tues–Fri 11am–6pm, Sat–Sun and holidays 3–5pm.

MUSEU DA IMAGEM E DO SOM [SOUND AND IMAGE MUSEUM], Praça Rui Barbosa 1, near Praça XV. Tel. 262-0309, ext. 181.

For an introduction to Brazilian classical and folk music, visit the Museu da

Imagem e do Som. The museum also houses a noncommercial movie theater, and numerous photographs and modern paintings.

Admission: 50¢.

Open: Mon–Fri noon–6pm.

VILA RISO, Estrada da Gávea 728. Tel. 322-1444.

This museum, located near the Gávea Golf Club in São Conrado is a restoration of a colonial-era *fazenda* (farm). Employees don colonial garb, and will take you on a 3½-hour tour that includes lunch. The tour takes you through the old-fashioned gardens and presents a medley of Brazilian theatrical music dating from the 1860s to the First World War. Lunch is buffet style, and includes feijoada and churrasco. You must make a reservation to take this tour, which is offered daily. Arrangements will also be made for pickup and return to your hotel.

Admission (including lunch): $50.

Open: Tues 12:30–4pm.

COOL FOR KIDS

THE BEACH OR A GREAT POOL   Kids love to run free, and they especially love a great swimming pool. From a kid's perspective, the best pools in Rio are at the Sheraton and the Inter-Continental. As for the beach of choice, any one will do; for smaller tots, the Sheraton beach is the most accessible.

PÃO DE AÇUCAR   Kids don't care much about views, but the gondola ride is always popular.

CORCOVADO   Again it's not the view, but the train ride that will appeal to the kids.

SANTA TERESA

If you want to get a representative taste of old Rio and you only have a limited time available after visiting the obligatory sights of Corcovado and Pão de Açúcar, go to Santa Teresa. This hilly neighborhood near the center of town was settled early in Rio's history, primarily by the well-to-do who sought the elevation as a refuge from the heat and noise below. The architectural integrity of the neighborhood is remarkable. Private homes, some extremely lavish, and small commercial buildings preserve a pre-20th-century scale throughout the area, and picturesque narrow streets wind dramatically among the rising slopes.

The main attractions in Santa Teresa, beyond the place itself—which merits a long drive, or better yet, a good old-fashioned constitutional—are a restaurant called the Bar do Arnaudo, and a museum, the Chácara do Céu, the former private residence of a wealthy industrialist that houses the art treasures of his rich and selective collection.

In the past, when one wanted to introduce a friend to the charms of Santa Teresa, there was no question that the way to get there was via the old *bonde,* the streetcar trolley that leaves from near the Largo da Carioca and rides above Lapa along the old aqueduct. But the bonde, especially where tourists are concerned, has been the object of considerable controversy in recent years. Gangs of young marauders have apparently found the trolley an easy target for their muggings, and the incidents are said to have occurred with alarming frequency in recent years. Because the trains were open on all sides to allow for the constant boarding and getting off while the train remained in motion, they were particularly vulnerable to these lightning assaults. Today police ride shotgun to discourage the bold assailants, who have always operated in broad daylight. The trains, moreover, are always packed, and the citizens of Rio, in growing outrage at the street crime epidemic, have been increasingly coming to the aid of assault victims, a case where the remedy is at times more ugly than the offense.

It is difficult to make a judgment as to whether a tourist ought or ought not to ride the bonde, though I'm tempted to answer in the affirmative, if for no other reason than that the train's bad reputation has made the authorities and passengers more alert, a condition that is not favorable to thievery. Nevertheless, tourists often stand out, and in the minds of the muggers, are likely to represent fairly risk-free targets. In conclusion, I personally believe that one can ride the bonde these days without great risk if you keep a low profile, leave your valuables in your hotel, and follow the lead of the thousands of passengers who ride the train daily without incident.

THE CHÁCARA DO CÉU MUSEUM If you opt for the experience of the trolley ride, ask the driver to leave you off near the Chácara do Céu Museum, Rua Murtinho Nobre 93 (tel. 224-8981). The walk is somewhat circuitous, and will take you down one of the many stairways cut into the hillside, but the museum sits on a rise at the end of this dead-end street, and there are signs that indicate the way. By bus, take the no. 206 or 214 from the downtown bus terminal, Menezes Cortes, to Rua Dias de Barras and follow the signs. The word *chácara* in Portuguese conveys the image of a gentleman farmer's country home, and *céu* means sky or heaven. This former home of the industrialist Raymundo de Casto Maia, however, has more of the Bauhaus about it than the barnyard. The home is very modern, and the grounds are landscaped and beautiful, but urban in their inspiration, not rural.

The modernist influence pervades the mansion in its design, its furnishings, and its art, one of the best small collections of impressionist and modern paintings in the country. While of a later vintage, the collection here has a force similar to that of the Frick in New York City, but on a much reduced scale of grandeur. The studies of Don Quixote in colored pencil by Cândido Portinari occupy an entire room. The work of other greats, Brazilian and foreign, are distributed throughout the mansion. They include canvases by Di Cavilcanti, Monet, Degas, Matisse, Miró, Modigliani, and Picasso. The library is the warmest room in the house, which almost seems to have been conceived as a gallery rather than as part of a dwelling. A large ground-floor space is given over to some very whimsical exhibitions, such as bathroom interiors of the past—complete with all the fixtures—were juxtaposed with those of the present. Prints, catalogs, and postcard reproductions of the collection are sold in the lobby. The museum is open Tuesday through Saturday from 2 to 5pm, and on Sunday from noon till 4:30pm. Admission is $1. If you arrive by cab, make sure you have your driver wait, since it will be difficult to hail a cab in this vicinity for the return trip.

The **Bar do Arnaudo,** Rua Almirante Alexandrino 316 (tel. 252-7246), is the perfect place for refreshments or lunch before wandering over to the Chácara do Céu. The bar is located near the **Largo de Guimarães,** Santa Teresa's main square, also easily accessible by trolley or bus. The bar is a traditional rendezvous for artists whose works are often displayed on the walls. See the review in Section 8 of Chapter 5, "Rio Dining," for full details.

HISTORICAL RIO

Rio has no "old town" per se. Yet there are numerous monuments to its past scattered throughout the downtown section and surrounding areas. And there are several architectural relics that date, in whole or part, from the early 17th century. Of primary interest are several churches and monasteries, a few palaces and government buildings, the city's oldest parks and public squares, and one or two blocks of buildings where the architectural integrity of a particular era is more or less preserved intact. See also the walking tour that follows this section.

Since most sites of historical interest are located downtown, it would be wise to get some picture in your mind of how the center city is laid out. The two major boulevards are named **Avenida Rio Branco** (running north-south) and **Avenida Presidente Vargas** (which runs east-west). These two grand avenidas are products of 20th-century urban renewal. First came Rio Branco (originally Avenida Central), which was conceived and executed in order to embellish the city with a fin-de-siècle elegance typical of large European capitals—and to avoid being outshined by the beautification of its major rival in South America, Buenos Aires. Before the city's expansion westward into what were at that time the rural and fishing communities of Copacabana and Ipanema, Avenida Rio Branco was the Champs-Elysées of Rio, along which were arrayed the city's most fashionable cafés and shops. It was also along Rio Branco that the great samba schools first paraded at Carnival time. Avenida Presidente Vargas wasn't built until the 1940s, but it, too, was to transform the face of the city.

Many of the city's older buildings and narrow streets were demolished when these two thoroughfares were constructed, and old neighborhoods were also destroyed, emptying downtown Rio of its former residential populations. The two wide avenues intersect dramatically at a point that at one time was near the center of the old colonial city. It is therefore near this intersection that most of the buildings, streets, and plazas of historical interest can still be found—those narrow lanes and cobblestone squares that, through good fortune as much as good planning, were spared from the wheel of progress.

HOW TO GET DOWNTOWN   Getting to the Centro from the Zona Sul is relatively easy. Take a cab by all means, if that is your preference. The *frescão* air-conditioned buses or the public buses heading for "Castelo" can take you directly to the Menezes Cortes terminal on Rua São José very close to where this tour begins. But remember that Rio also has a modern and safe subway system that runs from Botafogo with many downtown stops. You can get to the Botafogo station by cab or bus. Regardless of your mode of transportation, the best place to begin your exploration is probably Praça XV, near the waterfront (this is also the starting point for the walking tour you'll find later in this section).

A PRELUDE   If you're riding the subway, get off at the **Cinelândia** stop. Cinelândia means movieland, and there are several fine old movie palaces in this area. Films tend not to be dubbed, but play in their language of origin, with subtitles in Portuguese. This is also the neighborhood for downtown singles bars, both gay and straight.

When you alight from the train, follow the exit signs to Rua Santa Luzia and head in the direction of the waterfront. At the end of this street at no. 490 is the **Igreja Santa Luzia** (tel. 220-4367). This gem of the baroque era, built in 1752, was freshly painted recently in striking stucco blue, and there is no better example of that golden age in the city than this delightful little church. Patrons of Saint Luzia celebrate her December 13 feast day by washing their eyes in the church's holy water, believed to possess miraculous properties.

THE NATIONAL HISTORY MUSEUM   If you were thinking of lunch at the **Alba Mar,** the seafood restaurant occupying the old octagonal market depot on the wharf, cross the wide Avenida Presidente Antônio Carlos at this point and walk toward the water. On the way, you will pass the **Museu Histórico Nacional,** Praça Marechal Âncora s/n (tel. 240-2092), open Tuesday through Friday from 10am to 5:30pm and on weekends and holidays from 2:30 to 5:30pm. The permanent exhibition at the National History Museum is called "Colonization and Dependence," organized in modules with maps, coins, and navigational equipment, and emphasizing Brazil's historic orientation toward the sea and trade during that era. Other exhibits document the effects on Brazil of various economic cycles from slave labor through the discovery of gold and diamonds, and from the planting of coffee down to the urbanization and industrialization of the current day. Museum admission is 75¢.

OTHER DOWNTOWN ATTRACTIONS   Among the antiquities to be seen in the immediate vicinity of the Praça XV are two churches across the busy **Avenida Primeiro de Março.** The old cathedral, **Nossa Senhora do Carmo da Antiga Sé** (1752), was used first by Carmelite monks, and it became the royal, then the imperial, chapel, and finally cathedral of the city (it has now been replaced by the ultramodern Nova Catedral, near the Largo da Carioca). The 1822 coronation of Dom Pedro I as Brazil's first emperor took place in the old cathedral, which contains a golden rose given to Princesa Isabel by Pope Leo XIII. Next door is the quaint **Convento do Carmo,** connected to its church by Rio's only remaining public oratory under the tiled roof of an arch hewed from stone. The altar and much of the carving, including the portals, are by the important 18th-century sculptor Mestre Valentim da Fonseca e Silva, the illegitimate son of a Portuguese nobleman and a slave.

The **Rua do Ouvidor** has a degree of lore associated with it. It is a street that has appeared often in Brazilian literature. *Ouvidores* were pretty colonial magistrates who worked for the crown, and, as such, bedeviled the people of that era with their authority and their corruption. Today it's a banking street.

For blocks around on both sides of Avenida Rio Branco, which the Rua do Ouvidor crosses, there are shop-filled streets that are tempting whether you're in the mood to browse the merchandise or just want a distracting walk and some inner-city atmosphere.

The **Igreja Nossa Senhora de Candelária** is a treasure that was earmarked for demolition in initial construction plans of the Avenida Rio Branco. Fortunately a sober judgment saved the church, which remains on a little plaza of its own in the center of the avenue. Donations from sailors built this church in 1775 to commemorate a terrible shipwreck, scenes from which are vividly depicted by panels on the church's dome. Outside, behind the church, Avenida Vargas stretches beyond view in the direction of São Cristóvão and the Zona Norte. This was also the starting point for the Carnival parades that took place after the construction of the enormous avenue, until 1984 when an official parade ground was inaugurated on the other side of town.

SÃO BENTO MONASTERY   Two other sites of historic interest are located on this end of Avenida Rio Branco, the **Praça Mauá,** an old dockside square that has seen its share of history, and an early monastery, the **Mosteiro do São Bento** (tel. 291-7122), which is also mentioned in the walking tour that follows. The monastery complex is an unadulterated example of early-17th-century church and convent architecture, dating from the mid-1600s and built on the side of a *ladeira,* a steep incline overlooking the bay. To enter the monastery, take the elevator at no. 40 Rua Dom Gerado—and you must be appropriately dressed (no shorts or halters). Enjoy a moment of quiet meditation on the lovely grounds and visit above all the rococo chapel with the gold-leaf interior. Look also for the 17th-century paintings of Friar Ricardo do Pilar, including *O Salvador* (*The Savior*), which hangs in the sacristy. Open daily from 2:30 to 6pm, except Sunday, when there are masses at 7:15 and 10am.

THE LARGO DA CARIOCA   This is Carioca Square, a crossroad for streetlife in the city (there is a Metro stop right on the square). The first thing you will probably want to do when you get here is to check out the vendors and the entertainers who fill the square and line the neighboring blocks.

On a low rise overlooking the largo is the **Convento do Santo Antônio** and its church, built between 1608 and 1615 and notable for the decorative use of *azulejos,* those white Portuguese tiles that are hand-painted using only the color blue. Directly next door is the **Igreja São Francisco da Penitência,** on the corner of Rua Uruguaiana, a street noted for its bargain shopping. The church, which was built in 1773, is of the later baroque period, with an elaborately carved wooden altar and ceiling murals by José de Oliveira that are worth pondering.

Heading east toward the Avenida Rio Branco, you will see the **Teatro Municipal,** a small-scale replica of the Paris Opéra, set back on the Praça Floriano. This is Rio's temple of high culture, which has hosted the Brazilian arts as well as many international performers since opening in 1909. Check the box office while you're here to see if there's something going on you'd like to see. And also check out the **Café do Teatro,** if only to ogle the movie-epic decor.

Practically across from the theater at Avenida Rio Branco 199 is the **Museu Nacional de Belas Artes,** the Museum of Fine Arts (tel. 240-9869), Rio's most important art museum. The collection of Brazilian paintings provides a comprehensive visual account of the country's artistic development, and of its social and cultural history as well. Of contemporary interest is the painting *Café* by the Brazilian modernist Cândido Portinari. The museum is open Tuesday to Friday from 10am to 7pm, and on Saturday, Sunday, and holidays from 2 to 6pm. Admission 50¢, free on Sunday.

LAPA   Down from the Fine Arts Museum along Avenida Rio Branco toward the massive War Memorial is the Rua do Passeio. Here begins the neighborhood of Lapa. To the immediate left, as one enters, is the **Passeio Público,** Rio's oldest park, which once began at the water's edge before landfill pushed back the bay. The park is a bit of a no-man's-land at this point, in need of some care and regular tending, but its basic look is captivating because the landscaping dates from 1775 when public gardens reflected a very different view of nature than they do today.

The **Largo da Lapa** is the neighborhood's central square. Here the **Sala Cecília Meirelles,** a concert hall, can be seen at no. 47. This is a favorite place to hear classical orchestral and chamber music in Rio. A little farther along, at Av. Mem de Sá 15, is the **Asa Branca gafieira,** a music hall of a different type which is described more fully in the section on nightlife. The Asa Branca building is one of many in the neighborhood dating from the middle of the last century that have had their exteriors lovingly restored. Lapa was once a bohemian quarter and hub of Rio's cabaret life. Something of that era seems to linger in the air, making Lapa a delightful place for an unstructured stroll.

If your consumer curiosity is piqued, drop in at the Mesbla department store, Brazil's largest chain, and look around. Make sure you check out the store's rooftop restaurant.

AQUEDUCTO DA CARIOCA   From the Largo da Lapa, walk up Avenida República do Paraguai and cross under the aqueduct, officially the Aqueduto da Carioca, but known simply as **os arcos** (the arches). To remedy the shortage of fresh water within the city proper, the aqueduct was begun in 1724, linking the springs of hilly Santa Teresa with a public fountain in what is now the Largo da Carioca. Since 1896, when tracks were laid, the Lapa arches have shouldered a **trolley-car line,** the only one that still functions in Rio. Today passengers follow the ancient route of the water from the terminal on the Avenida República do Chile, near the Largo da Carioca, up through the winding streets of Santa Teresa.

NOVA CATEDRAL   The large conical dome that dominates the horizon beyond the arches is not a nuclear power plant, though use of this design in an urban setting seems grimly in pace with the times. What is strange, however, is that the city's Nova Catedral (New Cathedral), on Avenida República do Chile just above the Largo da Carioca, should have assumed such a shape. The building is massive, the exterior segmented by four huge stained-glass windows, and it has a standing-room capacity of 20,000 worshipers.

The Nova Catedral stands on flattened terrain that was once a hill, the Morro do Santo Antônio. In Rio, urban renewal and slum clearance has on several occasions taken the form of removing the entire hill occupied by a *favela,* or poor neighborhood, and using the earth for landfill somewhere else, usually a nice upper-class neighborhood. Thus did the hill of Santo Antônio become the *aterro* (landfill) of Flamengo Park, which was completed in 1960.

From the Largo da Carioca you can take the subway in either direction, depending on the next environment you wish to explore.

THE ZONA NORTE   The **Feira Nordestinho** is held every Sunday morning from 6am till 1pm in São Cristóvão, an old neighborhood of the Zona Norte near downtown. Other attractions that could bring you to the area are a visit to an **escola de samba** (samba school) rehearsal, or a soccer game at **Maracanã Stadium.**

There are several other traditional points of interest in and around São Cristóvão. Take the subway to the São Cristóvão stop, where you will be visiting the nearby **Quinta da Boa Vista,** a royal residence for all of Brazil's monarchs. The pink-and-white mansion was built in 1803 by a wealthy Portuguese colonial named Lopes, and bestowed on Dom João VI and the royal family when they arrived in 1808. Dom João was the architect of Brazil's major cultural institutions, including the country's first museum, now installed in the old palace. The entrance hall to the museum contains the Bêndego meteorite, which was discovered in the state of Bahia in 1888, perhaps the world's largest at almost 12,000 pounds. Displayed throughout are all the elements of a natural history museum as they pertain to the Brazilian experience: birds, mammals, reptiles, insects, plants, minerals, prehistoric relics, and artifacts of the country's various indigenous cultures. There is a separate **Museu de Faúna,** a museum of Brazilian fauna, at the Quinta da Boa Vista as well. The National Museum (tel. 264-8262) is open Tuesday through Sunday, from 10am to 4:45pm; admission is 50¢.

The **Jardim Zoológico** (the zoo; tel. 254-2024) is located on the grounds of the Quinta da Boa Vista—which means, incidentally, the country house with the nice view. The grounds are what you would expect from what was once a private royal park, including an elegantly geometric garden filled with sophisticated marble statuary. Brazil has many birds and animal species that are not found in North America, or even elsewhere on its own continent. Those who plan a trip from Rio to the Amazon region will have ample opportunity to view these creatures. If not, Rio's zoo is a very good place for an introduction to the country's unique birds and animals. There are capybaras and boas, jaguars and monkeys, tapirs and toucans, and much, much more. The zoo is open from 8am till 4:30pm Tuesday to Sunday; admission is $1.

Although the **Igreja Nossa Senhora da Penha,** in Penha, is distant from downtown, true lovers of church architecture, as well as adventurous train buffs, might find the trip worthwhile. Our Lady of Penha sits high on a hill, where 365 steps cut from the rock ascend to the church door. Some penitents make the climb on their knees in a gesture of atonement or thanksgiving (a funicular transports those who cannot or do not wish to negotiate the steps). Inside the church are hung crutches and plastic facsimiles of body parts, the votive offerings of those who have been delivered from their suffering by the intercession of Our Lady. This particular form of devotion seems peculiar to the Roman church in the Portuguese- and Spanish-speaking countries.

If you don't go to Penha by cab or car, you could try the suburban train, the Leopoldina line. Pick up the train at the Barão de Mauá station in São Cristóvão, or take it all the way to the Penha neighborhood.

BETWEEN DOWNTOWN & THE ZONA SUL If you had headed back toward the Zona Sul from your downtown tour, you could make a stop at the Glória subway station and visit the octagonal church called **Nossa Senhora da Glória do Outeiro** (Our Lady of Glory on the Knoll). This famous society church, built in 1714, is located behind the Glória Hotel at Praça da Glória 135 (tel. 225-2869), and is open to the public Monday to Friday from 8am to noon and 1 to 5pm. Emperor Pedro II was married in Our Lady of Glória, and his daughter, the Crown Princess Isabel, was baptized there. The Glória's interior also contains carvings by Mestre Valentim, most notably the main altar. Access to the church's collection of sacred art can be arranged by contacting one of the priests. On August 15 the church is ablaze with decorative lights in honor of the Feast of the Assumption, and provides a striking sight against the darkened background of the surrounding mountains.

If you want to get a closer look at the War Memorial, the **Monumento dos Mortos da II Guerra,** this would be a good opportunity. Walk from the church to the Praça Paris, a park that was indeed laid out in Parisian style with formal hedges, fountain, and reflecting pools. Do not attempt to cross the Avenida Beira Mar—instead locate the nearest underpass or overpass. (Please keep in mind that pedestrians are always in season from the point of view of any Carioca who is behind the wheel of a usually speeding automobile.) There is a small museum next to the War Memorial that explains Brazil's role in the Italian campaign during World War II.

Toward downtown from the memorial, but still in Flamengo Park, is the **Museu de Arte Moderna** (the Modern Art Museum; tel. 210-2188), or MAM as it is known locally. The building and the grounds are of more interest than the collection, much of which was destroyed by a fire in 1978. The MAM is in the process of reacquisition of works, and is used primarily as a site for visiting exhibitions. It's open Tuesday through Sunday from noon to 6pm; admission is 50¢. Films are shown daily, and there is also a reliable restaurant on the premises.

Opposite the Catete subway stop at Rua do Catete 153 (entrance on Rua Silveira Martíns) is the **Museu da República** (Museum of the Republic) (tel. 225-4302), which occupies the Catete Palace, formerly the official residence of Brazil's presidents until the transfer of the country's capital to Brasília in 1960. Getúlio Vargas committed suicide here in 1954 while still in office, and the bedroom where his body was found has been preserved. The collection begins where the National History Museum leaves off, with the founding of the republic. There are exhibits of presidential memorabilia and furnishings. Admission is free.

WALKING TOUR—Downtown Rio

Start: Praça XV.
Finish: Rua da Carioca.
Time: 2 to 3 hours, depending on how much time you linger at a given locale.
Best Times: Sunday afternoons, if you are accompanied by a native. The streets are empty, and most of the cultural points of interest are open. If you want to end your tour at a *pé sujo*—a typical downtown bar—you'll have to take this tour during the week. Most pés sujos themselves are only open Monday to Friday until 8pm.
Worst Times: Monday, when all the museums in Rio are closed.

1. **Praça XV** is Rio's oldest square, originally (and still frequently) called the Largo do Paço (Plaza of the Court), where the Brazilian royal family resided until the declaration of the republic on November 15, 1889. The palace is open Tuesday to Sunday from 11am to 6:30pm, and the admission is 50¢.

    Across the street from the largo is the:
2. **Arco de Telles,** a tiny archway leading down a narrow street called the Travessa da Conceicão. Here by the street's entrance at no. 6 is the *pé sujo* Arco de Telles bar, and nearby at no. 11, but on the opposite end of the social spectrum, the English Bar. The Cantina Mezzogiorno at no. 24 is also well spoken of, while the street itself is a rare example in Rio of an environment left over from the colonial period.

    Walk to the end of the street, turning left on the historic Rua do Ouvidor. Turn right immediately onto the Rua do Rosário. On the corner of the next street, drop in at the:
3. **Igreja N. S. da Lapa dos Mercadores** (Rua dos Mercadores 36), an ecclesiastical gem built in 1750.

    The Rua do Rosário, still going away from the Praça XV, leads into the Rua Visconde de Itaborai, which you may follow to the end, turning one block to the left onto the Avenida Primeiro de Março. Stop at no. 66, the:
4. **Centro Cultural Banco do Brasil,** a multicultural center in the huge former headquarters of Brazil's largest bank, which includes an art gallery, venues for film, video, and art, and a theater with regular performances (tickets $3.50).

    Backtrack a half block along the Primeiro de Março, and cross over to the:
5. **Igreja N. S. de Candelária,** one of Rio's most traditional churches (see p. 122 for more detail).

    From the church, you have the option of making a detour to the:
6. **São Bento Monastery.** Follow the Avenida Premeiro de Março away from downtown till it dead-ends at the Rua Dom Gerado. Along the great wall before you, look for the entrance to the elevator, or stairway. The grounds of São Bento are an island of tranquillity along Rio's noisy waterfront. On Sunday at 10am, the monks accompany the mass in Gregorian chant.

    Retrace your steps again to Candelária, and go two blocks to the right to the Rua da Quitanda.

REFUELING STOP This colorful *pé sujo* at no. 83, the **Bar Monteiro,** which is a popular haunt of artists and bankers.

Continue on to the Rua do Ouvidor, Rio's oldest commercial street, and turn right, crossing the wide Avenida Rio Branco until you come to the:
7. **Rua Uruguaiana,** center of Rio's most inexpensive clothing stores, converted recently to a quasi-pedestrian mall, with only a narrow delivery lane down the center. To the right is the zone referred to as the **Sahara,** the least expensive stores in the possession of a new wave of Middle Eastern immigrants. After strolling the street, walk away from the Sahara until you reach the:
8. **Rua da Carioca,** where again you are faced with two choices. To the right is the Largo da Carioca, the Igreja São Francisco, the Teatro Municipal, the Museu de Belas Artes, and the bonde, Rio's only remaining streetcar which rides above the Lapa aqueduct and on to the neighborhood of Santa Teresa (where you will find one of Rio's best small art collections in the Chácara do Céu, and probably its best

small restaurant/bar where northeast Brazilian food is served, the Bar do Arnaudo).

Our tour, however, goes off to the left for a walk along historic Rua da Carioca, and a final:

REFUELING STOP at the **Bar Luís,** a favorite downtown hangout for journalists, featuring a menu of German dishes.

2. ORGANIZED TOURS

CITY TOURS Rio has many companies that package tours, big and small, and may in general be booked directly through your hotel. Some typical tour packages are:

Corcovado and the Tijuca Forest, taking in all the major overlooks, including Corcovado, the principal attractions of the forest and the beaches of Barra, Leblon, and Ipanema.

Pão de Açúcar and City Tour, including the beaches of the Zona Sul, Sugar Loaf, and downtown sights like the Lapa aqueduct, the sambadrome, and Maracanã Stadium.

Rio by Night might include a big production show and a tour of several nightclubs and discos.

If you're looking for this type of guided tour, the first place to inquire is at the **porter's desk of your own hotel.** Many hotels actually provide their own buses and itineraries.

Among local tour operators, **Blumar/Brazil Nuts Rio,** Rua Visconde de Pirajá 580, Subsolo 108/109, in Ipanema (tel. 021/511-3636), is a dynamic young company in partnership with a major U.S. tour operator, specializing in adventure packages, Brazilian musical and cultural circuits, resort destination services, sports-oriented tours (such as the Rio Marathon, for which they are the exclusive agents), and, in the corporate sphere, technical and incentive group visits.

Other companies that are reliable and experienced are **South American Turismo, Ltda.,** Rua Hilário de Gouveia 36, 5th floor (tel. 021/235-1490); **Kontik-Franstur,** Av. Atlântica 2316A (tel. 021/255-2442); and **Gray Line,** Av. Niemeyer 121, Suite 208 (tel. 021/274-7146).

For a custom-tailored nature/outdoor activity tour, contact **Expeditours,** Rua Visconde de Pirajá 414 (tel. 021/287-9697). Expeditours specializes in tours to the Amazon and Pantanal, but also has a fleet of vans and tour guides in Rio who can give you a more personalized view of the city.

Since 1983, Prof. Carlos Roquette has been conducting all-day **cultural walking tours,** covering Rio's historical and cultural attractions. Professor Roquette, who speaks English and French in addition to his native Portuguese, helps bring interested visitors into intimate contact with the details of Rio's architectural and artistic patrimony. Tour bookings may be made via Professor Roquette's 24-hour a day telephone line, 322-4872. The cost of the tour is $20 per person.

Brazil Nuts (1150 Post Rd., Fairfield, CT 06430; tel. 203/259-7900, or toll free 800/553-9959), offers a "Music and Beaches" tour in which their staff personally escorts behind-the-scenes visits to Rio of particular interest to aficionados of contemporary Brazilian music. Any Brazil Nuts tour is highly recommended.

GEMSTONE & JEWELRY WORKSHOP TOUR One of the great visual attractions in Brazil—beyond its natural grandeur and historic patrimony—are the dozens of varieties of gemstones that are scooped from the country's mineral-rich earth. You don't have to fancy finished jewelry to appreciate the mystical attraction of the brilliant colored crystals, known as semiprecious stones for decades, but now—given their value and scarcity—referred to more appropriately as gemstones. In recognition of their general appeal, the H. Stern company has organized a tour of their lapidary workshops that allows you to witness craftsmen as they cut and polish the

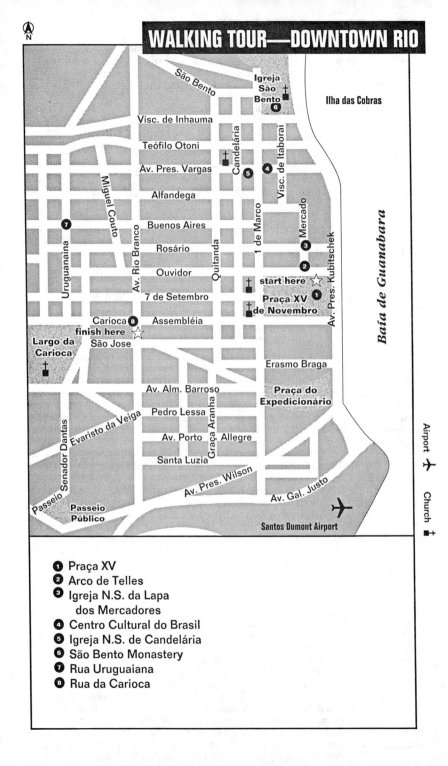

WALKING TOUR—DOWNTOWN RIO

1. Praça XV
2. Arco de Telles
3. Igreja N.S. da Lapa
   dos Mercadores
4. Centro Cultural do Brasil
5. Igreja N.S. de Candelária
6. São Bento Monastery
7. Rua Uruguaiana
8. Rua da Carioca

stones, design and construct their settings in gold and silver, and assemble the finished jewelry into rings, necklaces, and bracelets. The tour takes about 15 minutes and is conducted in one of seven different languages with the use of headphones. Don't forget to visit the small museum on completion of the tour to see some of the world's largest uncut gemstones, and the fascinating displays of polished gems as well, particularly the dozens of tourmalines in their many varieties of shapes and colors.

The free tour takes place during business hours in the **H. Stern Building,** located in Ipanema at Rua Visconde de Pirajá 490. H. Stern will even provide you with round-trip transportation—by private car or taxi—between the workshop and your hotel. Just contact a representative at one of the company's many outlet stores in hotels throughout Copacabana or elsewhere in the city, and arrangements for the tour will be made in a prompt and obliging manner. Clearly the tour is a form of sophisticated promotion, and the company would naturally like to attract your business. After completing the tour, you will be invited to a jewelry showroom or a large and well-stocked souvenir shop, but there is absolutely no pressure to buy. Anyone with the slightest curiosity about gemstones—where they come from, how they are mined, and how they are milled into priceless stones—will definitely find the H. Stern tour of great value.

3. SPECIAL & FREE EVENTS

CARNIVAL

No other country in the world has a national holiday as elaborate or as all-consuming as Carnival in Brazil. Nor as long! For over a week, all normal activity grinds to a halt throughout the country as Brazilians everywhere, from the tiniest backwater hamlets to the most sophisticated urban centers, take to the streets to reenact a pre-Lenten ritual that has been celebrated with a special zeal in Brazil for over a hundred years. And nowhere is the event staged with more panache or grandeur than in Rio de Janeiro—so much so, in fact, that for many non-Brazilians, the city and the event are fused into a single reality.

The official time span for the revelry is only four days, from Friday evening until noon of Ash Wednesday, which generally falls in mid- to late February, though rarely in early March. But in actuality the organized festivities are spaced over at least a two-week period. And for those who are its principal participants—members of the neighborhood associations called escolas de samba—Carnival is virtually a year-long preoccupation. In August each *escola* settles on the theme it will enact through song and dance during the Carnival parades. By November, intense rehearsals are in full swing, and the associations' seamstresses are working overtime to create costumes consistent with the chosen theme for as many as 4,000 members. The theme songs also have to be written, and recordings are aired by Christmas so that the public already has them committed to memory by the time Carnival rolls around.

The parades are the yearly celebration's most formal element. And they are certainly tremendous spectacles. Each year the samba schools attract thousands of visitors to Rio, and their performances are beamed over television to every corner of Brazil with all the hype and pomp of the Super Bowl.

But Carnival is not merely a commercial creation for the consumption of tourists and TV audiences. Carnival is a state of mind that infects the entire culture. Or better, it is a state of collective mindlessness, because it's anything but cerebral. All Cariocas—excepting those killjoys who yearly flee the city to escape the madness—take to the streets by day and attend the mass parties by night. These may be the ritzy, glitzy balls of the elite, or the frenzied dances of the poor, held in tin-covered pavilions in the most wretched of favelas. No matter! The spirit of total release from the psychological prisons of daily existence—whatever the social class of the participant—is what unites all the citizenry in a momentary utopia of euphoria and abandon. For many, the letdown is swift and inevitable. As the song "Manha de Carnival" ("Carnival Morning") from *Black Orpheus* puts it, "Tudo se acabar na segunda-feira" ("On Monday [following Ash Wednesday], everything comes to an end") and it's back to business as usual for another year. But then again, it really isn't the end, but the beginning. There's always next year's Carnival to look forward to.

THE STREET CARNIVAL A strong argument can be made that the best part of Carnival is also its simplest, most accessible element—dancing through the streets in the company of perfect strangers. Life affords few opportunities to be linked with fellow humans who are not of one's acquaintance in such moments of uncensored goodwill. After this experience, the evasions of daily life (the avoidance of eye contact in elevators, for example) will seem just that much more absurd.

The streets of Copacabana, Leme, Ipanema, and Leblon—to name only those neighborhoods where most foreign visitors are lodged during Carnival—are a constant swirl of activity from early in the afternoon until dawn. Mornings, in contrast, are silent and calm, not only in these bairros, but throughout the rest of the city as well. Even during Carnival people have to sleep sometime. After lunch, which may have to be in your hotel since many of your favorite restaurants will be closed, the pockets of revelers begin to form. On designated blocks, **bandas** (the traditional neighborhood bands) take up their positions as the evening draws near. Then the bands begin to play and march through the streets, attracting hundreds of revelers in their wake. Some people are dressed in *fantasias* (as costumes are called), others not. There are no dress codes. Many men are in drag; others play the fool. Women wear next to nothing and vamp as if their lives depended on the most erotic displays imaginable. Many people dress in beachwear or shorts—which are reasonable choices given the high temperatures and humidity of the Brazilian summer.

The basic dance step of the samba is not difficult. Essentially you jump up and down with your hands above your head to the driving rhythm of the percussion bands. As for the more complex steps, just watch and imitate. Who knows, you might be a natural. The one thing you can't do is stand around and watch shyly from the sidelines. The only human behavior—other than violence, of course—that is frowned upon during Carnival is timidity. And remember, you don't need a ticket to be a part of Carnival in the streets: It's one worthwhile experience that's completely free.

The best-known *bandas* and their jumping-off points are as follows: the **Banda do Leme,** on Rua Gustavo Sampaio, behind the Meridien Hotel; the **Banda da Vergonha do Posto 6** (the Shameful Band from Post 6), near the Rio Palace Hotel; and the **Banda de Ipanema,** Praça General Osório, site of the weekly Hippie Fair. Practically every block in these neighborhoods has its own band, however, and there's nothing to prevent you from hopping from one to another for as long as your energy holds out.

THE BALLS The traditional Carnival balls are to the upper and middle classes what street Carnival is to the *povo*—the people. The other distinctions are that the balls require tickets—from as little as $15 to as much as $100 per person—and their general atmosphere is even more lavish and erotic than anything taking place on the streets. Some participants at the balls wear costumes of extraordinary complexity and beauty, costumes whose costs can range into the thousands of dollars. Most participants, however, wear as little as possible. Nudity or near nudity is the order of the night. Ballrooms are swollen to capacity with revelers dancing back-to-back and belly-to-belly, and the music never stops until morning. These events are not for the prudish—you will get no fair hearing if your bottom is pinched. The major balls are as follows:

The **Hawaiian Ball** is the event that kicks off Carnival each year. It takes place on Friday night a week before Carnival at the Iate Clube do Rio de Janeiro, Rio's yacht club, on Avenida Pasteur in Botafogo, where tickets may be purchased directly. The

---

IMPRESSIONS

I'm Charley's aunt from Brazil, where the nuts come from.
—BRANDON THOMAS, *CHARLEY'S AUNT,* 1892

celebrants spend much of the evening outdoors dancing under the sky on the club's beautifully landscaped grounds.

On Thursday night—a day before official Carnival begins—one of the city's most traditional balls, the **Vermelho e Preto** (Red and Black) is hosted by Flamengo, Rio's most popular soccer club. While relatively cheap at about $30 a couple, the ball has a reputation for being among the raunchiest of them all.

The **Pão de Açúcar Ball,** perhaps Carnival's most fashionable, takes place on Friday night high above the city on Urca Hill. Tickets may be purchased for approximately $75 per person at the office of the event's organizers at Rua Visconde de Pirajá 414, Room 909, in Ipanema (tel. 287-7749).

Other traditional balls, like the **Champagne Ball** and the **Gala Gay** (one of several homosexually oriented events), are scheduled in Rio's major showcase houses, like the Scala in Leblon or the Help discotheque in Copacabana. Travel agencies specializing in booking the Carnival trade are the best sources for where these events will be scheduled in a given year.

Most of the major hotels, like the Copacabana Palace's **Golden Room Ball** on Monday night, produce their own spectaculars for those who want to celebrate close to home.

THE PARADES The **Passarela do Samba** is Carnival's main event. On Sunday and Monday nights, the year's 16 most prominent **escolas de samba**—the voluntary samba clubs that tend to be integrated into the very fabric of all Rio's blue-collar and *favela* neighborhoods—compete for first prize in the spectacular parades staged downtown in the **Sambódromo.** Tickets are required to view the parades in this special stadium that was inaugurated in 1984. And several grandstands are reserved exclusively for tourists, whose tickets are usually included in the packages they purchase at home before arriving in Rio. Otherwise, tickets are sold at offices of the Banco Meridional, Rua da Alfâdesa 18, 6th floor (tel. 271-9508). The best source of information on all Carnival activities is the event's major sponsor, **Riotur** (tel. 021/297-7117 or 242-8000). As a last resort, tickets may be purchased from scalpers who buy them by the lots when they first go on sale, and later do a land-office business with the tourists. Needless to say, a scalper's ticket will cost you more than face value. But remember, you shouldn't accept their first offer; a good round of bargaining can be as satisfactory to a scalper as a high markup.

The parades are scheduled to begin on each of the two evenings at 7pm, but they rarely get off before 9pm and can run until noon of the following day. The logistics involved in coordinating the productions are awe-inspiring. The schools can each involve the participation of 3,000 to 4,000 members organized into as many as a hundred separate components.

Each school's performance conforms to an *enredo*—a theme which is generally political or patriotic—and tells a story as the dancers and musicians strut their stuff in the 45 minutes allotted per school.

Each parade begins with the **abre-ala**, a float that is the sampler or title page of the whole ensemble, followed up by the **comissão de frente**, traditionally the school's directors and honchos who, rather than dance, would execute a series of formal salutations to the audience. Many schools have departed from the traditional use of the *comissão* component in recent years, using it to showcase celebrities or even to create laughs—as when one school put burros in its front line. Next comes the body of the school, with everyone in lavish *fantasia*, the costume that reflects its theme.

From here the school is divided into its various components, the group's dancers who whirl and twirl in unison, including the **ala das baianas,** the women in the traditional costumes of Bahia; the flag bearer and dance master, a couple who execute a formal choreography; individual dancers and musicians, whose steps will knock your socks off if anything does; and the **bateria,** the percussion band with the force of a locomotive, numbering as many as 300 musicians, that drives the whole machine. Each element in the parade is judged and given a score. The winner then appears for a curtain call at the victory parade scheduled for the Saturday after Ash Wednesday. This is Carnival's finale.

The Passarela do Samba is only one of several official competitions. The less important schools, called *blocos,* parade along Avenida Rio Branco practically all week long. Some can number as many as 10,000 participants in a single, joyous spectacle of mass celebration. Others, like the *frevo* and *rancho* schools, reenact regional or historical versions of Carnival. These events are free and very crowded, so leave your valuables in the hotel.

The best way to reach downtown during Carnival—when traffic crawls, at best, at a snail's pace—is to take the Metro, which runs 24 hours a day during this period only. It's perfectly safe, and cheap, but don't forget to purchase round-trip tickets so you don't have to stand on line for the return.

MACUMBA

Macumba is the name of the spiritist religion as it is practiced in Rio and its environs. In Bahia you will hear the term *candomblé,* while in São Paulo the term *umbanda* is used. All of these practices are similar, if not entirely the same in all their rituals.

Many tour agencies in Rio include a macumba rite in their list of sightseeing activities. The tourist should be aware, however, that these events are not genuine. Anyone who has a genuine interest in witnessing or learning more about macumba should try to strike up an acquaintance with a true practitioner—and these are not lacking in the city—and try to tag along informally. Only in this way are you likely to get a look at the real thing, which is not only impressive as a religious ceremony, but allows you to hear some of the most inspired drum music you will ever hear in your life.

4. SPORTS & RECREATION

SPECTATOR SPORTS

HORSE RACING Across the street from the Tívoli amusement park is a racetrack called the **Jockey Club.** Fans of the ponies will enjoy the grandstand restaurant (tel. 297-6655 for reservations) along with the races, which take place every Monday and Thursday night and on Saturday and Sunday afternoons. Handicappers should check the sports pages of the *Jornal do Brazil.* The track only costs about 25¢ to enter, $1 for the enclosed grandstands (where no one dressed in shorts is admitted). Bets are taken for win (*vencedor*) and place (*place*) only.

SOCCER **Maracanã** is the name of Rio's legendary soccer stadium, built to hold as many as 200,000 people. Sports fans are the only ones likely to spend their time in Rio at a soccer match. But since soccer is Brazil's middle name, the true sports fanatic is very likely to be tempted for the opportunity to see the game played at its very best, in that freewheeling, individual style that has made Brazilian players both feared and admired by their opponents throughout the world. The game of the week takes place on Sunday at 5pm.

There is a subway station at Maracanã, and you could go there on your own and be assured of getting a ticket. But given the size of both the stadium and the crowds, I strongly suggest that you book a tour for this particular activity. The cost will be somewhat higher than if you did it on your own, but you'll be assured of the best and most comfortable seats, transportation to and from your hotel, and most important, a reliable escort who will help you negotiate the large crowds and the unfamiliar turf. Most tour companies provide game packages to Maracanã, which can usually be booked through your hotel.

Maracanã Stadium is also used to host superconcerts and other special events. Frank Sinatra has performed there, and the pope once said mass in Maracanã before a crowd of 180,000. In addition to its soccer field, Maracanã also has a total sports complex, with facilities for Brazil's other professional or Olympic sports, including swimming, volleyball, and basketball. The gymnasium, called the Maracanazinho (Little Maracanã), holds 20,000 people and also serves as a concert hall for top names in music from home and abroad.

RECREATION

Cariocas make full use of the miles of beachfront for staying in shape; for more organized exercise activities like Nautilus, aerobics, or dance, consult the daily newspapers, or your hotel staff. Such enterprises proliferate throughout the Zona Sul.

For jogging, hiking, biking, or simply for a stroll along a wooded path, the most popular park setting in Rio is the **Estrada das Paineiras.** The entrance to the path is in Cosme Velho, on the way up to Corcovado. The 8km (4.8-mile) strip ends at the Alto da Boa Vista. Along the way, you will pass several little waterfalls, suitable for showering and with innumerable vendors nearby hawking beverages and snacks.

GOLF On weekdays, for a greens fee that fluctuates frequently, you may play the links of the **Gávea Golf Club** (tel. 322-4141). Your hotel can make a reservation on your behalf.

TENNIS Among Rio's hotels (see Chapter 4), only the Sheraton, the Inter-Continental, and the Nacional have tennis courts. There are also courts open to the public at the Barra Shopping Center, Av. das Américas 4666, in Barra da Tijuca (tel. 325-3233).

WATER SPORTS Whether your fancy turns to sailing, deep-sea fishing, or diving, your best bet for information on rental programs is through the **Marina da Glória** (tel. 205-6447).

A number of agencies are now offering white-water rafting expeditions along the Rio Paraibuna, about 1½ hour's distance from Petrópolis. The rafting takes you over numerous small falls—some with drops of up to 15 feet—and takes about 4½ hours to descend the river. The excursion, which costs about $58 per person, including transportation and lunch, can be booked in Rio through **Klemperer Turismo** (tel. 021/252-8170), or through their main offices in Petrópolis, Av. Afrânio de Mello Franco 333 (tel. 0242/43-4052).

5. SAVVY SHOPPING

Rio is a giant marketplace, filled with shops and shopping malls, souvenir stores and street fairs. Shopping in Rio can be a search for bargains in clothes or shoes at a fashionable boutique near your hotel. Or it can be an opportunity to explore the popular culture up close by wandering from stall to stall at one of the open-air markets that are regularly scheduled at various points throughout the city. But whether you approach shopping as an end in itself, or as a means to explore Rio off the beaten track, you are likely to find many items that will please your eye and tempt your purse.

Because of Brazil's status as a developing nation, many items that U.S. residents purchase there, including gemstones and jewelry, may be duty-free. A list of exempt items can be obtained from the U.S. Customs Service. Shops in Brazil tend to be open Monday through Friday from 9am till 6 or 7pm, and on Saturday until 1pm. Shopping malls generally remain open till 10pm. Most, but not all, stores are closed on Sunday, which is a day for street fairs at several locations in the city.

Avenida Nossa Senhora de Copacabana, which runs parallel to the ocean one block in, is the major shopping street in the Copacabana neighborhood. Copacabana, with its 300,000 residents, has been called a ghetto for the rich, and in Rio it's billed as the most densely populated neighborhood in the world. This street is a scene of animated street life from early in the morning till late at night, and contains shops of every type, including its own share of fancy boutiques. To experience and enjoy in full, you should stroll along one end to the other.

While you are walking around downtown, you'll certainly want to poke your head into any number of stores that strike your fancy. For the opposite of Ipanema chic, wander over to **Rua Uruguaiana** and its surrounding streets, and you'll see many clothing stores, and perhaps score a real bargain.

SHOPPING A TO Z
ANTIQUES

Serious antique buffs might want to take in an auction. There are several convenient **auction houses** in Ipanema and Copacabana, like the Investirarte, located in the Cassino Atlântica mall, attached to the Rio Palace Hotel. Check the Saturday and Sunday editions of the local newspapers *O Globo* or *Jornal do Brasil* under *"Leilão,"* the Portuguese word for auction. (See also "Markets," below, for information on the Feira de Antiguidades.)

ART

BATISTA AND MADY, Rua Pacheco Leão 1270. Tel. 227-8702 or 294-6715 for an appointment.

For an opportunity to see some interesting primitives and wood carvings, and possibly meet a charming pair of international artists, visit the studio of Batista and Mady.

KOSMOS, Rua do Rosário 155.

This is a shop specializing in old engravings and prints of the city, like those of Jean-Baptiste Debret, the French artist who has left an amazing pictorial record of early-19th-century Rio.

FASHIONS

Many travelers to Rio, particularly women, find the city's clothing fashions much to their tastes and very pleasantly affordable when compared with prices at home. The principal street for fashions is **Rua Visconde de Pirajá,** in Ipanema, which is lined with boutiques from one end to the other. Many fine shops are also located on the side streets of both Ipanema and Leblon. The main items of interest are formal and sports apparel, shoes and sandals, and swimwear. The favorite fabrics for dresses and outfits—generally in the $30 to $100 range—are cotton, linen, jersey, and silk. Acrylic knit dresses, ideal for traveling, are also quite popular. Tops, skirts, and pants made of smooth and often multitoned leather, are more expensive. Well-made sandals and pumps of many styles cost between $10 and $20, while highly styled dress shoes in soft, sculpted leather are between $50 and $75.

For women's clothing try **Mariazinha,** Rua Visconde de Pirajá 365A (tel. 287-5348), next to the **Forum,** a gallery of several shops, including **La Bagagerie, Elle et Lui** for both sexes, and **Soft Shoes** for footwear.

EDUARDO GUINLE, Rua Visconde de Pirajá 514A. Tel. 259-6346.

This conservative store specializes in preppy-style shirts, cotton (from $15) and linen (from $37). Open Sunday to Friday from 9am to 7pm, and Saturday from 9am to 4pm.

MR. CAT, Rua Visconde de Pirajá 414. Tel. 267-5645.

At midscale in men's shoe prices, there is Mr. Cat. The store's relatively svelte wing tips with leather soles and heels are priced at $60; from there prices scale downward for a wide variety of other styles, including the Brazilian version of the "topsider." All shoes are packaged in an attractive flannel sack with string tie, a trademark of the Mr. Cat chain whose six branches in Rio are located mostly in the shopping centers. Open Monday to Friday from 9am to 8pm, and Saturday from 9am to 3pm.

MR. WONDERFUL, Rua Visconde de Pirajá 503A. Tel. 274-6898.

This is where designer Luís Freitas began to showcase his fashions in the late 1960s. Today, Mr. Freitas exploits the "nerd" look, his mannequins dressed in Panama hats, pastel bermudas, and loud fifties-style polo shirts suggest a young Truman Capote dressed for a summer barbecue. The shop's large, uncluttered space, with lighting in blue neon and cult rock music blasting (Pearl when I visited recently) is also worthy of a peek. Open Monday to Friday from 9am to 8pm, and Saturday from 9am to 3pm.

MUNI'S, Rua Visconde de Pirajá 430A. Tel. 287-8299.

This is a popular footwear chain with 13 branches throughout the city. You might say it's the Buster Browns of Rio, a good place to come for inexpensive shoes and beachwear like clogs and sandals.

PETIT HOMME, in the 444 shopping center. Tel. 521-5244.

One-of-a-kind continental designs for boys aged 2 to 16 can be purchased at Petit Homme in the 444 gallery. Featured are white linen, silk, and Panama suits ($160 to $210), trousers ($73), and shirts ($37). Open Sunday to Friday from 9am to 7pm, and Saturday from 9am to 2pm.

The store has an affiliate (tel. 541-3793) on the first floor of Rio Shopping—just beyond the Copacabana tunnel heading toward Botafogo—that's open Monday to Saturday from 10am to 10pm.

POLO RALPH LAUREN, Rua Visconde de Pirajá 401A. Tel. 267-2741.

The Polo shop, two short blocks from the beachfront Caesar Park, specializes in sportswear for men and women. Fine shirts and shorts for men are priced in the $35 to $40 range, and women's skirts and blouses begin at $45 and $63, respectively. Open Monday to Friday from 9:30am to 8pm, and Saturday from 9:30am to 2pm.

TOULIN, Rua Visconde de Pirajá 540. Tel. 239-2195.

This chain store, with some 15 branch outlets dispersed throughout the city and state of Rio de Janeiro, features fashion apparel for the youthful set. I went in there to price skateboard components for my son, and decided that our own goods were both of better quality and cheaper. But I did admire the denim sportswear, baggy shorts, and much more among the attractive apparel. Toulin is open Monday to Saturday from 9am to 8pm.

Z-BRA, Orlegario Maciel 511, loja 203, Barra da Tijuca. Tel. 399-2963.

Z-Bra specializes in swimwear and sportswear for women. The shop is located in Barra near Pepe beach, a meeting space for the young and fashionable. Therefore, you can be sure of finding the latest in bikinis and casual wear at Z-Bra.

FOOD

CARREFOUR, Av. das Américas 5150.

Carrefour is a gigantic supermarket and home center. Anyone with a passion for large supermarkets, and sufficient time in Rio to warrant the visit, ought to visit Carrefour just for the experience. Row after row of edible commodities, fresh, packaged, and canned, will dazzle your eyes and set your mouth watering. Students of labels and packaging techniques will thrill to the overwhelming selection of goods to browse and admire. On a practical note, pick up a few large bottles of mineral water or beverage of your choice to stock the fridge in your hotel room rather than paying those outrageous minibar prices. While you're there, especially if you're feeling a bit homesick, check out the branch of the "golden arches." Open Monday to Saturday from 8am to 10pm.

GEMSTONES

Brazil is said to produce 90% of the world's colored gemstones. Furthermore, the low cost of labor in Brazil means that stones and finished jewels purchased in the country are 20% to 40% cheaper than comparable products elsewhere. For this reason, and because of the stones' intrinsic beauty, visitors to Brazil are often excited by the prospect of finding attractive gemstones, set in traditional jewelry or by themselves, to carry home as investments and as remembrances of their trip. The visitor in Rio, the country's gemstone capital, can be forgiven for thinking that practically all Brazilians deal in gemstones, so aggressively are the precious rocks marketed to arriving tourists. This misconception can make the task of a reliable gemstone purchase that much more difficult. Assuming you are not a gemological expert, how do you know you are getting a stone that's worth what you're paying for it? In fact, how do you know if you're even getting the stone you think you're paying for?

These potential dilemmas can best be remedied by purchasing your stones and jewelry from one of Rio's major gem dealers, who stand behind their products and provide buyers with certificates of appraisal and other safeguards like credit, exchange, or repurchase guarantees. The two largest and best-known jewelers in Brazil are the H. Stern Company and Amsterdam Sauer, the Hertz and Avis of Brazilian gemstones. Both enterprises are vertically integrated companies, which means that they handle all phases of the gemstone operation from mining through retailing. You won't have any trouble finding retail outlets for either company. Their stores are located at the airports, in all the major hotels, and at many other points throughout the city.

Brazilian jewelers offer all the world's precious stones at reduced prices, including diamonds, rubies, and sapphires. But the best deals are to be had on those gems that come from Brazil's own mines. These are amethyst, aquamarine, citrine, emerald, opal, topaz, and tourmaline. The price per carat of a given stone depends on numerous factors, not the least of which is its visual beauty—a quality that is difficult to gauge. In general, the fixed criteria of a gem's worth are based on a stone's color (both its shade and degree of transparency) and on its clarity or absence of flaws. In some cases, however, as with cat's-eye tourmalines or star sapphires, the flaws are considered intrinsic to the stone's beauty and value. The major characteristics for each of the Brazilian stones—including what some believe are their healing and mythical properties—are listed below:

Amethyst is the most highly prized quartz variety of gemstone. Colors range from pale lilac to rich purple. Believed to protect against blood disease and drunkenness, the amethyst signifies purity and is the birthstone for February.

Aquamarine, next to emerald, is the most highly prized of the beryls. It ranges from pale to deep blue, the price often depending on the depth of its shading. Frequently free of flaws, the aquamarine is said to calm the nerves, and to revive a lagging marriage. Sailors have long worn the stone as protective amulets. Aquamarine is the birthstone for March.

Citrine is quartz that grades from smoky brown to deep yellow. It looks like precious topaz, but costs far less, so you must be particularly careful when purchasing the latter stone. Still, the citrine is beautiful in its own right, and is believed to have powers to aid failing eyesight.

Emerald is the most valuable of the beryls, and has been in fashion for millennia. A fine stone of good color—deep green with no tint of blue or yellow—and flaw free can cost $50,000 a carat. Emeralds are believed to strengthen the memory and to protect against temptation and seduction. The emerald is the birthstone for May.

Opal, composed of silicone oxide, is called the queen of gems. The most popular are white with fireflies of red, gold, blue, purple, and green. The rarest and costliest are black, harlequin patterned. The opal is considered bad luck, unless it is your birthstone, which it is for those born in October.

Topaz is brilliant and sparkling. The most important color range is from yellow to brown, with rich sherry-brown the most expensive—up to $1,000 a carat. The gem also comes in pink (the rare imperial topaz) and in blue, which is becoming increasingly popular as aquamarines get more and more expensive. Said to heal insomnia, the topaz is also worn as a ring to guard against untimely death. The topaz is the birthstone for November.

Tourmaline comes in virtually any color you can imagine, but the most popular is emerald green. Some crystals have two or three color bands. These are called watermelon tourmalines because they are almost always green on the outside and pink in the center. Tourmalines are believed to attract goodwill and friendship, and are the alternative birthstone for October.

In all, there are about 90 different types of gemstones, though only 20 are of particular interest to jewelers. The names of some of these other stones you may see offered for sale are garnet, agate, hermatite, and amazonite.

AMSTERDAM SAUER, Rua Mexico 41. Tel. 220-8332.
Amsterdam Sauer is H. Stern's closest competitor. The company also has many outlets throughout Rio, including those at the Rio Palace, Meridien, and Caesar Park hotels. Founder Jules Roger Sauer's background is remarkably similar to that of Hans Stern (he also just managed to flee Europe on the eve of World War II). Sauer is the author of the excellent illustrated book *Brazil: Paradise of Gemstones,* which is

printed in seven languages including English (available in bookstores throughout Rio for about $10). The New York office, at 580 Fifth Ave. (tel. 212/869-5558), does no retail business, but services North American clients and handles the company's export business.

H. STERN AND COMPANY, Rua Visconde de Pirajá 490. Tel. 259-7442.

The headquarters for H. Stern and Company is the modern 18-story building in Ipanema. The company, founded by Hans Stern, a refugee from Nazi Germany and a brilliant success story, now has 170 stores and retail centers throughout Brazil and in 13 countries worldwide—including New York City, at 645 Fifth Ave. (tel. 212/688-0300), which exists primarily to service North American clients who have made their purchases in Brazil. Stern makes the following warranty for his products: "If we say something is perfect, it is perfect. If we say it is genuine, it is genuine." See the "Gemstone & Jewelry Workshop Tour" information in Section 2 for details on the company's free tour of its workshops.

GIFTS/SOUVENIRS

Brazil, like any other country, has what would have to be considered its traditional souvenirs. Typical of the tchotchkes are butterfly trays, carvings, stuffed snakes, and, or course, T-shirts.

The most typical of all Brazilian souvenirs is the **figa,** a good-luck charm in the shape of a fist with the thumb between the second and third fingers, available in a variety of materials from carved wood and stone to silver. According to tradition, however, the charm is only potent if you have received the figa as a present. It is therefore a nice, simple gift for the folks back home.

Most of the souvenir trade is centered in Copacabana, between Rua Paula Freitas and the Praça do Lido, primarily along Avenida Nossa Senhora de Copacabana. Look for **Macumba Souvenir** and **Liane.** Other popular souvenir shops are **Foclore,** Av. Atlântica 1782, for Native American artifacts, and **Copacabana Couros e Artesanatos,** Rua Fernando Mendes 45A, for leather goods, especially in crocodile.

XYZ, in the 444 shopping center. Tel. 521-4097.

XYZ features T-shirts and very hip accessories, like little lipstick cases of colorful molded leather with mirrors inside and designer plastic eyeglass cases. This would be an ideal place to buy some typically Brazilian contemporary items for your preteen and teenage kids and friends.

XYZ also has a branch in Copacabana on the Rua Barata Ribeiro 611 (tel. 236-7334). Open Monday to Friday from 9am to 8pm, on Saturday from 9am to 2pm.

MALLS/SHOPPING CENTERS

Over the past 10 years the shopping-mall phenomenon has exploded throughout Rio. This occurrence doesn't seem to have reduced the consumer movement in neighbor-hood shops, but rather to have added a new dimension to the city's shopping habits. The malls, for example, tend to open later than most neighborhood shops. They also provide free and ample parking, which is always a challenge in heavily populated areas like Ipanema and Copacabana.

BARRA SHOPPING, Av. das Américas 4666, Barra da Tijuca.

Barra Shopping is said to be the largest shopping center in South America, with 322 shops, all under the same roof. In addition to large department stores like Sears and Mesbla, there are dozens of restaurants and lunch counters, and even an amusement center with rides and video games for the children. Barra can also boast Rio's only ice-skating rink. Shuttle buses run between 40 of the major hotels and the shopping center on a fixed schedule. The first bus leaves from Leme at about 10:15am, and the final bus of the evening returns at 9pm. For details on scheduling, check at the porter's desk of your hotel. Barra is about a 30-minute cab or car ride from Copacabana. The stores are open Monday through Saturday from 10am to 10pm; the entertainment and recreational areas are open daily from 10am to midnight.

CASA SHOPPING, Rua Alvorado 2150, in Barra da Tijuca.

Casa Shopping is the newest shopping center in Rio. Tiles, tubs, wallpaper, and furnishings—everything you need for home design is here in many shops that all have first-floor entrances on the street. There are also numerous restaurants, including the famous Rodeio, and several cinemas. The open-air antiques fair also takes place here on Sunday. The stores are open Monday to Saturday from 10am to 10pm, while entertainment and recreational areas are open daily from 10am to midnight.

GALERIA 444, between Rua Maria Quitéria and Rua Garcia.

Going toward Leblon is the Galeria 444, an arcade of shops and galleries, including Bum Bum for bikinis and beachwear, and Benetton, with men's and women's apparel. The Brazilian airline VASP also has a ticket office here.

QUARTIER IPANEMA, Rua Visconde de Pirajá 414.

Directly across the street from Polo Ralph Lauren, this large complex houses dozens of shops and boutiques catering to every need and price range.

RIO DESIGN CENTER, Av. Ataulfo de Paiva 270, Leblon.

This is where Cariocas go when they want the latest in home decorations and designer furnishings.

RIO SUL, Av. Lauro Muller 116, in Botafogo.

Rio Sul is the closest full-size shopping center to Copacabana, located on the other side of the Túnel Novo at the end of Avenida Princesa Isabel. In addition to the many boutiques, there is a toy store and a branch of both Mesbla and Lojas Americanas, the Brazilian equivalent of Woolworths. Rio Sul also operates a free bus service to and from many major hotels. Open Monday to Saturday from 10am to 10pm.

SHOPPING DA GÁVEA, Rua Marquês de São Vicente 52, Gávea.

Gávea is an inland neighborhood bordered by Leblon and the Jockey Club racetrack. Because of the Catholic University there, it is somewhat a college neighborhood. Rua Marquês de São Vicente is a main drag, a westward extension of Avenida Jardim Bôtanico. Shopping da Gávea is a very toney mall, with high-fashion shops, art galleries, and showrooms of designer furnishings. Of special interest is the branch of **John Somer,** Brazilian manufacturers of fine pewter, the word for which in Portuguese is *estanho* (literally, "tin," the principal metal used to make the product).

MARKETS

Open-air fruit and vegetable markets take place throughout Rio's neighborhoods on a rotating basis. They usually begin at dawn and are over around midday. For color, smell, and general kaleidoscopic crowd activity, nothing in the day-to-day world of the Cariocas surpasses these markets as public spectacles. Every minute you spend at one of these markets is an education, whether to study and taste the produce or to watch the hearty *favelodos* as they dismantle the stalls and load them on the festively painted flat-bed trucks. The whole event has the energy of a circus coming to town.

In **Copacabana,** there are open-air markets on Wednesday on Rua Domingos Ferreira, on Thursday on Rua Belford Roxo and Rua Ronald de Carvalho (close to Avenida Princesa Isabel), and on Sunday on Rua Decio Vilares (near the Praça Edmundo Bittencourt). **Leme** has its market on Monday on Rua Gustavo Sampaio. The **Ipanema** street markets are on Monday on Henrique Dumont, on Tuesday at Praça General Osório, and on Friday at Praça da Paz. And the **Leblon** market is on Thursday on Rua General Urquiza.

There is a weekly antiques market, **Feira de Antiguidades,** on Saturday from 9am to 5pm near the Praça XV, downtown. Among the more transportable items are stamps, coins, and antique weapons. The Passeio Público **stamp and coin markets** are on Sunday mornings. A smaller antiques fair of more recent vintage also takes place on Sunday in Barra da Tijuca on the grounds of the Casa Shopping mall from 10am to 6pm. The well-regarded **Rodeio Churrascaria** is also located in Casa Shopping.

FEIRA DO NORDESTINHO (NORTHEAST FAIR), Campo do São Cristóvão.

The Feira Nordestinho (Northeast Fair) is the other Sunday street market of major interest. Much less artsy than its counterpart in Ipanema, the Northeast Fair caters more to the everyday needs of working people and is also somewhat of a weekly popular festival. Many of the stalls sell food typical of Brazil's northeastern states, and there are always many groups and individuals playing regional music as well. While the Hippie Fair may be a more suitable place to buy souvenirs for friends and family, you should think of the Northeast Fair as a cultural event, and a very entertaining one at that, although you will no doubt find something to purchase in the hundreds and hundreds of booths that spread out in all directions. The fair's one drawback is its location in the Campo do São Cristóvão on the Zona Norte side of downtown, near the National Museum at the Quinta da Boa Vista. The most direct route is by cab through the Rebouças Tunnel, the same centrally located tunnel you will take to get to Corcovado. The fair runs on Sunday from 6am to 1pm.

FLOWER MARKET, Praça Olavo Bilac.

The center of the flower market is downtown, off Rua Gonçalves Dias, near the Rua Uruguaina Metro stop. For fancy floral arrangements or corsages, there is a flower shop at the Copacabana Palace Hotel on Copacabana beach.

Generally, it is forbidden to enter the U.S. with botanical or agricultural products from abroad. But there is at least one plant that U.S. Customs allows, the **pau d'agua**. At some point during your stay in Brazil you are bound to see someone at a flower stall or on the street selling what looks like the segmented and leafless limb of a tree. These are *pau d'aguas*, or water sticks. You take it home, stick it in water, and it sprouts into the most amazing tropical plant—the waxy, palmlike fronds grow right out of the stalk in great profusion.

HIPPIE FAIR, Praça General Osório.

The Hippie Fair, or Feirarte as it is also known, occupies every inch of the spacious Praça General Osório in Ipanema on Sunday all year round. At about 9am the artists and artisans begin to mount their booths and displays, and they remain there throughout the day until sunset. Paintings and wood carvings occupy one large section, and as is generally the case with open-air art markets, you have to search carefully for anything original among all the dross. There are many stalls selling costume jewelry, predominantly silver pieces, but also bone, beads, and of course, gemstones, both loose and in settings. Leather goods are also much in evidence, primarily belts and handbags, as well as wallets, sandals, and portmanteaux. Check the stitching before making any leather purchases. Other items of interest are handmade toys and cooking utensils, hammocks, and musical instruments. Most of the vendors know enough English to be able to bargain. Never accept the first price, unless you just can't imagine getting it any cheaper.

SPORTING GOODS

DOURADA PESCA, Rua Aristides Espinola 121. Tel. 294-3998.

Around the corner from La Mole restaurant in Baixo Leblon, I found an unusual store, the Dourado Pesca. In front of the store, the sidewalk was covered with baskets of every shape and size, only a small percentage of which possessed any character to speak of. Inside, however, I discovered that this store could serve as a supply center for anyone who comes to Rio with the idea of camping (or fishing) and may be in need of some additional gear or equipment. It's open Monday through Saturday from 9am to 6pm.

6. EVENING ENTERTAINMENT

Do Cariocas ever sleep? This is a question you may find yourself asking after spending any time at all in Rio de Janeiro. Practically any night of the week, no matter where you are in the city, the restaurants are filled and the clubs and bars are jumping. *Movimento* the Brazilians call it—motion. Movimento plays as important a role in the daily life cycle of Cariocas as the *praia* (beach). During the week, of course, there is not as much movimento as there is on the weekends, when favorite nightspots are filled to the rafters and pulsating with the *papo* (table talk) and steamy rhythms of whatever music happens to be occupying the same air space as the animated conversation.

And music is an inevitable ingredient of Rio's nightlife. If there is no band around to make the music for them, Brazilians will make their own. Key chains, matchboxes, the edge of a table—whatever. These are the instruments that Cariocas will employ for the spontaneous *batucadas* (rhythm jams) that break out from table to table wherever Cariocas gather to let down their hair.

And song. Brazilians love to sing—especially the great samba tunes of yesterday and today. They love to "join in," whether at clubs or concerts, the lack of inhibition being practically universal in this country of Carnival, where people of all backgrounds are taught from childhood to feel free about singing and dancing in public.

Things don't really begin to happen at night in Rio until after midnight. After work, people go home to *tomar banho e descansar* ("take a shower and rest up") for the long night's festivities ahead. By around 10pm the restaurants and clubs slowly begin to fill, and most of them then remain open until the last customer toasts the dawn for the final time. Sunday and Monday nights are the slowest, depending on the time of year. Tuesday and Wednesday are so-so. By Thursday night the clubs are jumping all over town. Friday and Saturday nights are out-a-sight.

THE PERFORMING ARTS

The **Teatro Municipal,** Praça do Floriano, Centro (tel. 210-2463), stages concerts, opera, and ballet during its year-round season. Check newspapers for current programs.

Other venues for classical music are the **Sala Cecília Meirelles,** Largo da Lapa 47, Centro (tel. 232-9714), and the **Sala Nicoláu Copérnico,** Rua Padre Leonel Franca 240, in Gávea (tel. 274-0096), in the Planetarium.

For dance, classical and modern, there is the **Teatro Villa-Lobos,** Av. Princesa Isabel 440, in Leme (tel. 275-6695).

SAMBA

When Antônio Carlos Jobim wrote the tune "Só Danço Samba" ("I Just Dance Samba"), he was expressing the almost-universal preference of his compatriots for a music and dance form that is truly Brazilian. But the samba also owes much to drum rhythms brought from Africa by the country's original slaves. This music had a religious significance, used in the spiritist rituals that are known today as candomblé, macumba, and umbanda. Drum music is central to the frenetic supplications pressed upon the gods to descend and take possession of the faithful who worship them. As each devotee is "mounted" by his or her god, they whirl and swoon until falling to the ground in a state of blissful exhaustion. The samba is the secular and popular form of music and dance that has evolved from the chanting and gyrations of these religious practices.

Samba is also the centerpiece of Carnival. If you go to Rio during Carnival, you will experience samba in its most magnificent manifestations. If, however, your trip to Rio occurs during some other time of the year, you can still sample the samba culture in a more or less authentic form, depending on time, degree of interest, and individual taste.

The **escolas de samba** (samba schools) rehearsals are a nontouristy way to check out the samba scene. To get the real flavor of the samba schools, you must see them rehearse in their own spaces, all of which are located at various points in the Zona Norte. The most convenient from the Zona Sul are **Unidos de Vila Isabel,** Rua Maxwell 174, Vila Isabel (tel. 268-7052), every Saturday after 10pm; **Mangueira,** in the Palacio do Samba, Rua Visconde de Niterói 1072, near Maracaná Stadium (tel. 234-4129), Friday through Sunday at 10pm; and **Salgueiro,** Silva Teles 104 in Tijuca (tel. 236-5564), on Saturday at 10pm. Both rehearsal spots are relatively close to downtown. For an organized, escorted tour to a samba school rehearsal, contact Brazil Nuts/Rio (tel. 021/511-3636).

THE CLUB & MUSIC SCENE

As if to tune you up for the night ahead, most deluxe and first-class hotels have small samba groups circulating in their restaurants and at poolside during lunch. And at cocktail hour in the hotel bars there is usually a piano player to take your requests.

Restaurants that are also clubs feature cabaret-style shows with music and dance. And nightclubs offer supper along with their full-blown stage productions.

Samba and jazz clubs take up the slack during the wee hours, and the main discos and dance halls also feature live bands, and you are sure to find a place suitable to your particular brand of foot stomping.

Traditionally, many nightclubs in Rio admitted couples only, though this is no longer a hard-and-fast rule. You should check at the porter's desk of your hotel as to whether or not a particular club allows singles to enter. All clubs with live music charge an "artistic cover," generally between $3 and $8, and sometimes a minimum as well. Nightclubs are more expensive, beginning at $10 and going up to $50 for organized tours, which include dinner and a drink or two.

NIGHTCLUBS

It's hard to tell whether the following shows are actually popular with the tourists or not. They are passed off as authentic portraits, in song and dance, of everything folkloric in Brazil, from Carnival to candomblé. And though these shows are created for and aggressively marketed to the tourist, the impresarios then turn around and claim: "This is what the tourists want." Needless to say, you'll find few locals at these shows. It is, sadly, as close as many tourists get to Brazilian culture. They're not to my taste, but if you like big productions à la Vegas and Atlantic City, here they are—though, to be frank, they're not even that good.

The **Beija Flor** Carnival show at Pão de Açúcar every Monday night has already been described in the section on Rio's sights. Compared with Carnival, or a genuine samba school rehearsal, however, the show has all the drama and authenticity of a TV game show.

The other big production shows are **Oba-Oba,** Rua Humanitá 110, in Botafogo (tel. 286-9848), and **Plataforma 1,** Rua Adalberto Ferreira 32, in Leblon (tel. 274-4022).

A DESGARRADA, Rua Barão da Torre 667, Ipanema. Tel. 239-5746.

The only club in Rio to showcase the traditional Portuguese *fado* is A Desgarrada. The menu here also features Portuguese cooking. Open Monday through Saturday from 8pm onward, with nightly shows beginning after 10:30pm.

Admission: Artistic cover charge $5.

SCALA I & II, Av. Afrânio de Mello Franco 292, in Leblon. Tel. 239-4448.

At the Scala I, the show is like something left over from the heyday of Batista's Cuba: gaudy, tawdry, and slightly amateurish, but with none of the raunchy eroticism those pre-Castro spectacles were renowned for. There is a fair amount of topless nudity, usually confined to the *mulatas,* many of whom are indeed strikingly beautiful. If you go at all, it's advisable to skip the meal and the tour, and just go on your own to catch the show. The Scala II, on the other hand, is a showcase on occasion for top Brazilian and international talent. The show begins around 11pm and lasts for about two hours, after which there is dancing till 4am.

Admission: $50, including dinner and transportation.

JAZZ

Jazz is alive and well, and living in Rio. Whether your preference is for bebop, modern, or Latin, you're likely to find a group playing somewhere in the city that suits your tastes, especially if you're willing to make the rounds of the various clubs. Check the entertainment section of the local newspapers under "Música para Ouvir" (listening music) for name groups—Brazilian and international—that are making the scene.

The bars at the Rio Palace, Meridien, and Sheraton hotels feature live jazz on a regular basis. Another club where live jazz can be heard regularly is **Biblo's,** Av. Epitácio Pessoa 1484 (tel. 521-2645).

CANECÃO, Av. Venceslau Brás 214, in Botafogo. Tel. 295-3044.

Canecão, located opposite the Rio Sul Shopping Mall, is really a concert hall that plays host to both pop entertainers and well-known jazz ensembles. Canecão can seat more than 2,000 people, and is a supper club as well. In addition to the featured act, there is also continuous music.

CHIKO'S BAR, Av. Epitácio Pessoa 1560, in Lagoa. Tel. 287-3514.

Every night of the week there's a combo playing, for this is one of the most popular bars in town for both couples and singles. You may not know the musicians' names, but the music is hot and professional. If you stick around until the early-morning hours, you may witness a real old-fashioned jam session, as jazzmen drift in from their gigs all over town and play at their best for their friends and themselves. You can also eat a full dinner at Chiko's, or dine in the attached Castelo da Lagoa restaurant.

JAZZMANIA, Rua Rainha Elizabeth 769, in Ipanema. Tel. 287-0085.

Jazzmania is considered one of the best jazz clubs in Rio. Located over the Barril 1800, a large beachfront café, Jazzmania always features some top talent from the Brazilian or international jazz milieu. Here you can saturate yourself with the most sophisticated modern jazz being played in the world today.

PEOPLE, Av. Bartolomeu Mitre 370, in Leblon. Tel. 294-0547.

People has a glitzy, new wave interior and is a favorite nightspot for dance and music. It's located down the block from the Saborearte restaurant.

DANCE CLUBS

Those who like to get their exercise on the dance floor will find ample opportunity in Rio to cut a rug in whatever tempo and style suits their mood or taste. There's no sense showing up at any of these spots much before 11pm. Most clubs will remain open till 2am on slow days, and till dawn on the weekends.

Nothing since the heyday of *bossa nova* in the mid-sixties has been as hot in Brazil as a new dance sensation called the **lambada** that swept such world capitals as Paris and New York as well. The word *lambada* might best translate into English as "whiplash"; indeed this image provides a suitable description of the lambada's signature motion. Performed at its best, the lambada is wild and sensual, requiring well-conditioned and well-practiced dancers. Most people can manage the lambada's basic sway and the syncopated side step, which seem so familiar for the simple reason they have been recycled from an earlier time when Havana was the playground of the Caribbean. As one version of this tale is told, the lambada has been simmering for some time in the bistros of the Brazilian slums, influenced by scores of merengue and *bolero* records that became available dirt cheap in the record stores when all things Cuban, including music, fell into official disfavor here after the rise of Fidel Castro. And while lambada is super hot throughout the Brazilian northeast, where many clubs are devoted exclusively to the dance, it is also popular in most of Rio's traditional dance halls, called *gafieiras* (see below).

ASA BRANCA, Rua Mem de Sá 15, in Lapa. Tel. 252-4428.

The Asa Branca, is a throwback to the Big Band era of the 1940s. The warm-up house band gets the patrons in the mood for the big show, usually some major Brazilian talent. The place opens at 10pm, and the show begins about midnight.

Admission: $5–$10, depending on the headliner.

CARINHOSO, Rua Visconde de Pirajá 22. Tel. 287-3579.

Carinhoso is on the Copacabana end of Ipanema. There is a restaurant and two bands nightly.

Admission: Artistic cover $5.

UN, DEUX, TROIS, Av. Bartolomeu Mitre 123, in Leblon. Tel. 239-0198.

Un, Deux, Trois has a restaurant downstairs and a supper club with orchestra upstairs. You must make separate reservations on weekends if you want to dine and dance.

Admission: Artistic cover $5.

GAFIEIRAS

Gafieiras are old-fashioned dance halls. The best are those that retain their links to the popular culture and attract a cross section of social and economic classes. The bands play all the old standards, Brazilian and otherwise, and you wouldn't expect to see any of the musicians playing at society weddings.

Among the best are **Estudantina,** Praça Tiradentes 79, Centro (tel. 232-1149), open Thursday through Saturday; **Forro Forrado,** Rua do Catete 235, in Catete (tel. 245-0524), open Thursday through Sunday; and the **Elite Club,** Rua Frei Caneca 4, Centro (tel. 232-3217), open Friday through Sunday nights.

Gafieiras generally open around 10pm, and cost about $1 at the door.

DISCOS

There are some discos, generally quite popular, which restrict entrance to members or those who acquire temporary membership through their four- or five-star hotels.

Of all the private discos, the **Hippopotamus,** Rua Barão da Torre 354, in Ipanema (tel. 247-0351), was the hottest spot recently, followed by the **Palace Club** in the Rio Palace Hotel (tel. 255-7070), and **Rio Jazz Club** in the Hotel Meridien (tel. 275-1122). A "special invitation" to the Hippopotamus can sometimes be arranged through a five-star hotel.

BABILÔNIA, Av. Afrânio de Mello Franco 296 in Leblon. Tel. 239-4448.
The hot disco in Rio entering the 90s, is Babilônia. Teenyboppers enjoy the chem-free Sunday matinee from 4 till 8pm; normal operating hours are Wednesday through Sunday from 10:30pm till dawn.
Admission: $3.

BIBLO'S, Av. Epitácio Pessoa 1484, in Lagoa. Tel. 521-2645.
In addition to being a place to hear music, Biblo's is also a disco and a meeting place for singles.
Admission: $3.

BIERKLAUSS, Av. Rio Branco 277, Centro. Tel. 220-1298.
The new downtown swing spot for any of the city's office workers who want to start the weekend early—say on Monday night—is Bierklauss. Tables of single ladies wait patiently for the browsing Romeos, who cruise the premises on foot, to suggest a pas de deux. There's always some bouncy tune being served up live by the resident 10-piece orchestra. And as the boys well know, if you order your libations from the bar, you don't have to pay the 10% service charge.
Admission: $3.50 Mon, Wed, and Sat; $5 Thurs; $6 Fri and Sun.

CALÍGOLA, Prudente de Morais, at Praça Gen. Osório, in Ipanema. Tel. 287-7146.
This was Rio's number-one disco throughout the late eighties, and it's still a favorite of both Carioca and international high society. Located on the bottom floor of the same building that houses Le Streghe Italian restaurant, the dance floor at Calígola is designed like a pit in the Colosseum, and surrounded by columns and other details to recall Imperial Rome. Open seven nights a week.
Admission: $7.50.

CIRCUS, Rua General Urquiza 102, in Leblon. Tel. 274-7895.
Circus, located above the Bella Blu Pizzaria, is a popular disco with the younger set.
Admission: $2.

HELP, Av. Atlântica 3432, in Copacabana. Tel. 521-1296.
Help has the reputation of being a wild spot, for a mostly younger crowd and hungry single males who feast on the B-girls who hang out there.
Admission: $2.

RESUMO DA ÓPERA, Av. Borges de Medeiros 1426. Tel. 274-5895.

Located on the Ipanema side of the Lagoa, where the greatest concentration of Rio's most sophisticated houses of the night are to be found, the Resumo da Ópera has enjoyed top-dog status among the city's discos since the dawn of the current decade. Come late and stay early. Open Wednesday to Sunday from 10pm to 5am.
Admission: Around $3–$5.

ZOOM, Praça São Conrado 20, in São Conrado. Tel. 322-4179.
Zoom is the newest disco popular with the younger set. It's informal but not quite as raunchy as Help. It occupies the same building as the Pescador Restaurant.
Admission: $3.

KARAOKÉ

This is a craze which has ignited throughout Brazil. The house provides the music (mostly tapes, but sometimes live) and you provide the song. Karaoké clubs can be found in most of the country's major cities. In Rio the clubs to try are **Canja,** Av. Ataulfo de Paiva 375, in Leblon (tel. 287-0335); **Limelight,** Rua Ministro Viveiros de Castro 93, in Copacabana (tel. 542-3596); and **Manga Rosa,** Rua 19 de Fevereiro 94, in Botafogo (tel. 266-4996). These clubs, which usually close on Monday, charge about $3 cover and impose a $3 minimum.

THE BAR SCENE

ACADEMIA DA CACHAÇA, Rua Conde Bernadotte 26, Loja C. No phone.
On the popular front is a unique cocktail bar called the Academia da Cachaça, located across from the Casa Sendas supermarket and near the intersection with Rua José Linhares. To be even more precise, Conde Bernadotte is a small diagonal street about four blocks in from the beach, from the vicinity of the Marina Palace Hotel.
The specialty at the Academia, a pleasingly gaudy little place incongruously set in a small shopping mall, is cachaça—or pinga, as the sugarcane distillate is more commonly called. In all, about 50 varieties of the potent libation from various pinga-producing regions are offered on the bar's drink menu, priced between 60¢ and $1.50 a shot. Twelve blends of caipirinha cocktails—including kiwi and *caju* (the cashew fruit)—are also offered. On the snack menu are many *petiscos*, or appetizers, in the $1.50 to $5 range, from nuts and raisins to lobster bits, fried manioc to meatballs.

PIANO BARS

Almost all the major hotels, including the Inter-Continental, Caesar Park, Miramar, and Othon Palace, have piano bars, where you can enjoy your drinks in an environment where music is confined—at least during the week—to the background.

GAY NIGHTLIFE

Much of gay male nightlife centers around the **Galeria Alaska,** Av. Nossa Senhora de Copacabana 1241, where there are several bars and a drag (transvestite) theater. A section of the beach in Copacabana that is popular with gays fronts the Copacabana Palace Hotel, while in Ipanema it's the stretch of beach between Rua Farme de Amoedo and Rua Vinícius de Morales. There are additional gay bars and discos near Cinelândia, the downtown movie-theater district.

RED LIGHT DISTRICT & EROTICA

Rio's most respectable red-light district is located in Copacabana off Avenida Atlântica, between Avenida Princesa Isabel and the Praça Lido. These blocks contain numerous pickup bars, some of which, like the **Erotika,** Av. Prado Júnior 63 (tel. 237-9370), have erotic stage shows. Single men sitting at night in cafés along this section of Avenida Atlântica will almost certainly be approached by streetwalkers.

CHAPTER 7

EXCURSIONS FROM RIO

1. DAY-TRIPS
2. THE COSTA DO SOL
3. THE COSTA VERDE

Cariocas themselves, at least those who have the means, seldom spend the weekends or holidays in Rio. The beaches of Copacabana and Ipanema tend to fill up rapidly on Saturday and Sunday, a scene which can be quite pleasing and exciting to the tourist, but less appealing to the full-time resident. Travelers spending more than a week in or around Rio might easily include one of the following side trips in their itinerary. To escape the crowds, people generally head—depending on the season—in one of three directions. The two nearby beach options are the Costa do Sol and the Costa Verde. Those seeking relief from the hottest days of summer in January and February might opt, however, for the mountain regions, rather than the shore, where the heat and the action during the high season can be quite intense.

In any event, all of the locales described in this chapter are year-round destinations, more or less frequented depending on the season. Lodging and food prices tend to accompany the highs and lows of the season. The relative isolation and calm of the low season (most of the year) will cost you less than during those times of the year when the spas fill up with vacationers: summer, winter school vacation during the month of July, and some major holidays. The choice, then, is between the people scene of the high season, when the clubs are jumping, or the privacy scene of the low season, when you can have the towns and beaches much more to yourself. So as not to give a totally misleading impression, however, there is always *something* going on in most of these destinations, especially on the weekends, throughout the year.

1. DAY-TRIPS

NITERÓI

A short ferry ride away, Niterói, the former capital of the state of Rio de Janeiro, is Rio's neighbor city across the bay. Ferries and hydrofoils leave regularly from the dock near Praça XV in downtown Rio. There is also frequent bus service across the bay bridge, leaving from the Rodoviária Novo Rio in São Cristóvão.

Bus no. 33 from the Niterói ferry terminal will take you to the bay beaches of **Icaraí, São Francisco,** and **Jurujuba.** The ride is picturesque, but the beaches (like those on the other side of the bay) are less than pristine. There is a beautiful view of the Rio shoreline, however, especially from the beaches known as **Adam** and **Eve** (Adão and Eva). Beyond Jurujuba is the 16th-century fort (*fortaleza*) of Santa Cruz, one of Brazil's oldest fortifications, open daily from 8am till 4pm.

Bus no. 38 from the ferry terminal carries passengers to the spectacular ocean beaches of **Piratininga, Itaipú,** and **Itacoatiara,** about a 45-minute ride from Niterói. In Itaipú, there is an archeology museum in the ruins of the 18th-century convent of Santa Teresa. To the east of Niterói and its nearby beaches lies the Costa do Sol, which is described in Section 2.

PETRÓPOLIS

When Cariocas want to exchange the seaside landscape for the mountains, this is one of the closest and most popular destinations. The tradition was started by Pedro I, who bought a farm there in the 1830s, and was continued by his son, Pedro II, who so loved the more temperate climate in Petrópolis that he moved the country's capital there during the summer months, or during those times when Rio was rife with disease and epidemics. Much of the court followed the emperor's example, so there are many mansions with large gardens left from the empire period in a town that is today a mixture of modern textile plants and narrow cobblestone streets. Petrópolis is only 66km (41 miles) from Rio, reached by a dramatic climb along a steep mountain road with many stunning views of the surrounding mountains and valleys.

Buses leave Rio for Petrópolis frequently from the downtown Menezes Cortes bus terminal, and the cost is minimal, about $3 each way. The telephone area code for Petrópolis is 0242.

WHAT TO SEE & DO

Cotton knitwear is the principal product of industrial Petrópolis, and reasonable bargains can be had on *malhas* (*mahl*-yaz), as the garments are called, along the Rua Teresa.

The first sight of general interest, just before entering Petrópolis, is **Quitandinha,** once Brazil's most fashionable casino, before gambling was abolished in 1946. Today the place is a middling resort, slated to become an apart-hotel sometime in the near future. But the grounds and the buildings in the grand Norman style are worthy of a look for the old Hollywoodesque glamour they still reflect.

MUSEU IMPERIAL, Rua da Imperatriz 220. Tel. 42-7012.

In the town itself, the emperor's former palace now houses the crown jewels and other royal possessions, including an early telephone given to Pedro by Alexander Graham Bell. In appearance the palace remains much as it was during the occupancy of the imperial family.

Admission: 50¢.
Open: Tues–Sun noon–5:30pm.

PALÁCIO CRISTAL, Praça da Confluência. No phone.

The Palácio Cristal (Crystal Palace) was built by Dom Pedro II's son-in-law, the Conde D'Eu, a Frenchman who imported the structure from his native country to house the great flower exhibition of 1884.

Admission: 50¢.
Open: Tues–Sun 9am–5pm.

SANTOS DUMONT HOUSE, Rua do Encanto 124. Tel. 42-1618.

The house of Brazilian aviation pioneer Santos Dumont is an architectural oddity. Dumont had this house built at a time in his life when mystical obsessions had outdistanced his earlier scientific curiosity. He believed, for example, that he should always lead with his left foot when walking up stairs. The staircases in his houses were deliberately designed to accommodate this eccentricity. Nevertheless, Dumont was a man of indubitable genius, and many displays of his inventions in the house attest to this fact.

Admission: $1.
Open: Tues–Fri 9am–5pm, Sat–Sun 11am–5pm.

WHERE TO DINE

Within the town, the best restaurants are on Rua João Pessoa and Rua do Imperador.

Full tea is served from 8am till 10pm at the **Florália** restaurant in the Samabaia neighborhood, on Rua Maéstro Otâvio Maul 1700 (tel. 43-6050), which includes tea, toast, honey, jam, and cakes for $3. Next door to the tea garden is the **Floralia** nursery, with a permanent exhibition of orchids, as well as many other plants and flowers. Cuttings (called *mudas* in Portuguese) may be purchased.

LA BELLE MEUNIERE, Estrada União Industrial 2189. Tel. 21-1573.

Cuisine: FRENCH. **Reservations:** Not needed.
$ Prices: Appetizers $3–$6.50; main courses $5–$11. No credit cards.
Open: Daily noon–5pm and 8pm–midnight.

This is one of those reliable French eateries that produces quality meals from the best the local market has to offer. A good dish of trout with peanuts can be had for $10 at La Belle Meunière, 10km (6 miles) from the center of Petrópolis.

O SÍTIO DAS FLORES, Rua João Ferreira 341, casa 4. No phone.
Cuisine: CONTINENTAL. **Reservations:** Not needed.
$ Prices: Appetizers $2–$5; main courses $5–$11. No credit cards.
Open: Wed–Sun 1–11pm.

This country cottage belongs to painter Silvio Flores and his wife, Regina, and part of the premises have been transformed into a very good restaurant, one very popular among the jaded cognoscenti, particularly certain journalists of my acquaintance who like to flee the urban madness below on a given quiet Sunday afternoon. You might start your meal at poolside (don't forget your swim gear) with a baked potato stuffed with shrimp and melted cheese ($2.50). For your main course, choose from a variety of offerings like filet with mustard sauce ($7), chicken curry ($5), or a canard à l'orange ($5.50). The coffee, by the way, is not only homemade, but homegrown.

The Sítio das Flores is hard to find. You turn off the Rio-Petrópolis highway about 200 feet beyond the Motel Italo. Although the restaurant is close by, from here it is best to ask directions.

TERESÓPOLIS

Centered around Teresópolis is the **Parque Nacional da Serra dos Orgãos** (Sierra of the Organs National Park), so named because the surrounding mountains have the appearance of a pipe organ. The huge park boasts numerous trails to hike and peaks to scale.

Teresópolis is located beyond Petrópolis, 95km (58 miles) from Rio. On the way, be sure to stop at the **Mirante do Soberbo,** an overlook with a panoramic view of the Guanabara Bay and the surrounding peaks, including the **Dedo de Deus** (God's Finger), a prominent rock formation rising to an elevation of several thousand feet. There are many ponds and waterfalls in the park for bathing, and stable horses may be rented there at the **Pracinha do Alto.**

The night and street life in Teresópolis itself is centered around the area known as **A Várzea.**

As is the case for Petrópolis, the Teresópolis buses leave regularly from Rio's downtown bus station. Many tour companies offer day-trip excursions that take in both towns and their environs.

WHERE TO STAY

ROSA DOS VENTOS, km 22 Estrada Teresópolis–Novo Friburgo. Tel. and fax 021/742-8833. Telex 21/34958. 40 rms A/C MINIBAR TV TEL
$ Rates: $110–$135 single; $120–$145 double. AE, MC, V.

Situated in the mountains of the Serra do Mar an hour and a half from downtown Rio, the Rosa dos Ventos hotel offers a fresh-air alternative to the smog and noise of the city. Rooms are spread among three separate chalets which stand above the beautiful Campanha Valley, and enhance the hotel's atmosphere of isolation and tranquillity. In all, there are four separate restaurants at the hotel, plus a piano bar and a poolside cocktail area. The Rosa dos Ventos is the only Brazilian establishment listed in the prestigious French guide *Relais & Châteaux.*

WHERE TO DINE

TABERNA ALPINA, Rua Duque de Caxias 131. Tel. 742-0123.
Cuisine: INTERNATIONAL/GERMAN. **Reservations:** Not accepted.
$ Prices: Appetizers $3–$5; main courses $5–$12. No credit cards.

Open: Daily 11am–midnight.

The Taberna Alpina offers a good Spanish-style codfish plate for $12, a reasonable price given the heights to which that increasingly rare sea denizen has risen. The standby meals here, however, are the typical German dishes, like schnitzel and saurbraten.

NOVA FRIBURGO

High in the mountains, approximately 150km (93 miles) from Rio, is Nova Friburgo, a town originally settled by Swiss immigrants, and today a favorite summer retreat for Cariocas wishing to escape the summer swelter of the city. Nova Friburgo is a three-hour bus ride from Rio. Many chalets in the **Cônego** suburb still attest to the influence of European colonization, as does the elegant layout of the city's principal squares.

An energetic and steep climb up to the **Pico da Caledônia** offers a magnificent view of the valley, the city to one side and a lake district to the other. A different perspective can be viewed from the Morro da Cruz, reached by cable car from the Praça dos Suspiros.

Near Friburgo are two small towns that were only electrified in 1984 and retain the ambience of rural Brazil. First is **Lumiar,** 36km (22 miles) away, reached from the Rio-Friburgo highway by exiting at Mury. A further 6km (3½ miles) along on a dirt road is **São Pedro.** Both towns are hospitable to visitors. You can also take a dip in the local swimming hole, the *poço feio* (ugly well).

There are more than 30 quality hotels and inns in the region. Most offer full board for guests, and their restaurants are also open to the public.

ITACURUÇA

This beach resort town is actually the first stop along the **Costa Verde.** Only 82km (51 miles) from Rio's Barra da Tijuca, a trip to Itacuruça can also be considered a legitimate one-day excursion. One favorite activity is to cruise the clear blue waters of Sepitiba Bay in a coastal sloop (called a *saveiro*) and visit some of the many offshore islands. The transparent waters are excellent for snorkeling to see the many colorful varieties of tropical fish that make the bay their home. In Rio, **Sepetiba Turisma,** Av. Nossa Senhora de Copacabana 605 (tel. 021/235-2893), offers a cruise of the bay from 10am to 4:30pm that embarks from Itacuruça on Saturday, Sunday, and Monday. The cost, about $20, includes fruit on board and lunch on the Ilha de Jaguanum, but drinks are separate. Transportation by bus to and from your hotel can also be arranged by the tour agency.

On the way to Itacuruça you will pass **Pedra de Guaratiba,** where two of Rio's most popular out-of-town restaurants are located, **Cândido's** and **476** (for details, see Chapter 5).

2. THE COSTA DO SOL

East and north of Rio, along the shoreline, are a number of towns that have come to be known collectively as the Costa do Sol. The Sun Coast begins at the beaches near Niterói, passes through Búzios, the best known of its resort towns, and goes on to its most distant point, Macaé, 187km (116 miles) from Rio.

BÚZIOS

Once a rustic fishing village, **Armação dos Búzios** (the official name) is now most often referred to as the St. Tropez of Brazil. Ironically, it was the French actress Brigitte Bardot who really put Búzios on the map. Bardot, one of the most popular international stars of the 1950s, sought in Búzios a refuge from publicity during frequent vacations to Brazil. In her wake, many others among the rich and famous began to "discover" Búzios, transforming the simple coastal hamlet into one of the chicest of all Brazilian summer colonies and side-trip destinations.

GETTING THERE   The town sits on a small peninsula, approximately 170km (105 miles) from Rio de Janeiro, and is most easily accessible by car, cab, or even air taxi.

If you were going to rent a car at all in Brazil, this might be the time to do it. Not only will you be able to explore the whole length of the Costa do Sol on your way to and from Búzios, but once you've settled in there, you'll find it very convenient to have your own transportation for getting around from beach to beach or restaurant to restaurant. Your hotel in Rio can provide a **private car and driver** for the 2½-hour drive, or you can hire a **radio cab** to take you there as well. Needless to say, the cab will not wait, but you will be required to underwrite the cost of its return to Rio nonetheless—in all, a very expensive proposition. Finding a cab to take you back could be a problem, but not an insurmountable one.

A number of **tour agencies** make the run between Rio and Búzios on a regular basis. See Section 2, "Organized Tours," in Chapter 6 for details. In Búzios itself, try **Ekoda**. Ekoda may be contacted in Rio at Rua Mexico 11, Suite 1502 (tel. 021/240-7067), or in Búzios at Manoel Turibio de Faria 293, store no. 3 (tel. 0246/23-1490).

Still another option is to take a **bus** for about $2 from Rio to nearby Cabo Frio, which is only a 30-minute cab ride into Búzios. A public bus also runs between the two locales, and when combined with the bus from Rio this is by far the cheapest way to get to the spa. If you have reservations at one of the better inns, they will sometimes arrange to meet you in Cabo Frio, especially if more than one person is involved.

The fastest way to get to Búzios is by **air taxi**. One company, **Costair** (tel. 021/253-0441), makes the trip in about 40 minutes, leaving from Rio's downtown Santos Dumont Airport and landing in Búzios on a dirt strip in the middle of a great marsh. The $112 round-trip flight is worth it alone for the close-up view of Pão de Açúcar as the plane negotiates the curve of Guanabara Bay on takeoff and landing. The view on the way down the coast isn't half bad either.

WHAT TO SEE & DO

The center of the old fishing village is still somewhat intact, but is now surrounded by some of the fanciest boutiques and inns this side of Ipanema. One local lady, a British expatriate, attributed to Búzios the character of St. Tropez of 20 to 30 years past. "Totally disorganized," she claimed, by which she meant informal and not overly self-conscious as yet of being the great watering hole of the society set.

The principal center of Búzios from the standpoint of its concentration of fashionable shops, fine restaurants, and first-class pousadas, is the **Armação,** a term that loosely designates an area of several blocks, but primarily the establishments found on and around the Rua das Pedras. The street has another official name, but is known traditionally as the Street of Stones because of its unusual paving surface. Most of the streets in Búzios that are not simply dirt roads are paved with cobblestones. But on the Rua das Pedras you'll still see the colonial-era paving method of using large, thick flagstones, which stick up at every imaginable angle, forcing all vehicles to amble slowly down this long block at the speed of a walking horse.

Beyond the Armação area is the undeveloped point of the Búzios peninsula, and some of the most beautiful and unspoiled natural beach environments you will find in this part of Brazil. Unlike Cape Cod, say, or other U.S. Atlantic Ocean–beach communities for that matter, which are essentially flat with contiguous networks of elevated dunes, Búzios is hilly, with lush vegetation. The vistas in the hills beyond the town are breathtaking in spots, and uniformly beautiful. Try to arrange for a car with a very good suspension system when touring these backroads and undeveloped areas of Búzios—or at least prepare yourself for a jolting ride.

As for the nightlife, most of the clubs and bars are concentrated within several blocks of each other. You won't have any trouble finding the latest "in" spot once you are there.

WHERE TO STAY

Many top-rated inns—some 50 in all—can be found scattered among the surrounding hills and beaches, which are for the most part a 15-minute to half-hour walk from the Armação.

BARRACUDA, A Ponta da Sapata, Manguinhos. Tel. and fax 0246/23-1314. 21 rms. A/C MINIBAR TV TEL
$ Rates (including breakfast): $111–$140 double. AE.
The Barracuda, one of the best *pousadas* (inns) in the region, consists of gorgeous vine-covered bungalows, very comfortably furnished with all the amenities. Each bungalow has an attached terrace with a hammock overlooking the water. The inn has a particularly attractive pool and patio area, and the much-praised Tartaruga beach is over the hill about 200 meters (650 ft.) away.

BYBLOS, Morro do Humaita 8, Búzios. Tel. and fax 0246/23-1162. Telex 247/409. 15 suites. A/C MINIBAR TEL
$ Rates: From $82 standard double; from $107 deluxe double. AE.
Another classy hilltop hideaway, Byblos has beautiful suites, and a wide poolside patio for languishing away those lazy weekend afternoons against an incomparable scenic backdrop. The inn is conveniently located near some of Búzios' best beaches.

ESTALAGEM, Rua das Pedras 156, Búzios. Tel. 0246/23-1243. Fax 021/294-6787. 7 rms.
$ Rates: High season $55 double without A/C, $65 double with A/C. Low season $35 double without A/C, $45 double with A/C. No credit cards.
The Estalagem, an inn, restaurant, and music bar, is the property of an American rock and jazz bassist, Bruce Henry. A regular flow of visiting musicians adds zest to the scene. In season there is live music at the Estalagem every night, and in the off-season, only over the major holiday weekends. The inn's room, each painted brightly in white and blue, all open onto a courtyard, where the goings-on are always lively. There is also a sidewalk café on what is the most colorful street in Búzios.

A Special Island Resort

NAS ROCAS, Ilha Rasa, km 7.5. Tel. 0246/23-1303, or 021/251-0001 in Rio for reservations. Fax 0246/29-1289. Telex 247/248. 80 suites. A/C MINIBAR TV TEL
$ Rates (including half board): $138–$173 single; $190–$224 double. AE, DC, MC, V.
At the entrance to the Búzios peninsula, on the bank of a narrow river, is the reception center for the island resort of Nas Rocas. A seven-minute ride by trawler takes you across the inlet to the private island where coffee exporter and hotel impresario Umberto Modiano has created a tamer version of the Club Med–style resort. Nas Rocas occupies the entire island, which can be circled by footpath at a comfortable pace in no more than 45 minutes. Nas Rocas is totally self-contained, providing lodging, all meals, aquatic sports from windsurfing to snorkeling, tennis, and a variety of organized activities from pool games to exercise classes, and even a schooner for island-hopping and tours of the coastal beaches.

There are 80 two-room suites in 40 separate and attractive bungalows, which overlook the inlet or the open sea. Food is served buffet style, with a minimum of two main dishes—usually fish and meat—and all the trimmings.

The grounds on the island are resplendent with flowers. The decorative plants are all imported to the island from the mainland, and are lovingly tended by Sr. Hélio, the principal gardener, who receives ample assistance from many of the resort staff of 240 workers. The primitive, native growth on the nonlandscaped sections of the island is equally attractive. Botanists, whether professional or amateur, are welcome to tag along with Sr. Hélio, who will be happy to share his knowledge of Brazilian flora as he makes his daily rounds.

Taxi and bus transportation is available to take you into Búzios, which is actually 10km (six miles) farther down the peninsula. Or you can rent a dune buggy, a very popular mode of transportation in these parts. To get to Búzios proper from Nas Rocas, you cross over a single-lane bridge with an extremely acute curve in the shape of a camel's hump. Then you pass through the village of **Manguinhos,** a ramshackle affair not without its charm—really a strip of houses, cafés, stores, and markets. The 27 beaches of the area (or is it 36? no one seems to know for sure!) begin in this municipality.

WHERE TO DINE

Búzios is considered a Brazilian culinary capital second only to São Paulo and Rio, though on a much smaller scale to be sure. It also has many less fancy establishments, as is befitting a beach town, including the usual array of beachside cabanas serving fresh seafood at reasonable prices.

AU CHEVAL BLANC, Av. José Bento Ribeiro Dantas 181, Armação. Tel. 23-1445.

Cuisine: FRENCH. **Reservations:** Recommended for dinner.
$ Prices: Appetizers $4–$8.75; main courses $7.50–$23.25. No credit cards.
Open: Wed–Mon noon–midnight.

The Au Cheval Blanc is the elegant choice for dining when in Búzios. Chef Paul Blancpain has created a menu that alternates between classic French preparations and traditional Brazilian dishes. For starters, try one of the house specialties, blini de camarões ($7.50), or a dozen fresh oysters on the half shell ($8.75). After that you can choose from mouquecas, fish filets, shrimp, lobster (these are the most expensive dishes by half again as much as any others), frog, filet mignon, chicken, pork, and even steak tartare ($13.25, and only served at lunch).

LE STREGHE, Av. José Bento Ribeiro Dantas 201. No phone.

Cuisine: ITALIAN. **Reservations:** Recommended for dinner.
$ Prices: Appetizers $3–$10; main courses $6–$20. AE, MC, V.
Open: Wed–Mon noon–midnight.

This is the original Le Streghe, a longtime Búzios favorite. And you get the same fine Italian food here as at the companion restaurant in Ipanema, where the menu and prices are the same. See Chapter 5 for more details.

OTHER COSTA DO SOL DESTINATIONS

One could devote many weeks in Brazil just getting to know the stretch of coastline and string of beaches between Niterói and Macaé. The main route to follow is RJ 106, which is picked up outside of Niterói. The road runs north of the *lagos fluminenses*, great lagoons high in saline content from which the region's principal product, salt, is harvested.

At Bacaxa there is a turnoff that leads to **Saquarema,** a resort town surrounded by beautiful beaches where Brazil's surfing championships are held annually. There are many inns in the area, and the **Pousada do Holandés,** Av. Vila Mar 374, on the Praia de Itauna (no phone), comes highly recommended.

The next major port of call along RJ 106 is **Araruama,** which fronts the immense lagoon of the same name. Here, in contrast to Saquarema, the waters are calm and the sands said to possess medicinal properties.

Cabo Frio, one of Rio's most traditional weekend spots, is worth a detour. It is the region's largest town, filled with restaurants, hotels, and many campsites on or near neighboring beaches. After Cabo Frio—which means Cape Cold, a historical reference to the cool climate that has attracted Cariocas for generations—RJ 106 turns abruptly north toward the small port town of **Barra de São João,** where there is a church dating from 1630, the Capela de São João Batista, and the birthplace of poet Casimiro de Abeu, whose house is now a museum and library.

Farther on is the tranquil village of **Rio das Ostras,** renowned for its shellfish, and finally **Macaé,** a municipality that stretches from the ocean to the nearby mountains, embracing in between a historical district of colonial-era plantations.

3. THE COSTA VERDE

The Costa Verde (Green Coast) is below Rio to the south and west, and stretches along the Rio-Santos highway (BR 101) to the town of Paraty near the border with the state of São Paulo, some 300km (185 miles) away. Green is far too pedestrian a word to describe the spectrum of colors that envelop the traveler along this route, now curving and winding over mountainous terrain clad in every shade of luscious jungle vegetation, now hugging the shores of the island-cluttered bays whose waters glisten with such subtle tones that only a brilliant colorist would dare to give them names. Call them green if you must, even emerald in a burst of promotional zeal. But in the end, the eye will register a thousand variations.

Sit where you will in your car or bus on this journey. You will not miss the show. There are no obstructed views, so total is the spectacular scenery in which you are immersed. On one side are the hills and rock outcroppings that in places reach their extremities, dripping with verdure, to the very edges of the water. Elsewhere this same swollen topography has been cleared into rolling pastures and cultivated fields. Frozen on their surfaces, in the form of ancient corrals and *fazenda* houses, is the vision of an agricultural past. In some places only the scent of the sea is present, so you breathe more deeply and savor the pleasing, salty freshness of the air. But water is rarely out of sight for long as you speed by the succession of graceful coves with their impeccable strands, the horizon of the sea everywhere interrupted with a numberless multiplication of islands in every size and shape. And you think, "I must stop here on the way back, no there . . . oh, but definitely there."

The true miracle of this landscape is that it continues even beyond Paraty, virtually to the gates of the belching industrial zone that surrounds São Paulo. The whole journey to São Paulo along the Rio-Santos road takes about seven hours, taking only pit stops into account. A week by stagecoach would be a more reasonable pace. Here we will only take the trip as far as the preserved colonial town of Paraty. In Chapter 10, on São Paulo, we will work our way back as far as the beach resort of Ubatuba. Rio's Costa Verde segment of this excursion is divided into three distinct environments, and three major towns. First is the Baia de Sepitiba, with the town of Mangaratiba. Next comes Angra dos Reis, which embraces the Baia da Ilha Grande. And finally there is Paraty itself.

MANGARATIBA

What distinguishes Mangaratiba is not the town so much as its surrounding beaches. The great scenery of the Costa Verde really begins from this point onward. The fact that Mangaratiba is not a resort town may make it all the more attractive to those who value peace and quiet on uncrowded beaches more than the hordes of people and organized fun of resort areas. Or if you want, have your cake and eat it, too, stay at the nearby **Frade Portogalo,** about 20km (12 miles) farther south, and use Mangaratiba as the base for your unstructured explorations.

There is a daily ferry from Mangaratiba to **Ilha Grande,** the largest of the offshore islands, which in the mornings continues on to Angra dos Reis (see below). Also nearby is the village of **Itacuruça,** where *saveiro* cruises may be booked for exploration of the other 36 islands of Sepitiba Bay.

ECOTOURISM ON ILHA GRANDE

Ilha Grande is an ecological preserve and hikers' haven one and a half hour's drive up the coast from Rio to Mangaratiba, then another hour to cross the bay by public ferry ($4 each way). Assuming an early arrival at the island's principal village, Vila Abraão, a filling breakfast of fruit, cheese, bread, juice, and coffee can be gotten for about $3 a head at the **Pousada Mar da Tranquilidade,** up the main path from the beach.

For those sedentary hedonists who have come to Ilha Grande for the beach life alone, there are various boat taxis that will take you to the more remote Praia das Palmas, from which a pristine ocean strand called Lopes Mendes can be reached following a 15-minute stroll through the forest. Highly recommended for the more athletically minded is the five-mile hike to the Praia das Palmas over the hilly, wooded terrain that separates the two beach environments.

There are in this dense stretch of Atlantic forest a great number of wildlife species to be seen, from monkeys to eagles, not to mention a rich and varied census of plants and trees. This is a vigorous walk, moderately rough going in a few places, but an excellent outing for anyone in reasonably good shape. Bugs aren't much of a problem during the heat of the day, but head cover is imperative to protect against the sun.

Guide Vitor Barros de Araujo conducts this tour for **Expeditours,** from Rio, Rua Visconde de Pirajá 414, Ipanema (tel. 021/287-9697; fax 021/521-4388). Depending on the number of people, and how much you wish to spend, Vitor can arrange for a private boat crossing to Ilha Grande, which frees you from the fixed ferry schedule, and allows you to spend more time on the island. The price per person, in a group of from six to 10 is $60, healthy box lunch included. Consult with Expeditours as well about their hikes in Rio's Tijuca Park, and treks by mule or dirt bike over 60 miles of hilly backcountry between Angra dos Reis and Bocaina.

WHERE TO STAY

CLUB MEDITERRANEE, Estrada Rio-Santos, km 55, Village Rio das Pedras. Tel. and fax 021/789-1635, or toll free 800/CLUB-MED in the U.S. Telex 21/31404. A/C MINIBAR

$ Rates: Weekly (Sun–Sun) $756 adult, $370 child (4–11), $189 baby (2–3). AE, DC, V.

Rio das Pedras is 60 miles from Rio, and fronts the island-dotted bay of Angra dos Reis. The grounds are suitably tropical, spread over a five-by-seven-mile area, and facing a crescent-shaped beach the length of three football fields. Double-occupancy rooms are in colonial bungalows overlooking either the gardens or the beach. Each room has two full-size beds, and a private bath with a shower room. Electrical outlets are 220 volts.

Dining/Entertainment: There is a main dining room at the village center, and two specialty restaurants serving continental and regional Brazilian dishes. An open-air cocktail lounge surrounds the pool, and guests are entertained nightly at a theater and nightclub.

Services: Transfers from Rio airport, laundry service, excursion desk.

Facilities: Ideal conditions for windsurfing, sailing, and waterskiing. Nine tennis courts, including three indoor. Two squash courts, volleyball, basketball, soccer, and handball. Arts-and-crafts workshops, and Mini/Kids-Clubs for kids 6 to 9 and 10 to 12.

HOTEL FRADE PORTOGALO, BR 101 norte, km 71, Angra dos Reis. Tel. 0243/65-1022, or 021/267-7375 in Rio for reservations. Fax 0243/65-0947. 100 rms. A/C MINIBAR TV TEL

$ Rates: $85 single; $100 double. AE, DC, MC, V.

On the Rio-Santos road at the kilometer 71 marker is the Hotel Frade Portogalo, high on a hill overlooking the bay. A novel chair lift carries guests from the pool area down to a little village of attached condos, where there is a French restaurant, a boat marina, and a beach. The accommodations at this hotel are first class.

HOTEL PIERRE, Praia da Bica, Ilha de Itacuruça. Tel. 0234/788-1560. Fax 0234/788-1016. 51 rms. A/C MINIBAR TV TEL

$ Rates (including full board): $135 single; 150 double. No credit cards.

The luxury Hotel Pierre on the island of Itacuruça, opposite Coroa Grande, is reached by a five-minute boat ride. This is one of the great weekend getaway spots within comfortable commuting distance of Rio. Come here to lay back, or play hard; both options are offered. There's a seaside restaurant with a panoramic view, three swimming pools, steam bath and sauna, a jogging track in the woods, and much more.

POUSADA MAR DA TRANQUILIDADE, Vila do Abraão. Tel. 0243/780-1861. 15 rms.

$ Rates: $35 double. No credit cards.

The Pousada Mar da Tranquilidade is located in Abraão, the principal hamlet on Ilha Grande, and the point of debarkation for the ferryboat. The inn is simple, comfortable and clean, the best option on the island for those not wishing to camp or find simpler accommodations in one of the fishing hamlets. Reservations are necessary.

PARATY

The only blemish along the road from Angra to Paraty (which you'll also see spelled Parati) is Brazil's first nuclear power plant, near Cunhambebe, the very existence of which sends shudders up the spines of Brazilian ecologists who worry about the potential for radioactive pollution of the nearby waters. Other than that, the scenery is the same delicious ensemble of sea and mountains that characterized the earlier stage of the journey, a visual backdrop that is never tiresome.

You'll enter Paraty through an access road, and the scene along it is typical of rural Brazil everywhere. There are always groups of shirtless men hanging out in front of the many open-fronted commercial shops, while others are driving by in a variety of conveyances, from rickety trucks to horsecarts to bicycles. The side streets are all unpaved, and bare-bottomed toddlers play in the mud while their mothers with babes in arms sit in the open doorways. These are the folk that Brazil's history has always left in its wake, even in a town like Paraty, which was always relatively prosperous, a veritable power during colonial days, now a thriving tourist attraction.

THE STORY OF PARATY   Paraty's harbor was deep enough and just the right scale for ships of the colonial days, which called there often to load their holds with precious stones and gold from nearby Minas, and later the coffee and sugarcane that was cultivated so successfully on the surrounding hills. The cane cultivation led to the creation of an ancillary industry, the production of *aguardente de cana*, the archaic name for what is today generally known as pinga or cachaça. Actually, cachaça was originally distilled from honey, while only cana or pinga came from sugarcane alcohol. Paraty, in any case, became the pinga capital of Brazil, and is still considered to produce the highest-quality sugarcane brandy in the country.

The heart of Paraty today is a seven-square-block area set on a jutting neck of land between harbor and river, that might easily have been plucked from the mid-1700s and placed in the present, so authentic is the preservation of its buildings and streets. Development ceased in Paraty when a new road was laid in 1723 from the mine fields and plantations of Minas to Rio that bypassed the once-active port. And so Paraty slept for almost two and a half centuries in virtual isolation from the rest of the country. But it never decayed, sustaining itself on local agriculture, fishing, and, as always, on the production of pinga. A new road connecting the town to Angra in the 1950s opened Paraty anew, first to artists and bohemians, who were captivated by the tranquillity and ambience of the place, and lately to the casual tourist.

TOURIST INFORMATION   The old jailhouse, next to the Igreja Santa Rita, has a desk where you can get a program of the latest happenings in town, and also a gift shop with some attractive and well-made craft items. It's open daily from 9am till 4pm (tel. 0243/71-1266).

WHAT TO SEE & DO

The historic core of Paraty has now been declared a national monument by Brazil and a world treasure by UNESCO. Motor-vehicle traffic has been banned from its narrow, stone-paved streets. Many of the historical buildings are private homes, but a fair number also house shops and inns, though the air of commercialization remains extremely faint despite the obvious gentrification. Paraty is so genuine in its every detail that even the effete bohemian would still feel at ease here, and the artist no less inspired.

It hardly bears mentioning that one must visit Paraty in the daytime, although I highly recommend an overnight in one of the superb inns. It doesn't take more than a couple of hours to see the entire town, including the interesting slave's church, the **Igreja do Rosário** (1725), on the Rua do Comércio across from the post office. Note the statue of St. Benedict.

The **harbor** is very quiet, and at the dock are moored the colorful fishing craft that today carry tourists on excursions around the bay.

There are several interesting festivals held in Paraty every year. The most important is the **Festa do Divino,** a religious festival of great significance in Portuguese culture dating from the 13th century, and preserved in Paraty from its own colonial past. The festival culminates on Pentecost Sunday, after 10 days of diverse events, sacred and profane, including medieval pageantry with songs and processions, craft fairs and sporting competitions. The **Festival da Pinga,** a kind of Brazilian Oktoberfest, takes place from the 22nd to the 24th of August. Holy Week and Carnival are two other important periods of celebration.

Numerous *saveiros* also cruise the waters off Paraty to take in a panorama of sights that can best be viewed from the sea. Paraty was protected by several strong fortifications, which remain as a historical testament to the days when a million tons of gold were shipped from its wharves. It is also claimed that there are, in all, 65 islands and 300 beaches that may be visited near the town.

Also visible from the water, at Boa Vista, is the steam-driven mill of the Quero Essa pinga factory.

The schooner **Soberano da Costa** makes a daily cruise of the bay, which includes stopovers for swimming, leaving at noon and returning at 4:30pm. Two pinga factories, the **Engenho Murycana** and the **Engenho Quero Essa,** both located on colonial *fazendas,* may be visited by land.

WHERE TO STAY

Within its historic district Paraty offers lodgings in some of the most attractive inns in all of Brazil. For **camping,** there is the nearby Praia do Jabaquara.

Moderate

MERCADO DE POUSO, Rua Dona Rita 43, Paraty. Tel. 243/71-1114.
Telex 21/35632. 22 rms. MINIBAR TEL
$ Rates: $50–$65 double. AE, DC, MC.
The Estalagem Mercado de Pouso is found on the opposite side of town from the Porto Paraty, with its back to the wharf and the splendid Santa Rita Church to its front. The rooms and suites are all under thick-beamed ceilings, with views of interior gardens, or in ateliers over the tile rooftops of neighboring buildings—in all, an extraordinarily beautiful interior environment.

POUSADA PADIEIRO, Rua do Comércio 74, Paraty. Tel. 0243/71-1370.
Fax 0243/71-1139. 24 rms. A/C MINIBAR TV TEL
$ Rates: $80 double. AE.
Typical of the inns in Paraty, the Pousada Padieiro provides the kind of inner space that makes it hard to leave the hotel. There's a nice reading room for those who've come away for the weekend with a great book they haven't had time to read under normal circumstances. The inn also has a pleasant garden and a sauna. When you do go out, the Padieiro can arrange a slow cruise of the bay in a native craft called a *saveiro.*

POUSADA PORTO PARATY, Rua do Comércio 01, Paraty. Tel. 0243/71-1205. Fax 0243/71-2111. Telex 21/31034. 48 rms. A/C MINIBAR TV TEL
$ Rates: $70 single; $80–$100 double. CB, DC, MC.
The Frade's Pousada Porto Paraty is an elegant establishment, located on the extreme edge of the town near the river and behind the Igreja Nossa Senhora dos Remédios. The inn has a swimming pool and a gorgeous outdoor patio and garden.

Reservations are made in Rio (tel. 021/267-7375), and transportation is offered by the Frade company, which provides regular bus shuttle service from Rio to all of its hotels along the Costa Verde.

Budget

HOTEL SOLAR DOS GERÁNIOS, Praça da Matriz, Paraty. Tel. 0243/71-1550. 20 rms (some with bath).
$ Rates: $20 double. No credit cards.
The Hotel Solar dos Gerános is a Swiss-run inn occupying a building with much of the original interior intact, including a massive stone stairway that leads to a second-floor corridor with a number of very simple rooms without baths. The inn is

also filled with antique furnishings, collected by the owners and left in their unfinished state, a condition that strangely enhances their aesthetic appeal.

WHERE TO DINE

All the better inns in Paraty, including those listed above, have their own excellent restaurants. For a good home-cooked Brazilian meal of steak or chicken breast with all the usual side dishes, try the **Restaurante Santa Rita,** across from the Igreja Santa Rita at the corner of Rua da Matriz. For $4 or $5 per person, including beverage, you can eat simply but extremely well.

A fancier choice is the **Restaurante Ancoradouro,** Rua Dona Geralda 345 (tel. 71-1394), around the corner from the Pousada Mercado de Pouso. The menu is international, and main courses fall in the $5 to $10 range.

The **Do Lixo Ao Luxo,** on Rua do Comércio (tel. 71-1124), is a combination bar, restaurant, and antiques shop. The name means "From the Garbage to the Rich," and the colonial-era goods, including cast-iron cooking stoves, are certainly expensive and very beautiful.

CHAPTER 8

MINAS GERAIS & THE HISTORICAL CITIES

- **WHAT'S SPECIAL ABOUT MINAS GERAIS & THE HISTORICAL CITIES**
1. **BELO HORIZONTE**
2. **THE HISTORICAL CITIES**

The name Minas Gerais means General Mines, a rather prosaic term for a state that has contributed so much not only to Brazil's public coffers, but also to the country's artistic, architectural, and political heritage. Geologically, Minas—as the state is called for short—is both favored and ancient. Folded among the layers of its mountainous surface is one of the world's largest reserves of iron ore, so many billions of tons as to make numbers irrelevant and boggle the imagination. Iron, along with cattle and coffee production in the western and northern plains, is the real wealth of Minas today, but it was gold and gem fever that fed the territory's initial exploration and settlement from the late 1600s until well into the 19th century.

Minas also produces much of the Brazil's harvest of precious stones. In this case, the word "harvest" is no metaphor. Early on in the colonial days, stories began to circulate that emeralds were strewn all over the rocky ground in that unexplored region, just waiting for the courageous to go there and gather them up. Minas's reputation as the "Land of the Emeralds" spurred many adventurers to penetrate its forbidden terrain, where the Native American culture still dominated, in search of this easy wealth. The problem was, it was actually the less valuable gemstones that were out in the open, so that what the first pioneers, the *bandeirantes,* took for emeralds were really green tourmalines. Even today a high percentage of Brazil's precious stones are chipped from the surface rocks (if not found actually lying at their feet) by individual prospectors, not mined on an industrial scale. One result is that no one can begin to approximate the size of a given year's production, or the amount of wealth it generates.

It would take many more generations before Brazil's great emerald deposits would be discovered. But when the bandeirantes wound their way up the valley of the Rio das Velhas, they found a substance with a duller sheen but an even better market. Nuggets of pure gold, which washed from shallow deposits in the hills of the Serra da Mantiqueira and the Serra do Espinhaço, could be panned from this and other rivers by the bucketful in a single day, or scratched with minimal labor from right beneath the crust of the earth. Instead of emeralds, by 1693 the pioneers had stumbled onto the greatest gold deposits the world had ever known. Some 25 years later it was discovered that Minas also contained diamonds, so vast in quantity that they could be found clinging to the roots of bushes that were plucked from the ground.

From that time on, sugar would no longer be king in Brazil, nor Salvador the center of the country's power and culture. This was the beginning of the Gold Cycle that was to last 100 years. Fortune hunters flocked to Minas by the tens of thousands, and in their wake came the artists and artisans who spun gold into baroque opulence,

WHAT'S SPECIAL ABOUT MINAS GERAIS & THE HISTORICAL CITIES

Ace Attractions
☐ Belo Horizonte, the state's capital.
☐ The Historical Cities—Ouro Preto, Congonhas, and Sabara.

After Dark
☐ Belo Horizonte, one of Brazil's most cosmopolitan cities, boasts a great restaurant and club scene in the Savassi neighborhood.

Events
☐ Brazil's most elaborate Easter celebration, held in Ouro Preto each year.

Art and Architecture
☐ Ouro Preto, designated an International Treasure by UNESCO, a living museum of baroque art and architecture.
☐ The work of the artist Aleijardinho, found in Congonhas and Sabara as well as Ouro Preto.

Crafts and Gemstones
☐ Gems of great quality are snapped up at bargain prices in and around Ouro Preto.
☐ Carvings in soapstone are typical of the region.

creating the great art and architectural treasures that adorn the *cidades históricas,* the historical cities of Minas, to which thousands today still flock to visit and admire.

SEEING THE REGION

A traveler with two weeks or more to spend in Brazil might want to consider the following itinerary. Stay the first week in Rio, and then rent a car and head north toward Minas. The main artery is the 040 highway, which goes via Petrópolis. Spend the first day and night near São João del Rei and Tiradentes. Then travel on to B.H. and use the city as a base for side trips to the principal historical cities, with a possible overnight in Ouro Preto. To return, leave the car at the airport in B.H. and fly back to Rio for your last night or two in the country.

Those with less time to spare can still take in the historical cities by flying the air shuttle, called the **Ponte Aérea** (literally, air bridge) from Rio's international airport to B.H., a flight that takes only 50 minutes. The cost of a round-trip ticket is approximately $192. Then contact a local agency directly at the airport and book a standard bus tour. You can see all the sights—somewhat hurriedly, to be sure—in a day and a half, and be back in Rio within 48 hours. Those visitors planning to wander a bit more widely through the country are encouraged to purchase the VARIG Air Pass. Normally I would not consider recommending such a frenetic sightseeing pace for anyone in Brazil (that is, in Rio) on a limited stay. But the baroque wonders of Minas are so spectacular that I will suspend my better judgment in this and a handful of other special cases.

1. BELO HORIZONTE

250 miles NW of Rio

GETTING THERE   By Plane   Belo Horizonte is serviced by two airports, with most out-of-state flights landing at Lagoa Santa, some 39km (24 miles) from the city.

By Train   Travelers partial to railroads can reserve passage for about $67 each on the twice-weekly train from Rio.

By Bus   Long-distance buses arrive regularly in B.H. from most of Brazil's major cities. At $10.50 each way, the standard bus (run by Util Turismo; tel. 271-4522) is the cheapest mode of transportation from Rio to B.H., and the journey takes about seven hours. The more comfortable *leito,* with reclining seats, charges $22.50 for the ride from Rio, and is particularly recommended for night travel. It's run by Viação Cometa (tel. 201-5611).

By Car   The BR 040 highway links Rio to Belo Horizonte via Petrópolis.

Belo Horizonte is Brazil's fourth-largest city, with a metropolitan population of 2,049,000 inhabitants. Known as "B.H." ("bay-a-*gah*") or Belo, it was a planned city, constructed in a spacious valley and inaugurated in 1897 as the state's capital to replace Ouro Preto, which had outgrown its pinched-in boundaries. Today B.H. has the graceful appearance of a provincial center, the gridlike organization of its streets broken up by ample shade trees, architectural diversity, and the gentle rising and falling of the terrain. There is about B.H. an unmistakable air of sophistication and dignity that one comes to associate with residents of this remarkable state. And while the beachless city is not promoted heavily as a destination for tourists, it is not lacking in urban amenities, which take the form of animated café life and excellent eating.

ORIENTATION

ARRIVING   Special cabs, run by **Coopertramo** (tel. 443-2288), make the one-hour run from the Confins airport to downtown for $28, and to the Savassi for $36. An airport bus (operated by **Empresa Zé Zé Turismo Ltd.;** tel. 271-1335) makes the trip to B.H. every hour for $1.25. An executive bus runs between the JK Bus Terminal and the airport every hour for $5.75. Services include a VIP waiting room at the bus station and beverage service on the bus. The executive service is run by Empresa Util Turismo (tel. 271-4522).

INFORMATION   **Turminas,** the state's tourist authority, runs an information counter at the Confins airport, or you can check in at their main offices, the Centro de Apoio Turístico, Av. Bias Fortes 50, in the Lourdes neighborhood (tel. 031/212-2134). The office is open Monday through Friday from noon to 6pm.

BeloTur, Rua Paraiba 330, 19th floor (Centro) (tel. 031/220-5500; fax 031/224-6629), the city's excellent municipal tourist office, operates information booths at the Praça Sete, which is at the corner of Rua Rio de Janeiro (tel. 212-1400, ext. 355), and at the Rodoviária (bus station) on Praça Rio Branco (tel. 212-1400, ext. 404). These booths are open Monday through Friday from 8am to 10pm and on weekends from 9am to 5pm. The information booth at Confins Airport functions seven days a week from 8am to 6pm; English is spoken. The **Alô Belo** tourism information line (tel. 220-1310) operates Monday through Friday from 8am to 6pm.

CITY LAYOUT   The urban core of the city is belted by the **Avenida do Contorno,** which encircles its periphery and greatly enhances the movement of traffic from one neighborhood to another. The principal boulevard, **Avenida Afonso Pena,** divides the city at its middle, and at dead center an enormous green space, the **Parque Municipal,** occupies 200 of B.H.'s choicest acres.

You probably won't find the name **Savassi** on a city map, but the name indicates four square blocks where the best dining and nightlife in B.H. are to be found. Most of the restaurants listed below are located in the Savassi.

The best way to get a quick visual orientation of the city and its environs is to visit the **mirante** (overlook) in the neighborhood of Mangabeiras, reached by following Avenida Afonso Pena east (the direction away from Pampulha). The overlook occupies one corner of a park with picnic and recreational facilities. But the trip out here is really for the vista of the surrounding mountains which, row after row, seem to stretch on to infinity.

WHAT TO SEE & DO

While there are no major attractions in B.H.—the city is a place where it's simply nice to just hang out—there are numerous museums, parks, and points of interest for those who are so inclined.

MUSEU DE MINERALOGIA, Rua da Bahia 1149. Tel. 238-4203.

The Museu de Mineralogia (Mineralogy Museum) is in an old municipal building (ca. 1910), one of the few examples of Manueline Neo-Gothic architecture in Brazil. Some 98% of the 2,500 samples on exhibit come from the mines and hills of Minas Gerais. There are four exhibition rooms with displays of dozens of minerals and gemstones, organized according to their geological families. For those who can read Portuguese, there are printed explanations of the minerals' chemical composition, occurrence in nature, uses, and the locations of major veins within the state, in Brazil, and in the world.

Admission: Free.
Open: Daily 9am–5pm.

MUSEU HISTÓRICO ABLIO BARRETO, Rua Bernardo Mascarenhas. Tel. 335-9243.

The Museu Histórico Ablio Barreto (History Museum), in the Cidade Jardim residential neighborhood, occupies the only structure—an old *fazenda* house—that remains from the days when Belo Horizonte was known as Arraial do Curral D' El Rey. Built in 1833, the abobe house is itself an integral part of the exhibit, most of which documents the process of the new city replacing the old settlement.

Admission: Free.
Open: Wed–Mon 10am–5pm.

CENTRO DE ARTESANATO MINEIRO, Av. Afonso Pena 1537. Tel. 222-2544.

This is the place to go for well-made and reasonably priced craft items gathered from all over the state. The Craft Center is located close to the major hotels in the Palácio das Artes on the edge of the Municipal Park. Very modern and well organized, the shop features the best of Minas's soapstone statuary (lovely but very difficult to transport without breaking), yellow tinware, baskets, rugs, and wood carvings, all of exceptionally high quality and imaginative design.

Open: Mon–Fri 9am–9pm, Sat 9am–1pm.

PAMPULHA

The futuristic suburb of Pampulha was, in effect, a prototype of Brasília, promoted, designed, and constructed by virtually the same cast of characters who were to later create the new Brazilian capital. The principal in both cases was the then mayor of B.H., and later president, Juscelino Kubitschek, who in 1939 enlisted some of the country's most creative talent, including architect Oscar Niemeyer, landscape artist Roberto Burle Marx, and painter Cândido Portinari. The project involved the transformation of the area surrounding an existing reservoir into a modern residential and recreational district. The plans included the building of a chapel, sporting clubs, restaurants, and a casino. The **Capelinha de São Francisco de Assis,** designed by Niemeyer and decorated with *azulejo* tiles and murals by Portinari, considered now to be some of the artist's masterworks, remained unconsecrated for years, a reaction to both the aesthetic modernism and the leftist political views of the artists by the city's conservative clergy.

MUSEUM OF MODERN ART, Av. Octacílio Negrão de Lima 16585. Tel. 443-4533.

After gambling was outlawed in Brazil following World War II, the casino was converted into the city's Museum of Modern Art. As with most of the project's buildings, this, too, was designed by Niemeyer, and the gardens were laid out by Marx. Pampulha lies about 10km (six miles) to the west of the city, a 20-minute ride by cab or car, and is also reachable by frequent bus service.

Admission: Free.
Open: Daily 8am–6pm.

WHERE TO STAY

Strangely, for a city as charming as Belo Horizonte, the city's best hotel, the Brasilton, is located 10 miles out of town in Contagem, Brazil's third-largest industrial district.

The hotels downtown are a bit disappointing, but in recent years, a number of small hotels, built on the continental scale, and staffed accordingly, have begun to appear in the Savassi and along its margins. B.H.'s downtown hub is relatively small, and all the hotels there tend to be within walking distance of each other, and of the principal transportation terminals serving the airport.

EXPENSIVE

BRASILTON, Rodovia Fernão Dias at km 365, Contagem. Tel. 031/396-1100. Fax 031/396-1144. Telex 31/1860. 143 rms. A/C MINIBAR TV TEL
$ Rates: $80–$90 single; $90–$115 double. AE, DC, MC, V.

Belo's best hotel is the Brasilton, actually located about 25 minutes from downtown in the heavily industrialized suburb of Contagem. The hotel was no doubt built as an oasis for traveling businesspeople. And really, while the location is somewhat bizarre, the hotel's internal environment is so pleasant that you won't care or notice for a minute that you are surrounded by industrial enterprises (which are not on a particularly gigantic scale, in any event). There are also plenty of trees, stores, and open spaces in the vicinity—it's not the cold and smelly industrial-park look of the New Jersey Turnpike by any means.

The handsome white stucco facade of the two-story Brasilton suggests a stylized pueblo, square in shape, where most of the rooms overlook the pool and landscaped patio of a large interior courtyard. Off the central yard are the enclosed public spaces, including a smartly decorated lobby, restaurant, and various discreet seating environments. The medium-sized rooms all have small balconies. Overall, the Brasilton conveys a relaxed and resortlike atmosphere, despite its popularity among corporate clients as a venue for business meetings and weekend seminars.

Facilities: Sports facilities at the hotel include swimming, tennis, volleyball, and soccer courts, as well as a sauna and a recreational game room.

OTHON PALACE, Av. Afonso Pena 1050, Belo Horizonte. Tel. 031/226-7844. Fax 031/212-2318. Telex 31/2052. 304 rms. A/C MINIBAR TV TEL
$ Rates: $77–$85 single; $93–$102 double. AE, DC, MC, V.

The Othon Palace is Belo's only five-star hotel, and by far the best of the downtown selection. It's a fully equipped high-rise in the shape of a concave cylinder, which faces the Municipal Park. The hotel's public spaces are decorated in marble and tiles, with earth-tone colors predominating. Rooms are large, with big windows and separate sitting areas.

Dining/Entertainment: The principal restaurant, serving international cuisine, and the bar are on the third floor.

Services: Laundry service, in-house travel agency.

Facilities: An outdoor pool (which can be heated when the mercury dips) is located on the 25th floor, along with a dining terrace. In addition, there's a beauty shop, a gift boutique, and a parking garage.

MODERATE

HOTEL DEL REY, Praça Afonso Arinos 60, Belo Horizonte. Tel. 031/273-2211. Fax 031/273-1804. Telex 31/1033. 213 rms. A/C MINIBAR TV TEL
$ Rates: $65–$77 single; $73–$81 double. AE, DC, MC, V.

The Del Rey is between downtown and the Savassi, across the street from the Museum of Mineralogy, in a tree-lined residential neighborhood. This is a full-service hotel, equipped with a restaurant, a beauty salon, and parking facilities. The restaurant serves an executive buffet Monday through Friday for $7. Rooms appear spacious and comfortable, and each is furnished with an individual safe.

REAL PALACE HOTEL, Rua Espírito Santo 901, Belo Horizonte. Tel. 031/273-3111. Fax 031/273-2646. Telex 31/3733. 256 rms. A/C MINIBAR TV TEL
$ Rates: $75 single; $90 double. AE, MC, V.

The Real Palace Hotel is another of B.H.'s four-star hotels with a three-star appearance. The rooms here cost slightly more than the comparable Del Rey. The

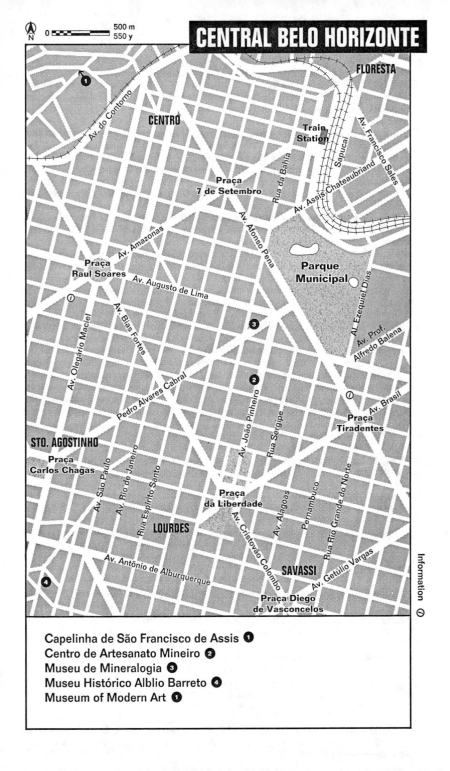

CENTRAL BELO HORIZONTE

Capelinha de São Francisco de Assis ❶
Centro de Artesanato Mineiro ❷
Museu de Mineralogia ❸
Museu Histórico Alblio Barreto ❹
Museum of Modern Art ❶

standard rooms are on the lower floors, but they are similar in size and detail to the so-called luxury rooms.

TERMINAL CENTER HOTEL, Av. Amazonas 1445, with an entrance on Rua Rio Grande do Sul 856, Belo Horizonte. Tel. 031/337-9555. Fax 031/275-3955. Telex 31/5573. 150 rms. A/C MINIBAR TV TEL
$ Rates: $75–$80 double. V.

The entrance to the Terminal Center Hotel is actually around the corner on Rua Rio Grande do Sul, and the large, brand new building is located across from the Terminal Turistico JK, the bus terminal for the airport bus (the *executivo*). The hotel is slated to provide 450 rooms, but only the first few floors are currently in operation, while the remainder are still being fitted out. The standard double is quite small, if cozy and well furnished. Among its facilities, the hotel offers a pool, a restaurant, and parking.

WEMBLEY PALACE, Rua Espírito Santo 201, Belo Horizonte. Tel. 031/201-6966. Fax 031/224-9946. Telex 31/3019. 105 rms. A/C MINIBAR TV TEL
$ Rates: $55 single; $72 double. AE, DC.

The rooms here are good-sized, and better furnished than those of rival hotels in the same category. The luxury rooms have separate sitting areas, and all units have individual safes.

In Savassi

CLASSIC HOTEL, Rua da Bahia 2727, Belo Horizonte. Tel. 031/225-0082. Fax 031/223-5769. Telex 39/2739. 46 rms. A/C MINIBAR TV TEL
$ Rates: $55 single; $60 double. AE, DC, MC, V.

This eight-story hotel, brand new in 1992, is one of the best bets for anyone wanting a room near the city. The Classic would be an excellent choice for a visiting business traveler, or a tourist. And the Savassi location is a bonus rather than an incentive for staying here. The hotel's special quality is first experienced in the tasteful, spacious lobby. The same attention to comfort and decor carries over to the large, agreeable rooms. Among the Classic's attractive facilities is a second-floor restaurant, with contiguous veranda.

HOTEL BOULEVARD, Av. Getúlio Vargas 1640, Belo Horizonte. Tel. 031/223-9000. Fax 031/225-8438. Telex 31/5029. 44 rms. A/C MINIBAR TV TEL
$ Rates: $73 single; $89 double. AE, DC, MC, V.

The Hotel Boulevard occupies a relatively new and attractive building on the fringe of the entertainment district. The Boulevard's rooms are all in the deluxe category, quite spacious with sleeping and seating areas separated by dividers. Rooms with twin beds are even larger than those with doubles, and furnishings throughout are comfortably modern. A wall of windows in each room looks out over the streets of this elegant neighborhood.

HOTEL CASA DOS MUNICÍPIOS, Rua Rio Grande do Norte 1017, Belo Horizonte. Tel. 031/226-5177. Telex 31/1782. 16 rms. MINIBAR TV TEL
$ Rates: $32 single; $40 double; $36 suite for one, $46 suite for two. V.

A small, slightly bohemian-looking hideaway called the Hotel Casa dos Municípios is located right in the heart of the Savassi district. Apparently the sprawling old mansion once did house some municipal administrative entity, but has long since been converted into this rooming house–style lodging. The rooms are located off a network of inner courts and corridors, and the suites here are largest and most attractive of the rooms. Other rooms are smallish, but have their charm as well. There is a pool and parking.

PALMEIRAS DA LIBERDADE HOTEL, Rua Sergipe 893, Belo Horizonte. Tel. 031/212-7422. Fax 031/212-7894. Telex 39/1130. 62 rms. A/C MINIBAR TV TEL

$ Rates: $45 single; $55 double. AE, DC, MC, V.

Another relatively new Savassi hotel, the Palmeiras da Liberdade, faces the coconut palm–lined Praça da Liberdade in a serene mixed commercial and residential neighborhood. Rooms are smallish, but efficiently modular to use the space well. The window shutters are a nice touch. Live music entertains diners daily at lunchtime.

SAVASSI HOTEL, Rua Sergipe 939, Belo Horizonte. Tel. 031/212-3266.
Fax 031/212-3628. Telex 31/3073. 78 rms. A/C MINIBAR TV TEL

$ Rates: $54–$64 single; $69–$77 double; $84 suite. AE, DC, MC, V.

Rooms at the Savassi Hotel are decorated in green felt and wood trim, like billiard or card tables, and suggest the atmosphere of a private men's club. Suites here are really double rooms, with separate sleeping and living areas. There is a pool with multileveled deck on the rooftop; the space is limited but the ambience, with its assorted chaises and umbrella-sheltered café tables, is very suitable for lounging over cocktails at the end of the day.

BUDGET

In many ways the following hotels are superior to their more pretentious rivals, if for no other reason than that the rooms are about half the price, while most of the services, including a restaurant, are still provided.

AMBASSY HOTEL, Rua dos Caetés 633, Belo Horizonte. Tel. 031/201-6019. Telex 31/6017. 69 rms (all with bath). A/C MINIBAR TV TEL

$ Rates: $32 single; $42 double. AE, MC.

The Ambassy Hotel offers spacious rooms with the usual amenities, except TVs are optional and may be rented for a fee. The old triangular building at a busy intersection of the downtown shopping district has a certain charm.

HOTEL ESPLANADA, Av. Santos Dumont 304, Belo Horizonte. Tel. 031/273-5311. 121 rms (60 with bath).

$ Rates: $16 single without bath, $20 single with bath; $20 double without bath, $30 double with bath. No credit cards.

The Hotel Esplanada is near the bus station where you catch the airport bus. Rooms with bath are called *apartamentos*. The simpler rooms, called *quartos*, have neither attached bathrooms nor TVs, but are very adequate for those on a limited budget or who would rather spend their money on something other than a hotel room.

A Youth Hostel

ALBERQUE DA JUVENTUDE POUSADA BEAGA, Rua dos Timbiras 2330, in Lourdes, Belo Horizonte. Tel. and fax 031/275-3592. Telex 39/1931.

$ Rates: $5 members, $6 nonmembers. No credit cards.

This youth hostel, conveniently located near most of the in-town action, has a reputation for modern facilities and great breakfasts. Towel and sheet rentals are available, and there is a washing machine on the premises.

WHERE TO DINE

One needs no other justification for traveling in Minas Gerais than the opportunity to sample the state's superb cuisine, **comida mineira,** popular throughout Brazil, but best in the kitchens of its origin. The favorite ingredients of a meal in Minas are pork, black beans, kale, and a cornmeal mush called **angu.** Two dishes you are sure to encounter everywhere throughout the state are **tutu com linguiça e couve,** a dish of country sausage, mashed beans, and kale, and **feijão tropeiro,** a stir-fry of pork and sausage, beans, eggs, and crackling (fried pork rinds). Many of the Mineiro dishes have their origins in the slave and laboring cultures, but have been fine-tuned over the years into the most palate-pleasing of country fare. Another staple found on most tables is **pão de queijo,** little puff balls of soft cheese bread (bet you can't eat just one!). The desserts, like **doce de leite,** and cheese, **quejo mineiro,** of Minas are also justly celebrated by Brazilians everywhere. One favorite dessert is to eat the cheese with a slice of **goiabada** (guava paste) on a **pãozinho,** the classic bread roll universally available no matter where you travel in Brazil.

There are many fine restaurants in Belo Horizonte, whether you favor comida mineira or more familiar international fare. And the *bom e barato* standard (good and cheap) of Brazilian restaurant food is as much in evidence throughout B.H. as in any other region of the country.

EXPENSIVE

CAFE IDEAL, Rua dos Inconfidentes 312. Tel. 223-9986

Cuisine: TRADITIONAL FRENCH. **Reservations:** Recommended for dinner.
$ Prices: Appetizers $6–$8; main courses $8–$15. No credit cards.
Open: Mon–Fri noon–3pm and 7pm–midnight, Sat noon–midnight, Sun noon–5pm.

One of B.H.'s most popular French restaurants, the Café Ideal is mounted within an unusual and elegant space. The restaurant occupies two floors in the narrow building, but the upstairs bar is really nothing more than an extended catwalk. The ceiling is extremely high, and a portion of the wall has been left in its unrenovated state, creating the effect of a large abstract expressionist canvas. The menu contains many classic French dishes, and specialized in several preparations of filet mignon. Not only a good choice for an excellent meal, the Café Ideal provides the right atmosphere for an intimate cocktail as well.

O PATO SELVAGEM, Rua Alvarenga Peixoto 900. Tel. 337-1752.

Cuisine: NOUVELLE. **Reservations:** Recommended.
$ Prices: Appetizers $2.25–$7.50; main courses $7.50–$15. No credit cards.
Open: Dinner Mon–Sat 7pm–2am.

O Pato Selvagem is located in the Lourdes neighborhood that borders the Savassi, and is one of the more subtle and tastefully decorated restaurants you will see in B.H. Tables occupy the several ground-floor rooms of a converted private house, but the symmetry of the space—bathed in a background of off-pink and soft lighting—is broken up by the placement of false columns and niches containing small statuary. The wall art is also exceptional. O Pato Selvagem serves correspondingly imaginative dishes in the "new Brazilian" style, which borrows from French tradition where necessary, but remains deeply rooted in the unique flavors and ingredients of the native culture. The restaurant's names means "the wild duck," so it is not surprising to find the fowl of that species prominent among offerings on the menu. One unusual dish that is flavorfully pungent combines duck with a caviar and salmon sauce au poivre.

VITELO'S, Rua Rio Grande do Norte 1007. Tel. 226-8131.

Cuisine: STEAK. **Reservations:** Recommended for dinner.
$ Prices: Appetizers $2–$5; main courses $21–$28. AE.
Open: Mon–Sat noon–3pm and 7pm–12:30am, Sun noon–5pm.

Possibly Belo Horizonte's best restaurant, this is certainly its best steakhouse. The service at Vitelo's is exquisite, but the beef outshines the pomp and circumstance. Prices are high, but a slab of meat, deftly carved directly onto your plate from a skewer, is more than enough for two. The *fraldinha* ($21), a very tender cut from the cow's underside, was absolutely heavenly.

BUDGET

BARTOLOMEU, Av. Olegário Maciel 1741. Tel. 335-3709.

Cuisine: CONTINENTAL. **Reservations:** Not needed.
$ Prices: Appetizers $2–$3.25; main courses $4.25–$7. No credit cards.

Open: Dinner Mon–Fri 6pm–late; Sat–Sun 11am until the wee hours.

The Bartolomeu, in Lourdes, is a popular spot for Belo's café society. A nice feature of the Bartolomeu is that you can call ahead for take-out. The restaurant serves a *feijoada* every Saturday for $5.50. The small *picanha* steak, the popular house specialty, is $4.25.

BUONA TAVOLA, Rua Santa Rita Durão 309. Tel. 227-6155.
   Cuisine: ITALIAN. **Reservations:** Not needed.
$ Prices: Appetizers $2–$5; main courses $6.50–$8.75. AE, MC, V.
   Open: Mon 6pm–midnight, Tues–Sat noon–3pm and 6:30pm–2am, Sun noon–6pm.

Buona Tavola is an Italian restaurant owned by the proprietor of the Chico Mineiro, and open during the same hours. Fettuccine da casa costs $6.50, while other pasta and meat dishes range between $3 and $6. An unusual shrimp lasagne is $8.75. The restaurant is quite small, with only about 10 tables.

CHEZ BASTIÃO, Rua Alagoas 642. Tel. 226-5694.
   Cuisine: COMIDA MINEIRA. **Reservations:** Not needed.
$ Prices: Appetizers $3.25–$16 (highest price is for shrimp); main courses $6–$8.75. AE, DC,
   Open: Mon–Sat 11am until the last customer is ready to leave, Sun 11am–2am.

Chez Bastião is the favorite restaurant of my guide from Turminas, as much for the food as for the animated atmosphere. The food and menu prices are similar to those of Chico Mineiro, which is directly next door. The house specialty among the continental dishes is the Stroganoff ($5.25).

CHICO MINEIRO, Rua Alagoas 626. Tel. 222-6027.
   Cuisine: COMIDA MINEIRA. **Reservations:** Not needed.
$ Prices: Appetizers $2.25–$4.75; main courses $4.50–$9. No credit cards.
   Open: Lunch Mon–Fri 11:30am–3pm, Sat 11:30am–6pm; dinner Fri–Sat 6pm–2am, Sun 11am–midnight.

Chico Mineiro, in the heart of the Savassi, serves down-home, authentic comida mineira, the country-style food of central Brazil. The principal dishes are *tutu, tropeiro,* and *galinha* (chicken). The restaurant's interior is divided into several partitioned rooms, amply paneled in wood, with indirect ceiling lighting and checkered tablecloths. There are also some 10 tables outside on the sidewalk. Your meal with beverage and tip will cost between $4 and $7.

CUCINA ITALIANA–PROVINCIA DI SALERNO, Rua Maranhão 18. Tel. 224-2205.
   Cuisine: ITALIAN. **Reservations:** Not accepted.
$ Price: Appetizers $3.50–$5.50; main courses $5–$12. No credit cards.
   Open: Tues–Sat 6pm–2am, Sun noon–5pm.

This is a new location for the ever-popular Cucina Italiana. The stuffed eggplant is very tasty for starters. And for the main dish, if pasta is your fancy, try something on the imaginative side like *fettuccine a caviar* ($7.75), or a filling rib-sticker like the roast goat ($8.25).

DEGRAU, Av. Alfonso Pena 4221. Tel. 225-7362.
   Cuisine: INTERNATIONAL. **Reservations:** Not needed.
$ Prices: Appetizers $1–$4; main courses $3.25–$7. No credit cards.
   Open: Daily 9am–4am.

The Degrau is what Brazilians refer to as a *restaurante popular,* which translates roughly as a "restaurant for the masses." Located on the way to the *mirante,* right below the Praça do Papa, where an outdoor altar was built for a mass celebrated by the visiting Pope John Paul II a few years back, the Degrau has a long menu and seating for hundreds. Many young people are attracted by the ambience and inexpensive food. The filet Degrau ($7) is the big draw.

   Directly across the street is the **Brunela,** a restaurant that is a mirror image of the Degrau, but with a different name.

DONA LUCINHA, Rua Padre Odorico 38, Savassi. Tel. 227-0562.
   Cuisine: COMIDA MINEIRA. **Reservations:** Not needed.

$ Prices: All-you-can-eat buffet $7. No credit cards.
Open: Lunch daily noon–3pm; dinner daily 6pm–midnight. May be open later on weekends.

Dona Lucinha lives on a farm in the countryside, where she raised her 11 children. She first opened a restaurant in her hometown, which made her reputation. So she opened a second establishment in the city. In it she offers one of the most complete and mouth-watering buffets of authentic regional dishes that I have tasted in Brazil. The dishes come in two styles, "fazenda" (ranch-style), and "tropeiro" (traditional-style), and you may serve yourself from both. If you include the salads, the relishes, and the homemade liquors, there are over 50 items to choose from, 20 of which are hot dishes—many of which you will not see in the more touristic restaurants.

PETISQUEIRA DO GALO, Av. Olegário Maciel 1516, in Lourdes. Tel. 335-5773.
Cuisine: COMIDA MINEIRA. **Reservations:** Not needed.
$ Prices: Appetizers 30¢–$4.75; main courses $5–$10. AE, DC, MC.
Open: Mon–Fri 11am–midnight, Sat–Sun 9am–6pm.

Only rarely does one encounter comida mineira that is prepared under the watchful eye of a true gourmet, a person whose passion for eating is complemented by his or her skills in the kitchen. Such is the case of Senhor Targino Lima, part owner and full-time inspiration of Petisqueira do Galo. Simple in its setting—an unadorned veranda—as a workingman's lunch pail, the Petisqueira is nonetheless cited by the Brazilian guide *Quatro Rodas* as one of the two finest restaurants in all Belo Horizonte. Actually, there is nothing "fine" about the Petisqueira, unless one is referring to the quality of the service, and the above-average presentation of the edibles. The food itself is just plain good, and so plentiful as to encourage the latent gluttony in anyone, like the author, who springs from old-world peasant stock. Every time the waiter moved to refill my plate, I demurred but never resisted his offer. My meal consisted of *lombo* (baked pork), *couve* (greens), *feijão tropeiro* (beans and fried manioc flour), and rice; all of which was ringed by tomato slices and topped off with a fried egg. Prior to the main course, I had consumed several meat-and-cheese pastries that were as good as any Indian samosas or Argentine empanadas I'd ever tasted. The tab for this feast, including several rounds of beer? About seven bucks a head.

TAVARES, Rua Santa Catarina 64. Tel. 286-1780.
Cuisine: GAME. **Reservations:** Not needed.
$ Prices: Appetizers $1–$4; main courses $5.25–$9. No credit cards.
Open: Mon–Sat 11am–midnight, Sun 11am–5pm.

Tavares, located in a back alley off the Praça Raul Soares, is assuredly Belo Horizonte's most unusual restaurant, serving a variety of game meats that are sure to intrigue the true carnivore. Also a "popular" restaurant, the Tavares is well worn but not unclean. A lunch here can be the starting point for an exploration of the downtown shops and open-air markets, one of which takes place daily on the neighboring plaza. The specialties include *viado* (deer), *capibara* (a giant member of the rodentia order of mammals, which has been likened to a 200-pound guinea pig), *cordorna* (quail), and *jacaré* (alligator). Less exotic is the rabbit ($6.75), a house specialty.

TIP TOP, Rua Rio de Janeiro 1754. Tel. 275-1880.
Cuisine: GERMAN/INTERNATIONAL. **Reservations:** Not needed.
$ Prices: Appetizers $1.50–$2.75; main courses $3.50–$5.50. AE.
Open: Daily 10am–2am.

The Tip Top is located in the Lourdes neighborhood, which is contiguous to Savassi. Other than the fact that it's much larger, the Tip Top has the same deli ambience as the Trianon (see below). The restaurant is very well attended on Sunday evenings in particular, a favorite time for denizens of the city to hang out and relax before the beginning of a new work week. Some house favorites are goulash with spaetzle ($3.50), and kasseler with sauerkraut ($5.25).

TRIANON, Rua Alagoas 730. Tel. 224-2005.
Cuisine: GERMAN. **Reservations:** Not needed.

$ Prices: Appetizers $1–$4; main courses $3–$6. No credit cards.
Open: Daily 11am–2am.
The Trianon is a thoroughly charming and fancy delicatessen. Forest green is the predominant color of the trim and furnishings, including the Vienna-style marble-topped tables on wrought-iron bases and green barrel-backed chairs. A large refrigerator counter runs the length of the room, which is part shop for delicacies, wines, and liquors, and part restaurant. German specialties—meats and cheeses—are displayed in the deli counter, and German dishes like pigs' knuckles with sauerkraut ($5) and sausage with potato ($5) add a special dimension to an extensive menu.

EVENING ENTERTAINMENT

Just for the novelty of it, you ought to pay at least one call on the **Chalézinho,** Rua Paraíba 1455, corner of Cristóvão Colombo (tel. 221-2170). Housed on the second and third floors of an A-frame that looks like someone's ski cottage, the Chalézinho offers the most varied menu for cocktails, coffee concoctions, and teas of any place I know of in Brazil. Some typical libations are the *café do bigode*—cognac, lime, coffee, and whipped cream ($1.25)—and the Ze Lamparina cocktail—whisky, Campari, and champagne ($2). For munching, try an order of the cheese-filled "micro pastries" ($1.50). A more elaborate fondue of meat or cheese can be had for $12.50. No credit cards are accepted.

The **Cervejaria Brasil, Rua** Aimorés 78 (tel. 225-1099), has long been a popular hangout in B.H. The menu features over 15 varieties of beer—which is rare in Brazil, where the available brew is usually limited to three or four domestic labels. The snack of choice here is the *picanha na chapa*—cubes of barbecued beef ($15 for two or three persons). Half of this space, which is very large, is under cover, the other half in the open air like a genuine beer garden. No credit cards are accepted, and it's open daily from 11am to 2am.

Under the same ownership, and right next door is the **Cervejaria Brasil Bar,** Rua Aimorés 108 (tel. 221-8336), a café-bar, spread over two floors. Considerably fancier than its sibling down the sidewalk, the "Bar" has walls hung with the striking black-and-white prints of some excellent local photographers. On the menu are literally dozens of *tira gostos*—appetizers priced from $1.50 to $3.25 each—and many "refreições," dinners in the $6 range. The Cervejaria Brasil does not accept credit cards, and it's open Monday to Friday from 6pm to 2am, and Saturday and Sunday from noon to 2am.

There are many good clubs in and around the Savassi, like the **Tom Marrom,** Rua Inconfidentes 1141 (tel. 224-3728), a singles bar that charges a $6.50 minimum per person on Friday and Saturday. **Upstairs,** Rua Tomé de Souza 935 (tel. 226-6783), is the city's "in" dance spot for the moment. Upstairs is only open to the public on Thursday, Friday, and Saturday nights, after 10:30pm. There is a $2.50 cover per

---

A ONE-OF-A-KIND WATERING HOLE

A must for any true fan of Brazilian *cachaça* (cane brandy) is the **Alambique,** Av. Raja Gabaglia 3200 (tel. 334-5873). The chalet-style building in which this moonshine still (*alambique*) is housed is located high above the city on the edge of town. (Take bus no. 3901—Vera Cruz–Estrela D'Avila—to get there.) The Alambique is what Brazilians call a *cachacaría*, a place to imbibe the native firewater, but it is also an *armazem*, a store whose shelves are filled with 120 different brands of fazenda-brewed cachaça. The house label is *Cachaça German*, which sells for 45¢ a swig; the best in the house is Havana, at $3 a shot. There are snacks, *tira gostos*, on hand to absorb the libation's worst effects, or if you want to eat *comida caipira*, country cooking, call ahead for a reservation. Monday night would be a good time to come here; there is live country music from 9pm till midnight.

person, and no minimum. The **Fabrica do Macarrão** (Spaghetti Factory; tel. 461-1762), Praça Duque de Caxas 69, in Santa Thereza, is a *gafieira* with live shows, open on Friday, Saturday, and Sunday after 8pm.

For live cabaret, there's the **Cabaré Mineiro,** Rua Gonçalves Dias 54 (tel. 227-5860), with a different show every night, including political theater. Wednesday nights are for karaokê, in which the audience provides the vocals, singing along to taped musical backup. The bar is open Wednesday through Sunday, and the show begins after 9pm. There is a $2.50 cover charge per person.

The L'Apogèe Club Privé, Rua Antônio de Albuquerque 729 (tel. 227-5133), attracts large crowds of beautiful people on the weekends. The club is open Tuesday through Saturday after 8pm, and there is live music every night. The cover is $6 for men, $2.50 for women, with a minimum of $4 per person. The bar opens at 6:30 for happy hour. Valet parking is available, and all major credit cards are accepted.

The down-and-dirty dive of the moment, also immensely popular, is **Dominus,** Rua Padre Odorico 95 in the Savassi (tel. 227-8607), just down the block from the Dona Lucinha restaurant. Three separate floors, one of which is a rooftop beer garden, provide entertainment to suit a variety of moods and tastes, from jazz and blues to rock and live cabaret. Pick up your *cartela*—punch ticket—at the door; the waiter records your consumption, and you pay on departure. Drinks are cheap, 75¢ a draft, $1.25 for Heineken, and $1.40 for a caipirinha. Open Wednesday, Thursday, and Sunday from 10pm to 1am; Friday and Saturday from 10pm to 6am. Thursday, Friday, and Saturday, there is a cover of $1.75 per person, and on Saturday, $3.50 minimum as well.

2. THE HISTORICAL CITIES

For their first 200 years in Brazil, colonists confined their settlements to the country's coastal lands. They looked on the mountainous interior as impassable and uninhabitable. Late in the 17th century, however, word slowly drifted back to the coast that the crude and antisocial slave hunters known as *bandeirantes* had discovered gold in those inhospitable hills. Within a short time the wealth that flowed from those early grubstakes attracted hordes of settlers to the virgin territory, and the rude camps of the prospectors were transformed almost overnight into the glittering pinnacles of baroque culture that are known today as the historical cities of Minas Gerais.

The cities we will visit are Sabará, Congonhas do Campo, Ouro Preto, and Mariana; they're near Belo Horizonte, and therefore most accessible to the majority of international tourists who are likely to visit them, preferring no doubt to fly to the capital of Minas rather than coming to the state by car. A car trip, on the other hand, would take the traveler from Rio first to São João del Rei and Tiradentes, will only be covered in passing.

The historical cities of Minas are living tableaux of Brazil's Gold Cycle, which occurred throughout the 1700s, but touched the fringes of two other centuries as well, running from the 1690s to the early 1800s, by which time the auriferous flow from the mines had slowed to a trickle. The principal attractions of the historical cities are the scores of churches, residences, and commercial structures that have been preserved from those times, and the artistry with which the facades and interiors of those churches were decorated by a dozen great artists, most notable of whom were the sculptor Antônio Francisco Lisboa (called Aleijadinho) and the painter Manuel da Costa Atraide. The work of these and many other remarkable artists can be seen in each of the four cities herein described.

Of the cities themselves, Ouro Preto is by far the most important for two related, if contradictory, reasons. As the territory's, and later the state's, capital for 150 years, the town grew to splendid proportions during its reign of power, the hilly streets crowned with one baroque architectural treasure after another. The transfer of its power to Belo Horizonte nearly a century ago, moreover, ensured the preservation of Ouro Preto's characteristic appearance, so that it remains today frozen in a state of near perfection, a veritable living mirror of the period of its former grandeur, little diluted by the developments of the 19th and 20th centuries.

While all the historical cities enjoyed a bountiful prosperity during the Gold Cycle, the heel of Portuguese colonial rule pressed most deeply in Brazil on the backs of the mining towns, whose people were taxed beyond endurance. This oppression in time gave rise to Brazil's first great republican movement, the Inconfidência Mineira, which was hatched and nurtured in Ouro Preto, and ultimately led to the martyrdom of the patriot Ensign Joaquim José da Silva Xavier, known to posterity as Tiradentes. The moving story of Tiradentes's conspiracy and ultimate betrayal is etched into the hearts of all Brazilian schoolchildren. An ample record of this simple man and his movement is also preserved in museums and historical sites, both in Ouro Preto and throughout the entire region.

SABARÁ

Sabará is the closest of the historical cities to B.H., only 11 short miles (18km) from the municipal limits. And what a treasure of the baroque period it is. Sabará contains at least a dozen sites that reward the eye and nurture the imagination. The town is worthy of a full day's visit in its own right.

WHAT TO SEE & DO

Whether you arrive by bus or car, you will most likely enter through the mountain pass where Sabará is set in a winding valley, like a jewel among the surrounding slopes, at the point where its two rivers are joined. The principal canal is the fabled **Rio das Velhas,** at one time saturated with gold, and still panned by diehard prospectors who can even today eke out a living in this anachronistic profession. The other is a tributary called the **Rio Sabará.** The name Sabará, incidentally, is the somewhat twisted adaptation of a Native American word that meant the "great rock that shines," a poetic reference perhaps to the precious metal for which the tribe in question had no use, but that was to ultimately cause its extinction.

Begin your sightseeing on **Rua Dom Pedro II,** a street, flanked by crooked alleys, that most completely preserves the 18th-century flavor of the town. Number 72, known as the House of Dona Sofia, and today the town's library, is a noble example of the grand town houses of the day. The old manor house at no. 200 is the Town Hall, housed in the **Solar do Padre Correia** (1773), once the pride of a wealthy priest, with a private oratory where delicate carved paneling is leafed in gold veneer. The facade of the house was renovated with certain early-19th-century embellishments, like the window balconies with individual iron railings, but in the rear the details of the earlier century are retained around the doors and windows. There you can also see what remains of the stables and the slave quarters. Such architectural details of the past abound in Sabará. As the poet Carlos Drummond de Andrade put it: "It is all inexorably colonial: benches, windows, locks, street lamps." The building may be visited during business hours, Monday through Friday.

TEATRINHO ELIZABETANO, Rua Dom Pedro II s/n. Tel. 671-1522, ext. 241.

The Teatrinho (1819) is the diminutive theater that was the town's opera house. With only 47 small boxes, the seating area is the same size as the stage. And the acoustics, if you wish to experiment with a note or two, are said to be perfect. Of special interest is the hand-painted curtain with its faded scene of old Sabará by the Austrian artist George Grimm.

Admission: Free.

Open: Tues–Sun 8–11am and 1–6pm.

IGREJA DO ROSÁRIO, Praça do Rosário.

Praça do Rosário contains what in Brazil is a rare sight, a church that is totally preserved in an unfinished state. The Igreja do Rosário was to be constructed around an existing chapel (1713), and financed by slaves from the pennies they were able to beg as donations. The project, begun in 1767, dragged on interminably, and was finally short-circuited by the dispersion of the slaves following their emancipation in 1888. When it was suggested in this century that the thick stone walls ought to be demolished or the church completed, the town historian said the idea was like "sculpting arms for the *Venus de Milo.*"

Admission: Free.

Open: Daily 1–5pm.

MUSEU DO OURO, in the Intendência, Rua da Intendência. Tel. 671-1848.

The Museu do Ouro (Gold Museum) is located in the Intendência, or Smelting House building (1732). Here a representative of the Portuguese crown resided with his family and collected the odious tax, called the *quinto,* the one-fifth of all gold mined in Brazil that was sent to the royal coffers in Lisbon. The interior of the museum is arranged like a private house of the period. There are many interesting period paintings, furnishings, religious carvings, and mining and smelting tools of that era.

Admission: 35¢.

Open: Tues–Sun 8am–5pm.

IGREJA NOSSA SENHORA DO CARMO, Rua do Carmo. Tel. 671-1523.

Among Sabará's most important churches is the Igreja Nossa Senhora do Carmo, begun in 1763. The sculptor Aleijadinho played an important role in the decorative finishing of this church. He is responsible for the portal, the pulpits, and the choir loft, and some of his most famous wood statuary occupies niches and altars throughout, including the images of the four Evangelists, and the 12th-century English mystic, St. Simon Stock, whose dying words, "Holy Mary, Mother of God, pray for us sinners now, and at the hour of our death," were incorporated by papal authority into the Hail, Mary, the principal prayer of the Catholic rosary. The church also contains many beautiful panel paintings, some of which are attributed to Atraide.

At **Rua do Carmo 153** is the house where, according to custom, Aleijadinho lived during his years in Sabará, from 1770 to 1783.

Admission: 40¢.

Open: Tues–Sat noon–5:30pm.

MATRIZ DE NOSSA SENHORA DA CONCEIÇÃO, Praça Getúlio Vargas. Tel. 671-1724.

The Matriz de Nossa Senhora da Conceição, begun in 1700 and completed in 1710, is as plain on the outside as the Church of Carmo is ornate. On the inside the opposite is true. Carmo is all simplicity, and Conceição is a festival of lavish carvings, sheathed in gold lamé. Leading to the sacristy is the famous "Chinese Door," which like much of the interior is said to be the work of artists brought to Sabará from the Portuguese colony of Macau off the Chinese mainland. The church is located out of town, along a road that leads to the Belgo-Mineira steel plant, and can be reached by city bus or a 10-minute cab ride.

Admission: 35¢.

Open: Tues noon–6pm, Wed–Sun 8am–6pm.

CAPELA DE NOSSA SENHORA DO O, Largo de N. S. da Conceição s/n. Tel. 671-1724.

Undoubtedly of Chinese influence is the tiny Capela de Nossa Senhora do O, slightly farther out along the road to the steel plant. Built in 1698, the church's official name is Our Lady of Maternity (in Portuguese, literally, Our Lady of the Expectant Birth). The "O" comes from the initial sound uttered during the recitation of a litany on the feast day of this divine aspect of the Blessed Virgin, celebrated in the days before Christmas since the time of the Council of Toledo in the year 656. Again the unadorned exterior masks the ornate, gold-covered carvings within. And many figures in the panel paintings, including the burros, have almond-shaped eyes.

Admission: 35¢.

Open: Daily 8am–noon and 2–6pm.

CONGONHAS

Congonhas do Campo (Hollies of the Field) takes its name from a plant used for making tea that is commonly found growing on the hillsides of this town, which occupies an undulating valley at an elevation of over 3,000 feet. Late in life, the sculptor Aleijadinho came to Congonhas and produced what many critics claim was his masterpiece, 12 statues of the Prophets carved in soapstone that adorn the terrace of a local shrine, the Santuário do Bom Jesus de Matosinhos.

Congonhas is connected by access road to the BR 040 highway, approximately 45 miles (72km) from Belo Horizonte. Rich in iron ore deposits, Congonhas continues its evolution as an active mining community. As a result, much of its colonial aspect has been lost. Congonhas today is typical of country towns in the interior of the state, and as such, offers a view of Brazilian life not to be found in the big cities. With Congonhas only an hour or so by car or bus from B.H., a side trip there, even without the major attraction of the Aleijadinho statuary, would be worthwhile to capture the flavor of small-town life in Minas.

WHAT TO SEE & DO

Congonhas has several graceful 19th-century churches. But beyond the shrine, the only reason to linger in the town is to explore the densely packed streets in search of souvenirs and some good home-cooking à la mineira. The journey to Ouro Preto from Congonhas, while not that long, takes a good hour and 45 minutes by car through some lovely farming country, and even longer by bus, which stops often on the circuitous route.

Congonhas is at its most animated during the annual celebrations of **Semana Santa** (Holy Week), when its religious processions and enactment of the Crucifixion make the city one of the biggest tourist attractions in the state of Minas Gerais.

THE STORY OF ALEIJADINHO In 1730 a slave named Isabel bore her Portuguese master, Manuel Francisco Lisboa, a son who, on the day of his baptism, was freed by his father and named Antônio. Manuel was a master-builder and church architect who encouraged the boy to develop his talents for carving in the workshops of local craftsmen. At the age of 47 the amiable and highly successful Antônio, whose work had already added great beauty to many churches of the region, was stricken by a crippling disease for which medical historians have been unable to provide a definitive diagnosis, their speculations running from a form of leprosy to rheumatoid arthritis. The disease deformed the artist's fingers and toes, and twisted the features of his face into a grotesque mask. It was due to this condition that Lisboa earned the nickname Aleijadinho, the little cripple. For almost another 40 years the artist continued to work, never slacking his pace, and creating some of his most powerful images with mallet and chisel strapped to his wrists by leather thongs. Despite the pain and mental anguish Lisboa suffered during his final years, art historians are astounded by the fact that as his own body deteriorated, the artist's carved figures became more and more robust and powerful, culminating in the work created in Congonhas while in his early 70s. Perhaps the choice of soapstone as the medium for the Prophets, and cedar for some 76 life-size Passion figures sculpted by Aleijadinho in his atelier, both comparatively soft materials, were the artist's only concession to the ravages of his disability. It is a mistake, however, to emphasize the artist's handicap in the evaluation of his work, which is considered to be as great as anything produced during his lifetime by contemporary artists throughout the entire world.

O SANTUÁRIO DO BOM JESUS DE MATOSINHOS On the top of a hill, the Morro do Maranhão, O Santuário do Bom Jesus de Matosinhos (Shrine of the Good Jesus of Matosinhos) dominates the landscape of Congonhas do Campo. The church itself (1757), with its twin towers and exterior carvings, is undeniably baroque. Steps leading to the main portal cross an ample terrace, bordered by a stone wall along which are strategically spaced the *Profetas* (Prophets) of Aleijadinho. Sloping down the hill away from the church is a broad stone patio, planted with tall, dramatic coconut palms, where six small devotional chapels house life-size wooden statues that depict scenes from the Passion of Christ. The interior of the church, heavily laden with carved arches, altars, and pulpits, all bathed in a hue of a golden tint, also contains work by Aleijadinho and Atraide. The whole ensemble was inspired by a shrine in Braga, Portugal, similar in detail but grander in scale.

The 12 Old Testament prophets were executed by Aleijadinho from 1800 to 1815. While taken as a whole the statues project a balletic movement, their true power and uniqueness can only be fully grasped by studying each work individually, to decipher its unique allegorical meaning. The Passion statues were all carved between 1796 and 1799. The construction of the chapels was plagued by economic delays for many decades, and only about half of the works were painted by Atraide and displayed during Aleijadinho's lifetime. The remaining half were not completed until late in the 19th century.

OURO PRETO

The title "Cultural Heritage of Mankind" was conferred on the city of Ouro Preto by UNESCO in 1980. Founded in 1711 as Vila Rica do Albuquerque, Ouro Preto today contains the largest homogeneous collection of baroque architecture in Brazil. In a country oversaturated with baroque and colonial-era buildings, that's saying a lot.

Ouro Preto is 62 miles (100km) from Belo Horizonte, and may be reached by frequent buses. Direct bus service from Rio de Janeiro is also available, but should be booked several days in advance to assure a seat. Like Congonhas, Ouro Preto sits high in the mountains, at an elevation of over 3,000 feet, so the climate is somewhat mild, temperatures ranging from 2°C (37°F) to 28°C (82°F). The highest point, at over 5,600 feet, is the landmark **Pico de Itacolomi.** There is no valley to speak of in Ouro Preto. Human structures occupy all the available space on the tightly packed hills, which are etched with a network of winding and narrow stone streets that follow the steep contours of the land across a dozen diminutive bridges over streams that empty from the surrounding heights, opening here and there into many small plazas, each of which is crowned with a graceful church.

Ouro Preto is not only a place to see, but also a place to experience. To be able to take in at a comfortable pace all the individual sights, as well as imbibe something of the general ambience, a two- to three-day visit is recommended. The town contains many churches, some 13 in all, plus a dozen chapels and a score of colonial fountains, not to mention the many secular buildings of visual and historic importance as well.

As is the case with Congonhas, Easter Week in Ouro Preto is a time of great celebration and pageantry.

WHAT TO SEE & DO

Churches, churches, and more churches—each one packed with religious art and enriched by its own unique history and legend. (Keep in mind that all the churches in Ouro Preto are closed on Monday.) Add to these the other historical buildings and museums, restaurants and inns, craft shops and events, and there's plenty to keep a visitor occupied and satisfied for days on end. Little noted is the fact that Ouro Preto is also a college town, filled with student *repúblicas,* similar to fraternity and sorority houses, where there is always a spare bed for a youthful comrade from abroad. At night the college students gather in the squares and in their cafés, and on occasion create a festive air when they serenade the city with their ballads.

LOCAL GUIDES & MAPS   The best way to see all the sights is in the company of a guide, one who is employed and trained by the city. These uniformed guides, who are hired from their offices at Praça Tiradentes 41 (tel. 551-1544, ext. 269), charge about $15 for four hours, and are excellent sources of information on the art, history, and lore of the city.

One among only a handful of English-speaking guides is a young man named Pedro Paulo Pinto Junior, who may be reached at 551-1706.

If you're looking for a mature, responsible driver, try Jair (tel. 551-2123 or 551-3304).

A map, stylized but useful, can also be purchased at the guide office for about $1, showing all the main streets and the placement of the principal sights.

THE TOP ATTRACTIONS   To visit the first two churches you will probably want to take a cab, as they are located on the fringes of town. Otherwise, unless health prohibits—the streets are often quite steep and the climbs can be arduous—most of the other places of interest are centered within walking distance of the main square, the Praça Tiradentes.

One of the early *bandeirantes* in the area, a Padre Faria, ordered a chapel built in

1701 in the vicinity of the earliest mines. The chapel, the **Capela do Padre Faria,** is located in the oldest section of the early settlement that predates the founding of the city. The towerless church contains a bell that was rung, in prohibition of a local order, on Tiradentes's execution day. Inside, the church is extremely ornate, the main and two side altars both richly veneered in gold. The vestment cabinet is the oldest in the city, and the colors for the dome mural, *The Coronation of Mary,* painted in 1727, were all mixed from natural elements: the red from *sangue-de-boi* (bull's blood), a kind of fruit; yellow from egg yolk; brown from a mixture of banana juice with the root of a vine. Water damage has all but destroyed other ceiling panels, a reality that underscores the terrible burden Brazil faces with maintaining its priceless art treasures in a country where resources for such projects are understandably scarce. Open 8am till noon Tuesday through Sunday.

The nearby **Rua Santa Rita** is Ouro Preto's oldest street, with its original paving stones called *pé-de-muleque,* the Brazilian term for peanut brittle. Some early slave houses can be seen along this street, which is still one of the poorest sections of the city. Of special interest are the roadside excavations where some of the earliest gold diggings in the city were made. They remain as cavities cut in the sides of embankments, overgrown with vegetation but otherwise unaltered.

Built in 1723 entirely of granite from Mount Itacolomi, **Santa Efigênia** is also known as Our Lady of the Rosary, whose image (attributed to Aleijadinho) occupies a niche over the portal. Both Our Lady of the Rosary and Saint Efigênia (a Christian Nubian princess) were patrons of the slaves, whose church this was. Legend has it that slave women hid purloined gold dust in their hair, and then washed the mineral out in fonts at the church door, to provide a fund for artists who worked on the church. Open to visitors from 8am to noon Tuesday through Sunday.

Matriz de Nossa Senhora da Conceição is Ouro Preto's largest church, dating from 1727. It was designed by Manuel Francisco Lisboa, who also created the first altar on the right (one of eight side altars), beneath which his son, Aleijadinho, is buried. The church was not completed until the early 1800s, and the interior decor alternates between the carved wood of the baroque period and the later rococo style which made use of molded plaster. A side door in the church leads to the **Aleijadinho Museum,** which includes the artist's sculpture of São Francisco de Paula. The statue's head is of carved soapstone, and painted. To this day it is not understood how Aleijadinho got the paint to adhere to the cold, smooth surface of the stone. The museum and church are open from 8 to 11:30am and 1:30 to 5pm. The museum is closed Mondays.

The **Igreja do Pilar** is the richest church in OUro Preto, on the charming square in the middle of the city, dating from 1711. Over 1,000 pounds of gold, and almost the equivalent in silver, add an almost blinding glitter to the carvings, much of which were the creation of Aleijadinho's father, his uncle (Antônio Francisco Pombal), and the artist's principal mentor, Francisco Xavier de Brito.

The church of **São Francisco de Assis,** located near the town's principal square, the Praça Tiradentes, is considered the jewel of Ouro Preto. It was designed by Aleijadinho and commissioned by the local military command in 1765. The facade, with its great medallion in soapstone, is one of the finest of Aleijadinho's works of this kind, carved entirely by his own hands without the assistance of his students or associates. The ceiling painting in the central nave is a rococo creation by Atraide.

Praça Tiradentes was the principal plaza of old Vila Rica, as it is Ouro Preto's main square today. On one end is the old Governor's Palace; at the other, the former legislative chambers and jail. Both buildings currently house museums. Until well into the 19th century the slave market and the public whipping post were both located in this square, which remains a picture of the past, with its stone pavement and border of colonial buildings. At the center of the square is a statue of Tiradentes, marking the spot where the martyr's severed head was displayed in a cage following his execution.

Born near the current town that bears his name, Joaquim José da Silva Xavier learned the trade of dentistry and denture-making from his godfather, and was thus nicknamed Tiradentes, the tooth-puller. The career he was to pursue, however, was in the state's militia, never rising above the rank of ensign, a position equivalent to second lieutenant. An ardent lover of freedom, Tiradentes espoused the republican cause at a time when all of Europe and the Americas were inflamed with a hatred of monarchic despotism. He helped to form a movement throughout Minas, centered in Ouro Preto, that came to be known as the Inconfidência Mineira, the "No-Confidence Movement of Minas." Along with numerous coconspirators, Tiradentes planned a revolt against Portuguese rule, but the conspiracy was betrayed in 1789 by one of its own members. Tiradentes assumed total responsibility for the conspiracy, whose other members were imprisoned or exiled to Portugal and the Portuguese colonies in Africa. Tiradentes himself was hanged three years later in Rio de Janeiro, his body quartered, the separate pieces of his corpse carried to various locales in Minas where he had spoken vehemently against the crown. His salted head was placed in Ouro Preto's main square, where after a short time it was stolen by friends. According to legend, the patriot's cranium was filled with gold dust and surreptitiously buried somewhere near the old Vila Rica, though the location was never revealed.

The **Museu de Mineralogia** (Mineral Museum), Praça Tiradentes (tel. 551-1666), containing some 20,000 pieces, uncut gems and minerals, both precious and common, from the region has been installed in what was the **Palácio do Governador** (Governor's Palace) in Minas Gerais from 1746 to 1897. The building was constructed in 1740 by Manuel Francisco Lisboa. In addition to the mineral collection, there is a gracious chapel in the palace that is worth visiting. Open Tuesday through Sunday from noon to 6pm. Admission is 75¢.

The exhibition rooms of the **Museu dos Inconfidentes** (tel. 551-1121) are filled with cultural artifacts of the colonial period, from arms to implements of torture used to punish the slaves, from plate and furnishings to the ubiquitous samples of religous art and liturgical paraphernalia. The two most important exhibits are the Aleijadinho Room, with the articulated statue of St. George, which was mounted on horseback and used during public processions honoring the saint, and the monument to the Inconfidentes, an austere mausoleum containing the remains of many of the revolutionaries. Open daily from noon to 5:30pm; admission is 75¢.

A GEM SHOP **Brazil Gems,** Praça Tiradentes 74 (tel. 551-2976), allows you to watch the lapidaries at work in the back room of the shop as they grind, cut, polish, and mount the sparkling gemstones. The shop speciality is the dazzling imperial topaz. Open daily from 9am to 8pm.

WHERE TO STAY

A number of the colonial-era dwellings have been converted into *pousadas,* inns of the bed-and-breakfast variety. You'll have to choose whether to stay close to the center of the town, within walking distance of many restaurants and other attractions, or in the outlying districts where your options will also include a number of resort-style hotels.

Expensive

LUXOR POUSADA, Praça Antônio Dias 10, Ouro Preto. Tel. 031/551-2244. Telex 31/2948. 16 rms. MINIBAR TV TEL
$ Rates: $69–$77 single; $76–$85 double. AE, DC, MC, V.
On the high end of the comfort spectrum, and across the street from the spectacular Matriz de Nossa Senhora de Conceição, is the Luxor Pousada. This inn occupies an old town house, and has only 16 rooms, but they are first class all the way. The rooms are decorated in a colonial simplicity that is totally harmonious with Vila Rica tradition. There is a small restaurant in the cellar where guests also eat their breakfasts, under a beamed ceiling and surrounded by a foundation wall of stone.

Moderate

GRANDE HOTEL DE OURO PRETO, Rua Senador Pocha Lagoa 164, Ouro Preto. Tel. 031/551-1488. Telex 31/2951. 17 rms, 17 suites. MINIBAR TV TEL
$ Rates: $33 single; $47 double; $66 suite for two. AE, DC, MC, V.
Formerly a state-run hotel, the Grande Hotel de Ouro Preto, has one of the best

locations in the small city. Only a block from the central plaza, the Praça Tiradentes, and within easy reach of the largest number of shops and restaurants, the Grande Hotel is a choice to be reckoned with. The Grande Hotel is the only modern structure in the city, designed by Oscar Niemeyer—and not one of his successes by any means. Surrounded by inspirational architecture like that of Ouro Preto, the man seems to have missed the point.

HOTEL ESTRADA DAS MINAS GERAIS, Rodovia dos Inconfidentes, km 87, Ouro Preto. Tel. 031/551-2122. Fax 031/551-2709. Telex 31/6133. 40 rms. MINIBAR TV TEL

$ Rates: $31–$45 single; $65–$78 double. AE, DC, MC, V.

The Hotel Estrada das Minas Gerais, about five miles outside the city in the hills off the highway, is the largest and fanciest hotel in Ouro Preto, in a beautifully landscaped resortlike setting on a scenic overlook. The hotel has a large pool and a tennis court, and also a fine restaurant, popular with guests and nonguests alike. Some of the rooms are in separate bungalows.

POUSADA MONDEGO, Largo do Coimbra 38, Ouro Preto. Tel. 031/551-2040. Fax 031/551-3094. Telex 39/2453. 27 rms. MINIBAR TV TEL

$ Rates: $55–$65 single; $71–$76 double. AE, DC, MC, V.

The Pousada Mondego is a first-class inn, filled with charm and sophistication. The inn also occupies a privileged spot, directly in front of the Igreja São Francisco de Assis, and is only a block above Tiradentes Square. Rooms at the Mondego vary in size and configuration. Some are atticlike, beneath the gables; others have special views and balconies. All are comfortable and homey.

The Mondego is in its final stages of completion. The restaurant, where guests eat a delicious breakfast in the morning, ought to be functioning by the time this edition goes to press. An art gallery and *cave* (barroom) are also being installed. Parking facilities are available.

POUSO DO CHICO REY, Rua Brigadeiro Musqueira 90, Ouro Preto. Tel. 031/551-1274. 6 rms (3 with bath).

$ Rates (including breakfast): $25 single; $28 double; $35 apt with bath. No credit cards.

The Pouso do Chico Rey is another lovely little inn, this time on a side street very near the Praça Tiradentes. There are three rooms and three apartments, the difference being that only the latter have baths. The several attractive public rooms at various levels give the inn a genuine "house" feeling.

Budget

POUSADA DA GALERIA PANORAMA BARROCO, Rua Conseilheiro Quitiliano 722, Ouro Preto. Tel. 031/551-3366. 6 rms (2 with bath).

$ Rates (including breakfast): $6–$7 single; $12 double. No credit cards.

American owner Peter Peterkin and his wife Lucia describe their place as "simply a B&B in an old house." It's really a most eccentric old establishment, three stories crammed with objets d'art and kitsch, perched dramatically over a steep hill where the grounds and view are a knockout. As for staying here, you will find, as Peter puts it, "a comfortable bed, a substantial breakfast, a secure room, and a relaxed environment." There is also a telescope for stargazing and a library with books in English on local flora and fauna, gems, history, and anthropology. Use of their washing machine is extra, as are excursions they will organize for sightseeing or gem-buying in their four-wheel-drive Land Cruiser. The house is a 10-minute walk from the Praça Tiradentes, or you can catch a bus from the stop just beyond their front door.

POUSADA NELLO NUNO, Rua Camilo de Brito 59, Ouro Preto. Tel. 031/551-3375. 3 rms.

$ Rates: $8 single; $14 double; $30 three-room suite. No credit cards.

The Nello Nuno is also more B&B than pousada—you are actually in someone's home. At night you can hang out with the owners, eat some snacks, and drink a bit of wine.

RECANTO DAS MINAS, Rua Manganes 287, Ouro Preto. Tel. 031/551-3003. Telex 39/1667. 36 rms (32 with bath). MINIBAR TEL
$ Rates: $20 single or double without bath; $25 single with bath and TV; $35 double with bath and TV. No credit cards.

About a mile and a quarter outside of town in the São Cristóvão neighborhood, on the road back to Belo Horizonte, is the Recanto das Minas. The hotel is reached by turning onto a dirt road at the sign and traveling half a mile or so to the top of the hill. There is a restaurant and a small swimming pool.

WHERE TO DINE

CASA DO OUVIDOR, Rua Direita 42. Tel. 551-2141.
   Cuisine: COMIDA MINEIRA/INTERNATIONAL. **Reservations:** Not needed.
$ Prices: Appetizers $3–$4; main courses $4.50–$7.75. No credit cards.
   Open: Lunch daily 11am–4pm; dinner daily 6pm–midnight.

One of the most popular restaurants in Ouro Preto is the Casa do Ouvidor, located on the second floor. There is always a good crowd in here on a given day, a blend of locals and tourists. Begin the meal with a pipping-hot bowl of *caldo verde* ($3.50) to fend off the foggy dews of this cool and cloudy town. The *feijão tropeiro,* that great mixture of pork, mashed beans, and sausage, topped with a fried egg, is a delicious stomach stuffer. Brazilian drinks like caipirinhas are only about $1 each.

CASA GRANDE, Praça Tiradentes 84. Tel. 551-2976.
   Cuisine: REGIONAL. **Reservations:** Not needed.
$ Prices: Appetizers $2–$5; main courses $4–$5.50. No credit cards.
   Open: Lunch daily 11am–4pm; dinner daily 6–11pm.

This attractive space is fitted into the ground floor of an old colonial house that opens right onto the Praça Tiradentes. The large, continual flow of customers during the lunch hours is a testimonial to the Casa Grande's menu. One popular specialty is the fresh river fish, transported here from the legendary Rio São Francisco.

RELICÁRIO 1800, Praça Tiradentes 64. Tel. 551-2855.
   Cuisine: CONTINENTAL. **Reservations:** Recommended for dinner.
$ Prices: Appetizers $3–$4; main courses $7–$8. AE, DC, MC, V.
   Open: Lunch daily 11am–4pm; dinner daily 7pm–midnight.

The Relicário 1800 occupies a "senzala," an old basement slave quarters that has been made over into an attractive first-class restaurant. The *frango ao molho prado* ($7) is made from hens that the owner herself has raised. On Saturday, a succulent feijoada ($7) is served. Live classical guitar accompanies the meals most evenings. Black beans are always on hand as a side dish here.

RESTAURANTE VILA RICA, Praça Tiradentes 132. Tel. 551-2342.
   Cuisine: REGIONAL. **Reservations:** Not needed.
$ Prices: Appetizers $1.75–$5; main courses $3.50–$5. No credit cards.
   Open: Daily 11am–10pm.

Pizza is the popular choice at the Vila Rica, along with many beef dishes prepared in a variety of *modas brasileiras.* The ham-and-cheese omelet is a real bargain ($1.75).

TABERNA LUXOR, in the Luxor Pousada, Praça Antônio Dias 10. Tel. 551-2244.
   Cuisine: FRENCH. **Reservations:** Recommended for dinner.
$ Prices: Appetizers $3.50–$5; main courses $8–$10. AE, DC, MC, V.
   Open: Lunch daily noon–3pm; dinner daily 7pm–midnight.

The Luxor restaurant has an excellent reputation. Many of the dishes are served flambéed, like the Siberian steak, flamed in vodka and served with a creamy mushroom sauce ($8.50).

TACHA DO OURO, Rua Conde de Bobadela 76. Tel. 551-2407.
   Cuisine: REGIONAL. **Reservations:** Not needed.
$ Prices: Appetizers $3–$5.50; main courses $4–$12; buffet $5. AE, DC, MC, V.
   Open: Lunch daily 11am–3pm; dinner daily 7–10pm.

When a group of 25 or more has booked lunch or dinner at the Tacha do Ouro, the owner puts out an excellent buffet. Otherwise, you will dine from the à la carte menu.

Regional dishes on this menu, like *tutu a mineiro* and *feijão tropeiro* are very reasonably priced in the $3 to $4 range.

TAVERNA DO CHAFARIZ, Rua São José 167. Tel. 551-2828.
   Cuisine: REGIONAL BUFFET. **Reservations:** Not needed.
$ Prices: Buffet $5. No credit cards.
   Open: Dinner daily 7pm–midnight.
There are always at least five hot main courses, and a generous number of side dishes as well, for the buffet served up in this family-owned restaurant that has been functioning in this same house for almost 40 years.

EVENING ENTERTAINMENT

Two nightlife options, one elegant, the other more plebeian, are recommended for any visitor staying over in Ouro Preto.
   The **Acaso 85,** Largo do Rosário 85 (tel. 551-2397), is a den of the local society. The interior space, like the Relicário 1800, was also once a basement, but there the comparison ends. This space is multileveled and cavernous, with ceilings that could easily measure 30 feet in height. The Acaso should be treated as a pre- or postdinner wine or cocktail club. There are snacks to nosh on, steak bits ($3.50), assorted cold cuts ($3.50), and a cheese plate ($2), but no meals are served. Most drinks are priced between $1.50 and $4.25; a good bottle of domestic cabernet goes for $5.75. Open Tuesday, Wednesday, and Sunday from 7pm to midnight, and Thursday through Saturday from 7pm to 3am. No credit cards.
   For a taste of the old student days, and some good live balladeering by Brazilian folksingers, try the **Sagarana,** Rua Conde de Bobadela 94 (tel. 551-2032). The place was packed with American college students when I was last in Ouro Preto, youngsters down from São Paulo where they were in the university. Their hosts among the local Brazilian students had "turned them on" to this place. Open from 6pm to 2am Thursday through Saturday. There is an artistic cover of $1.

AN EXCURSION TO MARIANA

The neighboring town of Mariana is only about a 20-minute car ride from the Praça Tiradentes, leaving via the street that runs to the right of the Mineral Museum. Like Congonhas, Mariana is still a very active mining town, and while the town is the oldest in the state (1698), it, too, has lost much of its former colonial appearance. The town sits in a little valley, and the surrounding hills are today worked mostly for the iron deposits, as well as the veins of quartz and manganese.
   The principal attraction is the cathedral, **A Sé de Mariana** (1709), Praça Cládio Manuel da Costa, containing an organ operated by hand bellows and work by Atraide (a native of the town) and the Lisboas, *père et fils.* Other works of these artists may be seen in the **Igreja de Nossa Senhora de Carmo** (1784) and the **Igreja de São Francisco** (1762), which are right next to each other on the Praça João Pinheiro.
   On the same square is the **Casa de Câmara e Cadeia** (1784), the old council chambers and jailhouse, now the town hall, with some interesting portraits of Portuguese monarchs and Dom Pedro II.
   On the road between Ouro Preto and Mariana you will pass the **Minas de Passagem,** the state's second-oldest gold mine. For an entrance fee of $6.50 for adults and $5.50 for children under 12, you can tour the mine and its processing plant.

OTHER DESTINATIONS AROUND MINAS

There is so much more to this historic, economically powerful, and sophisticated state that cannot be adequately included in this edition of the guide. Several locales, given their significance, at least deserve honorable mention and brief descriptions.
   The diamond and gemstone towns are located to the north and east of Belo Horizonte. **Diamantina,** 182 miles from the state capital, is the most important from a historical point of view. Here diamonds were discovered in the early 1700s, and, as with the other great cities of the baroque period, much has been preserved from that time. **Teôfilo Otoni** and **Governador Valadares** are the centers of the

contemporary gem trade, and anyone serious about gems—whether commercially or academically—will naturally be drawn to these towns, which are on the way to Salvador, the Bahian capital.

Minas contains hundreds of prehistoric caverns, called *grutas* in Portuguese. The closest to Belo is **Lapinha,** 35 miles away, while the more famous caves at **Maquiné** are about 75 miles distant. In both cases, visitors may descend into the several lighted chambers. The greatest of these caves, in the northern part of the state near Montalvania, contain primitive drawings and fossil finds said to rival in importance the great caves of Lascaux in France. But they have yet to be fully explored scientifically, and are not open to the public.

And Minas is still so much more than all this. It is the great Rio São Francisco, the river artery of interior travel and communication in Brazil for many generations before the construction of adequate roads, the hot springs at Caldas, and other towns on the border of São Paulo state.

SÃO JOÃO DEL REI   Those who follow political developments in South America may remember reading about this town during Brazil's 1985 elections for the country's first civilian president in over 20 years. A native of São João, Tancredo Neves, won the election, but died before he could take office. In addition to being a town of historic importance, containing many relics of the colonial past, the town has become somewhat of a monument to Tancredo, in whom many Brazilians placed great hopes for democratic and economic reforms.

The tourist office in São João houses a small **museum** with the only known portrait of Aleijadinho. The **John Somers pewter factory** is also located here.

TIRADENTES   While I was visiting Minas Gerais, the driver who accompanied me from the state tourist office, Turminas, mentioned that he was a native of São João. He told me of a very pleasant hike he has often taken in the company of friends after a night of drinking and fellowship in the local cafés, especially when the sky is clear and the moon bright and shining. They walk slowly along a path through the hills that connects São João to the nearby village of Tiradentes, about seven miles distant, timing it so that they arrive at dawn. A cure for whatever may ail you, says he. This may not be the most conventional way to visit Tiradentes, but with the orientation of a reliable local, it's certainly an option for anyone with the time and inclination. When I get to São João this excursion will be tops on my own list. Tiradentes, incidentally, is said to be a very authentic 18th-century town, and today a center for crafts.

CHAPTER 9

BRASÍLIA & GOIÁS

1. BRASÍLIA
2. EXPLORING GOIÁS & GOIÁS VELHO

The land for Brazil's new capital, Brasília, was carved from Goiás, a central state in the heart of the country. Brasília, the Distrito Federal (Federal District), occupies a tableland some 3,500 feet above sea level near the western border of Minas Gerais. Both the state and the capital are worth visiting, the former for its wide-open spaces, scenic beauty, and medicinal hot springs; the latter as a phenomenon of contemporary civil engineering, a planned city of monumental scope that symbolizes Brazil's contradictory vision of its own future, a perplexing blend of daring and self-aggrandizement.

1. BRASÍLIA

690 miles NW of Rio

GETTING THERE   By Plane   The Ponte Aérea air shuttle links both São Paulo and Rio with Brasília on frequent daily flights of 2½ hours from either city. The one-way fare from Rio is approximately $170; from São Paulo, $164.

By Train   A passenger train connects the capital to São Paulo. The *Trem Bandeirante* leaves Brasília Friday at 8:25pm, arriving in São Paulo, via Campinas, 24 hours later. For train information call 233-7044.

By Bus   Buses run daily from both Rio (20 hours) and São Paulo (15 hours).

By Car   You can now drive from Rio de Janeiro on BR 040 to Brasília, and then on to Belém along the Belém-Brasília highway, which has only been paved in recent years. There is also a direct highway, BR 050, from São Paulo.

ESSENTIALS   Brasília is laid out very logically, once you catch on to the numbering system. There are no street addresses per se. All locations are designated by block numbers in both the northern or southern sectors. These major directional sectors are further divided into subsectors, where specific activities are concentrated. Thus there are special sectors for shopping, hotels, sports and cultural activities, businesses, embassies, and banking. A quick glance at a map is sufficient to become oriented. I recommend the *Carta Turística de Brasília* put out by the tourist office, the Departamento de Turismo, Setor de Difusão Cultural, 3rd floor, Wing A (tel. 061/321-3318).

It is possible to walk around the city, which—I stress again—is deceptively large, but not terribly convenient. There are few sidewalks, though local residents have cut paths through the grounds of various buildings and malls. Strollers must be very careful of the traffic, however, as motorists are not accustomed to seeing many pedestrians.

When compared with the settlement of the United States, Brazil's experience could not have been less similar. Nor is there any reason to expect a parallel development in two countries of such distinct cultural origins, not to mention climatic and geographical differences, merely because both are great in size and owe their respective existences to the same impulses of 16th-century European mercantile expansion. Still, comparisons are inevitably made between these two New World colossi, often by Brazilian scholars themselves. Brazil, they point out, had no Manifest Destiny to spur exploration and settlement of its vast interior spaces, nor was there the equivalent of a Homestead Act to motivate settlers with the incentive of cheap land. For these and other reasons, settlement in Brazil was limited to the long but narrow strip of coastal lands, where even today 80% of the population make their homes within 50 miles of the sea. In place of a Manifest Destiny, the long-standing Brazilian vision—one that goes back two centuries or more—was to open up the interior by creating a new capital in the country's geographical center.

The *planalto* in Goiás, a plateau of rolling grasslands, had already been selected by a government commission in 1892 as the preferred site for the new capital. But the political will to make this vision a reality was missing until Brazilians in 1956 elected as their president a physician-turned-politician, the former mayor of Belo Horizonte and governor of Minas Gerais, Juscelino Kubitschek de Oliveira. During his campaign, Juscelino promised Brazilians he would fulfill the long-delayed vision of the past: He pledged to build the capital during his term of office, despite the enormous costs and the seemingly insurmountable logistical obstacles, not the least of which was the lack of roads connecting the target site with the developed cities to its east.

Soon after Juscelino's election, construction of the new capital was begun, the first stage scheduled for completion by 1960, before the expiration of the new president's term of office. At the time, Brazil's presidents could only serve a single term, and the rush was entirely appropriate—it is not uncommon in Brazil for a project initiated by one administration to be abandoned by its successor. Even while a highway (BR 040) was being cut into the prairie, heavy building materials were airlifted to the site by giant cargo planes, and buildings began to rise amid the isolation of the plains before the caravans of trucks could arrive to carry on the later stages of the project. Thousands of unskilled workers poured from the crowded slums of the big cities and the ruined backwaters of the northeastern badlands to grasp the employment opportunity of a lifetime. They soon re-created their shantytown existence on the periphery of the new city, as poverty in Brazil is the inevitable companion of progress.

Juscelino adopted the layout of city planner Lúcio Costa, to construct an ultramodern metropolis of marble, glass, and steel in the form of a bow and arrow. (You will also hear the metaphor of an airplane used to describe the layout, but this is a later invention.) Along the bow would be block after block of apartment buildings facing interior pedestrian malls, with access roads connecting to neighboring *quadras* and to the principal avenues. There would be little need for traffic signals in Brasília, since most principal roads were to be expressways, linked by cloverleafs. And where these roads intersected, they would do so via underpaths and bridges. It was also, for some strange reason, to be a city virtually without sidewalks, despite the fact that distances between buildings—especially in the government and administrative areas—can be quite long. The arrow segment would divide the city into southern and northern sectors, and would be the line along which the government buildings and decorative monuments were to be constructed. For this task, Juscelino called upon his old collaborator from the Pampulha project in Belo Horizonte, Oscar Niemeyer, to design the congress, the presidential offices, the Palace of Justice, and a new cathedral, among other ambitious architectural projections.

Brasília was inaugurated on schedule. On April 21, 1960, the seat of the Brazilian government was officially moved from Rio de Janeiro and installed in the cold and futuristic buildings of Brasília, to the accompanying groans of those in the federal bureaucracy who were called upon to move there. Juscelino did his best to sugarcoat the transition, offering economic incentives in the form of doubled salaries and heavily subsidized rents. Resistance to the move remained strong for many years, particularly in the diplomatic community, as most embassies clung to Rio's golden strands until the dust of construction settled somewhat in the new capital, and residence in the city became bearable with the gradual establishment of services, restaurants, and cultural distractions. An additional inhibiting factor was that many of the buildings and roadways were built in such haste that they quickly began to deteriorate. Many had to be rebuilt before the city could claim to be truly ready to receive the tens of thousands of residents the government hoped to attract there.

When I first went to Brazil in 1964, opinions about the new capital were already polarized in the extreme. I fell in with the hostile camp. Photos of Brasília did not inspire my curiosity to visit the place, and so I didn't. It was not until 1987 that I

CENTRAL BRASÍLIA

↻ N

To Urban Military Sector ← **1**
To Bus/Train Station ↓

North Banking Sector

North Commercial Sector

North Hotel Sector

South Banking Sector

South Commercial Sector

South Hotel Sector

Eixo Monumental

Eixo Rodoviário Norte

Eixo Rodoviário Sul

Esplanada dos Ministérios

Av. das Nações

Praça dos Três Poderes

Parque Recreativo de Brasília

To Airport →

705 705 305
704 704 304
703 703 303
702 702 302
203
103 205
102 105
402
202 403
203
102 202
103
104 303
304 705
305 704
306 903
307 902
901

903 905
907 904
906
908
911

A Espada **1**
Catedral **2**
Congresso Nacional **3**
Itamarati **4**
Memorial JK **5**
National Theater **6**

O Santuário São João Bosco **7**
Palácio Planalto **8**
Praça dos Três Poderes **9**
Rodoviária **10**
Torre de Televisão **11**

Church ✝   Information ⓘ

finally traveled to Brasília, the only destination in Brazil I looked upon as an onerous obligation while in the process of researching this guide. In many ways I'm glad I waited so long, because in the ensuing quarter century Brasília has become a genuine city, not the sterile construction site I was urged to visit in the 1960s. But I have also changed my mind somewhat about the look of the place. True, it still strikes me as a vision of an intergalactic settlement, but the buildings are more sympathetic and humane when seen three-dimensionally than when viewed in the flat medium of still photography or even moving pictures. I now realize that to appreciate the aesthetic of Brasília—as opposed to the daring and folly of its mere conception—you have to go there, and that the trip is worthwhile on two accounts: first, to grasp the monumental vision and something of the yearning in the Brazilian soul for the fulfillment of a destiny forestalled; and second, because Brasília has a population of over 400,000 and is now a true city in its own right, with genuine urban nuances despite a layout that favors vehicular over pedestrian traffic. Furthermore, when you are in Brasília you get an unexpected bonus. For you are also in Goiás, and within striking distance of one of that state's most striking attractions, the former capital city of Goiás Velho (see Section 2, below).

WHAT TO SEE & DO

It is not unusual for tourists to see all of Brasília in a single day. Many don't even bother to spend the night there, arriving at the airport on a flight that leaves Rio as early as 6:30am and returning that same evening after having seen all the obligatory sights. Tour companies all offer basically the same excursion, which may be booked directly at the airport without advance reservations. Or cars, with or without drivers, may be hired from the airport for the day. Anyone wishing to spend more time in the capital can easily—and cheaply—get around by public bus. Many buses, like those marked "Aeroporto," "Três Poderes/Universidade de Brasília," and "Avenida das Nações," make wide loops of the city and its environs, and in many ways are preferable in atmosphere to the sometimes-smarmy group tour.

THE EIXO MONUMENTAL   Walking is somewhat easier along the Eixo Monumental (Monument Row), a five-mile-long strip running from the new combined bus/train station at one end of the central "arrow" to the **Praça dos Três Poderes** (Plaza of the Three Powers) at the other. The strip is about 1,000 feet wide, separated by two roadways, along which all the principal ministry buildings and monuments are located.

Many of the buildings may be visited during business hours (Brasília is a formal town, so women visitors to official buildings must wear dresses, and men, sport jackets). The most interesting of these buildings are the **Palácio Planalto** (presidential offices), the **Congresso Nacional** (the House and Senate Chambers), **Itamarati** (Foreign Ministry), and the **Catedral,** all designed by Niemeyer and all near the Praça dos Três Poderes. Also of interest are the many modern sculptures in and near the praça, including *The Meteorite* by Bruno Giorgi above the Itamarati water mirror—it reflects the building's vaulted facade, and is a much-photographed symbol for the city. Itamarati, unlike the other offices, receives visitors only twice a day, at 10am and again at 4pm.

Brasília is also famous for its dried flowers, whose many varieties grow abundantly in the semiarid scrublands beyond the metropolitan oasis. The flowers may be seen and purchased in an open-air market that functions weekdays on the plaza opposite the cathedral.

THE OBSERVATION PLATFORM   Near the center of the esplanade is the old **Rodoviária,** the original bus station, across from the **National Theater,** which still serves as a terminus for city buses and where the tourist office maintains an information center and the Bureau of Indian Affairs (FUNAI) has a gift shop of Native American artifacts.

Directly to the south is the **Torre de Televisão,** a 600-foot television transmission tower with an observation platform at an altitude of 250 feet, from which there is an excellent panoramic view of the entire city. Access to the platform by elevator is free.

A crafts fair is held at the base of the tower on Saturday, Sunday, and holidays from 8am till 6pm. Most of the so-called Hippie Fairs I've wandered into during my travels throughout Brazil have been routinely disappointing. What I've seen for the most part are shoddy, mass-produced "crafts," banal and derivative artwork, and a few uninspiring items of everyday usage. But the Brasília Fair impressed me. One tends to forget that the Federal District is surrounded by a gigantic, and long-settled rural zone, all those little cities in the state of Goiás only a day's donkey ride away have yet to be spoiled by fame and fortune. Their social economies seem conducive to higher standards of quality, especially in the production of handcrafts. True, most of the stuff on sale—garden statuary, great cachepots, huge bouquets of dried flowers, bronzes, and wood carvings—are too large or too delicate to transport in your luggage. But the visual appeal of the well-attended fair could be consumed on the spot, as could the delicious *pamonha* (see "Where to Dine," below) that I bought for about 35¢, made from fresh ground corn, not from meal or flour. This event could be convenient for overnight guests, since the tower is within walking distance of the hotel sectors.

MEMORIAL JK At the far end of the Eixo Monumental, nearest to the new bus/train station, is the Memorial JK. Juscelino Kubitschek was also commonly referred to as *Jota Ka,* the Portuguese letters for the initials in his name. And this is his memorial, the latest addition to Monument Row, also designed by Oscar Niemeyer. Like so much of the architect's work, the memorial is deceptively simple on the outside and stunning within, suggesting the stylized burial chamber of an ancient pharaoh. The monument was paid for by the *candangos,* the name given to the construction workers who built Brasília and who revered the former president. Juscelino died in an auto wreck, somewhat mysteriously believe many Brazilians, who are often given to mystical and conspiratorial speculations in the face of the bizarre coincidences that seem to bedevil the country's political and economic development.

Within the chamber is a photo gallery documenting Juscelino's career and the building of the capital, as well as a reproduction of his presidential library. Unfortunately, all the exhibits are labeled only in Portuguese. Withal, the former president is portrayed in larger-than-life terms, mythologized with imperial exaggerations as the great *Fundador,* the founder of Brasília. Every Rome must have its Romulus.

As if to deflate somewhat this overreaching for immortality, a sardonic rumor circulates the city. It is said that the progressive Niemeyer added a crescent cap to the platform tower where a statue of JK guards the entrance to the tomb, and that at a certain time of the year the sun casts its shadow through this crescent and forms a perfect hammer and sickle. Indeed such is the way it appears to the disinterested observer, though I include the tale here more as a sample of Brazilian wit at its best, than as a literal fact.

THE SWORD Near the Memorial JK is the Setor Militar Urbano (Urban Military Sector), where outside the headquarters building on the Praça Duque de Caxias is a monument called **A Espada** (The Sword). The monument warrants attention both for its design and its acoustics. If you look closely at the monument's interior curve, you will notice that it is subtly, but unmistakably, shaped in the outline of an owl's head. To test the unique acoustic effect, you need a companion. If each of you takes up positions at opposite ends of the monument's wide mouth, you may talk across the considerable distance in a conversational tone and understand perfectly what each other is saying.

O SANTUÁRIO SÃO JOÃO BOSCO Like so many modern structures that rely on the building materials of metal and glass, this box-shaped church conveys an initial impression of tawdriness and slipshod design. One is so used to admiring great churches in the set forms of medieval tastes—their enormity, and their stonework combining the opposites of bulk and grace. Here again, as with so much of Brazil's modern architecture, the effect is reserved for the building's interior. The church is sheathed in small panes of stained glass, all in shades of blue. From inside the church by day, the walls seem like perfect reproductions of a starlit sky.

NEARBY ATTRACTIONS Scrublands, called the **cerrado,** surround Brasília, which is built by the banks of an artificial lake. Only when you get outside the city do you fully grasp the scale of the capital as an engineering feat, independent of personal views about "planned cities," and futuristic ones at that!

Even if your time in the city is limited, a drive along the perimeter of the 50-mile-long **Lake Paranoá** should not be missed. If you recross the bridge along the road that heads toward the airport and then turn in the opposite direction, you will soon be traveling with the lake on your left. In about 20 minutes you come to a shrine and overlook known as the **Ermida Dom Bosco.** The view of the city here from the opposite shore is quite spectacular, because it allows you to really capture the contrast between the self-contained island community and the sea of uninhabited plains that encircle it.

And while the shrine to Dom Bosco is not much in and of itself, the saint's story is worth retelling. A hundred years before the creation of Brasília the monk had a dream which revealed to him the map coordinates where "a great lake will be excavated that will flow forever." This, the faithful believe, was a prediction of the exact site where Brasília would be built.

SHOPPING There are several commercial sectors throughout the city. One principal complex not far from the Hotel Sector is the **Conjunto Nacional,** across from the National Theater. In addition to the many stores—including a branch of H. Stern—there are a number of Woolworth-style lunch counters, where for about $2.50 you can get the hot plate of the day. There are also movie theaters located in this shopping center.

The **Galeria dos Estados** is a 200-yard-long mall that links the central commercial district with the banking sector, and contains craft shops representing most of Brazil's states. Stirred perhaps by a spirit of interregional competition, the crafts here are of generally high quality.

Park Shopping is the newest addition to Brasília's mallmania, located in the ambiguously labeled Setor de Areas Isoladas Sudoeste (Southwestern Isolated Areas), about six miles from the center of town. The mall not only houses the city's most fashionable boutiques, plus many eateries, both the sit-down and fast-food varieties, it also has its own kiddie amusement park, eight movie theaters, and an ice-skating rink.

WHERE TO STAY

Practically every hotel in Brasília is located in either the southern or the northern hotel sector (Setor Hoteleiro Sul/Norte). The two sectors face each other across the city's central esplanade, which runs from east to west and along which all the city's monuments and futuristic government buildings are located. All the hotels are within walking distance of each other, and their addresses—block and lot number—are superfluous. Even the distinction of north or south seems irrelevant, given the proximity of one zone to the other in the case of the hotel sector.

EXPENSIVE

CARLTON, South Hotel Sector, Brasília. Tel. 061/224-8819. Fax 061/226-8109. Telex 61/1981. 192 rms. A/C MINIBAR TV TEL
$ Rates: $83–$97 single; $93–$107 double. AE, DC, MC, V.
The Carlton is smaller but newer than the Nacional, and the building itself is more interesting architecturally than most of the other hotels in Brasília, which tend to be slab-style high-rises. The lobby area occupies a one-story breezeway which joins the principal tower, where the rooms are located, with a smaller building which houses indoor parking and a host of public facilities, including an attractive rooftop pool. There are four bars in the Carlton, and La Fontaine restaurant, which features international cuisine. Rooms are decorated in blond wood trim and beige tones, and have color TV with satellite reception of the CNN American television network. Other attractions include golf and tennis privileges at local clubs, sauna, hairdresser and barber services, boutiques, and a travel agency on the premises.

ERON, Hotel Sector North, Brasília. Tel. 061/321-1777. Fax 061/226-2698. Telex 61/1422. 187 rms. A/C MINIBAR TV TEL
$ Rates: $70 single; $90 double. AE, DC, MC, V.

Slightly more care has gone into the decor (and perhaps maintenance) of the Eron's corridors and public areas than to those of its rivals in the same price range. The rooms are only moderate in size, the furnishings clean-lined and modern. The hotel's most unique feature is the glass-sided elevator, compatible with the glass-and-steel appearance of the building, which runs up the front facade. On the 29th floor a rooftop restaurant encased in floor-to-ceiling windows offers a panoramic view and serves international cuisine. The public facilities include a pool, tennis court, a bar and Italian restaurant off the lobby, a discotheque, and a variety of shops for gifts and necessities.

NACIONAL, South Hotel Sector, Brasília. Tel. 061/321-7575. Fax 061/223-9213. Telex 61/1062. 346 rms. A/C MINIBAR TV TEL
$ Rates: $65–$70 single; $80–$90 double. AE, DC, MC, V.
The Nacional, the oldest of the upper-bracket hotels, has a spacious lobby and public spaces, with dining rooms, bars, and a swimming-pool deck off the main floor. The otherwise undecorated corridors are in plain wood paneling with carpets that have seen better days, but at least testify to the hotel's heavy traffic and popularity. The service is often friendly, and always courteous and correct, a feature which no doubt accounts for much of the hotel's repeat business and popularity with touring groups. Several shops, including a small branch of the jeweler H. Stern, are off the lobby. The hotel is one of the city's largest, with rooms ranging in price according to their decor and height in the building—and therefore the view they afford of the city. The deluxe rooms, with the better views, have all been recently redecorated with new furnishings, bath fixtures, and carpets.

SÃO MARCO, South Hotel Sector, Brasília. Tel. 061/321-8484. Fax 061/223-6552. Telex 61/3744. 256 rms. A/C MINIBAR TV TEL
$ Rates: $85 single; $90–$100 double. AE, DC, MC, V.
One of Brasília's newest five-star hotels is the São Marco. The rooms have small balconies, and next to each bathroom is a separate dressing area with a second sink. Some units have small kitchenettes and rent on an apart-hotel basis. The rooftop restaurant and cocktail area are appealing, and the pool deck offers an excellent view of the city.

MODERATE

BITTAR PLAZA, North Hotel Sector, Brasília. Tel. 061/225-7077. Fax 061/225-7109. Telex 61/2254. 77 rms. A/C MINIBAR TV TEL
$ Rates: Ground floor $30 single, $33 double; aboveground floor $37 single, $54 double. AE, DC, MC, V.
The Bittar Plaza is a brand-new hotel where the least expensive rooms are located below ground level—well vented, but essentially windowless. Large and well lit, they don't create an automatically claustrophobic reaction, and they're unusually low priced for the degree of comfort and the location. Aboveground rooms are even nicer. Another of the Bittar's appealing features is its appearance of solidity. Unlike much of the construction in Brasília, this building seems like it was made to last. The in-house restaurant offers a well-rounded menu with meals in the $5 to $7 range, with many less expensive appetizers and beer at around $1 a bottle.

BRISTOL, South Hotel Sector, Brasília. Tel. 061/321-6162. Fax 061/321-2690. Telex 61/3443. 141 rms. A/C MINIBAR TV TEL
$ Rates: $62 single; $77 double; $85 suite. AE, DC, MC, V.
The Bristol has a single price range for all rooms, but the best accommodations are in the corners of the building; these units are slightly larger and have balconies. Each suite has a separate sitting room, two baths, and two verandas. The pool area is small, but seems like an agreeable place to sit and have a drink or take the sun.

GARVEY PARK, North Hotel Sector, Brasília. Tel. 061/223-9800. Fax 061/223-4170. Telex 61/2199. 350 rms. A/C MINIBAR TV TEL
$ Rates: $75 single; $85 double. AE, DC, MC, V.
The Garvey Park is really one of the more pleasant tourist-quality hotels in Brasília. While it occupies one of the city's taller buildings, and can house more than 350

guests, there is something self-contained and resortlike about this hotel. Deluxe rooms are very spacious, equipped with couches that divide the space in the manner of an executive suite. Other hotel amenities include an attractive mezzanine-level pool and patio area, an elegant little restaurant, and a wraparound commercial gallery where 130 tiny shops and counters are housed.

HOTEL DIPLOMAT, North Hotel Sector, Brasília. Tel. 061/225-2010.
Telex 61/3307. 44 rms. A/C MINIBAR TV TEL
$ Rates: $40 single; $50 double. AE, DC, MC, V.
The Hotel Diplomat has spacious, comfortable rooms spread over three floors. In addition to the Diplomat's Flash restaurant, where one may eat a palatable meal, the hotel offers three in-house entertainment options, two nightclubs (one with live music for ballroom dancing, the other a discotheque), plus a karaoké, where guests sing to backup recordings and entertain each other.

PHENÍCIA, South Hotel Sector, Brasília. Tel. 061/224-3125. Fax 061/225-1406. Telex 61/2254. 130 rms. A/C MINIBAR TV TEL
$ Rates: $55 single; $70 double. AE, DC, MC, V.
A slightly less expensive selection among the four-star hotels is the Phenícia. The rooms are airy and comfortable, and the hotel offers a full range of services, including a restaurant.

SAINT PAUL, South Hotel Sector, Brasília. Tel. 061/321-4342. Fax 061/224-3935. Telex 61/3721. 274 rms. A/C MINIBAR TV TEL
$ Rates: $48 single; $60 double. AE, DC, MC, V.
The St. Paul offers very large rooms, furnished and decorated in the Scandinavian mode, with balconies. All rooms have TVs that offer in-house movies. The hotel is large and has a restaurant, bar, and nightclub on the premises, as well as a health club with sauna and a beauty shop.

BUDGET

Since everything in Brasília is organized into sectors, it will come as no surprise that there is also a special section of private homes whose owners rent out rooms— **pensions.** It is located in the South Sector on Quadras 703 through 705, quite close, incidentally to the hotel sector. The prices for these accommodations are definitely lower than for rooms in the hotel sector, and can even be negotiated. Since this service is informal, there are no phone numbers to call. You must simply show up in the area and make the necessary inquiries.

On Brasília's light-industrial fringe is a neighborhood known as **SIA** (Setor Industrial e Abastecimento), where most of Brasília's cheaper hotels are located and are much preferred, I am told, by visiting *mochileiros*—backpackers or tourists on a shoestring. These hotels are clustered in a common area, and while their setting is somewhat stark, the accommodations are for the most part clean and pleasant. Rates are also considerably cheaper than the more highly rated establishments in the city's more central hotel sector.

AQUÁRIUS, SIA Sul, Brasília. Tel. 061/233-7122. Telex 61/1862. 50 rms (all with bath). A/C MINIBAR TV TEL
$ Rates: $28 single; $35 double. AE, DC, MC, V.
My personal favorite for its homey atmosphere and tidy informality was the Aquárius, where the aroma of home-style feijoada wafted from a simple dining room filled with boarders.

OLYMPUS, SIA Sul, Brasília. Tel. 061/234-5131. Telex 61/1760. 70 rms. A/C MINIBAR TV TEL
$ Rates: $18 single; $27 double; $29 twin. AE, DC, MC, V.
In appearance, the Olympus suggests a spaceship (and one in need of some minor bodywork, at that). But the rooms are clean, and the price is right.

SIA PARK, SIA Sul, Brasília. Tel. 061/233-3131. Telex 61/3609. 50 rms.
A/C MINIBAR TV TEL
$ Rates: $20 single; $25 double. AE, DC, MC, V.
The SIA Park is a modest three-star establishment, offering many comforts from air conditioning to color TV in the rooms, plus an in-house restaurant and bar.

WHERE TO DINE

Eating out is about the favorite pastime for residents of Brasília, and so an abundance of restaurants, specializing in many varieties of food, is available. Pick up the **"Guia Gastronômico de Brasília"** (Gastronomic Guide to Brasília), a pamphlet available from the tourist balcony at the airport or bus stations on your arrival in the city. Several score restaurants are listed according to type, with their addresses and phone numbers.

The *pamonha* is the Brazilian version of the corn tamale, and not to be missed by lovers of cornmeal and native fast foods. Though usually filled with cheese or meat, there is also a sweet variety. Pamonha stands abound throughout the city. To find one, just ask a cabbie or doorman where to get the best pamonha in the city and I'm sure he will have several suggestions.

AROUND THE CITY

While restaurants are located throughout the city, they also tend to be concentrated in specific *quadras*. First, here are a few places that are not in designated restaurant or entertainment areas.

CHURRASCO DO LAGO, on the banks of the artificial lake. Tel. 223-9266.
Cuisine: BARBECUE. **Reservations:** Not needed.
$ Prices: Appetizers $3–$5; main courses $5–$15; rodízio $12. AE, DC, MC, V.
Open: Daily 11am–midnight.
The perennial choice for a blowout barbecue meal in Brasília is the Churrasco do Lago, located on the banks of the artificial lake. You can order the all-you-can-eat *rodízio* or something "lighter" from the à la carte menu, like the mixed grill ($9).

COMIDA CASEIRA, 104 North. Tel. 225-7798.
Cuisine: SALAD BAR. **Reservations:** Not needed.
$ Prices: Salads average 75¢ per 100 grams (3½ oz.). No credit cards.
Open: Lunch daily lunch 11:30am–3pm; dinner daily 7pm–midnight.
An interesting alternative is the self-service Comida Caseira (which means home-cooking). Hot and cold trays offer more than 40 dishes daily, including many salads, and you pay by the weight of your meal.

ESQUINA MINEIRA, 704 North. Tel. 274-9695.
Cuisine: COMIDA MINEIRA. **Reservations:** Not needed.
$ Prices: Appetizers $1.50–$3.25; main courses $4.50–$7. No credit cards.
Open: Tues–Sat 11:30am–11pm, Sun 11am–4pm.
For Brazilian food, especially for those who still want a taste of Minas Gerais country cooking, there is the Esquina Mineira, which is near one of the principal avenues, Via W3N (there's nothing like the warm, personal touch of a street with a name like an abbreviated ZIP Code!). Dishes are served in a rustic atmosphere on checkered cloth-covered tables, and are inexpensive.

FLORENTINO, 402 South. Tel. 223-7577.
Cuisine: FRENCH. **Reservations:** Recommended.
$ Prices: Appetizers $3–$12; main courses $9–$17. DC, MC.
Open: Daily 11:30am until the last customer leaves.
The Florentino is one of the better restaurants in town, where you will eat French-style food, elegantly served, in the company of diplomats and politicians.

THE CENTRO COMERCIAL GILBERTO SALOMÃO

Located across the lake on the South Peninsula not far from the airport is the main culinary and entertainment center of Brasília. On the weekends its spacious outdoor and open-air restaurants are filled to overflowing. And in addition to a number of fine restaurants, there are a variety of nightclubs and movie houses as well. To get there, just tell your driver you want to go to the Gilberto Salomão. It's a 10-minute cab ride, and 30 minutes on the airport bus.

BIERFASS, Gilberto Salomão. Tel. 248-1519.
   Cuisine: GERMAN/INTERNATIONAL. **Reservations:** Not accepted.
   $ Prices: Appetizers $3–$5; main courses $6–$8; shrimp and codfish $12–$15. AE, MC, V.
   Open: Mon–Fri 6pm until the customers leave, Sat–Sun noon until the customers leave.

The *Bierfass* is just what its name implies—a large and informal beer garden. The menu is extensive, but there are in fact only a few German dishes. It's an after-work as well as a weekend hangout.

GAF, Gilberto Salomão. Tel. 248-1754.
   Cuisine: FRENCH. **Reservations:** Recommended.
   $ Prices: Main courses $9–$21. AE, DC, MC.
   Open: Lunch Mon–Fri 6pm–3am, Sat noon–5pm and 7pm–3am.

Among the better, nonweekend-oriented restaurants here is the GAF, where you go for the food, not the action. Similar in style and quality to the Florentino, the GAF also serves nouvelle French cooking. The low range covers pasta or fish, and the more costly dishes are the better cuts of meat and shellfish.

EASY EXCURSIONS FROM BRASÍLIA

Brasília is also surrounded—at some distance—by the so-called satellite cities, suburban towns that were settled first by the construction workers for whom there were no accommodations in the new capital. By law, Brasília's population is not to exceed 500,000 inhabitants, and most of the housing there was planned for residents of middle- and upper-income levels. Thus 15km (nine miles) from the city is the satellite city **Núcleo dos Bandeirantes.** From everything I had heard about the wild shantytown cities of the laborers, I had expected a giant slum, but I found a quiet and orderly suburban town.

Going beyond Núcleo dos Bandeirantes for another half hour or so, you will come to **Catetinho,** the original campsite where a rustic house was built for Juscelino and other high-ranking visitors who came to Brasília on periodic inspection tours while work was still in progress. The grounds around the camp have been made into a park and picnic site, and the simple house, with its assortment of mementos, is also open to the public.

Some 75 miles from Brasília, and easily accessible by bus, is the town of **Cristalina,** which, as its name implies, is a center for gemstones in the state of Goiás. Most of the shops dealing in gems, jewelry, and precious metals are located on the Praça José Adamian and Rua da Saudade.

2. EXPLORING GOIÁS & GOIÁS VELHO

The inhabitants of Goiás have a button that promotes their state. It says: "ESTADO SOLUÇÃO"—in a country where many states are considered *estados problemas,* the Goiânos are saying, "Here in Goiás, we have found the solution." Of course, it helps that in all of this immense territory that cuts through the center of Brazil and occupies its core, there are only five million inhabitants. No doubt the existence of wide-open spaces with plenty of elbow room for all explains the pride and euphoria of its citizens, and also adds to the allure of the state from the visitor's point of view. The climate, too, is near perfection. Rarely is it too hot or too cold.

Seen from the air, Goiás is a green land of low, bushy vegetation, rolling plains alternating with chains of small mountains. The state is cattle country, and the open land is a great range, reminiscent of the American West of the past century. In the towns, especially the small country towns, you are as likely to see the inhabitants on horseback as in Jeeps or pickup trucks. Along Goiás's western border with the neighboring state of Mato Grosso is one of Brazil's great rivers, the **Araguaia,** whose waters are filled with many fish, whose sandy banks furnish recreational beaches for hundreds of miles, and whose forested margins provide a haven for wildlife.

The capital of Goiás is **Goiânia,** a city of more than 700,000 residents, located some 125 miles from Brasília. Like Belo Horizonte, Goiânia was a planned city, inaugurated in 1933, and it, too, replaced its state's former colonial capital, Goiás Velho, a city worth a visit for those who have the time to travel the roughly 175-mile distance from Brasília.

GOIÁS VELHO

Founded in 1727, the pioneer settlement of Goiás (the "Velho" is a recent addition, as in "Old Sacramento") quickly evolved into an important regional center in west-central Brazil, and until 1937 remained the capital of the territory, and later the state, which bears the same name. Like Ouro Preto, whose history it parallels in many details, Goiás was a mining town during days of the great Brazilian gold rush of the 18th century. Also like Ouro Preto, the city of Goiás lacked the geographical setting—it was laid out in a small valley and penned in by many hills and mountains—that would have allowed its transformation into a modern state capital. The planned city of Goiânia was built to fulfill this role, and Goiás then ceased to be a center of trade and political decision-making in the state, a factor that also contributed to the preservation of its colonial appearance.

Unlike Ouro Preto, however, Goiás is a colonial-era town which has yet to fully develop and exploit its architectural and cultural patrimony. While Ouro Preto is hardly commercialized to the point of being unpleasant, the old section of the city of Goiás is equally pristine and, for the time being, totally noncommercialized. There are no fancy *pousadas* or boutiques. Tack shops and general stores, *boutequims* and small cafés exist in place of their gentrified equivalents. The general flavor of Goiás is of a municipal center for the many working farms and ranches in the wide-open spaces that surround the town. Riders on horseback and donkey carts are not part of some sideshow catering to tourists—they are integral means of transportation still in use by local cowpokes and tradesmen.

Most of the colonial structures are located in one large neighborhood in the city, which otherwise has the look of a typical town of the Brazilian interior—full of two-story stucco buildings in fading pastels, and narrow, wobbly streets, whatever their paving surface or lack thereof. Most of the colonial buildings, however, are whitewashed and of the dreamy baroque design that is the great human-made visual legacy of the 1700s throughout Brazil. There are, for example, seven baroque-era churches in Goiás. And while there is no hoopla associated with the historical legacy, the considerable number of old structures are lovingly preserved, many of them still in use as residences and others transformed into museums open to the public.

GETTING THERE Goiás Velho is 90 miles (145km) from Goiânia along Highway 070, and approximately 150 miles from Brasília on Highway 060 (via Anápolis). Buses run frequently along the Goiânia route, only half paved, and then on from the old capital to the river towns along the Araguaia. There is also a dirt landing strip in Goiás, not far from the center of town. Over the years the poorer folk of town have built their simple wood-frame houses along both sides of the runway. And the strip has become front yard, playground, and soccer field for the local residents. To land there, the pilot must call ahead to the police chief and request that the local constabulary *limpar a pista*—clear the strip of toddlers, chickens, and stray mutts—so the plane can make its approach and land safely. It was most amusing to observe the police cars patrolling the margins of the runway as I was about to land there on a visit in a small plane that had been provided by the state government. The people lined the strip or stood watching from their doorways as we circled the field and came in for a landing. The arrival was something of an occasion at this infrequently used airport facility.

WHAT TO SEE & DO

One could just "be" in Goiás for several days, walking through the streets, absorbing the unself-conscious historical atmosphere, riding on horseback or hiking in the backlands, and generally going native.

Those on a more restricted time schedule (as I was, unfortunately) will want to be sure to see the **Igreja de Nossa Senhora da Boa Morte,** built in 1779 and today a museum of sacred art. In addition to a fascinating collection of antique processional paraphernalia, all in handcrafted silver, the church is the principal repository of the work of José Joaquim da Veiga Valle (1806–74), a sculptor who carved statues in wood. His favorite subjects were Our Lady and St. Sebastian—to whom there is much devotion in rural Goiás—and there are several examples of these figures, along with many others to be seen in the museum. The interior of the building is unusually appealing in its rustic simplicity. The altars are also of carved wood, utilitarian rather than elaborate, and the main chapel (where most of Veiga Valle's work is on display) is filled with soft, sacred music, piped in on tape. A little gift shop at the entrance to the museum sells record albums of both religious and Native American music, and very plain but attractive earthenware.

The **Museu das Bandeiras,** off the Largo do Chafariz, is the secular counterpoint to the museum of sacred art. This plain, rectangular building was constructed in 1761 to house both the local legislature and the jail. On the ground floor, where the jail was located, the walls are nearly five feet thick, and entry to the cells was only through a trapdoor located in the 15-foot ceilings. The second floor, with a number of display cases containing artifacts of the early colonial period, was the venue of the local government. What recommends this building above all else is its remarkable state of preservation, allowing a clear view of both the method of construction and the nature of the building materials used at the time.

The **Palácio Conde dos Arcos** (1755) housed the residence and the offices of the governors from the colonial through republican eras. The two-story building is a warren of rooms, atriums, and courtyards. Furniture of state, plate, and numerous wall hangings and photographs are on display throughout.

WHERE TO STAY

There are few hotels in Goiás, but with the exception of Easter time, when the city fills up with visitors who come to attend the elaborate Semana Santa (Holy Week) festivities, the number of beds is sufficient to handle the normal tourist flow. Pensions and private homes take care of the overflow. The banks of the Bagagem and Bacalhau rivers are favorite sites for camping.

In addition to the listing below, three other hotels, with a total of 43 rooms among them, include the **Hotel Alegrama,** on Rua Morete Forgia (tel. 062/371-1947); the **Hotel Rio Vermelho,** Rua 2 no. 01 (tel. 062/371-1866), in the Jardim Vila Boa neighborhood; and the **Hotel Serrano,** Avenida Dr. Deusdete Ferreira de Moura (tel. 062/371-1981). All three hotels offer rooms for less than $10 or $15.

VILA BOA, Morro do Chapéu do Padre km 1, Goiás Velho. Tel. 062/371-1000. 33 rms (all with bath). A/C MINIBAR TV TEL
$ Rates (including breakfast): $22 single; $29 double. AE, MC.
The Vila Boa is a state-run hotel, but one that is in excellent condition. The hotel, which sits on a hill, has a pool and restaurant. From the stately, building-length terrace you may look out at both the nearby city and the surrounding countryside of green-covered mountains. Each of the rooms has a small balcony.

WHERE TO DINE

There is a very good restaurant in the Hotel Vila Boa. Other recommended eating spots are the **Toka Churrascaria,** Rua Americano do Brasil 17 (tel. 371-1408), where you can savor the local beefsteaks for about $4 an order. The **Restaurante Sobradinho,** Rua Prof. Alcides Jube 05 (tel. 371-1361), also serves regional food.

CHAPTER 10

SÃO PAULO

São Paulo, Brazil's largest and economically most important city, always suffers the misfortune of being compared unfavorably with Rio de Janeiro, its older, more attractive urban sibling. Whole mythologies have grown up to help natives and residents of both cities, locked in fierce familial rivalry, define and protect their respective identities. A cascade of clichés pour from the mouths of Cariocas and Paulistanos alike, in their persistent, urgent attempts at self-definition and self-justification. The suspect generalizations that are the by-product of this squabbling unfortunately find their way into travel articles and guidebooks. We are assured, according to these set scripts, that Rio is sensual, laid-back, and perhaps slightly irresponsible. "When do those Cariocas work? They always seem to be on the beach," one frequently hears. São Paulo residents, on the other hand, are said to be driven and dynamic, if a bit dull. "Those Paulistanos don't know how to enjoy life. They're workaholics," so the other side claims. There are a dozen other facile characterizations, rarely on target. For someone standing in a neutral corner in either city, the people do not seem so different. They both seem to work and play hard; perhaps that's a general Brazilian quality. The conditions under which the inhabitants of the two cities live, work, and play, however, are quite different. And in fact it isn't difficult to identify the major features that distinguish Brazil's two leading cities.

São Paulo's inferiority complex is based on its location—far from the nearest beach. The city, which is after all the largest in all of South America and therefore has something to feel superior about, has not been of particular interest to most international visitors, who come to Brazil on holiday adventures rather than commercial ventures.

Rio, the seashore city, is the destination of choice for the vast majority of Brazil's foreign tourists, while São Paulo, because of its industrial importance, gets hordes of international corporate visitors. This standoff from the São Paulo point of view is unfair and unacceptable. The metropolis does not want to be known exclusively as a business destination, and so is starting to fight back with positive images of its attractions rather than with futile attempts to detract from Rio's undeniable beauty and favored status. São Paulo is beginning to bill itself as what it is: with around 10,000,000 inhabitants, the third-largest—and possibly the fastest-growing—city in the world. People who love big cities are therefore likely to find much to their liking when they visit this one.

WHAT'S SPECIAL ABOUT SÃO PAULO

Gastronomy
- ☐ Most Brazilians consider São Paulo the gastronomical capital of Brazil.

The Performing Arts
- ☐ São Paulo is also the center of theater in Brazil, both traditional and avant-garde.

Ace Attractions
- ☐ The Butantã Snake Institute, where poisonous snakes are milked of their venom to produce antidotes.
- ☐ The Bienal, the internationally famous art festival hosted by São Paulo during odd-numbered years.

A BIT OF BACKGROUND   São Paulo is the home of Brazil's urban scene in its highest development, and Rio in this sense is indeed somewhat provincial. Power and wealth are concentrated in São Paulo. Half of Brazil's industrial output comes from this single state—and most of this economic might encircles the city of São Paulo itself, as close and intimate as the rings around Saturn. In Osasco and the so-called ABC towns—Santo André, São Bernardo, and São Caetano—the giant multinational corporations have planted scores of factories from which a powerful labor movement has emerged in recent years as the heartbeat and conscience of Brazil's fledgling and precarious experiment with democracy.

Along with Minas Gerais and Rio Grande do Sul—though ever in the forefront—since the mid-19th century São Paulo has dominated Brazilian politics, first with its coffee wealth, and now with both coffee and industry. It is an oft-stated truism that São Paulo by itself would be as powerful as many contemporary European nations. But the one time São Paulo actually did try to exert its sovereignty over that of the nation—during the revolution of 1932—it was soundly defeated. It may be a source of Brazilian pride to imagine an entity as powerful as the state of São Paulo standing alone today, able to compete with the best of the industrial giants. But the real challenge in Brazil is, and has always been, trying to overcome the patterns of uneven development that have plagued the nation during the entire 500 years of its existence. The inability of Brazilians to imagine São Paulo not as a separate nation, but as an inspiration and model for the rest of the country's internal development is reflected in the repetitious political instability that has characterized Brazilian governments since the end of the empire in 1889.

But São Paulo has also been a bit of a hothouse. The state actually managed for a long time to determine who could settle within its boundaries and who couldn't. A great effort during the early part of this century was made to attract "white" Europeans—an instant labor force already accustomed to, and trained for, an industrial reality—and to stem the flow of Brazilians from the impoverished states in northeastern Brazil. Jorge Amado, whose writing taken as a whole is a kind of biography of Brazilian life and times of the 20th century—particularly life in the northeast—portrays a touching migration scene in the as yet untranslated novel *Seara Vermelha*. In the scene, which takes place in the 1930s, the São Paulo state government has set up a public-health station in the town of Pirapora, in the neighboring state of Minas Gerais. A train line then linked São Paulo to this southernmost river landing of the Rio São Francisco, the great inland commercial and passenger waterway serving to link the towns of the Brazilian interior since the earliest

---

IMPRESSIONS

Several immense Madrids breaking half the horizon.
—RUDYARD KIPLING, *BRAZILIAN SKETCHES*, 1927

The locomotive which pulls the rest of Brazil.
—LOCAL SAYING, QUOTED BY JOHN GUNTHER, *INSIDE SOUTH AMERICA*, 1967.

colonial times. Here in Pirapora, in Amado's novel the doctors give free railway passage to the able-bodied and turn away the infirm from entering their state, which had already become a kind of promised land in the minds of the displaced peasants from the old semifeudal estates to the north.

Today, with a functioning, if not always state-of-the-art, network of roads and buses, such a policy of limited internal migration, never defensible, is also no longer possible in Brazil. In recent decades the *nordestinos* have literally invaded São Paulo (not to mention Bahia and the vast western and Amazon territories), extending in leaps the city's ever-widening periphery. They are indeed the force from which labor is recruited for the city's powerful industrial plants. Those for whom no jobs are available bide their time in the shantytowns, the ubiquitous poverty satellites typical of all of Brazil's modern cities, and survive by the skin of their teeth.

The city of São Paulo does not project poverty as its predominant image, however. Rather, one's eye runs along a skyline of gray concrete high-rise buildings, which seem to be replicated to infinity along the horizon. Dispersed among the high-rises throughout the city are a great variety of private homes, shopping centers, public parks, vest-pocket squares, and old neighborhoods of a smaller and more attractive scale, which invite closer inspection by true aficionados of inner-city life. Fortunately, São Paulo, which already sits at an altitude of over 2,500 feet above sea level, is also in many places a hilly city, a terrain feature which breaks up a certain feeling of architectural monotony.

1. ORIENTATION

São Paulo is not what you would call a pretty city. The urban rat race everywhere has long been motorized, and São Paulo is no exception. There can be monster traffic jams, and a lot of slow-motion driving, with (depending on the winds) the poor air quality that results from such concentrations of fuel exhaust. But neither is São Paulo a city where you go just to see skyscrapers, a few museums, the famous Butantã snake farm, or some other promotional attraction. It is a place to go and hang out, café-hop, shop, or walk the streets by day, eat out and boogie by night. There is a quasi-bohemian Italian neighborhood with coffeehouses and pizza joints, scores of intimate *nordestino* hangouts—tiny hole-in-the-wall bars and outdoor cafés where you can go anytime of day for great Brazilian draft beer and a quick snack—Japanese fairs and restaurants galore, and the same potential as elsewhere in Brazil to meet and spend time with such a group of convivial Brazilians as your time, luck, and initiative allow.

ARRIVING & DEPARTING

All roads in Brazil, by air or land—and such passenger trains as continue to run—lead to São Paulo.

Should you require the services of a travel agency while in São Paulo, I would recommend the **Agência Intersul,** Av. Ipiranga 318, bloco B, 16th floor (tel. 011/231-1899), a half block away, and across the street from the Hilton Hotel. Should any red tape or complications interfere with your domestic Brazilian air travel plans, consult here with Luisa, a straight-shooter who will do her best to clear the path for you.

BY PLANE From Rio, the VARIG air shuttle (Ponte Aérea; tel. 240-1130) takes you from inner city to inner city, from Santos Dumont Airport in downtown Rio to Congonhas in the midst of São Paulo. The 55-minute flights leave every half hour from 5:20am until 10:30pm and cost around $85 each way. You don't need a reservation unless you desire a specific flight. Ticketing arrangements for air travel in Brazil are relatively uncomplicated. The top hotels generally have, if not a ticketing representative among their lobby concessions, certainly a travel and tour agency. This agency will perform this service for you, sometimes only for a token fee.

The **airport bus** runs at 25-minute intervals during peak hours, and every 45 minutes or so in the dead of night, between São Paulo's two airports—Congonhas (domestic flights) and Garulhos (international flights)—and a downtown terminal at the Praça da República. A separate line operates directly between the two airports, with a brief layover at the Rodoviária, the city's principal bus terminal. The fare is $3 to $8.50. The cab fare from Garulhos (where most international visitors are likely to land) to downtown São Paulo is $27.

BY TRAIN   Train service is available to and from any point deep within the southwestern state of Mato Grosso do Sul, home of the Pantanal, the vast and—according to concerned ecologists—the rapidly vanishing marshland retreat of the bulk of Brazil's remaining wildlife. The journey to Corumbá, on the border with Paraguay, near the great river of the same name, takes about two days, accounting for a switch in trains in Baurú, in the interior of the state of São Paulo—and the usual delays.

The *Trem Bandeirante* leaves Brasília at 10:50pm on Friday night and arrives in São Paulo at 7:20pm the following evening. One-way fare is $87, and a full cabin costs approximately $235.

BY BUS   Express buses run frequently between Rio and São Paulo, and there is bus service to the economic capital from even the most remote points throughout the country. One reliable carrier is **Empresa Camarata** (tel. 299-0177), with buses leaving from the bus terminal Rodoviária Tiete (Av. Cruziero do Sul 1800; tel. 235-0322) every hour between 5:30am and 1am. Fare for the ordinary bus is $22 one way to or from Rio; the *leito,* with reclining seats, costs $45 each way. The last departing leito is at 11:45pm.

BY CAR   The quick car route to São Paulo from Rio is along the Via Dutra (BR 116), a toll road (token charge). The trip can be made safely in about six hours. The scenic route along the Rio-Santos highway (BR 101) follows the shoreline and is recommended for more relaxed touring. More description on this route can be found in Chapter 7, "Excursions from Rio."

TOURIST INFORMATION

All major entry points—airport, bus, and train stations—have **tourist information counters,** many open seven days a week from 8am to 11pm, and they always have a full complement of specialists on hand to meet the arrival of all international flights. Ask these folk, who will certainly speak English and who are highly professional, helpful, and well informed, for their recommendations about maps, hotels, bus routes, and whatever other logistical information you need. If you want to get to your hotel by public bus, for example, these are the people to ask for a clear and detailed route.

The city of São Paulo operates eight information booths throughout the city, one of which is conveniently located on the Praça da República (tel. 267-8307, ext. 581), open daily from 9am till 6pm. There is also a post office window at this booth, open Monday to Friday 9am to noon and 1 to 4pm.

The **São Paulo Convention and Visitors Bureau,** Rua Alameda Campinas, 5th floor (tel. 011/289-9397), is an in-town option for tourist information, open Monday through Friday from 9am to 6pm. Operating two offices downtown for information in addition to the reception counters they staff at the airports and bus/train stations is the **State Secretary of Sports and Tourism.** The office at Av. São Luis 115 (tel. 011/257-7248), is open weekdays from 8am to 6pm, while the sixth-floor office at Praça Antônio Prado 9 (tel. 011/229-3011), keeps hours on weekdays between 9am and 5pm.

CITY LAYOUT
NEIGHBORHOODS IN BRIEF

Centro   Downtown São Paulo has a little of everything—hotels, restaurants, movies, shops, and street life.

Bexiga Officially know as Bela Vista, this is a neighborhood of Italian restaurants and cafés, within easy walking distance of downtown.

Avenida Paulista The Fifth Avenue of São Paulo, with the MASP (Modern Art Museum) and the city's most elegant shops. Off the avenue is the tiny Trianon Park, where the city's best hotels are located.

The Jardims Jardim América, Jardim Paulista, Jardim Europa—these are São Paulo's most sophisticated neighborhoods, where the city's best nightclubs, bars, and restaurants are found.

Liberdade São Paulo's Asian neighborhood, known for its Japanese restaurants and Sunday craft fair.

Butantã Home not only to the famous snake institute, but also to the University of São Paulo, and therefore many student bars and restaurants.

Ibirapuera São Paulo's Central Park, a huge green space within the city, very popular on the weekends. On the edge of the park, along the avenue of the same name is the **Sambão,** a nightlife zone known for its samba bars.

STREET MAPS

São Paulo Is All, a free and otherwise useful government map and guide you are likely to be given at a tourist information point, is not adequate. Outside the old center city the map only shows the main arteries and thoroughfares, and not the hundreds of side streets you will need to search out in order to really get around. Furthermore, much of what you will want to see or do is outside the old center, even though you are likely to be staying in or near downtown, eating there at some point, and certainly visiting this section for one reason or another during your stay. Ask the tourist information people for a copy of the **Mapa Gastronômico de São Paulo** (Guide to São Paulo's Restaurants). The many restaurants listed and described on this map are also pinpointed by number on a detailed street layout which covers most—though no all—of São Paulo's neighborhoods. I would appreciate learning from any reader the name of an even better and more detailed map of the city, with index, and information on where it may be purchased.

2. GETTING AROUND

BY PUBLIC TRANSPORTATION São Paulo's **subway** system is in its infancy. There are two short lines currently in operation. The north-south line runs between the neighborhoods of Jabaquara and Vila Guilherme. An east-west line runs from one stop beyond the downtown Praça da República to Penha. Two other lines are currently being planned and constructed. The trains are new, the stations cavernous and clean, and the few trains crowded at all times of the day. But it's a good, cheap way to get around to a limited number of destinations. The fare is 40¢ and a book of 10 tickets costs $3.50; trains run from 5am to midnight daily.

Street crime is a problem for any big city, and São Paulo is no exception. City bus travel is only advised for those visitors who have some knowledge of Portuguese.

BY TAXI Taxis are abundant, and your best bet is a radio cab. The fare is slightly more than the common cab, but you are less likely to be hustled.

BY CAR One hears in São Paulo constant reference to a disturbing statistic: that every third inhabitant owns a car. Since São Paulo is both the Detroit and the Los Angeles of Brazil, this allegation is entirely plausible. City residents are close to the source of automobile manufacture, on the industrial edge of their city, and their geographically enormous metropolis is interconnected by many streets, avenues, freeways, and beltways. The automobile is clearly the favored mode of transportation, providing a strong argument in favor of taxi travel for all but the most intrepid and adaptable urban denizens, who might risk renting a car.

For car rentals, make arrangements with an international company prior to arrival. You'll find the rates much cheaper if you do. Local representatives of these companies are: **Hertz** (tel. 255-8055), **Avis** (tel. 256-4433), **National** (tel. 533-2133), and **Budget** (tel. 256-4355).

FAST FACTS: SÃO PAULO

American Express The American Express representative in São Paulo is the Kontik Franstur Travel Agency, Rua Marconi 71, 3rd floor (tel. 259-4211), open Monday to Friday from 9am to 6pm, and Saturday till noon.

Area Code The São Paulo area code is 011.

Babysitters Most hotels maintain lists of reliable babysitters. Or you could try contacting an agency called Vereda Brasilis (tel. and fax 011/34-7621). Agency owner Cláudia Rodrigues da Cunha operates a kind of "gal Friday" service, and offers to facilitate in making contacts and opening doors for visiting business persons.

Bookstores The Livraria Siciliana, Rua Barão de Itapetininga 227, (tel. 225-6641), near the São Paulo Hilton, has a good selection of paperbacks and magazines in English. The store, part of a chain with 27 affiliates in and around São Paulo, is open Monday through Saturday from 8am till 10pm. Bookshelves at Kosmos, located downtown at Av. São Luís 162 (tel. 258-3244), are filled with colorful and quality printed works on Brazilian wildlife, including one lovely volume entitled *Birds of Brazil.*

Car Rentals See "Getting Around," earlier in this chapter.

Climate See "When to Go" in Chapter 2.

Currency See "Information, Entry Requirements & Money" in Chapter 2.

Currency Exchange With the introduction of a new rate of exchange called the *dólar turismo*—the tourist dollar—it is now often most convenient to exchange money right at your hotel, rather than going in search of a *câmbio* that trades in the quasi-legal *paralelo*—or black market. Still, with Brazil's history of wild swings in the currency market, it's always good to have a fallback option. For this purpose, check out a travel agency near the Hilton and the Edifício Itália called Casa Faro, Rua São Luís 157 (tel. 257-7077), where dollars are exchanged for cruzeiros at the parallel rate through a window in the back of the shop.

Dentist Consult your local consulate. Open all night for emergencies is the Dental Office Tutoia, Rua Tutoia 70 (tel. 885-3755), in the Paraíso neighborhood.

Doctors Consult your local consulate. The Omni-Assistencial clinic, Rua Frederico Chopin 264/278 (tel. 813-4000), is conveniently located in Jardim Paulista.

Drugstores Twenty-four-hour drugstores include Centro 1, Av. Rio Branco 54 (tel. 223-0689), located downtown, and, in the Jardins, Jardim 1, Rua Augusta 2699 (tel. 883-0319), and Jardim 4, Av. Paulista 2103 (tel. 251-0206).

Embassies and Consulates All embassies in Brazil are located in the nation's capital, Brasília. Consulates of some English-speaking countries are: U.S., Rua Padre João Manuel 933 (tel. 881-2318); Great Britain, Av. Paulista 1938 (tel. 287-7722); Australia, Av. Morvan Dias de Figueiredo 1400 (tel. 954-4517); and Canada, Av. Paulista 854 (tel. 287-2122).

Emergencies See "Doctor" and "Dentist," above, or "Hospitals," below.

Eyeglasses Near downtown and the Jardins in the Cerqueira Cesar district is Mitani, Rua Augusta 2178 (tel. 853-5211).

Hairdressers and Barbers There are experienced and creative unisex stylists at Beka, Rua Oscar Freire 530 (tel. 881-0355); De La Lastra, Rua Bela Cintra 2245 (tel. 852-3566), is a full-service beauty shop. Both are located in Cerqueira Cesar.

Holidays See "When to Go" in Chapter 2.

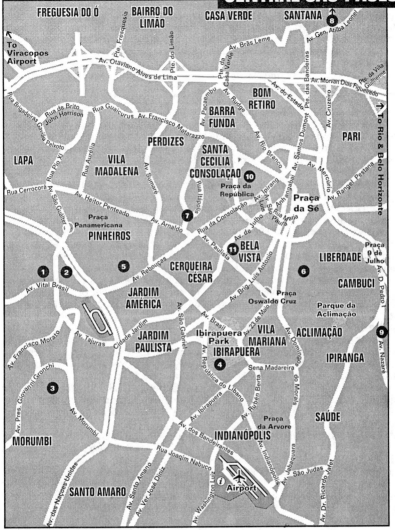

Butantã Snake Institute **1**
Casa do Bandeirante **2**
Fundação Maria Luiza & Oscar Americano **3**
Ibirapuera Park **4**
Museu da Casa Brasileira **5**
Museu da Imigração Japonesa **6**
Museum of Brazilian Art **7**
Parque Florestal **8**
Paulista Museum **9**
Praça da República **10**
São Paulo Museum of Art (MASP) **11**

Hospitals   The Albert Einstein, Av. Albert Einstein 627 (tel. 845-1233), is considered the best hospital in the city. You must have medical insurance to be treated there. The best heart specialists in Brazil are found at the Instituto do Coração (INCOR), Av. Dr. Eneias Carvalho de Aguiar 255 (tel. 282-7766).

Information   See "Tourist Information," earlier in this chapter.

Laundry and Dry Cleaning   The UÓSH, a self-service laundry, Av. Ipiranga 200, stores 33 and 35 (tel. 256-5444), open from 8am to 7pm Monday through Saturday, is located right across the street from the Hilton. VIP, Av. Morumbi 775 (tel. 542-9566), is a full-service dry cleaner. Probably the best bet for speed and reliability is to use your hotel service.

Libraries   The downtown Biblioteca Mário de Andrade, Rua da Consolação 94 (tel. 239-3459), is the largest library in São Paulo, with a comfortable reading room filled with interesting maps and rare books. The University of São Paulo library, Estudos Brasileiros, is on Av. Prof. Mello Morais 1235, bloco D (tel. 813-3222), in Butantã.

Lost Property   Property lost on the subway and public buses is brought to the central post office. See below.

Luggage Storage and Lockers   Storage facilities are available at Tiete Bus Terminal, Av. Cruzeiro do Sul 1800 (tel. 235-0322), in Vila Guilherme.

Newspapers and Magazines   The two newspapers of record in São Paulo are the *Folha de São Paulo,* and the *Estado de São Paulo,* known as the *Folha* and *Estadão* respectively. *Veja* magazine publishes a weekly calendar of events and restaurant reviews, available on all newsstands.

Photographic Needs   The Color Center (tel. 543-1424) is in the Shopping Center Ibirapuera, Av. Ibirapuera 3103, in Indianópolis. Or try one of the stores of the chain Photóptica, one branch of which is downtown on Rua Cons. Crispiniano 49/57 (tel. 239-4122).

Police   See "Safety," below.

Post Office   The central post office is downtown on Av. São João s/n (tel. 831-5522), open Monday through Friday from 8am to 10pm. For express deliveries anywhere in Brazil, go to the SEDEX window, which closes at 5pm. You may also make long-distance calls, and send telegrams from the post office.

Radio   For "MPB," Brazilian pop, try Cultura, 103.3 FM; Rádio USP (the university station), 93.7 FM; or Eldorado, 92.9 FM. Classical stations are Cultura, 103.3 FM and 1200 AM, and Eldorado, 700 AM. For Brazilian country music, try Rádio Capital, 1120 AM.

Religious Services   Catholic mass may be heard in English at N. S. Help of Christians, Rua Vigário João de Pontes 200 (tel. 247-7455). Jewish services in English are held by a North American rabbi at the Congregação Israelita Paulista, Rua Antônio Carlos 653 (tel. 256-7811). The Episcopal church is St. Paul's, Rua Com. Elias Zarzur 1239 (tel. 246-0383). For nondenominational Protestant services, there is the Fellowship Community Church, Rua Carlos Sampaio 107 (tel. 287-2294). There is a Mormon temple on Rua Teófilo de Carvalho 285 (tel. 843-1848).

Restrooms   Airports, hotel lobbies, commercial establishments, and good restaurants all have impeccably clean restrooms; in Brazil no one will deny you your right to use the plumbing when the need arises.

Safety   The Civil Police goes by the name DEATUR. They operate a special Tourist Police Station downtown, Av. São Luís 115 (tel. 231-0044 or 254-3561). To report a lost passport, call CEPOL (tel. 254-3121 or 227-2569), open 24 hours a day.

Shoe Repairs   Try Renovadora de Calçados Genaro, Rua José Maria Lisboa 196 (tel. 885-2758), in Cerqueira Cesar.

Taxes   All hotels and restaurants levy a 10% service charge.

Taxis   See "Getting Around," earlier in this chapter.

Telegrams and Telexes   For telegrams, see "Post Office," above. Telexes may be sent from most hotels.

Television   Major networks are Manchete, Globo, Bandeirantes, Record, and TV-SBT. Many first-class hotels offer CNN. Bandeirantes often carries major international sporting events, like heavyweight prize fights, World Series games, and the Super Bowl.

Transit Information   Dial 194.

Useful Telephone Numbers   Police, 190; first aid/ambulance, 192; fire, 193; 24-hour drugstores, 139; time, 130; weather, 132; long-distance information, 121; lost and found documents, 159; directory assistance, 102.

3. ACCOMMODATIONS

Perhaps because São Paulo caters to so many high-ranking corporate visitors, its hotels are among the best and the most expensive in Brazil. For the business traveler—or anyone else willing to pay the price—São Paulo's deluxe hotels offer the finest in rooms, services, facilities, and food. Many moderately priced hotels also offer fine accommodations and service.

VERY EXPENSIVE

The narrow, energetic Rua Augusta is promoted in most of the tourist literature as an attraction in itself. It is a long, commercial street crammed with shops, boutiques, and restaurants, and several of São Paulo's top hotels.

CA'D'ORO, Rua Augusta 129, São Paulo. Tel. 011/256-8011. Fax 011/ 231-0359. Telex 11/21765. 290 rms, 50 suites. A/C MINIBAR TV TEL
$ Rates: $120–$135 single; $150–$180 double. AE, DC, MC, V.
The Ca'd'Oro is a hotel cast in the tradition of European elegance of some bygone era. The building is set back from the street and guests enter the lobby under a canopy lined with the flags of many nations. The many alcoves off the lobby are filled with rococo statuary and prints of Renaissance figures. Also on the first floor is a cocktail area with high-backed upholstered chairs set before a large working fireplace. The adjacent room houses the hotel's popular and very formal Italian restaurant. There are two pools at the Ca'd'Oro, one set in a patio separating the main building from an annex, the other on the roof under a glass dome, with adjoining bar. There are 340 rooms and suites split between the old and new wings, the former furnished in heavy old-world style, the latter with modern pieces.

CAESAR PARK HOTEL, Rua Augusta 1508, São Paulo. Tel. 011/285-6622. Fax 011/288-6146. Telex 11/22539. 177 rms. A/C MINIBAR TV TEL
$ Rates: $230–$295 single; $255–$325 double. AE, DC, MC, V.
São Paulo also has its Caesar Park Hotel, the choice for those who prefer quiet elegance over the splashiness of the newer deluxe properties. The lobby is small and dark, the many pigeon-holed shelves behind the reception desk more suggestive of a fin-de-siècle apothecary th   hotel. A certain snobbishness pervades the atmosphere, encouraged vicariously b)   : aloof posture of the reception personnel. Behind the lobby on the main floor are several boutiques, a French restaurant, and a sushi bar. On the roof is an open-air pool encircled by a wooden sunning deck, a bar, and a restaurant for more informal meals. The rooms are furnished with queen-size beds, and plush oversize sofas.

HOTEL MOFAREJ SHERATON, Alameida Santos 1437, São Paulo. Tel. 011/284-5544. Fax 011/289-8670. Telex 11/34170. 248 rms. A/C MINIBAR TV TEL
$ Rates: $200–$210 single; $235–$250 double. AE, DC, MC, V.
One of the city's most elegant hotels is set on a hill behind the small Trianon Park, a botanical relic of the brush and tree species that once covered the land where all the city's human structures now stand. The sleek and well-toned Hotel Mofarej Sheraton looks like the ideal background for a fashion-magazine cover photo. The hotel's most striking feature is the lobby and atrium which sits beneath a many-paned skylight dome. The finely decorated rooms are spacious, trimmed in

polished hardwood, with tasteful artwork and artifacts adorning the gallerylike walls. Deluxe rooms have two double beds and sitting areas with couches and armchairs.

MAKSOUD PLAZA, Alameida Campinas 150, São Paulo. Tel. 011/251-2233. Fax 011/251-4202. Telex 11/30026. 416 rms. A/C MINIBAR TV TEL
$ Rates: $175–$250 single; $225–$275 double. AE, DC, MC, V.

The Maksoud Plaza is a rectangle of glass and steel built around a vast atrium that runs the full length of the 22-story building. The huge space is dominated by a great hanging sculpture of stainless steel and surrounded by balconies which are hung with living greenery. The four elevators travel up one side of the interior through transparent columns which view the atrium from three sides. Like the Sheraton, the Maksoud is in a neighborhood which conveys an atmosphere of chicness, calm, and security. There are six restaurants at the Maksoud Plaza, representing the cuisine of several nationalities, including Scandinavian, French, Brazilian, and Japanese. The lobby bar specializes in drinks made from cachaça. The rooms are entered from walkways that overlook the atrium. Accommodations are large and swank, with blond wood furnishings and beige broadlooms, and baths are equipped with separate temperature control for the showers.

SÃO PAULO HILTON, Av. Ipiranga 165, São Paulo. Tel. 011/256-0033. Fax 011/257-3137. Telex 11/21981. 407 rms. A/C MINIBAR TV TEL
$ Rates: $160–$190 superior single, $235 top-class single; $190–$220 superior double, $255 top-class double. AE, DC, MC, V.

The place to stay for those who have the means and desire to purchase additional privacy and services, has to be in "top class" at the São Paulo Hilton.
The top three floors of the circular 33-story hotel are reserved for top-class clients, who use special elevator keys to arrive at their private floors, take breakfast and cocktails in a private lounge stocked with liquor, fresh coffee, food, and international newspapers and magazines—all yours for the asking—and are attended by a staff of charming hosts and hostesses from 7am till 10pm every day.

The top-class rooms, however, as attractive as they are, are not so different from the other accommodations in the Hilton. This is good news for anyone booked into the Hilton by a group or package tour, since they will also get the Hilton comfort and service, but at a reduced group rate. Like all Brazilian five-star hotels, the Hilton is a self-contained environment, with several fine restaurants and bars, a steam room and pool, and an attached arcade of shops and boutiques for convenient shopping.

There are certain drawbacks to any hotel. For the Hilton it may be the location, the slightly shabby area of the old downtown, which is nonetheless still the one appealing visual hub of the city from an architectural point of view. At night the demimonde plays out its drama of low-grade sin and sleaze disturbingly or—depending on your perspective—intriguingly near the enclave where the circular Hilton Tower stands as a recognizable landmark along the horizon of the cityscape. This scene of the back streets has no immediate bearing on the comings and goings at the Hilton, most of which are by car or taxi. One is repeatedly warned, almost to the point of inducing a state of reckless curiosity, to foresake the paths of the Praça da República at night and not to wander among the crowds of prostitutes, toughs, and transvestites who decorate the street corners a block or two behind the Hilton.

A block or so from the Hilton at Av. Ipiranga 344 is the Edifício Itália, São Paulo's tallest building. The view from the observation deck on the 41st floor is free and about the best in the city. You can get the same scenic view from the rooftop bar, or from one of two restaurants as well (tel. 257-6566).

TRANSAMÉRICA, Av. Nações Unidas 18,591, São Paulo. Tel. 011/523-4511. Fax 011/523-8700. Telex 11/61197. 211 rms. A/C MINIBAR TV TEL
$ Rates: $165–$195 single; $185–$225 double. AE, DC, MC, V.

For a hotel with a resortlike atmosphere half an hour from the center of town there is the Transamérica. The environs are modified industrial, but the point again here is what happens inside, not outside, the hotel. The Transamérica is a horizontal complex which opened in 1985 and is set on sprawling grounds with many outdoor sports facilities, including a putting green, jogging track, large outdoor pool with outdoor café, and a regulation soccer field. The hotel also offers several fine tennis courts, and, as host to many national tennis tournaments, is considered the Forest Hills of Brazil. The Transamérica is truly an oasis for sports-minded executives who want to lodge close to the industrial scene. The hotel also provides many other comforts, including an elegant restaurant off the lobby, which is bordered by fresh flowers, changed daily. Accommodations, in beige and green color schemes, still have that just-out-of-the-package look, with queen-size beds, designer furnishings, and ceramic-tile baths.

MODERATE

DELLA VOLPE GARDEN HOTEL, Rua Frei Caneca 199, São Paulo. Tel. 011/285-5388. Fax 011/288-8710. Telex 11/35473. 133 rms. A/C MINIBAR TV TEL

$ Rates: $150 single or double. Discounts available. AE, DC, MC, V.

Given the voluptuous, neoclassical—or better—pop-classical decor, you might need sunglasses to get through the lobby of São Paulo's newest luxury hotel, all aglitter in metallic shades of brass and gold. The rooms, however, are toned down considerably, besides being quite spacious and comfortable in an overstuffed sort of way. With L-shaped alcoves, the rooms give the impression of being suites. All bathrooms have tubs equipped with Jacuzzis, and luxury rooms have separate showers as well. Other hotel amenities include a small pool under a greenhouse roof, and an equally diminutive jogging track on the roof, 10 stories up. The hotel is located only a few hundred feet from the fashionable Avenida Paulista, and may still be offering its five-star rooms for four-star prices with a 30% discount available through the reservations department.

HOTEL BOURBON, Av. Vieira de Carvalho 99, São Paulo. Tel. 011/223-2244. Fax 011/255-8181. Telex 11/37993. 111 rms. A/C MINIBAR TV TEL

$ Rates: Weekdays $120 single; $135 double. Weekends $95 single, $110 double. AE, DC, MC, V.

On an elegant old street, not too far from the Praça da República, are a number of still very fine hotels and restaurants to fit all budgets. At the top of the list is the old Hotel Bourbon. It's not easy to book a room here during the week, because the hotel is a traditional favorite of business travelers and has a clientele that keeps returning. One of the hotel's attractions is its moderately priced restaurant, serving quality meals costing an average of $10, not including drinks and service.

NIKKEY PALACE, Rua Galvão Bueno 425, São Paulo. Tel. 011/270-8511. Fax 011/270-6614. Telex 11/35187. 100 rms. A/C MINIBAR TV TEL

$ Rates: $75–$100 single; $95–$125 double. AE, DC, MC, V.

In the Liberdade neighborhood are a number of hotels that cater primarily to groups of Asian tourists and business travelers, but are a viable option for anyone who wants to soak up a little Asian atmosphere Brazil style. The Nikkey Palace is by far the best of the lot, a most charming and relatively small hotel with 100 rooms, delicately decorated in the austere good taste for which the Japanese are known. The hotel's Japanese restaurant has three separate environments: a salon with tables, a sushi bar, and a half-dozen private rooms behind walls and sliding doors of rice paper. A thermal pool/sauna room is also typically Japanese in design. Rooms are simply but comfortably furnished, and offer all the amenities.

VILA RICA, Av. Vieira de Carvalho 167, São Paulo. Tel. 011/220-7111. Telex 11/21465. 61 rms. A/C MINIBAR TV TEL

$ Rates: $45 single; $50 double. AE, DC, V.

The Vila Rica is a moderately priced option. The small scale of the hotel is one of its appealing attributes, as is its location on a wide boulevard, a block from the Praça de República, that's lined with innumerable reasonably priced eateries and shops.

BUDGET

AMAZONAS, Av. Vieira de Carvalho 32, São Paulo. Tel. 011/220-4111. 32 rms. MINIBAR TV TEL

$ Rates: $20 single; $25 double; $25–$29 room with A/C. DC, V.

A small and genuinely inexpensive but totally acceptable hotel is the Amazonas. Air-conditioned rooms, which are standard with all the other São Paulo hotels mentioned in this guide, are slightly higher.

BANRI, Rua Galvão Bueno 209, São Paulo. Tel. 011/270-8877. 55 rms. A/C MINIBAR TV TEL

$ Rates: $25 single with regular bath, $27 single with furo bath; $32 double with regular bath, $35 double with furo bath. No credit cards.

The Banri is modest, impeccably clean, and comfortable. Some of the rooms have *furo* baths—Japanese-style bathtubs, higher than they are long, in which a bather kneels in chest-deep water.

FUJI PALACE, Largo da Polvora 120, São Paulo. Tel. 011/278-7466. Fax 011/279-9041. Telex 11/26055. 75 rms. A/C MINIBAR TV TEL

$ Rates: $45 single; $50 double. AE, DC, MC, V.

The Fuji Palace is midway in size and price between the other selections in Liberdade. The deluxe rooms are larger and better furnished.

HOTEL SAN REMO, Rua Santa Efigênia 163, São Paulo. Tel. 011/229-8198. 40 rms. TV TEL

$ Rates: $11 single without bath, $15 single with bath; $15 double without bath, $20 double with bath. No credit cards.

This is the hotel that the tourist information people at the booth on the Praça da República most recommend to travelers on a shoestring budget who are looking for safe, clean, cheap digs in São Paulo.

HOTEL TERMINUS, Av. Ipiranga 741, São Paulo. Tel. 011/222-2266. Telex 11/30975 70 rms. A/C MINIBAR TV TEL

$ Rates: $28–$31 single; $35–$39 double. AE, DC, MC, V.

The Hotel Terminus is a very presentable three-star establishment with rooms on the north end of the Praça da República. There's a slightly Middle-European air about this place, with its homey accommodations and old-fashioned apartment-style balconies. The Terminus is located near several movie houses showing first-run Hollywood films, perhaps a month behind their U.S. schedules. Across the street are a McDonald's and the Brazilian equivalent in fast-food service, Bob's. There is a subway stop right on the nearby plaza, and on Sunday, the crafts fair described below.

A YOUTH HOSTEL

There is an **Albergue da Juventude Primavera,** Rua Mariz e Barros 346 (tel. 215-3144), in Vila Mariana that charges $5 per night for one of 36 dorm-style beds. You can take the subway or bus no. 407M from the Praça da República to the Jardim da Glória. The APAJ (Association of Paulista Youth Hostels), Rua Jandaia 154 (tel. 35-3077), in Bela Vista is open Monday to Friday from 9am to 6pm.

4. DINING

The number-one pastime for residents of large cities is, and probably always will be, eating out. In response to this powerful popular demand for culinary variety, São Paulo embraces within its city limits literally thousands of restaurants. This does not mean to say that every place listed is going to serve you some gourmet delight. Hardly! In most cases you'll get what you pay for—sometimes a little bit more, in others a little bit less. The size of your bill will in most cases reflect the amount of love and labor that have gone into your meal.

You could visit São Paulo, never eat in one of the restaurants mentioned in this guide, and not register the slightest dissatisfaction with your culinary experience. That's one of the great advantages of any big city. People who eat out a lot develop pretty good tastes in restaurant food, and bad restaurants don't tend to stay in business very long. So, bon appétit—now we can eat. Enjoy, and write to tell me about all your favorites—especially the inexpensive ones. Everybody loves a good deal.

EXPENSIVE

MARQUÊŞ DE MARIALVA, Rua Haddock Lobo 1583. Tel. 852-1805.
Cuisine: PORTUGUESE. **Reservations:** Recommended.
$ Prices: Appetizers $5–$15; main courses $14–$25. AE, DC, MC, V.
Open: Lunch Tues–Sun noon–3pm; dinner Tues–Sun 7:30pm–1am.

If there is such a thing as a gourmet Portuguese restaurant, the elegant Marquês de Marialva deserves that soubriquet. Owner Senhor Batalha has transferred a good deal of Lisbon's continental charm to this lovely establishment. What more civilized way to begin a meal of genuine Portuguese cuisine than with a glass of smooth, extra-dry port wine ($3.75). Soup must surely follow, especially when the menu offers *caldo verde* ($4.75), that creamy stock of finely chopped collard greens and potatoes reduced to purée with virgin olive oil and served with smoked sausage, and with slabs of corn bread on the side. The arroz de frutos do mar ($14) is a kind of subtle paella, a superb casserole of seafoods—shrimp, octopus, squid, and clams—steamed in their own juices over a bed of rice. Another Portuguese favorite is the porco a alentejana ($18.50), cubes of tender pork sautéed with clams. You cannot wash a meal down with better wine than that which springs from the stony backcountry of Portugal, and the acaio I sampled, a tangy vinho verde ($12 per bottle), was no exception. From the circulating dessert tray, I selected the eggs lamprey ($4.25), a mouth-melting confection of egg layers cooked in sugar syrup, filled with cream, and served on a bed of angel hair.

TATINI, Rua Batatais 558. Tel. 885-7601.
Cuisine: ITALIAN. **Reservations:** Recommended.
$ Prices: Appetizers $6–$15; main courses $10–$25. AE, DC, MC, V.
Open: Lunch Tues–Fri noon–3pm, dinner Tues–Fri 7pm–2am; Sat–Sun 11:30am–2am.

Tatini is the restaurant I liked the best, for its charm, its service, and its food. The restaurant is located on the ground floor of a white-brick high-rise apartment building on a tree-lined street in the old and elegant neighborhood of Jardim Paulista.

Many dishes from the selection of more than a hundred on the menu are prepared at tableside. The genial proprietor, Mario Tatini, who gracefully circulates among the tables, came to Brazil from Tuscany. Many of the dishes he creates were inspired by that Italian region.

The last time I ate at Tatini, our meal began with a dozen delicious oysters, grilled on the spit and flavored slightly with bacon ($11). For a second appetizer, we tried the *funghi*, wild mushrooms sautéed in garlic and oil ($8.50). Then came the pasta, a fettuccine bathed in a creamy artichoke sauce ($13); and in lieu of a salad, a crispy arugula crêpe ($11). The pheasant en croûte ($18.50), kept tender and sweet in its light pastry envelope, was one of those memorable main courses that more than surpassed our expecations. The final treat of the meal was a dessert called *sorvete quente* ($6), a delicious concoction of "hot" ice cream with fruit. The waiter prepares a special blend of cold fruits and cognac in a hot chafing dish, and spoons the mixture over fluffy vanilla ice cream. You could die!

MODERATE

ALFAMA DOS MARINHEIROS, Av. Pamplona 1285. Tel. 884-9203.
Cuisine: PORTUGUESE. **Reservations:** Recommended, especially for fado show.
$ Prices: Appetizers $3.50–$14; main courses $8–$24. AE, DC, MC, V.
Open: Tues–Sun 7pm–1am.

For excellent Portuguese-style cuisine, and authentic fado singers straight from the banks of the Tagus in Lisbon, there is the Alfama dos Marinheiros. The broiled seafood platter, in addition to being a beautiful presentation of a fisherman's harvest, is fit for the palate of the most discerning diners. Giant shrimp, *sardinhas* (the Portuguese kind, which are much larger than the variety that gets canned), octopus, squid, and crayfish fill the serving dish to overflowing, at a cost of $36 for two.

Affable proprietor Jerônimo Gomes imports the best fado talent from Portugal. There are fado shows Tuesday through Sunday, beginning after 9pm. You can catch the show over drinks for an artistic cover charge of $10 per person, or have a meal and pay only a $5 cover. Reservations are desirable on show nights.

EDUARDO'S, Rua Nestor Pestana 80, at the Praça Franklin Roosevelt. Tel. 257-0500.
   Cuisine: BRAZILIAN/INTERNATIONAL. **Reservations:** Not needed.
$ Prices: Appetizers $3–$5; main courses $6.50–$12 ($25 for large shrimp). AE, DC, MC, V.
   Open: Daily 11am–6pm.
Two blocks away from the Hilton is Eduardo's, one of those mid-priced, reliable Brazilian luncheon restaurants with a big menu. The Saturday feijoada is only $5.50. Eduardo's has six locations throughout the city.

MEXILHÃO, Rua 13 de Maio 626. Tel. 284-0895.
   Cuisine: SEAFOOD. **Reservations:** Not needed.
$ Prices: Appetizers $3–$12; main courses $5.70–$30. AE, DC, MC, V.
   Open: Lunch daily 11:30am–3pm; dinner daily 6:30pm–1am.
The Mexilhão is a moderately priced seafood restaurant of high repute, located across the street from La Távola. Tanks of live crustaceans greet guests at the door. The average main course costs about $8.50, if you stick to fish. Lobster and shrimp dishes have become luxuries and are priced accordingly.

RUBAYAT, Av. Vieira de Carvalho 166. Tel. 222-8333.
   Cuisine: BARBECUE. **Reservations:** Not needed.
$ Prices: Appetizers $3–$7; main courses $8.75–$21.50. AE, DC, MC, V.
   Open: Lunch daily 11:30am–3pm; dinner daily 6:30pm–midnight.
The Rubayat is a churrascaria, with an accompanying snack bar. The barbecue is not served rodízio style. The restaurant has an attached snack bar with a separate entrance, specializing in salgadinhos.

TAIZAN, Rua Galvão Bueno 554. Tel. 278-9498.
   Cuisine: CHINESE. **Reservations:** Not needed.
$ Prices: Appetizers $1.25–$15; main courses $12.50–$36. AE, DC, MC, V.
   Open: Wed–Mon 11am–11pm.
Taizan has a reputation for both excellent, medium-priced meals and good service. With its red-and-white tiled facade, the restaurant is very visible here in the Japanese quarter. Elaborate, multicourse meals account for the high end of their menu spectrum.

LA TÁVOLA, Rua 13 de Maio 621. Tel. 288-5673.
   Cuisine: ITALIAN. **Reservations:** Not needed.
$ Prices: Appetizers $2–$12; main courses $5–$19. AE, DC, MC, V.
   Open: Lunch daily 11:30am–4pm; dinner daily 6:30pm–1am.
La Távola is a large, lively, and popular restaurant specializing in fresh pasta dishes combined with bits of sausage, beef, olives, vegetables, and herbs. Roast goat is also a favorite, as is *rondelli*—pasta filled with ricotta and mozzarella cheese. Flaming braziers are also much in evidence at La Távola, as waiters energetically put the finishing touches on dishes at tableside. The house red wine is robust and reasonable at $6 a bottle.

BUDGET

FAMÍLIA MANCINI, Rua Avanhandava 81. Tel. 256-4320.
   Cuisine: ITALIAN. **Reservations:** Not needed.
$ Prices: Appetizers $2–$6; main courses $5–$11.50. AE, DC, MC, V.

Open: Lunch daily 11:30am–3pm; dinner daily 5:30pm–midnight.

The Família Mancini is a São Paulo institution among Italian restaurants, also within the orbit of the Hilton Hotel. In this brightly decorated café that suggests a rural cantina, you first serve yourself from the antipasto salad bar (and pay by the weight—75¢ per 100 grams, or 3½ ounces), then order one of the many inexpensive hot dishes.

O GATO QUE RI, Largo do Arouche 37/41. Tel. 221-2699.
  Cuisine: PIZZA/INTERNATIONAL. **Reservations:** Not needed.
$ Prices: Pizza $3.50–$7.50; main courses $3–$4.25. No credit cards.
  Open: Lunch daily 11am–3pm; dinner daily 6pm–midnight.

Near the permanent flower stands is the O Gato Que Ri (The Laughing Cat), one of those wonderful and popular restaurants with white-tile walls and coarse white cotton tablecloths, where you can happily eat what can only be described as the Brazilian equivalent of American diner food. If you had one of these meals at a truck stop, you'd walk away smiling. There are more than 50 varieties of pasta on the menu.

SINO BRASILEIRO, Rua Doutor Alberto Torres 39, in Perdizes. Tel. 67-4653.
  Cuisine: CHINESE. **Reservations:** Not needed.
$ Prices: Appetizers $2–$4; main courses $4–$6. No credit cards.
  Open: Lunch Tues–Sun noon–4:40pm; dinner Tues–Sun 6:30pm–midnight.

Sino Brasileiro offers several regional varieties of Chinese cooking, from the bland and crunchy Cantonese to the fiery Szechuan. The hot-and-sour soup and the double-sautéed pork were excellent, as were the spring rolls and the shrimp with cashews. The restaurant is colorfully decorated, and occupies the downstairs rooms of a large and old stone house, conceivably once the mansion of a prosperous coffee family from the end of the last century.

TORRE DO BEXIGA, Rua 13 de Maio 848. Tel. 289-7364.
  Cuisine: ITALIAN. **Reservations:** Not needed.
$ Prices: Pizza $3.80–$10.50. DC, MC, V.
  Open: Daily 7pm–2am.

On a different scale, but likewise tasty when your mood turns to pizza, is the Torre do Bexiga. Bexiga is the neighborhood for Italian restaurants, fringed with cafés and rock and video clubs that indicate the presence of a local bohemian and youth culture. Pizza at the Torre do Bexiga comes with dozens of unique and imaginative toppings: meats, cheeses, vegetables—and bananas. Pizza with bananas? That's what I said until I tasted it. Delicious!

You won't find the term "Bexiga" on your map, incidentally. The word is a nickname (it means pockmarked!) for the neighborhood that spans parts of Bela Vista and Morro dos Ingleses, and is concentrated primarily on Rua 13 de Maio between Rua Santo Antônio and Avenida Brigadeiro Luís Antônio.

TSUBAKI, in the Nikkey Palace Hotel, Rua Galvão Bueno 425. Tel. 270-1420.
  Cuisine: JAPANESE. **Reservations:** Not required.
$ Prices: Appetizers $2–$5; main courses $4–$25. AE, DC, MC, V.
  Open: Lunch daily 11am–3pm; dinner daily 6pm–midnight.

For Japanese food, try the Tsubaki, downstairs at the Nikkey Palace Hotel. The top sushi platter costs $9, the sashimi about $11. I had tempura soba, a great bowl of beef-noodle soup with a half-dozen big pieces of tempura for $6, including a serving of hot saké. Some of the Tsubaki's special features include a typical Japanese garden, tatami rooms, and a saké service for individuals and groups.

SPECIALTY DINING

LOCAL FAVORITES Bolinha, Av. Cidade Jardim 53 (tel. 852-9526), is said to serve the best feijoada in São Paulo, for $20 per person. It's open daily from 11am to midnight for lunch or dinner.

HOTEL DINING   The Hilton Hotel has an excellent, and reasonably priced restaurant called **The Harvest,** Av. Ipiranga 165 (tel. 256-0033). I have dined well here on several occasions, most recently on trout, which with cocktail and dessert came to less than $15. Also at the Hilton is a chic nightspot called the **London Pub,** where a popular buffet-style feijoada is featured every Saturday.

LIGHT, CASUAL & FAST FOOD   Several Greenwich Village–style coffeehouses are located on Rua 13 de Maio—for example, the **Café do Bexiga** at no. 76 and the nearby **Bar Café Socaite** (tel. 259-6562).

The **Almanara,** Av. Vieira de Carvalho 109, next to the Hotel Bourbon, is a bright-looking Arab fast-food restaurant for Middle-Eastern specialties.

VEGETARIAN FARE   For vegetarian meals in the haute cuisine tradition of the health-food movement, try the **Cheiro Verde,** Rua Peixoto Gomide 1413 (tel. 289-6853). Lunch is served daily from noon to 3pm, and dinner daily from 7 to 10:30pm.

5. ATTRACTIONS

SUGGESTED ITINERARIES

IF YOU HAVE ONE DAY   If that day is Sunday, go to the fairs at the Praça da República and the Praça da Liberdade during the day. If not, go to the Butantã Snake Institute in the morning, and stroll around the Liberdade neighborhood in the afternoon. Find a suitable Asian restaurant for lunch along Liberdade's principal artery, Rua Galvão Bueno. Eat dinner at Tatini, then go to Clyde's or Star Dust for some live music.

IF YOU HAVE TWO DAYS   Spend your first day as recommended above, then, on Day 2, stroll around your hotel's neighborhood in the morning after breakfast to get a sense of the city's layout and street life. If one of your two days is a Saturday, go to either Bolinha or the London Pub (at the Hilton) for the feijoada at lunchtime. In the afternoon, go to the Fundação Maria Luiza e Oscar Americano, a very appealing small art museum. Do Portuguese food for dinner at the Marquês de Marialva or the Alfama dos Marinheiros, and stay to hear the fado singers. Go to a club on the Sambão (Avenida Ibirapuera) after that for a samba workout if you still have the energy.

IF YOU HAVE THREE DAYS   Follow the suggestions above for your first two days. On your third, take the suburban train to the town of Americana, settled by Confederate war veterans (see "A Nearby Attraction," below). When you return in the late afternoon or early evening, sample the Italian fare in the Bexiga for dinner that night.

THE TOP ATTRACTIONS

Ibirapuera Park is a richly endowed and self-contained environment, offering a number of diversions. First of all, it's an immense green zone in a city of concrete. The shimmering leaves from a forest of eucalyptus trees shade acres of well-tended lawns and lakes. Scattered throughout the park are a number of important exhibition halls and popular attractions. São Paulo's biannual art show, the **Bienal**—an art event of international renown—takes place in the **Pereira Pavilion** during odd-numbered years. The **Japanese Pavilion** (open Saturday, Sunday, and holidays; admission 50¢) is an exact replica of Japan's Katsura Palace, and a **Planetarium** (tel. 544-4606) offers weekend shows (reputed to be quite good) at 4, 6, and 8pm, and on Tuesday and Thursday evenings there are also shows at 8pm. The price per entrance is around $1. The **Folklore Museum** (tel. 544-4212), the **Aviation Museum** (tel. 570-3915), and the **Modern Art Museum** (tel. 549-9688) are also on the grounds of the park. Admission for each is between 50¢ and $1.

The **Museu dos Presépios,** formerly in the park and famous for its collection of crèches and Nativity scenes, has now moved to the **Museu de Arte Sacra,** Av. Tiradentes 676 (tel. 227-7694). Free admission.

SÃO PAULO MUSEUM OF ART [MASP], Av. Paulista 1578. Tel. 251-5644.

The great art collections of Brazil are in São Paulo. Art lovers and mavens can take a quick course in Brazilian art at this museum, wherein hang the works of the important Brazilian artists and sculptors, along with a rich selection of work by such masters as Raphael, Velázquez, Rubens, Rembrandt, Hals, Renoir, and Toulouse-Lautrec.

Admission: $1; free on Thurs. Tickets for special exhibitions are higher.
Open: Tues–Fri 1–5pm, Sat–Sun 2–6pm.

FUNDAÇÃO MARIA LUIZA AND OSCAR AMERICANO, Av. Morumbi 3700. Tel. 842-0077.

Examples of the work of two important 20th-century Brazilian painters, Portinari and Di Cavalcanti, can also be seen more intimately at the Fundação Maria Luiza and Oscar Americano, in the neighborhood of Morumbi. This former house of the industrialist/philanthropist Oscar Americano and his socialite wife is today a tidbit-sized museum and park, with several beautiful collections, including first-rate paintings, plates, furnishings, and fascinating memorabilia of the Brazilian royal family.

A small and genteel tearoom serves *chá completo*—black tea with a variety of cakes, for $5.

Admission: $1.
Open: Tues–Fri 11am–5pm, Sat–Sun 10am–5pm.

MUSEU DA CASA BRASILEIRA, Av. Brig. Faria Lima 774. Tel. 210-2564.

The Museu da Casa Brasileira (Museum of the Brazilian Home) is another former mansion, whose collection of furnishings and photographs gives a retrospective view of Brazilian domestic elegance over the centuries.

Admission: Free.
Open: Tues–Sat 1–5pm.

CASA DO BANDEIRANTE, Praça Monteiro Lobato. Tel. 211-0920.

The Casa do Bandeirante (Pioneer House), a short distance from the Butantã Snake Institute, is a re-creation of the rustic and sparsely furnished frontier homestead (with house, outbuildings, and farm equipment) of an 18th-century pioneer family, or *bandeirantes*. The bandeirantes were companies of adventurers, each of which followed a single standard, or *bandeira*. In their quest for mineral wealth and slaves, they explored all of Brazil, and in the earliest times settled the interiors of São Paulo and Minas Gerais.

Admission: Free.
Open: Tues–Sun 9am–5pm.

MUSEU DA IMIGRAÇÃO JAPONESA, Rua São Joaquim 381. Tel. 279-5465.

The small but elegantly designed museum, at the corner of Rua Galvão Bueno, tells the story of the mass Japanese immigration to Brazil that has taken place during much of this century. Look for the home-carved baseball bats!

Admission: 75¢ adults, 50¢ children under 12.
Open: Tues–Sun 1:30–5:30pm.

COOL FOR KIDS

BUTANTÃ SNAKE INSTITUTE, Av. Dr. Vital Brasil 1500, in Butantã. Tel. 211-8211.

One of the favorite sights in all São Paulo, for kids and adults alike, is the Butantã Snake Institute. To be frank, the big attraction seems to be watching the snakes catch

? DID YOU KNOW . . . ?

- São Paulo is Brazil's largest city (third largest in the world), and also the nation's industrial powerhouse.
- São Paulo is the largest Japanese city outside of Japan, and the largest Italian city outside of Italy.
- São Paulo will celebrate its 440th birthday in 1994.
- Independence from Portugal was declared in São Paulo by Brazil's first emperor, Pedro I, with his famous "Cry of Ipiranga."
- The first soccer game in Brazil took place in São Paulo around the turn of the century. The players were British.
- São Paulo's wealth originally came from its coffee plantations; the state is still the largest coffee-exporting entity in the world.
- The Tropic of Cancer passes directly through São Paulo's city limits.

their live prey at feeding time. Small white mice—the really cute kind—circle the snake pits along the walls, stepping over so many motionless snakes as still as garden hoses, until one springs, encircles its prey, and so forth. Antidotes to poisonous snakebites are produced here and are shipped on demand to hospitals around the world. In addition to the snake pit and the lovely tropical grounds, the institute has halls with exhibits, including live and stuffed venomous reptiles, spiders, and tarantulas. The museum is a point of environmental education involving poisonous animals. Its theme is "There are no villains in nature."

Admission: $1 adults, 50¢ children.
Open: Tues–Sun 9am–4:45pm.

A NEARBY ATTRACTION A bit of U.S. Civil War history is preserved about 80 miles from São Paulo in **Americana,** a town founded and settled by Confederate refugees. There are still a number of descendants of the original families, and with many, English is still the language spoken at home. Their cemetery, located about six miles out of town on the Anhanguera highway, is filled with headstones bearing American surnames. Among the contributions to Brazilian culture of the *confederados,* as they were known, were improved agricultural techniques throughout the region, and the introduction of watermelons as a cash crop. *The Last Colony of the Confederacy,* by Eugene C. Harter, published in 1985 by the University Press of the University of Mississippi, is a fascinating account of the trials and tribulations of these defeated Confederates who chose exile in the tropics over life in the postwar South of the Reconstruction period.

ORGANIZED TOURS

The city of São Paulo offers a selection of city bus tours every Sunday. Each three-hour tour visits approximately 40 sites, and is accompanied by several bilingual guides. The buses depart from the Praça da República every half hour between 9:30 and 10:30am. There are also two three-hour **São Paulo Verde** excursions every Sunday departing at 9:30 and 10am from the same locale, which tour the São Paulo parks and greenbelt. Tickets are $1.25 for adults, and 75¢ for children, students, and seniors, and may be purchased at any tourist information post. The central post is on Avenida Ipiranga, near where the buses depart (tel. 267-2122, ext. 640).

6. SPORTS & RECREATION

SPECTATOR SPORTS **Soccer** can be seen at the **Pacaembu Stadium,** Praça Charles Miller s/n (tel. 575-5666, ext. 241), or at the **Morumbi Stadium,** Praça Roberto Gomes Pedrosa s/n (tel. 842-3377). Tickets are between $2 and $5. Check the sports pages of a local newspaper for schedules.

Horse racing takes place Monday, Wednesday, and Thursday at 7:30pm, and Saturday and Sunday at 2:30pm at the **São Paulo Jockey Club,** Av. Lineu de Paula Machado 1263 (tel. 211-4011). Admission is approximately 50¢ and $2 to the clubhouse where there is a restaurant/bar.

Fans of **auto racing** can see some of the best Formula One drivers in the world at the **Interlagos Racetrack,** Av. Sen. Teófilo Vilela 315 (tel. 521-9911). Admission to the track is $5.

RECREATION   **Tennis** buffs can stay at the Hotel Transamérica, which probably has the best courts in the city. Rental facilities also exist, like **Play Ténis** at two locations, Av. Imaraes 923 or Av. Irae 411 (tel. 241-8353). These courts are open Monday through Saturday from 6am to midnight at a fee of $5 per hour. Equipment may be rented, and parking is available.

The best place to **jog** in São Paulo is in **Ibirapuera Park,** entrance off Avenida Pedro Alvares Cabral (tel. 544-2511). The park opens daily from 6am to 10pm. Showers and other sporting facilities are available on the park grounds.

The **São Paulo Golf Club** is a public course whose entrance is at Praça Dom Francisco Souza 540 in the suburb of Santo Amaro (tel. 521-9660). The course is open Monday to Friday from 8am to 6pm, and Saturday and Sunday from 8am to noon.

7. SAVVY SHOPPING

GREAT SHOPPING STREETS   The **Rua do Arouche,** which runs diagonally off the small square Praça da República toward Avenida Ipiranga, is lined with shops selling shoes and leather goods, reportedly at good prices. The chic clothing shops are on **Rua Augusta** (which crosses **Avenida Paulista**), which—if such a scattered urban sprawl as São Paulo can be said to have one—is the city's principal avenue.

FAIRS & MARKETS   The Praça da República hosts a **Crafts Fair** every Sunday from around 8am till late in the afternoon. The major traffic is in gemstones, jewelry, paintings, and leather goods. But there are also dozens of single-item vendors, novelty hawkers, and hurdy-gurdy men with trained birds instead of monkeys. This square is really an elegant little tropical garden, green and shady, full of winding sidewalks which suddenly become bridges and cross small bodies of water. A lot of buying and selling goes on, so there's a real market atmosphere—a very good place to buy souvenirs for yourself and your friends.

One of the more unique gift possibilities I saw here was the attractive and delicate work of **Danilo Blanco,** who makes diminutive boxes and containers from laminated bits of horn and bone, each with its own tiny lid, and often some detail in inlaid wood. Danilo operates his own booth at the fair, but can also be reached at his home phone (tel. 841-1596). The work of a pair of "primitive" painters also caught my eye, **Neuza Leodora** and **Alcides Pinto da Fonseca.** In a field of mediocrity, the equivalent of roadside nudes and Last Suppers in velvet, the individuality and freshness of their respective canvases stood out in bold relief. The couple shares a studio in the suburb of Osasco at Av. Maria Campos 544. To visit them, by appointment, call 702-9712.

The **Oriental Crafts Fair** on the Praça da Liberdade, the heart of the city's Asian neighborhood, is held every Sunday from noon till 10pm. The booths offer a mix of items, from tooled leather belts and bags to practical kitchenware made from wood or bamboo. There are also artists and musicians, and a man who sells very imaginative papier-mâché puppets. The food stands are plentiful and sell an appealing variety of Asian street snacks.

Also in the daytime on Sunday is the **Bexiga Flea Market,** in the Bexiga square. You go to this not so much to buy—though there are many attractive and useful artifacts being recycled—but to experience the urban flea market environment in São Paulo.

A **flower and produce market** is held in Pacaembu Stadium, Praça Charles Miller, every Tuesday, Thursday, Friday, and Saturday. The sights and sounds of a Brazilian open-air food market are an education and a visual treat. Don't be shy about asking someone the name of an unfamiliar fruit or vegetable. You may even be invited to have a taste.

A SPECIAL EMPORIUM   One afternoon while walking in the Jardim América neighborhood, I came upon a very smart-looking boutique, which turned out to be the retail outlet for a small manufacturer of perfumes, soaps, and bathing lotions. Not that I know much about such commodities, but to be frank, what initially impressed me was the packaging and presentation of the products. As it turns out, the beauty line of the **Empório Nacional,** Rua Pinheiros 650 (tel. 881-0088), is well regarded in the local fashion world, and indeed, the items I purchased there as gifts were highly praised by the recipients.

A FAVORITE BOOKSTORE   Near Avenida Ipiranga, I stumbled onto a bookstore that has a branch I am familiar with in downtown Rio, known for its fine hardbacks, art volumes, and old prints. At the São Paulo **Kosmos,** Av. São Luís 162 (tel. 258-3244), I was impressed with several colorful and quality printed works on Brazilian wildlife, including a book entitled *Birds of Brazil;* the fact that the Kosmos had a few copies of *Frommer's Brazil* on their shelves also did not pass unnoticed.

A STOP FOR SWEET TOOTHS   **Brunella** is the name of a sweetshop that is on the lips of many Paulistas. The chain—soon to open a branch in Miami—fabricates 70 types of gooey delectables daily. One conveniently located store is on Av. Imaraes 268 (tel. 240-6248), behind the Ibirapuera Shopping Center.

8. EVENING ENTERTAINMENT

THE PERFORMING ARTS

The principal venue for symphonic music, ballet, and opera, in season, is the **Teatro Municipal,** Praça Ramos de Azevedo s/n, modeled on a theater in Paris, and recently renovated. Free concerts are often performed at the **Memorial da América Latina,** Rua Mario de Andrade 664 (tel. 823-9611). Theater and cabaret are alive and well in São Paulo. For current listings, consult the monthly tourism magazine, *São Paulo This Month,* available at tourist information counters and in most hotels.

THE CLUB & MUSIC SCENE

RUA FRANZ SCHUBERT

On this small street, about 200 yards in length, six of São Paulo's most popular nightclubs are to be found, including **Kremlin, Tramp,** the **Cotton Club,** and **Marco Polo.** The other two are described below.

LIMELIGHT, Rua Franz Schubert 93. Tel. 210-7892.
   To enter São Paulo's hottest disco at the moment, you must be very presentable, if not dazzling, to get by the platoon of bouncers in black tie who scrutinize all supplicants from their side of the roped-off sidewalk. Such is the tribute extracted from those who want to be seen with all the others who want to be seen at the apex of the nighttime social whirl. Open Tuesday through Saturday from 9pm until the last dancer on the floor has to be shot at dawn. Tuesday and Wednesday are singles nights; otherwise couples only.
   Admission: Tues–Fri $11, Sat $13.

STAR DUST, Rua Franz Schubert 135. Tel. 210-5283.
   This is the chic club that caters to the over-40 dance-band set. Star Dust has all the overtones of a New York nightclub from the fifties and early sixties. A full supper menu is available, sole Véronique ($17), a sole filet in a grape-and-almond sauce being the dish most requested. Your host and head piano man, Alan, is a most interesting chap, a White Russian Jew brought up in China, having migrated to Brazil 35 years ago via Tel Aviv. No singles. Open Tuesday through Saturday from 8pm to 4am.

Admission: Tues–Thurs $8.50, Fri–Sat $11.50.

JARDIM AMÉRICA

Another cluster of clubs and discotheques can be found within the confines of the Jardim América neighborhood, some of which are exclusively singles spots on designated nights of the week.

HOUSE, Rua Manoel Guedes 110. Tel. 883-7041.
A second-floor piano bar and restaurant separate the disco on the first floor, featuring golden rock oldies, from that on the third floor where the sound is acid rock, with MTV videos as a sidelight. Open Wednesday through Saturday from 11pm to 4am.
Admission: $4.

ROCK DREAMS, Alameda Tiete 580. Tel. 883-1707.
Rock Dreams, a London-style pub with a 1950s decor, opens Tuesday through Sunday from 7:30pm to 2am. The bill of fare is rock, soft, hard, and everything in between. Also known for its good sandwiches.
Admission: Fri–Sat $12.50, other nights $7.50.

ST. PAUL, Alameda Lorena 1717. Tel. 282-7697.
The St. Paul, which is closed Sunday and Monday, caters to three separate crowds during the week: over-30s on Thursday, younger singles on Tuesday and Wednesday, and couples on Friday and Saturday. The scene starts late, the bar is always crowded, and a supper menu is available.
Admission: Tues–Wed $4; Thurs $12 for men, $8 for women; Fri–Sat $8.

OTHER NIGHTLIFE AREAS

Avenida Ibirapuera, between República do Líbano (which runs along one side of Ibirapuera Park) and Avenida dos Bandeirantes, is strictly for after dark. A string of bars and clubs, like **Moema Samba,** at no. 2124 (tel. 549-3744), line the avenue. Most feature (generally) live samba music. The scene is dancing—these are not the honky-tonk shows with scantily clad mulatto beauties.
There are also goings-on after dark in the **Bexiga,** which offers options from coffee shops to video theaters to punk-rock clubs.

THE BAR SCENE

Scores of bars in São Paulo provide ports of call for neighborhood denizens and after-work encounters. Here's a small sampling of the city's watering spots.

CLYDE'S, Rua da Mata 70. Tel. 883-0300.
Clyde's is presumably patterned after its infamous namesake on M Street in Georgetown, Washington, D.C., from whose bar the author of this guide once plied the local worthies with such libations as were then in fashion during the early sixties.
This Clyde's, primarily a singles bar, might provide an oasis in São Paulo for nostalgic Yanks who want a bowl of two-beer chili or a slice of apple pie to offset the occasional feijoada.
There is live music every day of the week after 9:30pm, which sometimes passes as a reasonable facsimile of Willie Nelson and Co. Open daily from 6pm to 4am; happy hour is 6 to 9pm Monday through Friday. There's a $3 cover charge.

SPAZIO PIRANDELLO, Rua Augusta 311. Tel. 256-5245.
Newly remodeled with a large collection of mirrors, and under new management, the café of preference for the city's intellectuals is Spazio Pirandello, near the São Paulo Hilton, and practically on top of the Ca'd'Oro Hotel. Here you are likely to rub elbows with luminaries from among the local stars of stage and screen, or out-of-work college professors at work on their umpteenth unpublished novel. Open

Tuesday through Sunday from 8pm to 3am. Closed between December 23 and January 3.

VICTORIA PUB, Alameda Lorena 1604. Tel. 881-3822.
  Enjoying more than 10 years of success as an after-work hangout is this English-style bar, the Victoria Pub, open Monday through Saturday after 8pm. Getting in will cost you $3 a head, and the minimum consumption is $5 per person.

FOR GAY WOMEN

SEGREDUS, Rua Santo Antônio 922. Tel. 259-2492.
  Not far from the Spazio Pirandello is the unassuming storefront facade of Segredus, a lesbian nightspot charging a modest $2.50 for minimum consumption, with a nightly floor show of dancers and transvestites. Open Friday through Sunday from 11:30pm to 5 or 6am.

9. AN EXCURSION TO A MOUNTAIN RETREAT IN CAMPOS DO JORDÃO

When Paulistanos want fresh air and cooler temperatures, they don't have to go far. The environs of São Paulo are mountainous, and the majestic Serra Mar (Ocean Range) runs the length of the state's coastline, making any trip to the sea an excursion through the mountains as well. A favorite inland mountain spa, however—both during the summer vacation months of mid-December through February, and in the winter school-holiday month of July—is Campos do Jordão, about a two-hour car ride from São Paulo heading east along the BR 116 highway toward Rio. The three-hour bus ride from São Paulo costs about $2.

July is the coldest month in Campos do Jordão, when the mercury frequently hovers at the frost line overnight but warms up to a comfortable afternoon temperature of 50°F to 60°F on many days. Visually, this resort town is not so unlike its counterparts in New England, though architecturally it copies the alpine style, reflecting the European origins of many of its inhabitants. Narrow, winding roads climb the surrounding peaks, revealing around every curve the drive of a fine hotel or, at roadside, a chalet-style inn, all set among the towering evergreens of a dense conifer forest. By late March the few hardwood trees—mostly maples seemingly so out of place in this country of predominantly tropical vegetation—already display autumnal coloring and cover small patches of ground everywhere with their fallen leaves.

Campos do Jordão is entered through a formal portal which opens into the town's commercial center. Beyond this neighborhood, called Abernéssia, are the more swank sections of Juaguaribe and Capivari, where most of the shops, boutiques, and restaurants are located. Local crafts include products of the *malha* cottage industry—handmade pullovers and cardigans, a reminder of the town's frequent sweater-weather climate. But the greatest resource of the town is its pure mountain air, kept crisp and healthy at its protected mile-high altitude.

For further information, or to make reservations for Campos do Jordão directly in São Paulo, call **Campostur,** Rua 7 de Abril 404, 6th floor (tel. 0122/255-1156).

WHAT TO SEE & DO

The **Festival de Inverno** (Winter Carnival) occupies the entire month of July each year, when special events and festivities are scheduled for every day. Classical musicians flock to Campos do Jordão in July, and chamber music concerts are a big part of the scene.

The **Parque Florestal** is located in a remote corner of the town, along a mountain dirt road where cows graze freely among the trees on forested hillsides. The park has a trout hatchery, and many of these speckled beauties can be seen swimming in the local streams. There is also a working water-powered sawmill, and many separate picnic environments. You can rent horses at a stable near the park's entrance, and the local terrain and relatively open woods seem ideal for riding. Hiking and backpacking are also popular pastimes in the surrounding countryside.

The town also has a **mountain train** that makes hour-long excursions to a nearby village lower down the slopes, São José dos Campos.

A ski lift off a main square carries interested sightseers to a local mountaintop, the **Morro do Elefante,** for a panoramic view of the town and the surrounding Paraiba valley.

WHERE TO STAY

There are more than 50 hotels of differing categories in the region. Most include full board with their rates, so guests tend to eat "at home" while in Campos do Jordão.

Authorization to stay in the local youth hostel, the **Casa Azul,** may be obtained through the tourist office at the bus station.

EXPENSIVE

HOTEL E RESTAURANT VILA REGINA, Av. Emilio Lang Júnior 443, Campos do Jordão. Tel. 0122/63-1036. 28 rms. MINIBAR TV TEL
$ Rates (including full board): $105 double. AE, MC.
The Vila Regina is typical of the mid-range inns in Campos do Jordão, with modern and comfortable rooms. The restaurant is decorated hunting-lodge style, and specializes in baked trout along with a host of other international and Italian dishes. As an apéritif, try a Negroni—a cocktail made from sweet vermouth, Campari, and gin, served ice cold with a lemon wedge. You may ask for a refill.

OROTUR GARDEN HOTEL, Rua Sen. Roberto Simonsen 231, Campos do Jordão. Tel. 0122/62-1078. Telex 122/329. 61 rms. MINIBAR TV TEL
$ Rates (including full board): $154 double. AE, DC, MC.
The Orotur Garden Hotel has long been a watering hole of an elite clientele from São Paulo. This is a first-class establishment, nestled in the hills in a gorgeous setting. The table d'hôte may be the best in town.

VILA INGLESA, Rua Sen. Roberto Simonsen 3500, Campos do Jordão. Tel. 0122/63-1955. Fax 0122/63-2699. Telex 122/399. 54 rms. MINIBAR TV TEL
$ Rates (including full board): $147 double. AE, DC.
The Vila Inglesa is Campos do Jordão's other deluxe mountain spa. Rooms here are homey and have all the comforts. The hotel's kitchen is also reputed to serve up good and varied dishes.

BUDGET

CANTINHO DE PORTUGAL, Rua Alexandre Sirim 127, Campos do Jordão. Tel. 0122/63-2449. 23 rms (all with bath). MINIBAR TV
$ Rates (including continental breakfast): $25–$35 double. No credit cards.
This large Bavarian-style structure sits by the side of the road on the outskirts of town. The digs are very comfortable. The Cantinho is the best bet for bargain hunters.

WHERE TO DINE

Trout and fondue are the food specialties of the region. The **Só Queijo,** Av. Macedo Soares 642 (tel. 63-1910), is an attractive restaurant in a colonial-style building, which in addition to the regional specialties, also serves crêpes and steaks.

Willy's Confeitaria, Av. Macedo Soares 183 (tel. 63-1015), has an informal café atmosphere, and serves meals and desserts.

For French cuisine there is the **Casa d'Irene,** Rua Raul Mesquita 83 (tel. 63-1115), offering pâté maison, escargot, rabbit, and steak au poivre.

10. AN EXCURSION TO THE SEASHORE

UBATUBA

A logical place to visit after a stay in Campos do Jordão, especially for those touring independently by car or bus, is the coastal town of Ubatuba. The drive down the winding sierra to the shore at this point—via Taubaté and São Luís do Paraitinga— can be an unforgettable journey. Especially beyond this latter town, the roads curve through the hills like spirals, and become as narrow as logging trails in places. A perpetual mist hangs in these mountains, further slowing your forward progress to the pace of a caravan. After some three hours of occasionally breathtaking descent, you reach a flat coastal strip with 73 beaches, all incorporated into the municipal sphere of a resort town called Ubatuba.

The myriad beaches stretch over a distance of 72km (45 miles) in both directions from Ubatuba, which has a year-round population of 35,000. The word *ubatuba,* incidentally, is indigenous and literally means "place where the shafts grow," referring to the poles used by the earlier inhabitants to fashion their fishing spears. During Carnival—which always falls during the week before the Catholic penitential season of Lent—Ubatuba's population swells to some 400,000 souls. All these visitors during this particular time of the year, the majority of whom hail from Rio and São Paulo, come for the same singular reason: to escape Carnival. Clearly, Brazilians are not universally fond of their national festival.

By the same token, the Carnival time is not the time for foreign visitors to visit Ubatuba, which can be better appreciated as an off-season resort, when the vacation crowds have diminished and the hotel rates plummet to half of what is charged during the high season—December through February, and in July.

WHAT TO SEE & DO

You could spend your entire time in Ubatuba trying to figure out which of the 73 beaches is the most perfect according to your own criteria. If, however, the sun should fail you on a given day, or if your peripatetic rhythms prevent you from staying prone in the tanning position for more than a few hours at a time, there are a number of touring and activity options which might appeal.

Of historical interest is the colonial-era town of **Paraty** (see Chapter 7, "Excursions from Rio," for a more detailed description of this town), only 70km (43 miles) up the coast toward Rio. There are a number of **ruins** in the area: an old coffee plantation's slave quarters, Brazil's first glass factory, and a fort built at the turn of the century on nearby Anchieta Island, now a wildlife sanctuary, a 10-minute boat ride from the mainland.

A full range of **aquatic sports** from skindiving to sailing are also available. The tourist agency **Ubatur,** Rua Flamenguinho 17, on the Saco da Ribeira beach (tel. 0124/42-0388), offers tours, schooner excursions, equipment, and a boat, and car-rental services.

WHERE TO STAY

As with many Brazilian resort areas, you have the option of staying close to the center of activity or in relative seclusion, according to the dictates of your mood and constitution.

HOTEL VILLAGE TROPICAL, at the edge of Enseada beach, Ubatuba. Tel. 0124/42-0055. 24 rms. A/C MINIBAR TV TEL
$ Rates (including breakfast): In season $70 single, $78 double; off-season $30 single, $35 double. No credit cards.
The two-story building has interior courtyards and open-air corridors filled with plants, like a Brazilian ranchhouse. There is also a beautifully planted *quintal* (yard) between the hotel and the beach, but no pool.

MEDITERRÂNEO, Enseada beach, Ubatuba. Tel. 0124/42-0112. Fax 0124/42-0535. Telex 124/743. 30 rms. A/C MINIBAR TV TEL
$ Rates (including breakfast): $54–$108 single; $60–$120 double. No credit cards.
The Mediterrâneo is true to its name, architecturally speaking. The grand white facade with the awninged windows is certainly imbued with a look of the European Riviera. Set against verdant riding hills and surrounded by tropical vegetation and lawns, the hotel looks out over the breathtaking sea. Steps from a large story-high terrace with a pool lead down to the beach, where tables, chairs, and umbrellas have been placed for the convenience of guests. The hotel restaurant serves lunch and dinner, with meat courses averaging $11 to $12, fish courses from $10 to $13, and shrimp dishes around $17.

TORREMOLINOS, Rua Domingos Della Mónica Barbosa 37, at Enseada beach, Ubatuba. Tel. 0124/42-0625. Fax 0124/42-0600. Telex 124/771. 37 rms. A/C MINIBAR TV TEL
$ Rates: $70 single; $80 double. AE, DC, MC, V.
One choice for a remote, resort-style hotel is the Torremolinos. This modern, three-story beachfront hotel has the look of a Frank Lloyd Wright original. Most of the brightly decorated rooms face the ocean and open onto small balconies. Two pools—one for adults, the other for children—and a large tiled patio area with chaise lounges and umbrellas, separate the hotel from the sandy beach. The hotel has a restaurant and a poolside snack bar, and is about a 15-minute car ride from Ubatuba.

UBATUBA PALACE HOTEL, Rua Coronel Domiciano 500, Ubatuba. Tel. 0124/32-1500, or 011/280-8496 in São Paulo for reservations. Telex 124/741. 59 rms. A/C MINIBAR TV TEL
$ Rates (including half board): In season $90–$100 double; off-season $25 per person. AE, DC, MC, V.
The in-town hotel of choice has to be the Ubatuba Palace. This venerable hotel is a block from the Avenida das Praias, the town's principal oceanfront thoroughfare, where the evening promenade takes place and where nightlife is centered in the avenue's many cafés, restaurants, and beer gardens.
The rooms at the Ubatuba Palace all have deep-green louvered doors, and front on common balconies which offer a view of the town. Furnishings are comfortable and attractive in a *fazenda* (ranchhouse) style, right down to the pious placement of crucifixes over the queen-size beds. The hotel's several two-room suites are huge, with private balconies.
It will require no hardship to eat in the Ubatuba Palace dining room, where the food, ranging in price from $6 to $15 à la carte, is of genuine gourmet quality. The shrimp crêpe, with its creamy sauce, will melt in your mouth. The hotel also offers a very attractive pool and lounging area, and a steam room.
Surrounding this hotel is a warren of small streets filled with craft shops and stores of every variety, laid out among the obligatory church-dominated plazas and small parks. The overall effect of municipal Ubatuba, however, is of an informal beach town where people in bathing costumes are in a constant parade either toward or away from the beachfront.

SANTOS & GUARUJÁ

Santos, located about 45 miles from São Paulo, is Brazil's largest and most active port city. Traditionally Santos, and now the nearby island of **Guarujá,** have been the principal beach resorts for the landlocked Paulistanos. Practically every weekend, the season and weather permitting, the urbanites flee São Paulo in droves and head for the beach, by car, train, bus, and even plane. Santos—one of Brazil's wealthiest cities, if somewhat industrialized—has the most modern facilities. In recent years, however, visitors have departed the in-town beaches of Santos for the more pristine strands of neighboring Guarujá. Buses leave regularly from the downtown bus station, and a free passenger ferry connects Santos with Guarujá, and buses shuttle bathers from there to the various beaches.

CHAPTER 11

THE SOUTH

Iguaçu Falls is the second most popular destination for North American travelers in Brazil after Rio de Janeiro. No wonder! The falls are truly one of the world's great natural phenomena, and are understandably the main attraction in Brazil's southern region, but by no means the only one. Southern Brazil is totally distinct in its population, climate, geography, history, and culture from the rest of the country. The three states of Paraná, Santa Catarina, and Rio Grande do Sul are located along Brazil's most active border with its Spanish-speaking neighbors, touching as a whole the frontiers of Paraguay, Argentina, and Uruguay. Generations of conflict and several wars were fought before the existing boundaries of the region were agreed upon, as Uruguay was finally created by compromise as a buffer between South America's largest and most powerful nations, Brazil and Argentina.

The early settlers here, Spaniards and Portuguese, alternately lived in peaceful coexistence and fought each other for control of the territory, while the Jesuits built dozens of missions to protect the native peoples from annihilation and enslavement by both parties. The ruins of these missions in the Sete Povos district of Rio Grande, and Missiones in Argentina, are a striking testament to this historical period. To strengthen their hold in the south, the Portuguese further colonized the area with former mercenaries from their armies who came from the Azores Islands. These later arrivals mixed with the earlier Spanish and Portuguese settlers and formed the bedrock of the *gaucho* culture as it exists today. And while the Spanish presence in southern Brazil is now somewhat invisible, the influence can still be felt, especially when the population is compared with that of Brazil's other regions. During the 19th century great waves of German and Italian immigrants settled throughout the south. They, too, have left a strong mark on the region. Today their descendants are fully assimilated as Brazilians, and yet many families, particularly the Germans, remain bilingual and retain other cultural characteristics, notably their work ethic and a preference for alpine-style architecture.

Southern Brazil is both agrarian and industrial, prosperous, and highly developed. Modern cities are centers of textile and shoe manufacturing. Great expanses of prairie lands, *pampas*, primarily in Rio Grande do Sul, nourish the herds of cattle that provide the nation's main source of beef. Grains, soybeans, and coffee are grown in abundance throughout the region, both on small, private holdings and on enormous tenant-farmed estates. The interiors of Paraná and Santa Catarina are heavily forested, and home to Brazil's pulp and paper industries, while among the eastern hills of Rio Grande do Sul the viticulture brought a century ago by the Italians flourishes, and today produces wine for all Brazil. As with the coastal lands to the north, the mountain range known as the Great Escarpment accompanies the shoreline, never far from the sea. But in the south the climate is temperate; frosts are frequent during the winter, but snow is rare. Summer, from November through May, is warm and dry along the shore, and humid in the subtropical interior.

WHAT'S SPECIAL ABOUT SOUTHERN BRAZIL

Beaches
- ☐ The Ilha de Santa Catarina, occupied in part by the city of Florianópolis, is home to some of the most popular resort beaches in Brazil.

Events/Festivals
- ☐ The Brazilian Film Festival, held every March in the Rio Grande do Sul town of Gramado.
- ☐ The *Festa da Uva* (Wine Festival), celebrated in February or early March in towns throughout Rio Grande do Sul's wine region, like Bento Gonçalves and Caxias do Sul.

Monuments
- ☐ The ruins of seven colonial mission villages, on Rio Grande do Sul's western border with Argentina.

Natural Spectacles
- ☐ One of the country's most spectacular natural settings, Iguaçu Falls.

- ☐ The little-visited canyon of Itaimbezinho.
- ☐ The stretch of Atlantic forest between Curitiba and the coastal port city of Paranaguá—a vast, magnificently beautiful ecological preserve and outdoor recreation resource.

Regional Food
- ☐ A not-to-be-missed regional dish called *barreado*, found only in the coastal region south of Curitiba, in towns like Morretes and Antonina.
- ☐ On the Ilha de Santa Catarina many restaurants serve a meal called *sequência de camarão*—a round-robin of shrimp dishes.
- ☐ Shrimp caught near Florianópolis, just about the best in all Brazil.

1. IGUAÇU FALLS

390 miles W of Curitiba; 205 miles E of Asunción, Paraguay

GETTING THERE By Plane The falls are such a popular attraction—at least on the Brazilian side—that there is an international **airport** near Foz do Iguaçu receiving several daily 1¾-hour flights from Rio, via São Paulo, and from other points within Brazil as well. Round-trip airfare from Rio, for those who do not have a VARIG Air Pass, is approximately $310. A smaller airport on the Argentine side handles that country's domestic flights. There is regular service from Buenos Aires, and the flying time is an hour and a half. If all goes according to plan, a new international airport on the outskirts of Ciudad del Este, Paraguay, will be in full operation by 1994.

By Bus There is frequent bus service to Foz do Iguaçu from all major metropolitan centers throughout Brazil. The trip from Rio takes 23 hours, from Curitiba 12 hours. For those who wish to continue on to Asunción by land, regular bus service is also available. The trip takes about 4½ hours, with an additional two-hour delay for border crossing. Make sure that you have the appropriate documentation and visas if you wish to travel in Argentina or Paraguay beyond the border towns.

By Car BR 116 runs all the way from Rio, via São Paulo, to Curitiba. From there, motorists to Foz do Iguaçu may travel BR 277, while those heading south to Santa Catarina or Rio Grande do Sul will follow either BR 116, for the inland route, or BR 101 along the coast.

ESSENTIALS In the city of Foz do Iguaçu, the Argentine Consul maintains offices at Travessa Eduardo Bianchi 26 (tel. 74-2877), and the Paraguayan Consul, at Rua Bartolomeo de Gusmão 480 (tel. 72-1169). The city of Foz also maintains a **tourist**

information center—FOZTUR, at Rua Almirante Barroso 1065 (tel. 74-2196), and a special three-digit *teletur* number (139) for information, suggestions, and complaints.

Rising from an obscure spring on the outskirts of Curitiba, capital of Paraná state, the Iguaçu River flows from the high coastal plateau 4,000 feet above sea level, not immediately toward the nearby Atlantic, but inland, seeking the great valley that drains the Andes watershed to the south, merging its waters first with the mighty Paraná and ultimately with the Plata far to the south. The Iguaçu winds along its westerly course for nearly 800 river miles, and is fed by many streams hardly more impressive than that of its own source. As the Iguaçu approaches the Paraná, the final stretch of the river forms a border between Brazil and Argentina, cutting through the last great expanse of Atlantic rain forest that remains in South America. On both sides of the border, the forest—over 500,000 acres in all—has been converted to national park lands, providing a preserve for more than 2,000 varieties of vegetation and habitat for a large population of native fauna, including 400 bird species and innumerable reptiles and insects. The awesome beauty and power of the forest cannot be deducted from a mere census of its animal and plant life, which meld into a visual symphony of color, texture, and sound that has to be experienced to be felt and appreciated.

About seven miles above its mouth (*foz*), the Iguaçu widens its bed to a span of some two miles, and here drops precipitously over a 200-foot-high cliff, forming an interconnected curtain of 275 cataracts. Mist rises from the bottom like boiling steam, and more than one moistened rainbow hovers in midair between the river bottom and the wide, curly lip of the enormous basin. Andorinhos, related to the sparrow, flock like pigeons throughout the canyon, and dart behind the sheets of falling water to perches on the rocky walls where they make their nests. There is something primordial, if not timeless, in the contrast between the placid upper river against its silent backdrop, the lush rain forest, and the naked, rocky canyon of the river below, seething with agitation from the tons of fallen water.

As the end approaches, the river achieves its moment of glory with an unanticipated and thunderous crescendo, only to be absorbed a few miles downstream in meek submission by the dominating currents of the much larger Paraná. During its last seven miles, the once-proud Iguaçu, having shed its dazzling forest plumage, is paraded like the condemned past the tawdry border towns and frontier markers of three nations—Argentina, Brazil, and Paraguay—which seem to mock both the river's moment of greatness and its ignominious end.

There is a primary distinction between the Brazilian and Argentine vistas of the Iguaçu Falls. Since most of the cataracts are on the Argentina side, the Brazilian view is more sweeping, more panoramic. Keep in mind that the full expanse of the falls is nearly 1½ miles in width. Only from the air, moreover, can all 275 cataracts that line the curving wall of the upper river be seen. The greater your distance from the falls, the more remote and abstract they appear, and their drama diminishes correspondingly. This is not to say that the falls seen from the Brazilian side are devoid of dramatic detail. Hardly! But the system of catwalks and paths on the Argentina side provides the visitor with a powerfully intimate experience, as you follow the outline of the river wall, alternately walking from the edge of one cataract to another. Each view has its compelling validity; and so both must be experienced for you to claim you have really seen the Iguaçu Falls.

By far the most appealing of the three border towns is **Foz do Iguaçu** on the Brazilian side. Over the past decade Foz (as the town is called by locals) has grown in population from about 40,000 to 200,000 inhabitants, a boom resulting from the construction of the Itaipú Dam, the world's largest hydroelectric power station. A survey of the city's hotels, restaurants, and other attractions follows. On the Paraguayan side is **Ciudad del Este,** about which there is also more to say below. **Puerto Iguazu,** on the Argentinian side, is a town very much in formation, given a boost by the inauguration of a new bridge linking the town with the Brazilian mainland.

The word *iguaçu* means "great waters" in the Guarani language, a prosaic understatement to say the least. The first European credited with having seen the falls was the Spaniard Don Alvar Nuñez Cabeza de Vaca, who in 1541 led an expedition from the coast of what is currently Santa Catarina state in Brazil to what is now Asunción in Paraguay. The redoubtable hidalgo (whose last name translates as Señor Cow's Head) rechristened the wonder as the Falls of Santa Maria, but the Guarani name has held firm.

Earlier in this century the pioneer Brazilian aviator Alberto Santos Dumont mounted a wooden tower to better observe the phenomenon. To reassure his nervous hosts—who owned the Brazil side of the falls at that time, but would have never dreamed of doing anything quite so bold as their guest—the melancholy Dumont cracked what was probably the only joke of his life, saying, "Heights don't intimidate me."

Eleanor Roosevelt is another historical personage whose reaction on first seeing the falls is much quoted. Moved no doubt by feelings of loyalty to her native New York, the First Lady was heard to muse, "Poor Niagara."

The Iguaçu Falls have a wet season and a dry season. The rains fall in the winter months, April through July, and so the volume of water crashing over the cliffs is greatest during that season, and the weather is mild, though it can be quite chilly in the vicinity of the falls themselves. During the autumn and summer months the temperatures climb to their subtropical warmest, with humidity and mosquitoes to match, and the water flow is cut by a third during the driest periods. In 1977 the falls dried up for the only time in recorded history. And in 1983 the flooding was so severe that much of the vegetation surrounding the cataracts, as well as a network of catwalks that allows visitors a spectacular close-up view of the falls from numerous vantage points, was completely destroyed. Many moviegoers learned of Iguaçu for the first time in 1986 when they saw *The Mission,* which was filmed on the Argentine side.

Finally, a note on pronunciation. The accent at the bottom of the letter *c* in Iguaçu is called a *cedilha* (cedilla in Spanish). This letter always precedes the vowels *a, o,* or *u,* and is pronounced like an *s.* On occasion Brazilians employ the spelling Iguassú. The double *s* in Portuguese is also pronounced like a so-called soft *s.*

WHAT TO SEE & DO

To view the falls and the region's other sights at a comfortable pace, a visit of at least two, and preferably three days is recommended. The first two days can be spent getting to know the falls from the Brazilian side, with side-trip excursions to the Itaipú Dam, the town of Foz do Iguaçu, and possibly Ciudad del Este, formerly Puerto Stroessner, in Paraguay. The final day can then be reserved for a visit to the Argentine side, where you will want to spend a minimum of four to five hours wandering the various paths and catwalks both above and below the falls. The trip to and from the Argentine side will also consume a certain amount of time, which is why a full day is suggested for this excursion.

THE BRAZILIAN SIDE

GETTING THERE Let's assume that you will be arriving at the international airport and staying at one of the dozens of hotels located in or around Foz do Iguaçu. By way of orientation, the airport sits at about the midpoint between the falls and the city, which are linked by a modern highway and are 16 miles apart. In addition to **taxis,** which will carry you to the city for about $12, there is a **local bus,** which costs only 25¢, but the driver will refuse to take you if you are loaded down with baggage. During the high season—the summer months and the July winter school holiday—buses run hourly from 8am to 6pm between the city bus terminal (on Avenida Juscelino Kubitschek) and the falls. In the off-season buses run every two hours. The one-way fare is about 30¢, plus an additional $2 to enter the **Parque Nacional do Iguaçu** (Iguaçu National Park). Operating hours for the park are 8am and 7pm. Keep in mind that the park entrance is still a good five miles from the area where the falls can be viewed. Some buses stop at the entrance to the park, while others continue on to the falls.

The tour of the Brazilian falls can very easily be self-guided. There is no need to incur the extra expense of a special agency tour. Spend the extra money on cab fare, if you want the most convenient transportation; for an added $3 per hour the driver will even wait for you.

THE PARK MUSEUM   A brief visit to the museum, especially for those who wish to learn something of the forest's ecosystem, is worthwhile. Displays include cases of stuffed fauna native to the forest, including the *tamanduá,* a tropical anteater; the tapir, the largest of the South American mammals, weighing more than 600 pounds (they resemble a swine, but are related to the rhinoceros); the paca, a large spotted rodent, also known as the water hare; as well as innumerable bird species, the most striking of which is the tucano with its curved beak and its cobalt-blue eyes. A separate room contains wood samples culled from the forest's many varieties of trees. The wood of the *pinheiro,* the giant pine of southern Brazil, is notable for its orange tint, strength, and lack of knots along the trunk, as the leafy growth, like that of a coconut palm, is confined in mature trees only to the crown. Placards and photographs document the history of the falls, though legends are only in Portuguese. There are some striking photos from the 1977 drought and the 1983 floods.

THE BRAZILIAN VIEW OF THE FALLS   A clearly marked stairway opposite the famous Hotel das Cataratas leads to a mile-long path that accompanies the river upstream. This walk offers a spectacular view of the falls across the lower river, which has narrowed at this point to channel width. The high ground to the land side is matted with dense forest growth, and if you're lucky (as was I, getting a good look at a colorful paca), you may sight a creature or two flitting through the underbrush. As you walk, a wider and wider horizon of crashing waters opens to view, until you reach the end of the trail near a tall elevator tower. The descent has been gradual, with many viewing stations along the way, but here you are actually below the first step of the Brazilian falls. A screened-in catwalk set on stone pillars leads through clouds of boiling mists to the very rim of a lower cataract, and the view here is a breathtaking experience. Depending on the time of year, you can expect to be soaked or merely dampened while walking on this catwalk. During steamy weather, the shower can be welcome and refreshing; otherwise, bring rain gear or rent an outfit from the enterprising vendors along the trail. The elevator lifts you back to road level. Before leaving the tower, however, the energetic may climb a metal ladder, hand over hand, to a viewing platform for a final appreciation of the wide canyon, and the "great waters" of the Iguaçu.

ORGANIZED TOURS   Once on the roadway you will see a stand operated by **Helisul,** offering seven-minute overflights of the falls by helicopter. The fee is roughly $38, slightly less if you pay in cruzeiros, assuming you have exchanged at a favorable parallel-market rate. Farther up the road is a concession offering **boat rides** on the upper river, which operates only under favorable conditions, depending on weather and volume of water.

Buses for the return trip to Foz leave from a nearby parking area, or you can return along the road, by foot, for refreshments at the Hotel das Cataratas and a walk around the spacious grounds. Be sure to notice the statue of Alberto Santos Dumont near the trail's end. The inscription on the pedestal implies that Petitsantos himself, the patron saint of Brazilian aviation, deserves credit for the idea of removing the lands surrounding Iguaçu from private hands and converting them into a public trust.

A 1½-hour-long guided tour of the forest environment is offered by a private company, Ilhado Sol Turismo (tel. 74-4224; fax 0455/74-4717). Their concession, **Macuco Boat Safari,** is located beyond the park entrance going toward the falls. The 1½-mile (2.5-km) walk through the woods terminates at the edge of the river and includes a boat ride in the vicinity of the nearest falls. Unlike federal parks in the U.S. and Canada, access to the lands of the Iguaçu Park is limited. You cannot just walk about at will, but must have special permits or be accompanied by a park official. No camping, fishing, or hunting is allowed in the park. The Macuco tour is one of the few easily available means for actually penetrating, however superficially, the interior of the preserve.

The tour is highly recommended, moreover, not only for this opportunity to intimately experience a fragment of the fabled Atlantic forest, but for the boat ride that provides a thrilling climax to the excursion. To be truthful, when my party climbed aboard the aluminum skiff, I did not expect more than a gentle cruise on the river below the falls, one perhaps that offered a squinting view of the crashing waters still far upstream. Fortunately, the guides who steer these craft, propelled by powerful outboards, are quite skilled. As we approached the falls—nowhere within view I might add—the water began to fever into powerful, corrugated swells. Suddenly, all hands, seasoned salts and brave souls alike, gripped the gunwales for dear life, as the boatman executed a sweeping curve against the raging currents that drew off our collective breaths and left us gasping. If sheepish grins were currency, our boat possessed a priceless cargo as we motored back to pier and calmer waters. For $20 a person, this tour packs a fair punch.

The same company now offers two other regular trips. The **Bertoni Cruise** leaves Porto Meira—the old ferry landing in use before Brazil and Argentina were linked here by bridge—by riverboat, and drifts slowly up the Paraná River to Paraguay. Here passengers disembark on the riverbank, then climb for 20 minutes through the woods to reach the house of a late-19th-century utopian scientist named Santiago Bertoni. The home and outbuildings of the eccentric Swiss immigrant have been preserved in a perilous state of authenticity, and are filled with dusty volumes, specimen jars, and the scattered paraphernalia pertaining to Ex Silvis, Bertoni's publishing imprint, which produced scores of tomes devoted to the Guarani culture and the local flora that were sought by fellow naturalists all over the world. The excursion costs $15, and usually takes about 3½ hours; an on-board beverage service is included.

River anglers might be tempted by Macuco's third organized excursion, the **Dourado Fishing Trip.** The dourado is a large species, similar to a salmon, and is usually fished from the end of February through September while drifting down rapids with live eel as bait. The 4½-hour trip costs $65 per person, tackle and bait included.

FOZ DO IGUAÇU   The city of Foz is itself an attraction. In fact, staying in town should be considered seriously by those who prefer urban over resort environments. The Hotel das Cataratas, the only hotel on the Brazilian side with a view of the falls, is in great demand. Indeed, it's getting increasingly difficult to get a reservation at this favored locale unless the booking is made well in advance. Most tourists are placed in one of several first-class resort-style hotels that are located on the Rodovia das Cataratas (Highway of the Cataracts) that links the national park with the city.

The advantage of the city is its street life, as well as the numerous shops and restaurants. After a day of touring, the city offers the possibility of another, less structured excursion. Foz is small enough to walk around in without getting lost while hunting for the restaurant that best fits your mood (as opposed to being limited to a single hotel dining room) and to search out the nightlife centered in a small but appealing selection of crowded cafés, bars, and discotheques. If you are lucky, there may even be a street fair going on during your visit. The fairs are animated by live music, and many stands selling excellent crafts and foods, representing all three nations.

THE ARGENTINE SIDE

The **Oficina de Información Turístico,** Ave. Victoria Aguirre 311 (tel. 0757/20-800), maintains a visitor center in Puerto Iguazú, open Monday through Saturday from 9am to 5pm, and on Sunday till noon.

When visiting the Argentine national park, (open daily from 8am to 6pm; admission $2), using the services of a tour company makes considerable sense, especially if your time is limited. Rather than hassle the logistics as an individual—not the least of which is the border crossing—you can leave all these details to the tour guide. By all means carry your passport with you when crossing into either Paraguay or Argentina. Visas are not generally required for day-trips into these particular border areas, but in the case of Argentina this is not always so. Better check with an Argentine consulate before traveling to Iguaçu to avoid disappointment. Or consult with the consulate in Foz itself.

Until the completion of the Tancredo Neves Bridge, which links Foz with Puerto Iguazú, the crossing was made by ferry, and involved taking a bus or taxi to Porto Meira near Foz, crossing the river and negotiating Customs on both sides of the border, then taking another bus or cab to the Argentine park. Now you can go directly to the Argentine falls by a single means of transportation—a tour bus, for example, or even by cab or rented car if you want to go it alone. Most hotels can help you book a tour to the Argentine side, and the better hotels usually provide the service themselves. Your only concern is to make sure there is sufficient time to walk freely along the many trails both above and below the falls, and to see everything you want to see, including the famous **Garganta do Diabo** (Devil's Throat), the largest single waterfall in the world in terms of its volume of water flow per second.

The entrance to the Argentine **Parque Nacional de Iguazú** is about 12 miles beyond the town of Puerto Iguazú. A good place to begin your exploration, however, is several miles beyond the entrance at **Puerto Canoas,** which is serviced by park buses. Here a half-mile (1-km) catwalk leads to the edge of the Devil's Throat Falls, which straddles the imaginary frontier line in the river between Brazil and Argentina. Along this walk there are signs everywhere of the damage wrought by the devastating flood in 1983—the ruins of the original catwalk provide a particularly humbling reminder of nature's dark and angry side. Otherwise, on a given day, you are enveloped in the overwhelming beauty of the place, where so many strands of the great outdoors are woven into a single tableau. On one extreme there is the serenity of the shallow river beneath your feet, gently flowing among the dozens of fragmented islets that sustain the catwalk. On the other, and just as near at hand, is the din of the falls, as those same quiet waters unleash their latent energy by spilling over the U-shaped chasm and crashing on the rocks below. Where there is vegetation, the setting is not manicured but well tended, a subtropical forest transformed into a cross between an English and a Japanese garden. Greens and earthy browns are the dominant hues, as all the flora seems to blend into a single continuous plant. As you pass beneath the treetops, a flock of a hundred parakeets will suddenly take to flight. And in their season (May and June) the air can be saturated with brightly painted butterflies (there are 500 known species in the forest). From the overlook at the Devil's Throat, the catwalk continues on for another mile and a half, back toward the park's main parking lots, and here descends to the river bottom. Below there is a trail that takes you along the river's edge and across the several islands beneath the jungle canopy. Several pools beneath the more gentle falls are suitable for bathing, and meditating on the endless thundering echo of the cascading waters.

THE MISSIONS The Argentines in Mission Province have yet to exploit an appealing regionalism that might draw many an admiring visitor to this far northern corner of their country. One can understand and respect their ambivalence, given that tourism can rapidly deprive a sleepy, homespun economy of its long-prized unself-consciousness and anonymity. But Hollywood resolved that issue when an audience probably numbering in the tens of millions saw a movie called *The Mission* a few years back and most were "blown away" by the grandeur of the Iguaçu Falls. Increasing numbers of international visitors come to Iguaçu every year, some of whom want to see what, besides the falls, remains of the missions portrayed in the popular movie as well.

Numerous were the missions built in these parts by the Jesuit fathers and their Guarani followers in those early colonial times. The ruins of at least four of these original missions are within a three- to four-hour drive of Foz do Iguaçu. Personally I was only able to make a rapid inspection tour of the major ruin, **San Ignácio,** along National Route 12 (Ruta 12), which took me through the intriguing middle portion of Argentina's Mission Province. Intriguing because the good road passed through an area of forest reclamation and, not unexpectedly, a thriving pulp and lumber industry represented by dozens of roadside sawmills and then on through productive grazing and agricultural lands, interspersed by several small towns that I would have stopped in if traveling at a more relaxed pace.

The ruins of San Ignácio Mission lie adjacent to a town of the same name, by far the most pristine and pastoral of all I saw that day. Here you are close to the regional capital of Posadas, where I am told good lodgings are available for anyone wanting to make an overnight of this excursion. At the entrance to the ruin, I met a team of local officials who presided over a beguiling museum whose exhibits serve as a prelude to touring the ruins. Inside are 10 separate rooms or environments where, in an impressive mixture of media and creative styles, the story of the San Ignácio Mission is recounted. In the first hall, you pass through a forest of fabric, populated by cartoon-faced animals suspended all around you, all stitched up like puffy pillows. The inner courtyard of a large home is duplicated, piled with crates and sea chests that suggest the close link between domestic and mercantile life in those times. One odd room contains nothing but two bizarre mannequins in period costume confronting each other across a large globe of the world, and watched over by a wall portrait of their king, Philip II. The final room is devoted to artists' reconstructions of the ruins in models and dioramas and to documents that refer to fragments of the tale of those who built this place and lived here.

Within the confines of the vast park where the actual ruins lay, the curators have added few touches—a few signs or placards being all that was necessary, since the stones can speak so eloquently on their own behalf. The entire site spreads over at least 100 acres, much of it now returned to open field. But there remains the entire walled outline of the immense church, begun in the late 1600s and destroyed by fire in 1810. In places, the original paving-stone floor is well preserved. Many impressive details carved in stone remain around portals and window casings, on walls and on the base of what had been the baptismal font. Within this space lived 4,500 souls, mostly Native Americans, in 76 *vivendas* (long stone houses), of which the ruins of 36 remain.

Buses leave the Argentine border town of Puerto Iguazú at two-hour intervals and take about five hours to San Ignácio; if you leave early enough, you could make the return trip in one long day. The other less well-preserved mission sites to be found along Route 2 below San Ignácio, en route to Posadas, are named Loreto, Santa Ana, and Candelária. Still more mission ruins are to be found scattered throughout the province, and in neighboring Paraguay as well.

Another option would be to **rent a car.** Cars can be rented at the airport in Foz do Iguaçu at Naipu Locadora (tel. 22-2229). The cost for an overnight rental as far as Posadas and back is about $70, including gas. If you do rent a vehicle in Brazil to drive within Argentina or Paraguay, make sure you get one that burns gasoline, not alcohol—which is only sold in Brazil.

A GEM MINE On the way back from San Ignácio, I stopped at a gemstone mine called **Mina Selva Irupe,** in an area called Wanda. Here a guide walked me through an open pit mine where geodes have been left in place and cracked open to display the formation of colored crystals, mostly amethyst and citrine beneath an outer crust of agate. Of the 105 types of agate, 27, I was told, are present in the Irupe mine fields. There was no fee for the tour, which more than justifies a digression here, especially if you've never seen exactly how rock crystals "grow." A very fancy and well-stocked jewelry and rock outlet forms part of the mine complex, along with a small outdoor café.

THE ITAIPÚ DAM Itaipú is the artificial equivalent of Iguaçu. A dam, after all, is simply a variation on nature's waterfalls, a technique for concentrating the power of water and converting it to energy. Itaipú is an impressive achievement of Brazil's world-class civil engineering skills. When all the dam's 18 turbines are completed, it will provide the country with fully one-third of its electricity. Switch on a light in Rio or São Paulo, and then in your mind trace the illumination back to the molecules of water from the Rio Paraná that are squeezed through a massive concrete keyhole a few miles outside the town of Foz do Iguaçu. Enough concrete was used, it is said, to pave a two-lane road from Lisbon to Moscow.

The price tag for this binational effort—touted as a joint venture between Paraguay and Brazil—has risen into the billions, with Brazil picking up most of the tab as well as draining off most of the power. But the cost to nature has been even greater. The trade-off for the power station involved flooding the Paraná valley above the dam, and obliterating **Sete Quedas** (Seven Falls), a natural wonder that the *Guinness Book of World Records* once listed as the greatest of all the world's waterfalls. The flooding also created an enormous lake, and transformed the ecosystem of the river valley for many miles above the dam—whether for good or ill, it is yet too early for environmentalists to determine conclusively.

To head off its environmental critics, whose voices in Brazil are muted at best, the Itaipú administrators have launched a massive public relations effort to draw the public to the site as a tourist attraction. A slick 35mm color film and high-quality printed material make the case for the defense, the dam versus nature. Unless you are attuned to environmental issues, or to the impact of mass technology on nature, you would never suspect that there was even a potential problem if the technocrats involved in this and similar projects were not so eager to defend themselves. The issue for the tourist, however, is not necessarily to defend or support the dam, but whether or not it is worthwhile to visit as a bona fide attraction.

In its favor, the Itaipú film (available in several languages, including English) is a persuasive, if one-sided, documentary which focuses mostly on the fascinating technical challenges that accompanied the excavation and construction of the project. A bus tour takes visitors across the top of the dam, and to an overlook from which there is a close-up view of the waters as they rush through the locks. The tour is free, so there is no reason to engage a tour company, which is only performing the service of taking you to and from the site. Efficient public transportation, needed to support the project's 13,000 employees, runs frequently from nearby Foz to the administrative area, where the tour begins.

An ecologically oriented museum has been added to the Itaipú tour, open Monday from 2 to 5pm and Tuesday through Saturday from 9 to 11:30am and 2 to 5pm. Called the **Ecomuseu**, the brand-new building contains well-mounted displays of the region's flora and fauna, as well as numerous artifacts of indigenous inhabitants from pre-Columbian and colonial times. One mission of the Ecomuseu is to study and preserve from extinction certain regional species like the *cachorro vinagre,* a wild dog, and the *loboguara,* a wolf, which are threatened by the march of local development. During my visit there, packets of tree seeds were available for the taking; I have since raised certain exotic Brazilian trees like bonzai, as houseplants, since they will not tolerate a deep frost and cannot be planted outside.

PARAGUAY

I found **Ciudad del Este** much grown since my last visit, when the city was still known as Puerto Stroessner, so named in honor of the longtime dictator who was finally removed in a palace coup. As with Foz, the growth here has been explosive, due in large part to the wealth created in the region by the construction of the Itaipú Dam. In a short space of time, the Paraguayan border town—a free port—has lost much of its sordid appearance as a Third World bazaar. New construction everywhere apes the Brazilian style across the river in perfect imitation. Even the kids and teenagers here now look and act like their modern Brazilian counterparts in dress and manner, down to the sensual "check it out" sway of their bodies as they amble along. Boys lug heavy ghetto blasters on their shoulders and sport fashionable military haircuts, complete with "white sidewalls." And girls are done up in career fashions with padded shoulders, hair heavily coiffed, and perched on precarious spiked heels.

The patina of prosperity stretches farther beyond the city's outskirts than during my earlier visit. A side trip to neighboring Puerto Franco in search of the Paraguayan version of the "marker of the three frontiers" left me with an impression at total variance from that formed when I had last been here. Gone was the red brick-surfaced road, replaced by a wide, four-lane asphalt strip that runs roughly parallel to the Rio Paraná, the river generally out of view but the high-rise skyline of Foz visible along the horizon. At Puerto Franco, I turned off the four-lane and drove through a fair-size town, one that—judging from several spruced up cafés in evidence and a pretty, stucco-pink hotel—has already become accustomed to the overflow crowds from Ciudad del Este that wander somewhat afield in search of a slightly more authentic vision of life in Paraguay.

Beyond the town the road soon turns to jagged cobblestone, then dirt, first smooth then deeply rutted. Despite the poor surface, public buses passed in both directions, and the houses here are by no means of the poorest class. Though simple, and mostly of board-and-batten construction, they appear solid and well maintained, as are the grounds and cultivated gardens that surround them.

You drive along slowly by necessity, but also to scout for the entrance that takes you down to the river and to the Paraguayan marker where the three frontiers form a three-pointed star at the conjunction of the Rio Iguaçu with the Rio Paraná. All of my attempts to descend some likely side road failed, as each time the way ended in a planted field or became unpassable for some other reason. Finally, I gave up and returned to Ciudad del Este, where I succumbed to the magnetic pull of the marketplace. Among the good purchases I made were two recorded tapes, one Brazilian *forró* music, the other Paraguayan harp, for $1.50 apiece.

TRÊS FRONTEIRAS

The mark of the three frontiers is an unusual sight, but also not for everybody, especially if going there cuts into time that could be spent at the two national parks. At the point where the Rio Iguaçu flows into the Paraná, the corners of the three nations meet. Each country has erected a triangular marker painted in the colors of its national flag, and standing behind whichever one you choose to visit, all three obelisks can be seen simultaneously. The Brazilian marker is found at the end of a road outside Foz going away from the falls, while the Argentine marker is across the river on the outskirts of Puerto Iguazú. The Paraguayan marker is less accessible, at the end of a remote road beyond Puerto Franco.

ORGANIZED TOURS

Cassino Turismo, Rua Almirante Barroso 505 (tel. 0455/74-3367; fax 0455/72-3088), is a reliable tour company. The company offers many tour packages, at both individual and group rates. These include the nearby attractions, the falls, gambling casinos in both Argentina and Paraguay, as well as several overnight excursions to Asunción, the Argentine mission ruins, and a day-trip which combines a visit to a gemstone mine and a *mate* (herbal tea) plantation in Paraguay.

SHOPPING

There are several shops along the Rodovia das Cataratas that are worth popping into to browse among the wares. One complex is located at the kilometer 2.5 marker, and includes several interesting stores. The **Artesanato de Facas** (tel. 72-1340) sells handcrafted knives, including machetes, very reasonably priced from $5 to $15, leather sheaths included.

The **Artesanato e Chocolate Três Fronteiras** is the largest gift shop in Foz on the Rodovia das Cataratas, at km 11 (tel. 74-3002). The store is filled with bric-a-brac of the butterfly-tray variety, but the real attraction is the homemade chocolate, 70 delicious varieties—the bittersweet with cashews is particularly mouth-watering.

Along the main drag of Foz do Iguaçu, there is a very interesting bookstore with an international flavor, **Kunda,** Rua Almirante Barroso 34E (tel. 74-1894). Primarily a university book shop, the Kunda also stocks some guidebooks, and paperback works in both English and French.

WHERE TO STAY

There are more than 120 hotels of all categories in and around Foz do Iguaçu.

EXPENSIVE

HOTEL BOURBON, Rodovia das Cataratas km 2.5, outside Foz do Iguaçu. Tel. 0455/23-1313. Fax 0455/74-1110. Telex 455/247. 181 rms. A/C MINIBAR TV TEL

$ Rates: $87–$114 single; $98–$132 double. AE, DC, MC, V.

The five-star Hotel Bourbon is slightly more than a mile from town. The building is a three-pronged star, three stories high. The decor is very plush, but the rooms are spacious and comfortable. There is a large outdoor pool area, and the grounds are enormous, about a square mile in all. The hotel is ideal for those who want a resort atmosphere and still wish to be relatively close to town, which is within walking distance if you enjoy stretching your legs.

HOTEL DAS CATARATAS, in Iguaçu National Park. Tel. 0455/23-2266.
Fax 0455/74-2382. Telex 455/113. 200 rms. A/C MINIBAR TV TEL
$ Rates: $81–$113 single; $90–$126 double. AE, DC, MC, V.

Hotel das Cataratas, located on the grounds of Iguaçu National Park, is the area's best-known hotel, and most in demand. This is the only hotel on the Brazilian side with a view of the falls—and a commanding view it is. The hotel is also a classic of colonial design. The main section is shaped like a squared-off U, in rosy-pink stucco and white trim. There is an elegant covered veranda along the front of the building, spanning the entrance.

The rooms are large, and fitted in heavy ranchhouse furnishings of the Brazilian mission period. The front rooms face the falls and the rear rooms overlook the manicured grounds, which are all the more striking against the background of the encroaching rain forest. Both vistas are equally beautiful. All rooms offer heat or air conditioning, according to season. There is a swimming pool and some sports facilities on the grounds, where numerous animals can be seen walking about at their leisure, including emas or rheas, a close relative of the ostrich. Be forewarned: The emas have been known to eat guests' room keys and watches left loose on poolside tables.

One drawback of the hotel is that you are as far away from the action in town as you can be, and there are no special recreational facilities here—no health club or sauna, no discotheque. Of course, this is not a problem for most guests, for whom Iguaçu is essentially an overnight destination. And after all, most international tourists come to see the falls, and that's why they stay at the Hotel das Cataratas.

Reservations are an absolute necessity, made as far in advance of arrival as possible. This can be done through any VARIG office, since the airline owns and operates the hotel.

HOTEL INTERNACIONAL FOZ, Rua Almirante Barroso 345, Foz do Iguaçu. Tel. 0455/23-1414. Fax 0455/74-5201. Telex 455/167. A/C MINIBAR TV TEL
$ Rates: $120 single; $132 double. AE, DC, MC, V.

The best in-town hotel is the brand-new five-star Hotel Internacional Foz. The building is a round high-rise tower, where all rooms are set spokelike off circular corridors. The hotel has every facility, including restaurant, bar, and nightclub, as well as a barbershop and beauty parlor, gift shops, and a sauna. An outdoor pool area is at ground level, with a lawn for sunning and tent tops that shade a sitting area. The building is centrally located, but in a quiet corner of the town. Avenida Brasil, the town's principal avenue, is only a block away, and there you will find many shops and the offices of the major Brazilian airlines. The hotel is within walking distance of all restaurants and other in-town points of interest.

MODERATE

HOTEL SAN MARTIN, Rodovia das Cataratas km 17, Foz do Iguaçu. Tel. 0455/23-2323. Fax 0455/74-3207. Telex 455/248. 142 rms. A/C MINIBAR TV TEL
$ Rates: $63 single; $69 double. AE, DC, MC, V.

The Hotel San Martin is near the entrance of the Iguaçu National Park. A massive central chalet with exposed interior beams dominates the hotel's structure and houses its public spaces—lobby, restaurant, disco, game room, and gift shops. The rooms are modern and appealing, with all the usual amenities, including full bath. The hotel's grounds, with swimming pool and outdoor barbecue area, do not overlook the river, but the left bank of the Iguaçu is within strolling distance from here.

LIDER PALACE, Av. Juscelino Kubitschek 3146, Foz do Iguaçu. Tel. 0455/22-2121. Fax 0455/22-2121. Telex 455/447. 111 rms and suites. A/C MINIBAR TV TEL
$ Rates: $56 single; $72 double. AE, DC, MC, V.

The Lider Palace is a brand-new, reasonably priced four-star hotel on the far side of town away from the falls, near the bridge leading to Ciudad del Este. The hotel welcomes you with a large, comfortable lobby, a feature not much in fashion in new hotel construction these days. The lobby café is ideal for a snack break or lunch, say a plate of beef filet tips with farofa and a cold beer ($4.25). The Lider caters with equal grace to commercial travelers and tourists, who blend into a single community at day's end around the hotel's large pool and patio area. Rooms are adequate in every way, though in no way fancy.

RAFAHIN PALACE HOTEL, Rodovia BR 277 km 727, Foz do Iguaçu. Tel. 0455/22-3434. Fax 0455/22-3131. Telex 455/453. 93 rms. A/C MINIBAR TV TEL
$ Rates: $55 single; $75 double. AE, DC, MC, V.
On the road from Foz to the state capital, Curitiba, is the Rafahin Palace Hotel. This is a medium-priced hotel, perfect for families traveling with small children. The hostelry is set on large, parklike grounds with sporting and playground facilities and a small but interesting zoo. The hotel boasts a barbecue restaurant that can accommodate 2,000 patrons, and serves churrasco rodízio style for a very reasonable $4.50 per person.

BUDGET

ALBERGUE DA JUVENTUDE, on the Fazenda Picui do Sul, São Miguel do Iguaçu. Tel. 0455/233-2746. 60 beds; 2 rms (both with bath).
$ Rates: $2.50 per person for a bed; $15 double room. No credit cards.
Some 27 miles outside Foz do Iguaçu is the Albergue da Juventude youth hostel. Two dorms on this old farm can accommodate up to 30 women and an equal number of men. There are also two more expensive "suites" available, and no age limit.

FOZ PRESIDENTE HOTEL, Rua Xavier da Silva 918, Foz do Iguaçu. Tel. 0455/74-5155. Fax 0455/74-5155. Telex 455/351. 36 rms. A/C MINIBAR TV TEL
$ Rates: $30 single; $37 double. AE, V.
The Foz Presidente is located around the corner from the Hotel Internacional Foz (see the review above, under "Expensive"). The Presidente is what Brazilians refer to as a "family hotel"—clean, well run, inexpensive, and no frills. The rooms are of good size and airy. A large backyard area, surrounded by a high wall, has a pool and sitting area.

LUZ HOTEL, Rua Almirante Barroso—Travessa B, Foz do Iguaçu. Tel. 0455/74-4311. 37 rms (all with bath). A/C TV TEL
$ Rates: $15 single; $18 double. No credit cards.
Near the old in-town bus station is a budget hotel popular with European tourists. The owner of the Luz Hotel, Pedro Grad Roth, a Brazilian of German extraction, prides himself in running a tight ship. Rooms are strictly no frills, but they are spotless and the showers work.
Under the same ownership and similarly priced is the **Sun Hotel,** Ave. Juscelino Kubitschek 1895 (tel. 0455/73-4343).

WHERE TO DINE

ABAETE, Rua Almirante Barroso 893. Tel. 74-3084.
Cuisine: BRAZILIAN/INTERNATIONAL. **Reservations:** Not needed.
$ Prices: Appetizers $3.25–$5.50; main courses $5.50–$10. AE, DC, MC, V.
Open: Lunch daily 11:30am–3pm; dinner daily 7–11pm.
Abaete has a very attractive red-brick interior, and serves both international and Brazilian dishes, including paella, codfish, shellfish, and the Bahian specialty vatapá.

AL BADIYA, Rua Almirante Barroso 893. Tel. 72-1112.
Cuisine: MIDDLE EASTERN. **Reservations:** Not needed.
$ Prices: Appetizers $3.25–$7; main courses $4.50–$16.50. AE, DC, MC.
Open: Lunch daily noon–3pm; dinner daily 7pm–midnight.

An unexpected novelty in dining here is the Al Badiya, an Arabian restaurant that serves its Middle Eastern delights *rodízio* style. (There is a large population of Arab descent in Foz, and if you're out for a drive around town, be sure to go past the very large and ornate mosque and cultural center that serves the Islamic community.) The round-robin meal includes 10 typical dishes, and you more than get your money's worth.

BUFALO BRANCO, Rua Rebouças 550, at the corner of Rua Taroba. Tel. 74-5115.
Cuisine: BARBECUE. **Reservations:** Not needed.
$ Prices: Complete meal $10. AE, DC, MC, V.
Open: Daily noon–midnight.

The favorite meal in Foz is *churrasco* (barbecued meat), and the town's newest and most elegant steakhouse is the Bufalo Branco. Maître d'Jair, a warm and well-polished professional, will seat you and attend to your smallest need. The salad course is self-service, and I recommend the tender *palmito* (hearts of palm), as much as you can load on your plate without embarrassment. The meats, in many varieties and as much as you desire, are served French style at your table. All meats are raised locally, and the best among them to my taste were the slightly salty *picanha* with its band of fat like a T-bone, and the buttery filet mignon.

CENTRO GASTRONÔMICO RAFAIN, Av. Brasil 157. Tel. 23-2233.
Cuisine: BRAZILIAN/INTERNATIONAL. **Reservations:** Not needed.
$ Prices: Main à la carte courses $4.25–$8; buffet $7. No credit cards.
Open: Restaurant lunch daily 11:30am–3pm; dinner daily 6:30pm–midnight. Café daily 11:30am–midnight.

One of the more appealing places, both to eat and to hang out in the downtown section of Foz, is the Centro Gastronômico Rafain. The Rafain family is well represented in both the local hotel and restaurant sectors, but the Centro Gastronômico has to be their flagship establishment. The very modern complex offers a range of environments: an interior dining room for sophisticated meals, several fast-food counters, and an outdoor café that stays open late. In addition to the à la carte menu, there is an above-average buffet served daily, offering two hot meat dishes, 10 or more salad platters, rice and pasta, and a half-dozen tasty desserts, not to mention numerous fruits and compotes. Outside, in separate stalls, there is a pizza stand, bake shop, ice-cream parlor, and a *pastel* counter selling these meat, shrimp, and cheese pies, all open 18 hours a day. The open-air café serves sandwiches, hamburgers, and draft beer.

CHURRASCARIA CABEÇA DE BOI, Av. Brasil 1325. Tel. 74-1168.
Cuisine: BARBECUE. **Reservations:** Not needed.
$ Prices: Complete meal $10. AE.
Open: Lunch daily 11:30am–4pm; dinner daily 6:30pm–midnight. **Closed:** Christmas.

This restaurant is a cavernous barbecue palace serving locally produced meats from the owner's *fazenda* (ranch). Service is buffet style, and you may return to the groaning board as often as you'd like. In addition to pork, lamb, fowl, and half a dozen cuts of beef, there are many salads and side dishes, including a large baked *dourado* to carve from. The golden-hued dourado is fished from the Rio Paraná and is considered a delicacy of the region. The restaurant holds 500 diners and provides live-music entertainment.

DU CHEFF RESTAURANTE, in the San Rafael Hotel, Rua Almirante Barroso 683. Tel. 23-1611.
Cuisine: FRENCH/SEAFOOD. **Reservations:** Not needed.
$ Prices: Appetizers $3.50–$8.75; main courses $5–$18. AE, DC, MC, V.
Open: Lunch daily 11:30am–4pm; dinner daily 7pm–midnight.

For a change of pace from the town's ubiquitous barbecue fare, try the Du Cheff, in the heart of Foz's downtown district, one of the better eateries in the city. I dined elegantly there on *sopa do mar,* a seafood stew awash with large chunks of shell and fin fish ($9.25) and a plate of creamy fettuccine Alfredo, with fresh fruit and ice cream for dessert.

GALETERIA LA MAMA, Av. das Cataratas 1301. Tel. 74-3272.

Cuisine: ITALIAN. **Reservations:** Not needed.

$ Prices: Buffet $10. AE, MC, V.

Open: Lunch daily 11:30am–3pm; dinner daily 7–11pm.

The rodízio here is called *Santa Felicidade,* and consists entirely of Italian specialties. In all, a team of waiters haul 13 courses to your table, including soup and dessert. There are pasta and meat dishes, salads and polenta, among others. The restaurant is often filled with visitors on upscale bus tours. There is live music—heavy on lighthearted Andean panpipes and harp—and the food is very palatable.

RAFAIN CHURRASCARIA DAS CATARATAS, Rodovia das Cataratas km 6.5. Tel. 23-1177.

Cuisine: BARBECUE. **Reservations:** Not needed.

$ Prices: Buffet $12. AE, V.

Open: Lunch daily 11:30am–4pm; dinner daily 7pm–midnight.

This restaurant, which provides a live samba show of music and dance (except on Sunday), can seat 1,500 diners and is self-service, with 10 varieties of meats, other hot and cold platters, and a choice of 25 different desserts.

SPECIALTY DINING

Hotel Dining

The Hotel Internacional is not only the best hotel in downtown Foz, but it has the best dining room as well, plus a ground-floor restaurant specializing in pasta and pizza.

LA CUISINE DU CIEL, in the Hotel Internacional, Rua Almirante Barroso 345. Tel. 23-1414.

Cuisine: FRENCH. **Reservations:** Recommended.

$ Prices: Appetizers $5–$10; main courses $11–$26. AE, DC, MC, V.

Open: Dinner daily 8:30pm–2am.

This is a beautiful rooftop restaurant, with a grand view over the surrounding city, serving traditional French cuisine. This is the choice for elegant dining in Foz for such classics as canard à l'orange, steak au poive, tournedos, or lapin bourguignon.

TRATTORIA VIA VENETO, in the Hotel Internacional, Rua Almirante Barroso 345. Tel. 23-1414.

Cuisine: ITALIAN/PIZZA. **Reservations:** Not needed.

$ Prices: Appetizers $2.50–$4; main courses $4–$7; pizza $4–$5. AE, DC, MC, V.

Open: Lunch daily noon–3pm; dinner daily 7pm–midnight.

This better-than-average pizza restaurant enjoys pleasant surroundings on the ground floor of the Hotel Internacional. The pizza menu offers a variety of toppings, like pizza calabreza—mozzarella, calabreza sausage, onion, and olives ($4). The insalata alla romana ($3.25) is a platter of tasty mixed vegetables.

An Argentine Steakhouse

RESTAURANTE ST. GEORGE, Av. Córdoba 148, Puerto Iguazú. Tel. 0757/20-633.

Cuisine: STEAK/INTERNATIONAL. **Reservations:** Not needed.

$ Prices: Appetizers $2–$7; main courses $5–$20. No credit cards.

Open: Dinner daily 7:30–midnight.

Puerto Iguazú is a neatly ordered and tranquil border town, most of which is brand new. The St. George occupies the ground floor and veranda of a hotel by the same name, overlooking a principal boulevard where the sidewalks are rolled up by 9pm. The chorizo steak ($6) was very flavorful, holding up the high reputation of Argentine beef. Surubí, one of the large local river fish, is a generous serving at $6.50.

The local beer, Quilmes, is quite good, but considerably more dear, at $2.50 for three-quarters of a liter, than its Brazilian counterpart, but a bargain by American standards. An excellent dessert is the large chunk of homemade bread pudding ($2.20), which is almost a meal in itself.

EVENING ENTERTAINMENT

OBA, OBA RAFAIN SAMBA FOZ, Rodovia das Cataratas km 6.5. Tel. 74-2720.

In a separate annex next to the Rafain Churrascaria, the show Oba, Oba Rafain Samba Foz holds forth every night of the year, from roughly 11 at night till 1 in the morning. This is the traditional Brazilian samba and folklore show that you might see in Rio, Salvador, or São Paulo, with lots of nudity, but—in this case—on the scale of a cabaret rather than a full-blown stage show. Standout performances included an excellent demonstration of *capoeira*—the uniquely Brazilian martial-art dance form, a pair of very funny percussionist-clowns, and a couple of female hip-shakers who could put a Cuisinart out of business. Audience participation is encouraged, which is to say that obliging men are invited to come up on stage and rub bellies and bottoms with some member of the chorus line, who on one occasion "turns out" to be a transvestite.

Prices: $12.

PLAZA FOZ, BR 277 km 726. Tel. 73-4370 or 22-1643.

Foz has added a lively nightlife dimension since my last visit. You can see a show with some of the best production values in all Brazil at the Plaza Foz, just out of town on the highway. The theme of the show is the three frontiers, which the troupe executes in a series of dance and musical numbers. These range from distinctive Paraguayan harp compositions and contradances, to the sultry tango as it might be performed at some back-street bistro in the Buenos Aires demimonde, to the ever-vivacious, joy-giving rhythms of the samba. The two-hour show culminates in a mini-carnival with the audience joining the cast for a spontaneous finale. The auditorium is set up nightclub style, and drinks and appetizers may be ordered throughout the evening. The show begins after 11pm Tuesday through Sunday.

Prices: $20 ticket, $25 ticket with hotel transfer, $30 ticket with transfer and dinner at a churrascaria.

2. PARANÁ

The Brazilian state immediately south of São Paulo is Paraná. Along its wide western border with Argentina and Paraguay is the state's most famous attraction, Iguaçu Falls. Paraná's eastern coast is limited to a mere 60 miles in width, encompassing the mouths of two tidal estuaries, the immense Bay of Paranaguá, and that of the smaller Bay of Guaratuba. The city of Paranaguá is Brazil's second-largest port and first in volume of agricultural exports. Two traditional products continue to dominate the state's agricultural production, coffee and *erva-mate,* the bitter herbal tea that has long been the favorite beverage of the southern populations. The capital city of Paraná, called Curitiba, like that of São Paulo, is located 60 miles inland, high on the *planalto,* where the coastal tablelands flatten out to an altitude of over 4,000 feet above sea level. Visually, the Paraná countryside and coastal plains alike are stunningly beautiful. Even today the state justifies the praise it once received from a 19th-century visitor, the French botanist Saint-Hilaire, who referred to Paraná as the "earthly paradise of Brazil."

CURITIBA

Paraná's capital is a large city in miniature. All the ingredients of a genuine urban environment are there, limited in volume and spread, but true to proportion and scale. The city is tidy and compact, combining modern high-rises with monumental government buildings of an earlier era, the tree-lined streets and boulevards spaced with numerous parks, plazas, and promenades. The effect is more Swiss than Brazilian.

To risk some generalizations about the population of Curitiba, the city's denizens seem to possess a rare blend of formality and warmth, spiced with a subtle humor that often escapes unexpectedly. Curitiba is a university town, and the seat of Paraná's government, as well as center for the state's professional and business life. Men typically go about in jacket and tie, and women are dressed formally in the fashion of the day. In all, Curitiba offers an atmosphere of urbane sophistication, combining provincial intimacy with animated street life, and a fair selection of historical and cultural attractions. Visitors touring Brazil more or less at leisure might find a layover in Curitiba for three or four days much to their taste.

INFORMATION & ASSISTANCE   If you require the services in Curitiba of a competent and companionable guide, call **Josefina Bicaia** (tel. 041/232-8355). Jo is a registered guide with 16 years of experience in leading groups, large and small, primarily throughout southern Brazil. One of her regular clients is IBM. Paraná's state tourist agency—the **Secretaria Especial de Esportes e Turismo**—maintains offices on the third floor of the Edifício Caetano Munhoz da Rocha, Rua Dep. Mario de Barros s/n (tel. 041/254-7273), and can provide you with any number of attractive brochures and publications. For a travel agency in the private sector, try **Lenatur,** Rua Des. Westphalen 2005, Suite 15 (tel. 041/233-7797). Proprietor and guiding light Maria Helena Rocha de Oliveira will organize tours not only in and around Curitiba, but to Paraná's neighboring Spanish-speaking countries, Argentina, Uruguay, and Paraguay as well.

WHAT TO SEE & DO

Curitiba itself is the principal sight, a city that can be easily explored by foot from end to end. But there are several specific points of interest that are worth noting.

Since many of the city's tourist-grade hotels are located near the **Praça Osório,** this small park is a good place to begin a walking tour. Walk easterly along the pedestrian promenade called the Rua das Flores and turn left on Avenida Marechal Floriano Peixoto until reaching the **Praça Tiradentes,** the original hub from which Curitiba grew outward. The blocks bordering this square are narrower and more irregular than those in the newer parts of town, and it is among these streets that you will find the city's historic sector. A number of 18th-century public spaces and churches may be visited, including the **Romário Martins House,** the **Igreja São Francisco,** the city's two oldest buildings, and the **Praça Garibaldi,** also surrounded by historic buildings, and site of a craft fair every Sunday.

Continue on in a northerly direction from the Praça Garibaldi and turn right on Rua Carlos Cavalcanti. After several blocks you will come to the large park called the **Passeio Público,** a peaceful green zone in the heart of the city with boating on interconnected ponds, islands filled with monkeys, gardens, a zoo, and a small aquarium—even a bucolic park-restaurant called Pascuale. Return along Rua Presidente Faria to Rua das Flores.

Rua das Flores, a wide pedestrian mall several blocks long, is the evening gathering place for Curitiba's residents. Both sides of the promenade are lined with shops and cafés, not to mention the several florists and flower stands from which the mall derives its name. The cafés along the section of the strip called Avenida Luz Xavier has been dubbed the **Boca Maldita** (Devil's Tongue) for it is here that the various currents of the city's population—politicians, bankers, artists, and intellectuals—meet and exchange ideas, argue politics, or bemoan world events from the Brazilian perspective.

WHERE TO STAY

Most of Curitiba's better hotels are located near Praça Osório and Rua das Flores.

Expensive

ARAUCÁRIA FLAT HOTEL, Rua Doutor Faivre 846, Curitiba. Tel. 041/ 262-3030. Fax 041/262-3030. Telex 41/6417. 84 suites. A/C MINIBAR TV TEL

$ Rates: $70, $79, or $87 suite daily; $275, $300, or $390 suite weekly. AE, DC, MC, V.

This is Curitiba's only in-town five-star hotel. It is located away from the center between the cross streets Rua Nilo Cairo and Rua Com. Macedo. All units are suites, varying slightly in size, and have kitchen alcoves with separate sink, fridge, and hotplate burners. The Araucária is really a residential hotel and has the appearance of being a fashionable address in town, and houses one of the city's best (and most expensive) restaurants.

DUOMO PARK, Rua Visconde do Rio Branco 1710, Curitiba. Tel. 041/ 225-3545. Fax 041/224-1816. Telex 41/2425. 48 rms. A/C MINIBAR TV TEL

$ Rates: $82–$108 single room or suite; $94–$116 double room or suite. AE, DC, MC, V.

The executive Duomo Park is probably Curitiba's best hotel. The Duomo Park's clientele seems made up mostly of corporate travelers in Curitiba on a temporary basis to represent the interests of this or that major multinational concern. Despite its business orientation, rates here are quite reasonable. The two-room suites are very swank and spacious. While the Duomo Park does not have any leisure facilities, like a swimming pool or health club, it does provide an excellent breakfast, superior service, and a rare degree of pure comfort. The hotel is also centrally located, only two blocks from the Praça Osório.

SLAVIERO PALACE HOTEL, Rua Senador Alencar Guimarães 50, Curiti-ba. Tel. 041/222-8722. Telex 41/6155. 110 rms. A/C MINIBAR TV TEL

$ Rates: $80–$90 single; $90–$100 double. AE, DC, MC, V.

The Slaviero Palace Hotel is located on a block-long pedestrian alley of its own, two blocks from Rua das Flores. The hotel is modern and well maintained, offering rooms at half the normal rates on the weekends since Curitiba's hotels tend to be used primarily on weekdays by travelers doing business in the capital. The discounted room includes a free feijoada on Saturday. Both the rooms and interior spaces of this four-star hotel are pleasant and fully equipped. Le Doyen restaurant serves good international food.

Moderate

HOTEL PROMENADE, Rua Mariano Torres 976, Curitiba. Tel. 041/224-3022. Fax 041/234-2927. Telex 41/35298. 80 rms. MINIBAR TV TEL

$ Rates: $60–$72 standard room; $72–$80 deluxe room. AE, DC, MC, V.

Curitiba's newest first-class hotel is the very attractive and tourist-oriented Hotel Promenade, on the corner of the city's principal thoroughfare, Avenida 7 de Setembro. The long, rectangular rooms are bright and nicely appointed in blond wood-trimmed, Formica-topped furnishings. Deluxe rooms contain an alcove with a convertible couch that opens into an extra double bed. The standard room is smaller, without the alcove, and is not air-conditioned, which seems odd but is probably not a great inconvenience even in the summertime, given Curitiba's high altitude above sea level. Leisure amenities at the Promenade include a small thermal pool on the roof, and also a formal à la carte dining room.

TOURIST UNIVERSO HOTEL, Praça Osório 63, Curitiba. Tel. 041/223-5816. Telex 41/5031. 48 rms. A/C MINIBAR TV TEL

$ Rates: $30–$41 single; $37–$53 double. AE, DC, MC, V.

Directly on the square is the Tourist Universo Hotel, which has very serviceable and inexpensive accommodations. The rooms have mock-colonial furnishings and gallery-white walls; those facing the front have large windows and are very bright. The house restaurant, called the Debret, serves an excellent Wednesday feijoada for $5.50.

Budget

CURITIBA PALACE HOTEL, Rua Ermelino de Leão 45. Tel. 041/224-1222. Telex 41/5220. 71 rms. A/C MINIBAR TV TEL

$ Rates: $31–$35 single; $32–$41 double. No credit cards.

In this modern red-brick building, all rooms facing the street have balconies, and the rooms themselves are crisply decorated, with queen-size beds. As with most hotels in the region, rooms can be heated or air-conditioned, depending on the time of year. The hotel also has its own restaurant and inside parking facilities.

HOTEL PARANÁ SUITE, Rua Lourenço Pinto 452, Curitiba. Tel. 041/223-8282. Fax 041/322-4242. Telex 41/6095. 115 suites. MINIBAR TV TEL
$ Rates: $50 single suite; $60 double suite. AE, DC, MC, V.
Hotel Paraná Suite is near Avenida 7 de Setembro, where many office and government buildings are located on the outer ring of the urban center. The suites each contain two separate rooms, plus a small kitchen. Deluxe suites are air-conditioned, but otherwise the same. There is a pool, and a restaurant where meals range in price from $7 to $12.

HOTEL PRESIDENTE, Rua Des. Westphalen 33, Curitiba. Tel. 041/232-4122. Fax 041/234-1706. Telex 41/5537. A/C MINIBAR TV TEL
$ Rates: $29–$38 standard room; $33–$46 superior room. AE, DC, MC, V.
One block east of the Boca Maldita, and near the Praça Zacarias, is the Hotel Presidente, a hotel that receives many groups. The superior rooms here are much lighter and larger than the standards, and definitely worth the few extra dollars. The Presidente has what is said to be a very reliable and moderately priced restaurant.

Nearby Places to Stay

HOTEL PARANÁ GOLF, BR 376 km 24.5, on the road to Joinvile, Curitiba. Tel. 041/282-5566. Fax 041/225-7778. Telex 41/6095. 34 rms. A/C MINIBAR TV TEL
$ Rates (including full board and greens fees): $100 single; $120 double. AE, DC, MC, V.
Visiting execs who want to keep their golf game sharp ought to consider this brand-new hotel on the outskirts of Curitiba. The hotel, which looks like a farm in the Pennsylvania Dutch country, also has a tennis court, swimming pool, and a convention hall that will accommodate up to 500 participants.

IGUAÇU CAMPESTRE, BR 116 km 396. Tel. 041/262-5315. Fax 041/262-5775. Telex 41/5943. 47 rms. A/C MINIBAR TV TEL
$ Rates: $65 single; $75 double. AE, DC, MC, V.
The Iguaçu Campestre is a small, luxury motel outside the city on the road that connects Curitiba with São Paulo to the north. Each of the rooms has its own walled-in outdoor garden and attached carport. As public transportation to the suburbs is infrequent, it would indeed be advisable to have a car while staying at the Iguaçu Campestre. If given adequate notice, however, the staff will pick you up at the Curitiba airport. This hotel is one of the few in Curitiba that has a swimming pool.

WHERE TO DINE

BAVARIUM PARK, Rua Mateus Leme 4248. Tel. 253-4396.
  Cuisine: VARIED. **Reservations:** Not needed.
$ Prices: Appetizers $1–$6; main courses $3–$12. AE, V.
  Open: Daily 11am–midnight.
The vast Bavarium Park must contain an inner space approaching 12,000 square feet. Beneath its high, alpine-style roof, 3,500 to 4,000 people can be seated. The space is divided into various multileveled environments containing a formal German restaurant, a beer hall, a barbecue house, and a pizza parlor.

DOM ANTÔNIO, Av. Manoel Ribas 6121. Tel. 273-3131.
  Cuisine: ITALIAN. **Reservations:** Not needed.
$ Prices: Complete meal around $7. No credit cards.
  Open: Lunch daily 11:30am–3pm; dinner Mon–Sat 7pm until the last customer leaves.
The main gastronomic quarter in Curitiba is located in a suburb called Santa Felicidade. It was settled initially by Italian truck farmers, and today the wide principal avenue is lined with restaurants, most of which serve Italian food. Dom Antônio is enormous, an eclectic octagonal palazzo strung between two medieval-

looking fortifications, complete with stone towers. The interior is cavernous, as up to 2,000 diners can be accommodated for the *rodízio di pasta*—a continuous round of 11 different homemade pasta and meat dishes. House wines are the product of the owner's own small farms. The rodízio, without beverage, is slightly more than $4 per person.

KAMIKAZE, Av. Manoel Ribas 6354. Tel. 272-1575.
   Cuisine: JAPANESE. **Reservations:** Not needed.
$ Prices: Appetizers $2–$5; main courses $4–$11. No credit cards.
   Open: Lunch Tues–Sun 11:30am–3pm; dinner Tues–Sat 7pm–2am.
The Kamikaze has a reputation for serving the best Japanese food in the city. The owner, a former Zen master, recently arrived from Japan where he lived a contemplative monastic existence for many years, is particularly hospitable to Americans. The average meal, including saké, is about $10.

RESTAURANTE MALI, Rua Francisco Torres 427. Tel. 264-9152.
   Cuisine: JAPANESE. **Reservations:** Not needed.
$ Prices: Appetizers $1.75–$4; main courses $6–$10. No credit cards.
   Open: Lunch Tues–Sun 11am–2pm; dinner Tues–Sun 7–11pm.
Restaurante Mali, despite its name, is a neighborhood Japanese restaurant. The neighborhood in question is quiet and residential, and is within reasonable walking distance of the central hotel sector. The Mali offers standard Japanese fare, including sushi. Servings are large, however, and one plate generally will be sufficient for two people.

WARSOVIA, Av. Batel 2059. Tel. 242-3423.
   Cuisine: POLISH. **Reservations:** Not needed.
$ Prices: Appetizers $1.50–$3.50; main courses $3.50–$8. No credit cards.
   Open: Lunch Tues–Sun 11:30am–2pm; dinner Tues–Sat 7–11pm.
This is the only restaurant in Curitiba serving Polish food. Typical plates include pirogi, kasha, bigos, cabbage soup, and borscht, with feijoada and barreado (a regional specialty) also featured on the menu. The average price per diner is between $4 and $7, including beverage and dessert.

THE PARANÁ COAST

A visit to the bay towns on the Paraná coast is an absolute must for anyone who has traveled as far as Curitiba. Paranaguá, Morretes, and Antonina are the three signal destinations on this excursion. From Curitiba, you can travel to the shore by rail or by highway. The best option is to do both, staying overnight in the sleepy port town of Antonina. If this is not possible, you can also visit all three locales in a single day—somewhat hurriedly—by bus alone, or even by combining bus and rail, assuming a bit of prior planning to ensure good transportation connections.

   Take the early-morning **train** (leaving at 7 or 8:30am) from the railroad station (*ferroviária*) in Curitiba (on Avenida Afonso Camargo) to Paranaguá. The descent is one of the most dramatic and breathtaking railway rides you will ever experience. The construction of the track is considered to be as daring an engineering feat as any ever attempted in the world. As you descend the steep and rugged hills toward the sea, you pass over 41 bridges and viaducts, some of which seem suspended in midair, and through 14 tunnels carved from the mountainous rock. One bridge spans a river chasm some 350 feet wide, and the Viaduto do Carvalho hangs 2,000 feet above the valley floor. Make sure you pick a clear day for the descent, because in addition to the thrills, the scenery is unforgettable.

   The trip down to Paranaguá by train takes 3 to 3½ hours and the number of passengers is limited, so either get to the station at least an hour before departure, or (preferably) buy your ticket a day in advance. For information on departure times and fares, call 234-8411. The same trip by car or bus can be as short as an hour and a half.

PARANAGUÁ

You needn't spend much time in Paranaguá itself. The town is a sprawling, active port, and even though it's one of Brazil's oldest cities (founded in 1585), what remains of the past is too scattered about to visit conveniently. Besides, your time can be better spent in the two more interesting towns up the bay.

One popular attraction in Paranaguá, however, is the **Archeology and Popular Art Museum,** Rua XV de Novembro 562, located in the small historical quarter. Open Tuesday through Friday from 1 till 5pm and Saturday through Monday from noon to 5pm, the museum occupies a building that briefly housed a Jesuit high school from 1755 to 1759, when the Society of Jesus—trying to protect the Native Americans from extermination—was summarily expelled from Brazil by order of the Marquês de Pombal, the most powerful prime minister and statesman Portugal has ever known.

The **waterfront market** in Paranaguá—which is a free port for Paraguay—can be very animated, and is worth a visit if time permits.

En Route to Morretes

From Paranaguá, take the bus from the end of the beach, Rua João Estevam (tel. 422-0504) to Morretes. You will begin the trip on BR 277, and turn off onto the charming **Estrada da Graciosa,** which traverses the marshy lowlands at the headwater of the Paranaguá estuary, continues along the foothills of the Marumbi mountains across the **Marumbi State Park,** and then connects with the BR 116, which goes on to Curitiba. There is good camping, hiking, and climbing throughout the region.

Morretes itself is at the headwater, where the Rio Nhundiaquara meets the tidal waters of the bay. The Paranaguá train also stops at Morretes, and on Sunday only, a special train runs from Curitiba via Morretes and on to Antonina.

MORRETES

In Morretes, walk around to savor the ambience of this quiet river town. Also keep an eye out for announcements of musical events, especially fandango dances. The **fandango** is a regional favorite of the Paranaense coastal inhabitants, first introduced by the Spanish in colonial times, who for many years exercised considerable influence on the local culture.

Where to Stay

PORTO REAL PALACE HOTEL, Rua Visconde do Rio Branco 85. Tel. 041/462-1344. 11 rms. A/C MINIBAR TV TEL

$ Rates: From $10 small room or suite; $20 double suite. No credit cards.

This small hotel in a white stucco building, with its gaudy and overdecorated lobby, and its contrastingly immaculate, uncluttered white-walled corridors, is a very romantic spot. The $20-a-night suite is a steal, well furnished with a sitting room, two baths, and a very light, front-facing bedroom off a small balcony. Several smaller rooms and suites are also available.

Where to Dine

Only on the Paranaense coast can you eat **barreado,** probably the best-kept culinary secret in Brazil. The dish was first prepared by the poor folk along the Paraná coast as a Carnival meal, one that would provide food for several days and require little tending while it cooked. Barreado is a kind of ragoût, a stringy beef stew. The secret to the dish's unforgettable taste, however, is in its unique preparation. The ingredients—beef, salt pork, and herbs—are placed in successive layers in a large urn-shaped clay pot. The pot is then *barreada,* (sealed). First a banana leaf is tied across the opening, then the cover is placed on the mouth of the pot and hermetically sealed, using a paste of ashes and *farinha* (manioc flour). The pot is then placed in the oven of a wood stove and cooked at a low, steady temperature through the night. The finished barreado is served in bowls, with farinha, fried bananas, orange slices, and rice. And to drink, a fine glass of Morretes cachaça. The result is an unambiguous culinary rival of Brazil's other great national and regional specialties, feijoada and the moquecas of Bahia.

Many restaurants throughout the region serve barreado, a couple of which are listed below.

CASA DO BARREADO, Largo José Pereira. No phone.
   Cuisine: BARREADO/SEAFOOD. **Reservations:** Not needed.
$ Prices: Appetizers $1.75–$3; main courses $4–$12; barreado $5. No credit
   cards.
   Open: Mon and Wed–Fri 11am–3:30pm, Sat–Sun 6–10pm.
The owner of the Casa do Barreado prides himself on the cleanliness of his open
kitchen, and on the barreado produced therein, which he also sells frozen to
customers down for the weekend who pick up a few servings on the way to their
summer cottages. If you choose to eat your meal here, however, sit on the restaurant's
covered patio, which overlooks the river. Try the other typical dish of the region, fish
with shrimp sauce; you can have a sampling with the barreado for $4.50.

NHUNDIAQUARA HOTEL, Rua General Carneiro 13. Tel. 462-1228.
   Cuisine: BARREADO/REGIONAL. **Reservations:** Not needed.
$ Prices: Appetizers $1.50–$3; main courses $3–$7; barreado $4. MC, V.
   Open: Dec–Mar, daily 11am–10pm; Apr–Nov, daily 11am–5pm.
Stop at the Nhundiaquara Hotel for a glass of the aged and golden cachaça that is the
town's principal product. The hotel also serves a fine barreado with all the trimmings.

ANTONINA

Heading back toward the bay along PR 408 for another 10 miles (this is a state road;
the PR stands for Paraná), you will come to Antonina, once a vital port in its own right
but now virtually retired from the pages of active economic history. There is
something magical about Antonina, the old wharf with its simple municipal market,
the all-embracing presence of the upper bay, the well-worn buildings—a treasure of
scale and antiquity.
   Since the decline of its port, Antonina now functions as a weekend retreat for city
folk, but the town remains a genuine backwater, not a resort. Even the infrastructure
of the old port, which now stands dormant on the outskirts of the village, seems
benign, like an industrial ghost town, more dignified and monumental in repose
perhaps than it ever was as an active waterfront. Studies are now under way to
determine how to ensure the preservation of the old port buildings and to what end
they should be employed.
   Beyond the old port is a popular beach and summer community called **Ponta da
Pita,** with many more restaurants and bayside cafés.

Where to Stay

**REGENCY CAPELA ANTONINA, Praça Cel. Macedo 208. Tel. 041/432-
   1357.** 37 rms. A/C TEL
$ Rates: Weekend $36 single, $45 double; weekday $21 single, $31 double.
   Off-season rates include half board. No credit cards.
This is the best hotel in Antonina. The setting is almost perfect: One side faces the bay
and the other a quiet plaza and an old colonial church. The hotel grounds were once a
Jesuit mission, and the current structures were constructed among the remaining
ruins. Beyond the aesthetic, the practical accoutrements required by urban weekenders are not lacking. There is a good pool and fine tennis court. The overall impression
of the hotel is of a comfortable, country boardinghouse. Some rooms face the water
and have balconies.

Where to Dine

There are several very appealing restaurants right on the old wharf. **Tia Rosinha,**
Rua Cons. Antônio Prade 54 (tel. 432-1503), is a family-run place opposite the old
municipal market. The restaurant specializes in seafood, but barreado is also a regular
menu item. Tia Rosinha is open daily and closes in the early evening. The most
expensive meal in the restaurant is about $6.
   Among the market stalls themselves, look for a hole-in-the-wall called **Sant'Ana,**
where, if you're hungry, order the house special, including a crab appetizer, fish filet,
shrimp in sauce, breaded shrimp, shellfish in sauce, fried, breaded bananas, and salad
for the princely sum of $3.50. Out on the old port road is the much fancier

Restaurante Buganvil, Avenida Matarazzo (tel. 432-1434), with a full and impressive menu, featuring barreado, seafood, and various cuts of meat. Open daily for lunch, and on weekends for dinner.

VILA VELHA

A second day-trip from Curitiba involves a visit to the **Vila Velha Park,** where the combined forces of time and nature have carved from glacial sandstone deposits some two dozen massive rock formations, many of which stand alone in open fields like monumental stabiles. There are several hiking trails in the park, a public swimming pool, and three deep craters filled with water, into one of which an elevator descends for a close-up look at the vegetation-covered walls and the placid bottom.

Vila Velha is reached by taking the road to Ponta Grossa, a large inland city about 75 miles west of Curitiba.

About 15 miles outside the capital city there is the old water-driven mill of a former *erva-mate* plantation. The mill is open to the public, and worth visiting to learn something of Paraná's rich *mate* economic cycle, and about the somewhat elaborate production and processing of the plant.

3. SANTA CATARINA

In its dimensions, Santa Catarina state is the reverse of Paraná, its neighbor to the north. Santa Catarina has a coastline 300 miles long and only the narrowest frontier with Argentina to the west. The state is also relatively small, like Brazil's northeastern states. In the northeast, however, the interiors of the states are parched with badlands. Santa Catarina's interior is a mixture of bucolic and prosperous farm country, rich hilly pastures, and great forest lands. In fact the state possesses the largest forested areas in all of southern Brazil.

The state's population derives primarily from three distinct ethnic groups: Azorean Portuguese, German, and Italian. Even today each group seems to dominate its respective region or regions, as if Santa Catarina were consciously organized into cantons, like Switzerland. The Azoreans were the first to arrive, and then as now were primarily fishermen. Predictably, they settled on an island, the island of Santa Catarina, where today the state's capital, Florianópolis, is located. Throughout the 19th century Germans and Italians came in large numbers and settled on interior lands to farm. They established family holdings and duplicated the mixed-farming methods they had brought with them from Europe. Some 60% of the state's population still lives in rural areas and is involved in agriculture.

Santa Catarina also has its urban side, and can claim the fourth-largest industrial output of all Brazil's 26 states. Cities like Joinvile and Blumenau, founded as rural German colonies in the mid-19th century, have evolved into robust factory towns. In the large urban centers much of the German influence in local society has disappeared, blending into the general Brazilian reality, the few remaining visible signs of the culture reduced to its commercial components: beer festivals, restaurants, and cabaret entertainment. In the countryside the opposite is true: There is a healthy rural Germanness in the small towns and on the farms, where tradition is honored naturally, without fanfare or self-consciousness. The same can be said about the Azorean way of life in the fishing villages, and the Italian customs as they continue to be practiced in the valley of the Itajaí and the wine district to the west. A traveler in Santa Catarina, therefore, who truly wishes to experience what the state tourist authority quite accurately portrays as its remarkable ethnic diversity, must avoid the cities and wander in the countryside.

As is typical along the Brazilian coast, the mountains are not far from the sea. And the rise is sudden, climbing over 4,000 feet at one point in the short distance of five miles. Much of the state's farmland is highly domesticated and picturesque, a subtropical version, yet similar in feeling to the European countryside. Here, too, as in Europe, there are winter frosts. The only town in Brazil that receives regular dustings of snow, São Joaquim, is in these hills.

Despite its inland attractions, most tourist movement in Santa Catarina is confined to the state's seashore. A traveler with limited time who is touring several locales in southern Brazil, for example, will almost certainly want to include Florianópolis, the state's island capital, in his or her itinerary. The only problem is that once you've been there, you are likely to have a typical reaction, wishing you could stay longer.

The island of Santa Catarina itself has 42 beaches, a strand for every taste, pocketbook, and age group. And the coast northward, toward the turnoff road for Blumenau, is dotted with fine seashore watering holes and fashionable beach resorts.

FLORIANÓPOLIS

The capital occupies the central third of Santa Catarina Island, which is 25 miles long from north to south, with a six-mile girth at its widest point. The link to the mainland is made easily via two public bridges, one of which is Brazil's largest suspension bridge, of similar late-19th-century design to that of the Brooklyn, Manhattan, and Williamsburg bridges that span the East River in New York City.

WHAT TO SEE & DO

The island is a large beach community, with a limited urban atmosphere, uncrowded and slow-paced except during the summer months of January and February when it fills up with seasonal residents and visitors. In addition to the bay and ocean beaches, there is also a large lagoon, the **Lagoa da Conceição,** several exhilarating vistas from hillside overlooks like the **Morro das Sete Voltas,** and the preserved remains or ruins of three old fortifications from the colonial period. The shoreline is divided into three sections, the north, south, and east coasts.

After choosing a hotel, you can tour the island by public transportation, cab, or rented car. The most famous and fashionable beaches are those on the northern shore, **Jureré, Canasvieiras, Ponta das Canas,** and **Inglesses.** Many of the island's best hotels are found along these beaches, and there are many houses available for short-term rentals.

On the opposite (southern) end of the island are the more rustic and utilitarian beaches. Here you will find the still-active Azorean fishing community, and delight at the colorful, wedding-cake designs of the old houses and the simplicity of the churches, both so reminiscent of what their forebears left behind in distant Portugal.

The most historic section, the birthplace of the Azorean colony, is **Ribeirão da Ilha,** on the bay side.

On the eastern shore, the stretch of the island most exposed to the sea is **Joaquina beach,** where national and international surf championships take place each year. On other nearby beaches, like **Barra da Lagoa,** you can watch the fishermen work their nets and pull large catches of mullet from the sea with the aid of many cooperative hands. Also near the eastern shore, the **Lagoa da Conceição** accompanies the coast for several miles, surrounded by a network of enormous dunes. There are many excellent seafood restaurants on the road that encircles the lagoon, where the specialty is a *sequência,* a succession of shrimp and other seafood platters that allows you to sample everything from the daily catch.

The road around the lagoon has several names, each of which designates a particular activity. **Avenida das Rendeiras** is lined with small wooden shacks where female descendants of the original Azorean islanders pursue the ancient handwork of their race, the creation of *renda de bilro,* bobbin-lace cloth for table coverings, clothes, or for whatever other use you may wish.

Each year on a weekend in mid-June the **Festa da Tainha** takes place on the Barra da Lagoa beach. *Tainha* means mullet, the most abundant of the fishes in these waters. Temporary restaurants are set up the length of the beach, where the mullet, shrimp, and other specialties are prepared in a variety of ways. The event also includes folkloric presentations like *brincadeira de boi,* a benign version of *farra do boi,* a somewhat barbaric ritual which is outlawed, but still widely practiced throughout Santa Catarina in local festivals. Originally a farra do boi was a game of running the bulls. For some years now, however, the game has degenerated. The bull, having come to symbolize a demon, is slowly tortured to death by the participants. The activity, which has Brazilian ecologists and local authorities up in arms, was once confined to

Holy Week, but is now practiced frequently, and even accompanies other celebrations, like baptisms and birthdays.

INFORMATION & TOURS For information in general about hotels and events, contact **SANTUR,** the state tourism bureau, Rua Felipe Schmidt 21, 9th floor (tel. 0482/24-6300), open from 8am to 8pm daily. They also operate an information booth at the airport, open daily from 8am to noon and from 2 to 6pm. The American Express representative in Florianópolis is **Ilhatur,** Rua Felipe Schmidt 27 (tel. 0482/23-6333; fax 0482/23-6921). The agency can arrange transportation to and from the airport, and a variety of tours of the region.

WHERE TO STAY

The most appealing lodgings in Florianópolis are the hotels and resorts that occupy favored positions along the beaches or in the hills.

The **Centro** or downtown section of Florianópolis is located only a few minutes from the island's airport. The principal square is called Praça XV, notable for its century-old fig tree. A circular bench surrounds the tree, which serves as a kind of tribal function as a meeting place for locals, or a quiet spot for reading the daily paper. There are several first-class hotels in this area, and on the side streets that look out over the water.

Downtown

CASTELMAR HOTEL, Rua Felipe Schmidt 200, Florianópolis. Tel. 0482/ 24-3228. Fax 0482/22-3126. Telex 482/322. 192 suites. A/C MINIBAR TV TEL
$ Rates: $115 single; $125 double. AE, DC, MC, V.
The Castelmar Hotel, on a hill several blocks from the water, has a very adequate restaurant, where for about $12 you can eat *camarão a catupiry,* a tasty cheese-and-shrimp casserole. All accommodations are relatively spacious, with separate sleeping and living areas; some suites have two bedrooms. A middling walk around the curve of the bay from the hotel will bring you to a residential beach neighborhood along Avenida Jornalista Rubens de Arruda Ramos, where there is constant late-night activity all week in a selection of restaurants, bars, and nightclubs along the strip.

HOTEL BAIA NORTE, Av. Beira Mar Norte, Florianópolis. Tel. 0482/23-3144. Fax 0482/22-8227. Telex 481-041. 113 rms. A/C MINIBAR TV TEL
$ Rates: $65 single; $70 double. AE, DC, MC, V.
This attractive, five-story hotel overlooking the bay is a good bargain for anyone wanting comfortable accommodations in downtown Florianópolis. All rooms are equipped with an in-house video channel.

HOTEL DIPLOMATA, Av. Paulo Fontes 800, Florianópolis. Tel. 0482/23-4455. Fax 0482/22-7082. Telex 482/543 100 rms. A/C MINIBAR TV TEL
$ Rates: $95 single; $105 double. AE, DC, MC, V.
The Hotel Diplomata overlooks the old metal bridge that connects the city with the continent on the opposite shore. All rooms have queen-size beds. The hotel has a small pool and a piano bar, as well as a beauty salon and a sauna.

Near the Beach

COSTÃO DO SANTINHO, Praia do Santinho, Florianópolis. Tel. 0482/24-6300. Telex 481/005. 44 units (with a total of 250 projected). A/C MINIBAR TV TEL
$ Rates: High season $180 two-room unit; $220 three-room unit. AE, DC, MC, V. 30% low-season discount.
This well-designed, condo-style cluster of buildings fronts a lovely, uncrowded ocean beach, approximately a mile long, and behind which only a few rustic bars have sprouted along the dunes. The intention of the owners is to create a small resort village here, oriented toward sports and recreation (with a gym, health spa, and hiking trails) and catering primarily to families. A large restaurant is already in operation, as well as a cabana bar where I sampled some breaded shrimp ($5)—fat, fresh, and juicy—that were among the best I've ever eaten. The nightly buffet ($10) served in the restaurant is also excellent.

JURERÉ PRAIA HOTEL, Alameda 1 s/n, Florianópolis. Tel. 0482/82-1108. Fax 0482/82-1644. Telex 482/219. 58 cabanas. A/C MINIBAR TV TEL

$ Rates: High season (Dec 15–Mar 15) $1,840 cabana per week; off-season from $185 cabana per night. AE, DC, MC, V.

The Jureré Praia Hotel has 58 cabanas, rented for a minimum of one week during the summer but available for overnights during the off-season, and then at a fair discount depending on your ability to negotiate. The cabanas are very unusual in design, made from high-tech building materials: exposed steel I-beams, and arched metal roofs that look like segments cut from giant industrial drums. What could have been a design disaster somehow works very well, probably because all the building materials are first-rate. The interiors also have modern furnishings, and feature large living rooms, dining areas with attached kitchenettes, and separate bedrooms. Each also contains a full bath, pots, pans, and full table service. According to the management, some of the units will accommodate as many as 10 people. Outside there is an attached carport in the front, and in the backyard, a patio with a brick barbecue grill. The spacious grounds overlook the protected Jureré beach, and are very well tended. The hotel has its own supermarket, restaurant, swimming pool, tennis court, and equipment for a full range of water sports.

MARIA DO MAR, Rodovia Vigílio Várzea, Florianópolis. Tel. 0482/33-3009. Telex 482/319. 85 rms. A/C MINIBAR TV TEL

$ Rates: $55 single; $65 double. AE, DC, MC, V.

The Maria do Mar is located in Saco Grande, a hillside neighborhood facing the northern bay, near the Praia de Cacupé. This is a new hotel, rustic in design, all in brick and timber, and occupying a beautiful natural hillside setting. The general environs of the Maria do Mar are sparsely populated, and the area seems perfect for long leisurely walks. The rooms are attractive and reasonably priced.

Praia das Canasvieiras

This is one of the most developed and popular of the ocean beaches on the island. Visitors on a shoestring budget can arrive here from the airport by public bus for about 80¢, and choose from a wide selection of simple boardinghouses and beach hotels for a fraction of what they would have to pay in a first-class establishment.

Another option for visitors who wish to prolong their stay on the Ilha de Santa Catarina is to consider renting a house. The sign ALUGA-SE CASA (house for rent) is ubiquitous throughout the island, and some real bargains can be found near the Lagoa da Conceição.

WHERE TO DINE

HOTEL DIPLOMATA RESTAURANT, Av. Paulo Fontes 800. Tel. 22-3247.
   Cuisine: INTERNATIONAL. **Reservations:** Not needed.
$ Prices: Appetizers $1.75–$8; main courses $9–$15. AE, DC, MC, V.
   Open: Lunch daily noon–3pm; dinner daily 7pm–1am.

The sequência de camarão is pricey here ($41), but what a way to go. And besides, the maître d' insists that there's plenty for at least two persons. The meal begins with a seafood broth and a crab appetizer; then come four shrimp dishes, a sautéed fish filet, and, of course, dessert, something like passion-fruit pudding. If that doesn't appeal, you can try the delicious shrimp in mustard sauce with mashed potatoes ($15).

LINDACAP, Rua Felipe Schmidt 178. Tel. 24-0558.
   Cuisine: SEAFOOD/INTERNATIONAL. **Reservations:** Not needed.
$ Prices: Appetizers $2–$6; main courses $6–$11. AE.
   Open: Lunch daily 10am–3:30pm; dinner daily 6–11:30pm.

For in-town dining, the Lindacap offers a panoramic view of the bay. It's what residents consider a traditional restaurant. The specialty of the house is *tainha*, mullet served with ova, the fish's egg sack, which is fried in manioc flour, at $6. Other favorites are *marreco* (domesticated wild duck with stuffing) at $7, and *rabada ensopada* (oxtail stew) for $4.50.

MIGUELÃO, Av. das Rendeiras 1001. Tel. 32-0024.
   Cuisine: SEAFOOD. **Reservations:** Not needed.

$ Prices: Appetizers $2–$6; main courses $4–$9. No credit cards.
   Open: Daily 10am–midnight.

On the lake, try the Miguelão, for a round-robin of shrimp dishes. Your meals begins with *bolinhos de ciri* (crabcake balls) and *caldo de camarão* (a stocky shrimp soup). Then come the platters: breaded shrimp, shrimp with garlic, and steamed shrimp, to name a few. The local *pinga* (sugarcane liquor) is clear white and goes very well with the meal or as an apéritif. You can eat and drink to your total satisfaction for about $12 per person.

PETITE SUISSE, Jururé Internacional. Tel. 82-1173.
   Cuisine: FRENCH/INTERNATIONAL. **Reservations:** Recommended for dinner.
$ Prices: Appetizers $3.50–$8; main courses $6–$16. No credit cards.
   Open: Oct–Easter, daily 10am–midnight; off-season, lunch Thurs–Sun noon–3pm, dinner Thurs–Sun 7–11pm.

The Petite Suisse occupies a chalet-style building that looks out over the beach. Above and beyond the restaurant's normal à la carte selections, there is a "special menu" offering such delights as a mixed grill with steamed potatoes, all coated with melted cheese and accompanied by a shrimp cocktail and a salad ($15); filet Madagascar flambée ($15); or fondue Oriental, lean beef cooked in boiling boullion ($15).

4. RIO GRANDE DO SUL

A native of Rio Grande do Sul is called a *gaucho* (ga-oo-shoo). The same term is used to describe the very unique cowboy culture of the pampas, that great expanse of grasslands stretching across southern Brazil through Uruguay and into northern Argentina. Vast herds of cattle still roam throughout this rangeland, providing meat and leather for much of Brazil's domestic consumption and for export as well. And the cowboy, with his lonesome ways, still has a function here, despite being portrayed most often in his Sunday finery: dressed in baggy pantaloons and white linen shirt with red kerchief, and shod in high pleated boots with silver stirrups. As long as cattle roam freely, grazing in nature's pastures, there will be gauchos to round them up and drive them to market. The image of the solitary gaucho in the saddle, sipping *chimarrão* (sugarless mate tea) through a silver straw (a *bomba*) from a dried gourd called a *cuia* is not just a nostalgic re-creation of the past to entertain the tourist trade, but has a strong basis in reality, and accounts for the fiercely independent nature of the state's political history.

Border settlers, like those in Rio Grande do Sul, had to be active in defense of their territory until the respective Spanish and Portuguese authorities could finally settle on their permanent boundaries. Not surprisingly, the influence of the Spanish throughout Rio Grande do Sul is extensive, if subtle; even the Portuguese spoken here has a more clipped cadence, like castellano, very different from the lilting accent of the Cariocas in Rio. Originally the rangelands were divided into vast *latifúndios* (landed estates) and society was ruled by local *caudillos* (strongmen) and populists, some of whom, like Getúlio Vargas and João Goulart, rose to national prominence and power. Even today large landowners still wield the real power in the state. And while Rio Grande do Sul has also evolved in modern times to become the nation's most literate state, with considerable industrial might added to its traditional agrarian economy, a strong hint of gaucho individualism and hauteur still flavors the land.

The macho culture of the south was tempered—but by no means displaced—by the heavy influx of European immigrants in the last century, primarily Germans and Italians. The regions settled by these people are today the favorite attractions of visitors to the state. Which is not to say one should avoid the pampas. Hardly! Travelers with the time and inclination to explore the state could do no better than to wander at will among the villages of the range country, and travel all the way to São Borjas, birthplace of Vargas and Goulart, the state's western frontier with Argentina. Furthermore, a truly sentimental journey can be made among the ruins of the Jesuit

Native American missions dating from the 17th century. The ruins, called the *Sete Povos das Missões Orientais* (Seven Settlements of the Eastern Missions) are found in São Borjas, and in the surrounding district at São Nicolau, São Lourenço, São Miguel, São Luíz, São Ângelo, and São João. The most extensive and best preserved of the ruins is in São Miguel.

Nonetheless, the mainline of tourism in Rio Grande do Sul is in the serra, the hill country, which is much closer to Porto Alegre, the state's capital and principal entry point for air and bus arrivals. Porto Alegre holds no major appeal for the casual tourist; it is a large and not particularly attractive city. But 70 miles inland, however, is some extraordinarily scenic landscape, rivaling anything you will see elsewhere in Brazil, a country whose reservoir of natural beauty seems at times infinite. Our tour will take us first to Gramado and Canela, the ideal base for either a brief or extended stay in the region. From there we explore the *colônias,* where descendants of Italian immigrants produce virtually all of Brazil's table wine. Visits to the wineries and sampling of the wares is much encouraged. Other excursions will include a day-trip to Itaimbezinho, the "Grand Canyon of Brazil," a visit to an art treasure in Caxias do Sul, and a stopover in Torres, the state's most popular beach town.

PORTO ALEGRE

The capital of Rio Grande do Sul emerged from a settlement originally built below the confluence of five rivers, on the Rio Guaiba. Although Porto Alegre is a deep-water port, and one of Brazil's busiest, the open sea is more than 150 miles distant, reached by crossing the Lagoa dos Patos, the largest freshwater lagoon in South America. The city was built on two levels: The upper town contains the oldest sections, while the waterfront and commercial district are on the lower level, much of it on landfill. A pleasant vantage point with a good view of the Guaiba estuary is on the **Morro de Santa Teresa.**

Porto Alegre is connected to other major Brazilian centers by regular air and bus service.

SHOPPING For excellent craft items gathered from every corner of Rio Grande do Sul, try the **Casa do Artesão,** Julio de Kastilhos 144 (tel. 26-3055), which is open from 9am to 6pm. Here you will find both individual and craft art, painting, bolos, whips, sheepskin rugs, and ponchos.

Another choice would be **Souvenirs Pampas,** Rua Alberto Birus 554 (tel. 25-9766).

WHERE TO STAY

PLAZA SÃO RAFAEL, Av. Alberto Bins 514, Porto Alegre. Tel. 0512/21-6100. Fax 0512/21-6883. Telex 51/1339. 284 rms. A/C MINIBAR TV TEL
$ Rates: $91 single; $101 double. AE, DC, MC, V.
This is the only five-star hotel in the city. Both the suites and standard accommodations are large and well appointed, with attractive furnishings. The standard rooms also have separate alcoves with a table and seating area. The best rooms offer views of the river.

HOTEL PRAÇA DA MATRIZ, Largo João Amorim do Albuquerque 72, Porto Alegre. Tel. 0512/25-5772. 22 rms. MINIBAR TV TEL
$ Rates: $15 single; $21 double. No credit cards.
Located on a square lined with trees and government buildings, this hotel is the perfect stop for an overnight in Porto Alegre if your tastes can accommodate the unadorned as well as the inexpensive simultaneously. The hotel occupies an old colonial house, and offers large, clean rooms. The general atmosphere is seedy in a very graceful sort of way. The hotel's interior has many nooks and unexpected stairways, and some rooms open onto a catwalk of connected verandas overlooking an interior courtyard.

WHERE TO DINE

BARRANCO, Av. Protásio Alves 1576. Tel. 31-6172.

Cuisine: BARBECUE. **Reservations:** Not needed.
$ Prices: Appetizers $1–$4; main courses $7–$12. AE, DC, MC, V.
Open: Daily 11am–2am.
Barranco is famous in Porto Alegre for its churrasco in the $7 to $10 range. The meal includes a large variety of salads.

CHURRASCARIA SACÍ, Av. Parque Cacique 891. Tel. 33-9020.
Cuisine: BARBECUE. **Reservations:** Not needed.
$ Prices: Complete meal $8. No credit cards.
Open: Lunch daily noon–3pm; dinner daily 7–11pm.
This restaurant is located in the city's soccer stadium, and provides all you can eat for about $8.

LE BON GOURMET, in the Plaza São Rafael Hotel, Av. Alberto Bins 514. Tel. 21-6100.
Cuisine: FRENCH/BARBECUE. **Reservations:** Not accepted.
$ Prices: Appetizers $2.75–$7.25; main courses $9–$15. AE.
Open: Lunch daily noon–2:30pm; dinner daily 7:30–11pm.
This is one of the city's best restaurants. The service is French and formal, and the à la carte menu is changed every three months. The restaurant also features five daily platters and churrasco, including nine varieties of meat with side dishes, for $7 in its churrascaria section, Capitão Rodrigo.

The **Alfred Coffee Shop,** in the same hotel, is a pleasant rooftop restaurant with an excellent view of the city, ideal for lunch.

PORTOVELHO, Rua Andrade Neves 42. Tel. 25-6398.
Cuisine: INTERNATIONAL. **Reservations:** Not needed.
$ Prices: Appetizers $2–$6.50; main courses $5–$11. AE, DC.
Open: Lunch daily 11:30am–3pm; dinner daily 7–11:30pm.
Portovelho is a popular luncheon spot for businessmen and government officials. The lunch buffet features half a dozen hot dishes and another dozen cold platters and salads. The cost, with beverage, is about $7.

GRAMADO & CANELA

These two picturesque mountain towns stand side by side, high in the Serra Gaucha. Gramado can be reached by two routes: via Novo Hamburgo on BR 116, the faster and more industrialized highway, and via Taquara, the slower and more scenic way over state roads. The distance is roughly 75 miles along either route, adding another five miles for Canela. Originally both Gramado and Canela were immigrant colonies, the Germans arriving in the first quarter, and the Italians in the third quarter, of the 19th century.

Throughout their growth and development, both towns have shown a preference for Bavarian styling in their architecture, and so comparison with kindred towns in Europe has become inevitable, though the similarities are at best superficial. The area surrounding Gramado and Canela, which also includes the towns of Nova Petrópolis and São Francisco de Paula (which are of similar pedigree) is known as the Região das Hortâncias (Region of the Hydrangeas). Indeed the large and fragrant pom-pom-shaped flower seems to grow everywhere, both as ornamental bordering for roads and pathways and in wild clusters in the fields and woods. Gramado and Canela in particular are "in" spots, favorite summer and winter spas for the well-heeled. And Gramado hosts the very chic Brazilian National Film Festival every March, drawing to the town many of Brazil's top entertainment and film industry personalities, in addition to hordes of distinguished and sophisticated moviegoers.

WHAT TO SEE & DO

There are surprisingly many excursions that can be made around the Region of the Hydrangeas, including at least one "must-see" spot, the Canyon of Itaimbezinho.

AROUND CANELA The **Parque Cascada do Caracol** is located five miles from Canela, and can be reached by a public bus called the "Caracol Circular," with four departures a day from the village. The park is a popular campsite, but the main attraction for day-trippers is a view of the narrow but dramatic cataract with a sheer drop of over 400 feet. At the entrance to the park you are likely to see several vendors standing behind large pots of boiling water. The pots are used to cook *pinhões*, the large pine nuts that are stripped from the volleyball-size cones of the towering *pinheiro*, the emblematic tree of the region. The boiled nuts are very tasty, similar in taste and consistency to roasted chestnuts.

There are two other points of interest near the falls. First is **Ferradura Point**, which is reached by traveling an additional five miles beyond the park along a dirt road to an overlook of the same canyon, which has descended to a depth of over 1,200 feet here. The Rio Caí, which can be seen at the bottom flowing between the narrow canyon walls, seems pencil-thin from this high perch. A trek down a woodsy path to see the **Araucária Milenar** (Thousand-Year-Old Pine) is also worthwhile. Whatever the actual age of the phenomenon (estimates are between 500 and 700 years), how often do you get a chance to see a tree 150 feet tall, with a circumference of almost 40 feet at the base of the trunk?

The **Parque Kurt Mentz** was donated to the town by a local figure from his own extensive holdings as a 500-acre conifer preserve. The main reason to visit this park is for its three *mirantes*, vantage points from which to view Canela in its lovely valley setting. The three hills have colorful names—Dedão (big toe), Pelado (naked), and Queimado (scorched earth)—and endless vistas over wild, orchid-grown hills, apple orchards, and vineyards.

AROUND GRAMADO Like Campos do Jordão, the mountain retreat near São Paulo, Gramado is a town that caters to a year-round stream of weekend and seasonal visitors. Throughout the year the town hosts several important festivals and cultural events. The **Festa da Colônia** in January commemorates Gramado's Italian and German immigrant origins with traditional music and food. The annual **Brazilian Film Festival** takes place in March. The **Feira de Gramado** is the winter version of the Festa da Colônia, scheduled in June of each year. In September there is a major crafts fair, the **Feira Nacional de Artesanato.** And during July of even-numbered years Gramado hosts an **International Music Festival.**

Gramado is a pretty village, where several good hotels, restaurants, and shops are all within convenient walking distance of each other.

ITAIMBEZINHO The morning we left for Itaimbezinho, my host played down the side trip. We were going to some national park, about an hour and a half from Gramado, "through cowboy country." The trip was visually stimulating. We sped along over the hardtop that crossed over the undulating rangeland, where *fazendeiros* (ranchers) punched cattle for the country's meat market. The first town we came to was São João de Paula, a kind of regional depot for grains and meat bound for distribution elsewhere. As we neared the city, the sides of the road were festooned with huge flower-bearing hedges—ice-blue and pale-pink hydrangeas burned black by a recent frost which, though it was only late March, a cold front from Argentina had brought in its wake.

Beyond the municipality the road turned into a bumpy dirt surface. The landscape was simple and stunning, the way uniform grasslands and rolling hills can be, with groves of *pinheiros* (crown-topped pines) springing up here and there in the vicinity of solitary farmhouses, or away in fields where they provide shade for the grazing cattle. At one point we were startled by a wolf, which bolted across the road in front of us. After a further gut-wrenching drive of about 30 minutes, with my host making few concessions to the rocks and potholes, we drove through a one-road settlement, intriguingly rustic right down to its single visible symbol of world civilization, the ubiquitous Coca-Cola sign tacked to the side of a wood-frame building. A bit farther on, the road forked to the left, but we entered to the right under a sign which announced the **Parque Nacional de Aparados da Serra** (loosely translated as the National Park of the Sheered-Off Cliffs). We drove along for another several hundred yards over the unimproved road, surrounded by grass and scrub, parked the car, and walked into a field. In a few seconds I understood fully why we had come. It was not visible even a few feet behind us where we had parked, but I was suddenly standing on the edge of a vast, deep canyon, utterly spectacular in its scope and dimensions. Itaimbezinho—at that point only about 25 miles from the Atlantic coast—is almost four miles in length, between 2,000 feet and a mile and a quarter wide, and at its deepest point 1½ miles down to the stream-size river that runs the length of the canyon floor.

The canyon walls were covered with many species of trees and plants, one striking for the beach-umbrella size of its deep-green leaves. Perhaps the most extraordinary thing about the place—besides being able to drive within 10 feet of its edge without barriers or warning signs—is the total lack of a commercializing presence there. The canyon is still in a totally pristine state. The park contains thousands of acres, and during our three hours there we only encountered four other carloads of visitors. The park, I was told, is primarily used by serious campers and backpackers. No one, however, traveling as far as Gramado, should fail to take this side trip, even if only as a half-day excursion.

ORGANIZED TOURS Sergatur (Serra Gaucha Turismo Ltda.), Rua Garibaldi 152 (tel. 054/286-2087), offers accompanied tours throughout both the Region of the Hydrangeas and the wine country (see below). The company provides transportation and a guide for three-hour city tours of Canela and Gramado for about $15, and the same for full-day tours of Itaimbezinho or the wine country, both of which cost around $45 per person.

SHOPPING There are two products created in and around Gramado, both available in its many excellent shops, that are of exceptionally high quality: hand-knit sweaters and home-style chocolate.

WHERE TO STAY

Between them Gramado and Canela boast some 60 hotels, ranging from sprawling first-class resorts to cozy Swiss-style boardinghouses offering home-cooked meals.

In Canela

There's a new five-star hotel in Canela that I've yet to visit but that has been recommended to me. The **Continental Serra,** Estrada do Caracol 220 (tel. 054/282-2100; telex 54/1046), offers singles for $75 and doubles for $85, all with minibars, televisions, and telephones.

GRANDE HOTEL CANELA, Rua Getúlio Vargas 300, Canela. Tel. 054/ 282-1285. Telex 54/3846. MINIBAR TV TEL
$ Rates: $35 double; $45 suite. DC, MC, V.
This is a family-run establishment in the old-world tradition. The lodge is set on landscaped grounds overlooking a private pond, where fishing is allowed in season. A large lobby has a fireplace, fronted by comfortable armchairs. The Grande Hotel is not fancy, but has an appealing domestic atmosphere. The hotel does not charge the usual 10% service tax.

LAJE DE PEDRA, Av. Presidente Kennedy, Canela. Tel. 054/282-1530. Fax 054/282-1532. Telex 54/2226. 250 rms. MINIBAR TV TEL
$ Rates: $110 single; $120 double. Off-season discounts available. AE, DC, MC, V.
The best address in Canela, and perhaps in the entire region, is the Laje de Pedra. The immense complex of horizontal halls and wings is perched at the edge of a mountain wall about 3,000 feet above sea level, and overlooks the valley of the Rio Caí. From several vantage points both within the hotel and on the grounds, the view of the valley seems to roll on to infinity, primitive and uncultivated in certain areas and quite settled in others. In every case it is breathtaking and superb. A favorite area for viewing the scenery is a spacious lounge off the main lobby, enclosed by floor-to-ceiling windows and warmed by a communal fireplace that is in regular evening use from March to August when the nighttime temperatures descend into the 40s and 30s, and sometimes lower.

After a day touring the countryside—where the opportunities for hiking and horseback riding should not be overlooked—the Laje de Pedra offers several choices for filling up the evening hours. If your visit is during the cool winter months, head first for the tearoom—a *mate* tearoom, that is. The waiters will instruct you to place the ground and moistened *mate* leaves vertically in your *cuia,* leaving a space from top to bottom free in the gourd to receive the boiling water. You can refill the cuia up to a dozen times, with the fifth or sixth refilling said to be the most flavorful—that is, assuming you acquire a taste for *chimarrão* in the process. An option for the cocktail hour is a Swiss-style *cave* for wine and fondue. This is wine country, after all. You can dine on the premises or in town, and then stay up half the night in the typical Brazilian fashion, partying in the hotel's swinging discotheque. Other facilities include a large park with woods and a pool, which is heated during times when temperatures are low. The rooms here are charming, and have small balconies; but make sure to request one that faces the scenic valley.

VILA SUZANA PARQUE HOTEL, Rul Cel. Theobaldo Fleck 15, Canela. Tel. 054/282-2020. Telex 54/3777. 19 cabins.
$ Rates (including breakfast): $85 for up to four. AE, DC, MC, V.
This is another of Canela's first-class lodgings. The hotel has 19 separate white stucco cabins, with bedrooms and living areas. Each also contains a working fireplace, and wood is provided gratis by the management. The bungalows can accommodate up to four people, and the breakfast includes several varieties of sausage and other hot dishes.

In Gramado

The hotels in Gramado are all located on, or not terribly far from, the town's two main streets. Gramado also has several excellent hotels in the less expensive price categories.

HOTEL DAS HORTÊNSIAS, Rua Bela Vista 83, Gramado. Tel. 054/286-1057. 16 rms. MINIBAR TV
$ Rates: $57 single or double. AE, DC, MC, V.
The Hotel das Hortênsias is one of the most attractive buildings in town, a cross between a Spanish mission and a Swiss inn. Located near the entrance to Gramado's beautiful public park in the heart of town, the hotel does not allow children under 12 and bars groups, to preserve the tranquil setting, they say.

HOTEL SERRA AZUL, Rua Garibaldi 152, Gramado. Tel. 054/286-1082. Fax 054/286-3374. Telex 54/2427. 152 rms. MINIBAR TV TEL
$ Rates: $57–$60 single; $75–$85 double. AE, DC, MC, V.
This in-town four-star hotel is located right off Gramado's principal cross street, Avenida Cel. Diniz. The fully equipped Hotel Serra Azul is an excellent choice for those who like to take their evening constitutional in the midst of boutiques and craft shops, and also for those attending the numerous screenings during the film festival—the principal theater is only a few doors from the lobby entrance of the Serra Azul.

HOTEL SERRANO, Rua Costa e Silva 1112, Gramado. Tel. 054/286-1332. Telex 54/1041. 84 rms. MINIBAR TV TEL
$ Rates: $50–$55 standard room; $65–$75 deluxe room. AE, DC, MC, V.
Overlooking the town on a nearby hill is the Hotel Serrano, the most modern of Gramado's hotels, including convention facilities for up to 1,000 participants. The hotel is self-contained, with all the requisite four-star features from restaurant to swimming pool.

HOTEL VOVÓ CAROLINA, Av. Borges de Medeiros 3129, Gramado. Tel. 054/286-2433. 18 rms. MINIBAR TV TEL
$ Rates: $23 single; $29 double. No credit cards.
This simple but very adequate hotel is right on Gramado's main street. There is no service charge.

PARQUE HOTEL, Rua Leopoldo Rosenfeld 818, Gramado. Tel. 054/286-2588. Fax 26 rms. MINIBAR
$ Rates: $17 single; $20 double. No credit cards.
The Parque Hotel has 26 rooms, 13 of which are heated and have TVs; the other 13 are housed in separate cabins overlooking a small lake. There is no service charge.

WHERE TO DINE

Most of the restaurants in the area are located in Gramado itself.

Visitors might want to try a regional specialty called *café colonial,* a late lunch consisting of many small dishes, including pastries and meat pies. There are several restaurants in Gramado that serve café colonial exclusively.

GASTHOF EDELWEISS, Rua da Carrière, at the corner of Rua João Leopoldo Lied. Tel. 286-1861.
   Cuisine: GERMAN. **Reservations:** Not needed.
$ Prices: Appetizers $1.75–$4.50; main courses $6–$12. No credit cards.
   Open: Lunch daily 11am–3pm; dinner daily 7–11pm.

The Gasthof Edelweiss, as the name implies, offers German specialties, as well as fresh trout. The restaurant also overlooks the Lago Negro, the town's so-called Black Lake, and is decorated with many excellent graphic artworks collected by owner Clécio Gobbi on his many trips to far corners of the world. With beer, a large platter of German viands goes for about $10.

ST. HUBERTUS, Rua da Carrière 974. Tel. 286-1273.
   Cuisine: FONDUE/INTERNATIONAL. **Reservations:** Not accepted.
$ Prices: Appetizers $2.50–$5; main courses $7–$14. DC, MC.
   Open: Lunch daily noon–2:30pm; dinner daily 7pm–midnight.

The St. Hubertus specializes in fondue, but has a full selection of international dishes as well. A large curved window in the homey dining room looks out on a lake. An extra-large fireplace adds atmosphere and warmth in winter months.

THE WINE COUNTRY

Ideally, you will have several days to tour the wine country. If not, you can still see quite a bit of the area by taking a day-trip from Gramado or Canela, either by private car or with an organized tour. You will begin by heading toward Caxias do Sul, the "capital" of the wine region and one of the state's principal industrial cities.

NOVA PETRÓPOLIS

Along the way, be sure to stop over in Nova Petrópolis, a community that retains much of its German flavor, especially on farms in the outlying districts where Portuguese is still the second language of the inhabitants. Whether or not you stop, the drive is a particularly scenic one, with many enchanting views of mountain passes, clusters of houses and outbuildings, and fields cultivated up and down the hillsides.

Where to Stay

RECANTO SUIÇO, Av. XV de Novembro 2195, Nova Petrópolis. Tel. 054/281-1229. 14 rms. MINIBAR TV
$ Rates (including full board): $55 single or double. AE, DC, MC, V.

This is a real country inn, in an alpine-style home that would not be out of place practically anywhere east of the Rhine. The rooms are very personalized and charming, and the daily rate includes all three meals—a combination of Swiss and Brazilian home-cooking, according to the owner.

CAXIAS DO SUL

The most important reason for stopping in Caxias do Sul, the third-largest city in Rio Grande do Sul, is for a quick pilgrimage to **São Pelegrino,** at the intersection of Avenida Rio Branco and Avenida Itália, to see the amazing work of the Italian artist Aldo Locatelli (1915–62). The interior of the church is lush with Locatelli's dynamic murals. Locatelli was a vivid colorist, and a modernist in every way, so each scene in the larger-than-life panels of the artist's stations of the cross explodes with emotion. The ceiling murals also—especially of the Creation and the Last Judgment—are paradigms of the expressionist vision. This collection of Locatelli's work is truly one of the great hidden treasures of modern art to be found anywhere in Brazil.

The art of wine making is also not overlooked in the environs of Caxias do Sul, where an annual **Festa da Uva** (Wine Festival) draws tens of thousands of participants to the city in late February and early March to celebrate the annual harvest. The rest of the year many **adegas** (wineries) are open to the public for tours of the facilities and, of course, a little *degustação* (sampling of the produce). Outside of Caxias at km 143 on the Rodovia BR 116 is the **Castelo Lacave** (tel. 222-4822). Tastings and tours are scheduled Monday through Saturday at 9, 10, and 11am and at 2, 3, and 4pm.

Where to Stay

SAMUARA ALFRED, RS 122, km 10, Caxias do Sul. Tel. 054/225-2222.
  Telex 54/2409. 81 rms. MINIBAR TV TEL
$ Rates: $43 single; $49 double. AE, DC, MC, V.
Five miles from Caxias do Sul on the road to Farroupilha is a resort worth knowing about, especially for anyone interested in visiting the region during the wine festival. The Samuara is a resort occupying 1,000 acres of parkland, complete with its own private lake for boating and fishing. A large pool (enclosed in glass and heated in the winter) is centered on a wide patio overlooking the countryside.

Good bargains in footwear can be had in nearby Farroupilha, center of the state's shoe industry.

BENTO GONÇALVES

The next stop on our tour of the wine country is the town of Bento Gonçalves, founded by Italian immigrants who began to settle in the region after 1875. These original colonists came from wine-growing backgrounds, and brought with them all the necessary skills to transplant that tradition in the hills of the Serra Gaucha. Their descendants are today the backbone of the Brazilian wine industry, most of which is centered in these few towns of the wine country. Bento is one of the most productive and charming of these towns. A visit to Bento's small but lovingly tended museum, the **Museu do Imigrante**, Rua Erny Dreher 127 (tel. 252-1088), can provide an informed introduction to the experience of Italians who came to Brazil.

Where to Stay

HOTEL DALL'ONDER, Rua Erny Dreher 197, Bento Gonçalves. Tel. 054/252-3555. Telex 54/3767. 150 rms. A/C MINIBAR TV TEL
$ Rates: $27–$31 single; $33–$39 double. AE, DC, MC, V.
A good hotel choice in town is the relatively large Hotel Dall'Onder, located in the *cidade alta,* the upper section of this town built on many hills.

Where to Dine

IPIRANGA, Rua Olayo Bilac 403, cidade alta. Tel. 252-3278.
  Cuisine: BARBECUE. **Reservations:** Not needed.
$ Prices: Appetizers $1–$4; main courses $3–$7. No credit cards.
  Open: Lunch daily 11:30am–2:30pm; dinner daily 7–11pm.
The Ipiranga restaurant is typical of the *galetos* (barbecue houses) found throughout the state. Begin your meal with a healthy, stocky chicken soup, Brazil's famous *canja,* and then try the churrasco. The meat served here is excellent. With a good bottle of wine, dessert, and coffee, the meal will cost around $15 for two.

DEGUSTAÇÃO

The 1,350 wine-growing families throughout this district participate in a cooperative called the **Cooperativa Vinícola Aurora,** Rua Olayo Bilac 500 (tel. 252-4111). The winery offers 40-minute tours and wine tasting in its cellars, with a 20% discount on all purchases. From December through March the hours are 8 to 11am and 3:15 to 5:15pm Monday through Friday, and till 5pm on Saturday and Sunday; from April to November, morning hours only. Here, as in all the wineries, ask to sample the best wines, in the case of the Aurora, the merlot and the cabernet franc, in either white or red.

A third *adega* to visit, if you desire additional background for your survey of the region's wines, is in the town of Garibaldi. The **Forestier** complex is located off Rodovia RS 470 at km 62.2 (tel. 262-1811). As you enter the grounds, all around you are plantings of experimental vines. The tour includes a 20-minute video, followed by wine sampling.

TORRES

The most popular beach resort on the coast of Rio Grande do Sul is the municipality of Torres. The beaches are very crowded during the summer season and all but deserted during the six cold months of the off-season. There are many hotels in all price ranges, and camping is also popular the length of the coast. In all candor, however, neither the beach nor the big cities are the reasons one comes to Rio Grande do Sul.

CHAPTER 12

SALVADOR, BAHIA

Mention Salvador, Bahia, to the average Brazilian and you are likely to elicit an unexpected outpouring of sentiment and national pride. The state of Bahia, and Salvador, its capital city, are as deeply symbolic to Brazilians as Plymouth Rock is to many Americans. And like the Puritan colony, Bahia was not the only cradle of its nation's formative culture, but it was the most significant. Bahia is also the gateway to Brazil's legendary northeast, while Salvador is the region's main entrance and still its most fascinating city.

A BIT OF BACKGROUND Beyond its role as a national symbol, Bahia's story and reality could not be more distinct from that of Yankee New England. Bahia, for example, was settled almost 100 years before the Puritans established their colony. The state's name was bestowed by Cabral's expeditionaries, who anchored in the harbor on November 1, 1501, and christened it Bahia de Todos os Santos (All Saints Bay), in honor of the feast being celebrated that day on the Catholic liturgical calendar. In time the name was shortened by popular usage to simply Bahia, often referring to both state and city at the same time. The initial settlement on the right bank of the bay, then as now called Salvador, was established in 1549, by which time tiny Portugal, with a population of barely two million souls, made its decision to colonize the new continent and defend it from the predatory intentions of the French and the Dutch, who had never reconciled to the papacy's decision in the Treaty of Tordesillas to divide South America exclusively between the Spanish and the Portuguese.

By the late 1600s—when Daniel Defoe was writing some of the first novels in the English language—Salvador was already well known to European readers of the day, ever hungry for adventurous accounts of fortune seekers in the New World "plantations," and of sea dogs and piracy on the high seas. In *Robinson Crusoe*, Defoe's best-known book, the hero, an English seaman and adventurer, is living the life of a prosperous tobacco planter in Portuguese Bahia early in the 17th century. Just prior to his famous shipwreck on an uninhabited island, Crusoe has embarked from Bahia as a principal investor on a speculative voyage to the Ivory Coast of Africa, directly across the ocean at that longitude, to trade sugar and tobacco for slaves and gold.

While Defoe's story is the imaginary portrait of a failed "slaver," he might just as well have written of the many more successful ventures in that trade. The Portuguese, already hampered by their small numbers, nevertheless displayed a special distaste for physical labor when they inhabited the colonies of their new empire. And so their dependancy on slaves—both Native American and African—to work their fields was even greater than their counterparts in the colonies to the north. In the long run, enslavement of the Native Americans proved problematic. To some extent they were protected by the missionaries, but as a last resort to subjugations, they could slip off

WHAT'S SPECIAL ABOUT SALVADOR

Beaches

- ☐ Salvador's ocean beaches stretch from the edge of downtown in Barra to the most distant suburb of Itapoã, the city's most pristine and picturesque strand some 10 miles to the north.

Architecture

- ☐ No city in Brazil has a greater number of architectural relics, literally thousands of buildings built before 1800.
- ☐ Many of Salvador's churches are the most ornate and sparkling of Brazil's treasures from the baroque era. The churches of Bonfim, São Francisco, Carmo, and Rosário are must-see attractions.

Events/Festivals

- ☐ Carnival in Bahia, Brazil at its most ecstatic.
- ☐ The Festival of Bonfim, on the third Sunday of January, one of the world's great popular religious events.

Ace Attractions

- ☐ The historic district of Pelourinho, which has been declared on "international treasure" by UNESCO.
- ☐ The island of Itaparica.
- ☐ The colonial town of Cachoeira.

---

into the deep and still-familiar forest and hope to evade the hunters. But the Africans were trapped. In time, some of these slaves also escaped into the "bush" and created independent villages, but for most, the choices were to work or die. It did not take long under these conditions for the slaves to outnumber their masters, but neither element was so dominant in Bahia as to obscure the other. Both currents were strong, and they survive today as very separate realities in Salvador—the European descendants still represent power and privilege; the blacks, marginal in economic terms, are creators of a viable subsistence economy and a rich popular culture that has only been integrated commercially around its smoother edges.

Visually, Salvador today reflects this division. On the 30-minute drive into town from the very modern airport, it is easy to observe the city's social organization. Along the outer rings are the squatters' camps, called *invasões* (invasions), hovels filled with refugees from yet another cycle of droughts and failed harvests somewhere in the interior. The city's middle parts are suburbs of the working poor, tightly packed wood or brick bungalows—exclusively occupied by blacks. Sometimes the details of the street scenes can remind one of Africa—for instance, when you see a file of turbaned women, balancing water cans and bundles on their heads, disappear from the main road down some dirt pathway into their village. The inner city, however, suggests not Africa, but Lisbon. Here the Portuguese masters of the colonial era built their mansions, their sturdy countinghouses and massive fortifications, their scores of elaborately ornamented churches. And it is here today—as well as along the nearly 70 miles of Salvador's shoreline—that their descendants have built their villas and their modern city, in the midst of an architectural preserve that includes more than 20,000 structures built before 1800. Nowhere else in the Americas can you see, almost routinely, so many churches and other structures that date from the 1600s, and astoundingly, even the 1500s.

While the contrast between the city's two dominant and coexisting cultures may be stark in strict economic terms, the common ground they occupy is also great. In religion, food, music, art, and popular celebrations, both influences are strongly felt, and through these activities the population of Salvador has achieved a kind of cultural synthesis, a common trunk that thrives despite the dissimilar roots that feed it. Catholicism and *candomblé*, the drumbeat and the ballad, African street food and Iberian shellfish stews, folk art and fine art—all overlap their boundaries in Salvador, where at its best, tolerance and compromise, not bigotry and confrontation, are the operative ingredients of the day-to-day social contract.

Salvador's relative social harmony can perhaps be attributed to several factors. Food, fish, and fresh fruit in particular, seem superabundant. By outward appearances, even the poor seem well fed and physically robust. But there are also in Salvador certain intangibles of life that are available and free to all, not the least of which are the perpetually sunny climate, the miles of excellent public beaches, and the tradition of street celebrations, spontaneous and organized, dozens of which occur throughout the year. "That man is the richest," observed Thoreau, "whose pleasures are the cheapest."

Religion, also, is of central importance in the daily lives of many Bahians. Catholicism began as the colony's official religion, and has left a remarkable artistic legacy in Salvador. The city is justifiably proud of its many fine churches, which represent a collective monument to the energy, spiritualism, and high aesthetic expression achieved during both the early colonial and the baroque eras. In the shadows of the state religion, however, the slaves managed to preserve and enrich their own spiritual traditions. It was coincidently the case that their particular animist faith—today known as candomblé—and Catholicism were both religions that revered many saintly personages. The slaves therefore were able to cleverly disguise the practice of their traditional beliefs. Each of their spirits and gods was identified with either the diety of Catholicism or with one of the many saints. So when a slave—or later, a descendant of slaves—was seen to pray to Saint Anne or Saint George, for example, what was not perceived was that he or she was also seeking communion with the African spirits that had been "syncretized" with the holy figures of the dominant religion. The open practice of "pure" candomblé—which had never ceased to be practiced behind closed doors in the slave quarters or the shantytowns— was not legally permitted until early in this century. Today in Salvador alone, it is said that the temples of candomblé number some 4,000, and are now almost as popular with the descendants of the masters as with those whose forebears were in bondage.

The tourist, too, in Salvador, will find that the best the city has to offer is there, either for the taking or at a price that is more than reasonable. The beaches, the historical sites, the city streets, the outdoor markets, the open-air cafés, the island-studded bay, the movable feast of sights, sounds, and flavors—this is the Salvador more and more international visitors are discovering every year, the great "secret" that Brazilians themselves have known since the city was first founded almost 450 years ago.

1. ORIENTATION

ARRIVING

BY PLANE   Salvador is one of six Brazilian cities (along with Rio, São Paulo, Manaus, Belém, and Recife) that can be reached by direct flight on VARIG Airlines from the United States. Salvador-bound flights embark from Miami only. As of this writing there is one nonstop flight to Salvador each week, on Sunday. (Confirm this and all scheduling information directly with the airline or with your travel agent at the time of travel. Schedules, as well as fares, change frequently.) There are several direct flights daily from Rio to Salvador. The two cities are about 990 ground miles apart, and flying time is roughly an hour and a half, at a cost of approximately $426 round-trip.

Airport taxis to most downtown destinations or beach hotels is $20 (or $30 at night). Two reliable companies are **Coometas** (tel. 244-4500) and **Contas** (tel. 245-6311).

Airport buses ($1) run to various locations, including the Praça da Sé, Campo Grande, Barra, and Rio Vermelho.

BY BUS   There is ample bus service from Rio to Salvador, via both interior and coastal routes, a trip that will take a minimum of 24 hours and cost between $30 and

$45, depending on whether you travel by express "sleeper," or on the local carrier. The bus station, Rodoviária de Salvador, is located on the Avenida Tancredo Neves in Iguatemi (tel. 358-0124).

BY CAR   To arrive from Rio, take the inland route via BR 116, or the longer coastal route via BR 101.

TOURIST INFORMATION

The state tourist board is called **Bahiatursa,** which has several information centers at key points throughout Salvador. Bahiatursa's main branch is in the Centro de Convençoẽs (tel. 071/371-1522), in the Praiade Armação neighborhood, en route to the airport. It's open from 8am to 6pm. Other branches can be found at the airport (tel. 240-1244), open daily from 8am to 10pm; and in the lower city at the Mercado Modelo, Praça Cairú (tel. 241-0242), open from 8am to 6pm. Bahiatursa can furnish you with practical, up-to-the-minute information on such matters as tours, English-language guides, cultural events, and so forth. The Bahiatursa representative in New York City is located at 33 E. 33rd St., 10th floor, c/o Helena Laufer (tel. 212/725-6153; fax 212/725-6242).

CITY LAYOUT

Salvador's geographic layout is similar to Rio's, but also the mirror opposite. Both are cities built at the mouth and along the shores of immense bays. But while Rio occupies the lower bank of the estuary and curves around to the ocean beaches to the south, Salvador was built on the upper bank and has expanded up the northern seashore. Also, both cities combine coastal strips and high grounds. But in Salvador, the two levels—at least in the oldest part of town—are more distinct, forming a lower city of wharfs, warehouses, and commercial buildings, and an upper city which sits on a cliff 250 feet above the waterfront, connected to it by steep inclines called *ladeiras,* and by the **Elevador Lacerda,** a complex of municipal elevators that carries passengers quickly between the two levels. With only 1.5 million inhabitants, Salvador is also considerably smaller than Rio, and easier to get around in. The beaches in Salvador, too, begin in the bay where, in most cases, swimming is not recommended, and stretch out for many miles along the ocean on a strip called the **orla.** The great arch of land that surrounds the bay, beyond Salvador's city limits, is called the **recôncavo,** and it was here that the plantation system first took root in Brazilian colonial times.

MAIN ARTERIES & STREETS   Visitors need to know three street names to be able to negotiate the better part of Salvador that is of interest to them: the **Avenida 7 de Setembro** runs all the way from Barra to the Pelourinho; the **Avenida Presidente Vargas** and **Avenida Otávio Mangabeira** between them run the length of the oceanfront orla.

STREET MAPS   The tourist agency, Bahiatursa, sells a map of the city for about $1, which is adequate to gain an overview of the urban layout. But if you plan to do any serious exploration, buy a copy of the more detailed **Planta de Salvador,** put out by the Brazilian tour-guide company Quatro Rodas, available at bookstores and newsstands.

2. GETTING AROUND

BY PUBLIC TRANSPORTATION   Buses are the principal means of mass transit in Salvador. The destinations and routes of the various lines are clearly marked on the

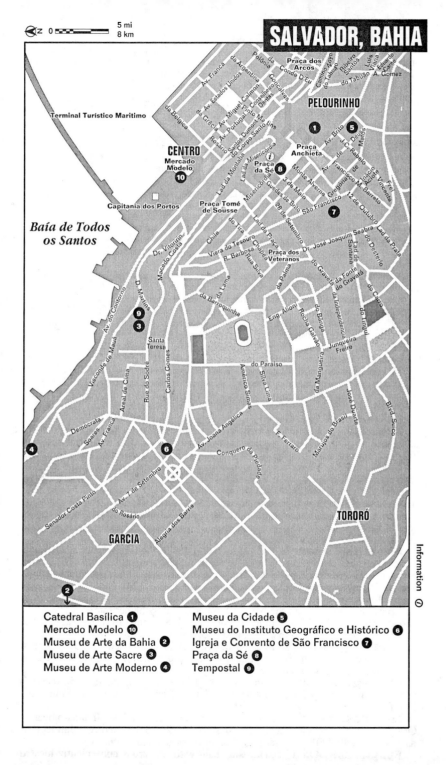

SALVADOR, BAHIA

5 mi
8 km

Terminal Turístico Marítimo

PELOURINHO

CENTRO

Mercado Modelo **⑩**

Capitania dos Portos

Baía de Todos os Santos

Praça dos Arcos

Praça Anchieta

Praça da Sé **⑧**

Praça Tomé de Sousse

Praça dos Veteranos

Santa Teresa

do Paraíso

TORORÓ

GARCIA

Information ⊙

Catedral Basílica **①**	Museu da Cidade **⑤**
Mercado Modelo **⑩**	Museu do Instituto Geográfico e Histórico **⑥**
Museu de Arte da Bahia **②**	Igreja e Convento de São Francisco **⑦**
Museu de Arte Sacre **③**	Praça da Sé **⑧**
Museu de Arte Moderno **④**	Tempostal **⑨**

windshields of public buses. With the aid of a good city map, you may reliably depend on the buses to get around the city. They feel safe, and while drivers speed right along, there are many stops and the routes tend to be circuitous, and so they are not the fastest way to get around the city. The fare is approximately 30¢.

BY TAXI For those with limited time in the city, taxis are the most efficient way to cover ground quickly. Fares are cheaper than in Rio, and drivers less likely to hassle you about running on the meter.

BY CAR **Galo Rent A Car,** Av. 7 de Setembro 3564 (tel. 247-6011), rents cars in a variety of models, with or without drivers. The agency also rents boats. Another agency which caters to tourists is **Locadora Centerauto,** Av. Dorival Caymmi 1012 in Itapoã (tel. 249-1930). **Hertz** (tel. 204-1296 or 245-0448) and **Avis** (tel. 204-1330 or 237-0154) both have rental booths at Salvador's Dois de Julho International Airport.

FAST FACTS SALVADOR

American Express There's an office at the Itaigarra Shopping Mall in Pituba, next to the Banco Econômico, Av. Antônio C. Magalhães 542 (tel. 358-3443).

Area Code Salvador's telephone area code is 071.

Babysitters Two agencies offer this service: Deixe Com A Gente ("leave it to us"), Rua Horacio Hurpia 802, in Graça (tel. 235-2001), for children 1 to 7 years old; or Deixe Conmigo ("leave it to me"), Rua do Carmo 15, in Carmo (tel. 243-5767), for kids up to 10 years old.

Bookstores Livraria Guauna, Av. 7 de Setembro 1448, Centro (tel. 321-8397), is open Monday through Friday from 8:30am to 6:30pm, Saturday till noon. The hours for Livraria Planeta, Rua da Independência 46, Centro (tel. 243-2333), are Monday to Friday from 8am to noon and 2 to 6pm, Saturday till noon. Both stores devote ample shelf space to titles in English.

Car Rentals See "Getting Around," earlier in this chapter.

Climate Throughout the year, average temperatures hover between the 70s and the high 80s. Cool sea breezes ensure pleasant days even in hottest summer. Tropical rainstorms are possible anytime of year in Salvador. Most typically there will be a sudden and tempestuous downpour for an hour or so, and then the sun will return and reclaim all signs of moisture within minutes. On occasion, squalls, like tropical monsoons, will close the city in for several days of gloomy, rainy weather. If there is one region in Brazil, however, where you can almost count on having some sun during your vacation, it is the northeast. And Salvador is no exception to this general rule.

Crime See "Safety," below.

Currency Exchange The Banco do Brazil is the official place to exchange currency at the tourism rate. There's a branch at the airport (tel. 204-1276), open Monday to Friday from 8am to 9:30pm, and Saturday and Sunday from 9am to 4pm. The bank's downtown office is on Av. Estados Unidos 561, 2nd floor (tel. 242-2333), open Monday to Friday from 10am to 4pm. Most hotels are also authorized to exchange currency, though the bank may offer a slightly higher rate.

Dentist The Clínica Campo Grande, Av. 7 de Setembro 1417 (tel. 321-2322 or 321-2996), functions 24 hours daily, and is centrally located.

Doctor The Clínica Manoel Barreto, Rua da Graça 208 (tel. 247-5555), is open around the clock. Generally speaking, it is wise to consult one's hotel for a reliable doctor in the event of an emergency.

Drugstores Santana, in the Tancredo Neves Bus Terminal (tel. 358-0559), is open 24 hours, as is Estrela Galdina, Av. Manoel Dias da Silva 326, in Pituba (tel. 248-4340).

Emergencies The CATO (Clínica de Acidentados Traumatologia e Ortopedia) has two clinics, Av. Barros Reis 376 (tel. 244-3575), and Av. Manoel Dias da Silva (tel. 240-7901). The telephone number for first aid is 192.

Eyeglasses Ótica Teixeira is a chain with numerous conveniently located outlets, including Av. 7 de Setembro 942, Centro (tel. 321-1564), and Rua Guedes de Brito 1 on the Praça da Sé (tel. 243-1848), open Monday to Friday 8am to 6pm, Saturday till noon.

Hairdressers and Barbers   Your best bet here is any four- or five-star hotel, because they'll be more likely to speak some English, as well as have the experience of cutting or styling hair for non-Brazilians.

Holidays   See "When to Go" in Chapter 2.

Hospitals   The Hospital Alicana, Av. Juracy Magalhães Jr. 2096, in Rio Vermelho (tel. 358-0555), is not only the newest and most modern in Salvador, but considered one of the best in all South America.

Hotlines   Dial Turismo 131 for information on hotels, restaurants, films, etc.

Information   See "Tourist Information," earlier in this chapter.

Laundry and Dry Cleaning   For dry cleaning, there's Clipper Azul, Rua Afonso Celso 532 (tel. 245-8751), in Barra, open Monday through Friday from 8am to noon and 1 to 6pm, Saturday from 9am to 1pm. There is also a Laundromat on the same street at no. 109, loja 3 (no phone), open Monday through Saturday from 8am to 6pm.

Libraries   The main library is the Biblioteca Central, Av. Gen. Labatut 27 (tel. 247-7414), open Monday through Saturday from 8am to 8pm. Another important library is the Biblioteca Anisio Teixeira, Av. 7 de Setembro 105 (tel. 243-7426), open Monday to Friday from 8am to 6pm.

Lost Property   There is no specific service. You can try the main post office (dial 159) or the Civil Police (dial 197).

Luggage Storage and Lockers   There are a limited number of lockers at the airport and the bus terminal.

Newspapers and Magazines   The three most important dailies in Salvador are *A Tarde, Correiro da Bahia,* and *Jornal da Bahia.*

Photographic Needs   Try Foto Wang, Av. 7 de Setembro 3577, loja 13, Barra (tel. 245-4963), open Monday through Friday from 8:15am to 7pm, and on Saturday from 8:15am to 3pm.

Police   To contact the Civil Police, dial 197; for the Military Police, dial 190.

Post Office   There are branches scattered all over the city, including in the airport and at the bus terminal. The airport post office (tel. 204-1094) is open Monday through Saturday from 8am to 6pm, and Sunday and holidays from 8am to noon. In Campo Grande there's a branch on Rua Visconde de São Lourenço 66, in the Forte de São Pedro (tel. 240-6222), open Monday through Friday from 8am to 6pm, and Saturday from 8am to noon.

Radio   For Brazilian pop music, tune in to Globo, 90.1 FM; Transamérica, 100.1; or Itapoã, 97.5. For jazz and classical music, try Educadora, 107.5.

Religious Services   There are scores of Catholic churches throughout Salvador. The Sunday masses at N. S. do Rosário dos Pretos (no phone), on the Largo do Pelourinho, between 8am and 2pm, have interesting Afro-Brazilian overtones. The Anglican church is Igreja Bom Pastor, Rua Ceará 30, in Pituba (tel. 248-3428), with a Sunday mass at 7pm. Baptists have a service at 9am on Sunday near Campo Grande, Associação Batista, Forte de São Pedro (tel. 321-6568). The Lutheran church is in Federação, Rua Prof. Aristides Novis 7 (tel. 247-3440), and there is a Sunday service at 7pm. Presbyterian services are held Sunday at 9:30am in Nazaré on Rua da Mangueira 17 (tel. 243-5858). The Methodist church is in Rio Vermelho, Av. Juracy Magalhães Jr. s/n (tel. 240-2362), and two services are held there every Sunday, one at 9am, another at 7pm. Jewish services are held Friday at 6:30pm and Saturday at 8am in Campo da Polvara, Rua do Carmo 60 (tel. 321-4204).

Restrooms   Any first-class hotel, decent restaurant, or cultural institution is likely to have clean facilities that you would be welcome to use.

Safety   As is the case with most large cities of the world, street crime in Salvador has increased steadily over recent years. Tourists who stand out, or needlessly call attention to themselves, are more vulnerable under such circumstances. Be particularly careful in the Pelourinho district, and don't wander around empty streets, especially after dark. In general, Bahians are a friendly sort, and you shouldn't have any difficulties if you use your head. There's a special police unit which concerns itself with the safety of tourists, the Delegacia de Protecção ao Turista (tel. 242-2885).

Shoe Repairs　Try Waldemer Calçados, Av. Princesa Isabel 645 (tel. 245-8665), in Barra.

Taxes　Most hotels and restaurants will affix a 10% service charge to your bill. You may also have to pay an airport exit tax, if it was not included in the price of your ticket.

Taxis　See "Getting Around," earlier in this chapter.

Telegrams and Telex　Telegrams may be sent from any post office (see above). Virtually every tourist-quality hotel has a telex machine, and will send and receive your message for a fee.

Television　Globo is channel 11; Manchete, channel 4; SBT, channel 5; Bandeirantes, channel 7; and Educadora, channel 2. Most major sporting events, including American sports specials, are carried on Bandeirantes. The famous Brazilian soap operas run nightly on most stations.

Transit Information　Dial 158.

3. ACCOMMODATIONS

Hotel construction in Salvador has yet to catch up with the city's rising popularity as a destination for a new generation of international visitors, mostly traveling from the demanding European and North American markets. One result is that hotel resources sometimes seem strained, and service can suffer. Standards in Salvador are not quite on a par with those of more tourist-sensitized Rio or more sophisticated São Paulo. One senses that Salvadorans are trying to adjust to a new dimension in tourism, and that the necessary fine-tuning will follow this adjustment.

EXPENSIVE

With the exception of the Hotel da Bahia, all of Salvador's other luxury hotels are on the orla, the strip of suburban ocean beaches.

BAHIA OTHON PALACE HOTEL, Av. Presidente Vargas 2456, Salvador, Bahia. Tel. 071/247-1044. Fax 071/245-4877. Telex 71/1217. 277 rms. A/C MINIBAR TV TEL

$ Rates: $120–$156 single; $130–$170 double. AE, DC, MC, V.

A stone's throw away from the Salvador Praia (listed below) is the delightful Othon Palace. Its lobby is one of grand conception, quite consciously a vaulted cathedral, but the lines are more square than curved, and the materials are thoroughly contemporary. Near the entrance, two floors are offset, with shops on each level. A succession of high arches deliberately creates the effect of a cloister yard and leads to the reception area. The building itself is brown-tinted, the two 12-story wings meeting in a V, a design that provides all rooms with views of the sea. The pool area is built on a platform that slightly overhangs a rocky stretch of the shoreline, where the elevation is no more than 15 feet above the water. A trail leads to a nearby beach.

The rooms are very large, and the walls are decorated with tiles. The cabinetry and bed alike are curvaceous and shiny, like Asian furniture. The headboards are rattan, and the floors are of polished stone. Each room has a small balcony with teak floorboards, and lattice shutters. Blue-tile baths have tubs with shower curtains. The hotel's bright coffee shop with blue-checkered cloth-covered tables overlooks the pool, and serves a full lunch for about $7.50.

ENSEADA DAS LAJES, Av. Oceânica 511, Morro da Paciência, Salvador, Bahia. Tel. 071/336-1027. 9 rms. A/C MINIBAR TV TEL

$ Rates: $160, $180, or $200 double. No 10% service charge. AE, V.

The Enseada das Lajes, a former private villa tucked away on a hill called the Morro da Paciência, has been converted into a small hotel of distinction by the same family that once resided there. Each guest room has walls of polished red brick and wood-plank floors, but no two rooms are furnished or decorated alike. Each is large and light, and contains several stunning antique pieces. One bathroom has a sunken tub and a separate shower with a curtain of lace. Venerable brass fixtures operate the plumbing. There is no lobby to speak of, but several large public spaces, including an atrium garden, an inviting lounge, and a glass-enclosed veranda restaurant with rattan tables and chairs and a superb view of the sea. The hotel has a pool and patio, lovely grounds set on a sloping hillside, and access to several quiet, rocky coves on the shore below.

HOTEL DA BAHIA, Praça 2 de Julho 2, Salvador, Bahia. Tel. 071/321-9922. Fax 071/321-9725. Telex 71/1136. 292 rms. A/C MINIBAR TV TEL
$ Rates: $80–$115 single; $90–$115 double. AE, DC, MC, V.

The Hotel da Bahia is across from the Campo Grande park, midway between downtown and the neighborhood of Barra. The attractive 10-story Mediterranean-style building was completely renovated in 1984, and upgraded in the process to a five-star hotel. In addition to the attractive standard rooms, white in decor with dark-wood furnishings, the hotel has a variety of luxury rooms with large verandas, and two duplex suites, complete with wooden decks and private dip pools. The high-ceilinged lobby has stuffed leather chairs, several boutiques, and a travel agency. The large pool and patio on the second level overlook the park, where on occasion public fairs are staged, like the Spring Festival in early October with music, plus craft and food stands.

HOTEL SOFITEL QUATRO RODAS, Rua do Passárgada, Salvador, Bahia. Tel. 071/249-1041. Fax 071/249-6946. Telex 71/2449. 196 rms. A/C MINIBAR TV TEL
$ Rates: $105–$115 twin; $125–$140 double. AE, DC, MC, V.

About 15 miles from downtown in Itapoã, the Hotel Quatro Rodas sits on 14 acres of beachland thickly planted with coconut palms. The lobby and public rooms are large and elaborately decorated with plants and old farm equipment. There is a happy hour in the piano bar every night at 6pm. A small working water mill provides both the theme and the centerpiece for the hotel's restaurant. Outside, there is a small natural lake on the grounds, and boats for the guests to paddle. The beach itself, considered Salvador's best, is about a five-minute walk over a path that cuts beneath the palms. The rooms all look out on the sea over a landscape of dunes and beach vegetation. Standard rooms have twin beds, and deluxe accommodations have two large double beds. Rooms are spacious, with clean lines, whitewashed walls, and carpeted floors. Baths are also large, and have tubs with showers. There are three tennis courts on the grounds, and a large swimming pool and sunning area.

MERIDIEN, Rua Fonte do Boi 216, Salvador, Bahia. Tel. 071/248-8011. Fax 071/248-8902. Telex 71/1029. 426 rms. A/C MINIBAR TV TEL
$ Rates: $115 single; $130 double. AE, DC, MC, V.
Salvador's premier beach hotel, the Meridien, is a luxury establishment along the beach, in Rio Vermelho, immediately following the Paciência. The Meridien is Salvador's largest hotel, and chic in the French mold, boasting of both a superior restaurant, the rooftop St. Honoré, and a popular discotheque, Régine's. All the hotel's rooms face the sea, since the tall high-rise building occupies the point of a small peninsula. The decor in the rooms is subtle—peach is the dominant shade—and the furnishings, like the maroon jug-shaped lamps, are modern and tasteful. Original art decorates the walls, and all rooms have small balconies with long views of neighboring beaches. Other facilities include a large pool and patio, sauna, and tennis courts.

SALVADOR PRAIA HOTEL, Av. Presidente Vargas 2338, Salvador,

Bahia. Tel. 071/245-5033. Fax 071/245-5003. Telex 71/1430. 164 rms. A/C MINIBAR TV TEL
$ Rates: $115–$125 single; $125–$140 double. AE, DC, MC, V.
This hotel is in Ondina, the first of the ocean-beach neighborhoods, along a stretch of coast that is more rocky than sandy. Nevertheless, the Salvador Praia is blessed with a small private sand beach on its own grounds. The hotel's rooms are painted in languid shades of café au lait, with polished wood furniture and original oil paintings. Each bath is tiled in marble from floor to ceiling, with a stall shower but no tub. Outside, overlooking the beach, is a large pool and sun deck area adjacent to an equally spacious shaded terrace. The hotel's breakfast room sparkles, and has some strange, but quite good, surreal art.

MODERATE

BAHIA PARK HOTEL, Praça Augusto Sévero, Rio Vermelho, Salvador, Bahia. Tel. 071/248-6588. Fax 071/248-7111. Telex 71/3357. 56 rms. A/C MINIBAR TV TEL
$ Rates: $58 standard room; $64 deluxe room. AE, DC, MC, V.
Shades of brown dominate the room decor here. The headboards are unusual—detached from the bed, they hang from the wall. The rooms' stark design and use of abstract paintings is appealing, and the bathrooms have marble sinks, tile floors, and large stall showers. The rooftop terrace is very simpatico; it has only a dip pool, but a spectacular view of Rio Vermelho and its environs. One major defect of the Bahia Park is that roughly half the rooms in effect have no windows, because the glass is covered by a metallic facade fixed to the building's front, creating not only an intrusive feature, but one that is totally unnecessary architecturally or functionally.

GRANDE HOTEL DA BARRA, Av. 7 de Setembro 3564, Salvador, Bahia. Tel. 071/247-6011. Fax 071/247-6223. Telex 71/2300. 117 rms. A/C MINIBAR TV TEL
$ Rates: $75 single; $95 double. AE, DC, MC, V.
At the Grande Hotel da Barra, half the rooms are classified as standards and occupy an older building off the street. The deluxe rooms are in a newer building nearer the water, attached by glass-enclosed walkways to the hotel's older components. The standard rooms are large, with enough space for several extra armchairs, and have big baths, tiled in blue from floor to ceiling. The deluxe accommodations are newer and smaller, and they all have balconies with views of either the sea or a very private interior courtyard pool.

HOTEL BAHIA DO SOL, Av. 7 de Setembro 2209, Salvador, Bahia. Tel. 071/247-7211. Telex 71/1849. 90 rms. A/C MINIBAR TV TEL
$ Rates: $50 single; $70 double. AE, DC, MC, V.
The Hotel Bahia do Sol is on the downtown side of the Avenida 7 de Setembro between Barra and Campo Grande, along the so-called Vitória Corredor. The building has wooden shutter shades, a feature quite typical of apartment buildings in the tropics. The shades shut out the light but allow ventilation, a nice feature for people who like to sleep without air conditioning. The walls of the rooms are papered, while bright heavy-textured fabric is used for the bedspreads. The furniture is modular, constructed of hardwood, with white Formica surfaces. The baths are large with attractive turquoise-colored tile walls, seashell pedestal sinks, and mirrors framed in wood. Off the lobby is an atrium garden and a restaurant-bar set in the rear of the building, distant from the street.

MARAZUL, Av. 7 de Setembro 3937, Salvador, Bahia. Tel. 071/235-2110. Fax 071/235-2121. Telex 71/2119. 125 rms. A/C MINIBAR TV TEL
$ Rates: $75 single; $95 double. AE, DC, MC, V.
The Marazul is across the street from both the Porto da Barra beach and another old fort, the Forte de Santa Maria. The hotel is a relatively new, nine-story modern building of glass and molded concrete. A terrace at mezzanine level with a small but stylish pool on a raised teak deck overhangs the street, but looks through the tops of palms to the water beyond. The rooms are no-nonsense modern, with large double

beds, and built-in hardwood furniture, all in light earth tones (except for the dark brown blackout curtains). The baths are fully tiled, and in the ceiling is a single recessed light.

PRAIAMAR, Av. 7 de Setembro 3577, Salvador, Bahia. Tel. 071/247-7011. Telex 71/1871. 174 rms. A/C MINIBAR TV TEL
$ Rates: $75 single; $95 double. AE, DC, MC, V.

The pleasant and sturdy Praiamar has a nice diagonal view of the old Barra fort. Rooms are of medium size, and all very day-room bright with bedspreads and other highlights in orange and with solid furnishings. Added to green carpets and floral-patterned tiles in the baths, it sounds garish, but the decorators somehow carry off their statement with good effect.

VILA VELHA, Av. 7 de Setembro 1971, Salvador, Bahia. Tel. 071/247-8722. Telex 71/1500. 98 rms. A/C MINIBAR TV TEL
$ Rates: $50 single; $60 double. AE, DC, MC, V.

The Vila Velha is an older hotel, but well maintained and newly redecorated. The rooms are mid-sized but have large bathrooms with powder-blue tiles and marble-topped sinks. The rooms don't face the front or back, but the sides of the building, and all have good lateral views.

BUDGET

Students and impecunious writers favor the cheaper hotels—by no means fleabags—in the old city, like the **Hotel Pelourinho,** at Rua Alfredo de Brito 20, in the Largo do Pelourinho (tel. 071/242-4144), and off such inner-city plazas as the Praça Anchieta and the Terreiro de Jesus.

YOUTH HOSTELS There are several *albergues* (youth hostels) spread around Salvador. The fee per night for a bed is $5; sheets and towels may be rented for a token amount. In Barra there is the **Senzala,** Rua Florianópolis 134 (tel. 071/247-5678), and in Pituba, the **Casa Grande,** Rua Minas Gerais 122 (tel. 071/248-0527).

4. DINING

Bahian food is the most unique and varied of all regional cooking in Brazil. The use of many spices and herbs along with coconut milk and an African palm oil called **dendê** make it so. The cuisine owes much to African tradition, and to the improvisational abilities of the early slaves, whose choice of ingredients was limited to a catch from the sea or the master's unwanted leftovers. Out of this adversity has come a great school of cooking.

Many a restaurant meal in Salvador will begin with **casquinha de siri,** a concoction of white crabmeat mixed with dendê (palm oil), onions, and tomatoes, and served in its own shell with a sauce, and topped with sprinkles of grated parmesan cheese. **Moquecas,** fish or shellfish stews cooked in earthen pots, are the city's culinary emblem. Moquecas should be made with the freshest ingredients from the sea, and are flavored by hot chiles and dendê, but are seldom overly spicy right from the kitchen. **Molho de pimenta,** a hot sauce of chile paste and dendê, is always present on the table, and can be added according to taste for those who savor truly "hot" food. Cooked with coconut milk instead of dendê, a moqueca becomes an **ensopada.**

Bahians have two favorite chicken dishes, the first a stew called **xim xim** (pronounced "shing shing"), with ingredients that vary from cook to cook. The preparation can include ground peanuts, coconut, mint, fish, or squash, but the sauce is always thick, and the chicken well stewed and flavorful. **Galinha do molho pardo** is a freshly killed chicken served in a brown gravy from its own blood. This dish is a popular offering to the gods in *candomblé* rituals, where animal sacrifice is a central element in the liturgy. From here the dishes become even more exotic, like **efó,** beef tongue and shrimp stew, and **sarapatel,** a pork dish in which innards like tripe and other unmentionables are stewed in the pig's blood. Bahian-style **feijoada,** with red instead of black beans, should also not be overlooked.

As is usual throughout all Brazil, side dishes also play an important role in every Bahian meal. Commonly served as accompaniments are rice, **farofa de dendê** (manioc flour fried in palm oil), and **vatapá,** a very tasty porridge made primarily from bread, ground cashews and peanuts, dried shrimp, dendê, and the usual flavorings.

Bahian desserts are rich and much in demand. The most delicate are **quindim** and **papo de anjo,** egg-yolk custards, the first with coconut, served doused in sticky syrup. **Cocadas** are coconut candies, white or dark depending on whether regular or burnt brown sugar is used in their preparation.

Street food is sold everywhere in Salvador by Bahianas, women in traditional costume—wide skirts and lacy white blouses, turban-headed and bejeweled. These vendors once had to be sanctioned by their respective candomblé temples, where as devotees the young women were initiated into the culinary secrets of the sect. They learned how to make those bean-cake fritters called **acarajé,** which you will see boiling in oil on their improvised braziers. A dried bean called *fradinho,* similar to a black-eyed pea, ground and mixed with dendê, is the basic recipe. Salvadorans have as many opinions about who makes the perfect acarajés, as New Yorkers have about where to buy the best pizza. You can eat the acarajé by itself, or have it served stuffed with vatapá and shrimp and seasoned with hot pepper sauce. Some Salvadorans hold that the best acarajés are sold on the Praça de Santana, across from the Ad Libitum bar. The perfect beverage with this snack is **caldo de cana,** freshly squeezed sugarcane juice, which is also sold at this same location.

EXPENSIVE

CASA DA GAMBOA, Rua da Gamboa de Cima 51. Tel. 245-9777.
   Cuisine: BAHIAN. **Reservations:** Recommended for dinner.
   $ Prices: Appetizers $4–$15; main courses $9.50–$19. AE, DC, MC, V.
   Open: Lunch Mon–Sat noon–3pm; dinner Mon–Sat 7:30pm–midnight.

Since Bahian food is bound to represent a whole new taste for many visitors, it would be wise to sample the fare first at the Casa da Gamboa, where you will be assured of fine ingredients and fastidious preparation. This whitewashed old town house on a hill would be a perfect setting for any meal in Salvador, but ask to be seated near a window looking out over the bay, if possible. Order the moqueca of your choice, and the xim xim, too, if in company, along with vatapá, rice, and farofa, and then settle back with an apéritif, say a fruit batida (fresh-squeezed mango, passion fruit, or maracujá) with cachaça cane brandy. The fish moqueca ($7.75) is an excellent bargain, while the grilled lobster ($5.50) is a special and reasonably priced treat. Sample as many desserts as you have appetite for—but don't miss the heavenly quindim and one or more of proprietor Dona Conceição's homemade liqueurs. If you decide you've enjoyed the experience, you will have many other opportunities in the city to satisfy and widen your newly acquired tastes. Salvadorans with discerning tastes, like author Jorge Amado, always come to the Casa da Gamboa, however, when they want a particularly special Bahian meal. Depending on your selections and bar bill, the meal will cost you between $15 and $25 per person.

RESTAURANTE BARGAÇO, Rua P. Quadra 43. Tel. 231-5141.
   Cuisine: SEAFOOD. **Reservations:** Recommended for dinner.
   $ Prices: Appetizers $4.50–$7.50; main courses $7.25–$18.50. AE.
   Open: Lunch daily 11:30am–3pm; dinner daily 7pm–1am.

The Restaurante Bargaço, in the Bocado Rio section (after Pituba beach on the orla), began as a simple beach-neighborhood fish house. Today the restaurant can boast the most chic clientele in the city. Upper-class Salvadorans from cabinet ministers on down dine regularly on the fine seafood of the Bargaço. Most of the tables are at an outdoor covered patio. For appetizers there are generous portions of crab and lobster meat, grilled shrimp and raw oysters, at about $7 a platter. The principal main courses are several varieties of ensopadas, mariscadas, and fish stews simmered in coconut milk, which arrive at the table still bubbling and cost an average of $15. The Bargaço is on a back street near the convention center complex—not easy to find on your own, but most cab drivers will know how to get there.

ST. HONORE, in the Meridien Hotel, Rua Fonte do Boi 216. Tel. 248-8011.
 Cuisine: FRENCH. **Reservations:** Recommended.
$ Prices: Appetizers $8–$23; main courses $12–$16.50. AE, DC, MC, V.
 Open: Dinner Tues–Sat 7pm–midnight.

For French cooking, and one of the best views of both town and sea in Salvador, there is the rooftop St. Honoré. While not quite on a scale of conception or performance with the equivalent category of restaurant in Rio or São Paulo, the St. Honoré comes close enough, and has an atmosphere that is refreshingly relaxed, rather than stiffly formal as is commonly the case where French service is imposed. Surprisingly, the St. Honoré is not that expensive. So if you want to treat yourself to some genuine designer food as a break from *comida baiana,* say les raviolis de fruit de mer au gingembre ($7.75), and la cuisse de lapin à la crème moutarde ($15.50), this is a recommended spot to consider.

MODERATE

BABY BEEF, Av. Carlos Antônio Magalhães. Tel. 358-0811.
 Cuisine: STEAK. **Reservations:** Not needed.
$ Prices: Appetizers $1.50–$4.50; main courses $4.25–$13. AE, DC, MC, V.
 Open: Lunch daily 11:30am–4pm; dinner daily 6pm–midnight.
For fine cuts of beef, Salvadorans favor Baby Beef, next to the giant Hipermercado Paes Mendonça. Filet, T-bone, beefsteak, pork, and lamb are the specialties, served in a sophisticated atmosphere.

EL MESÓN ESPANHOL, Rua Alfredo Brito 11, at the entrance to the Pelourinho. Tel. 321-3523.
 Cuisine: SPANISH. **Reservations:** Not needed.
$ Prices: Appetizers $2.50–$3.75; main courses $6–$20. No credit cards.
 Open: Mon–Sat noon–11pm, Sun 7:30–11pm.

Tucked away on the second floor behind floor-to-ceiling windows, the way a back-street Spanish restaurant ought to be, El Mesón serves up a mouth-watering and succulent paella a marisacada (fresh shellfish cooked in a pilaf of rice) at a price of $19 for two (or even more).

TAMBORIL, Av. Otávio Mangabeira. Tel. 231-5820.
 Cuisine: SEAFOOD. **Reservations:** Not needed.
$ Prices: Appetizers $6.50–$9.50; main courses $7.50–$26. No credit cards.
 Open: Daily 11am–midnight.
Near the convention center is the Tamboril, in the Boca do Rio stretch of the orla, opposite the old Air Club field, now fallow real estate awaiting the right moment for development. The Tamboril is a typical beachside seafood restaurant with an informal and spacious dining area. The restaurant's menu is extensive, including all the local fish specialties. Normally a reasonably inexpensive joint, I last caught the Tamboril during the hiatus in the shellfish season, a three-month period when gathering these delicacies is curtailed by law. Thus, prices listed here are somewhat inflated. You can make a meal of the *entradas* (appetizers), served in generous portions, and save a few bucks.

BUDGET

EXTUDO, Rua Lido Mesquita 6, in Rio Vermelho. Tel. 237-4669.
 Cuisine: INTERNATIONAL. **Reservations:** Not needed.
$ Prices: Appetizers $3–$5; main courses $4–$8. No credit cards.
 Open: Tues–Sun noon–2am; sometimes open later on weekends.
All the meals in Extudo have names that are takeoffs on book titles, with many of the greats of international literature represented. Meals here are bargain-priced, and the sauces are said to be excellent. A very popular hangout for gourmands with light purses.

MARCO BARBACOA, Av. Oceânica 345. Tel. 247-6151.
Cuisine: PERUVIAN/BAHIAN/INTERNATIONAL. **Reservations:** Not needed.
$ **Prices:** Appetizers $1.25–$3.25; main courses $3.50–$8.25. AE, MC.
Open: Lunch Mon–Sat 11:30am–3 or 4pm; dinner Mon–Sat 7pm–midnight; Sun all day.

Owner Marco Barbacoa, an amiable bear of a gent, lives up to his wanderer's name. A Sephardi whose father fled Romania for Peru, Marco made his way to Salvador as a youngster, and is now a Brazilian dyed-in-the-wool. How he came to open this restaurant, I did not discover, nor what were the other talents and accomplishments he may have accumulated along the way. But it was clear after one long and exceedingly pleasant seating, that this establishment bearing his name, the responsibility for which his wife, Tania, shares in full, is an uncommon eatery fed by many currents. Peruvian ceviche, kreplach, tamales, steaks, bobó . . . and much, much more.

To say this was the best restaurant I ate in during a recent stay in Bahia—at any price—would be no exaggeration. Thus Marco Barbacoa is not only a bargain, it's a real find. The chicken and rice, saturated in a paste of fresh coriander ($5) was particularly inventive. The grilled chicken ($5.50) was somehow elevated beyond its Rotarian earnestness to a level of the first rank, not only by the homemade barbecue sauce, but by some intrinsic magic. The picanha steak ($7), imported from Argentina where the best beef is bred, was butter on the tongue, and balm to the palate. There was a *bobó de camarão* ($6) of perfect flavor and consistency. And not to be forgotten for most honorable mention were the couvert of snappy fresh carrot and celery sticks (served with a homemade mayonnaise, and unmolested by ice that makes them soggy); the warm, oven-fresh bread; and the house trademark, a salmon mousse one could be forgiven for consuming in gobs.

PHILIPPE CAMARÃO, Rua Alexandre Gusmão 104, in Rio Vermelho. Tel. 235-1596.
Cuisine: FRENCH/SEAFOOD. **Reservations:** Not needed.
$ **Prices:** Appetizers $2.50–$7.75; main courses $5.50–$9. AE, DC.
Open: Sun–Thurs noon–1am, Fri–Sat noon–3am.
Philippe Camarão is an in-spot, a hangout for singles, night owls, beats, and bookworms. And the restaurant seems to have an environment suitable to every mood or species attracted to its portals. There's a taproom, a salon, a sit-down restaurant, and a veranda with a view. The house specialty? *Camarão* (shrimp), of course.

SPECIALTY DINING

DINNER & FOLKLORE SHOWS

SENAC, Largo do Pelourinho 13/19. Tel. 321-5502.
Cuisine: BAHIAN. **Reservations:** Not needed.
$ **Prices:** Buffet $10. No credit cards.
Open: Lunch daily noon–3pm; dinner daily 7–10:30pm.
SENAC is an acronym for Serviço de Educação Nacional de Artes Culinarias, the state-run restaurant school where young chefs get their training. The SENAC occupies a grand old building and serves its meals buffet style in a formal atmosphere, a reproduction of a dining room for heads of state. More than a dozen regional dishes are kept hot in steam trays on a central table, and guests can serve themselves. There is a separate table with more than 20 desserts, including sweets and fresh fruit. Here you can sample the more exotic offerings, like *efó* or *sarapatel,* relatively risk-free in small doses. Drinks are served by waiters and are charged for separately. After the meal, you can stay for the folklore show staged outdoors in the yard behind the building. Patrons may order the *seia,* coffee or hot chocolate with sweets, alone for $2 between 5 and 8pm.

SOLAR DO UNHÃO, Av. do Contorno. Tel. 321-5551.
Cuisine: BAHIAN. **Reservations:** Recommended.
$ **Prices:** Buffet and show $18. AE, DC, MC, V.
Open: Daily 8pm–midnight.

The Solar do Unhão, the popular restaurant/cabaret set in this colonial *engenho* (sugarcane mill), puts on the best tourist show in town. The young dancers and musicians are all earnest, and well rehearsed, but what makes this show special is the extraordinary display of *capoeira*—the acrobatic martial-art form Brazil's slaves brought with them from Africa. Groups and individuals usually arrive around eight, serve themselves to a reasonably good buffet of typical Bahian dishes, then settle in for the show, which begins about 10pm.

FAST FOOD

Paes Mondonça operates a chain of fast-food joints throughout Salvador, featuring the usual fare borrowed from the kitchens of the metropolis: grilled-cheese sandwiches, hot dogs, burgers, fries, even potato salad—all with a distinct Brazilian twist, of course. Locations include Barra, and Praça Cairú, near the Mercado Modelo.

OCEANFRONT DINING

Just over the municipal line to the north, beyond the beach of Itapoã, is the town of Lauro de Freitas. Two possible dining spots for anyone staying on that end of the beach are listed below.

LUA NOVA RESTAURANT, Terminal Turístico do Portão, Estrada do Coco km 8. Tel. 379-0801.
   Cuisine: BRAZILIAN/INTERNATIONAL. **Reservations:** Not needed.
$ **Prices:** Appetizers $1.25–$6.75; main courses $5–$13. No credit cards.
   Open: Daily 10am–midnight.
   The Terminal Turístico is a complex of several restaurants with craft shops, a formal garden, and a boat-ride concession for anyone who wishes to sail up the nearby river on a native jangada. The Lua Nova is one of those restaurants, and a spot suitable to many culinary or thirst-quenching agendas. The night I visited, we had already eaten. So we nibbled from a platter of delicious *bolinhos de aipím* (deep-fried pastry balls of manioc flour, filled with melted cheese for $2.25), and drank from owner Antônio Hirtz's special reserve of cachaça, in my case imbibed pure from a small dried-out gourd.

TORRE CHURRASCARIA, Estrada do Coco km 2. Tel. 378-1219.
   Cuisine: BARBECUE. **Reservations:** Not needed.
$ **Prices:** Appetizers $1.50–$4.75; main courses $5.75–$20. AE.
   Open: Daily 11:30am–midnight.
The Torre Churrascaria is a beachfront steakhouse, set amid the palms. The average selection—some tender cut of beef—runs about $14, but will easily feed two.

5. ATTRACTIONS

Salvador's most important sights and activities can be divided into five distinct groupings, each of which occupies a specific neighborhood or area within the city or on the bay, and represents either a full- or half-day excursion. First are the 30 miles of beaches along the orla and beyond. Second are the historical and religious sights, found primarily near the Pelourinho, the colonial district overlooking the bay from the edge of the cliff in the upper city. Third is the Itapagipe Peninsula, for a taste of the city's bayside ambience, including visits to Bonfim, the city's most important active church, and Monte Serrat, one of its oldest fortifications. Fourth is the neighborhood of Barra, between the orla and the city, with many medium-priced hotels and restaurants, and a center of café society and nightlife. Fifth is Itaparica, an incomparable island across the bay. The historic district and Barra are covered in walking tours later in this section; attractions around the bay are covered in Section 10, "Easy Excursions Around Bahia."

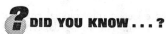

DID YOU KNOW . . . ?

- The great rhythm band, Olodum, which has toured and recorded with Paul Simon, is native to Salvador.
- A longtime resident of Salvador is the world-famous author Jorge Amado.
- Salvador was one of the favorite foreign haunts of Jean-Paul Sartre and Simone de Beauvoir during the sixties.
- Vinícius de Morais, who wrote the words to "The Girl from Ipanema," lived on Itaparica.
- Other rock and pop stars who once frequented Salvador and its environs were Janis Joplin, Mick Jagger, Jimmy Cliff, and David Byrne.
- Salvador was home to the first synagogue in the New World.
- The first American consulate in Brazil was also in Salvador.
- Salvador is the most African city in the New World.

SUGGESTED ITINERARIES

IF YOU HAVE ONE DAY   If you only have one day in Salvador, and you don't plan to spend it on the beach, walk through historic Pelourinho, and visit some of the churches and small museums within its periphery. Be sure to eat at the Casa da Gamboa to sample some first-rate Bahian food.

IF YOU HAVE TWO DAYS   Spend Day 1 as outlined above. On Day 2, make a pilgrimage to the church of Bonfim, stopping in on the Mercado Modelo and the São Joaquim open-air food market on the way. Eat a meal at Marco Barbacoa, or one of the other small restaurants in or around Barra, and then stick around for the nightlife.

IF YOU HAVE THREE DAYS   Follow the suggestions above for your first two days, then on Day 3, take a day-trip excursion to Itaparica or Cachoeira. If to the former, see if you can arrange to eat lunch at the Quinta Pitanga.

IF YOU HAVE FIVE DAYS OR MORE   If you chose Itaparica to visit on Day 3, then go to Cachoeira on Day 4, and eat lunch at the Pousada do Convento. Combine Day 4 and Day 5 and take an overnight excursion to either Itaparica or the Praia do Forte.

THE ORLA

Orla in Portuguese means "hem," and the area given this name in Salvador is precisely that seam of land on the city's northern coast that joins with some 15 miles of ocean frontage. Along this strip are found virtually all of Salvador's best hotels and its finest beaches. Most visitors who book their lodgings in Salvador in advance of arrival are likely to find themselves staying somewhere along the orla.

The **coastal beaches** begin where the neighborhood of Barra ends, and lead all the way to Itapoã, near the city limits. The rule of thumb in Bahia as far as good beaches is concerned is that the farther out you go, the better they get and the longer it takes to reach them, especially during weekend traffic jams. By this criterion, the good beaches begin more or less with **Pietá**, and include **Placaford** and finally **Itapoã** itself. The really super beaches today are considered to be even farther up the coast, from **Burroquinho** to **Praia do Forte**. Between them is **Arembepé,** once an international watering hole for the 1960s counterculture, which was frequented by giants of rock 'n' roll like Joplin and Jagger; now it has returned to its more sedate existence as a coastal resort and fishing village.

The beaches closer to the city, like **Ondina** and **Rio Vermelho,** may not be the largest or the most pristine, but they offer in places some lovely natural pools ringed by rock formations where bathing can be very intimate.

There is much nightlife in bars and restaurants throughout the quaint streets of these chic residential neighborhoods that overlook the water.

Along the entire run of strands lining the orla, the beaches continue to be shared by solitary fishermen, who work the shallows with their nets, or farther out, fish from sailing rafts of lashed logs, called *jangadas,* dozens of which can be seen at any given time bobbing just beyond the breakers.

THE ITAPAGIPE PENINSULA

This is a large codicil of land beyond the port jutting into Salvador's upper bay. Tourists have long been coming here to visit its most famous parts, Monte Serrat and Bonfim, but have seldom been taught to consider the peninsula as a whole as a place for a day's outing and exploration, rather than just a quick in-and-out by cab to visit the requisite sights.

The best time for a pilgrimage to the peninsula is on Saturday, and we begin our tour—at dawn if possible—with the colorful **Feira D'Agua de Meninos,** also known as the Open-Air Market of São Joaquim, about three miles up the bay from the Mercado Modelo in the lower city. While the market is mounted daily (6am to 6pm; on Sunday till 1pm), Saturday is the universal shopping day, and so finds the *feira* at its most animated. But why at dawn? For the same reason one went to the old Les Halles in Paris at daybreak—not for onion soup alone, but to witness the market as it awakens from the torpor of inactivity and is filled not with shoppers, but with porters carrying tons of produce to the individual stalls.

Nowhere else in Salvador will you see gathered in a single place such a cross section of inhabitants so typical of the northeast, a people with as great a variety of characteristics as any artist could imagine, much less distinguish. Many a wary *caboclo,* as the country folk are called, will stare back at you, puffing slowly on his or her pipe, as intensely as you stare at them. Most producers arrive with their goods by truck, and some still come by cart and on donkeys. But many more come by sea, on coastal sloops called *saveiros,* and beach or tie up in the little coves adjacent to the market grounds.

Here is the way to tour the bay, if you are bold. Bargain with the master of a sloop, someone going up the bay toward the colonial towns of Cachoeira or Maragogipe on the opposite shore, and ask him to carry you as a passenger. Then find a sloop making the return voyage, or take a swing through the *recôncavo* and come back to Salvador by bus.

With so much fruit and raw meat, the market has its rank and squishy sections, to be savored or avoided according to personal taste. There are also many stalls filled

---

 ## FROMMER'S FAVORITE
SALVADOR EXPERIENCES

Walking the Pelourinho　Stroll from one end to the other, beginning at the Terreiro de Jesus and ending up on the Praça de Santo Antônio. There is something unbelievably evocative of the colonial experience from the days when the New World was truly "new" for its European and African transplants.

Spending a Day on the Bay Side of the City　Allow plenty of time to soak up the color, flavors, and aromas of the São Joaquim market, and to explore around the back streets near the church of Bonfim.

Eating Bahian Food　This will win you over practically anywhere, but especially at the Casa da Gamboa or my new favorite, Marco Barbacoa.

Visiting Itaparica　Explore the island from tip to toe. And now that the Quinta Pitanga inn has been opened, you won't find a better place to eat in the whole region.

Hanging Out at a Bar, Café, or Beach Shack　There's just nothing like the Bahian pace of life to drive off the shadows of life in the fast lane.

with sacks of colorful spices, household items you won't find in either department stores or souvenir shops but which deserve the status of genuine folk craft, and pottery—dozens of tented shops selling brittle plate and knickknacks, underglazed and underfired, which you won't be able to resist but which will probably break long before you get home, or soon thereafter.

When you tire of the market, continue up the shoreline to the favorite of all the in-town beaches, near the **Praça da Boa Viagem.** The weekend scene here is very democratic and appealing, and there are dozens of beach-shack restaurants to satisfy hunger and thirst. Farther on along the shore you will arrive at the point of the peninsula, where the old 16th-century fort of Monte Serrat (not open to the public) commands the high ground and offers a wide, breezy view of both upper and lower bay. The nearby **Igreja do Monte Serrat,** farther out on the point, is a lovely miniature that dates from the 1500s and has the rude, hand-hewn pews to prove it.

From here the land makes a 90° bend and continues up the bay, and we will follow Rua Rio São Francisco (which becomes Rua Plínio de Lima) uphill toward the most fascinating of all Salvador's religious shrines, **Nosso Senhor do Bonfim,** a landmark in the daytime by virtue of its hillside perch, and by night as well, its outline traced in the light of a thousand bulbs.

To Catholics, Bonfim is Christ the Lord; to the fetishists he is Oxala, prince of the gods. The church of Bonfim somehow evolved into the great crossroads of both faiths. Once a year, in early January (see Section 6, "Special & Free Events") Bonfim is actually the focus of a major rite of the *candomblé*. Lest we forget the significance of Bonfim to the average Bahian, everywhere in the city, encircling people's wrists or fastened to the rear-view mirrors of taxis and buses, are thin streamers in various shades of pastel printed with the legend "LEMBRANÇA DO BONFIM" (souvenir of Bonfim). This ribbon is a good-luck charm common to adherents of both religions, and its presence is also much in evidence throughout the church, looped around crucifixes and candlesticks (which are electric, on the main altar) and pinned to the walls.

The faithful pray to Bonfim to be delivered from harm or illness. Promises are made, and fulfilled. A woman is seen carrying her baby, walking on her knees from the main entrance the full distance of the long central aisle, all the way to the altar. Other believers add their requests for special favors in the form of letters—often with accompanying photographs of loved ones for whom they wish to intercede—to the thousands of similar appeals that form a thick covering on the walls and ceiling of the Room of Miracles, to the rear of the church on the right-hand side. Also suspended everywhere in this room are the ex-votos—plaster and plastic models of limbs and organs, offered in thanks for miraculous cures. One man has pasted a note with some photocopied pictures, asking the Lord to help his brother stop drinking. There are few smiles on the faces in these photographs; people have their tough, everyday faces. The most devout—or perhaps just the most affluent—commission miracle painters, a profession unique to the city, to capture their hour of need on canvas, and these, too, are found hanging throughout this gallery of human hope.

Outside the church in the plaza are the milling squads of *capitães da areia* (beach urchins), so called by novelist Jorge Amado, a resident of the city and principal chronicler of its popular and sacred myths. The children are attracted by the thousands of tourists who visit Bonfim yearly, and are seeking alms for the here and now, while others inside plot their strategies for eternity. Across the street, toward the water, is a line of shops, including a juice bar that serves fresh-squeezed beverages in large plastic bags taped around long, thin straws. A road along the bay leads from here to the very desirable back-harbor neighborhood of Ribeira, a place to fantasize about when imagining where in Salvador you might want to live in your future life.

MUSEUMS

MUSEU DE ARTE SACRA, Rua do Sodré 276. Tel. 243-6310.
The Museu de Arte Sacra (Museum of Sacred Art) is probably the most important collection of art—religious or secular—in the city. The museum is housed in the

IMPRESSIONS

The Bahiano holds himself the cream of Brazilian cream.
—RICHARD BURTON, *EXPLORATIONS OF THE HIGHLANDS OF BRAZIL*, 1869

---

former 17th-century convent of the Barefoot Carmelites, and is a veritable cornucopia of religious-inspired art, much of it the old carved-wood images the Portuguese brought with them from the home country. Of the domestic work, there is a gilded reliquary by Aleijadinho.
Admission: 50¢.
Open: Tues–Fri 1–6pm.

TEMPOSTAL, Rua do Sodré 22, Largo Dois de Julho. Tel. 321-9685.
Across from the Museum of Sacred Art is Tempostal, a private museum devoted to postcards and stamps, as well as many other cultural artifacts of the Bahian past.
Admission: $1.
Open: Sat–Sun 2–6pm.

MUSEU DE ARTE DA BAHIA, Av. 7 de Setembro 2340. Tel. 235-9492.
This museum is an eclectic collection of paintings and furnishings from both Europe and Brazil, set in a restored colonial mansion.
Admission: 50¢.
Open: Tues–Sat 2–6pm.

MUSEU DE ARTE MODERNO, Av. do Contorno s/n. Tel. 243-6174.
The Museu de Arte Moderno (Modern Art Museum) is attached to the **Solar do Unhão,** a complex of colonial-era buildings that includes a popular restaurant, with entertainment, on Avenida do Contorno. The museum houses no permanent collection, but is open during exhibitions, as scheduled. There is a *son et lumière* focused on the buildings on many evenings.
Admission: Free.
Open: Tues–Sun 1–5pm.

MUSEU DO INSTITUTO GEOGRÁFICO E HISTÓRICO, Av. 7 de Setembro 94A. Tel. 241-2453.
Map and history buffs might enjoy browsing through the stately halls of the Museu do Instituto Geográfico e Histórico, located on the Praça da Piedade. One interesting exhibit shows the arms used during Brazil's war with Paraguay.
Admission: Free.
Open: Mon–Fri 2–5pm.

COOL FOR KIDS

Brazilian society does not cater to children in quite the same way we do in the northern reaches of the Americas. Thus kids tend to be more integrated into the same space and activities that engage the grown-ups. Those traveling to Salvador with children should consider spending most of their stay in a resort environment, either on the island of Itaparica or at the ecological preserve of Praia do Forte to the north. The beaches in these places are more contained, and certainly not urban like their counterparts in Salvador proper. There are also many activities in these locales which older children may find attractive, from beachside sports to windsurfing and horseback riding.

A STROLL THROUGH HISTORICAL SALVADOR

The greatest concentration of historical buildings in Salvador—a city where around every corner you might stumble upon a rare and ancient architectural gem—is found in the **Pelourinho.** Like so much of historical Brazil, the Pelourinho has been sanctified by UNESCO as an "international treasure," in this case "the most important area for colonial architecture in the Americas." It is good to keep in mind that while Salvador bloomed radiantly during the Belle Epoque of Brazil's baroque period (essentially the Gold Cycle of the 1700s), the city—Brazil's capital until 1763—was already the flower of the South Atlantic during the 1600s. And of all Brazil, only here in Salvador will you see the roman numerals XVI and XVII (denoting the 1500s and 1600s) so frequently associated with extant structures.

A tour of the Pelourinho district can begin at the **Praça da Sé,** a large public square adjacent to its smaller neighbor, the **Terreiro de Jesus,** from which you actually enter the Pelourinho. The Praça da Sé has its own architectural charm, bordered by the 18th-century former Palace of the Archbishop and the Igreja da Sé, but the real show on this square is its animated street scene. Someone is always performing here: a backcountry poet selling his work in a rudely printed chapbook; a magician who will wrap your watch in a handkerchief, smash it with a stone, and return it to you whole; or a pitchman swearing on his mother's grave that the weird gadget he is hawking "really works" and that you can't live without it. How will you resist the photographers who want to shoot your picture with one of those old box cameras that stand on skinny tripod legs like bashful cranes in a marsh?

From here you can approach the Pelourinho in one of two ways, entering the Terreiro de Jesus directly, or via a short back-street digression to visit Salvador's famous "church of gold," considered by many the most striking of all Brazil's baroque accomplishments. For the latter option, walk from the Praça da Sé up Rua Guedes de Brito, past the monumental gate of the Saldanha Palace, now housing the School of Arts and Crafts, and on to Rua São Francisco. Turning left here, proceed to the **Praça Anchieta** where you will find the **Igreja e Convento de São Francisco** (Church and Cloister of St. Francis), open all week during business hours, but closed Sunday afternoon. The church's uncomplicated facade contrasts mightily with the elaborately carved interior, where every chiseled surface is sheathed in brilliant gold. A wainscoting of *azulejos* (blue-and-white Portuguese tiles) lines the walls, each panel illustrating a signal episode from the life of St. Francis of Assisi. On the altar is an unexpected sight: A large, sensual carving of the candomblé goddess Iemanjá, syncretized with the Virgin Mary, is mounted on the prow of the main pulpit, a familiar gesture of Catholicism's compromise in Bahia with its pagan rival. A statue of St. Peter of Alcântara on the right lateral altar was one of Dom Pedro II's favorite works of sacred art. The cloisters themselves, covered walkways around an interior courtyard, may be visited by men in the company of a monk, but women may only view the tiled and colonnaded retreat through a wrought-iron gate.

Next to the convent church is the equally stunning **Igreja da Ordem Terceira de São Francisco** (Church of the Third Order of St. Francis), built in 1703. The exterior of this church is as unique and prized in Brazilian architecture as the glittering interior of its next-door neighbor. The intricately carved stone facade was covered with stucco for generations, and only discovered accidentally by workmen a few years back. The discovery is viewed as one of Brazil's greatest art finds, ever. A room inside the church filled with life-size statues is worth visiting.

Walk through the Praça Anchieta and you will enter the Terreiro de Jesus, one of the oldest squares of the original city, with some of its oldest churches, including the **Catedral Basílica,** originally a Jesuit church, dating from the mid-1600s and final resting place of Mem de Sá, the Portuguese governor-general who drove the French from Rio de Janeiro. The basilica is open Tuesday to Saturday from 9 to 10:30am and 2 to 5pm and on Sunday from 9 to 10am. The *terreiro* (sacred ground) itself is heavily shaded by broad-leafed almond and poinciana trees, and in its midst stands the city's original public water source, though the cast-iron fountain imported from France is of a later period.

The walk through the Pelourinho district—a lengthy succession of narrow, cobbled streets, opening every several blocks into small interior *largos* (squares)— should take about two hours, especially if you wander all the way to the Praça de Santo Antônio and stop frequently along the way to admire the buildings, singly or in ensemble, browse the shops and side streets, and take such refreshment as is necessary. The pavement is of rough stones, and the descent is steep in places, but to get the entire flavor of the old neighborhood, it's wise to go the distance. Begin by entering Rua Alfredo Brito, past the old medical college which today houses the Afro-Brazilian Museum and its collection of candomblé art and artifacts. In a few minutes you will come to the irregularly shaped **Largo do Pelourinho,** an archetype of the colonial square of its day with its fine old houses. Here stood the *pelourinho,* the public whipping post where slaves were punished in full view of the approving gentry. Legend has it that the victims of this cruelty were succored at the nearby Igreja do Rosário, the Slave's Church, a sweet sampler of the baroque style in its own right.

The Pelourinho circuit is much tramped by visitors to Salvador, but it is still best to stick to the straight and narrow of the route and avoid the back streets and alleys, where the darkened doorways of the poor are not a pretty sight and muggers have been known to intimidate tourists and fleece them of their purses and cameras. A more probable danger faces the gullible who fall victim to the sting of a hustler; he offers to change money at a rate you can't refuse, then disappears with your cash through the doorway of a respectable building, never to be seen again. Overall, it should be stressed that Salvador seems a safe place to stroll endlessly and at will, avoiding only the most obvious cul-de-sacs of poverty, and staying alert at points where tourists concentrate and make obvious and tempting targets.

Also on the Largo do Pelourinho are the SENAC cooking school and cultural center, about which more below, and the **Museu da Cidade** (City Museum), where scenes from candomblé ceremonies are displayed wax-museum style, with mannequins dressed in ritualistic garb and posed in a variety of trancelike postures. Continuing on to the bottom of the square, to a point where five lanes converge, go straight on along Rua Luís Viana, and climb the incline toward the **Largo do Carmo,** where in the mid-1600s the city's Créole population finally defeated and forced the surrender of the Dutch, who had by then occupied Salvador for some years. On the way, a set of stairs to the left leads to the **Igreja do Passo,** perched above the lower city and offering a wide view of the bay. On the largo itself is the **Igreja da Ordem Terciera do Carmo** (1585) with its museum, one of the city's several repositories of fine sacred art, also containing an illustrated key to the syncretization of the Christian saints with their counterparts among the African deities.

Here ends the obligatory tour of the Pelourinho, but the walk on to the plaza at the end of the slope is much recommended, for a more unstructured contemplation of the quieter zones of this neighborhood, where nonetheless steady restoration of all the charming little buildings is rapidly transforming the place into the Brazilian equivalent of a gentrified bohemia. The single lane changes names several times as you descend, from Rua do Carmo to Rua Joaquim Távora, and finally Rua Direita. At the end of this final stretch is the **Praça de Santo Antônio,** a shady, quiet corner of the city bordered by delightful cottages—nos. 6, 7, and 8, in coral pink, pale blue, and earthy yellow—have a storybook quality about them. The plaza dead-ends at the **Forte do Santo Antônio,** one of the many colonial fortifications that defended early Salvador from the encroachments of its foes, and where today a Popular Cultural Center has been installed that provides space for craftspeople and dancers, and for the *capoiera* studio of Mestre João Pequeno.

A STROLL THROUGH BARRA

Barra, on the opposite end of the bay from Itapagipe, might be characterized as a kind of Bahian Greenwich Village. Barra began as a neighborhood of wealthy planters, and in its decline became a bohemian quarter. Today it has been restored to some of its past glory, and is a favorite address of the professional set, young and not-so-young alike. Barra is also a neighborhood attuned to the sensibilities of tourists, as its numerous hotels can attest, and is furthermore the city's most concentrated zone of nightlife.

Anyone staying in or near Barra might want to consider all or part of the following walking-tour itinerary. Begin in Barra at the **Forte de Santo Antônio da Barra,** a fortress originally built in the early 1600s to defend against the Dutch invasion. Today the fort houses the **Hydrography Museum,** and can be entered on Tuesday, Wednesday, Friday, and Saturday from 11am to 5pm. From here, the walk will take you via **Avenida 7 de Setembro** (with several detours) as far as you wish to go into the heart of the city. Consult a map before you begin, and carry it with you to verify distances and landmarks along the way. The entire walk as outlined here could easily consume four or five hours.

From the Largo da Barra you begin a steady climb up Avenida 7 de Setembro past many of the city's better small hotels. The first detour is a brief stroll off to the right up **Rua da Graça,** a pleasing residential block where you'll see several old mansions with grounds that are overgrown with large trees, vines, and other vegetation similar to what you might see in an interior town of Louisiana. Look also for the facades of houses decorated with Portuguese tiles that portray colonial and plantation scenes.

Continuing back up Avenida 7 de Setembro you will come to the **Museu Carlos Costa Pinto,** at no. 2490 (tel. 247-6081), open Wednesday through Sunday from 1 to 7pm. The museum is a modern house with a collection of fine furnishings and jewelry—including the *balangadas,* gold and silver trinket jewelry of the slaves—that once belonged to a wealthy Brazilian family.

The next major point of interest along the avenida is **Campo Grande,** a large, formal park with a monumental column as its primary landmark. Behind the park, on Rua Forte de São Pedro, is the modern **Teatro Castro Alves,** a venue for theater, dance, and popular concerts. Beyond the park Avenida 7 de Setembro curves inland, rising to the upper city, while Avenida do Controno hugs the shore and leads to the lower city. The next stretch of the walk along Avenida 7 de Setembro takes you past a wide variety of shops and offices, until arriving at the **Praça da Piedade,** where you may continue on in one of two directions.

If you wish to walk toward the harbor—to the Lacerda municipal elevator, for example—continue to follow Avenida 7 de Setembro to the **Praça Castro Alves,** monument and tomb of the romantic poet. From here you enter **Rua Chile,** a street of shops, once the most fashionable commercial zone in the city. Walk until you come to the **Palácio Rio Branco,** originally the Governor's House, some portions of which date to 1549, and now a museum and headquarters of Bahiatursa. The palácio has been through many transformations, renovations, and expansions since the colonial governors first resided on this spot, and the bulk of the building is really fin de siècle, constructed around 1900. Whatever its age, the building is an impressive edifice, and very much worth a visit. Despite a fantastic mix of styles, the rooms open to the public reflect a grandness and splendor of detail found in the great palaces of European royalty. Among the attractive details are several striking panel paintings recently uncovered from beneath successive layers of thick oil paint. From here you can descend to the lower city by elevator or go on to the historic district.

If on arriving at the Praça da Piedade, however, you wish to explore something of the inner city, simply follow **Avenida Joana Angélica,** a principal thoroughfare through the neighborhood of **Burroquinho.** There are many pleasant discoveries to be made as you wander among the unpretentious back streets of this old commercial district. Turning left on **Rua da Independência,** which turns into **Rua do Gravatá,** walk until reaching the **Praça dos Veteranos** and then enter onto **Rua 28 de Setembro.** This route will lead you to within a block of the Praça da Sé, and you will have seen a perfectly charming part of Salvador that few tourists ever bother to visit, yet it's only several blocks away from the more frequented historical zone.

6. SPECIAL & FREE EVENTS

Salvadorans celebrate often, and not only in private. Their best parties are public and take place in the streets, some even on the water. The feasting begins on New Year's Day with the impressive boat procession of the **Festa do Nosso Senhor do Bom Jesus dos Navigantes** (Our Lord Patron of Sailors). Hundreds of boats, led by the archbishop himself, who accompanies the image of Christ, are festooned with flowers and banners, and sail from the cove opposite Conceição da Praia church in the lower city to the beach of Boa Viagem on the Itapagipe Peninsula. Rental boats are available to follow the procession by water.

January 6, the **Festa dos Reis** (Feast of the Magi) is a cause for some pre-Lenten street dancing. The third Sunday of January is reserved for one of the city's most traditional celebrations, the **Festa do Nosso Senhor do Bonfim.** This festival actually begins on the preceding Thursday, when priestesses of the candomblé, dressed in full regalia, wash the white steps of Bonfim church, which are considered the sacred stones of the god Oxala. The great Carnivallike parade to Bonfim takes place on Sunday, and on Monday the **Festa da Ribeira** brings to a close this particular cycle of outdoor celebrations, although the more modest **Festa de São Lázaro** on the last Sunday in January is the official end of the month's wild festivities.

Can February be far behind? By no means! After barely a breather, one of the great popular spiritual manifestations of the year is orchestrated on February 2, the **Festa de Iemanjá,** goddess of the sea and principal mother figure in the pantheon of candomblé dieties. This is a festival of fishermen who are seeking the protection of the goddess from storms and shoals in the practice of their craft. All of the trappings of the candomblé accompany this colorful water pageant—priests, priestesses, and devotees in their vestments and symbolic costumes, processions, drums, chanting, candles. Offerings deemed appropriate to one as vain as Iemanjá is thought to be, from cosmetics to jewelry, are floated out to sea all along the beach from Rio Vermelho to Itapoã in the hope they will find favor with Salvador's most beloved goddess.

Two Sundays before Carnival, which usually takes place in February, the **Festa do Rio Vermelho** pays special homage to St. Anne, mother of the Blessed Virgin. And then all hell breaks loose in Salvador as **Carnival** has come again, and is celebrated like nowhere else in Brazil. The Carnival of the slaves, incorporating music and dance that originated in the rites of the candomblé, was imported from Salvador and melded seamlessly throughout the country with the ancient pre-Lenten festivities that stemmed from Christian traditions. The practice of Carnival in Salvador, moreover, has not been completely commercialized, as in Rio. The spontaneous singing and dancing through the streets, behind sound trucks carrying live bands, is still more central to the event than the formal parades and competitions of the *blocos* and *escolas de samba* or the celebrations in private clubs.

Holy Week in Salvador is more of a religious festival than a party, though Easter time is also a major secular holiday weekend throughout Brazil and the country comes to a complete halt. With so many churches, the processions in Salvador are endless, and particularly medieval throughout the city's historic district.

On May 10, Salvadorans publicly celebrate the feast day of their patron saint, **St. Francis Xavier,** a tradition in the city that dates from the late 17th century.

June is the month of bonfires and fireworks, the apostolic feasts honoring **Sts. John and Peter.** June is also significant on the calendar of the candomblé, when all the gods are honored in rites spread over a 12-day period.

Finally a hiatus, until November, when the pre-Carnival festivities begin the celebratory cycle anew. The next-to-last Sunday in November is the public **Feast of São Nicodemo de Cachimbo,** then **St. Barbara's Day** on December 4, and the **Feast of the Immaculate Conception** on December 8, a major street event on the waterfront, especially near the Igreja Nossa Senhora da Conceição da Praia.

After Christmas begins the **Festa da Boa Viagem** once again, culminating on New Year's Day with the boat procession of Nosso Senhor dos Navigantes. And in Salvador, for the rest of the year, the beat goes on.

7. SPORTS & RECREATION

SPECTATOR SPORTS   The principal spectator sport in Salvador—as throughout Brazil generally—is **soccer.** The city's main stadium, Fonte Nova, in the Dique de Tororó neighborhood, holds 77,000 spectators. Ticket range in price from $2 to $6, and the schedules of games can be found in the daily newspapers.

RECREATION   Jogging markers, in kilometers, are found along the beachfront sidewalks in Barra. People tend to use the beach in the vicinity of Farol de Barra, the lighthouse, for every variety of personal, outdoor fitness training. The Meridien hotel has tennis courts, and the Sofitel Quatro Rodas resort can offer both tennis and golf. Most five-star hotels, like the Hotel da Bahia and the Meridien, have saunas and modern exercise facilities.

8. SAVVY SHOPPING

The streets of Salvador are filled with vendors. Half the people on the streets are out walking somewhere, while the other half seem to be selling something: handmade jewelry, "silver" charms, T-shirts, rosewood carvings, *balangandas* (copies of the baubles given in the past to favored female slaves), leather goods, percussion instruments, and of course, gemstones—raw, polished, strung, or set in rings, bracelets, or brooches. Some vendors sell, more or less officially, from stalls in the various plazas like the Praça da Sé, the Praça da Piedade, or the Praça Castro Alves, and many others spread their wares at curbside, while jewelry makers carry their goods pinned to cardboard placards and approach you as you stroll by. You can probably do all the shopping you require, for personal mementos and presents, without ever entering a store. And remember—never accept the first price. Try to pay half, or at most, two-thirds of the offered price.

For craft items of better quality, try the **Instituto Mauá,** Av. 7 de Setembro 261, in Barra (tel. 235-5440). This nonprofit organization is charged with the mission of protecting and supporting the state's traditional crafts, samples of which—including pots, lace, and baskets—are assembled here from various centers of handcraft manufacture from all over Bahia. There is no bargaining at the Instituto Mauá: All items have clearly marked price tags.

The **Mercado Modelo,** overlooking the harbor on the Praça Cairú, is a big disappointment as a craft market. It seems to exist today solely for tourists, and the quality of the goods is no better than that found on the streets, while the prices are considerably higher. The one advantage of the Mercado Modelo is that all the geegaw-style souvenirs are assembled here under a single roof. While you might reasonably forgo shopping at the Mercado Modelo, the building's two restaurants should not be ignored. The second-floor café with the large outdoor veranda is one of the more pleasant places to lunch, snack, or drink, while observing the lively harbor scene.

Many vendors will approach you with items crafted from silver—or a metal they claim to be silver. Unless you are expert in distinguishing true silver from its alloys, you're better off going to a legitimate shop, like **Gerson** in the Pelourinho at Rua do Carmo 26 (tel. 242-2133), which specializes in silver service and jewelry. The shop occupies several floors of a lovingly restored colonial building, and hostesses circulate continually, offering trays of fresh-squeezed juices while you browse. Gerson also has branches in Barra next to the Hotel Praia Mar, at the airport, and in **Iguatemi,** Salvador's principal shopping center, located on the Praça da Mariquita, Rio Vermelho.

H. Stern is also well represented in the city, with shops at the airport, shopping centers, and in the Othon and Meridien hotels, with probably the finest collection of colored gemstones and crystals in the city.

If there is one city in Brazil where art collectors might have some luck in acquiring first-rate **contemporary paintings,** it is Salvador, long a bohemian haven for practicing painters. The naive street art can be found displayed in the various plazas mentioned above. Galleries and artist studio shops also abound, particularly in Barra. The enigmatic **Carybé,** a kind of latter-day Debret, is an Argentine who through his anthropological drawings has become the chief interpreter of Bahia's folk culture, and has a studio at Rua Medeiros Neto 9. The equally popular **Mirabeau Sampaio,** sculptor and draftsman, has an atelier at Rua Ary Barboso 12. Serious collectors interested in contacting these or other artists to visit their studios should seek the assistance of an intermediary—**Tatu Tours** (see Section 10, below) can perform this service.

9. EVENING ENTERTAINMENT

THE PERFORMING ARTS

Wherever you travel in the city, whether on the beach or in the local square, you are bound to see boys, young and old, practicing what appears to be an acrobatic form of kung fu. This is called *capoeira*, and while it is a martial art, it is also an art form. According to legend, this form of foot fighting was brought to Brazil by the slaves. But since slaves were not allowed to fight among themselves, the masters outlawed the practice. To circumvent the ban, the men, so that they might both preserve the form and themselves, began to choreograph the steps, and over time transformed capoeira into a dance of ritualistic confrontation. The object is to not deliver the blows, but to sweep close to the opponent's head and body with the many varieties of kicks and feints. Each "fight" is between two dancers only, who are accompanied by the rhythmic music of a drum, a tambourine, and a *berimbau* (a gourd and bow strung with a single strand of wire), and by the chanted verse of a melancholy song, often related to a *briga de amor* (fight over a woman).

Capoeira can be viewed at tourist shows, in the capoeira academies themselves, which often have weekly performances as a means of fund-raising, and best of all, on the streets. Bahiatursa can provide the names of academies and the scheduling of their performances.

The preservation of candomblé and its related sects that exist throughout Brazil represents one of the great struggles and achievements of a people threatened with cultural annihilation in the modern age. To be sure, the African-derived religions have suffered many modifications since the first slaves were transported to Brazil. Over time these animist practices borrowed freely from both the dominant state religion, Catholicism, and from the myths and sensibilities of the indigenous peoples as well. Nonetheless, it is humbling to recollect just how much of the original African content is retained in the rites despite the overwhelming repression and the strong currents of assimilation to which the slaves and their ancestors were subjected: snatches of chanted language, like Yoruba, passed surreptitiously from one generation to another; the names and attributes of the various deities; the drum and percussion rhythms, so intimately related to the religion, and which have no peer in musicology; the transcendent body movements of the celebrants when possessed by their gods, which in the secular culture gave birth to the samba; the cuisine, special dishes prepared to satisfy the most demanding spirit.

Too often candomblé and macumba ceremonies are exploited by the tourism industry in Brazil, and served up to visitors as if they had no more significance than a TV variety show. It is precisely the color, music, and movement of the legitimate ceremonies, in fact, that encourage this tendency to view and present these practices to tourists as a form of entertainment. As a result, the rituals attended by most "outsiders" have a staged and artificial quality, as if their only purpose were to put on a good show for the foreigners, who in exchange are charged a healthy entrance fee.

There are at least two ways—beyond traditional research in libraries and museums—in which the visitor may make a more authentic connection with candomblé, if so motivated. The first is obvious: Befriend a believer, and convince him to quietly sponsor you as a guest during one of the regular services. The second is to go privately to a *terreiro,* as the temples are called, and meet the *mãe de santo* or the *pai de santo* (priestess or priest), and ask if you can tour the facilities, interesting in and of themselves. Many of these clerics (for want of a better term) will also be happy to throw the shells and read your fortune, one of the many services they provide their parishioners, though this will cost you a donation and you will probably need an interpreter if you don't speak Portuguese.

There are a few theaters where you can see candomblé and capoeira. The show at the **SENAC,** Largo do Pelourinho 19 (tel. 321-5502), is a dignified introduction to Bahian folkloric culture, including candomblé and capoeira. Earnest young artists and performers put on the show here, and their respect for the experiences they portray is communicated, even if these abstractions of culture are never as good as the real thing when witnessed at their most spontaneous and least self-conscious. A very polished show can be seen at the **Solar do Unhão,** on Avenida do Contorno (tel. 321-5551). See "Specialty Dining" in Section 4 for details.

THE CLUB & BAR SCENE

The hot spot for singles recently was the **Bar Ad Libitum,** Rua João Gomes 88, off the Largo de Santana (Praça Marechal Aguiar) in the beach neighborhood of Paciência, not far from Barra. Many deluxe and first-class hotels have nightclubs or discotheques; **Zodiac** at the Hotel Meridien is one of the most popular in the city. Thursday, Friday, and Saturday are the nights with the most action.

Many headliners, often natives of the city or region, play Salvador frequently. Names to look for are Gilberto Gil, Gal Costa, Maria Bethânia, and Caetano Veloso. A new sensational homegrown talent to watch for is singer Margareth Menezes, who often plays clubs and cabarets, but has recently broken through to the concert level.

There are numerous good bars scattered around town with music nightly by pianists or small combos. Notable is the **Bistro do Luís,** Rua Cons. Pedro Luís 369 (tel. 247-5900), in the fashionable Rio Vermelho neighborhood on the orla. The bistro is co-owned by Lisboan Luís Guedes and his American wife, Patricia, and is popular with luminaries of the Bahian art, music, and literary scenes. Habitués are said to include the artists Carybé and Carlos Bastos, whose works hang with those of many other painters, salon style, about the premises.

Salvador's Barra neighborhood is saturated with bars, dancerias, and nightclubs that come in and out of fashion from one season to another. The **Close-Up,** Rua Prof. Fernando Luís 12 (tel. 245-5763), has been around for a while; the other houses seem to change their names at least once a year. But the one constant to remember is that Barra is—and has been for many years—one of the hottest and most concentrated zones of nightlife in the city, with many clubs along both the Avenida 7 de Setembro and its side streets. So café- and bar-hopping is convenient here.

Many other good clubs are located throughout the city, and along the 15-mile stretch of the orla, from Barra to Itapoã.

Off the narrow alleys of the Pelourinho, for example, is a kind of back-street supper club, the **Banzo,** Largo José de Alencar 6, on the second floor (no phone). Here's where international castaways do their "wasting away" in Salvador. Reggae and jazz are the featured sounds. Closed Monday.

A popular *boutequim* for beer guzzlers and café philosophers of all stripes is the **Rio de Janeiro Bar,** Trav. Lidio Mesquita 6 (no phone), in Rio Vermelho, next to the Extudo restaurant. Open after 7pm, until the wee hours, Tuesday through Sunday.

Similar in spirit, yet a bit more socially mixed in its clientele, is the **Cantina da Lua,** Terreiro de Jesus 2 (tel. 321-0331), right at the entrance to the Pelourinho. Open from 10am to 10pm daily; the beer is 80¢ per large bottle. Banners suspended from the nearby basilica indicated that the bar's owner, Claudio Silva, was the *Cidadão Samba*—essentially, "jolly good fellow of the year" in some recent civic free-for-all. The Cantina is one of the great meeting spots in Salvador, especially on Tuesday nights when crowds flock to the square for the *bênção,* the weekly blessing dispensed from one of the local churches, then descend to the Largo do Pelourinho to hear Olodum—the great rhythm band—strut their stuff for nothing.

Not far from the Campo Grande park, midway between Barra and the Praça da Sé, is one of the most unique gin mills in all Salvador. To get to the **Bar Quintal do Raso da Catarina,** Av. 7 de Setembro 1370 (tel. 321-7987), you have to hazard several sets of stone steps that lead to the sunken backyard—*quintal*—once the pride of the shabby old town house that surrounds and hovers above it. Right off one of Salvador's principal avenues, this bar is among the most secluded and delicious spots in town. Closed on Sunday, the Bar Quintal is open Monday through Thursday from 6pm to 3am, and Friday and Saturday till 4am, if not later. There's a drink there, the *Principe Maluco* (crazy prince), which is the bargain booze find of the decade. Forty cents gets you a double shot of mellow Brazilian moonshine (cane brandy), nested in a little coaster with a slice of cinnamon-soaked lemon. For another buck and a half, you can nibble at an order of tasty, salty *queijo coalho*—grilled cheese slabs. The rickety chairs are filled with conspiring *artistes* and other assorted anarchists; guitars are strummed and art prints hang pell-mell from a clothesline. If they knew their hideout were in a tourist guide, they would desert the place in droves; so disguise yourselves accordingly.

On the more polished end of the nightlife spectrum is the **Cutty Sark,** Av. Otávio Mangabeira s/n (tel. 230-5385), in a small shopping mall called Flat Jardim de Alah, across from the Jardim de Alah beach. Bahianos apparently have all the rest they can handle on Sunday, because by Monday—about the biggest night of the week at Cutty Sark—the nocturnal festivities swing back into high gear. Some nights there's live music at this club, and the dancing is informal, betwixt and between the crowded tables.

In the summertime, the beach of Stella Maris is a popular place to hang, often near **Pandang, Pandang** (tel. 378-1015), "next to the abandoned hotel," and known for its well-chilled beer, natural foods, and fresh juices.

10. EASY EXCURSIONS AROUND BAHIA

Bahia is such a vast state, with so many attractions beyond the city limits of Salvador, that in future years the state's appeal may come to justify a guidebook of its own, just for the visitors from abroad. Brazilians already tour Bahia in its entirety, and have been doing so for years. Three locales, all within an hour or so of the capital city, are here given brief descriptions: the incomparable island of Itaparica, the Praia do Forte beach resort on the northern coast, and the old sugarcane capital of Cachoeira, nestled in an upper estuary of the bay of All Saints.

All Saints Bay has a life all its own, independent of the hustle and bustle of the city. There are supposedly 34 islands in the bay, with Itaparica by far the most important. Itaparica is a summer and weekend colony for Salvadorans, serviced frequently by passenger and car-ferries. But even on Itaparica you can see how different, and exquisitely so, life on the bay islands is from the urban intensity that is Salvador. Itaparica is treated as a sep   .te destination, below, where you will find details on the island's villages, beaches, hotels, and restaurants. But a day-trip is also strongly recommended for those on limited schedules, who nevertheless have a yen to get out on the bay as well as to see something of life outside the city.

A GOOD TOUR COMPANY   Two enterprising young Irishmen, enchanted by Salvador during their days of student globe-trotting, settled here over a decade ago, and now earn their keep escorting tourists around the city. Their company, **Tatu Tours,** Rua Afonso Celso 447, Sala 105 (tel. and fax 071/237-7562), has offices in Barra, and is one of the best options available for English-speaking tourists in need of a guide or an organized tour. Along with the usual "city tour," (car and driver for $25 per person, with a minimum of two people), and Bahia by night ($50 per person, including transportation, dinner, and show), their specialty is an all-day trip to Cachoeira ($100 per person). Co-owner Conor O'Sullivan calls this the "real Bahia just beyond the city limits." The day includes stops at various farms along the way, with Conor always choosing new spots to keep the tour fresh.

BAY EXCURSIONS   Full- and half-day excursions aboard fully equipped schooners (written *escuna* in Portuguese) cruise the bay and call at the islands. For information, contact **Itaparica Turismo,** Rua Manoel Dias da Silva 1211, Pituba (tel. 248-3187). The ships usually depart from the Mercado Modelo pier around 9am, then call at various islands, have lunch in a typical restaurant, then return around 5pm. The cost is $20 per person, $30 if you wish to be picked up and returned to your hotel.

Other companies that offer regular schooner excursions, for groups or private charter, are **L. R. Turismo,** Av. Otávio Mangabeira 2365 (tel. 248-3333), and **Kontik-Franstur,** Praça da Inglaterra 2 (tel. 242-0433).

Many of the smaller *saveiro* sloops moored near the Mercado Modelo are also available for private rental. Arrangements are made directly with the skippers of these craft.

ILHA DE MARÉ

An overnight excursion can be made to the Ilha de Maré, in the upper bay, on a small boat that leaves from Ribeira (Praça Gen. Osório) sometime in the morning between 9 and 11am. The boat makes calls on the island at the hamlets of Itamoabá, Praia Grande (a basket-weaving center), and Santana (known for its lace), and returns the following morning from Santana before dawn. There are no tourist facilities on the island, but you can bargain with a local for a bed or camp on the beach.

ITAPARICA

This is the largest island in All Saints Bay, straddling its mouth between the two opposing points of the mainland, Salvador to the east, and rural coastal Bahia to the west. Itaparica was once a center of the Brazilian whale fishery, but in recent years the island alternates between its off-season role as a backwater of fishing communities and small agricultural holdings, and its high-season function as a spa for escapees from Salvador who are well enough heeled to possess summer homes in this little corner of Eden. Itaparica also has a growing infrastructure of tourist facilities. The ideal vacation in Salvador, especially for the first-timer, is to split the time between the city and the island. The ferry service is so regular, and the crossing sufficiently brief—less than an hour—that you can easily consider a form of commuting between the two destinations.

Itaparica is long and relatively narrow, about 18 miles from tip to tip, with major settlements on each end, **Vila Itaparica** to the north and **Cacha Pregos** to the south. A third center of summer action, **Mar Grande,** is in the middle of the island, a settlement with its eye turned perpetually toward the Salvador skyline across the bay. Strung between these principal towns are fishing hamlets, beaches, and colonies of summer cottages: some extravagant, others quite simple. Inland, a large portion of the native population lives on small farms, and works the soil producing crops of *mandioca,* along with bananas, breadfruit, mango, cashews, and numerous other fruits typical of tropical Bahia. The interior network of rutted dirt roads is hard on motor vehicles, but the inhabitants travel distances on the backs of horses and burros, and occasionally a bicycle is seen among the throngs of folk who most often walk from place to place.

On the opposite shore, the *contra costa* is close to the western continent and linked by a bridge. Here are located forgotten villages, like **Baiacú,** whose inhabitants, their dugout canoes and houses of mud and wattle, suggest the disorienting image of an isolated African hamlet. And indeed, perhaps this and similar communities are the remnants of **quilombos,** the free towns established as early as the mid-1600s by runaway slaves. Uprisings accompanied the institution of slavery in Brazil from its inception. The greatest of all the quilombos, called **Palmares,** was established in the neighboring state of Alagoas, and it endured for a century, finally brought to heel only in 1869. The great leader of Palmares, Zumbi, is today an honored national figure in Brazil, particularly among adherents of the country's incipient civil rights, or Black Consciousness, movement.

To keep it simple, I will outline two separate day-trip excursions to the island of Itaparica. In both cases, you will get to spend two hours cruising the bay—an hour each way—which is by far the cheapest, least formal way of observing both harbor life and the outline of the city skyline from the vantage point of the bay itself.

FERRIES TO BOM DISPACHO The São Joaquim ferry leaves from its slip adjacent to the grounds of the Agua de Meninos market. This ferry, which costs about 50¢ or less each way for passengers, also carries motor vehicles, and disembarks at Bom Dispacho on the island of Itaparica. A small car is charged $5 one-way ($7.75 on Sunday), while a van cost $6.25 ($9.75 on Sunday). The ferry is large, loud, and unadorned except for a stand-up bar and a blaring TV in the main compartment. Most passengers hang dreamily over the rails when the weather is fair, and watch the endless harbor activity during the 50-minute crossing. The first ferry in the morning leaves at 6am, and boats run hourly until 10pm to midnight on weekends and holidays.

When you arrive at the Bom Dispacho terminal, you will have several transportation choices for touring the island. Most efficient and expensive are the private cars, about $10 an hour. The advantage here is that you will get a driver who is probably an Itaparica native and who can give you an excellent orientation in two to three hours, including a stop for lunch and a swim. The *kombi* is a VW van that carries half a dozen passengers to fixed destinations, like Mar Grande, or the town of Itaparica, for anywhere from $3 to $5. The public bus is a rickety affair, used mostly by the simpler folk, but it goes everywhere and is a wise and reasonable choice for the more self-reliant.

FERRIES TO MAR GRANDE Another boat, a passenger launch, leaves from a terminal behind the Mercado Modelo, every hour on the hour beginning about 8am, for the town of Mar Grande; the final boat returns late in the afternoon. In fact the launch's schedule is not fixed, and is subject to a variety of factors. It seldom sails, for example, before the boat is full. Ask the master when the last boat returns on the day of your crossing. And remember, if you miss it, you can always return via nearby Bom Dispacho. The one-way fare is less than $1, and the trip takes about an hour each way.

The advantage of the Mar Grande launch is that you arrive directly at the dock of the island's most fashionable beach town, and need travel no further for your pleasures if you so choose. Mar Grande has lovely beaches, and several excellent restaurants.

A GOOD TOUR COMPANY A very personable couple, Marilia and Bernard (she's Brazilian, he's French), head **ILHATUR,** Av. Lomanto Júnior s/n (tel. and fax 071/831-1711), on Itaparica. Anyone visiting the island, whether on a day-trip or overnight, might have an interest in any of the following ILHATUR programs. An eight-hour historical tour by car and foot covers pretty much the entire island, and includes lunch and drinks ($90 apiece for two, $60 for three, and $50 for from four to seven persons). A six- to eight-hour trekking and dugout canoe excursion covers the more remote interior or backshore locations on the island, and includes lunch on the beach ($35 apiece for two, $25 for three or more). Night, bicycle, and boat tours, plus information on house rentals, are also available through the agency.

WHERE TO STAY

Campers may pitch their tents for free on the **Praia de Areia,** a beach on the bay side between Vila Itaparica and Mar Grande.

In Mar Grande

POUSADA FAZENDA ARCO-IRIS, Estrada da Gamboa 102, Mar Grande. Tel. 071/883-1130. 15 rms (10 with bath). MINIBAR TV

$ Rates: $20 single; $30–$40 double. AE.

The Arco-Iris complex, including three separate bungalows, is centered around an old fazenda farmhouse, set on a 500-acre mango plantation. This is a delightful place, and the owner is an extremely gregarious and entertaining chap. The in-house Manga Rosa restaurant is open to the public, and serves reasonably priced, well-prepared dishes in the $4 to $16 range. Another of the inn's features is the availability of horses, and a huge area for riding. Five of the rooms are singles with shared bath, and there are fans in seven of the rooms.

In Vila Itaparica

Two other hotel options for the island are both in Vila Itaparica, the miniature city on the northern tip that has a mysteriously medieval air about it. No doubt the presence of several churches and chapels that are among the oldest in Brazil contributes to this feeling. In fact, the entire island is studded with antiquities and ruins, and Itaparica's relatively small size makes it ideal for unstructured exploration, adding an element of wonder and surprise to private discoveries.

HOTEL ICARAI, Praça da Piedade 03, Vila Itaparica. Tel. 071/831-1110. 20 rms (some with bath).

$ Rates: $15–$20 double. No credit cards.

This is a budget hotel with simple rooms, located on one of the most charming sites in the town, overlooking a delightful square and the waterfront.

QUINTA PITANGA, Rua Nova s/n, Vila Itaparica. Tel. 071/831-1554. 3 rms, 6 suites.

$ Rates (including all meals): $200 double. 30% discount off-season, May–Nov. No credit cards.

When artist James Valkus made his escape from New York City's fast lane of high-toned corporate art a few years back, he landed on his feet in Itaparica, imagining that he'd died and gone to heaven. In brief, he found an 18-room estate facing the bay, and turned it into a B&B. But what a B&B! The finished product would have been the envy of the gentry and nobility of ancient Rome, should they have had the good fortune to possess a weekend villa of this stamp in old Pompeii, and a genius of interior design like Jim Valkus to go with it. His interiors are singularly gorgeous, without ever lapsing into some cliché of fashion, conventional or otherwise. Billowing fabrics, original canvases, a chandelier of tiny lights fabricated from the pruned branches of a mango tree, and *objets* of every other species, each a sampler of taste and authenticity, all combine to delight the eye and the imagination in a spacious dwelling already made elegant by virtue of its classical dimensions—tall, wide windows; large, airy rooms and corridors.

A bevy of houseboys in livery—costumes that recall *A Thousand and One Nights*—glide about the premises, serving drinks and waiting at table during meals. How's the food? It doesn't get much better, thanks to Jim's protégé, Itaparica native Jacinto, who has (Valkus freely concedes) surpassed his mentor in the kitchen by several strides. If the lunch I sampled was typical (and I have every reason to believe it was, after hearing the glowing reports of a guest who had been there for three months), the Quinta Pitanga is not only the find of the decade in and around Salvador, but in all Brazil.

WHERE TO DINE

There are simple seafood restaurants all over the island, usually right on the shores of the sandy beaches. Nowhere on Itaparica are you ever far from a cold beer and a plate of fresh-caught shrimp sautéed in garlic and oil.

O MARINHEIRO, Estrada Beira Mar s/n, Ponta de Areia. Tel. 831-1490.
Cuisine: SEAFOOD. **Reservations:** Not needed.
$ Prices: Appetizers $1.50–$3.50; main courses $4–$12.
Open: Daily 11am–10pm.

This beachside restaurant is located on the road to Vila Itaparica. The house specialty is a shrimp dish called camarão a Paulista ($12). The traditional Portuguese soup, caldo verde, is also well reputed. Live music is offered every night during the summer months, December through March.

O TIMONEIRO, Estrada de Cacha Pregos, Berlinque beach. No phone.
Cuisine: BAHIAN/INTERNATIONAL. **Reservations:** Not needed.
$ Prices: Appetizers $2–$10; main courses $5–$18. No credit cards.
Open: Daily noon–10pm.

The Brazilian guide *Quatro Rodas* gives O Timoneiro a star for its consistently good food. That's quite an accomplishment, considering that the menu offers 70 different dishes, with specialties ranging from mixed-grill barbecues to Bahian fish moquecas.

PHILIPPE RESTAURANT, Praça de São Bento 53, Mar Grande. Tel. 833-1060.
Cuisine: SEAFOOD/INTERNATIONAL. **Reservations:** Not needed.
$ Prices: Appetizers $2–$3.50; main courses $6–$16. No credit cards.
Open: Daily 11am–midnight.

The Philippe Restaurant, opened under the guidance of a transplanted Frenchman and former employee of the island's Club Med (a playground for wealthy Brazilians and Argentines that studiously avoids promoting to the North American market), offers both local and French-inspired dishes. Two of the standby specialties at Philippe are the grilled lobster ($16) and the steak au poivre ($9).

PRAIA DO FORTE

Several years ago, before the coastal Coconut Road (BA 099) was paved, the beach at Praia do Forte, a once-quiet fishing village, was the lone weekend preserve of those who had the dune buggies or four-wheel-drive vehicles needed to get there. And while the beach has undergone some development since those halcyon days, mostly the region remains protected by an ecologically minded foundation which holds title to the shore and its surrounding lands, the former estate of a Portuguese nobleman. Garcia D'Avila once ruled virtually all of northeastern Brazil, and the ruins of the family castle, built in 1552—the only example of Renaissance architecture that remains in the country—are not far from the beach and worth a visit.

WHERE TO STAY

POUSADA PRAIA DO FORTE, Rua do Sol, Praia do Forte. Tel. and fax 071/835-1410. 18 cabanas. MINIBAR
$ Rates (including breakfast and dinner): $120 double. AE, DC, MC, V.
A slightly less expensive option than the listing below, this is a very comfortable beachfront property closer to the little village, where craft shops and café-restaurants are to be found. Dinner is also included at the pousada. Here you may lounge on the sand all day, and sip caipirinhas at poolside as the sun goes down.

PRAIA DO FORTE RESORT HOTEL, Estrada do Coco, Praia do Forte. Tel. 071/835-1110. Fax 071/832-2100. Telex 71/3897. 138 rms. MINIBAR
$ Rates (including breakfast and dinner): $170 double. AE, DC, MC, V.
This is a beautifully designed resort, which occupies one of the most favored beachfronts in all Brazil. The resort functions in a similar manner to the Club Med, with many programmed water and land activities, but at a somewhat more informal Brazilian pace. Rooms, incidentally, are designed in the native fashion, with high ceilings, open at the roofline, which allows for natural cooling and ventilation.

WHERE TO DINE

In nearby Arembepé, there's a restaurant that is a favorite of tour guide Conor O'Sullivan of Tatu Tours, because the seafood dishes are quite good, while the prices are much lower than those in the city.

MAR ABERTO, Largo de São Francisco, Arembepé. No phone.
Cuisine: SEAFOOD. **Reservations:** Not needed.
$ Prices: Appetizers $1.25–$3; main courses $5.50–$10.75. No credit cards.
Open: Sun–Thurs 10am–11pm, Fri–Sat 10am–2am.

Some of the bargain treats at the Mar Aberto—which means the "open sea"—are the shrimp in garlic and olive oil ($7), *ensopado de peixe* (fish stew in coconut milk, for $5.50), and the mixed ensopado of shrimp, lobster, and langostino ($10.75).

CACHOEIRA

Cachoeira is another of Brazil's colonial towns that has been declared a national monument. Once a major port and financial center for the sugarcane plantations, the town is located in the *recôncavo*, about 70 miles from Salvador. In 1624 the Portuguese colonials retired to Cachoeira, which became the de facto capital of Bahia during the two-year-long Dutch occupation of Salvador. The small provincial city is a showcase of colonial-era architecture, whose most remarkable buildings date from as early as the 16th and 17th centuries.

Many hotels and travel agencies in Salvador offer day-trips to Cachoeira, some of which transport visitors there via the bay on converted commercial schooners. Check with Bahiatursa for details.

CACHOEIRA'S BLACK HERITAGE Cachoeira is the unofficial seat of the candomblé religion—in the words of one tour guide, "what the Vatican is to Catholicism, and Mecca to Islam." Many important candomblé festivals take place in Cachoeira, like **Boa Morte** in mid-August, when the elite sorority called the Sisters of the Black Death, which began as a group of freed woman slaves, perform ancient rituals in honor of the death and assumption of the Virgin Mary.

OVERNIGHTS IN CACHOEIRA The state-run **Pousada do Convento,** on the Rua Inocêncio Boaventura (tel. 071/724-1716), offers double-occupancy accommodations for $35. (No credit cards are accepted.) The best time to visit Cachoeira under normal circumstances is on market days, Wednesday, Friday, and Saturday, when the streets are filled with vendors and shoppers.

THE NORTHEAST

The Brazilian northeast is a land of legends. *"O nordeste,* that's the real Brazil," say the citizens of the country's comfortable and developed south. And you might respond, "But isn't the nordeste the land of the dreaded *sertão*—the arid badlands, where sometimes there is no rain for an entire year, and cattle and people routinely die of starvation?" "Yes, of course, but do you know," you are instructed, "that despite the misery of the northeast, the underdevelopment, the high infant mortality, and all the other ills of the region, a quarter of the Brazilian population still lives there, though it is only 10% of the national territory? True, people leave all the time whenever the droughts are particularly prolonged, but at the first sign of rain, they all go back." Strange, this nordeste.

It was in the nordeste that the Portuguese staked their first claims in Brazil, planted their sugarcane, imported their slaves, and slaughtered male Native Americans. The mixed-race culture of the *caboclos* is what remains of that legacy. In the black-haired, bronze-faced caboclos you see a reflection of the earliest indigenous peoples. The amalgamation of their race and culture with that of their conquerers is their compromise with history, one that has endured in the sertão for over 4½ centuries. Yes, you think, this is the real Brazil.

The region's inhabitants, the *sertanejos,* are also often referred to as the *flagelados* (flagellants), with the unmistakable inference that their status as Brazil's sacrificial lambs is at least partially self-inflicted. And indeed, to modernists everywhere, even native Brazilians, the caboclos seem inscrutable, and their punishing way of life incomprehensible. And yet, the sertanejos are stubbornly committed to the unforgiving desert where they make their home. No other people anywhere, moreover, has embraced more fully the mystical elements of Catholicism. Out of this mysticism have sprung the greatest of all Brazilian legends, including the millenarian tragedies like the seige and destruction of the flagelado stronghold, Canudos, by the modernizing forces of the First Republic; and *coronelismo* (strongman rule) and *cangaceiros* (banditry), which go hand in hand, spawning such historic figures as Lampião and Padre Cícero, one a legendary gunslinger, the other a demagogue-priest, both mad as hatters, and as typical a human product of the sertão as the scrawny *caatinga* growth that covers the waterless backlands.

But the culture of the caboclo is only half the reality of northeastern Brazil. The rest of the story is told along the *litoral,* the extensive coastal plains that run from one end of the great Brazilian bulge to the other. While never prosperous like the south, the northeastern coastal cities were the setting for great political and intellectual movements which have their strong echoes in the Brazil of the present, as well as their historical and literary romance. Recife was the center of several bloody rebellions, providing its share of names for Brazil's pantheon of national heroes, like Frei Caneca, a republican priest who was executed under the first Brazilian Empire in the early 19th century. The northeast has also provided the nation with some of its greatest statesmen and poets, like Rui Barboso and Castro Alves.

WHAT'S SPECIAL ABOUT THE NORTHEAST

Great Towns and Cities
- ☐ Natal, a city of giant dunes, cooling sea breezes, and tropical dreams.
- ☐ Maceió, boasting some of the best beachfront hotels in Brazil, minus a lot of urban clutter.
- ☐ Recife is large and civilized, but its most appealing asset is the historic town of Olinda, just minutes north of the city limits.

Beaches and Resorts
- ☐ 14 great spas and resorts—the Hotel Genipabu in Natal, the Pratangy Village Hotel near Maceió, and the Portal de Ocapora and the Hotel Intermares near Recife.

- ☐ From Aracajú to São Luís, the coastline is one unbroken beachscape. Take your pick; you can't go wrong.

Regional Food
- ☐ Fresh seafood abounds along this infinite coastline. Dine al fresco on grilled red snapper or feast on shrimp still you cry "uncle."

Crafts
- ☐ Hammocks from Recife and Natal.
- ☐ Lace and embroidery from the Pontal da Barra neighborhood in Maceió.

It is within the four cities of this chapter—each the capital of a state—that we will confine our current tour, surveying an attraction of the northeast that has only just begun to catch the eye of the international traveler: a coastline that can boast some of the world's finest and most unspoiled beaches. Despite being in the equatorial zone, the northeastern coast is blessed with perpetually cooling sea breezes. The sunshine is equally constant, giving credence to the region's claim of year-round summer weather. But the beaches are not the only appealing features of the northeastern coast. The cities themselves—some small and provincial, others genuinely metropolitan and urbane—are each special in a multiplicity of ways. This is the time to visit the nordeste. Hotel and resort development has increased geometrically in the region over the past several years. But the coastline is so long, so rich with beachfront, that the atmosphere remains for the time being minimally touristic, and very fun-loving.

1. MACEIÓ

320 miles NE of Salvador

GETTING THERE   By Plane   Regularly scheduled flights by VARIG, Cruzeiro do Sul, VASP, and Transbrasil ply the northeast coast from one end to the other.

By Bus   The main bus station in Maceió is the **Terminal Rodoviária João Paulo II,** Avenida Leste/Oeste, a mile and a half from downtown in the Feitosa neighborhood (tel. 223-4432). The **Empresa Bom Fim** (tel. 221-5601) has three buses a day (each way) between Salvador and Maceió. A ticket for the 10-hour ride costs $20. The trip between Recife and Maceió, via a bus of the **Empresa Real Alagoas** (tel. 221-5055), takes four hours and costs $7.

By Car   The inland route up the coast follows BR 101 from Salvador to Maceió. A series of coastal roads hugs the actual shoreline, hopping from town to town. In some places, rivers impede the journey, and ferries may or may not be available.

ESSENTIALS   EMANTUR—the Alagoas state tourism bureau—maintains an information counter, meeting all flights at the airport (no phone). Or visitors may go directly to their headquarters at Av. Duque de Caxias 2014, downtown (tel. 221-8987), open Monday to Friday from 8am to 6pm. The city tourism office staffs a kiosk on the Pajuçara beach, open seven days a week from 8am to 7pm.

For assistance in airport transfers and guided tours, contact **Transamérica Turismo,** Av. Duque de Caxias 1436 (tel. 082/221-6992; fax 082/326-1610), and ask for Rosmario Santa Cruz.

Maceió is the capital of the coastal state of **Alagoas.** The story of how the state got its name is prosaic in the extreme. An early explorer, Pero Vaz da Caminha, commenting on the number of large inland lakes along the future state's coastline, included the following sentence in his report to the crown: *"Encontrei um lugar onde ha lagoas"* ("I have found a place where there are lakes"), and thus *"ha lagoas"* became Alagoas. Or so the story goes.

The state today is rare in what was once an entire region whose lands were saturated with sugarcane plantations. Sugarcane remains Alagoas's principal agricultural crop. The great green shoots of the cane are seen growing everywhere as you travel around the immediate environs of Maceió, and the very presence of the plants still embodies something of the atmosphere of Brazil's agrarian beginnings.

Maceió is one of the fastest-growing tourist destinations in Brazil. The state's coastline is a continuous and beautiful beach some 150 miles long. Among the cognoscenti, moreover, the beaches of Maceió are considered the best in all Brazil—though it's difficult to see how one would make such a judgment in a country where equally gorgeous beaches can be found from the mouth of the Amazon all the way to the Uruguayan border.

WHAT TO SEE & DO

Maceió, like Salvador, has an *orla,* a strip of in-town beaches where most of the city's tourist-quality hotels and restaurants are concentrated. The best of these, as would seem logical, are the strands that are farthest from the inner city, which remains an active and colorful sugar port with some of the historical flavor of the days when it first evolved in the mid-1600s as a plantation and sugar mill.

The prime beaches are **Pajuçara, Ponta Verde, Jatiúca,** and **Praia de Cruz das Almas.** Maceió occupies the tip of a curved peninsula, the ocean beaches on one shore and the great lagoon, **Lagoa do Mundaú,** on the other, immediately to the south of Maceió's downtown area. Beyond the lagoon is the **Região do Sul** (the southern beach zone), and to the north of the city, going toward Pernambuco state, are the beaches of the **Região do Norte,** both of which are described under "Easy Excursions," below.

The major attraction of the in-town beaches, beyond the obvious pleasures of sand and sea, is the sidewalk promenade that accompanies the contours of the shoreline. The wide pedestrian way, raised slightly above the sand and shaded by innumerable tropical trees, doubles as a jogging track by day and a center of nightlife when the sun goes down. All along the promenade, spaced every hundred yards or so, are sidewalk cafés—large stylized Native American huts with conical straw roofs, uniform in design according to a city plan. Each café, however, has its own regulars and its particular scene, one that often includes live music, and always tables full of friends in animated conversation.

On the southern fringe of the city's urban zone and waterfront begins the old surburban fishing village of **Pontal da Barra,** along the shores of the Lagoa do Mundaú. The village has a small and lovely town square, surrounded by old, low buildings and cottages. At the cottage windows, women weave their lace and display their artistic works for sale. Many rustic, but excellent, restaurants line the shores of the lagoon, specializing in seafoods purchased from the daily catch from its waters.

The art and charms of one needleworker here, **Teka the Lacemaker,** Travessa São Sebastião 56 (tel. 221-8383), were celebrated in a 1981 carnival samba called

"Teka Rendeira," by singer Martinho de Vila. The walls of Teka's shop are covered with photos of the rich and famous (including President Collor, a former mayor of Maceió), who have come here in recognition of her fame as both popular symbol and fine artisan. A friend purchased one fetching ensemble of Teka's for about $12, a hand-embroidered pair of bermudas with a top to match.

Boat and canoe excursions can be booked in Maceió for the popular cruises on the enormous lagoon, with its many islands and canals, and numerous other towns upstream along its banks (see below).

WHERE TO STAY
EXPENSIVE

HOTEL JATIÚCA, Lagoa de Anta 220, Maceió. Tel. 082/231-2555. Fax 082/235-2808. Telex 82/2302. 96 rms and suites. A/C MINIBAR TV TEL
$ Rates: $100–$124 single; $111–$138 double; $155 suite. AE, DC, MC, V.
This is a resort really, only 20 minutes from town, on a point overlooking Jatiúca beach. A long driveway leads to a separate lobby building, with a courtyard restaurant and pool to the rear. And laid out over the 15-acre grounds under a cover of much vegetation are four long two-story buildings with the hotel's rooms, and half a dozen other structures housing various facilities, all of which are interconnected by a network of covered brick pathways. The path, which also has walls of louvered shutters that open and close, crosses a small lagoon at one point as it meanders over the grounds down to the sand. No roadway need be crossed to reach the water, as is the case with the city's other hotels. In a rose stucco building near the edge of the sand is the cocktail bar and a restaurant, with banquettes along the walls, and large mullioned windows that slide open, the better to take in the seascape and the ocean air. Rooms at the Jatiúca are large, bright, and simply but tastefully decorated, and each opens onto a balcony.

MACEIÓ MAR HOTEL, Av. Alvaro de Otacílio 2991, Maceió. Tel. 082/ 231-8000. Fax 082/231-7085. Telex 82/3150. 128 rms. A/C MINIBAR TV TEL
$ Rates: $85–$105 single; $103–$128 double. AE, DC, MC, V.
The city's newest deluxe beach accommodations are in the Maceió Mar Hotel. All rooms have ocean views. The superior rooms are L-shaped and roomy and have balconies looking out over Ponta Verde beach. The standard rooms don't have balconies and are smaller, but they're still quite comfortable. Corridors and elevators have window walls, so that no matter where you walk within the hotel, you are in touch with the outdoors. The Maceió Mar is a full-service hotel, where facilities include a swimming pool, a restaurant, and two in-house bars.

MATSUBARA, Av. Roberto Brito 1551, Maceió. Tel. 082/235-3000. Fax 082/235-1660. Telex 82/2224. 110 rms. A/C MINIBAR TV TEL
$ Rates: $130–$160 single; $140–$175 double. Half-board rates available. AE, DC, MC, V.
✪ Maceió's only five-star hotel, the Matsubara is a paradigm of discreet good taste, and may just be the best small luxury hotel in Brazil. Every detail of design and organization in the Matsubara seems to have been consciously selected to blend and harmonize with its immediate surroundings, as well as with the overall image of the hotel. The building—an interconnected series of white blocks with protruding windows trimmed in brown—is a study in the creative applications to architecture of plain and solid geometry. All the forms are there, but their arrangement is never repetitious or banal. The hotel is located across from the Praia de Cruz das Almas, the farthest strand from the city, just now being developed by the hotel sector.

The Matsubara's bright atrium lobby is not huge by any means, but the space is ingeniously divided by barriers, mixed levels, plants, mirrors, and columns to create several distinct environments: a circular arrangement of green leather chairs; an informal café with rose-colored table linen, on a raised platform in a smart wood-dominated setting of its own; an excellent mezzanine restaurant behind an elegant wall of glass. The accommodations all have balconies, some quite generous depending on the category of the room. Decor in the rooms, light shades of blues and greens, maintains the standard of elegance set by the hotel in its public spaces. The best carpets, classically striped fabrics, fine wood, and decorative modern art are used to highlight the bedroom, while the bath is lined in speckled brown granite tile and has a sauna-type ceiling of tongue-and-groove wood battens.

The hotel's grounds occupy a somewhat narrow strip, but they stretch from oceanside way back to the lower slopes of a palm tree–covered hill. Behind the hotel are a large serpentine pool, two tennis courts, and basketball and volleyball facilities. And in the front courtyard is another pool which faces the beach. Both pools are set on patios ringed with recliners, and are served by their own bars. Another rare treat is the terrific steam room in the health club area.

MODERATE

TANI PLAZA HOTEL, Rua Ezechias Jerónimo da Rocha 247, Cruz das Almas, Maceió. Tel. 082/235-0774. Fax 082/235-3422. Telex 82/3244. 61 rms. A/C MINIBAR TV TEL

$ Rates: $56–$70 single; $64–$80 double. AE, DC, MC, V.

The Tani Plaza opened when this guide was between editions. And that's good news for anyone looking for a rare combination of location, value, and comfort during their visit to Maceió. The Tani Plaza is located so far out on the Cruz das Almas beach (the city's most undeveloped strand) that the avenue accompanying the oceanfront all the way from downtown stops a quarter of a mile before the hotel's rear gate, which is right on the sand. The hotel's actual entrance—not terribly easy to find—is off an internal avenue that runs out to the northern suburbs.

Several features make the Tani a very special hotel. The lobby is large and comfortable, and there are two pools on an immense inner court patio. The first-class rooms occupy a horseshoe of two-story wings, surrounding and overlooking the pool. Finally, as noted above, the grounds are right on the open sea. The hotel's restaurant, incidentally, has an extensive and separate Japanese menu in addition to a full international menu.

BUDGET

PONTA VERDE, Av. Alvaro Otacílio 2933, Maceió. Tel. 082/231-4040. Fax 082/231-8080. Telex 82/2368. 147 rms. A/C MINIBAR TV TEL

$ Rates: $29–$60 double. AE, DC, MC, V.

A very popular hotel all year round is the simple Ponta Verde, a 10-story tower across from the beach of the same name. Like most beaches on the stretch of coast from Maceió to above Recife, Ponta Verde has a reefline that follows the outline of the shore, about 200 yards out. At low tide a natural pool is formed between the coral rock and the land, and fishermen easily catch the trapped octopus at that time. The best rooms, which are large, face the sea. The hotel has a pool and restaurant, but limited facilities otherwise. What it does have is superfriendly service, fair comfort, and a great location opposite one of Maceió's most popular beaches by day and its nighttime promenade after dark.

A Youth Hostel

The city of Maceió has a very good *albergue da juventude* (youth hostel) called **Nossa Casa,** Rua Abdon Arroxelas 177 (tel. 231-2246), off the Ponta Verde beach. The cost per night, including breakfast, is $7 for members, and $8.50 for nonmembers. Towels and sheets may be rented for 50¢ apiece.

WHERE TO DINE

In addition to the recommendations below, two excellent choices are the Matsubara's **Blooming Garden** or the **Restaurante das Alagoas** in the Hotel Jatiúca.

BAR DO ALÍPIO, Av. Alípio Barbosa 321, Pontal da Barra. Tel. 221-5186.
   Cuisine: SEAFOOD. **Reservations:** Not needed.
$ Prices: Appetizers $3–$7.50; main courses $5–$8.50. AE, DC, MC, V.
   Open: Mon–Sat noon–midnight, Sun noon–7pm.

On the road that runs along the bank of the lagoon in Pontal da Barra there are many small restaurants with unpretentious exteriors and superior kitchens. A good choice is the Bar do Alípio, where the nearby lagoon is a steady and reliable supplier of fresh seafood. The *camarão moda da casa* is shrimp poached in a broth of herbs and coconut milk. Particularly good is the *carne de sol,* tender and tasty slices of sun-dried beef with side dishes of rice and *pirão,* a kind of grits made from *mandioca.* The prices, to the relief of many locals, are ridiculously low.

FIORELLA RISTORANTE, Av. Deputado João Lajes 239, Ponta Verde. Tel. 231-3039.

Cuisine: ITALIAN. **Reservations:** Recommended at dinner.

$ Prices: Appetizers $2–$8; main courses $5–$14. AE, DC, MC, V.

Open: Lunch daily 11:30am–3:30pm; dinner daily 6:30pm–midnight.

I'm not sure if Maceió is a haven for superior chefs and restaurateurs, or if I just happened upon the best eateries in town by good fortune. Anyway, Fiorella is another excellent choice for dining, either for lunch or dinner. The restaurant menu features more than 50 different dishes, with an accent on pasta and seafood. A nice light lunch might be made of Fiorella's top appetizer, the lobster salad with a mustard-cream sauce ($8).

GSTAAD, Av. Robert Kennedy 2167, Ponta Verde. Tel. 231-1202.

Cuisine: FRENCH/INTERNATIONAL. **Reservations:** Recommended.

$ Prices: Appetizers $9–$13; main courses $9–$17. AE, DC, MC.

Open: Daily 7pm until the last customer leaves.

Every town of any size has its salon, its prime-time watering hole where the local luminaries come to graze and conspire. In Maceió, that spot is Gstaad. No one really gets here until 10, and most don't arrive until midnight. Then, under a magic spell of light jazz—played smooth as silk by a tenor sax/piano duo—the waiters begin to mobilize and ply their stately craft. In one corner, a maître d' bends over a chafing dish. With an alchemist's zeal, he mixes a concoction that suddenly bursts into flames, serving up, in my case, scallops of beef, accompanied by three distinct sauces of mango, cream, and Madeira ($9.75). My dessert was prepared in the same spirit, an equally well-crafted crêpe Suzette ($5.50). After dinner, anyone who has a mind to may step downstairs to Middo, a disco of some sophistication that is part of the same complex.

REPUBLIC DO CAMARÃO, Av. Sandoval Arrochelas 670, Ponta Verde. Tel. 231-8262.

Cuisine: SEAFOOD. **Reservations:** Recommended at dinner and on weekends.

$ Prices: Shrimp cocktail $8.50; main courses $9–$17.50. DC.

Open: Lunch daily noon–3pm; dinner daily 7pm–midnight.

If you only have time for only one meal in Maceió, and you adore fresh shrimp, eat here. The owners have their own fleet of shrimp boats, so the supply is never interrupted nor stale. Each order consists of a half-pound of shelled shrimp. An excellent medium-priced dish (we ate two orders between three people and were full) is the *camarão a moda do chefe* ($10.50). The large shrimp come breaded, and strung along a skewer with pieces of cheese, onion, and pepper, all served in a bed of rice pilaf with a side order of shoestring potatoes. Sit on the pleasant veranda at lunch or inside the air-conditioned dining room and wash your meal down with two or three ice cold *chopps,* as the draft beer is called, and you might think that life in this troubled old world is a pretty nice gig.

EASY EXCURSIONS

A JANGADA SAILBOAT RIDE

A fleet of rustic sailing craft, called *jangadas,* awaits your pleasure on the in-town beach of Pajuçara, and will carry you and your party—for about $2 a head—to a bathing reef and sandbar about a mile offshore. At a designated anchorage, as many as 50 jangadas tie up gunwale to gunwale, while their passengers dive from the boats and swim in the clear, salty green water, and explore the coral-studded bottom. At least one craft among the fleet is a floating restaurant, from where a crew of agile "waiters" crosses from boat to boat, delivering platters of fried shrimp, and tropical drinks served in carved-out pineapples. Among purely touristic activities, the jangada ride receives high marks; but take adequate precautions against the sun's burning rays.

PASSEIO DE ESCUNA

The schooner ride aboard the *Lady Elvira* (tel. 326-1679), which departs from a small pier opposite the Bar do Alípio restaurant in Pontal da Barra, is also highly recommended. The morning cruise is scheduled from 9am to 1pm, but actually didn't sail until after 10am, and I don't think we got back much before 3pm; but no one was complaining. The water excursion itself is brief, a slow turn around the islands of the Mundaú lagoon, before heading toward the ocean breakers, and tying up right on the sandy bank of the hugh bar that separates the lagoon from the open sea. Here on the wide beach you can swim in either body of water, sunbathe, or walk for miles along the oceanfront. Or you can sit under the straw roof of the *barraca*—beach-shanty bar—and philosophize with your shipmates. Tickets for the cruise are $8 per person; the three large bottles of beer, and generous plate of grilled shrimp my companion and I consumed cost another $7.50.

EXPLORING THE LAGOON

Also worth visiting is the far shore of the lagoon, with its small houses and the look of a rural bayou culture, subsisting on fishing and small-scale agriculture. Here on the far shore was the old state capital, also the birthplace of Brazil's first president, Marechal Deodoro da Fonseca, whose name it now bears.

THE SOUTHERN REGION

The road to the Região do Sul is a pleasant ramble on the lakeside, passing homes and occasional bars—like the **Bar do Walter**—about nine miles from Maceió, where you can sit under a grove of trees drinking a cold beer and watching the comings and goings on the lagoon.

Around 15 miles from the city is the turnoff to the left for a prized ocean beach, the **Praia do Francês** (Frenchman's Beach). You'd think a name like that would refer to some recent resident, a well-liked or eccentric expatriate who had perhaps built the first home or restaurant on the beach. But the derivation is more remote, harking back to a national slight committed centuries ago by French smugglers who were raiding the coast of Alagoas for valuable brazilwood. Today the beach is a favorite weekend retreat for residents and vacationers alike. By contrast, weekdays at Frenchman's Beach are tranquil and all but deserted. The beach is wide and long, with clean white sand and tepid waters, and natural pools at low tide.

Six miles farther south is **Barra do São Miguel,** where Brazil's first bishop, Dom Pero Fernandes Sardinha, had the misfortune to be captured by a tribe of nonbelievers. These people of the Caetés sacrificed the poor bishop and, one assumes, as was customary in such cases, consumed him.

Where to Stay

VILLAGE BARRA HOTEL, Praia do Francês. Tel. 082/272-1207. Telex 82/2213. 18 rms. A/C MINIBAR TV TEL
$ Rates: $37 single; $55 double. AE, MC, V.

There is a very swank little hotel here on the beach, the brand-new and inexpensive Village Barra Hotel. The construction materials used here are both first rate and imaginative. For example, *jangada* logs are used as exposed support posts for a variety of structures.

MARECHAL DEODORO

To visit the old colonial capital, founded in 1612, we must head back toward Maceió for a bit and turn off away from the Praia do Francês exit toward the interior, heading up the opposite shore of the lagoon. All told, Marechal Deodoro is about 40 miles from the new capital. The banks of the lagoon here are remarkably hilly in places, so the town has several dramatic prospects with views high above the water. Most streets have never been modernized, and remain narrow and paved with stone. President Deodoro, who expelled Dom Pedro II and proclaimed the Republic of Brazil in 1889 with himself as first "president," was born here in a respectable, but by no means luxurious house. Deodoro is never spoken of in Brazil. He seems somewhat of a national embarrassment, best forgotten as the perpetrator of the country's first military coup. His home is now a modest museum, but not without its fascinations, including the family furnishings and memorabilia—mostly photographs and news clippings related to the marshal's career, first in the military, later as a statesman.

THE NORTHERN REGION

The Região do Norte covers a route that runs close to the ocean. One of several popular watering places is the **Balneário Paripueira,** 20 miles north of Maceió. The population zones to the north are closer to the ocean than they are immediately south of Maceió. These are old residential beaches with a standard blend, albeit Brazilian style, of year-rounders and summer folk. There is nothing built up or touristy about the area though. The small towns retain a rural character, and the beaches are shared by fishermen and bathers, snack bars and bathing beauties—in all, an appealing combination.

Where to Stay

PRATANGY VILLAGE HOTEL, Praia de Pratangy. Tel. 082/231-4549. Fax 082/231-5134. Telex 82/2295. 93 rms. A/C MINIBAR TV TEL
$ Rates: $150 double. AE, DC, MC, V.
About 30 km (18 miles) north of Maceió, a 20-minute car ride along AL 101 through several colorful coastal villages brings you to one of the newest and most stunning resort hotels in the northeast. Amid a lush grove of palms and banana trees, on a spit of land surrounded by a mangrove preserve, the sedate five-star facilities of the Pratangy have been installed. A large, attractive central building of red-brick houses the lobby, restaurant, and a variety of craft shops and services. Rooms are in separate duplex cabanas scattered about the property. A large contoured swimming pool borders an oasis of vegetation, etched with walking paths, one of which crosses a footbridge over the inland waters en route to the dunes and the ocean sea. Many programmed activities—games, exercise, shows, and nature walks—fill out the guests daily schedule.

---

2. RECIFE

505 miles N of Salvador, 175 miles N of Maceió

GETTING THERE By Plane See Section 1, "Maceió" earlier in this chapter. One VARIG flight per week connects Recife and Miami.

By Bus The main bus station, called the **TIP** (tel. 455-1503), is located in the neighborhood of Curado on BR 232 at km 15, a 20-minute subway ride from the downtown Central station. Buses run to and from Recife from every corner of Brazil.

By Car Anyone wishing to drive to Recife may follow BR 101 from the north or south, or BR 232 from the interior of the state of Pernambuco.

ESSENTIALS For general information on tourism activities and accommodations, contact Pernambuco state's tourism bureau. **EMPETUR,** Av. Conde de Boa Vista 700, in the Boa Vista neighborhood (tel. 081/231-7941). The agency also maintains information counters at the airport and bus station. The American Express representative in Recife is the **Souto Costa Travel Agency,** Rua Felix 666, in Boa Viagem (tel. 081/325-0305; fax 081/326-8776), offering the usual services and guided tours.

After having been expelled from Salvador in 1625, the Dutch reinvaded Brazil to the north, hoping to establish a foothold in the rich, sugar-producing lands above

Bahia. In 1630 forces of the Dutch West India Company occupied the colonial city of Olinda, the old capital of Pernambuco. But they built their own capital four miles to the south in a little village, called Recife, where the natural features of the coastline were more suitable to good defenses and a deep, working harbor.

By the mid-1630s the Dutch controlled most of the fertile coastal plains from the mouth of the Rio São Francisco—which divides Sergipe from Alagoas—all the way to Maranhão, almost to the mouth of the Amazon in the north. The invaders administered the conquered territory and maintained a monopoly on the trade in sugar, slaves, and dyewoods, but permitted the colonials free trade in all other commodities, and extended liberal credits to planters for the rebuilding of plantations and mills that had decayed or had been destroyed during the years of fighting.

The Dutch settled in for a long stay, as this was the height of their colonial expansion in both the New World and in Africa. Dutch settlements had also been established throughout the Caribbean and the Hudson Valley in New York, as well as along the coast of Angola, where they sought to gain control of the slave trade and the labor supply so necessary to their newly won sugar-producing lands in Brazil. From their base in Recife, the curious Dutch, under the leadership of the intelligent and energetic viceroy, Johan Maurits of Nassau-Siegen, began the first systematic and scientific study of the tropics. The Dutch colony was depicted on the excellent canvases of Albert Eckhout; Willem Piso isolated tropical diseases and concocted remedies for them; naturalist Georg Marcgraf collected flora, fauna, and geological samples. The Dutch adorned Recife with an aviary and both zoological and botanical gardens, and built the New World's first weather station and observatory in their colonial capital.

The native Brazilian population, however, never accepted the Dutch presence. Much of the conflict rested on religious scruples. The Dutch were Protestants, and the Portuguese Brazilians, Catholics. And never was sectarian hatred between the two faiths at a more fevered pitch than during those very years, when Europe was consumed by the near apocalyptic fires of the Thirty Years' War. But Portugal, having been absorbed by Spain through an accident of royal succession, was powerless to expel the invaders, and the renowned Spanish infantry was occupied in the service of the Holy Roman Emperor on the battlefields of Germany.

The native population, however, began a guerrilla operation to effect the expulsion through their own efforts. And while their motives were fired by religious zeal, this was also the first major step taken by the colonials toward the creation of a unified Brazilian nation. The combined forces of patriots from Salvador, Rio de Janeiro, and Pernambuco, with troops representing all three races in equal proportion, defeated the Dutch regulars in several important battles and laid seige to Recife. With the Netherlands suffering reverses in the European war, the homeland could not come to the aid of its colony. The Dutch were forced to surrender Recife in 1654 and leave Brazil, never to return again. But when the crown of Portugal was restored to the House of Bragança, and the Portuguese found themselves in an ironic alliance with the Netherlands against Spain, a Brazilian expedition was organized which sailed to Angola and successfully liberated Luanda from the Dutch occupation there.

The Dutch had found Recife a mere village of 150 huts, and left it a city of more than 2,000 houses, inhabited by Brazil's first truly commercial class, where the seeds of republicanism would one day grow to challenge the monarchist sentiments prevalent among the landed gentry. Of the Dutch legacy, little is visible in Recife today other than a few fortifications, different in no obvious way from the forts of their Portuguese contemporaries. The one indelible mark the Dutch left on Recife, however, was their choice of a building site. They had chosen a kind of terrain familiar to them from their homeland—land etched with waterways, including inlets, marshes, canals, and two rivers—and used their engineering skills to link into a single entity a peninsula, an island, and the mainland. The modern city of Recife occupies all three of these geographies, which are connected by such a large number of bridges that local boosters promote the city as the "Venice of Brazil."

Since 1989, Recife has become the new gateway to Brazil for many vacationing Europeans and Canadians, and some Americans as well. Tourists, to the tune of 2,000 a week, have suddenly become very visible here, particularly on the beach strip in Boa

Viagem and in the historic city of Olinda. For the moment, Miami is the only point of departure from the U.S. for direct air service.

WHAT TO SEE & DO

With a population of more than 1.5 million people, Recife is Brazil's fourth-largest city. Its name derives from the word *arrecife*, referring to the ubiquitous rocky reefs that lie not only off this city's shores, but off those of much of the northeastern coast. The municipality itself has a historic district set on its central peninsula, and on the mainland is the suburb of Boa Viagem, where the best hotels and beaches are found. The colonial city of Olinda is Recife's main attraction. Several excursions to more remote coastal beaches are also quite popular.

PÁTIO DE SÃO PEDRO This large, inner-city square in the Santo Antônio district, dating from the early 18th century, has yet to be beautified, a fact that may explain why it remains a popular meeting spot for Recife's youth, its artists and intellectuals. The broad cut-stone facade of the São Pedro dos Clérigos church with its imposing portal of carved rosewood (1782), and the square's other buildings of similar vintage and girth, create an atmosphere of shadows and forms reminiscent of town life as portrayed on the canvases of old masters. This is particularly so at night, when the square is filled with the mirthful laughter and chatter of its denizens who occupy the tables at several outdoor cafés. In one corner of the square is a stage, set high on scaffolding, where on weekends musicians jam and poets proclaim their latest pieces. The patio is also a center for handcrafts, with numerous shops both on the square and its surrounding side streets.

Many of Recife's other architectural treasures are located within walking distance of the Pátio de São Pedro, including the Dutch-built **Five-Points Fort** (1630), now a museum, the **Basílica de Nossa Senhora de Carmo** (1687) on Avenida Dantas Barreto, and the **Capela Dourada** (Golden Chapel of the Church of Santo Antônio) on Rua do Imperador.

MUSEU DO HOMEM DO NORDESTE The Museum of Inhabitants of the Northeast, Avenida 17 de Augusto 2187 (tel. 268-2000), is a complex on the outskirts of town near the zoo and the botanical gardens. The **Museu de Açúcar** (Sugar Museum) section documents Brazil's great sugar cycle, the first episode in the country's long-standing single-crop economy. The collection contains models of *engenhos* (mills), early processing equipment, and artifacts relating to sugar's domestic usage—the evolution of the sugar bowl, so to speak. Located quite appropriately in the same building is the **Museu Joaquim Nabuco.** Nabuco, a lawyer and native of the Pernambuco backcountry, was Brazil's most outspoken abolitionist. The interdependence of the sugar economy and the institution of slavery is self-evident. Preserved in the museum are examples of the instruments of torture used to bend recalcitrant slaves to the fulfillment of their role in the manifest vision of the sugar barons. Open Tuesday, Wednesday, and Friday 11am to 5pm; weekends and holidays 1 to 5pm. Equally interesting is the **Museu de Antropólogia** (Anthropology Museum), with its display of chapbook poetry and literature. This *literatura de cordel* represents the popular view of local history and heroes, in popular literary language. These crudely printed, but often delightfully illustrated, self-published pamphlets are still hawked in markets and squares throughout the northeast by earnest bards and balladeers.

BOA VIAGEM Avenida Boa Viagem is to Recife what Avenida Atlântica is to Rio de Janeiro and the *orla* is to Salvador: a shoreline drive on a long stretch of ocean frontage with the city's most enviable beachside residences, its best hotels, and the center of its conventional nightlife. On the weekends, however, the strands of Boa Viagem do not discriminate, and become the playground for all of Recife's citizens, as a glorious and colorful democratic hodge-podge flocks to the nearby shore and every square inch of sand, from the sidewalk to the waves of the washing tide, is packed with bodies.

Those who have the time and the means head for the more remote strands on the outskirts of the city, to the southern beaches of Piedade, Venda Grande, Candeias, and Barra de Jangada, or the northern beaches of Rio Doce, Janga, Pau Amarelo, and

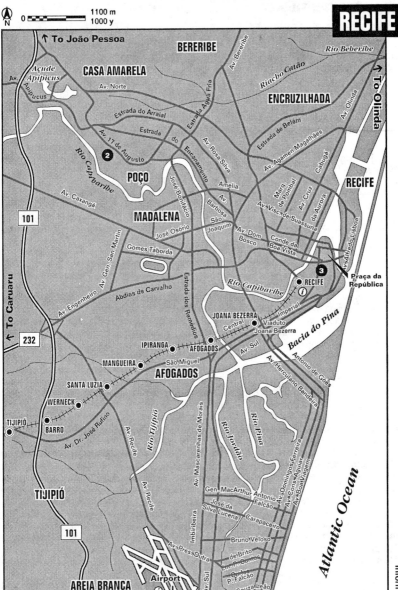

RECIFE

0 ⊢━━━━┥ 1100 m
0 ⊢━━━━┥ 1000 y

↑ To João Pessoa

BERERIBE

Rio Beberibe

CASA AMARELA

Açude Apipicus

ENCRUZILHADA

Av. Norte

Estrada do Arraial

Estrada do

Av. 17 de Augusto

Estrada de Belém

Rio Capibaribe

Av. Rosa Silva

Av. Agamen Magalhães

→ To Olinda

POÇO

Amelia

Av. Cabugá

RECIFE

Av. Caxangá

Av. Barbosa

Marq. de Pombal

Av. Cruz da Aurora

Av. Alfredo Lisboa

MADALENA

José Bonifácio

São Joaquim

Av. Visc. de Suassuna

José Osório

Gomes Táborda

Av. Dom Bosco

Conde da Boa Vista

3

● RECIFE

Praça da República

Av. Gen San Martin

Abdias de Carvalho

Estrada dos Remédios

Rio Capibaribe

i

Av. Engenheiro

Central

Av. Imperial

JOANA BEZERRA

Bacia do Pina

232

IPIRANGA

AFOGADOS

Viaduto Joana Bezerra

Av. Sul

Antonio de Góes

MANGUEIRA

São Miguel

AFOGADOS

Av. Herculano Bandeira

SANTA LUZIA

WERNECK

Rio Tijipió

Av. Dr. José Rufino

Av. Mascarenhas de Morais

Rio Jordão

Rio Pina

TIJIPIÓ

BARRO

Av. Recife

Av. Domingos Ferreira

Av. Cons. Aguiar

Av. Boa Viagem

TIJIPIÓ

Av. Recife

Gen. MacArthur

Antonio Falcão

José da Silva Lucena

Carapaceiro

101

Imbiribeira

Bruno Veloso

AREIA BRANCA

Av. Pres. Dutra

de Brito

Emir de Gama

Av. Sul

Airport

i

Cap. P. Falcão

Av. Barão de Souza Leão

1

To Maceió ↓

BOA VIAGEM

Atlantic Ocean

Information ⊙

Boa Viagem **1**
Museu do Homen do Nordeste **2**
　Museu de Açúcar
　Museu de Antropólogia
　Museu Joaquim Nabuco
Pátio de São Pedro **3**

Maria Farinha. As a general rule, the farther you travel from the city center, the cleaner and more deserted are the beaches, and the more dense their cover of palm trees.

All the beaches of Pernambuco, like those of Alagoas to the south, possess natural pools at low tide because of the rocky offshore ledge along the entire coastline that traps the ebbing water. And all the beaches have their populations of fishermen who ply the waters in their native log-lashed rafts, *jangadas,* and who are often willing to carry passengers for a reasonable fee.

A CERAMIC FACTORY TOUR One popular sidetrip on the outskirts of Recife is a visit to the factory where ceramicist Francisco Brennand manufactures his world-renowned tiles and garden statuary. The **Oficina Cerámica Francisco Brennand** (tel. 271-2623) is located on the Propriedade Santos Cosme e Damião in the suburb of Várzea. The factory would be difficult to find on your own, so the services of a guide or tour company are probably required. The attraction here is not so much the workshops where the objects are produced but the acres of formal gardens and showrooms where they are displayed in all their—in the case of the statuary—surreal and phallic splendor. The factory may be visited Monday to Friday during normal business hours.

A STROLL AROUND OLINDA

Every bit as striking and well preserved as Ouro Preto is Pernambuco's old colonial capital of Olinda, founded in 1537 and only four miles north of Recife. Unlike Ouro Preto, however, which remains a self-contained and viable municipal entity, Olinda has become a *dormitório* (bedroom community) for nearby Recife, as well as a center of fine dining, art and handcrafts, and nightlife. Notwithstanding the city's narrowed social and economic role, Olinda has not succumbed to theme-park status by any means. There's just too much authenticity, too many original structures scattered over its one square mile of hilly terrain overlooking the South Atlantic, for example, for the town to reflect only the glitter of its modern inhabitants.

Olinda is small enough to explore in its entirety by foot, an exercise made doubly enjoyable by restrictions placed on automobile traffic along its tight, winding lanes. The tour begins at the **Praça do Carmo,** where the stately, impoverished **Igreja do Carmo** (1588), the first Carmelite church in Brazil, sits on a mound a hundred feet above the square, undergoing a slow and expensive restoration.

Running off the square is Rua do São Francisco, where the **Convento da Nossa Senhora das Neves** (1585) has lovely panel paintings. It was the first Franciscan church in Brazil, and one of the few churches in Olinda open to the public during normal daytime hours. The street ends at Rua Bispo Coutinho, opening onto the Alto da Sé, a wide hill with a dramatic view of town and sea. The **Igreja da Sé** (1537) was the first seat of an archbishopric in Brazil. The nearby bishop's palace houses the **Museu de Arte Sacra** (tel. 429-0036) with its collection of paintings of the city as well as some of the country's oldest examples of sacred art. It's open Tuesday to Friday from 8am to noon and 2 to 6pm, and on weekends from 2 to 6pm. The **Convento da Conceição** at the far end of the street remains an active convent, and may be visited by applying at the gate.

The **Alto da Sé** itself, a large cone of a hill, is Olinda's outdoor party spot and permanent craft fair. Every evening and on Sunday afternoons, the alto begins to swell with people who come to shop, eat from the food stalls, and dance while they listen to musicians playing regional music. A spiritist temple, the **Tenda do Edu,** is off to one side on the alto, and is worth a visit if for no other reason than for the contrast it provides to the predominantly Catholic viewpoint of Olinda's history. Opposite the working convent is the **Largo da Misericórdia,** with a former academy, **Santa Getrudes,** and the Misericórdia church, with its golden wood-carved panels and Portuguese *azulejo* tiles with their allegoric illustrations. A further landmark of this square is the **Bica de São Pedro,** a public fountain from colonial days.

On **Rua Bernado Vieira de Melo** are the ruins of the old colonial senate where in 1710 the street's namesake, in a great, though premature, historic gesture, called for the establishment of a republic. The context was the so-called Peddler's War, an armed conflict pitting the sugar aristocracy of Olinda against the rising commercial bourgeoisie of Recife. Here you also find the **Mercado da Ribeira,** an arts and crafts market, open daily 9am to noon and 2 to 6pm.

The building of the **Museu de Arte Contemporânea,** Rua 13 de Maio (tel. 429-2587), has a history more interesting than the art collection it now houses. Built as a jail to confine clergy who ran afoul of the Inquisition in its later, tamer years of the 18th century, the building has the further dubious distinction of having been a slave market. The Inquisition in Brazil was never established as an institution, and its influence was minimal, directed primarily against licentious priests and New Christians—Jews forced to convert to Catholicism who were required to make periodic displays of their adherence to the "true faith." The museum is open Wednesday through Monday from 2:30 to 6pm.

The final "official" site on the walking tour is the **Monastery of São Bento** (1582), on Rua de São Bento, a continuation of Rua Bernado Vieira de Melo. The church is worth a visit to see the unique terra-cotta images, as is the monastery, which once sheltered Brazil's first law school. It's open daily from 8 to 11am and from 1 to 5pm. Interconnecting all the religious monuments are hundreds of houses, many from the 1600s, with their cartoon facades of stucco, heavily framed doors and windows, and balconies with wooden railings, among other charming architectural features.

WHERE TO STAY

Most visitors to Recife, by choice or because they are placed there by predetermined hotel packages, stay on the beach at Boa Viagem. Olinda now also has a first-class beach hotel to add to its several inns and pensions.

For students and other youthful travelers to the city there are newly established **youth hostels** that charge only $5 per night with breakfast. Inquiries about hostel availability, as well as general tourist information, should be made at **EMPETUR** (tel. 231-7941).

IN RECIFE
Expensive

MAR HOTEL, Rua Barão de Souza Leão 451, Recife. Tel. 081/341-5433.
Fax 081/341-7002. Telex 81/1073. 207 rms. A/C MINIBAR TV TEL
$ Rates: $125–$140 single; $140–$165 double. AE, DC, MC, V.
The Mar Hotel, located a block and a half from the Boa Viagem beach, has one of the most elaborate and gorgeous poolside environments of any hotel in Brazil. The pool is a mosaic of fountains and falls, separate compartments of water on split levels, plus islands and isthmuses of mottled flagstone with potted palm trees. The hotel's rooms are on the small side, but have balconies. Quilted bedspreads, modern armchairs, and rich, mineral-blue carpets add elegance to the rooms. There are good-size tubs in the marble-highlighted baths. The hotel, with its jet-age lobby in stainless steel and black leather, also has variety in its restaurants, including a sushi bar and the Mont Blanc, specializing in Swiss-German cuisine.

PETRIBU SHERATON, Av. Bernado Vieira de Melo 1624, Recife. Tel. 081/361-4511. Fax 081/361-4680. Telex 81/1825. 197 rms. A/C MINIBAR TV TEL
$ Rates: $120–$140 single; $135–$155 double. AE, DC, MC, V.
Recife has a brand-new luxury hotel, the Petribu Sheraton, with ocean-fronting rooms and located just two miles beyond the Piedade end of the Boa Viagem beach in the municipality of Jaboatão. The neighborhood is very mixed, with commercial services and large high-rise apartment buildings; it's anything but a center of tourism or nightlife. But there is nothing wrong with the area, especially once you are inside what is without doubt the prettiest hotel in Recife, and the only one in the city that can truly claim deluxe status. It must therefore be assumed that the current room rates are vaguely promotional, and will rise accordingly once the hotel has established itself.

The hotel's structure, as well as its interior decor, are really quite stunning. Someone has taken pains with the construction and design of this hotel, and it shows. The rooms are also very special; mine was one of the most comfortable I have had in

Brazil. It was spacious and stylish, had a solid tile floor (to reflect the hotel's location on the beach), a queen-size bed, and a small balcony facing the sea. The balcony is nice, because in Brazil, you often want to turn off the air conditioning at night, and swing open the balcony door—especially in the northeast—allowing the ocean breezes to naturally ventilate and cool the room.

As for public spaces, the top-floor restaurant is an absolute knockout. There's a large, attractive pool on an outdoor patio, one story above the beach, and a mezzanine with various shops, including a branch of the ubiquitous H. Stern. To top it off, the breakfast at the Petribu Sheraton is a real treat, a cut above what is served at most other hotels I've stayed at in Brazil.

RECIFE MONTE HOTEL, Rua dos Navegantes 363, Recife. Tel. 081/326-7422. Fax 081/326-2903. Telex 81/2139. 156 rms. A/C MINIBAR TV TEL
$ Rates: $115–$165 single; $130–$183 double. AE, DC, MC, V.
The Recife Monte is composed of a U-shaped block of three buildings overlooking a large, sumptuous courtyard pool. Sitting back a block off the beach, the hotel is well run and supercomfortable, and has all the facilities required of a luxury hotel. The rooms are decorated in soft yellows and light wood trim. Deluxe rooms have balconies with louvered double doors and white wood patio furniture. In addition to the separate coffee shop, bar, and nightclub, the hotel houses the respected Góvea restaurant.

RECIFE PALACE, Av. Boa Viagem 4070, Recife. Tel. 081/325-4044. Fax 081/326-8895. Telex 81/4528. 300 rms. A/C MINIBAR TV TEL
$ Rates: $97 single; $102 double; $107–$112 deluxe room. AE, CB, DC, MC, V.
The Recife Palace is a new luxury hotel equipped with all the five-star facilities, including a nightclub and a fine French restaurant. The hotel belongs to the same group that owns and runs the Rio Palace Hotel in Copacabana, and like its Rio counterpart, the Recife Palace caters equally well to tourists and business travelers who demand the best when away from home. The deluxe room, for example, is extra-large, creating a sense that the sleeping and sitting areas occupy very distinct spaces. The care with the hotel's construction and design can be seen even in the corridors, with their wooden ceilings and hardwood table tops suspended from the walls, decorated with attractive lamps and hand-thrown pottery. The service is also a cut above—discreet and professional.

Moderate

CASTELINHO PRAIA, Av. Boa Viagem 4520, Recife. Tel. 081/326-1186. Fax 081/465-1150. Telex 81/4670. A/C MINIBAR TV TEL
$ Rates: $50–$65 single; $55–$70 double. AE, DC, MC, V.
This is an especially attractive hotel. The former *casarão* (mansion) is a stone building with a red-tile roof and a large covered front porch with a red-painted railing. The standard accommodations are in the old main house, and the deluxe rooms are spread among several two-story outbuildings with views of either a backyard court or the patio pool deck which also faces the ocean. The rooms lack the extra attention to detail of the pricier establishments, being smaller and less elegantly furnished, but they are comfortable and modern in every way. The baths receive natural lighting from the corridors.

FATOR PALACE, Rua dos Navegantes 157, Recife. Tel. 081/326-7777. Fax 081/326-8753. Telex 81/4167. 200 rms. A/C MINIBAR TV TEL
$ Rates: $80–$85 single; $85–$90 double. AE, DC, MC, V.
Another relatively new beach hotel in Boa Viagem is the Fator Palace. The hotel opened in 1990, and is located about two blocks off the beachfront boulevard. The rooms at the Fator Palace appear very comfortable. And despite its fairly moderate price structure, there are many first-class facilities in this hotel, including separate adult and children's swimming pools, two restaurants, and a nightclub.

HOTEL CASA GRANDE & SENZALA, Av. Conselheiro Aguiar 5000, Recife. Tel. and fax 081/341-0366. Telex 81/3126. 50 rms. A/C MINIBAR TV TEL
$ Rates: $60–$65 single; $65–$75 double. AE, DC, MC, V.

Brick for brick, Recife's most charming hotel—or inn—has to be the Hotel Casa Grande & Senzala, located about three blocks in from the beach on one of the neighborhood's busier commercial thoroughfares (where, incidentally, many service shops and a post office may be found). Colonial in its decor and architecture, the Casa Grande & Senzala really embodies, spatially, something of the sensibility of the old sugar barons' manorial lifestyle. The sense of old-fashioned homeyness carries over to the accommodations; the rooms seem a lot more like guest quarters in a private home than the typical hotel room, however fancy or commodious. The Casa Grande restaurant, said to be quite good, serves regional specialties from the Pernambuco countryside.

HOTEL SAVARONI, Av. Boa Viagem 3772, Recife. Tel. 081/325-5077.
Fax 081/326-4900. Telex 81/1428. 70 rms. A/C MINIBAR TV TEL
$ Rates: $60–$65 single; $70–$75 double. AE, DC, MC, V.
This hotel has a pleasant and informal lobby restaurant with dried flowers on the tables. A compact, but appealing pool and sunning deck on the second floor has tables with bright-yellow umbrellas and a wide view of the sea. The hotel's rooms are entered through an alcove with a built-in carpeted bench and table. The same carpet motif continues on to the sleeping area, and the entire front wall is a large window, a section of which can be opened. The room is filled with light during the day, and has blackout and soundproofing curtains for nighttime. The bathroom has a round stall shower with a transparent curtain, and a frosted-glass wall that lets in light from the corridors.

OTHON PALACE, Av. Boa Viagem 3722, Recife. Tel. 081/326-7225. Fax
081/326-7661. Telex 81/3482. 218 rms. A/C MINIBAR TV TEL
$ Rates: $45–$50 single; $68–$76 double. AE, DC, MC, V.
The Othon Palace occupies a 17-story tower, directly across from the beach. Narrow wood-paneled and carpeted corridors open into spacious deluxe rooms where table tops and luggage racks are slabs of stone, suspended legless from the walls. Potted plants and cream-colored walls add warmth to each room, with its curved glass doorway leading to a balcony. Other features are a built-in bar with TV, and an extra-large bath tiled in brown from floor to ceiling. The standard rooms are slightly smaller, while their connecting corridors are correspondingly wider. The small rooftop pool and its deck seem to overhang the beach below. A second small pool occupies an interior courtyard, and the veranda off the entrance serves as an outdoor café and restaurant.

VILA RICA, Av. Boa Viagem 4308, Recife. Tel. and fax 081/326-5111.
Telex 81/1903. 102 rms. A/C MINIBAR TV TEL
$ Rates: $35–$40 single; $45–$50 double. AE, DC, MC, V.
The Vila Rica has launched what they refer to as a "new concept" in hotel accommodations, "eliminating all superfluous services," including bellhops. Room service will be replaced by a store, open around the clock, that will allow guests to purchase food items at market prices, and stock minibars in their rooms themselves. Those rooms, incidentally, have all undergone complete renovation as recently as two years ago.

VOYAGE, Rua Barão de Souza Leão 439, Recife. Tel. 081/341-7491. Fax
081/341-7002. Telex 81/1073. 100 rms. A/C MINIBAR TV TEL
$ Rates: $45–$50 single; $55–$60 double. AE, DC, MC, V.
The Voyage is a moderately priced hotel, next to the Hotel Mar and close to the beach. The rooms are housed in five two-story block buildings, with a mid-size pool and sun veranda occupying an interior patio. The rooms are functional and modern, and baths have a seat built into the wall and stall showers.

Budget

HOTEL SEA-VIEW, Rua dos Navegantes 101, Recife. Tel. 081/326-7238. 34 rms. A/C MINIBAR TV TEL

$ Rates: $35 single; $40 double. AE, DC, MC, V.

A block from Boa Viagem beach, the Hotel Sea-View is housed in a horizontal complex of two- and three-story buildings within sight and sound of the water, at the end of an alley lined with cafés and restaurants. Off the corridors of its mazelike interior are some rooms, small but tidy, furnished with compact captain's bed and built-in bureaus to make the most of the space.

IN OLINDA

POUSADA DOS QUATRO CANTOS, Av. Prudente de Morais 441, Olinda. Tel. 081/429-0220. Fax 081/429-1845. 15 rms (most with bath). A/C MINIBAR TV TEL

$ Rates: $15 single without bath, $20–$27 single with bath; $20 double without bath, $23–$30 double with bath; $63 suite. AE, MC, V.

Anyone pursuing more or less seriously their private version of a Graham Greene "lost-in-the-tropics" fantasy could not find a better place to hole up in Olinda than the Pousada dos Quatro Cantos. Formerly a planter's town house, the inn is located on the fringe of Olinda's most colorful, and only working-class, quarter. Within a block of the inn, the open doors and windows of several dozen unrestored colonial buildings reveal the stark existence of Olinda's poor minority who have thus far refused to sell out to the forces of gentrification. The carnival doings among these particular back streets are said to be the most uncommercialized within the historic city. In fact, the Pousada dos Quatro Cantos provides the perfect base for those who come to Olinda during carnival time. The inn has its own band and in-house carnival festivities behind the walls of its lovely central garden and patio, and also fields a *bloco*, or parade component, of its own, made up of staff and guests who participate in the local street parade. My favorite room here was Suite A, two large rooms side by side, each with tall colonial double doors that open onto a common veranda above the lushly planted courtyard.

POUSADA SÃO FRANCISCO, Rua do Sol 127, Olinda. Tel. 081/429-2109. Fax 081/429-4057. 40 rms. A/C MINIBAR TV TEL

$ Rates: $21 single; $24 double. AE, DC, MC, V.

The Pousada São Francisco is a much more modern facility than the Quatro Cantos, with a fair-size courtyard swimming pool, and rooms that, while fully equipped and comfortable, lack the personal touch of those at the Quatro Cantos. Given the spaciousness and comfort of the place, accommodations are a bargain.

SOFITEL QUATRO RODAS, Av. José Augusto Moreira 2200, Olinda. Tel. 081/431-2955. Fax 081/431-0670. Telex 81/1324. 204 rms. A/C MINIBAR TV TEL

$ Rates: $100–$110 single; $115–$135 double. AE, DC, MC, V.

The only luxury hotel in Olinda is the Quatro Rodas, and in reality the Quatro Rodas is also the only genuinely resort-style hotel in all of Recife, with its location right on the beach, and such aquatic and sporting activities as windsurfing, sailing on catamarans, tennis, and of course, freshwater swimming in the large pool. The hotel has a giant lobby, lush with plants, rustic antiques, and old farm equipment, the same theme that is duplicated in each of the chain's hotels. Facilities off the lobby include a live-music bar, a restaurant, and an outdoor barbecue snack bar. Superior and deluxe rooms differ only slightly in size, but are otherwise the same in details and furnishings. All rooms face the sea, and have balconies with crescent-shaped window lights above the door and either two double beds or one king-size bed.

WHERE TO DINE

Good restaurants are scattered throughout the large metropolitan area, but the greatest concentrations of eating spots are in Boa Viagem and Olinda. Northeastern cooking and seafood top the list of specialties in most restaurants.

IN RECIFE

There are many nightspots, restaurants, and *cervejarias*—beer gardens—near the Boa Viagem hotel district.

IL CASTELLO, Av. Domingos Ferreira 3980. Tel. 326-2757.
Cuisine: ITALIAN/INTERNATIONAL. **Reservations:** Not needed.
$ Prices: Appetizers $2.75–$11.50; main courses $5.95–$14.25. AE, DC, MC, V.
Open: Mon–Sat 7pm–1am, Sun noon–midnight.
Across the street from Porção, in a novel building whose design was inspired by a medieval castle, is the aptly named Il Castello, primarily a dinner spot for Italian cuisine. The restaurant also has a separate wine bar with many labels from which to choose, beginning around $6 a bottle. Pasta dishes are the specialty, and many of these are priced in the $4 range.

MARIA BONITA TROPICAL BAR, Rua Jack Ayres. Tel. 325-5402.
Cuisine: ECLECTIC. **Reservations:** Not needed.
$ Prices: Appetizers $2–$12; main courses $7–$14. AE, DC, MC.
Open: Dinner daily 6pm–midnight.
The straw-covered cabanas of the Maria Bonita Tropical Bar, opposite the Shopping Center Recife, make a pleasant setting for open-air dining. The eclectic menu offers a variety of items ranging from chicken Stroganoff to more typical Brazilian dishes like crab stew. Thursday to Saturday there is live music after 10pm. The name Maria Bonita refers to a bandit heroine and moll of the infamous Virgolino Ferreira da Silva, the gunslinger who terrorized the northeast with his gang, and who is known popularly as Lampião in recognition of his lightning tendency to shoot first and ask questions later.

MARRUÁ, Rua Ernesto de Paula Santos 183. Tel. 326-1656.
Cuisine: REGIONAL/STEAK. **Reservations:** Not needed.
$ Prices: Appetizers $3–$9; main courses $6.25–$16.75. AE, MC, V.
Open: Daily noon–midnight.
If you wish to experiment with regional dishes, try the Marruá, a block off the beach in Boa Viagem. You may select a sampling of preparations that might make up the evening supper of a typical northeastern family of the interior. The platters have colorful names like *munguza* (a cream of cornmeal soup), *pagoca (farofa* with bits of sun-dried beef), *macaxeira* (a variety of boiled cassava root), and *inhame* (taro-root yam). Another specialty of the house is the barbecued mixed grill, a variety of meats and sausages served on a skewer. International main courses may be ordered à la carte from the menu, and regional specialties are served buffet style, from terra-cotta chafing dishes.

PORÇÃO, Av. Domingos Ferreira 4215. Tel. 325-17140.
Cuisine: BARBECUE. **Reservations:** Not needed.
$ Prices: Rodízio (all you can eat) $13. AE, DC, MC, V.
Open: Daily 11am–1 or 2am, depending on the crowd.
This is a branch of one of Rio's best-loved churrascarias. This Porção, however, is much more elegant than any of its Carioca counterparts. In addition to a snazzy dining room holding 270 people, most at tables for eight, there is an intimate, handsomely decorated piano bar in a separate space. As for the food, you begin at a buffet salad bar, choosing from 22 different dishes, including *surubim,* a large freshwater fish, first baked, but then served cold. Once at your table, the waiters serve an endless round of 16 varieties of grilled meats, including the northeastern specialty *carne de sol;* and you may have as many repeats as you desire.

RESTAURANTE LOBSTER, Av. Rui Barbosa 1649. Tel. 268-5516.
Cuisine: SEAFOOD. **Reservations:** Not needed.
$ Prices: Appetizers $3–$12; main courses $7–$18. AE, MC.
Open: Daily 11am–midnight.
Located in Boa Viagem, the Restaurante Lobster is an elegant eating space where the large rectilinear room is made extra-bright by white walls and large windows. The

featured dish is the clawless Brazilian lobster, costing about $12. Dinner is accompanied nightly by piano music.

SANATORI GERAL, Av. Domingos Ferreira 2766. Tel. 326-3960.

   Cuisine: INTERNATIONAL. **Reservations:** Not needed.
$ **Prices:** Appetizers $3–$8; main courses $7–$15. AE, V.
   Open: Dinner Tues–Sat 7pm–midnight.

The Sanatori Geral is a supper club and dance hall on the outskirts of Recife. A live band plays regional and popular music Thursday through Saturday usually beginning after 11pm, and on Friday there is a floor show as well. Every night customers in the downstairs bar are serenaded by a singing guitar player.

TERTÚLIA, Av. Boa Viagem 4780. Tel. 325-2276.

   Cuisine: STEAK. **Reservations:** Not needed.
$ **Prices:** All-you-can-eat buffet $10; appetizers $1.50–$6.50; main courses $6–$12. AE, DC, MC, V.
   Open: Sun–Thurs 11am–1am, Fri–Sat 11am–2am.

Within its large enclosed dining room, the Tertúlia, somewhat of a beachfront institution, serves a modestly priced buffet nightly, comprising some 20 different dishes. Outside, facing the ocean, is a covered veranda, a good place to sit on your first night in Recife to take the measure of the crowded district. On the sidewalk at the edge of the sand, endless files of locals and tourists promenade, and hippie artisans sell their craftwares. On the veranda, you may order meals and side dishes from an à la carte menu, and of course, beer and other beverages.

IN OLINDA

BAR DA RAMPA, Av. Beira Mar 953.

   Cuisine: SEAFOOD.
$ **Prices:** Appetizers $2.75–$7; main courses $5.50–$14. No credit cards.
   Open: Daily 11am–midnight.

On the beach in Olinda is the Bar da Rampa, set in a cottage facing the long-settled oceanfront of the old colonial town. The specialties here are fresh-caught fish like *pescada,* a species of South Atlantic hake, broiled and served whole. Also tasty is the shrimp casserole.

L'ATELIER, Rua Bernado Vieira de Melo 91. Tel. 429-3099.

   Cuisine: FRENCH. **Reservations:** Recommended on weekends.
$ **Prices:** Appetizers $4–$6 (escargots $12.50); main courses $10–$15. No credit cards.
   Open: Dinner daily 7pm–midnight.

L'Atelier occupies a restored colonial house whose facade can be sampled as an aesthetic appetizer before you enter to eat. Diners sit in several rooms and alcoves on the first floor amid the tapestries and wall hangings produced by the two owner/craftsmen who live above the store. A backyard veranda contains additional tables, and there's a second level with a swimming pool, which guests sometimes use, especially during the wilder parties. L'Atelier serves the new French cooking—which is to say, well-crafted small portions—and is quite simply "the best restaurant in the northeast," says Brazil's premier travel guide, *Quatro Rodas.* But even more impressive is the lavish praise bestowed on the two French entrepreneurs, and reprinted on their brochure as a jacket blurb by the respected Brazilian sociologist Gilberto Freyre. Main courses are expensive for this region, but well compensated by the quality of the food and the atmosphere.

MOURISCO, Rua João Alfredo. Tel. 429-1390.

   Cuisine: REGIONAL/INTERNATIONAL. **Reservations:** Not accepted.
$ **Prices:** Appetizers $3–$9; main courses $6–$10. No credit cards.
   Open: Lunch Tues–Sun noon–4pm; dinner Tues–Sun 7pm–midnight.

The building housing the Mourisco is equally charming, while the restaurant itself is more traditional in the Luzo-Brazilian mold. The 400-year-old timber-framed stucco building is a masterpiece of rustic detail, with hand-hewn and planed wood trim and railings everywhere polished smooth by centuries of use. The elegant dining area, divided among several rooms, contrasts pleasingly with the backyard *choparía* (beer garden) with its shiny apple-red metal café tables and chairs. The menu is international, featuring steaks and seafood.

EVENING ENTERTAINMENT

A special event takes place every Friday night in Olinda, an all-night dance party called **Noites Olindences** at the Clube Atlântico on the town's main plaza (tel. 429-3616). The party begins at 11pm, and ends around six in the morning. The music changes hourly, embracing dance forms as varied as the merengue, waltz, and *forró,* the slinky, sensual northeastern dance.

EASY EXCURSIONS
IGARAÇU & ITAMARACA

About 20 miles north of Recife is the old colonial town of Igaraçu, settled in 1535 and full of architectural relics of its own, including the **Igreja Santos Cosme e Damião,** reputed to be the first church ever built in Brazil. Other notable attractions in the town are the country's first Masonic Temple, and a mile to the south on the Recife road, the **Engenho Monjope,** an early sugar plantation, preserved and open to the public.

Another 10 miles farther north is the island of Itamaraca, connected to the mainland by a causeway and bridge. A sign on the Itamaraca side boasts that "Adam and Eve spent their vacations on this island," which is prized for its 50 miles of beautiful beaches.

An interesting side trip off the island can be taken to an old settlement called **Vila Velha.** Traveling toward the water over six miles of very bad road, you ride through an old plantation where tenant farmers in rustic cottages still live closer to the rhythms of colonial life than to modern ways. At the end of trail is an old harbor town with a few buildings, one of which is now a restaurant.

Where to Stay

ORANGE PRAIA HOTEL, Av. do Forte, Itamaraca. Tel. 081/554-1170.
   54 rms. A/C MINIBAR TV TEL
$ Rates: $65–$85 single; $75–$95 double. AE, DC, MC, V.
Itamaraca now has a first-class tourist hotel to attract international visitors who come to Recife. The Orange Praia Hotel has large rooms that command a view of the beach and Fort Orange, a fortification built by the Dutch during their occupation of the coast. The hotel has many resort facilities, a big pool, sailing boats, and a lighter-than-air plane for those guests who wish to soar above it all.

MARIA FARINHA

Across the bay from Itamaraca is the traditional summer colony of Maria Farinha, located only about 10 minutes by car from the Hotel Quatro Rodas, and one of those delightful seaside villages that abound along the coast of Brazil.

Where to Stay

AMOARES, Rua Garoupa 525, Maria Farinha. Tel. 081/435-1208. Fax 081/435-1880. Telex 81/4546. 78 rms. A/C MINIBAR TV TEL
$ Rates: $70–$75 single; $75–$80 double. AE, DC, MC, V.
Amoares is a brand-new resort dedicated to aquatic sporting activities. The rooms, large, airy, and inviting, but not overloaded with furnishings, are divided among five separate blocks set on attractive landscaped grounds. A separate, central complex houses the reception area and other public spaces, including a large swimming pool with surrounding multileveled decking, enclosed restaurant, with saunas and disco-theque in the basement. Windsurfing, waterskiing, kayaking, diving, and boating and fishing in general, are among the organized activities at this sport's resort.

PORTO CANOAS, Praia de Nova Cruz, Maria Farinha. Tel. 081/341-4382. Fax 081/436-2220. 10 bungalows.

$ **Rates:** $35 double. No 10% service charge. No credit cards.

⭐ Your host, Julio Britto, is a convivial man with a lot of good energy. His property is informal, on the natural side of things, being right on the water and surrounded by a variety of ecosystems. The accommodations are in bungalows, each with a bedroom, living room, kitchen, bathroom, and veranda.

Ⓢ Several one-day excursions are offered, including a one-day boat ride in the mangrove bayou, with lunch ($20). The excursion may be purchased separately by anyone staying in Recife for $28, including round-trip transportation.

PORTO DE GALINHAS

About 40 miles (70km) south of Recife is a very special oceanside resort, near the small port town of Porto de Galinhas.

Where to Stay

HOTEL PONTAL DE OCAPORÃ, Porto de Galinhas. Tel. 081/224-4103.
Fax 081/224-2288. Telex 81/1339. 45 bungalows. A/C MINIBAR TV TEL
$ **Rates:** Off-season $65 double; in season $115–$125 double. AE, DC, MC, V.

⭐ The motto at the Hotel Pontal de Ocaporã makes a self-referential claim to the "the art of good living" in practice there. Normally, such promotional slogans are not to be taken seriously, but Ocaporã is the proverbial exception to the rule. Without reservation, I would have to list this exceptional operation with the top 10—perhaps even the top five—beach resorts I have visited in all Brazil. The spot itself, the simple landscaping of flower-bordered cobble paths etched through a park shaded by scores of palm trees, is simply stunning. The hotel's rooms are divided among clusters of duplex bungalows, and one or two larger garden-style apartment buildings, all roughly within 100 to 200 feet of an impeccably clean, white sandy beach. Every detail in the physical plant and ambience, from the very sensual pool area to the cheery lobby, is maintained in tip-top condition. And the rooms are definitely five-star quality, each opening onto a hammock-equipped veranda ventilated by the fresh breezes that waft off the sea.

Service in Brazil can be a problem in the more remote rural districts, where training is difficult to provide. Not so at the Ocaporã; the staff here is every bit as classy as the facilities, not only in their etiquette, but also in their good-natured spirit. When not grazing or sunbathing at poolside or on the strand, guests have the option of more active pursuits like dune-buggying, horseback riding, or soaring above the waves in an ultralight plane, in each case for a very reasonable fee.

As for the Ocaporã's restaurant, I ate an incredibly good lunch there, the house shrimp dish, priced at about $7. As a bonus, the nearby village of Porto de Galinhas provides an alternative locale for socializing and dining in several cafés and restaurants.

SOLAR PORTO DE GALINHAS, Porto de Galinhas. Tel. 081/325-0772.
Fax 081/325-1331 Telex 81/3215. 46 rms. A/C MINIBAR TV TEL
$ **Rates:** $50–$70 single; $70–$90 double. AE, DC, MC, V.

⭐ On the same magical stretch of beach as the resort described above is a moderately priced alternative, the Solar Porto de Galinhas—nothing fancy, but a solid sort of place, and very well managed. One of the advantages of this establishment is the restaurant, which comes highly recommended, not only for the seafood delicacies, but for the Saturday feijoada. You can come here for a day-trip, too; a guide will pick you up in your hotel in Recife, bring you to the hotel, where you'll be served lunch, and spend the day on the beach ($35 per person).

PRAIA PONTA DE SERRAMBI

Right up the beach from Porto de Galinhas is a similarly beautiful beach, where a brand-new deluxe hotel has just been inaugurated.

Where to Stay

INTERMARES VILLAGE, Praia Ponta de Serrambi. Tel. 081/527-1200.
Fax 081/527-1006. Telex 81/2452. 94 rms. A/C MINIBAR TV TEL

$ Rates: $150–$180 single; $180–$230 double. AE, DC, MC, V.

The InterMares, which means "between the seas," was literally a week away from opening when I visited there recently. Except for a few odd and ends in the finishing work which remained to be completed, the place was sparkling like a new toy at Christmas. A great white wall surrounds the many acres of ecologically preserved, coconut palm–studded grounds, so that the resort recalls something of the coastal fortifications that once protected this area in the years it was a great port of entry for slavers from Africa. The style of the many structures within the grounds is also colonial, all tropically brilliant in white stucco. If this resort has a theme—other than its self-proclaimed intention of drawing 80% of its clientele from a sophisticated international market—it is the emphasis here on active water sports: jetskiing, sailing, and motorboating, windsurfing, deep-sea diving, and much more. Each of the spacious and well-decorated rooms overlooks the ocean. And other facilities include a giant pool, sauna, a fine restaurant, and three bars.

FAZENDA NOVA & CARUARU

West of Recife some 75 miles distant is the town of Fazenda Nova, which visitors to the region will definitely want to visit during Holy Week. Outside the town is a vast open-air arena, a scaled-down reproduction of ancient Jerusalem, where a full-blown **Passion Play,** including the crucifixion of Christ, is reenacted every year.

A few miles from this Nova Jerusalem is the state craft capital, the town of **Caruaru,** with its famous weekend market for pottery, terra-cotta figurines, and other handmade items in wood, leather, and straw.

---

3. NATAL

675 miles N of Salvador, 180 miles N of Recife

GETTING THERE By Plane See Section 1 on Maceió, earlier in this chapter.

By Bus Natal's principal bus station, the **Rodoviária,** is located on the corner of Avenida Capitão-Mor Gouveia with Avenida Col. Estevam in the Lagoa Nova neighborhood. Among the companies servicing Natal are the **Empresa Napolis** (tel. 231-1074), with a bus departing for Recife at 11:50pm and costing $15; and **Empresa São Geraldo** (tel. 223-5343), with a bus for Maceió ($13) at 10pm, and one for Salvador at noon ($25).

By Car The coastal route from the south follows BR 101, and from the north, BR 304.

ESSENTIALS Natal has a **Centro de Turismo** at Rua Aderbal de Figueiredo 980, in Petrópolis (tel. 084/231-6729), open Monday through Saturday from 2 to 8pm. In addition to an information counter hosted by the state tourism bureau, the tourism center contains arts-and-crafts galleries, and a restaurant. The Rio Grande do Norte state tourism bureau is **EMPROTURN**, Via Costeira km 12 (tel. 084/219-3400), open 9am to 6pm Monday to Friday. EMPROTURN maintains a special tourism information hotline called Disque Turismo (tel. 221-1453).

Anyone wishing to book airport transfers or guided tours may contact one of the following agencies: **International Viagens e Turismo** (tel. 084/231-9946; fax 084/231-9947); **Solis Turismo** (tel. 084/221-1150; fax 084/221-2488); or **Nataltur** (tel. 084/222-5401; fax 084/221-5956).

Natal, a city of 500,000 inhabitants and capital of the state of **Rio Grande do Norte,** is quite simply the new fun capital of the *nordeste,* with the best beaches, the best food, and the best hotels. In fact, more new hotels have been built in Natal in recent years than in any other Brazilian city. And the building boom continues. Slated for completion along a newly developed six-mile stretch of beachfront immediately to the south of the city are 18 new hotels, a number of which are already open for business.

Natal has a long history of receiving foreign visitors. The city was an obligatory refueling point for aviation pioneers who flew the first mail runs between Europe and South America. And during World War II, thousands of Americans were stationed at a large air base outside the city, called the "Victory Trampoline," a major logistical link in the resupply route for Allied forces in North Africa.

WHAT TO SEE & DO

Natal has three major zones of interest: the city itself with its satellite beaches, and the more remote coastal beaches, both to the north and the south. Giant sand dunes embrace the town and continue on the length of its coastline. Considering its configuration, Natal itself must have been built on dunes very similar to those you will see along the virgin shoreline. The city begins at the water's edge on a spit of land between the Atlantic and the **Rio Potengi**, and climbs steeply upward to the downtown commercial and administrative center.

Along the river in the lower town is the waterfront, and Natal's oldest neighborhood, **Ribeira.** Nearby is the **Igreja de Santo Antônio,** known as the Rooster's Church, built in 1766. The next neighborhood going up the river is **Alecrim,** where every Friday from dawn till Saturday afternoon there is a popular outdoor fair covering 10 square blocks. The point where the river meets the sea is occupied by the **Forte dos Três Magos** (Fort of the Three Wise Men), which is open to the public. The fort was built and occupied by the Portuguese in 1598 as part of their system of coastal defenses to discourage the marauding of their European rivals. The official settlement of the town occurred the following year, on Christmas Day, and thus the name Natal.

On the ocean side of the fort in the lower town are Natal's oldest beaches, the **Praia do Forte, Praia do Meio, Praia dos Artistas** (a center for nightlife), and **Praia de Areia Preta,** with its many restaurants overlooking the rocky shore. From here the **Via Costeira** begins at the **Praia Mae Luíza** and travels for several miles along the coastal highway lined with new hotels to Ponta Negra, one of the most popular of Natal's outlying beaches.

The beaches continue along the southern shore, but the road jogs inland here and then back along the sea, through such summer beach communities as **Piragi do Norte.** Across the Potengi River to the north is another string of beaches, more primitive, with mountainous snow-white dunes that begin at the shore and travel inland for many miles. Both regions are described in "Easy Excursions," below.

WHERE TO STAY

Visitors have three basic choices for accommodations in the city proper. First are the hotels at the foot of the downtown section, along or close to the traditional beaches and the centers of nightlife and shoreside dining. Next are the new, self-contained resort hotels along the Via Costeira, with their miles of unspoiled beaches, yet still only a few minutes' ride from downtown by bus or taxi. Finally, there is an executive-style hotel in the upper city, where many more fine restaurants are located, as well as a number of bargain accommodations, less expensive because they aren't on the beach.

Wherever you decide to stay, there's no reason why you can't spend as much time as you like poolside at any hotel of your choice. Protocol requires that you order a drink or two, or a meal, if you take up table and pool space at a given hotel. But this is a reasonable and inexpensive way to experience a variety of different resort environments along the Via Costeira.

EXPENSIVE

IMIRA PLAZA, Via Costeira 4077, Natal. Tel. 084/222-4105. Fax 084/222-8422. Telex 84/2300. 118 rms. A/C MINIBAR TV TEL
$ Rates: $100 single or double. AE, DC, MC, V.

The Imira Plaza bills its location as the Parque das Dunas, in recognition of the surrounding hills of sand. The lobby opens onto an atrium bar and coffee shop. A terraced walkway, with a waterfall wall, wanders through a rock garden of pools filled with aquaculture plants. The rooms all face the sea and Dutch doors (the top sections have shutters that open) lead to large balconies perched over the dunes. The rooms contain two large beds with broad-striped cotton spreads. Baths with large open showers and marble-topped sinks have ceilings of cedar boards, which exude their inimitably fresh aroma. A pool area at the edge of the dunes drops off to the long and narrow beach below.

NOVOTEL LADEIRA DO SOL, Rua Fabricio Pedroza 915, Natal. Tel. 084/221-4204. Fax 084/221-4858. Telex 84/2612. 62 rms. A/C MINIBAR TV TEL

$ Rates: $90 single or double. AE, DC, MC, V.

One of Natal's nicest hotels is the Novotel Ladeira do Sol, on the ramp leading from the Praia dos Artistas to the upper town. The split-level lobby has a tile floor and a seating area with black, soft-leather couches and armchairs. On the lower level is a bar and cocktail lounge, and in the mezzanine, a restaurant where a delicious buffet is served at lunchtime daily. The hotel has rooms in standard and deluxe categories. The standard room has a double bed with a quilted spread, and light-yellow carpets on the floor. There is also a couch that can serve as an extra bed, and a pair of captain's chairs. These rooms face an interior open-air walkway. The deluxe rooms are similarly furnished, and all have balconies with hooks for hammocks, provided by the hotel on request. Other features are an imaginative interior garden and a two-level pool with a waterfall effect and a large patio.

MODERATE

BARREIRA ROXA PRAIA HOTEL, Via Costeira km 05, Natal. Tel. 084/222-1093. Telex 84/2351. 40 rms. A/C MINIBAR TV TEL

$ Rates: $40–$45 single; $48–$50 double. No credit cards.

Closest to the city along the Via Costeira, this spacious hotel is actually a school run by the state to train hotel staff for Natal's growing tourism sector. The best rooms have large balconies that look out beyond the large pool area to the ocean. Like all the hotels on this new strip, the Barreira Roxa sits directly on the beach, although much of the coast here alternates between rocky ledges and patches of sand. The hotel has a full complement of facilities, including restaurant, bar, and a lobby gift shop.

HOTEL MAINE, Av. Sen. Salgado Filho 1741, Lagoa Nova, Natal. Tel. 084/221-5775. Fax 084/221-5333. Telex 84/2611. 40 rms, 4 suites. A/C MINIBAR TV TEL

$ Rates: $79–$87 single; $94–$104 double; $130 suite. AE, DC, MC, V.

The recently constructed Hotel Maine replaces the Luxor Hotel—which closed unexpectedly—as Natal's only downtown, executive-style hotel. The hotel's name may strike a curious note. Maine, as it turns out, is the sister state of Rio Grande do Norte, and never was a more paradoxical affinity concocted, though various private organs within each state maintain the most cordial of relations. One of the Hotel Maine's most appealing features, along with its very comfortable accommodations, is its top-floor Augusta Restaurant, where some very fine dishes are prepared.

HOTEL VILA DO MAR, Via Costeira 4223, Natal. Tel. 084/222-3755. Fax 084/221-6017. Telex 84/2366. 210 rms. A/C MINIBAR TV TEL

$ Rates: $115 single; $140 double. DC, MC, V.

Hotel Vila do Mar comes closest of all the new hotels on the strip to creating a full-blown resort atmosphere. Two separate buildings, each with its own reception area, are linked by a wide, stone patio of salmon-colored bricks cut into the dunes, with a swimming pool bridged by a wooden walkway. The lobby in the main building has a greenhouse facade and a sloping glass roof, and looks out on the breaking waves. The sea—a mere 100 feet distant—is always in view from most points within the complex. Close to the pool is a separate structure with a bar and several shops. Another building is a breakfast room with a mock-thatch roof, straw fastened deftly to more reliable red roofing tiles. The main building and the annex together contain 210 rooms with small balconies, some of which face the water. With the built-in hardwood furniture and large box-frame bed, the rooms are designed for space and beachside comfort. Handmade baskets and pottery add a touch of intimacy to the decor, and baths are equipped with hairdryers and shampoo.

MARSOL, Via Costeira 1567, Natal. Tel. 084/221-2619. Fax 084/221-2619. Telex 84/2554. 60 rms. A/C MINIBAR TV TEL
$ Rates: $70–$80 single; $95–$105 double. AE, DC, MC, V.
At the Marsol the rooms occupy two stories. First-floor rooms open on stone- and brick-paved patios, with a colorful hammock, plus table and chairs, only 100 feet from the water's edge. Rooms have clean-lined, bunk-style beds with hardwood frames, and stone floors. The hotel's lobby and other public spaces occupy a central pagoda with a high ceiling of exposed timbers and a red-tile roof which opens onto a deck with two pools, one for children. The beach is a very private strand about 300 feet wide, the sand covered in places with natural growth typical of the local ecology.

NATAL MAR HOTEL, Via Costeira 8101, Natal. Tel. 084/219-2121. Fax 084/219-3131. Telex 84/2449. 149 rms. A/C MINIBAR TV TEL
$ Rates: $68–$89 single; $75–$100 double. DC, MC, V.
Cheek-by-jowl with the Praia da Ponta Negra is the Natal Mar Hotel, in a superb location on this prized beach. The hotel has two blocks of rooms with a central area occupied by a smallish pool and a seaside patio circled by white umbrella-covered tables and contoured modular recliners. The deluxe room is of suite size, with a large table and chairs occupying a partitioned space opposite which is a circular cut-out in the wall with a coffee table and more seating. These rooms have double beds and verandas that view the sea. And the tile baths offer the novelty of double sinks and windows of their own. The standard rooms have a similar decor but are smaller.

NATAL OTHON HOTEL, Av. Pres. Café Filho 822, Natal. Tel. 084/222-2055. Fax 084/222-2146. Telex 84/2102. 91 rms. A/C MINIBAR TV TEL
$ Rates: $55–$60 single; $65–$70 double. AE, DC, MC, V.
The well-placed hotel overlooks the old fort and the Praia do Meio beach. The first-class Natal Othon (formerly the Hotel Reis Magos) remains a bargain-priced establishment despite its complete renovation, spurred by competition from the newer hotels along the Via Costeira. The rooms are distributed among several two- and four-story buildings with curved exterior lines in white stucco. Deluxe rooms, all in white with stone floors, open either on the interior courtyard (with an extra-large pool) or have ocean views, seen through a curtain of swaying *coqueiros* from their balconies. Standard rooms have smaller beds, but are otherwise the same, and some standards on the higher floors have the best views in the hotel. Other facilities include a restaurant and a nightclub.

PARQUE DA COSTEIRA, Via Costeira km 7, Natal. Tel. 084/222-6147. Fax 084/222-1459. Telex 84/2701. 90 rms. A/C MINIBAR TV TEL
$ Rates: $110 single; $120 double. AE, DC, MC, V.
The newest of the hotels along Natal's ocean boulevard, the Parque da Costeira offers a few unique features, like clay tennis courts and a vast patio pool area. The hotel's rooms are painted a relaxing tone of green, and blend rattan furnishings with the solid stone floors that are typical of the region. From just about everywhere in the hotel, you can hear the continual and soothing roar of the sea.

WHERE TO DINE

When it comes to meals in Natal, often the best food and prices are found in the dining rooms of the many top hotels. Other fine restaurants can be found throughout the downtown area, and at the beaches along the coast to the north or south of the city. Restaurants located in the environs are described in the "Easy Excursions" section, below.

MODERATE

AUGUSTA RESTAURANT, in the Hotel Maine, Av. Sen. Salgado Filho 1741. Tel. 221-5775.
   Cuisine: FRENCH/INTERNATIONAL. **Reservations:** Recommended on weekends.
$ Prices: Appetizers $4.50–$15; main courses $6–$18. AE, DC, MC, V.
   Open: Lunch daily 11am–3pm; dinner daily 7pm–midnight.
Here in the Augusta, as with most restaurants in the Brazilian northeast, it is almost axiomatic to begin a meal with *pato de carangueijo* ($4), the breaded leg of the land crab found throughout the vast mangrove swamps that border the coastline from Bahia to Pará. For a more delicate appetizer, you could choose the smoked salmon ($15). Among the main courses, there's an intriguing dish, *camarão ao café* ($10), shrimp sautéed in butter, then flambéed in vermouth, into which mixture a white sauce spiked with coffee liqueur is prepared. Another excellent choice is the médaillons of filet mignon with mushrooms, in Madeira sauce ($7.50).

CAMARÕES, Av. Eng. Roberto Freire 2610, Punta Negra. Tel. 219-2424.
   Cuisine: SHRIMP. **Reservations:** Not needed.
$ Prices: Appetizers $3–$7; main courses $9–$10. No credit cards.
   Open: Lunch daily 11:30am–4pm; dinner Mon–Sat 6pm–midnight.
This shrimp house, across from the beach, occupies an apparently residential dwelling, and has tables with starched white tablecloths on a wraparound outside veranda, and an inside formal dining room. Camarões serves 14 different shrimp dishes, all of which cost around $9.50. There are also a few lobster dishes, priced at slightly over $10 each.

CARNE DO SOL, Rua Dionisio Fiqueira 799, Petrópolis. Tel. 222-9627.
   Cuisine: REGIONAL. **Reservations:** Not needed.
$ Prices: Appetizers $3–$8.50; main courses $6.75–$7.75. AE, DC, MC, V.
   Open: Daily 11am–11pm.
Just up the incline, above the downtown beachfront, Carne do Sol is probably one of the best bargains in Natal—plus the food is excellent. This is regional cooking of the northeast at its best. One incomparable main course is the sun-dried beef, rolled and filled with cheese, served with black-eyed peas, rice, baked mandioc root, and a farofa flavored with fresh coriander leaves.

CHAPLIN, Av. Pres. Café Filho 27. Tel. 222-0217.
   Cuisine: FRENCH/INTERNATIONAL. **Reservations:** Recommended on weekends.
$ Prices: Appetizers $2.50–$12; main courses $7–$17. AE.
   Open: Daily 11:30am–2am.
Considered by many local residents to be the fanciest restaurant in Natal, the Chaplin concentrates on many of the most traditional French preparations. The restaurant's signature main course, however, has very much of a Brazilian accent—the *camarão St. Jacques* ($15), breaded shrimp filled with creamy melted cheese.

COCO BEACH, Morro do Careca, at the far end of Punta Negra beach. Tel. 236-2404.
   Cuisine: SEAFOOD. **Reservations:** Not needed.
$ Prices: Most items $3.50–$10. No credit cards.
   Open: Daily 10am–midnight, much later on weekends.
To get to Coco Beach, we drove to the end of Punta Negra, then took off our shoes, and walked along the sand for the last 100 yards or so. The road crossing in the front of the restaurant was blocked off due to construction. But, arriving this way is really in

the spirit of this appealing and informal hangout, since many of the tables are scattered helter skelter on the beach anyway. Partners Rolf, formerly of Búzios, where he owned a place of the same name, and Jerry, an American most recently from Las Vegas, live with their families in the terraced condos that climb the hill behind and above the rustic beach bar. Their menu is very select. The specialties are barbecued red snapper (priced by size at $5.50, $7, or $8.75), and shrimp barbecued in garlic oil, also priced by size (large $9.25, medium $7.75). On Monday nights, there is live music at Coco Beach, usually authentic forró, right down to the tell-tale accordion.

MOQUECA CAPIXABA, Av. Gov. Silvio Pegroza 150. Tel. 221-3148.
   Cuisine: CAPIXABA. **Reservations:** Not needed.
$ Prices: Appetizers $1–$5; main courses $6.75–$11. No credit cards.
   Open: Daily 11:30am–midnight.
The Moqueca Capixaba is located on the edge of Natal's nightlife district along the downtown beachfront. The menu, which concentrates on specialties from the state of Espírito Santo, features more than 50 different dishes, including the famous capixaba moqueca, usually a seafood stew, cooked with coconut milk, and served in a ceramic pot straight from the oven, along with rice and a superb home-style *pirão*.

O CRUSTÁCEO, Rua Apodi 414A. Tel. 222-1122.
   Cuisine: SEAFOOD. **Reservations:** Not needed.
$ Prices: Appetizers 75¢–$3; main courses $5–$8. No credit cards.
   Open: Daily 11am–6pm.
O Crustáceo is an unpretentious hole-in-the-wall in Tirol, near the Avenida Prudente de Morais. It's not much to look at, but the food, billed as home-cooked seafood—shrimp, oysters, lobster, crab, and fish—is good and cheap. This is also a great place to sit and drink beer while consuming large quantities of *pastel de camarão*, little turnovers filled with shrimp cooked in a superb sauce of onions and tomatoes, a steal at about 50¢ each.

RAIZES, at the corner of Av. Campos Sales and Rua Mossoro. Tel. 222-7338.
   Cuisine: REGIONAL. **Reservations:** Not needed.
$ Prices: Appetizers $2–$3; main courses $5.25–$13.50; buffet $6–$25. AE.
   Open: Lunch daily 11am–3pm; dinner daily 6pm–11pm.
Raizes, in the Petrópolis section, offers in addition to its full à la carte menu, a *café sertanejo*, a rodízio of cheeses, juices, and cakes, plus tapioca and coffee, tea, or milk, for $4; and for $8, a *ceia nordestino*, a rodízio of 35 items, including homemade liquors, covering just about all the foods that are typical of the northeast region.

XIQUE XIQUE, Av. Afonso Pena 444. Tel. 222-4466.
   Cuisine: INTERNATIONAL. **Reservations:** Not needed.
$ Prices: Appetizers $3.25–$7.50; main courses $6–$13.50. AE, DC, MC, V.
   Open: Lunch Mon–Sat 11am–3pm; dinner Mon–Sat 6pm–midnight.
Xique Xique, in the nearby Tirol neighborhood, occupies a colonial-style house surrounded by a garden of lush tropical plants. There are several dining rooms inside, each decorated with the original art of a local artist, notably the landscapes and folkloric scenes of Milton Navarro. The specialties here are strictly international platters, meats, and seafood.

A HOT TIP

On weekends, when the sun is hot, and most people find themselves stretched out on the beach, who has time for a sit-down lunch when the munchies hit? Most Brazilians under these circumstances head for their favorite *barracas* on the sand to snack and quaff cold drafts. On Punta Negra beach, the in barracas are **Baixa Verde** and **Inácio.**

EVENING ENTERTAINMENT

Natal has a number of interesting supper clubs, one a hangout of the town's upper crust; several discos and cafés with live music; and two tourist joints, one with a quasi-amateur, but amusing, floor show, the other staging some well-rehearsed and energetic dance numbers.

The **Chaplin,** mentioned above under "Where to Dine," is Natal's high-society watering hole. The club also has one of the best locations in the city, at the circle where the roads to downtown and those leading to the traditional and the new beaches all meet, at the end of the Praia dos Artistas. Outdoors on a partially covered veranda is a *choparía,* an informal café. Indoors is a pub and a swank restaurant for formal dining and dancing.

A block or so from the Chaplin, on a strip of beach called the Praia do Meio, are a half-dozen cafés and restaurants, including the **Império do Rei,** Rua Café Filho 41 (tel. 219-2714), open daily from 11am till as long as there are customers to wait on. The corner café/restaurant sits above the sidewalk, where, on a veranda—partially in the open air, partially covered—a festive, animated crowd usually disports itself. Live music every night but Sunday, after 10pm.

MANDACARU, Av. do Jequi 201, in Neópolis (behind the Cidade Jardim Shopping Center). Tel. 217-3008.

In this gym-sized hall with a capacity for a gigantic crowd, a troupe of youngsters puts on a first-rate performance. To begin with, there's a medley of Brazilian music—popular and traditional—by the excellent band and vocalists. Then the spirited dancers go through a variety of choreographed interpretations of the regional dances that take their original inspiration from the rhythms of the Caribbean. After the show, which is more than worth the price of admission, the band plays on and the audience takes over the dance floor. The price of drinks is downright cheap, less than $1 for beer, and 50¢ for caipirinhas. Open Sunday to Wednesday from 9pm to 2am, and Thursday to Saturday till 4am; the show starts around 10:30pm.

Admission: $4.50.

ZÁS TRÁS, Rua Apodi 500, Tirol. Tel. 222-6589.

The Zás Trás is a popular cavern, seating up to 1,000 patrons, most of whom are Brazilian tourists there for the show, and to hear the *repentista,* a singer who makes up the verse as he goes along, managing to make a crack or compliment about every table and many individuals in the audience with his song, which goes on for 45 minutes. Natives of Natal come to the Zás Trás when the show is over, around 11pm to dance the forró to live music. Meals here are basic and not expensive, from $4 to $6.

Admission: $4.

LUA CHEIA

There's a tradition in Natal on the night of the full moon. Hundreds of people gather at the Punta Negra beach, and make an all-night party of it.

EASY EXCURSIONS
GENIPABÚ & THE NORTHERN BEACHES

North of the city, across the Rio Potengi, beginning with Genipabú, are the most extraordinary beaches and dunes, without a doubt among the very best in Brazil. On that same Potengi River, incidentally, author Antoine de Saint-Exupéry, as well as Charles Lindbergh and other early pioneers of aviation, once landed their hydroplanes during their South American mail runs.

A DUNE-BUGGY ADVENTURE If you are staying in Natal, one of the best ways to make your first visit to Genipabú is by renting a dune buggy with a driver and getting a full introduction to the attractions of the region over the course of an entire day. The rental cost for a buggy and driver is about $40 for a six-hour excursion.

For a buggy with a professional driver, contact the **APCBA** (Independent Association of Buggy Owners), Rua João Pessoa 267, Room 267 (tel. 235-1062). The association has a list of more than 50 qualified drivers, and will be happy to recommend someone who is safe and reliable. Or contact directly **Beto & Angela,** Av. Alexandrino de Alencar 1094 (tel. 222-5921). The couple, who are members of the association, have a fleet of cars. Ask for Beto to accompany you personally, if possible. He's a former banker turned beachcomber, excellent company, and an extremely responsible driver.

The driver will pick you up at your hotel in the morning, say, between 8:30 and 9am. The open dune buggy is most comfortable with a maximum of three people, including the driver. One passenger rides shotgun next to the driver, the other occupies a kind of rumble seat, in theory big enough for two, but actually bearable for one person alone. Since the buggy is a convertible with no top, be sure to apply plenty of sunscreen, and above all, wear a hat to protect your head from Natal's tropical sun.

Your driver now speeds through the city and then up along the river to the bridge where you cross the Rio Potengi, and turns off toward **Redinha.** If the day is really scorching, ask to stop at a roadside stand so you can buy a cooling drink of *agua de coco* (coconut water) served in its green shell with a straw. When you finish drinking, ask the vendor to slice the shell in quarters so you can eat the soft, unripened meat on the inside, a kind of coconut custard (this has the reverse name, *coco de agua*). Reaching the beach of Redinha you notice that you are merely on the other side of the river, viewing the port and the old fort from the opposite bank. Many small children are wading in the water on the river end of the beach, which curves northward and confronts the ocean head-on, continuing for many miles up the coast. The little village of Redinha, with its quaint buildings and country chapel, serves as a backdrop to the beach, where an animated urban crowd takes its pleasures on the weekends amid racing dune buggies, motorcycles, food stalls, and a classy-looking restaurant, the **Porto Belo,** overlooking the sand.

For additional excitement, there are kayaks for shooting the waves, rented for $2 an hour, and a contraption called a **triócolo a vela,** built of metal tubing in the triangular shape of a dragster, with three wheels, a mast, and mainsail. The single front wheel can turn, manipulated by foot pedals, and the vehicle is said to reach speeds nearing 40 m.p.h. on flat, hard sand. Getting the knack of the thing is easy for anyone who has sailed; otherwise you can give it a whirl in the company of an attendant, also for about $2 per hour.

But the real excitement begins when you head for Genipabú, for a roller-coaster ride of buggy-surfing by way of the giant dunes. The ride is a set piece, and should only be attempted with an experienced driver who knows the itinerary. Up and down the slopes of the dunes you race, making one hairpin turn after another. At one point the driver stops the buggy on a hill high above Lake Genipabú, a totally unexpected body of fresh water set among the dunes like the cone of an extinct volcano. A few tents line the margin of the shore below, campers who have come by way of an access road to this relatively isolated spot, only a 15-minute walk to the beach. After a few more thrilling slalom runs comes the pièce de résistance, a final dramatic descent down a 100-foot-high slope onto the beach at Genipabú.

Boys lead jackasses and small horses by the bridle, and will rent them if you wish to saddle up and wander the beach or explore the dunes further at a slower pace. But it's time for lunch, and there are a half-dozen bars and cafés on this beach, not to mention a fine restaurant nearby at the Hotel Genipabú. After lunch, the journey up the coast continues along the beach (see description under "A Jeep Safari Excursion," below).

Where to Stay

HOTEL GENIPABÚ, Estrada de Genipabú, Genipabú. Tel. 084/225-2063. Fax 084/231-4602. Telex 84/2604. 24 rms. MINIBAR TV
$ Rates: $50 double. MAP rates $10 extra. AE, DC, MC, V.
If you want to really relax in a beautiful spot, in a comfortable, inexpensive hotel with excellent food and service, the Hotel Genipabú is the place for you. Only 25km (15 miles) from downtown Natal, and a half-hour's drive from the airport, the hotel's owners/hosts Patrick (French) and Ana (Brazilian) Muller, who both speak excellent English, have constructed a delightful getaway refuge a stone's throw from the hustle bustle of the city.

The hotel, a two-story block of rooms, built in native style with heavy timbers and red roofing tiles, is perched high above the surrounding landscape. The rooms are modern, spacious, and well ventilated (with the aid of ceiling fans), and have balconies with hammocks. The central pool area also commands a magnificent view, virtually 360°, encompassing not only the lush environs, but the beach and ocean along the horizon. You can reach the beach, if you wish, by walking for about 25 minutes along the nearby access road. But the hotel staff will also transport you there and pick you up at your convenience. The Mullers have designed several interesting excursion packages for taking guests to more remote spots, since things are getting somewhat built up around Genipabú, which are described below. The breakfast here includes the rare option of eggs cooked to order, and for an additional $10, you can be on the Modified American Plan, adding either lunch or dinner.

POUSADA MAR AZUL, Praia de Genipabú, Genipabú. Tel. 084/225-2065. 9 rms (8 with bath).
$ Rates: $15–$20 double. No credit cards.
The Mar Azul is a pleasant, clean establishment, located right on the beach. Typical of a genuine inn, none of the rooms is uniform in size or accoutrements. The two best rooms, on the corners in the front, face the beach and have verandas with hammocks. Six units have minibars, and one is air-conditioned.

Where to Dine

There are many informal cafés and restaurants in the small village of Genipabú at the entrance to the beach. One that the Mullers recommend is **O Pedro** (tel. 225-2114). One that I recommend is their own restaurant at the Hotel Genipabú, specializing in regional and seafood dishes in the $6.50 to $9.25 range. The shrimp *catupiry* was outstanding.

A Jeep Safari Excursion

Patrick, or his brother-in-law, Antônio, will take you on a Jeep or buggy ride up the beach, a day-trip covering 100km (60 miles), including lunch—usually a seafood barbecue right on the sand at a cost of $40 per person.

To get to the northern beaches, your vehicle must cross the relatively narrow Ceará Mirim river, but there is no bridge. The ancient art of the ferryman is alive and well on the Ceará Mirim, however. Cars and buggies alike drive to the edge of the bank and board individual rafts, called *balsas,* that are poled to the other side by two men. From here to the beach you follow the dune route, past an occasional fisherman's house, planted like a lonely wooden cactus in a desert of white sand, with a few scrawny *coquiero* seedlings the owner hopes will one day grow into mature crop-bearing trees. In the distance, a lone rider or two on horseback paces slowly from somewhere in the interior toward the beach for some unknown purpose. Then its up the beach along the only "highway," the hard-packed sand at water's edge. The further you go, the more primitive and isolated the beaches become. My version of this ride went as far as the Praia do Muriu, where Antônio and I stopped at the **Restaurant da Guismar** (tel. 228-2082; open 7am to 6pm daily), the only access to which is along the beach, and ate cheese and shrimp *pasteis* (50¢), and drank cold beer.

Two Nights in Galinhos

The Mullers of the Hotel Genipabú have designed a three-day, two-night fantasy excursion to an isolated fishing village, Galinhos, 120 miles up the coast from Genipabú. Leaving in the early morning from their hotel where you have spent the night, the safari of several Jeeps and dune buggies snakes up the beach for seven hours, stopping frequently along the way. Arriving at Galinhos, separated from the mainland by a river, you must cross over by boat if the tide is too high to ford by vehicle. There are power and telephone hookups in the village, but no cars; and you spend the night in hammocks in the houses of local fishermen. You then return by bus, a two-hour drive, to the Genipabú hotel, where you spend one more night, including dinner. The price, including meals, is $400 per person.

REGIÃO DO SUL

South of Natal are a string of beaches—part summer and weekend colonies, part rural fishing villages—that are completely different in appearance and function than the more primitive and recreational beaches to the north. Also distinct from the north, the road here runs close to the sea, and so the ride with its many lovely views of coves and coastal boating is an end in itself, not merely a dull ride to the beach.

A popular destination here is **Pirangi do Norte**, not only a lovely beach but home to the world's largest cashew tree, a veritable phenomenon of nature. The tree, which can be visited in a little park of its own, has spread its branches in serpentine fashion along the ground, so that it occupies the terrain of a good-size house lot.

The **Marina Badaué** (tel. 222-9366) company offers a cruise of the southern waters off Pirangi and its neighboring beaches.

Where to Stay

It's easy to imagine wanting to prolong your stay in Pirangi, and the beach has just the right hotel to satisfy such an impulse.

HOTEL VILLAGE DO SOL, Praia do Pirangi do Norte, Pirangi. Tel. 084/238-2020. Telex 84/2672. 24 rms. A/C MINIBAR TV TEL
$ Rates: $55 double. AE, DC, MC, V.
A dozen bungalows are spaced on a well-landscaped and gently rising dune, surrounding a pool with patio and a very reputable restaurant. Each apartment has two rooms with three beds in all.

4. FORTALEZA

325 miles NW of Natal, 480 miles NW of Recife

GETTING THERE By Plane See Section 1 on Maceió, earlier in this chapter.

By Bus The city bus station, the Rodoviária, is located at the corner of Rua Oswaldo Studart with Avenida Borges de Melo in Fatima (tel. 272-1566). There is frequent bus service from Fortaleza to neighboring cities of the northeast, with connections in Recife and Salvador for more distant Brazilian destinations.

By Car BR 304 connects Fortaleza with Natal to the south, and Teresinha, to the north, the interior capital of neighboring Piauí state.

ESSENTIALS You'll find **EMCETUR** information counters at the airport (tel. 085/272-1325); the bus station, Terminal Rodoviário Eng. João Thomé, Av. Borges de Melo 1630 (tel. 085/227-4614); the Centro de Turismo, Rua Senador Pompeu 350 (tel. 085/231-3566); and along Avenida Presidente Kennedy at a kiosk near the Iracema Monument. There is also a tourist information hotline, called Disque Turismo; dial 1516.

The state of **Ceará** is a living metaphor for the contradictions besetting modern Brazil. Within the borders of the state, all the extremes of the country's paradoxical development are reflected. Ceara's interior remains backward. The *sertanejos* there still look more to the next world for solace to their misery than to the possibilities of real gain or satisfaction in the present world. The traditions of religious fanaticism are woven deeply into the fabric of rural Ceará, and the roots of that phenomenon run deep. Even as the troops of the first republic were obliterating one manifestation of millenarian power in Canudos, another was rising in the interior of Ceará, in the city of Juazeiro do Norte. In 1889 a woman received communion from a priest and the water was said to have turned to blood within her mouth. This and subsequent "miracles" were attributed to a simple parish curate, Padre Cícero Romão Batista. Padre Cícero went on to exert a powerful and reactionary influence over state and national politics for many years thereafter. And the shadow of his rule has yet to vanish from the barren core of the northeastern region.

On the modern end of the political spectrum is the new, forward-looking urban experience of cities like Fortaleza, Ceará's capital of 1.3 million inhabitants. Fortaleza has evolved into northeastern Brazil's most genuinely urban city, one where the savvy pragmatism of an urban middle class has neutralized certain trends and qualities that characterize even the larger and more prosperous cities in the region: the patrician provincialism of Salvador, and the suburban spread of Recife, for example.

WHAT TO SEE & DO

Fortaleza, like the other coastal cities of the region, has its perennial sunshine and sensual beach life, but it also has a special inner-city rhythm. Much of the street life takes place along the main drag of the in-town **Iracema** and **Meireles** beaches on Avenida Presidente Kennedy. The polluted waters here don't attract many bathers, but the beach is in constant use, primarily by joggers, walkers, and exercise activists. The sidewalks along the avenue are lined with hotels, cafés, restaurants, and nightspots. This is the playground for the city's residents, and for tourists and conventioneers who seem to be drawn here in great numbers throughout the year. At the far end of the beach the *jangada* fishermen land their rafts every afternoon and unload the day's catch.

Around the point is the closest good swimming at the **Praia do Futuro,** and farther south is the fishing village and weekend resort of **Prainha.**

The sweetest swimming within a reasonable distance is to the north, in **Cambuco.** The more remote beaches—some of which can only be reached by four-wheel-drive vehicle or even burro—like **Jericoacoara,** are many hours to the north, and are visited as overnight excursions from Fortaleza.

SHOPPING   Fortaleza is a center for both folk and artistic crafts. Popular with tourists and residents alike is the **Mercado Central,** a closed market occupying an entire block on Rua General Bezarril, downtown. The mercado has been operating since 1930 and shelters 600 stalls. Around the perimeter are dozens of hardware stores for those who wish to see what Brazilian tools are like or who wish to purchase a *facão*, as the large machetelike knives are called. Inside is a honeycomb of shops selling fabrics, ready-to-wear clothes, lace towels and tablecloths, and what are reputed to be the best hammocks in Brazil. An attractive and sturdy linen hammock can be purchased for about $15 to $25 from the **Depósito O Sousa,** stall numbers 505 and 515 (tel. 231-9713). Hammocks are called *redes* in Portuguese, and they come in a variety of qualities. The detail to look for is how the end loops are joined to the body of the cloth—the better hammocks are woven at this point, not sewn. The Mercado Central is open Monday through Saturday from 7am to 6pm.

Many of the better-crafted objects, whether lace (*filé*), straw (*palha*), ceramics (*cerâmica*), or macrame (*cipó*), are sold in individual shops along **Avenida Monsenhor Tabosa,** near the Hotel Praia Centro, between Rua Idlefonso and Avenida Dom Manuel. Two locations for artist-run shops are the government-sponsored **Centro de Turismo,** Rua Senador Pompeu 350, open during the high season on Saturday from 7am to 6:30pm and on Sunday from 8am to 1pm, and the **Central Cearense de Artesanato Luíza Távora,** on Avenida Santos Dumont, Monday through Saturday open from 9am to 6pm year round, and on Sunday as well during the high season. The Luíza Távora Center is a huge and remarkable structure: a tentlike roof, suspended by log rafters and purloins, with two large stucco wings that contain separate compartments for craftspeople selling primarily goods of leather, wood, and cloth. One man does those bottled sand paintings you see in all the markets and souvenir shops in the northeast, and which at first sight seem as though they must be trompe l'oeil, some illusion of what they would seem to be. But here you can watch one of these amazing artisans creating the image inside the bottle one grain of sand at a time—not only the set landscapes of house and palm trees, but commissioned works, like wedding portraits that he copies from photographs his clients provide.

WHERE TO STAY
MODERATE

ESPLANADA PRAIA HOTEL, Av. Presidente Kennedy 2000, Fortaleza. Tel. and fax 085/244-8555. Telex 85/1103. 244 rms. A/C MINIBAR TV TEL
$ Rates: $75–$80 single; $85–$90 double. AE, DC, V.

The Esplanada, along the Beira Mar, the in-town beachfront, is a five-star luxury hotel in all its details. The rooms in the 20-story hotel all face seaward, and in the shade of your private balcony you can sway to your heart's content in a rustic linen hammock, cooled by the steady breeze from the east despite the tropical heat. A pair of louvered sliding doors separates the balcony from the room with its modern decor and king-size bed. The hotel has a large deck with a pool on a platform that protrudes out over the sidewalk from the second floor. The Moringa Restaurant as well as the Esplanada's bar and nightclub are popular ports of call on most nights during the week.

HOTEL PRAIA CENTRO, Av. Monsenhor Tabosa 740, Fortaleza. Tel. and fax 085/211-1122. Telex 85/2070. 190 rms. A/C MINIBAR TV TEL
$ Rates: $60–$65 single; $70–$75 double. AE, DC, MC, V.
The Praia Centro looks like a five-star hotel but its rates are those of a midrange establishment. Perhaps it is because of the location of this striking high-rise, a large black square trimmed in white, propped up on a foundation of pillars. The Praia Centro may have a slight complex at not being across from the Iracema beach (despite the fact that you can't swim there) and at being tucked off on a secondary avenue a block from the sea. The explanation is likely implausible, but one need not plumb the mystery to enjoy this attractive hotel. The rooms are spacious almost to a fault, simply but flawlessly decorated. The hotel towers over the homes and businesses in its own neighborhood, and from the rooftop restaurant or the adjacent pool deck area there is a commanding view of the entire city, near and far. The hotel also runs a regularly scheduled and complementary shuttle bus to points along the Iracema and Futuro beaches.

BUDGET

HOTEL BEIRA MAR, Av. Presidente Kennedy 3130, Fortaleza. Tel. 085/244-9444. Telex 85/1852. 97 rms. A/C MINIBAR TV TEL
$ Rates: $40–$45 single; $50–$55 double. AE, DC, MC, V.
Centrally located on the beachfront and close to most of the nightlife action, the Beira Mar maintains near-capacity occupancy throughout the year since the management markets heavily to tourist and convention groups. As a result there is always a diverse, lively crowd on hand. The large outdoor patio in the courtyard is used for colorful shows and pageants, while guests view the events seated at tables around the swimming pool. Rooms are large and are decorated in modern and traditional designs. They are divided into standard rear units and standard and deluxe units that face the sea.

HOTEL PRAIA MAR, Av. Presidente Kennedy 3190, Fortaleza. Tel. 085/244-9455. Telex 85/1801. 34 rms. A/C MINIBAR TV TEL
$ Rates: $27 single; $35 double. AE, DC, MC, V.
This three-star hotel has some rooms which are cavernous and will accommodate up to four guests, all in separate beds. Some of the accommodations for single or double occupancy have king-size beds, and all rooms are furnished with simple elegance, and include such touches as potted plants, ceramic objects, and original art. The Praia Mar also has a bar and coffee shop.

A NEARBY PLACE TO STAY

HOTEL PRAIA VERDE, Av. Dioguinho 3860, Praia do Futuro, Forteleza. Tel. 085/234-5233. Telex 85/2027. 146 rms. A/C MINIBAR TV TEL
$ Rates: $66 single; $79 double; $81–$93 superdeluxe room. AE, DC, MC, V.
Only five miles from town the beaches are relatively undeveloped, except for occasional clusters of summer homes and oases like that of the resort Hotel Praia Verde, on the Praia do Futuro. The Praia Verde is a self-contained luxury hotel set right on the beach, about a hundred yards from the water. The walled-in complex consists of a square of two-story buildings built around an inner courtyard playground, with a mini-zoo—several cages of tropical birds and small animals. Other interior environments include a large patio with two circular swimming pools. Deluxe rooms occupy the ground floor, and superdeluxe accommodations are on the

second level. Both have hammock-equipped verandas. Rooms are spacious with king-size beds, and are decorated in pale-yellow tones and blond wood trim. Baths are also large, with walls in light-brown tiles, marble sink tops, and wood-framed mirrors. The Praia Verde also has its own restaurant, the Termidor, and an American bar.

WHERE TO DINE

Many restaurants and cafés can be found along the oceanfront Avenida Presidente Kennedy.

CHOPPILEQUE, Av. Presidente Kennedy 2560. Tel. 244-5637.
   Cuisine: SEAFOOD/INTERNATIONAL. **Reservations:** Not needed.
   $ Prices: Appetizers $2.75–$6; main courses $5.75–$13. AE, DC, MC, V.
   Open: Mon–Fri 8am–1am, Sat–Sun 8am–5am.

This is a popular eatery and nightspot with live music, where you'll dine under the roof of an open-air veranda, and the food is straightforward and tasty, with many seafood specialties, and, for light meals, pizza. Fortaleza is so cosmopolitan that a bar like Choppileque can stage live music all week long.

PEIXADA DO MEIO, Av. Presidente Kennedy 4632. Tel. 261-3390.
   Cuisine: SEAFOOD. **Reservations:** Not needed.
   $ Prices: Appetizers $2–$8; main courses $5–$14. No credit cards.
   Open: Daily 11am–2am.

Close to the source where the day's catch is sold each afternoon by the returning *jandadeiros* is the Peixada do Meio. The house specializes in rich stews of shrimp, oysters, octopus, and lobster.

RESTAURANT MIRANTE, in the Hotel Praia Centro, Av. Monsenhor Tabosa 740. Tel. 211-1122.
   Cuisine: INTERNATIONAL. **Reservations:** Recommended for dinner on weekends.
   $ Prices: Appetizers $3.50–$7; main courses $6–$16. AE, DC, MC, V.
   Open: Lunch daily 11:30am–3pm; dinner daily 6:30pm–midnight.

This excellent rooftop restaurant is a good choice for lunch, to take in the daylight view of the city. As for the meal, try the filet Praia Centro, a cut of prime beef braised at tableside in butter and cognac, to which thin slices of ham are added, making a very succulent dish. Add a good Brazilian claret and a dessert like coconut pudding, and the bill—with gratuity—comes to around $15 per person.

EVENING ENTERTAINMENT
FORRÓ

Dancing the forró is the passion of all northeasterners. Every Wednesday night, thousands flock to the outskirts of Fortaleza where the large forró dance halls are located.

The word is of uncertain derivation. Local myth has it that decades ago an American firm invited to Brazil to help install and manage local utilities would host a weekly dance "for all," a weird combination of sounds to the Brazilian ear yielding *forró* (the double *r* in Portuguese sounds like an *h*, sometimes raspy, sometimes not). While colorful, the story is no doubt apocryphal, a more likely derivation being the Brazilian slang word *forrobodó,* meaning riot, disorder, and ultimately, popular ball.

CLUBE DO VAQUEIRO, on the BR 116. No phone.

This extremely popular forró spot is out of town on the main highway, where the event is scheduled for Wednesday only.

OBÁ OBÁ, Av. Washington Soares 3199. Tel. 239-2820.

Obá Obá is on the main inland road between Aquiraz and Fortaleza, near the convention center, about a 15-minute ride from the capital. The expression *obá,* incidentally, is the Brazilian equivalent of "wow." The dance hall, which is also a restaurant, sits on grounds planted with ornamental tropical fruit trees, the pride of the owner, behind high stucco walls. The 400 rustic plywood tables and chairs are distributed beneath a high-roofed, open-air A-frame. In addition to the *forró* every

Wednesday night, there is dancing Friday through Sunday, and shows, sometimes with major national headliners.

A CASINO

CLUBE GUARANY, Rua Carlos Vasconcelos 390. Tel. 244-5847.

While not advertised openly as such, the Clube Guarany is a small-scale but genuine gambling casino, operating in the same semilegal penumbra as the black-market currency exchange. Housed in an old mansion, the casino also has a bistro restaurant and piano bar. But the grand hall is a casino, pure and simple, with roulette, craps, baccarat, and twenty-one. Gamblers are treated well here, with free drinks and canapés—and the best rate of exchange for your cruzeiros in the city.

EASY EXCURSIONS
PRAINHA

The Prainha beach is approximately 20 miles south of Fortaleza, and parallels the old capital of Ceará, **Aquiraz,** which is located about a mile inland. Unlike the beaches right outside the city, which are endless expanses of flat sand and scrub growth, Prainha, long a summer colony, dates from an earlier era and is more appealing to the eye with its groves of coconut palms, old stucco buildings, and vintage cottages. The old capital of Aquiraz is unusual on the northeastern coast, where most of the early cities were built upstream along riverbanks as protection against coastal pirates. The town is agreeably sleepy, with several small squares, old churches, and narrow back streets.

Where to Stay

PRAINHA SOLAR HOTEL, Rua Central, Prainha. Tel. 085/361-1000, ext. 156, or 085/239-1254 in Fortaleza for reservations. 15 rms. MINIBAR TV
$ Rates: $12–$15 single or double. No credit cards.

For lodgings at Prainha, a hundred yards from the beach is an ideal weekend hideaway, the Prainha Solar Hotel, opposite the area's center of lacemaking. Most of the rooms here are beach-house informal, but there are a couple of larger rooms on the second floor of a separate building overlooking the swimming pool that have balconies with hammocks, louvered doors and windows, and old-fashioned ceiling fans. With the doors and shutters open, the rooms are well ventilated with the most refreshing sea breezes.

THE NORTHERN BEACHES

Quite close to the city is the **Praia do Cambuco,** a 30-minute ride north of Fortaleza. For a token fee, you sit under an umbrella on chairs provided by the local beachside restaurant while a waiter brings your chilled beer in a Styrofoam container, and vendors circulate selling such delicacies as home-roasted cashew nuts. The swimming here is good, and other activities include a variety of excursions by buggy, horseback, or *jangada,* all of which may be rented on the beach. For a more formal meal, there is the **Restaurante Sal e Sol,** right on the beach.

JERICOACOARA

The new "in" side trip for the more adventuresome tourists is a stay—overnight or longer—at Jericoacoara. The state tourist bureau organizes overnight trips to this remote beach in four-wheel-drive minibuses, which cover the distance from Fortaleza in about seven hours. The itinerary includes "sand skiing" on the dunes, watching the sunset, then a moonlight walk and an evening of forró. The tour leaves the city at 7am on Saturday and returns Sunday night. For information, call 224-7660 during weekday business hours and 239-3407 on the weekend.

CHAPTER 14

THE AMAZON & THE PANTANAL

Before traveling to the Amazon, ask yourself: "Why am I going there?" and "What do I expect to see and do?" To be frank, many people will get more out of "exploring" the Amazon from the comfort of their own armchairs, perusing the vast body of literature that has been written about the region, than they will out of actually going there. The very idea of the Amazon conjures up fantasies of adventure in the remote and unspoiled rain forest, and a vision of Native American cultures clinging precariously to pre-Columbian, if not prehistoric, ways of life. The casual tourist to the Amazon region gets to experience little of this reality—a reality, moreover, at least where the Native Americans are concerned, that is rapidly vanishing.

To be sure, there are still vast unexplored areas in the rain forest and among the seemingly infinite number of tributaries that empty into the basin's major rivers. But these are accessible only to those with the time, money, desire, and skills necessary for such expeditions far from the lifelines of civilization. Few people, even the seemingly fit, are suited to the real adventures the Amazon still has to offer. Indeed, the greatest expeditionaries in the Amazon region through the years were studious naturalists, not men or women cut in the Rough Rider mold, although, come to think of it, TR himself did once hazard an exploration there, and the Brazilians named a previously undiscovered river after him for his efforts.

What, then, can the casual tourist hope to get out of a visit to the Amazon? Most visitors opt for a stay in one of the region's major cities, like **Manaus** or **Belém,** and fan out from there, under careful supervision, availing themselves of a range of boat trips and overnights into the nearby second-growth forest. Few of these tours involve roughing it, and some house their guests in first-class accommodations, built on floating platforms or in clearings near the riverbank. As for wildlife, you don't see much under these circumstances, though the existence of so many bird and animal species in the rain forest ensures you of seeing something. In my own neck of the woods, a Cub Scout once asked a woodsman/historian why the men on Benedict Arnold's expedition to Québec had to eat tallow candles for four days after their food supplies ran out, when they had guns to hunt with. The answer was that when you have so many people traipsing through the woods, making so much noise, you're not likely to see any critters in that area for weeks to come. The same answer applies to those who go on organized tours in the Amazon with great expectations of seeing the wildlife there.

Ruling out true adventure and intimate familiarization with the virgin forest—other than under the most controlled, even pampered conditions, except in rare cases—most tourists go to the Amazon to experience the cities for their unique river-town moodiness, and their settings, with the "jungle" as a mysterious, and

WHAT'S SPECIAL ABOUT THE AMAZON & THE PANTANAL

River Travel
- ☐ Hop a boat in Belém and spend four or five days pulling up stream to Manaus, with stopovers in other large river towns like Santarém.

River Lodges and Ecology Treks
- ☐ Numerous "jungle" lodges several hours by riverboat from Manaus, with comfort levels varying from the first-class Amazon Lodge to the more rustic Ariau Tower.
- ☐ Many outfitters and tour operators breaking new ground in the area of ecotourism.

Historic Attractions
- ☐ The turn-of-the-century architecture of Belém, evidence of the decline and fall of the rubber boom.

- ☐ Santarém, a city settled in part by former soldiers of the Confederate Army after the Civil War.
- ☐ A planned village near Santarém, Belterra, and a failed plantation, Fordlandia, built by Henry Ford in an attempt to revive the Brazilian rubber industry.

Wildlife
- ☐ Exotic birds and animals, even more abundant in the Pantanal than in the Amazon. One of Brazil's best resorts, the Pousada Caiman, offers both elegance in accommodations and dining, and a highly professional staff of scientists to guide your explorations.

---

the most part impenetrable, background. Even at that, even while staying at the best luxury hotels, all but the most intrepid travelers are likely to undergo some discomfort resulting from the climate, the bugs, the funky—albeit undeniably tasty—food, and the general informality of the tourist apparatus. Sound discouraging? It need not be so. To be forewarned is to be forearmed. There is still ample justification for a visit, assuming your trip is well planned, and you know what to expect.

The city of **Belém** is a delightful relic, with possibilities for several unique side trips. Upriver from Belém, about midway to Manaus, is the city of **Santarém**, settled in part by expatriate Confederates after the U.S. Civil War, and today an increasingly popular stopover for tourists who branch out beyond the more heavily visited of the Amazon's destinations. The most popular spot in the Amazon for Brazilians and foreigners alike remains **Manaus**, that astounding phenomenon, a semimodern metropolis on the margins of the rain forest and virtually disconnected from the rest of Brazil. Even today, the only reliable way to get to Manaus is by plane or boat, because trans-Amazonian roads are not only primitive—they are, at best, seasonal. Finally, there is **Rio Branco**, capital of Acre, a remote frontier state that is more than civilized enough to justify a visit, especially for the most adventuresome.

AMAZÔNIA ORIENTATION

Amazônia should not be confused with Amazonas, Brazil's largest state, of which Manaus is the capital. Amazônia is a vast basin of forests and wetlands occupying roughly half of the South American continent, embracing not only a substantial chunk of Brazil—estimates ranging as high as 57%—but also parts of the Guyanas, Suriname, Venezuela, Colombia, Bolivia, Ecuador, and Peru. Within Brazil itself, Amazônia embodies all of Amazonas, the remote states and territories of Acre, Rondônia, Roraima, and Amapá, and parts of Pará and Maranhão as well. Amazon is also the name given to the system of rivers and tributaries that stretches some 4,000 nautical miles from its several outlets on the Atlantic Ocean to its source, Lago Lauricocha, at an altitude approaching 13,000 feet in the Peruvian Andes, but only 90 miles from the Pacific coastline. Until it crosses into Brazilian territory, the river's principal trunk is called the Marañón, and thereafter the Solimões, itself fed by major and minor tributaries until joining the Rio Negro several miles upstream of Manaus at the famous Encontro das Aguas (Meeting of the Waters). The Solimões is a "live" river, full of silt and microorganisms that give the river its "whitish" color. The Rio Negro is a "dead" river, much less hospitable to water life, and is dark and clearer. When the two meet, they run parallel for several miles until the competing tones blend and form the pale-brownish Amazon, as it is called from here until it empties into the Atlantic.

From below Manaus until Santarém to the east, the river is so wide in places that from midstream neither bank can be seen. At the "narrows" near Santarém, the Amazon tapers and reaches its deepest point, 225 feet during the high-water season. The Amazon system, from source to mouth, is the longest river in the world, just barely outdistancing the Nile, and the largest river basin on earth by a substantial margin, containing 20% of the planet's fresh water. The forest is also believed to possess fully 10% of all the world's species of life-forms, including countless invertebrates, 2,500 fish and 50,000 plant species. And even more remarkable is the theory that as many as 85% of these species have yet to be identified and documented.

Among the European explorers, it was possibly Columbus himself, on his third voyage in 1498, who first set foot on the shores of South America and who noted in his journal that the presence of fresh water far into the Caribbean was evidence of a great river (the Orinoco in Venezuela), and "a very great continent, until today unknown." First of the Europeans actually to enter the Amazon from the Atlantic end was the great Genoan navigator's former subaltern, Vicente Pinzón, captain of the *Nina* on the 1492 voyage. Pinzón, returning with a fleet of his own in 1500, penetrated some 50 miles up one of the mouths of the Amazon. It was not until over 40 years later, however, that a European was finally to sail the length of the river. In 1541 an expedition left Quito, commanded by Francisco Pizarro's brother, Gonzalo, in search of precious spices. A year later, his forces decimated by battles with both the Native Americans and the elements, the younger Pizarro gave his lieutenant general, Francisco de Orellana, permission to take a party of men by ship and forage downstream for food to relieve the expedition. Orellana, who disregarded his orders, continued all the way to the Atlantic and returned to Spain. The account of this journey was recorded by his scrivener, Friar Gaspar de Carvajal, who chronicled, among many other hair-raising adventures, a battle with female warriors (or Amazons), a hallucination brought on by the heat, no doubt—at least scholars give little credence to the tale. But the name stuck.

IS THE AMAZON DISAPPEARING?

A great deal of controversy surrounds the development occurring throughout the Brazilian Amazon, and the impact of these activities on the region's ecology. At the core of the conflict may ultimately rest those two endlessly irreconcilable world views: the romantic and the pragmatic. To some—whether or not they actually wish to visit the region—the continued existence of the Amazon represents an almost transcendental vision. One instinctively rebels against the disappearance of the earth's remaining unsettled forests. To others, the Amazon represents the future, at best a solution to the problem of scarce land, but also a fulfillment of aspirations of national greatness, or merely the restless quest for the grail of instant riches—gold, oil, diamonds, whatever the land will yield.

Nature seems to have its own point of view, perhaps the most compelling. As the forest is cut—to make room for towns, mines, sprawling cattle spreads, factory farms, and the civil construction of dams and roads—the fertility of land seems to diminish very rapidly. You would think that land capable of sustaining the dense and varied growth of the Amazon forest would be capable of producing good hay for grazing or some kind of cash crop. This seldom appears to be the case. The topsoil of the forest floor is thin, easily eroded, and strangest of all, considering the plethora of decaying organic matter, low in nutrients. When land is cleared, often with the highest of motives—to give land to settlers and to produce food for the national belly—it often refuses new plantings and turns to dust. Perhaps nature is trying to tell us something. Or, as some would undoubtedly respond, we just haven't found the right technological key to maintain the growing cycle.

Of even greater concern globally than the impact of the rain forest's shrinkage on Brazil's internal affairs, are two significant issues, of which only the first has truly entered the public dialogue. Suddenly the term "greenhouse effect" is on everyone's lips. The theory is that the Amazon forest produces gases that block some portion of the sun's heat. A projected warming trend for the world's climate in the immediate future will result, the theory holds, from Amazon deforestation and the depletion of these protective gases. The other issue that has put the Amazon in the news with some frequency in recent times, is the plight of Brazil's remaining Native Americans, victims of the country's latest gold rush, which has reportedly spilled onto large tracts of tribal lands, and decimated much of the native population.

The controversy rages on, but on one point there is some modicum of consensus. Not a great deal of the Amazon Valley has thus far been developed or destroyed. The real issue here seems to be exactly how fast the forest is disappearing, not how much still remains. And about this there are endless debates. An excellent account of the state of the Amazon is a paperback book by Roger D. Stone, *Dreams of Amazônia* (Penguin, 1986). (For a list of additional recommended books on the Amazon, see Chapter 1.)

SPECIALTY TOURS

Within the general sphere of **ecological tourism,** things are looking up. In the marketplace—the travel market being no exception—"recognition" is everything. Owing to the factors described above, the United States, beginning in 1989, has witnessed a vast increase in media coverage on developments in the Amazon region. The words "rain forest" have probably been heard on newscasts or read in newspapers to an unprecedented degree during this period by the average American. Topical issues, however, come and go. Whether the Amazon's sudden fame is merely faddish in the popular mind or reflects a deeper ecological awakening remains to be seen. In the meantime, tour operators have responded quite imaginatively overall to the new tide of visitors this windfall of publicity has drawn to the region. Most people, including a small percentage of true naturalists as well as many among the ecologically informed, demand standards of hygiene and comfort not terribly remote from those they are accustomed to in their own habitats. They also demand authenticity and are willing to pay for it. Tour operators in response have designed their itineraries accordingly. One or two tours that have come to my attention are beginning to approach the line that separates spontaneous travel from programmed touring. The programmed tours, however, are appropriate for most visitors and have themselves been impressively upgraded to appeal to intelligent, nature-conscious individuals. From what I gather, the satisfaction rate seems to be running high. Many of these rain-forest excursions are described in this chapter, while a more detailed listing of the best facilitators operating in these specialty markets can be found in Chapter 2.

---

1. BELÉM

1,272 miles N of Brasília; 484 miles NW of São Luis; 2,070 miles NW of Rio

GETTING THERE   By Plane   There are only five Brazilian cities that may be reached on nonstop flights from the United States: Rio de Janeiro, São Paulo, Recife, Manaus, and Belém. The VARIG Belém-bound flight leaves from Miami on Sunday evenings and arrives in Belém six hours later, nonstop. As long as this flight continues in service, Belém can be considered a Brazilian destination in and of itself, three hours closer in flying time than Miami to Rio.

By Bus   Belém's bus station, the **Terminal Rodoviário,** is on the Praça do Operário in the São Bras neighborhood (tel. 228-0500). Buses regularly connect Belém with most major Brazilian cities to the south, but travelers should be forewarned that roads between Belém and other destinations are often washed out by periodic floods. Under the best of circumstances, bus travel takes 56 hours from São Paulo, 24 hours from Fortaleza, 36 hours from Brasília, and 12 hours from São Luís. Other major Amazonian centers (Manaus, Santarém, Porto Velho, and Rio Branco) can only be reached by air or water.

By Car The Belém-Brasília highway cuts through the rain forest in the remote central portion of Brazil, and connects these two terminal points. In theory, trucks and buses can make this run. In practice, the road is often unpassable due to rain damage or simply a general lack of maintenance. One hears stories of buses, en route to points within the Amazon region, sometimes delayed for days, if not weeks, while repairs are being made to bridges or the road's surface. One glance at the map will reveal that Pará is an enormous and sparsely settled state. Car travel to and from Belém, except for local excursions, is therefore not recommended.

ESSENTIALS The state tourist bureau, **Paratur,** maintains a tourist information center on Praça Kennedy (tel. 091/224-9633), providing visitors with maps, brochures, and timetables for river trips, both short and long. It's open Monday to Friday from 8am to 6pm. For guided help in getting around the city, contact **AGTURB** (Associação de Guias de Turismo de Belém), Av. Braz de Aguiar 612 (in the Equatorial Plaza Hotel), open Monday to Friday from 8am to noon, and 2 to 6pm; 8am to noon on Saturday. Or call the association's president, Nilma, at home (tel. 229-1850). I found one of the members of this group, guide Afonso Oliveira, to be very reliable. He can be contacted directly at 235-0718.

SPECIAL EVENTS **Círio** is Belém's most important festival. It takes place the second Sunday of October every year, and attracts as many as a million visitors to the city. The festival is both sacred and secular. The religious component involves a procession, accompanying a statue of Belém's patron saint, Our Lady of Nazaré, from the cathedral to the basilica. To local residents Círio is also a kind of Thanksgiving, a family day of feasting on traditional foods. The festivities go on for two weeks, until at the end of October the image of the saint is returned to her permanent niche.

Belém is really a splendid little city. Located barely 80 miles upriver from the Atlantic, Belém was never far removed from major ocean shipping lanes. Since its founding in 1616, Belém has prospered steadily in its role as depot for the natural wealth extracted ever since from Amazônia and distributed from its docksides to the markets of the world. When you talk of nature's plenty, the Amazon forest and its rivers are unsurpassed for providing great stores of fish, fruits, berries, nuts, wood, and innumerable derivatives, not the least of which are some remarkable handcrafts. The city was christened Saint Mary of Bethlehem of Grand Pará, because on the day the site was first consecrated by the formal act of its founder, Francisco Caldeira Castelo Branco, the church liturgical calendar indicated the feast of Santa Maria de Belém (Belém is the Portuguese for Bethlehem, the town of Christ's birth).

Belém was built on the shores of the Guajará estuary, which empties into the Rio Pará, the southernmost arm of the mighty Amazon from which it is separated by the country-sized delta island of Marajó. The Amazon's main branch is reached by boat, along a serpentine water route that never flows far from the edge of the forest. Much closer to Belém than the River Amazon is the Rio Tocantins, another of Brazil's giant internal waterways, springing from Goiás and joining with the Rio Pará in the immense Bay of Marajó that opens to the sea. **Pará** is also the name of the state of which Belém is the capital, a territorial landmass larger than most European countries, including France, Italy, and the British Isles. Most typically one hears the city referred to in its long form as Belém do Pará, as if to emphasize the distinction between this secular Bethlehem and its namesake in the Holy Land.

Architecturally, Belém is one of the most delightful and diverse of all Brazilian cities with colonial roots. In Belém, moreover, which has a perfectly wonderful historic quarter, it's not just what remains of the colonial period that catches the eye. Belém's days of splendor were actually much later, dating from Victorian times and running through the turn of the century. These years covered the Brazilian rubber boom, an economic miracle of relatively short duration that rested on an arbitrary fact of nature. The latex-producing trees called *hevea brasiliensis* existed in great numbers only in the Amazon forest. Owing to the forest's peculiar ecological ground rules, rubber trees do not grow there in clusters, but individually, often hundreds of feet from one another. Thousands of gatherers, each of whom tended massive plots, were required to tap the widely scattered trees. Despite a tremendous security effort to retain the country's rubber monopoly, seedlings were soon smuggled out of Brazil and domesticated in the far more efficient plantations of the British East Asian colonies.

But the short-lived rubber wealth transformed the cities of the Amazon, particularly Belém. From a prosperous backwater, Belém evolved into the genuine urban belle of the Amazon river towns. The stately *mangueiras* (mango trees) that line the avenues and plazas were planted then, their bushy forms and wide leaves providing excellent shade in a city where the average yearly temperature is 80°F. Public buildings and private houses followed the rapidly changing fashions of those days, from neoclassical to art nouveau to fin de siècle, with a fair dose of glass and cast-iron construction for bandstands, park gazebos, and markets. There are also many palazzos in the Italianate style remaining in Belém as testimony to the tastes and fortunes of the city's old rubber barons. Added to the buildings of the rubber-boom era are the many examples of what Brazilians call "pure Portuguese" architecture—colonial houses and commercial buildings with their characteristic billowy windows and portals, iron railings, and tile facades. And the ubiquitous baroque of the sacred structures, with unique equatorial signatures, is by no means lacking. Each shaded street in the center of Belém and each stark, sunny alley in the historic quarter along the waterfront is a visual treat for the professional stroller and amateur building buff.

The crown jewel of structures in Belém is the Teatro da Paz, a world-class monument to the human arts. The markets of Belém, like the nonstop Ver-O-Peso on the waterfront, are also in a class by themselves. In contrast to the urban scene is the life of the river and the people who live on its margins and depend on it for their livelihood. Many varieties of boat excursions are available for getting as close to the river culture as you may wish. And once you have exhausted the attractions of Belém and its environs, there are still the horizons of Marajó and Macapá to explore.

WHAT TO SEE & DO

A traveler's itinerary in Belém might justifiably consist of several days for getting to know the city, and several days to explore the environs, like the island of Marajó or Macapá, capital of Amapá, a city slightly to the north and west of Belém that straddles the equator.

A walking tour of Belém can begin at the **Praça da República** with a visit to the **Teatro da Paz.** Construction on this unabashedly classical temple was begun in 1869, and follows the Empire style then in fashion, inspired by a romantic rediscovery in the West of the ruins of Greek and Roman antiquity. The building houses several richly detailed spaces—rehearsal halls, foyers, a terrace, and salon for the entr'acte—but the theater itself outsparkles the undeniable loveliness of these other components. The auditorium is horseshoe-shaped, with three levels of boxes, a pit, a balcony, and high above, a gallery called Paradise. The decor is original in most details, notably the woven-straw armchairs and a spectacular floral wallpaper that from afar seems remarkably abstract. On a wall near the entrance are commemorative plaques memorializing great artists who have performed here. In 1918 the local press club so honored the presence of the Russian prima ballerina Anna Pavlova.

Since my last visit to Belém, the theater has opened a street-level gallery with its own entrance, available to the public for exhibitions of a wide variety, including a recent one a Cuban-Brazilian Friendship group had mounted on the life of Ernesto "Ché" Guevara.

Of further interest in the Praça da República itself are the **Bar do Parque,** an outdoor café on a raised platform, and the miniature "crystal palace," the **gazebo** built of cast iron and glass.

Going from the Praça da República toward the bay, descend along **Rua do Santo Antônio** toward the waterfront. Note the striking example of the art nouveau building named "F. de Castro," the one with the trendy América boutique. Continue on to the **Praça Mercês,** with its church; although much altered from the original, it still has its rude flooring of terra-cotta tiles. There are several buildings on the square in the "pure Portuguese" style, their facades sheathed in tiles. A block or two from the square is the wide boulevard along the pier, **Avenida Castilhos França,** and the vast stone apron where the public markets, including the permanent stalls of the Ver-O-Peso, are located.

The **Ver-O-Peso market** is a warren of stands, many of which remain open 24 hours a day, selling fruits and vegetables, snack foods, and many strange objects that have been salvaged from the creatures of the river or forest, or that have been prepared by human hands to dispel ill fortune or disease in all the many forms they can assault us. The market's name literally means "see the weight," but a more accurate translation might be "watch the scale," a local reference no doubt to the universal consumer complaint of the greengrocers' heavy thumbs. Endless streams of porters carry produce from the boats at dockside, which come and go all day and night, to their appropriate stalls and vendors.

Among the sights are the fetish potions used in the rites of the Afro-Umbanda religion, hundreds of vials for giving or repelling the evil eye, to induce virility, or for seduction. One little bottle had a printed label which in translation reads: "Strong potion to seduce your secret love and dominate her affections." On some stalls scores of little bags of powder are suspended by strings, each one a herbal remedy for whatever ails you, the traditional medicines being at least affordable to most of Belém's denizens, unlike modern pharmaceuticals, which are only for the affluent. There are withered roots and leaves for purposes not indicated by signs or labels, dried starfish and sea horses, deer's hooves and alligators' teeth, cocks' tails and the hard tongues and scales of the *pirarucu* fish, used as emery boards.

Emerging from this spectacle of strange smells and sights, you come to the great old market itself, a cast-iron marvel, painted marine gray and imported piece by piece from England, including the stately steeples that adorn each of its four corners. Inside is the fish fair. Here you will see the biggest, smelliest, ugliest fish in existence, all culled from the rivers of this land. Note the *mero,* a finny creature the size of a St. Bernard, with a huge round head to match.

Here and there on the dockside you might see green bundles of some rolled material, a yard or so in length, and tied like fasces, those symbols of a Roman magistrate's authority. These are giant leaves called *guarumã*—simply the "wrapping paper" people buy to carry their fish in.

From the Ver-O-Peso, we now enter the **Cidade Velha,** the older part of the city, stretching away from downtown and generally accompanying the shoreline of the bay. Immediately off the waterfront is the **Praça Frei Caetano Brandão,** also called the Largo da Sé because of the **Catedral,** an 18th-century church but completely restyled in the past century. It is from here that the procession for Círio begins during Belém's most important celebration. On the same square is the **Igreja do Santo Alexandre,** commissioned in the early 1800s by Jesuits, and built by unskilled Native American laborers, resulting in a primitive baroque effect most notable in the crude decorative touches, like the childlike carved flowers on the facade.

Leave the square along the **Travessa da Veiga,** a narrow lane left undisturbed since the colonial days. The street contains many period houses with smooth facades and balconies with iron grillwork. At the other end you come out onto Rua Siqueira Mendes and another square, the **Praça do Carmo,** which seems like a study of so many village squares found in any given town of the Brazilian interior. The layout of the garden is formal but modest, with stone-demarcated paths bordering sparse patches of grass and a few plants. What gives the square its stature and ancient quality, however, are the century-old mango trees that envelop the space in a blanket of shade.

At the far end of the praça is the **Igreja do Carmo,** a mixture of baroque and neoclassical design. From the church floor to the beginning of the great vault, the details like the main and side altars are all heavily carved in busy, intricate baroque. The vault and its paintings are of a latter period. One unsatisfactory explanation has it that the difference reflects the long delay and passage of time between the laying of the cornerstone and the church's finished form. But how came it that the altars were installed before the roof was on?

The old city covers a wide area, and has by far the highest concentration of colonial homes, buildings, and churches in all Belém. Yet practically whatever street you turn onto as you wander through this city seems to offer some vision of the past, one that is nonetheless generally well integrated into the present. Perhaps the presence of so many tree-lined streets provides a common denominator for the many ages that are so inexplicably—though not self-consciously—preserved in this city.

NEARBY ATTRACTIONS

There are three additional and important sights in Belém near downtown, going toward the suburbs and the airport. First is the **Basílica de Nossa Senhora da Nazaré,** Praça Justo Chermont, a church built in 1908 that sparkles with marble and stained glass, and is another of Belém's relics from the rubber boom.

MUSEU PARAENSE EMÍLIO GOELDI, Av. Magalhães Barata 376. Tel. 224-9233.

Not far from the basilica is the Museu Paraense Emílio Goeldi, a very special zoo and Native American museum. The museum has been in existence since 1866 when it was created to perform a naturalistic inventory of Amazonian resources, embracing the flora, fauna, rocks and minerals, geography, history, and indigenous cultures, and to mount exhibitions for the public. The Goeldi Museum continues to carry out the same mandate to this day. Surrounding the museum building are a zoo and an array of structures where the staff does its research. In the zoo, you will get what may be your only chance to see a manatee, the nearly extinct sea mammal of the Amazon, as well as cats, birds, monkeys, snakes, and other creatures native to the region. The museum itself contains a well-organized collection of Native American artifacts—weapons, headgear, funeral urns—photographs of contemporary tribes, and a reproduction of a typical native hut.
Admission: $1.25.
Open: Tues–Thurs and Sat 9am–noon and 2–5pm, Fri 9am–noon, Sun and holidays 8am–4:45pm.

BOSQUE RODRIGUES ALVES, Av. Almirante Barroso.

This park occupies a square block on the outskirts of the city where the original vegetation of rain forest is preserved.
Admission: Free.
Open: Tues–Sun 8am–5pm.

SHOPPING

Belém ships its high-quality pottery all over the world. Called **marajoara,** the style of the local ceramic crafts is derived from techniques and designs first produced by the Marajó tribe. An interesting morning or afternoon excursion can be made to the **Vila do Paracuri,** a suburb of Belém beyond the air force base, named for the small river that traverses it. You will need a guide or an astute cab driver to find this very rustic neighborhood with its unmarked and unpaved roads. The Paracuri River (really a stream) is the source of the mud from which scores of cottage artisans who live here make their pots. With every high tide, canoes ascend the Paracuri and dump mounds of mud along the riverbanks where the small factories are located. I entered one of the larger establishments, the **Olaria Rosemiro,** where some 30 potters and other workers are employed (*olaria* means pottery factory). The structure they occupy is wood-framed and thatch-roofed in part, and open along the sides. The workers follow a defined division of labor: Some scoop the mud from the shore and pound it into blocks, while others feed the blocks into a kind of mill to purify it and produce clay. Potters sit behind their foot-powered wheels and throw the variety of pieces—great jars, vases, bowls—that are the stock-in-trade of the house. Still others glaze the pots and fire them for the artists who by hand paint the old Native American designs on the finished surfaces.

In Belém, near the Praça da República, the state tourist bureau **Paratur,** Praça Kennedy (tel. 091/224-9633), maintains a craft shop where *marajoara* pottery may also be bought, in addition to Native American-made goods and other items in leather, straw, and wood. Paratur also maintains a tourist information center at this same location.

There's a factory making natural soaps and lotions on a Belém side street that produces cleansing and moisturizing aids, genuine natural craft products of such high quality that they are endorsed by a number of Brazil's reigning TV actresses. In addition to the **Artesanato Juruá** retail store across from the **La Em Casa Restaurant,** Av. Gov. José Malcher 390 (tel. 241-5970), there is a factory store on Rua Deodoro de Mendonça (tel. 229-7746), open weekdays and Saturday from 8:30am to 6:30pm, and closed daily during the siesta from half past noon till 2:30 in the afternoon.

WHERE TO STAY

Belém is not blessed with a surplus of good hotels, which means that any rapid increase in the city's popularity as a destination will stand to place a severe strain on the availability of acceptable lodgings. If you wish to visit the city during its major festival, Círio, in mid-October, make your reservations far in advance.

EXPENSIVE

EQUATORIAL PALACE HOTEL, Av. Braz de Aguiar 612, Belém. Tel. 091/241-2000. Fax 091/223-5222. Telex 91/1605. 211 rms. A/C MINIBAR TV TEL

$ Rates: $95–$100 standard single or double; $110–$120 deluxe single or double. AE, DC, MC, V.

⭐ The Equatorial Palace fronts a residential and chic commercial street shaded by mango trees and made agreeably quiet by the one-way traffic. This is an elegant hotel, and much more personal than the Hilton, but with far fewer facilities. What the hotel can boast, however, is a fine dining room, as reputable as any in the city, and beautifully appointed with its polished plank floor and cedar-boarded ceiling. On the hotel's roof is a very intimate pool and patio area similar to something you might find in the backyard of a well-off friend. While the Hilton may have the "ideal" room from the standpoint of maximum travel comfort, the accommodations at the Equatorial Palace are warmer and more homey.

HILTON, Av. Presidente Vargas 882, Belém. Tel. 091/223-6500. Fax 091/226-8761. Telex 91/2024. 361 rms. A/C MINIBAR TV TEL

$ Rates: $165–$185 single; $185–$205 double. AE, DC, MC, V.

⭐ By far the best hotel in Belém is the Hilton, which occupies a 19-story tower off Belém's principal square, the Praça da República, where the elegant old theater stands in its proud shell of white marble. The standards set by Brazil's Hilton hotels in facilities, decor, and services are only rarely duplicated by a handful of its competitors, and in Belém, the Hilton has no competitor. Naturally, the Hilton's rates reflect its dominant position among the city's hotels.

In addition to the extremely comfortable rooms, the Hilton serves excellent food in several restaurants and bars, and offers the perfect environment on its outdoor veranda for observing the scene and street life around the nearby Praça da República. The rooms are spacious and outfitted with large double beds, a generous seating area, and a TV that receives a U.S. satellite channel.

MODERATE

HOTEL EXCELSIOR GRÃO PARÁ, Praça da República 718, Belém. Tel. 091/222-3255. Fax 091/224-9744. Telex 91/1171. 136 rms. A/C MINIBAR TV TEL

$ Rates: $64–$72 rear room; $72–$80 front room. AE, DC, MC, V.

This was once the best hotel in Belém, and is still reliable as well as moderately priced. The small, utilitarian lobby reveals how tastes in the design of first-class hotels have changed with the years. Instead of the posh lobby boutiques of the newer establishments, a lone sales clerk sits behind a table attending to the sale of jewels and stones.

The Excelsior's rooms are a mixed bag. The rooms in the rear of the hotel are musty and dark, while those that face the square are superb. Front rooms have double doors of frosted glass that open onto, not a balcony, but a wrought-iron railing. The baths are large and comfortably old-fashioned, also with double windows which open to allow wide views as well as good circulation of air.

HOTEL ITAOCA, Av. Pres. Vargas 132, Belém. Tel. 091/241-3434. Fax 091/241-0891. Telex 91/0801. 36 rms.A/C MINIBAR TV TEL
$ Rates: $38–$42 single; $44–$50 double. AE, DC, MC, V.

The Itaoca combines the facade of a historic building with the interior of a small, well-run continental hotel. This is one of Belém's newest hotels, and the location, near the Praça da República, is ideal. Rooms here are as comfortable as those in the larger deluxe hotels. Among the facilities in the five-story structure is a small rooftop restaurant.

HOTEL SAGRES, Av. Gov. José Malcher 2927, Belém. Tel. 091/228-3999. Fax 091/226-8260. Telex 91/1662. 243 rms. A/C MINIBAR TV TEL
$ Rates: $50 single; $57 double. AE, DC, MC, V.

The interior of the Sagres looks something like a cruise ship. The rooms are not cabin-size, though, but large and very shipshape in appearance with clean wood-trimmed lines and gallery-white walls. The rooftop pool, where the nautical theme is even more pronounced, offers the best panoramic view of Belém.

NOVOTEL, Av. Bernardo Sayão 4804, Belém. Tel. 091/229-8011. Fax 091/229-8709. Telex 91/1241. 111 rms. A/C MINIBAR TV TEL **Transportation:** Hotel provides transfers from the airport.
$ Rates: $49 single; $54 double. AE, DC, MC, V.

Six miles from the center of town is the Novotel, which often caters to groups of visitors whose stay in Belém a week or more, and offers special package rates to these guests. The Novotel also provides transportation to and from the airport, an incentive owing perhaps to the hotel's location on the city outskirts.

Its location, right at the edge of the river, is also the hotel's most arresting feature. Another very agreeable facility is the courtyard with two pools and a large wooden deck that looks out on the river, where the pageant of passing boats is endless and fascinating. While rated a four-star establishment, the Novotel provides only a three-star room, either ascetic or spartan, depending on your viewpoint. Outside, at the Novotel's own pier, a launch seems to be ever in attendance, about to embark on one of the many water excursions the hotel offers its guests.

VILA RICA, Av. Julio Cesar 1777, Belém. Tel. and fax 091/233-4222. Telex 91/1585. 108 rms. A/C MINIBAR TV TEL
$ Rates (including breakfast): $50 single; $64 double. AE, DC, MC, V.

Near the airport, but also not terribly far from downtown Belém, is the Vila Rica, formerly known as the Seltom. This is a resort with sultry overtones (à la roadhouse from *The Night of the Iguana*) to retreat to after a hard day of meetings or just much running around town. The hotel offers great comfort and a laid-back ambience, but the peak attraction is the courtyard pool surrounded by tropical foliage.

BUDGET

HOTEL MILANO, Av. Pres. Vargas 640, Belém. Tel. 091/224-7045. 22 rms. A/C MINIBAR TV TEL
$ Rates: $17–$20. No credit cards.

The in-town bargain special for lodgings is probably the Hotel Milano. You can hobnob at the Hilton up the block, lounge there on the veranda bar where drink and snack prices are by no means outrageous, then retire to your minimal digs at $17 a night, rather than $185. You get what you pay for, but the rooms here are sound enough. The Milano's best rooms face either the Praça da República or Guajará Bay.

HOTEL REGENTE, Av. Gov. José Malcher 485, Belém. Tel. 091/224-0755. Fax 091/224-0343. Telex 91/1769. 188 rms. A/C MINIBAR TV TEL
$ Rates: $22–$24 rear room; $30–$35 front room. AE, DC, MC, V.

Away from the waterfront, going toward the Church of Nazaré, is the Hotel Regente. This very moderately priced hotel has large rooms, with glass-fronted walls and modern baths. The beds, however, are on the small side. The hotel has an excellent backyard pool, behind a very private high wall, and an appealing mezzanine bar.

TRANSAMAZÓNICO, Trav. da Indústria 17, Belém. Tel. 091/222-5232.
$ Rates: $2.30 single; $2.85 double. No credit cards.

Want to play George Orwell among the down-and-outers for a night? Or pretend you've been absorbed into a novel by Graham Greene, transformed for a few days into a seedy colonial who's lost his soul in the tropics? Suitable to either fantasy is the Transamazónico, a hotel that caters in real life to the near impoverished journeyman, the drifter, and the marginal commercial traveler. Seedy, threadbare . . . but clean as a whistle. Stark, well-lighted, and spartan rooms, but then again well sheltered and not without their ascetic, monkish overtones. This is the final rung on the ladder of respectability, with the street as the next stop. Let me reassure the wary that, for my own part, I sensed nothing threatening about being in this neighborhood. Clearly, this excursion is not for everyone.

WHERE TO DINE

Belém's cuisine is genuinely aboriginal, directly traceable to the long-standing diet of the continent's pre-Columbian inhabitants, just as Bahian food is known to derive from various African cultures. In both cases, of course, other influences have contributed to the evolution of the dishes served today. But the use of certain basic ingredients, like **tucupi** (fermented juice form the manioc root), **maniva** (the leaf of the manioc plant), and **jambú** (a green similar to Italian broccoli)—as is the case with *dendê* in Bahia—ensures that the respective cuisines retain much of their original character.

Snack foods and more informal meals are available throughout the city, but particularly at the tent-covered popular restaurants found throughout the stalls of the public markets. One favorite street food is *tacaca*, a very strong-flavored porridge laced with shrimp and *tucupi*. Ice cream made with unique Amazon fruits is also widely available in Belém. New fruits to look for at the market and taste are *açaí, popunha, murící, sapotí, buçuri, mangaba, taperebã, cupuaçu,* and *uxí.*

In addition to the recommendations below, the **O Teatro** restaurant at the Hilton is expensive, but recommended for its innovative dishes, like lobster and caviar topped with hollandaise sauce. The churrascaria at the Equatorial Palace Hotel is less expensive but equally recommended. **Augustu's,** Av. Almirante Barroso 439 (tel. 226-8317), is a popular restaurant near the Hotel Sagres.

LA EM CASA, Av. Gov. José Malcher 247. Tel. 225-0320.
    Cuisine: INTERNATIONAL/REGIONAL. **Reservations:** Recommended for dinner on weekends.
$ Prices: Appetizers $3.25–$8.25; main courses $6.50–$13. AE, DC, MC, V.
    Open: Lunch daily 11:30am–3pm; dinner daily 6:30pm–midnight.

La Em Casa is to Belém what the Casa da Gamboa is to Salvador. When you experiment with food as novel to the palate as the aboriginal food of Amazônia, it's best to find a restaurant that takes particular care in its choice of ingredients and with their final preparation. Some of the specialties served at La Em Casa are *pato no tucupi* (slices of roast duck stewed in *tucupi* sauce, with *jambú* leaves), *manicoba* (often referred to as the feijoada of the Amazon), a stew of minced *maniva* leaves with jerked beef, smoked pork, tongue, sausage, calves' and pigs' feet, tripe, and pigs' ear and tail, served with *feijão da colônia* (small white beans), and *pirarucu* (a gigantic river fish, salted like cod, and served in a variety of presentations). La Em Casa occupies an open-air veranda of a private house belonging to Dona Ana Maria Martins, a local society figure who opened the restaurant, and who personally supervises the kitchen.

A second restaurant at the same site is the enclosed and air-conditioned **O Outro,** where fine cooking in the international mold is the specialty.

MIRALHA, Av. Doca de Souza Franco 194. Tel. 241-4832.
    Cuisine: JAPANESE. **Reservations:** Not needed.

$ Prices: Main courses $4–$9.25. No credit cards.
Open: Dinner daily 7pm–1am.

For informal surroundings and eats, join the nightly scene at the Miralha. Down by the docks, and as colorful and festive as a night at a Montmartre beer garden à la Renoir, there are precisely three distinct scenes taking place here, often simultaneously. There are the diners, people who come for the home-style Japanese food; there's the café crowd drinking and chatting; and there's the music and dance crowd for when the band starts playing after 9pm most nights. The Miralha, in true beer-garden style, is spacious, half open-air, half covered under canvas or tin roofing, and crowded every night. MPB—*Música Popular Brasileira*—provides the musical currency, and the food is plentiful, tasty, and cheap. Two dishes we tried were the *haposai,* shrimp, chicken, and octopus in Asian veggies ($4), and the *yakisoba,* shrimp and chicken with noodles ($4).

O CÍRCULO MILITAR, Praça Frei Caetano Brandão. Tel. 223-4374.

Cuisine: SEAFOOD/INTERNATIONAL. **Reservations:** Recommended.
$ Prices: Appetizers $1.25–$9.50; main courses $7–$10.25. AE, DC, MC, V.
Open: Lunch daily 11:30am–2:30pm; dinner daily 7–10:30pm.

Attached to the Forte do Castelo is the restaurant O Círculo Militar, a former officer's club, but long open to the public. The old fort sits on the waterfront in the oldest section of Belém. In the restaurant, try to occupy a table by the window. Even at night, when visibility is necessarily curtailed, the sounds of life from the river continue. The constant putter-sputter signals the one-stroke engines of the flat-bottomed riverboats, spiritual kin to the *African Queen,* that glide by in endless procession, illuminated only by the night sky and their running lights.

River fish and forest game are the mainstay of the Círculo's menu, which extends to many varieties of standard Brazilian dishes as well, like filet mignon or roast chicken. One delicacy is the *casquinho de buçua,* a blend of farofa and tortoise meat. I must point out that many game meats—like tortoise and manatee—are illegally hunted throughout the Amazon, to the degree that the existence of these species is gravely endangered. Nonetheless, the habit of eating tortoise is deeply rooted in the region, and manatee, the large Amazon sea mammal, is a staple among the river dwellers in the bush. One result of this habit and demand is that these foods are still served by even respectable restaurants in Belém, although often requested discreetly and referred to euphemistically.

ROXY EXPRESS, Av. Senador Lemos 231, in Umarizal. Tel. 224-4514.

Cuisine: CONTINENTAL. **Reservations:** Not needed.
$ Prices: Appetizers $3.25–$6; main courses $5.50–$12. No credit cards.
Open: Dinner daily 7pm–midnight.

The Roxy is a new-wave video bar whose menu sports a nostalgic photo of Marilyn Monroe, and offers many steak and seafood platters with the names of movie stars: Grilled Filet of Fish Jane Fonda, Shrimp Francis Coppola, and Filet Fred Astaire. Despite this silly celebrity worship, the Roxy is attractive and said to have a good kitchen.

STEAK HOUSE HAKATA, Rua Dr. Moraes 314, in Nazaré. Tel. 224-8308.

Cuisine: JAPANESE. **Reservations:** Not needed.
$ Prices: Main courses $4–$10. No credit cards.
Open: Lunch Tues–Sun 11:30am–2:30pm; dinner Tues–Sun 6–11pm.

Occupying the old quarters of the Dutch restaurant, O Minho Holandês, is this very simple Japanese steakhouse. Actually, "steakhouse" is something of a misnomer. Most of the platters are served on the *chapa,* the metal griddle on which they are cooked. Expecting to find the Dutch restaurant on a recent visit, I ate here instead, and was the only non-Asian in the house. The camarão na chapa consisted of six luscious shrimp with a selection of Asian-style veggies ($8), which went well with a serving of warm saké ($3).

STEAK HOUSE OKADA, Rua Boaventura da Silva 1522. Tel. 241-4417.

Cuisine: JAPANESE. **Reservations:** Not needed.

$ Prices: Appetizers $1–$6; main courses $4–$15. No credit cards.

Open: Lunch daily noon–2:30pm; dinner daily 7pm–midnight.

If you're in the mood for classic Japanese dishes, you might try the Steak House Okada, between Alcindo Cacela and 9 de Janeiro. The most expensive dish on the menu was the sushi special.

EVENING ENTERTAINMENT

Popular dances from Brazil's deeply traditional rural outback have become the rage throughout Brazil and internationally as well. The *lambada* from the badlands of the northeast was all the rage in Paris and New York a few years back. Northern Brazil also has rich folkloric tradition, which has burst into the fashion scene of the region's urban centers. In Belém, the place to hear and dance this music is the **Sabor da Terra,** Av. Visc. de Souza Franco 685 (tel. 223-6820). There is a show at 8:30pm on Monday through Saturday nights, featuring *carimbo, xote, lundu,* and *siria,* folk dance with pop overtones. Closed Sunday. Other nightlife options in Belém include the always popular **Boite Lapinha,** Travessa Padre Eutíquio 3901 (tel. 229-3290), which features erotic shows and, of course, the **Miralha,** described above. A 10-minute cab ride from the Praça da República will bring you to **Maracaibo,** Av. Alcindo Cacela 1239 (tel. 222-4797), a big loft with a balcony, where there is live music Wednesday to Saturday from 9:30pm to 3 or 4am.

EASY EXCURSIONS

RIVER TOURS

River excursions from the port of Belém fall into two categories: local sightseeing tours and river journeys to other destinations. A number of companies offer day-trips in and around the harbor of Belém, often with visits up meandering *igarapés* or *igapós* (seasonally or permanently flooded creeks) for a peek at stilt houses and local village life, rubber and Brazil-nut trees, and the like. Such local excursions are organized by **CIATUR,** Av. Pres. Vargas 645 (tel. 228-0011); and **Gran-Pará Turismo,** Av. Pres. Vargas 676 (tel. 224-3233).

The standard river-tour excursion leaves from a dock on the Rio Guama at 9am (hotel pickup at 8:30am), and cruises the canals and creeks for three hours, giving you a close-up look at the river people and their lives ($15 per person, minimum three people). A nature excursion to the **Ilha dos Papagaios** leaves before dawn to arrive at this island by sunup, and see the great flocks of parrots before they disperse for the day ($15 per person, minimum three people).

Many companies operate cruises between Belém and other Amazon cities like Manaus, Macapá, and Soure in Marajó. The most comfortable ferryboats are operated by **ENASA,** a government company, with main offices at Av. Presidente Vargas 41 (tel. 223-3011), and ticket purchases directly on ENASA's pier off Avenida Castilhos França. The journey upstream to Manaus takes about six days, and only part of the time—owing to the width of the river—does the ship travel in sight of land. First-class passage may or may not be available; the company has been trying to sell its flagships to the private sector, and they have been mothballed for some time. Hammock space in the less fancy ships can be had for about $60, including meals—but you must supply the hammock. The discomfort, crowding, and poor sanitary conditions are free.

MOSQUEIROS

About an hour's drive from Belém is the island of Mosqueiros. The road surface there is for the most part quite good, and the landscape reflects the world of small landholders, subsistence farmers, and fishermen who inhabit the region. Most of the housing hasn't emerged much beyond the mud-and-wattle stage, because the cost of building materials is generally beyond the reach of even middle-class Brazilians. Yet, in other ways, history seems kind to these inhabitants. Their surroundings are lush, the forest bountiful in its own way, not always pliant, however, to the ways of humankind. The big cash crop seems to be the manioc root, the staff of life along the Amazon.

There are numerous beaches on the island of Mosqueiros, some that attract large crowds, a few sandy coves where privacy is yet possible, and a strand or two that serve as watering holes for vacationers and day-trippers. The high season here occurs from July till November, with January and February being the rainy season and the months of least activity at the beaches. A good place for lunch is the **Maresia,** Praia Chapeu Virado 19 (tel. 771-1463). The Maresia's owner, Carlos Alberto, serves fish platters for which I reserve the highest praise. One white-meated species is baked and comes to the table smothered in the most delicious sauce. Another local river fish is prepared as a *caldeirada,* a stew with vegetables served in its natural broth and accompanied by generous scoops of white rice and a manioc purée called *pirão.* The restaurant is open from 11 in the morning till 9 at night, seven days a week, all year.

Carlos Alberto is a genial host who organizes an excursion to the forested interior of the island that is said to be extremely popular with foreign tourists. The two-hour tour costs $20 per person and includes transportation from your hotel to a dock where you board a small fishing boat, then cruise up a wide creek into the forest to encounter much unspoiled nature and pretechnological village life. During the tour, you snack on shrimp and may drink either beer or soft drinks.

CIATUR (listed above) offers a day-trip excursion to Mosqueiros, leaving Belém at 9am and returning at 4pm, that includes lunch at Maresia, and a tour of the river beaches for $30 per person. Those looking for accommodations in Mosqueiros can try the **Hotel Ilha Bela,** Av. 16 de Novembro 409/463 (tel. 091/771-1448); $20 single, $30 double. No credit cards accepted.

MARAJÓ

An interesting two-day side trip can be made to the nearby country-size island of Marajó during the dry season, roughly from May through December. Tours may be booked through any of the agencies listed in "River Tours," above. One interesting way to organize the trip is to fly over and return by boat, economizing a bit on time, yet availing yourself of a pleasant river crossing as well. The best time to visit Marajó is over the weekend.

GETTING TO MARAJÓ BY FERRY Go to the bus terminal, Praça do Operário, in the São Bras neighborhood (tel. 228-0500). Buses leave for the ferry landing on Friday between 4 and 5am, depending on the tide, and return Sunday at 4pm. The 2½-hour crossing costs $10 each way.

FLYING TO MARAJÓ A seat on a small plane can be booked in the early morning on **TABA** (Transportes Aérea da Bacia Amazônica), Av. Gov. José Malcher 883 (tel. 223-6300), which has flights departing for Marajó from the international airport on Monday, Wednesday, and Friday at 7am. The one-way fare is $52. The half-hour flight is highly worthwhile, as you soar above the *mata,* the forest green, etched everywhere with rivulets and creeks.

The asphalt landing strip in **Soure,** capital of Marajó, is somewhat of a luxury for so small a town in the Brazilian interior, but in compensation for this unexpected symbol of the island's development, there are no cabs or buses to take you to the town's only hotel. For this reason—unless you are absolutely resigned to go it alone under all circumstances—it's advisable to book at least a portion of your Marajó visit through a tour company, like one of those listed above. If you do, you'll be met by a car belonging to the **Pousada Marajoara,** Quarta Avenida (tel. 091/741-1472), which provides perfectly adequate quarters for your overnight on Marajó. It's within walking distance of the waterfront, the center of town life, and has comfortable rooms, a swimming pool, and a good restaurant.

Many visitors to Marajó prefer to stay on one of the water buffalo ranches, like the **Bonjardim,** two hours further into the island by boat from Soure, though direct air access is also available, since every ranch of a reasonable size, like this one, can boast its private airfield. Great herds of water buffalo are raised on Marajó, and the first of this species apparently came to the island by accident, the result of a shipwreck. Bonjardim is a working spread, but also something of a dude ranch, with many outdoor activities programmed, like horseback riding, roundups, fishing and nature walks, and excellent home-cooking—much of the food provided in the form of butter, cheese, and meat by the same buffaloes. The Bonjardim has a booking office in Belém at Rua Tiradentes 392 (tel. 091/222-1380).

A new inn, the **Pousada dos Guaras** (tel. 091/241-0891), has opened on Marajó on Praia Grande in Salva Terra, a village across the Rio Paracanary from Soure. The inn is located on a 15-acre ecological preserve. There are five cabins with 20 guest rooms, each with a private thatch-roofed veranda. All rooms have air conditioning, and are equipped with full bathrooms. Meals in the restaurant run an average of $4.50. Bookings can be made in Belém through **Mururé Viagem e Turismo,** Av. Pres. Vargas 134 (tel. 233-0034), which offers a three-day package, including hotel pickup, ferry transport, and breakfast at $80 per person.

WHAT TO SEE & DO   Those who stay in Soure may also visit a **water buffalo ranch** on a tour organized by the Pousada Marajoara. The trip involves a ride on a comfortable riverboat with a bar to a typical ranch where you will be met at the dock by local cowpokes driving buffalo carts to carry you up to the house. You will then be served a few dairy snacks made from buffalo milk and treated to a rather stupid display of animal abuse that is passed off as a kind of rodeo.

My personal recommendation would be to forgo the ranch tour and spend your day at the remarkable **Araruana** beach. The Pousada Marajoara also organizes tours to this nearby beach, but they are of too limited duration given the beauty of the spectacle that awaits you. Your best bet would be to rent a bicycle in town and make the trip on your own. As you near the water, you will first have to cross the mangrove swamp on the half-mile-long wooden walkway that connects the access road to the beach. The *mangueiros* (mangroves) are those remarkable trees which have adapted to the ecologies of delta lands and savannas, flooded or dry depending on the season. The root systems grow in swirls above the ground, and so the thousands of trees seem like dainty ladies holding up their skirts as they cross through a puddle. Here in the mud, among the twisted roots, the funny, side-stepping *carangueijo* crab makes his home, and is gathered as a favorite food by rich and poor alike.

As you near the beach, you will get your first view of the roiling, boiling water. The surf is not high but amazingly agitated, like the ocean during a hurricane, owing to the location of the beach some 50 short miles below the mouth of the Amazon, where the inland and the ocean seas crash against each other.

The sun here, and throughout the region, is very hot, the bathing good, and the water warm and shallow a long way out. On the weekends the shanty restaurants are open, selling food and beverages. But there is no other development, and you can wander far down the beach for all the privacy you want. Stay away from the edge of the treeline, however. The insects are large and rapacious.

For the evening, you have basically two choices: You can stay at the Pousada Marajoara and participate in the organized follies, where guests are called upon to join a performer on the dance floor for a little jig and are then given certificates for being good sports, and so forth. Or you can go to the town square, opposite the dock where the ENASA boat is docked, and hang out in one of the two **outdoor cafés,** mixing with the locals and snacking on the savories. The little town is really quite charming, especially its main avenue lined with bulky mango trees, and the formal garden and walkway that accompanies the bank of the river. Soure is not old, having been laid out at the end of the last century by the same architect who designed Belo Horizonte, but it feels absolutely timeless.

If you choose to return by boat, you should already have made arrangements in Belém prior to coming to Marajó. The ENASA liner boards around 10pm for the return, at which time you can retire to your cabin or party all night in the discotheque, and arrive in Belém sometime early the following morning.

MACAPÁ

Another popular side trip from Belém is to the capital city of the Brazilian territory of Amapá, usually on a regularly scheduled flight with VARIG or another of the country's airlines, although a 12-hour boat trip is also available on the ENASA line.

The main attraction in Macapá is a more dramatic version of what you will see and hear at the beach on Marajó. Travelers come all the way to Macapá to witness the **pororoca,** the thundering sound made when the draining waters of the Amazon crash into the rushing tide of the Atlantic. The best time to experience the phenomenon is when the Amazon is high, roughly from July through December.

2. SANTARÉM

825 miles W of Belém

GETTING THERE   By Plane   Santarém is a stop on the daily VARIG run from Belém to Manaus. The VARIG information number in Belém is 224-3344. Santarém may be added free of charge as a fifth stopover on the VARIG four-stop air pass; the airline is trying to promote the city.

ESSENTIALS   Any of the following agencies or individual guides can provide you with a wide program of escorted services in and around Santarém. In general— barring the need for special food or equipment—the cost of a tour booking in Santarém is roughly $30 per person, per day. **Lago Verde Turismo,** Rua Galdino Veloso 664 (tel. 091/522-1645 or 522-2118), offers photo safaris, birdwatching expeditions, boat trips, plus tours of Belterra, Alter do Chão, national park lands, and to the mining towns and goldfields. Another Lago Verde specialty is sport fishing on the many small creeks and tributaries of the Tapajós. **Amazon Tours,** Travessa Turiano Meira 1084 (tel. 091/522-1098), offers nature walks and campouts within a private preserve of Amazon forest. **Gil Sirique** of the English School, Rua 24 de Outubro 1111 (tel. 091/522-5174), offers his services as a free-lance guide.

Tourists to the Amazon first learned of Santarém by traveling the river between Belém and Manaus (or vice versa). The trip takes from four to seven days depending on whether you go with or against the current, and on other such vagaries as time of year and a studied disinclination among the natives to be driven by the clock. The passion of these pioneering tourists was (as it remains for many today) to experience intimately the mode of transport most typically used by the people who live here as they travel throughout the region. Since all the big riverboats that make the Belém to Manaus run call in at Santarém, the exact midpoint between the two cities, word of this "other" large Amazon river town has gradually spread among a new wave of Brazil-bound visitors. Many of these visitors find it more convenient to avoid a long and potentially monotonous boat ride and arrive by plane, making use of a three-week air pass.

So, how do you spend the two or so days you've just economized by not taking the boat? Maybe you only spend two of them here, or maybe you decide to check it out more closely if you're not on a schedule and can carve out the time. There's a ton of history and nature surrounding this city, indeed some very curious facts. Santarém is booming, bursting its seams, growing fat as a staging area for the legions of prospectors reportedly wreaking havoc throughout the forest beyond the confines of this urban outpost.

Some Americans might actually be drawn to Santarém by genealogical ties. The town originally evolved from a Jesuit mission, established in the mid-1660s at the point where the waters of the Tapajós enter those of the Amazon. But Santarém apparently underwent a great spurt of growth, notably in agricultural technology, after the American Civil War when a colony of disgruntled Confederates settled here rather than face life in occupied Dixie. Families with Anglo-Saxon last names, and lingering American traditions, may still be found here, but the best account of the Confederate's tale that I have seen is in *The Last Colony of the Confederacy,* by Eugene C. Harter, published by the University of Mississippi Press.

Today, Santarém is at an agreeably schizophrenic stage in its development: big enough to have some character, a few colorful public places where crowds gather on the wharves, in markets and cafés, to work, to shop, and to socialize; yet also remote and insular, cut off from the world except by air or sea. Greater Santarém, home to 300,000 residents, grows daily, horizontally, chewing away at the wooded environs of the surrounding forest in ever widening circles. As for overland access to the remainder of Brazil, the so-called road to Cuiabá in Mato Grosso can hardly be said to be open. The route was laid out halfheartedly, and while passable segments exist, mostly the surface is washed out and unrepaired. Santarém's side streets are hardly more reliable for normal transit than the road to Cuiabá. They are narrow, deeply rutted, and cause traffic to slow to the uncomfortable and comic gait of a bouncing buckboard. Without doubt, automotive travel around Santarém is rough going, primitive, but the minor inconveniences are justly rewarded for those who venture forth.

WHAT TO SEE & DO

For a two-day layover in Santarém, there is just time enough to explore the town, languish a bit in a wharfside café, and take a single day-trip excursion chosen from among the three principal options. Logistically, it's the most that can be managed at anything short of a gymnast's pace.

For your day-trip, you might visit **Alter do Chão,** a small beach resort on an inland river "lake," two hour's distance by car; there are several all-day ecology and river tours routinely available, some including overnights in the forest; and lastly, an odd historical glitch straight from the annals of *Ripley's Believe It or Not,* an opportunity to visit the failed rubber plantation, **Fordlândia,** and the semiabandoned American-style company town, **Belterra,** founded in the 1920s by the Ford Motor Company only 50 miles outside Santarém. Any of these tours, described more fully below, can be booked in Santarém, or you can free-lance, using public transportation (miraculously, there are buses to most of these places) and direct bargaining with drivers and boat owners.

Finally, Santarém may be considered a gateway to the vast public lands of the rain forest, especially the **Parque Nacional de Amazonas** (Amazonas National Park), and the **Floresta Nacional de Tapajós** (Tapajós National Forest), by means of an expedition booked directly through one of the agencies mentioned above.

WHERE TO STAY

Occupying the most romantic spot of any hotel in Santarém is the completely run-down **Uirapiru,** Av. Adriano Pimental 140, facing the wharf and beyond that the point where the city's two large rivers meet and mingle their contrasting colors. I was told the hotel was about to be fully renovated and resurrected in a year or so. If it reopens, check it out for the location alone.

MODERATE

TROPICAL HOTEL SANTARÉM, Av. Mendonça Furtado 4120, Santarém. Tel. 091/522-1533. Fax 091/522-2631. Telex 91/5505. 122 rms. A/C MINIBAR TV TEL

$ Rates: $42 single; $45 double. AE, DC, MC, V.

The Tropical is Santarém's only deluxe hotel—which means the rooms are air-conditioned and very spacious, there is a big pool and patio area, and an in-house agency can book all your local tour and transportation needs. Among rooms, the best are those with balconies overlooking the pool area, with a view of the Rio Tapajós. The Tropical is on the outskirts of town, however, and is not maintained at the level of a four-star hotel, though the staff, in compensation, is very friendly and accommodating. The tropics are hard on everything, including buildings; if you don't keep after the details, you can get swamped by them. There is just too much unattended decay at the Tropical, given its rating.

BUDGET

BRASIL GRANDE HOTEL, Travessa 15 de Augusto 213, Santarém. Tel. 091/522-5660. 25 rms (20 with bath). MINIBAR TV

$ Rates: $2.75 single without bath; $4.25–$5.50 small standard room with bath; $12–$14 room with bath and A/C. No credit cards.

One in-town alternative is a nice family-run establishment, the Brasil Grande Hotel, set in a couple of blocks from the river. The owner is very proud of this relatively new hotel. It's nothing fancy, but the neatness of the place reflects attentive care. The best rooms are air-conditioned and have a comfortable appearance, including a full bath. Smaller standard singles are available, but these guests must make use of a communal bathroom, which, incidentally, was spotlessly clean. A bar and restaurant occupies one floor of the Grande Hotel, and the owner is in the process of adding more rooms.

CITY HOTEL, Travessa Francisco Correa 200, Santarém. Tel. 091/522-4719. 20 suites (all with bath). MINIBAR TV
$ Rates: $7.75 single; $15 double. No credit cards.

The City Hotel has suites that reminded me of rooms I'd stayed in 20 years ago on the Rossio in Lisbon—a positive recollection, I should add. Bargain rates add to the appeal.

SANTARÉM PALACE HOTEL, Av. Rui Barbosa 726. Tel. 091/522-1285. Telex 91/5526. 48 rms (47 with bath). A/C MINIBAR TV TEL
$ Rates: $20 single; $24 double. MC.
Overseen by resident manager Cslava Luczynski Souza, of Polish-Portuguese extraction, this hotel is solid, with no luxuries, and no doubt a reliable port-of-call for assorted transients of the middle classes, be they commercial travelers or Brazilian tourists. The double-bedded room I saw was large, clean, and unadorned. Half board is available in the hotel's own small dining room. You should definitely spend a few minutes chatting with Dona Cslava, who knows English, and ask her for a *suco de cacau*—a tasty juice made from the pulp of the cacao fruit.

WHERE TO DINE

The **Yana**, Av. Cuiabá 1854 (tel. 522-5515), serves regional food and natural fruit ice creams. I had a very generous cone of something called *tarerebá*, a pumpkin-colored ice cream, for about 50¢. This luncheonette is open seven days a week, from 9am till 11:30pm.

Other restaurants recommended to me by knowledgeable locals are the **Peixaria Cantogalo**, Travessa Silva Jardím 820 (tel. 522-1174), in the Aparecida neighborhood, and the **Restaurante Lago Verde**, Travessa Francisco Correa 125 (tel. 522-2354), which are both open daily for lunch and dinner and serve primarily fish and other regional dishes.

RESTAURANTE MASCOTE, Praça do Pescador 10. Tel. 522-5444.
Cuisine: INTERNATIONAL. **Reservations:** Not needed.
$ Prices: Appetizers $1–$3; main courses $3–$6. No credit cards.
Open: Daily 8am–midnight.

The Restaurante Mascote is the perfect lunch spot, an open-sided café on the waterfront, with white-linen-clad tables, and the same courteous, semiformal service that continental Portuguese culture implanted throughout all Brazil, and is still practiced everywhere from São Paulo to Santarém. The breeze blowing off the water ventilates the restaurant and relieves some of the steaminess of the rain-forest climate. On the menu, the chef's daily specials are recommended, priced generally in the $2 range, and from $3 to $4 on Saturday and Sunday when feijoada or *pato no tucupi* are the featured dishes. I ate reasonably tender beef filets, smothered in gravy and served with rice and mashed potatoes. During the midday siesta, the Mascote is a hangout for a group of professional pilots, who form the taxi-and-supply link to the interior for rainbow chasers and get-rich-quick adventurers of every stripe.

EVENING ENTERTAINMENT

Out of town, on the road to Alter do Chão is an open-air beer garden, where barbecued chicken is the featured dish. The **Mutunuy** has no phone, and you will probably require the company of a native to find the place on the Estrada Santarém–Curuá-Una, kilometer 6. When I joined a tour operator and her Danish clients for an evening at the Mutunuy, we were the only ones there. But the place was beautifully set in the midst of the woods, and suggested festive possibilities on perhaps any but a Monday night. The grilled chicken, *franguinho de leite,* is served on skewers for about $2 an order.

In Santarém itself, the most popular meeting place is said to be the **Mascotinho,** a wharfside bar directly opposite the old Hotel Uirapiru. Open daily after 4pm, the bar faces the Ponta Negra and the "meeting of the waters."

EASY EXCURSIONS

ALTER DO CHÃO   The 25-mile drive from Santarém can take almost two hours. I've seen better logging roads in the Maine wilderness than the dirt "highway" that provides the link. But I found every bump exhilarating given the incomparable beauty of the landscape.

Alter do Chão is a beach community of pretty summer cottages on the shore of Lago Verde, called a lake but really a river bay of turquoise water bisected by a sandy, tree-covered point. At the village center on a plaza set back from the point where the beach curves around a bend in the lake are a village chapel and a café-restaurant, accounting for Alter's only public buildings.

Cruise ships, such as those of the Royal Viking Line, often anchor mid-river and hold civilized beach parties complete with bonfire, six-piece dance band, and awning-covered booths dispensing cocktails and soft drinks. The local urchins join in with their feigned sad expressions begging Cokes and Pepsis, making out well enough to return home with aching tummies.

FORDLÂNDIA & BELTERRA   History buffs and lovers of the absurd will place a visit to Fordlândia/Belterra high among their excursion priorities while staying in Santarém. In the 1920s, Henry Ford believed he could standardize rubber production in the Amazon forest and return the Brazilian latex industry to a profitable and competitive position in relation to the plantations of East Asia. Ford's first attempt to fulfill this dream led to the construction of the **Fordlândia** plantation. This was followed by the creation of **Belterra,** in layout and appearance a prototypical American company town: orderly blocks of white-sided bungalows trimmed in green, a village square with a wooden church and a bandstand, and a hospital that was once the envy of all Amazônia. In all, 28,000 acres encompassing 3 million rubber trees were under production, and I do not know the details of why this enterprise ultimately failed. It appears to have been an early, and to some extent, an unheeded lesson on the limits of technological know-how to tame and civilize the Amazon Basin. Brazilian agencies today use Belterra as a research center, and thus this one-time and unexpected outpost of American industry remains in a state of excellent preservation. In the dry season, public buses from the center of Santarém make a daily run to Belterra, about 100 miles upstream along the Tapajós. For no rational explanation that I have been able to discover, there is a one-hour time difference between Santarém and Belterra, complicating a same-day return by public means. The transportation alternative is an informal and personalized tour by a knowledgeable guide, or with one of the other tour operators listed above.

A wide variety of ecological tours that provide relatively fresh and genuine encounters with the rain forest and its human culture may be booked in Santarém.

RIVER BEACHES   At low water, during the Amazon summer—July through December, when the river's sandy banks are exposed—local residents flock to the beaches. The most popular strands, **Maracanã** and **Vera Cruz,** begin right in town. Santarém has a wide front along the riverfront, and the beaches here are surprisingly extensive. The more private beaches, like Alter do Chão, and others more deserted along **Rio Arapiuns,** are out of town. Fish cookouts on the beaches, called *piracaias,* are frequent occurrences, and such an event is included in many organized excursions.

3. MANAUS

1,030 miles NW of Belém

GETTING THERE   By Plane   The **Eduardo Gomes International Airport** is located 10 miles from downtown Manaus. The city being a free port, all passengers must go through Customs here on departure, so you must be at the airport two hours before your flight leaves; the exit lines can be quite long. Transbrasil (tel. 621-1185), VASP (tel. 621-2017), and VARIG (tel. 621-1556) all have regular flights in and out of Manaus; telephone numbers listed here are their local numbers. If you arrive here on a VARIG Air Pass, you are entitled to a 15% discount at the Hotel Tropical, the best hotel in town. Buses run downtown from the airport; the fare is approximately 35¢. Taxis from the airport to downtown cost around $14; for a radio cab, call Radiotaxi (tel. 621-1578).

By Car or Bus   It's possible to get here by way of Porto Velho when the road is open, but it's not recommended.

By Boat   Wherever there is water in the Amazon, you can get there by boat. There is regular river traffic between the major towns and commercial centers. For information in Manaus on boat departures, contact the Harbor Master (Capitânia do Porto), Rua Mq. de Santa Cruz 264 (tel. 234-9662), or the shipping company ENASA, Rua Mal. Deodoro 61 (tel. 232-4280). In Santarém, you can also contact ENASA, Rua Sen. Lameira Bittencourt 459 (tel. 522-5855), regarding boat service from Santarém to Manaus.

ESSENTIALS   Information   EMANTUR, Amazonas state's tourism bureau, Av. Taruma 369 (tel. 234-5303), open Monday to Friday from 7:30am to 1:30pm, is an excellent source of up-to-date information on the cheaper hotels and rooming houses. A receptionist can provide this information by phone (tel. 234-5414) Monday to Friday from 8am to 6pm, Saturday till noon. The downtown EMANTUR information booth on Avenida Eduardo Ribeiro is open Monday to Friday from 9am to noon and 2 to 5pm, on Saturday from 9am to 2pm. Their airport information counter, located next to the VARIG desk, is open around the clock daily.

Climate   The climate in Manaus is most suited to visitors from March through June, the beginning of the dry season when the river's waters are still relatively high.

Bugs   There are many small, flying insects that will penetrate the otherwise hermetic security of even the city's finest hotels. Come to the Amazon prepared to tolerate a certain amount of insect annoyance. If you are prone to allergic reactions from insect bites, bring plenty of repellent or other appropriate medications. To lessen the impact of insects, most overnight river excursions are on sites along the Rio Negro, where the relatively antiseptic ecological conditions keep the bug population to a minimum. The flora is also less disturbed along the Negro, while the Solimões is known for its fishing. Only your physician—by consulting personal medical records and appropriate reference materials—can inform you as to the need for shots or other medication.

───────────

Manaus is the capital of the state of **Amazonas,** built up from an obscure river village only at the end of the last century as a result of the rubber boom. Amazonas state has a population of perhaps 1.2 million inhabitants, and yet represents some 20% of Brazil's national territory. After the fall of the Brazilian rubber market, Manaus foundered for half a century. To revive the city, Manaus was designated a free port by the Brazilian government in 1967, and since then government policy has encouraged the growth in the city of extensive assembly plants by major multinational firms, primarily in the consumer electronics field.

Manaus grew up on the hilly left bank of the Rio Negro, which is carved by an endless chain of creeks called *igarapés,* where water enters or recedes depending on the time of year. In July the river is at its highest, and December, its lowest, a difference of as much as 35 feet most years, sometimes more. Floating houses and stilt dwellings are the adaptations made by those who live near the riverbank in response to flood season. And while the city is some 1,000 water miles from the Atlantic, its general elevation is only 20 feet above sea level. With few historic buildings and a pattern of hodgepodge industrial development over the past 20 years, Manaus is not what you would call a pretty city. What Manaus does have in its favor is its location on the great river, and—despite the hivelike activity of its port and industrial suburbs—an eerie sense of isolation from the mainstream of civilization. Its distance from other regional centers in Brazil puts the Amazonian capital and its vast, sparsely populated surrounding territories somewhat in the same position as Alaska in the U.S. But of course the comparison does not extend to the climate. Manaus is hot and humid. The year-round mean temperature is 85°F, with September through November being the hottest months.

A stay of two or three days in Manaus is sufficient to see the city and a few of the better-known sights on the river, like the truly impressive "meeting of the waters," where the different-colored Rio Solimões and Rio Negro run parallel before mixing into the muddy brown of the Amazon. Manaus, of course, is also the major port of entry for visitors who wish to travel extensively on the river, taking advantage of the dozens of excursions and adventure tours that originate from the city, which are usually booked long in advance of arrival through specialty travel agents at home. The names of several respected travel agencies and tour operators active in these areas, with brief descriptions of their itineraries, are given below and in Chapter 2, along with U.S. travel agents and organizations that book specialty tours to Brazil, including adventure tours throughout the Amazon.

WHAT TO SEE & DO

One of the most popular nonriver sights in Manaus is the old **Teatro Amazonas,** an opera house that was opened in 1896, a cultural by-product of the city's newfound rubber wealth. The building is a synthesis of various styles, including baroque, neoclassical, and art nouveau. The structure beneath the facade is of cast iron which, along with all the other building and finishing materials, was imported from Europe. Renovations on both the exterior and interior of the theater have recently been completed at a cost of $8 million, and opera has been scheduled once again for performance within the walls of the Teatro Amazonas for the first time in decades.

Near the theater is the **Praça do Congresso,** a popular place for evening promenades.

The **Municipal Market** at dockside is an impressive cast-iron building, similar to the Belém market. And much of what can be seen in the Ver-O-Peso can be seen here as well.

An excellent source of Native American and artist crafts is the **ARPP-AM,** Av. Adolfo Dulk 165, in the Parque Acariquara section of Aleixo (tel. 244-2246). ARPP stands for Associação dos Artesãos de Arte Primitiva e Popular; that is, a league of artisans who work in primitive and popular media. The association is currently led by the brothers Andrade, Rogério, and Cláudio, and the address listed here is that of the suburban studio where Cláudio—a highly talented wood-carver—does his work. When I visited the studio, Cláudio showed me an album with photographs of association members' work, much of it quite appealing and unique. But the association also maintains contact with large numbers of tribal artisans, and offers for sale numerous objects of Native American artisanry, especially baskets, utensils, and masks. The best place to see the association's stock of craft items is not at Cláudio's studio, but on the floating pier in Manaus where they set up a stand whenever a cruise ship comes to port.

INSTITUTO NACIONAL DE PESQUISAS DA AMAZÔNIA, Estrada do Aleixo 1756. Tel. 236-5860.

INPA (Instituto Nacional de Pesquisas da Amazônia), the National Institute of Amazonian Research, is a government research facility outside Manaus that is worth visiting. It is necessary to enter through the main gate and get permission from the security police. Once inside the forested grounds, you immediately hear the music of the jungle, since the many trees provide a kind of urban refuge for great numbers of birds. INPA is also like a large college campus, with many buildings where scientists pursue the various branches of naturalistic studies relevant to gaining a greater understanding of the Amazon. You can see many different animals here as well, like the manatee and the *ariranha,* a very funny and animated Amazonian otter. Don't be surprised at the large numbers of Americans you see within the grounds. They are here serving on staff, sharing their ecological training in exchange for a rare opportunity for practical study in the world's largest remaining forest reserve.

While at INPA, try to arrange a brief tour of the sawmill belonging to the Centro de Pesquisa de Productos Florestais (Center for the Study of Forest Products) on the same grounds. Civil engineer Murilo Suano, head of the mill, not only showed me around, he then presented me with a dozen *amostras*—block-size pieces of exotic hardwoods—as souvenirs. One sample, true to its name—purple heart—was indeed beet purple in color, another wood was positively canary yellow, and many others were dense and dark like mahogony or ebony. Samples for as many as 70 species of Amazonian woods can be purchased at INPA, packed in well-made boxes with hinged tops, when available, for approximately $50 a box. Murilo explained that mill workers cut the samples during rare periods of downtime, in between their more significant experiments. And so demand for the sample boxes far outstrips the supply.

Admission: Free.
Open: Mon–Fri 8am–6pm, Sat 8am–noon.

MUSEU DE CIÊNCIAS NATURAIS, in Colônia Cachoeira Grande of the Conjunto Preto section of the Aleixo suburb. Tel. 244-2799.

A very small, but infinitely worthwhile, museum has recently opened on the outskirts of Manaus. Within a single, stucco-white exhibition hall, hundreds of stuffed fish and mammals, mounted butterflies and insects, are displayed in handsomely constructed cases. The taxidermy is first rate, and the effect dramatic and spellbinding as you confront at such close quarters the enormity and Stone Age appearance of some of these Amazonian specimens, especially the fish and the beetles. The seven-foot-long *pirarucu* is truly a sight to behold. In the center of the pavilion is a large fish tank, where many live species may also be seen through observation windows that line the walls. For anyone with the slightest interest in the natural history of the Amazon region, I cannot recommend too highly a visit to this thoroughly fascinating institution.

As if the collection of river and forest specimens were not enough, the Japanese director of the museum has also created a gift shop that sells the very best examples of Brazilian handcrafts I have ever seen gathered in a single locale in that country. Many of the crafts, in particular the baskets and bark drawings, are the products of still healthy Native American economies, the work of tribal artisans who continue to dwell in remote areas far from contact with the modern world. Prices at the gift shop are reasonable if not cheap, and marked in dollars.

Admission: $1.
Open: Tues–Sun 9am–5:30pm.

WHERE TO STAY

Manaus does not have an abundance of good hotels, and because of the generally higher cost of living in the city, you should expect to pay more here than for hotels of comparable quality in other Brazilian cities.

VERY EXPENSIVE

HOTEL TROPICAL, Estrada da Ponta Negra, Manaus. Tel. 092/238-5757. Fax 092/238-5221. Telex 92/2173. 605 rms. A/C MINIBAR TV TEL
$ Rates: $160–$190 single; $180–$210 double. AE, DC, MC, V.

By far the best hotel in Manaus—and one of the most luxurious resorts in Brazil—is the Hotel Tropical. For those who wish to be in the Amazon but remain insulated from its rough edges, the Hotel Tropical provides the perfect environment. The hotel even organizes all its own tours, including several options for overnights in the forest at the Tropical's very own first-class floating lodge.

Located near the airport approximately a 15-minute ride from the city, the Tropical sits on the bank of the Rio Negro, with its own access to one of Manaus's most popular beaches, and on acres of private, beautifully landscaped grounds that contain a small zoo, a playground, an enormous central courtyard with swimming pool, and tennis courts. Everything about the Tropical is voluptuous, including the somewhat oversize *fazenda*-style furnishings. Several of the public spaces are genuinely elegant, including a formal restaurant, the very masculine bar in polished hardwood and leather, and several lounges and seating areas off the lobby.

A succulent and very traditional feijoada, with all the trimmings including *batida* cocktails and black-bean broth, is served in the principal dining room every Saturday. Maintenance at the hotel is definitely among the best in all Brazil, perhaps because the Tropical is a star property belonging to VARIG Airlines, and it is always heavily booked. So make your reservations far in advance. For all its efficiency, the Tropical must still function within the framework of civil anarchy that has long characterized life in the Amazonian region. Hotel managers pull out their hair when telling how they've installed the most sophisticated communications system in the world, but it can function at just 30% of capacity because the city will only cede the hotel 45 phone lines. As a result, guests do on occasion experience delays when dialing out.

The Tropical is adding rooms, and many additions and improvements to the public spaces and outdoor and sporting areas are planned. Rooms are constantly being redecorated, and the pattern today is leading away from the colonial style to a more modern decor in an ample and light-bathed space.

Baths have bright tiles painted with floral motifs, and contain separate tub and stall shower. The standard and deluxe rooms differ only in their location within the hotel.

A shuttle bus connects the Tropical with downtown Manaus and the city's newest shopping center. There are two buses in the morning and two in the afternoon; the fare is $2.25 each way.

EXPENSIVE

DA VINCI HOTEL, Rua Belo Horizonte 240-A, Manaus. Tel. 092/611-1213. Fax 092/611-3721. Telex 92/1024. 116 rms. A/C MINIBAR TV TEL
$ Rates: $60–$71 standard room, $70–$81 standard room facing pool; $80–$97 deluxe room; $89–$105 extra-large executive room. AE, MC, V.

Away from the river, about 15 minutes from the city in Adrianópolis, one of its most affluent suburbs, is the Da Vinci Hotel. It's a hotel, not a plush resort like the Tropical, but it still provides elegant digs in Manaus.

There are four categories of rooms, distinguished by location, size, and to some degree, furnishings. The least expensive standard room does not suffer a decline in either comfort or the tastefulness of its decor. The room has a double bed, armchair, and deep-brown carpeted floors, and is of high-quality workmanship in its furnishings and finish. The regular deluxe room adds a balcony with plenty of elbow room, covered by a sloping tile roof, and sports two modern rocking chairs. A large set of double doors—part louvered slats, part mullioned windowpanes—separates the room from the balcony. The deluxe room also contains a couch, and all rooms display dried floral arrangements that have been fashioned into unique wall hangings.

A lovely sunken lobby is imaginatively divided into several discreet seating environments, each with individually styled armchairs, love seats, and tables—all of rattan and cane. Borders of living plants and vases of dried flowers, grasses, and leaves complete the effect. Both the bar and the restaurant off the lobby convey an air of sophistication, and outside there is a large pool area with two dozen patio tables with chairs, shaded by umbrellas.

HOTEL AMAZONAS, Praça Adelberto Valle, Manaus. Tel. 092/622-2233. Fax 092/622-2064. Telex 92/2277. 171 rms. A/C MINIBAR TV TEL
$ Rates: $52–$66 standard single or double; $66–$79 deluxe room. AE, DC, MC, V.

This hotel is right in town, close to both the free-port shopping district and the floating dock and market. Deluxe accommodations at the Amazonas are high-ceilinged rooms with good-sized balconies offering views of the active waterfront and the Rio Negro. The standard rooms are smaller and face the rear, with views over the back commercial streets. All rooms are furnished with cabinetry and surfaces in modern, straight-lined designs, with two single beds in the deluxe rooms and a double bed in the standards. The hotel has a large second-floor restaurant with voluminous black columns, heavy handmade, country-style tables and chairs, and a small courtyard pool with a hardwood deck and separate bar.

IMPERIAL HOTEL, Av. Getúlio Vargas 227, Manaus. Tel. 092/622-3112. Fax 092/622-1762. Telex 92/2231. 100 rms. A/C MINIBAR TV TEL

$ Rates: $83–$90 standard room; $93–$100 deluxe room. AE, DC, MC, V.

This hotel is a 10-story apartment-style building, located on one of Manaus's principal avenues. Rooms are of good size, approximately 12 feet by 15 feet, and comfortably furnished, some with large double beds, a couch, and a lace-covered table with chairs, while others have two single beds and an armchair. The hotel's second-floor restaurant is a pleasant room where food is served both à la carte and buffet style, and there is live music on Friday and Saturday nights. Behind the hotel is a midsize backyard, with a pool and a tile deck.

PLAZA HOTEL, Av. Getúlio Vargas 215, Manaus. Tel. 092/233-8900.
Fax 092/233-5125. Telex 92/2563. 80 rms. A/C MINIBAR TV TEL

$ Rates: $70–$77 single; $75–$82 double. AE, DC, MC, V.

The Plaza has been open since 1986. The deluxe rooms are small and set up like a Pullman suite to maximize the use of limited space. Some rooms have a single bed and a couch that opens to a second bed; other rooms are larger with double beds, tables, and chairs. The closets have doors that slide up and down like rolltop desks, and the bathrooms are also small, but equally well organized with marble corner sinks whose surfaces are large. The general decor of the hotel is attractive, and the corridors are wide, carpeted, and well painted—not dazzling, but well done. An atrium lobby leads to a mezzanine restaurant.

MODERATE

HOTEL CENTRAL, Rua Dr. Moreira 302, Manaus. Tel. 092/622-2600.
Telex 92/2765. 50 rms. A/C MINIBAR TV TEL

$ Rates: $32–$40 double. No credit cards.

Rooms here are spacious enough, with windows, double beds, and good old-fashioned baths with porcelain fixtures.

HOTEL INTERNATIONAL, Rua Dr. Moreira 168, Manaus. Tel. 092/234-1315. Fax 092/234-5396. Telex 92/2603. 39 rms. A/C MINIBAR TV TEL

$ Rates: $38–$46 standard room; $45–$53 deluxe room. AE, DC, MC, V.

A block from the Lord hotel is a street with several of the city's older medium-priced hotels, and the International is the best of the lot. Its deluxe rooms are large, and breezy when the windows are open, although all rooms are also equipped with individual air conditioners. The rooms contain two good-sized beds, and the floors are carpeted. Baths are tiled with decorative azulejos. The furnishings are definitely well used, but not in bad shape by any means.

HOTEL MÓNACO, Rua Sílva Ramos 20, Manaus. Tel. 092/622-3446. Fax 092/622-1415. Telex 92/2802. 90 rms. A/C MINIBAR TV TEL

$ Rates: $65 single or double. AE, DC, MC, V.

The Hotel Mónaco is near the Amazonas state tourism office, EMANTUR, on the city's downtown fringe, but still easily within walking distance of central Manaus and the Duty-Free Zone. The Mónaco has recently undergone a major renovation, and the newly decorated rooms are a great improvement over the old ones.

The hotel building itself is very attractive, and houses a fine restaurant, the Mirante (see "Where to Dine," below), and also serves as headquarters for **Rio Amazonas Turismo** (tel. 092/234-7308), a reliable tour agency operating actively throughout the Amazon.

THE LORD, Rua Macílio Dias 217, Manaus. Tel. 092/622-2844. Fax 092/234-0285. Telex 92/2278. 105 rms. A/C MINIBAR TEL TV

$ Rates: $62–$70 standard room; $72–$80 deluxe room. AE, DC, MC, V.

The best of the middle-bracket hotels is the Lord, though it has a few serious flaws, some of which are being corrected by the gradual renovation of the accommodations. The six-story building with a pseudomodern facade occupies a corner (with Rua Quintino Bocaiúva) on an active commercial street closed to traffic and recently converted to a pedestrian shopping mall. Many consumer shops selling crafts and electronic goods line the street. Rooms on the upper floors look out over the surrounding rooftops, and are pleasant enough, though the individual air conditioners make a terrible noise, forcing you to open the windows at night, which is not necessarily unpleasant. The hotel is well situated, quite near the central section of the waterfront, and has a reasonably spacious lobby—something lacking in most hotels of its class in Manaus. The attached bar is pleasant.

SOMBRA PALACE, Av. de Setembro 1325, Manaus. Tel. 092/234-8777. Telex 92/3058. 43 rms. A/C MINIBAR TV TEL
$ Rates: $30 single; $40 double. AE.

In the heart of downtown Manaus, the Sombra Palace can provide you with a very nice three-star room. The relatively new hotel has a well-constructed and well-maintained appearance. Rooms are spacious, with uniquely patterned parquet floors, and modern, yet homey furnishings.

BUDGET

HOTEL DONA JOANA, Rua dos Andrades 553, Manaus. Tel. 092/233-7553. 62 rms (all with bath). A/C MINIBAR TV
$ Rates: $15 double; $20 suite. No credit cards.

The Hotel Dona Joana has several plain but spacious air-conditioned suites with balconies. Standard rooms are smaller, but all have double beds, bathrooms, and Amazon River views. A simple open-air restaurant occupies the fourth floor, reached only by stairs since the Dona Joana has no elevators. The food served there, especially hot meals, is good, plentiful, and cheap. The hotel is spotless, has a pleasant, well-chilled lobby (not to be gainsaid in a city where the mean temperature is 86°F), and seems like a real bargain for the budget traveler in pricey Manaus.

HOTEL RIO BRANCO, Rua dos Andrades 484, Manaus. Tel. 092/233-4019. 36 rms (28 with bath). MINIBAR TV
$ Rates: $4–$5 room without fan or A/C; $7 room with fan; $9 room with A/C. No credit cards.

The style and layout of this hotel is more that of a boardinghouse than a hotel, and it's quite a find for budget travelers. The Rio Branco sits on a street that runs parallel to the river, a few blocks in, and upstream somewhat from Manaus's famous floating pier. Only the more expensive rooms have bathrooms.

KYOTO PLAZA HOTEL, Rua Dr. Moreira 232. Tel. 092/232-6552. 15 rms (all with bath). A/C MINIBAR TV TEL
$ Rates: $12 single; $20 double; $27 triple. AE, DC, MC.

The Kyoto Plaza is more of a *pensão* than a hotel. Rooms are small, without windows but otherwise adequate. Some rooms have single beds, others doubles, and all are air-conditioned.

WHERE TO DINE

The regional food in Manaus is the same as that in Belém. Such dishes as *pato no tucupi* (duck in fermented manioc sauce) and *tacaca* (the funky tapioca porridge served in a gourd, primarily as a street food) are readily available throughout the city. But the mainstay of the local diet is fish—*pirarucu, tambaqui,* and *tucunaré* are the most popular, but the list only begins with these. Despite the high cost of living in Manaus, restaurant food is not appreciably more expensive than elsewhere in Brazil.

MODERATE

LA BARCA, Rua Recife 684. Tel. 236-8544.
Cuisine: INTERNATIONAL. **Reservations:** Not needed.
$ Prices: Appetizers $3–$8; main courses $8–$15. AE, DC, MC.
Open: Lunch Mon–Sat 11:30am–3:30pm, Sun 11:30am–4pm; dinner daily 7:30pm–midnight.

La Barca, in an area called Parque 10, is a white stucco building, trimmed in dark hardwood and open on three sides, that looks like the veranda of a hacienda. This is probably the most sophisticated restaurant in Manaus. The tables are attractively set for elegant dining, and the menu is extensive, listing more than 100 plates, including many *iscas* (side dishes and appetizers). Best of all, meals are reasonably priced, and there's live music.

CAÇAROLA, Rua Maures 188. Tel. 233-3021.
Cuisine: SEAFOOD. **Reservations:** Not needed.
$ Prices: Appetizers $3–$5; main courses $5–$15. No credit cards.
Open: Lunch daily 11am–3pm; dinner daily 6pm–midnight.

One very popular fish restaurant, and one of the most expensive in Manaus, is the Caçarola, located on the outskirts of town in a modest suburb. The Caçarola has the atmosphere of a neighborhood outdoor café, nothing fancy; indeed, the chairs and tables are a bit rickety. But the restaurant has won its reputation on the basis of its kitchen, not its decor. All the typical fish dishes are served, in a variety of presentation, and the steak is also excellent.

FIORENTINA, Rua Recife 900. Tel. 232-3177.
Cuisine: ITALIAN. **Reservations:** Not needed.
$ Prices: Appetizers $3–$5; main courses $5–$12. No credit cards.
Open: Daily 11am–11:30pm.

Manaus has two branches of the Fiorentina restaurant. This one occupies an attractive brick and timber open-air lean-to on a busy intersection in the Adrianópolis neighborhood. The original Fiorentina is downtown at Praça Roosevelt 44 (tel. 232-1295), more popularly known as the Praça da Polícia because of the presence there of a Military Police barracks. The food at both locales is Italian, beginning with pizzas at around $4, pasta dishes at $3 to $4, and meat plates around $7. House specialties include Amazonian fish platters.

MIRANTE, in the Hotel Mónaco, Rua Sílva Ramos 20. Tel. 622-3446.
Cuisine: GRILLED MEATS. **Reservations:** Not needed.
$ Prices: Appetizers $2.75–$5.25; main courses $5.25–$11.50. MC, V.
Open: Lunch daily noon–4pm; dinner daily 6pm–midnight.

The Mirante overlooks Manaus from the 13th floor of the Hotel Mónaco, and definitely provides the best public rooftop view of the city. Food at the Mirante is excellent and moderately priced. Good bets are the *caldeirada* fish stew, made with *tambaqui* and served with rice and *pirão;* also the tasty and imaginative *frango cubano,* a tempura of chicken breast, banana, tomato, palmito, onion, and pineapple. With its small swimming pool to one side, the Mirante is a weekend meeting place, where many shutterbugs show up to record the magnificent Amazonian sunset.

PALHOÇA, Estrada da Ponta Negra. Tel. 238-3831.
Cuisine: INTERNATIONAL. **Reservations:** Not needed.
$ Prices: Appetizers $3–$4.75; main courses $5–$11. No credit cards.
Open: Dinner daily 6pm–midnight (usually open later on weekends).

Many of Manaus's favorite restaurants are located outside the city, along various suburban access roads. The Palhoça is such a place. A large, open-sided shed with a straw roof, the Palhoça serves a good mixed-grill barbecue for about $7.75.

PANORAMA, Blv. Rio Negro 199. Tel. 624-4226.
Cuisine: REGIONAL/INTERNATIONAL. **Reservations:** Not needed.
$ Prices: Appetizers $2–$4; main courses $4.50–$12. AE.
Open: Lunch daily 11am–3pm; dinner daily 6pm–midnight.

The Panorama actually overlooks the river from the nearby Educandos neighborhood. It's a popular institution in Manaus where an average meal costs about $7. Especially recommended are the *farofa de tambaqui,* chunks of fresh fish fried in farinha flour, preceded by an appetizer of *bolinhos de peixe,* fish cakes, and several rounds of caipirinhas. For dessert, try the delicious cream of *cupuaçu*—a favorite local fruit prepared like a custard.

TIMONEIRO, Rua Paraiba 07. Tel. 236-1679.
Cuisine: SEAFOOD. **Reservations:** Not needed.

$ Prices: Appetizers $3–$5; main courses $5–$12. DC, MC, V.
   Open: Mon–Fri 7pm–midnight, Sat–Sun 11am–midnight.
The Timoneiro is also in Parque 10. For native decor, this is the most attractive restaurant in Manaus. The large space is saturated with authentic artifacts of the Amazon Native American cultures, as well as taxidermic oddities like mummified alligators, strange fish, tortoise shells, and jaguar pelts. Bird cages in the parking lot are filled with chatty parrots and *arraras*. Specialties here are *tambaqui* barbecue, *tucunaré* stew, and filet of *pirarucu*. International platters are also available. Fresh fruits of the Amazon are recommended for dessert, especially the *capuaçu, tucuma, pupunha,* and *graviola.* The liquor made from graviola is strong and smooth, and makes an excellent apéritif. There is live music on weekends.

BUDGET

Strictly for local color, try the immense **Bar e Restaurante Central Natália,** Rua Rarroso 237, at the corner of Saldanha Marinho (tel. 233-8058), a very blue-collar dining spot with live music from Monday to Saturday. The Natália claims to serve a "delicious" feijoada at Saturday lunch. It's open daily from 11am.

GALO CARIJO, Rua dos Andrades 536. Tel. 233-0044.
   Cuisine: SEAFOOD. **Reservations:** Not needed.
$ Prices: Plates $1.50–$4. No credit cards.
   Open: Mon–Sat 11am–11pm.
Right down by the docks, the unadorned Galo Carijo is one of the most popular lunch spots and after-work hangouts in the city. The former status is owing to the inexpensive fish dishes, like the *jaraqui* ($2), a small fish served fried—you eat the whole thing, bones and all. As a café, the Galo Carijo's reputation rests on serving "the coldest beer in town."

RECANTO DA TIA, Rua Ferreira Pena 491. Tel. 234-2206.
   Cuisine: GRILLED MEATS. **Reservations:** Not needed.
$ Prices: Plates $2–$4. No credit cards.
   Open: Mon–Sat 7am–9pm.
The downtown Recanto da Tia is one of the real finds of my recent return to Manaus. The garden/patio atmosphere is extremely pleasant. And while there isn't that much to choose from on the menu, what there is is definitely good chow. I heartily recommend the grilled chicken, a large portion of boneless breast, served with mounds of rice and mashed potatoes ($3.25). A large bottle of beer (80¢) is the perfect accompaniment.

EVENING ENTERTAINMENT

Nightspots come and go with great rapidity in Manaus. Still popular after several years, however, is the supercrowded and very animated **Conciente Bar,** Av. Joaquim Nabuco 1425 (tel. 232-1425), open after 5pm Monday through Saturday, and not winding down until dawn on the weekends. Since it's located on the fringes of the city's red-light district, the streets surrounding the Conciente are a dangerous place to be walking late at night. To get there by cab from the Hotel Amazonas in the heart of the Duty-Free Zone costs about $2—off the meter. During my last visit, two musicians played guitar while singing standards and current hits, and dozens of couples squeezed onto the Conciente's small dance floor. Dozens more sat around small tables, drinking beer and keeping up a steady din of chatter, adding to the very agreeable bistro-style atmosphere.
   Also promising to hang in there for more than one edition of this guide is the brand-new, gigantic **Papagaio,** Estrada da Ponta Negra s/n (tel. 238-2014), right on the beach of the same name, and only a hundred yards or so beyond the gate of the Hotel Tropical. The multileveled environment at the Papagaio caters to a variety of tastes and pocketbooks. A tier of balconies functions as a restaurant, where manager/part owner Ivano Cordeiro (who speaks excellent English, by the way) has inaugurated a menu with some very tasty dishes ($5.25 to $8.25). The rest of the cavernous space, facing a bandstand and an ample dance floor, functions as a

nightclub and disco. The club is open Tuesday to Sunday from 5pm on, with shows Thursday through Saturday; men pay a cover charge of $4.50, women $1.75.

Ury's Bar, Estrada Torquato Tapajós 6100 (no phone), is a more exclusive nightspot on the margins of the city, along one of the roads that leads to the airport. By the look of it, it's a former residence, with a patio and pool behind—which apparently is available to guests sometimes but not others, according to the whims of management. Open Thursday through Saturday from 7pm to 4am, and offering live music.

Every Sunday evening on the **Praça da Saudade,** near the Hotel Mónaco, there is an outdoor fair with impromptu beer gardens mounted under tent tops, craft booths, children's rides, and lots of tempting food stands. Also extremely popular on the weekends is **Paulo's Bar,** Rua Nelson Batista Sales 102 (tel. 244-2479), in the suburb of Conjunto Preto.

EASY EXCURSIONS
A RIVER DAY-TRIP

The eight-hour river excursion organized by **Amazon Explorers,** Rua Quintino Bocaiúva 189 (tel. 092/232-3052), came highly recommended. I boarded the double-decker boat around 8am from the floating pier. (This pier is a considerable engineering accomplishment in itself, for it must not only accommodate many sizes of ships and boats, but also accompany the rise and fall of the river's seasonal water levels.) The company's excursion boat has a top deck, part of which is open to the sun, the other part covered by a permanent roof, with canvas side flaps for nighttime and inclement weather. Down below there is a bar and galley, four heads, and a souvenir stand selling T-shirts, hats, and suntan lotion.

As the boat glides from its slip into the **Rio Negro,** you get your first view of the city from the water. Most of the buildings sit on the high ground, well back from the river embankments. Since the river was low when I made the trip, I could see the outlines of the creeks and the high-water marks on the pilings and stone retaining walls. The shoreline houses (*palafitas*) stand like circus clowns on stilts high above the water. Boats are everywhere on the move, mostly canoes, some propelled by paddles, others by outboard motors. There are also the *barcos regionais,* the typically long and narrow barges with superstructures covering the entire deck. Like so many *Merrimacks,* these floating houses of the river traders seem to ride right on the surface of the water.

For the first few miles as you head downstream, you pass half a dozen giant platforms moored in midstream—floating gas stations. The shore is lined with sawmills; millions of board feet of sawed lumber stockpiled on land, millions more uncut in the form of saw logs floating in the river on the edges of the banks. Roughly an hour later you begin to pick up the silty coloring of the **Rio Solimões** as it joins the dark Rio Negro and flows alongside without mixing, as if each river still occupied its own separate channel: the "living" river and the "dead" river. This "meeting of the waters" stretches on for several miles, until the rivers have finally melded into the yellowish Amazon. But here you reverse course and begin to run up the Solimões, hoping to sight a few dolphins (*botos*) and sure enough—as if responding to a predetermined script—the rose- and gray-colored botos begin to surface and submerge as they accompany the lazy perambulation of the slow-moving boat.

There are several versions of the **legend of the botos.** The one you are most likely to hear is the sentimental myth, packaged for tourist consumption. The sociological version is both more realistic and more disturbing. First the romantic tale: On the nights of the full moon, when there is sure to be some festive celebration in the illuminated villages deep in the forest, the dolphins transform themselves into handsome young men and seduce the young maidens. Pregnancy follows, and the dolphin is held to be the unassailable culprit. The legend may have arisen, social scientists now believe, as a way to explain the high incidence of pregnancy among young girls who most often live in relative isolation from their potential suitors, and who were more likely the victims of incest.

The dolphins also figure in a more naturalistic, and less controversial, theory. All dolphins are believed to have originated as saltwater creatures. Their presence in the fresh water of the Amazon may indicate that South America was two landmasses, and the basin was a sea that once connected the Atlantic and the Pacific.

The vegetation you see along the banks of the Solimões as you sail on for almost two hours is all secondary growth. It can even be said to be sparse in places. You pass no settlements, but there are scattered farms at decent intervals at the edges of the shore. At each of these homesteads, a system of wooden pipes can be seen running from the water and disappearing over the embankment. These are the hollow branches of the *imbambeira,* a deciduous tree, linked together to make a conduit for carrying water to the fields and houses. For any real experience of the dense jungle, it would be necessary to travel many more hours above Manaus, you are told by your guide.

At a clearing where there is a single residence, you make your first stop. Past the dwelling, past a small garden plot where scrawny chickens are scratching the ground, past a few banana and mango trees, you follow a wooden boardwalk into the forest to a platform built over an *igapo,* a creek bed that is permanently flooded. Growing in the water are the giant lily pads, the *Victória régia,* today very much a symbol of the Amazon despite their being named to honor an English monarch. That crackling sound you hear beneath the lilies is the gnawing of piranhas and other small fish that feed on the plants and give them their perforated appearance.

Here, several hundred yards beyond the riverbank, the **jungle** begins to reappear. Wildlife is abundant, especially birds and butterflies. But you can see small alligators as you approach the platform, especially if you are quick of eye, as they slide off the mud banks into the safety of the water. Kingfishers dive for fish. Many other birds—blues, yellows, reds—dart among the branches or bounce along the water's edge as they feed, in what must be a particular treat for bird fanciers familiar with the names and habits of the various species. Flocks of black birds (called *anuns*) flit through the bulrushes and swamp cane as you retrace your steps to the river. When domesticated, they are said to talk as well as parrots.

For your second stop you visit a small village populated by migrants from the northeast. A *caboclo* (rural Brazilian) demonstrates how to tap a rubber tree. He tells you that he goes out at night with a head lantern like a miner's hat and taps all his trees. Then in the morning he gathers up the latex, which is rendered slowly in a little smokehouse over a fire using only green wood. When the substance coagulates, it is joined into large balls called *pelas,* which are collected by boat at riverside, along with the other produce like *cacão, mandioca,* and fruits grown by the little community. The caboclo is also an artisan, and some people buy his model canoes, delicately carved from rose wood. Others buy petrified piranhas or native-style jewelry. You'll walk into the village, a cluster of little wood buildings, including a diminutive clapboard chapel, to look at the cacão trees. The flowers grow almost stemless right from the trunk, and mature into a large green fruit with a funny shape like a pleated balloon. You'll also see the *castanheira* with its coconut-size *ouriço* which when opened expels anywhere from 25 to 30 Brazil nuts.

From here you begin the return trip. Lunch is served on the boat, a delicious home-cooked fish stew and a variety of side dishes. You can drink little cocktails of Amazon fruit juices with cachaça. A while later you stop at a swimming spot and everyone takes a cooling dip in the river, with much giggling and guffawing about the danger of piranhas. In fact, the fierce little fish seldom attacks humans, you are told, but a cow unfortunate enough to fall from a floating pen during the flood season can be consumed in seconds. You are back in Manaus by 3pm. The cost of the excursion is about $34 per person.

INFORMAL DAY-TRIPS

Below the market, on any given day there are dozens of boats tied up along the shore (or at the piers when the water is high) whose owners will take you on the river and cover pretty much the same attractions as the large companies. No lunch is served on these boats and there is no deck to walk around on, but you also aren't required to follow any formal program. The skipper will take you wherever you want to go—and may even have a few suggestions of his own. His fee should be no more than half of what the excursion boats charge.

OVERNIGHT RIVER TRIPS

Dozens of tour operators in Manaus, like **Rio Amazonas Turismo,** Rua Sílva Ramos 20 (tel. 234-7308), offer overnights in the jungle, usually at special "lodges" or "villages," located three to six hours from the city up the Rio Negro. Typically, these excursion packages offer one or two nights in comfortable accommodations, occasionally with hammocks for beds and a variety of daytime and evening programs. These include walks into the jungle, canoe trips up streams and creeks, and an alligator hunt, where flashlights are used to "freeze" the reptiles, which are then captured and released unharmed.

A package of three days and two nights runs from $270 to $320 per person, and two days and one night, from $190 to $260. Cheaper overnights are also available through numerous other tour operators in Manaus. These generally involve accommodations that are considerably more rustic than those offered by operators on the upper end of the market.

THE ARIAU JUNGLE TOWER

Rio Amazonas Turismo, the agency mentioned above, accepts prebooked tours directly up the Rio Negro from Manaus to the Ariau Jungle Tower—an ecologically oriented resort camp located at the junction of the river's main trunk and a tributary called the Ariau. A tour that includes a two-day stay at the "jungle tower" and all transfers leaves from the floating pier in downtown Manaus. The riverboat, aptly named the *Jacques Cousteau,* is a three-decker, complete with lounge and a hot tub-size soaking pool on the forecastle deck. (Manaus is always hot.) The trip upstream takes about four hours. In low-water periods, when the boat can't go all the way up to the hotel, passengers have to wade ashore to a kilometer-long (one-half mile) catwalk of saplings, trunks, and planks that span a marsh to the high ground, a marvel of engineering in the shipwreck tradition of the Swiss Family Robinson. Much of the walkway goes through relatively young woods; although there are few trees of any girth and fewer of any great height, the growth is thick, lush, and fecund.

At a fork in the catwalk is a multileveled tree-house village that blends seamlessly into the greenery, and consciously apes the look of a guerrilla band's clandestine jungle headquarters. The hotel's reception desk is centered on a platform supporting a three-story tower with a dozen guest rooms that overlook the Ariau. As you check in, you are likely to be welcomed with a drink and literally a host of howler and spider monkeys, green parrots, red and blue macaws, and—strangest of all—squeeky little coatis, who cruise the deck like house cats. While the rooms, with narrow bunk beds or double beds (the latter worth insisting on), offer some comforts, nothing at the lodge is really comfortable, nor is it supposed to be. One comes here for a dose of nature, and nature seldom provides much comfort of the domesticated sort. However, tabletop fans provide some relief from the stifling closeness and screens keep the biting insects at bay for the most part. Hot meals are provided as well.

In the afternoon, the tour continues with a trip up the *igarapé* in a shallow-draft skiff, cutting through the thick marsh grasses, scattering birds and nesting fowl, to a "typical house" of a rural river-dwelling family. The straw hut was surrounded by a field of mixed cultivation, with most of it manioc, the root-producing staple of the Amazonian diet. The hut itself is divided into two parts, including a kitchen shed that leans against one exterior wall, with a pit fireplace and mud floor, and a living quarters raised on wood pilings, presumably above the flood line. On my visit, its occupants were absent, but all their household utensils and bedding (hammocks and straw mattresses) were in place and in a nearby shed was the hand-fabricated machinery used in the processing of manioc into flour and tapioca.

The next stop is a settlement where tour members learn about the vegetation and the economy of the folk who live and work in the small community. After a short stop in a favorite cove to watch the incredible Amazonian sunset and dinner at the lodge, a nighttime ride out on the river for an alligator hunt is offered. Each time a critter is captured during the "hunt," it is passed up and down the boat for inspection and then returned to the water unharmed.

The following morning a swim from a sandy bank along the Rio Negro is likely to be planned, and after the noon meal, the tour returns to Manaus.

The tab for this worthwhile adventure is (assuming double occupancy at the lodge) $225 per person for two days and one night and $360 per person for four days and three nights. The single supplement is $25 a night, and children under 12 are half price.

POUSADA DOS GUANAVENAS

This is an independent first-class forest hotel about 150 miles from Manaus. The hotel, which has won several major architectural awards, was completely built with regional materials, and occupies a clearing near the riverbank. To get there, guests first travel to Itacoatiara by bus, and continue on by boat. Guests may also make special arrangements to arrive by seaplane. The hotel offers various packages from three to seven days. Each package includes full board and several guided jungle expeditions. The Guanavenas has offices in Manaus at Rua Ferreira Pena 755 (tel. 092/233-5558). Rates are available on request there or through your travel agent at home.

AN ECOLOGICAL SAFARI

One of the more interesting excursions out of Manaus for the ecologically minded traveler, but suitable for the general public as well, is a seven-day river tour aboard an 80-foot boat called the *Tuna*. The *Tuna* has every comfort, including 10 first-class, double-occupancy, air-conditioned cabins, each with private bath. Other features include a well-equipped kitchen, dining room, lounge, bar, and a library well stocked with titles about the Amazon's ecosystem. The *Tuna* cruises far up the Rio Negro, making calls at several research stations, where there are scientific lectures and videotape presentations. The safari costs $805 per person. A mini-safari of four days is also available for $435.

MORE JUNGLE OVERNIGHTS

Other options for jungle overnights roughly in the same price range as the Ariau Tower are the **Amazon Lodge** and the **Amazon Village,** both reachable in Manaus through **Nature Safaris,** Rua Leonardo Malcher 734 (tel. 092/622-4144; fax 092/622-1420). The lodge complex floats in the middle of Lake Juma, and is the more rustic of the two. The village, slightly pricier, provides the most deluxe digs available for a sojourn in the jungle.

ECOLOGICAL EXPEDITIONS

Now if it's real—or close-to-real—adventure you're after, Nature Safaris has introduced a relatively new excursion package on the travel market (which, along with the Amazon Lodge and Amazon Village, may also be booked in the U.S. through Brazil Nuts at their toll-free number, 800/553-9959). Nature Safaris can take you deep into the Amazon on an eight-day trek they call **Humboldt's Track,** named for the great German naturalist who explored this region from 1799 to 1804. You first embark from Manaus on a three-hour flight over the rain forest to the interior Amazon city of Gabriel da Cachoeira. From there you travel, sometimes by motorized canoe, other times by four-wheel-drive vehicle, to small villages and up obscure channels along the trail Humboldt followed, crossing the equator and visiting the three-nation border of Brazil, Colombia, and Venezuela on the way. This excursion costs $750, plus $350 additional round-trip airfare, and requires both pre- and postnight stays in Manaus (included in the price mentioned above).

Ecotour Expeditions, 39 Mt. Pleasant St., Suite 2 (P.O. Box 1066), Cambridge, MA 02238-1066 (tel. 617/876-5817, or toll free 800/688-1822 outside Massachusetts; fax 617/576-0552), operates expeditions in Brazil that focus on getting as close to the natural setting of the rain forest as possible, as well as on the issues surrounding tropical ecology. Owner Mark Baker offers four itineraries, and leads many of the expeditions himself. All tours are guided by scientist/ecologists, and are exploratory in nature. The characteristic of his tours, Mark says, is that they keep moving, and that each tour is fresh, covering new ground from the one that preceded it. Ecotours, whose maximum group size is 16 persons, attempts to disturb the native inhabitants and their environment as little as possible.

One 10-day itinerary, which costs $1,650 without airfare, but includes most meals, is a camping trip into the rain forest by way of the *igarapés,* the small creeks that line its surface like capillaries. This trip is usually offered between June and September when the rain has stopped, but the water level is still high enough to allow canoe travel within more remote areas of the forest. For information on Ecotours' other offerings, write or call for their brochure.

For those who already find themselves in Manaus, and who want to book a scientifically based tour of the forest, Mark Baker recommends they contact Moacir Fortes, who operates a small company called **Amazônia Expeditions** (tel. 092/232-7492). Writes Baker, "Mo operates his own tours on his own boat, the *Cichla Ocellaris,* the scientific name for the fish tucunaré. His trips are generally a week to 10 days in length, and are exploratory in the same way ours are. He goes into the Solimões and Negro, and wherever he thinks there might be interesting wildlife. Sometimes he has a scientist on board, but usually it is his own knowledge of the region that serves as the program of the trips."

AMAZON PADDLING

Nature Safaris, mentioned above, operates a canoe-and-camping trip into the forest, using the Amazon Lodge as a base. After spending the first night at the lodge, the group departs by canoe and paddles to a predetermined campsite. The second day, you go deeper into the forest, and find a new campsite, which will then serve as a base to explore the surrounding forest for the next two days. All meals are included, and you sleep in tents using special hammocks. The six-day package, including two overnights at the Amazon Lodge, costs $680 per person. Bookings for this tour may be made in the U.S. through Brazil Nuts (tel. toll free 800/553-9959).

Questers Worldwide Nature Tours, 257 Park Ave. South, New York, N.Y. 10010-7369 (tel. 212/673-3120, or toll free 800/468-8668; fax 212/473-0178), offers a comprehensive tour of the Amazon Basin, which departs from Miami four times a year. The first stop on the 16-day trip is Belém. From there the group travels to a buffalo ranch on Marajó by chartered plane. Then it's onward to field trips in Santarém, Manaus, and Iquitos. The 1993 departures are February 21, April 10, July 31, and October 23. The land portion of the tour costs $2,720; airfares are extra.

---

4. RIO BRANCO

870 miles SW of Manaus, 1,200 miles NW of Cuiabá

GETTING THERE   By Plane   The airport is barely 3 miles (5km) from the center of Rio Branco. A cab ride to town should cost you approximately $3.50 to $4. To call a cab from the airport for your return, dial 224-3242.

By Bus or Car   The only real road access is via Porto Velho, from Cuiabá along BR 364, but the only time of year that road travel is recommended is from July to September. The rest of the year the roads are very likely to be washed out by rain.

ESSENTIALS   ACRETUR travel agency, Rua Rui Barbosa 193, in the Rio Branco Hotel (tel. 068/224-2404), offers the following local excursions, among others. (Prices, they say, are negotiable, depending on the size of your group.) A visit to Plácido de Castro, including a boat ride to a working *seringal* (a rubber plantation), costs $100 per person. A visit to the *colônia* of the "five thousand" is $20 per person. A boat ride on the Rio Acre in a native craft called a *batelão* is $50 per person. And a visit to the historical city of Porto Acre—where an adventurer named Galvez once tried to establish an independent republic—is $50 per person. Galvez's story is retold with considerable humor by Brazilian novelist Márcio Souza in *The Emperor of the Amazon,* translated into English and available in paperback by Avon.

Rio Branco is the capital of Acre, a territory turned state in recent times, and one of the more remote corners of the rain forest that you may now visit with relative ease, especially if you take advantage of the Brazilian air pass. The small but tidy city is divided by the Rio Acre into two sections, with the older zone occupying the opposite bank of what is today the city center. Many original wooden houses line the streets of the old section, often in bad repair, and they are being rapidly replaced by dwellings of modern construction, brick walls faced with stucco. The wood houses reminded me of similar structures I'd seen in Paraguay, even to the detail of their faded painted exteriors, with soft colors obviously distilled from natural dyes.

As you wander the old section's streets, you're likely to come across an immense and historic shade tree that marks the site where Rio Branco's first settlers were said to have tied their boats in 1882. A simple snack bar next to the old tree provides a watering spot for visitors, and a place to view the surroundings from a deck overlooking the river.

It should be pointed out that Rio Branco is not yet prepared to accommodate large groups of tourists, especially those who demand international standards in lodgings and services. As a destination, Acre still appeals mostly to backpackers, and to those individuals willing to tolerate plain surroundings, the discomforting presence of exotic insects, and the city's occasionally scalding temperatures.

One perennial attraction of Rio Branco is that the city serves as a jumping-off point for visits to remote frontier towns where Brazil borders Bolivia and Peru. A good asphalt road covers the 56-mile (94-km) distance from Rio Branco to the town of Plácido de Castro on the Bolivian border. There are three buses a day that make the trip there, about two hours in each direction. You might find a cab driver to take you there and back for 400 cruzeiros (about $33). While a travel agency package tour to Plácido de Castro costs $100 per person, it also includes some organized sightseeing, like a boat ride to a rubber plantation, and a guide who can speak at least some halting English—which, of course, the cabbie cannot.

WHAT TO SEE & DO

The most popular "youth culture" excursion from Rio Branco is to the **Comunidade das Cinco Mil** (Community of the Five Thousand), where a religious sect performs a ritual involving the consumption of a psychotropic drug, called *daime*. The ritual traces its origin to an indigenous practice, but the community in question is made up primarily of latter-day Brazilians.

Needless to say, in Brazil the Community of the Five Thousand operates totally within the law, and even maintains a craft booth in downtown Rio Branco at the state sponsored **Fundação Cultural** (Rua Rui Barbosa s/n). Here they sell their own creations—beads, leather goods—mostly quite primitive, but not without their charm, as well as crafts produced by coreligionists from local Native American tribes with whom they maintain close contact.

The daime adherents are willing to accompany strangers to their colônia, only 11 miles (18km) from Rio Branco toward a town called Porto Acre. Interested parties may make all necessary inquiries at the Cultural Foundation craft booth. No fee is charged, but as the group lives communally, you will be expected to share in the costs of food (if you stay the night) and transport through in-kind or cash donations. Every travel agency in Rio Branco also offers a tour excursion to the daime encampment. Or you may go there on your own by public bus to Porto Acre, getting off before that town at a stop known as *o engenho*—the mill—where you leave the asphalt and travel an additional three miles along a dirt road by foot or thumb.

Another excursion the daime group will accompany you on is to an affiliated sect called *O Ceio do Mapiá*, located within a state forest reserve. This trip takes four days during the rainy season, when roads are closed and you must travel by boat the entire distance, or two and a half days in the dry season (June through December), when you travel by road to Boca do Acre (five hours), and from there by boat another two days to Mapiá. Again, there is no charge, but you must share in the expenses and carry any special foods you require, or accept the simple fare of rice, beans, and farofa that form the sectarians' staple diet.

WHERE TO STAY

Rio Branco is not blessed with an abundance of tourist-quality hotels. Those listed below are among the best, however.

PINHEIRO PALACE, Rua Rui Barbosa 38, Rio Branco. Tel. 068/224-7191. Fax 068/224-5726. Telex 68/2546. 42 rms. A/C MINIBAR TV TEL
$ Rates: $24 single; $35 double. AE, DC, MC, V.
Constructed in the late 1980s, the building possesses a distinct architecture, red oversized brick walls with wide pointing spaced between exposed concrete columns and beams. Front rooms have balconies facing this relatively quiet end of Rua Rui Barbosa, and for furnishings, trestle tables with shelves replace the traditional chest of drawers. The beds are standard-size twins, and rooms are fully air conditioned with private baths. Breakfast is served in a wall-enclosed patio and pool area, and the second-floor restaurant here is reputed to be one of the city's finest.

RIO BRANCO HOTEL, Rua Rui Barbosa 193, Rio Branco. Tel. 068/224-1785. Telex 68/2479. 40 rms. A/C MINIBAR TV TEL
$ Rates: $20 single; $30 double. AE, DC, MC, V.
Another hotel, slightly older but quite presentable, is the Rio Branco Hotel, located closer to the city center and around the corner from the principal downtown plaza. The hotel's corridors are nicely, if oddly, decorated with a mixture of local craft objects and old Hollywood posters and memorabilia. Midsized rooms with single beds face the street with small balconies, while larger interior rooms with two twins or double beds.

WHERE TO DINE

ANEXO BAR E RESTAURANTE, Rua Francisco Ribeiro 99. Tel. 224-1396.
Cuisine: INTERNATIONAL. **Reservations:** Not needed.
$ Prices: Appetizers $2–$5; main courses $5.50–$11. No credit cards.
Open: Lunch daily noon–3pm; dinner daily 5–10pm.
This is probably Rio Branco's fanciest restaurant. Crisp white linen covers the country-style antique tables, and service is on the formal side. A meal of chateaubriand, along with beer and coffee, comes to a total of $8.

O CASARÃO, Av. Brasil 110. Tel. 224-4793.
Cuisine: INTERNATIONAL. **Reservations:** Not needed.
$ Prices: Appetizers $2–$3.75; main courses $3.50–$6. No credit cards.
Open: Mon–Fri 7am–midnight, Sat–Sun 7am–3am (lunch served 11am–3pm; dinner served 6pm–10pm; side dishes available until 2am).
Both as an eatery and gathering spot, the most popular restaurant in town is the O Casarão. After Brazil's then foreign minister, the Baron of Rio Branco, purchased Acre from Bolivia at the beginning of this century, the old manse now housing this restaurant was built for the territory's first governor. A cool place to eat at night is on the Casarão's veranda, choosing among any number of relatively simple preparations. Chicken dishes are priced from $3 to $4, meat dishes from $3.50 to $4.50, and fish platters for $2.75 to $4.75. A special *bandeja do dia* (tray of the day), usually rice, beans, and meat, is available for about $2.50. Side dishes range from $2 to $3.75, and I recommend the grilled sausage—*calabreça na chapa*, $2.25 with a tall, cold beer, if you just want a light snack or supper. There is live music from Tuesday through Sunday.

5. THE PANTANAL

Five years ago, only the most committed naturalists and birdwatchers had ever heard of the Pantanal, a vast wildlife preserve occupying segments of two southern Brazilian states as well as sections of two bordering South American nations. **O Grande Pantanal** (the Great Wetlands), as the region is known, stretches over an area roughly 400 miles long and 200 miles wide, forming an ecological bridge among the states of Mato Grosso and Mato Grosso do Sul and the countries of Bolivia and Paraguay. Like the Amazon River Valley, the Pantanal is also a great basin through which numerous rivers drain en route to the Río de la Plata and the Atlantic Ocean to the south. Largest of these is the Rio Paraguay, which forms Brazil's southern frontier with its South American neighbors.

But the comparison with the Amazon stops with this hydrographic analogy. The Pantanal is not a forest but a plain, combining swamps and grazing lands during the dry season, April through November, and largely flooded during the rains, from December through March, when fishing is said to be as good as anywhere on the planet. The region is shared by huge populations of wildlife and the cattle herds belonging to ranchers with spreads of baronial proportions. During the rains, both cattle and wildlife take refuge on the pockets of high ground that are never covered by water. During these days the lion lies down with the lamb. Or more accurately, the jaguar and the deer cohabit in the thick undergrowth of these elevated mounds.

Tourists who visit the Pantanal are often those whose attention has been drawn in recent years to nature and to those conditions that threaten the stability and existence of species and natural habitats. This new consciousness has spawned a generation of amateur naturalists who come to the Pantanal to see the birds—of which there are some 600 species—and the animals like deer, capybaras, monkeys, rheas, alligators, and occasionally the more stealthful jaguar, which is relatively easy to sight on the open terrain. Most tourists come during the dry season, when access to the Pantanal is greatest, unless of course they wish to fish.

To get the most out of your visit to the Pantanal, I would strongly recommend booking a stay at an ecologically oriented ranch through one of the specialty agencies listed in Chapter 2. Below is an account of my own three-day stay at the **Pousada Caiman,** to which the capital city of Mato Grosso do Sul, **Campo Grande,** serves as the gateway. (My experience at this pousada turned out to be the best I have ever had at a Brazilian resort.) Those touring Brazil on a more restricted itinerary, via air pass for example, can still sample the fringes of the Pantanal by stopping over in **Cuiabá,** the capital of Mato Grosso state, and located only 60 miles from the beginning of the **Transpantaneira Highway** (described further on in this chapter).

CAMPO GRANDE

Campo Grande could be thought of as the Omaha of Brazil, a clean, midsize city built in the midst of a vast, flat plain, 2,000 feet above sea level. For many, though, Campo Grande is not a destination in its own right, but a mere stopover en route to an ecological dude ranch near the city of Miranda, another three hour's distance by road travel to the west. Campo Grande, while small and unspectacular, is one of those very livable and comfortable urban centers one is likely to find in prosperous agricultural areas, not unlike its American counterparts in the Midwest. In contrast with Rio Branco, with its precarious ruggedness and pervasive decay typical of a frontier town in the middle of the rain forest, Campo Grande is well kempt and well organized with a more temperate climate.

Avenida Afonso Pena is a wide thoroughfare divided by an ample grass covered median into two opposing lanes of traffic. Lining the stretch of avenue from the airport side of town and the city center, where a skyline of tall buildings can be seen at a mile's distance, are a mixture of homes and enterprises, including private houses, office buildings, high-rise apartments, stores, cafés, and service businesses, like car agencies and lumberyards. The Rua Barão do Rio Branco, which crosses Avenida Calogeras a block in from Afonso Pena, sports a promenade of wide sidewalks with one outdoor café after another for several blocks with only a narrow drive for vehicular traffic.

WHERE TO STAY

FRENÍCIA, Av. Calogeras 2262, Campo Grande. Tel. 067/383-2001. 38 rms. A/C MINIBAR TV TEL
$ Rates: $15–$20 single; $25–$30 double. AE, DC, MC, V.
The Frenícia is a small hotel on the edge of downtown. Clean and moderately priced, it is the kind of old-fashioned lodging favored by commercial travelers who make up the majority of the Frenícia's clientele. This hotel should not be overlooked by travelers looking for inexpensive digs in downtown Campo Grande.

INDAIA PARK HOTEL, Av. Afonso Pena 354, Campo Grande. Tel. 067/384-3858. Fax 067/721-0359. Telex 67/2122. 86 rms. A/C MINIBAR TV TEL

$ Rates: $30 single; $35 double; $40 suite. AE, MC.

Just beyond the Brazilian air force base surrounding Campo Grande's airport is the tourist-class Indaia Park Hotel. With a three-star hotel in Brazil, you take your chances. Depending on age and maintenance, you may find an establishment so classified to be anywhere from very comfortable to very disconcerting. The Indaia is of the former species, a little gem of a hotel, and as the Brazilians say, *com todo o conforto*—it has all the little comforts. The Indaia is also very professionally staffed. Helpful employees are much in evidence at every station of activity from the front desk to the public spaces, where the custodial crew seems in a state of perpetual motion, constantly cleaning and picking up after guests in the hotel's lobby, the pool area, and the restaurant. Rooms, while not splendiferous, are totally acceptable and comfortable in every way. And the hot water in the bathroom is hotter than that at any other provincial Brazilian hotel in which I've ever stayed.

JANDAIA, Rua Barão do Rio Branco, Campo Grande. Tel. 067/382-4081. Fax 067/382-4966. Telex 67/2257. 140 rms. A/C MINIBAR TV TEL

$ Rates: $45 single; $55 double. AE, DC, MC, V.

The Jandaia is a high-rise tower, on a promenade of wide sidewalks with one outdoor café after another and only a narrow drive for vehicular traffic. Various types of suites, from the elegant to the sublime, are available. The hotel offers a swimming pool with a panoramic view and a second-floor restaurant and American bar.

WHERE TO DINE

VITÓRIO'S, Av. Afonso Pena 1907. Tel. 384-5701.
  Cuisine: BARBECUE/INTERNATIONAL. **Reservations:** Not needed.
$ Prices: Appetizers $2–$5.50; main courses $4.50–$12. AE.
  Open: Sun–Thurs 7am–midnight, Fri–Sat 7am–2am.

Located downtown, Vitório's is a large continental café and steakhouse where live music, often Paraguayan, is played nightly from 7pm till midnight. Vitório's claims to be *O Rei do Picanha* (King of Flank Steak), and the mixed grill of barbecued meats, impaled on a skewer, comes to table on its own stand; the price, around $5.50.

THE PANTANAL & THE POUSADA CAIMAN RANCH

Transportation to the **Pousada Caiman** from Campo Grande, with a stop at the airport (often entailing a wait for guests arriving on various flights), is provided by the ranch's air-conditioned, 12-seat supervan. The landscape just outside Campo Grande is flat, and relatively featureless, spotted here and there with trees, but mostly fields in cultivation. Cattle ranching is in evidence everywhere. After about an hour's driving, the terrain transforms into a scene more or less resembling the American Southwest, in the sense that the low ground alternates frequently with monumental mounds, carved from some early geological formation by the forces of erosion. After the municipality of Anastácio, the *paisagem*, the landscape, changes again. There are no plantings visible, and fewer cattle. A thick wooded growth replaces the scrub and grasslands. Tall trees appear as you enter the partially forested lands of the southern Pantanal. Turning from the highway, a hard-packed road of reddened earth runs for about 36km (22 miles) past vast pastures with skinny white zebra cattle to the Pousada Caiman ranch.

The ranch occupies about one fourth of what had been a gigantic estate covering over half a million acres, and all the land still belongs to various branches of the same family. Past a wide wooden gate like the kind one has seen in a hundred cowboy movies, the commonplace of pasturelands was transformed into a dramatic passage for a mile or more beneath a tunnel of arching vegetation leading to a line of simple, semiattached cottages that housed cowpokes and their families, your first indication that the Pousada Caiman is a working ranch.

The lodge, a pink-tinted, horseshoe-shaped hacienda—while very much a ranchhouse—verges on the grand. The main public room, with its high cathedral ceiling and many sparkling rural artifacts, is a cross between a living room and a hotel lobby. Twelve guest rooms bordered by a covered cloister where hammocks hang before each door, ring the inner courtyard, at the center of which is a large swimming pool. As for the rooms, they are quite fancy and spacious, about 12 by 12 feet, and have two sets of shuttered windows, one facing the courtyard, the other an exterior garden, where the grounds are planted with beautiful shade trees.

The welcoming dinner I enjoyed was an excellent meal of rolled beef, mashed potatoes, rice, beans, and mixed salad—along with two bottles of good Brazilian red wine.

A MORNING ON HORSEBACK The first morning of my stay, we were awakened by the fierce clang of a bell at 6:15am, and were served a hearty breakfast. At 7:30am sharp—for everything here runs on an exact timetable, and as such is very un-Brazilian—we walked into the entry yard where a troop of horses was already awaiting us, tied to a long hitching post. Our guide for the morning, Antônio—like all the young people who were to accompany us here on our treks—had a college science degree, zoology and husbandry in his case.

The heat had already begun to rise off the moist grasslands, as we rode single file up a road that lead to certain far-flung pastures. Thanks to an overnight shower, a dozen varieties of wild flowers were scattered along the embankment.

By nine, we had seen two dozen bird species, including a comic toucan who streaked through the sky like a cartoon bird imitating a rocket ship. An enormous pair of *jaburu* storks with their black heads like executioners' masks, red swollen necks, and fat white bodies, eyed us cautiously from a puddle where they stood feeding. A partial listing of the ornithological roll call for that morning, included the *chaco chachalaca*, the southern screamer, the limpkin, the plumbeous ibis, the green ibis, the *jacana*, the wood stork, the snowy egret, the tiger heron, the black-bellied whistling duck, not to mention thick flights of parrots, blue and red macaws, and dozens of smaller birds. These were among the bird species we see over and over during the next two days. But we are also fortunate in our sightings of mammals, including a *tatu*, a kind of armadillo, and a white-lipped peccary, a species of wild pig.

AN AFTERNOON SAFARI Around three that afternoon, following another magnificent meal, and a couple of hours for rest or lounging around the pool, we set out again, this time by truck. Soon after leaving the populated zone of the ranch, with the help of our binoculars we immediately spot a variety of game in the fields: first a few tiny marsh deer; then a pair of long-legged rheas trucking for all they were worth to put some distance between us and them; and finally a family of pampas deer grazing in a far-off grove. Again, we saw marsh birds in abundance, ambling amid the swamp grass with no more apparent aim than inmates on the grounds of a madhouse. We also spooked a great flock of metallic blue macaws from their favorite pair of trees, and then stopped to watch two large storks perched on the lip of their giant nest built high in a tree and measuring about six feet in diameter and three feet in depth.

At a predetermined spot, we left the truck and walked into the woods among hordes of mosquitoes. Our mission now was to find monkeys, and we soon did. A half-dozen howlers looked down at us from the highest branches of a very tall tree, and made halfhearted territorial noises as we craned our necks below trying to keep them in view. Coming out of the woods, we approached a large watering hole encircled by more than a hundred crocodiles, most of whom posed frozen-still and slack-jawed on the shore like plastic lawn ornaments. Only when one of us walked to within 10 feet of an individual animal, would it spring to life, and waddle into the water, to join with many other pairs of floating eyes.

On our way back to the lodge, we continued to scan the horizon for animals and birds, usually spotting some new wildlife species and I pointed out a pack of wild dogs foraging in the earth for fallen fruit at the base of a distant tree. Enthralled by the stunning sunset, we arrived at the front yard of the pousada, thrilled with every aspect of the Pousada Caiman.

THE SECOND DAY The second day was in essence a repeat of the first. Our morning expedition was by truck, and in the afternoon we went by boat along the

Aquidauana River that runs through the ranch. On both occasions we saw many more animals and birds, and the shutterbugs among us were fully sated with photo opportunities. After the luncheon meal, a churrasco, we visited a modest museum in the courtyard to see a display of some of the area's varied natural history.

In all, I feel the Pousada Caiman gets rave reviews for having delivered at least as much as it promised, and much more than I expected. The double-occupancy cost is $150 per night per person; single occupancy is $175 per night, including all meals and transfers. You may book directly through **Roberto Klabin Hoteis e Turismo,** Rua Pedroso Alvarenga 1208, São Paulo (tel. 011/883-6566), or through any of several agencies listed in Chapter 2.

CUIABÁ

The capital of Mato Grosso grew up as a gold-rush town during the 1700s and remained relatively undeveloped until recently, when agricultural prosperity in the state transformed Cuiabá from a frontier town to a modern city. In the process the town lost most of its character and charm, and cannot be considered a destination in and of itself. It's not, however, a bad place to hang out for a couple of days, and to use as a base for a few brief forays into the nearby countryside, including the edges of the Pantanal.

When it is finished, the traveler will be able to visit much of the Pantanal on the **Transpantaneira,** a raised dirt highway that spans much of the wetlands from Poconé, a historical city 60 miles from the river city of Cuiabá, the capital of Mato Grosso on the border with Bolivia.

The state tourist office, **Turismat,** is located on the Praça da República 131 (tel. 065/322-5363).

WHERE TO STAY
Moderate

AÚREA PALACE HOTEL, Rua General Melo 63, Cuiabá. Tel. 065/322-3377. Telex 65/2476. 78 rms. A/C MINIBAR TV TEL
$ **Rates:** $38 single; $44 double. AE, DC, MC, V.
In addition to the Mato Grosso Palace, the town's other four-star establishment is the Aúrea Palace. The hotel has some character, but the rooms here are small, as are the beds, and the whole place could use a paint job. There is a small pool on ground level.

MATO GROSSO PALACE HOTEL, Rua Joaquim Murtilho 170, Cuiabá. Tel. 065/322-9254. Telex 65/3156. 149 rms. A/C MINIBAR TV TEL
$ **Rates:** $60–$65 standard room; $70–$75 deluxe room. AE, DC, MC, V.
The four-star Mato Grosso Palace Hotel, one of the best in Cuiabá, is located around the corner from the city's principal square, the Praça da República. The Palace Hotel has very comfortable rooms and other facilities, like a restaurant and bar, but no swimming pool.

Budget

HOTEL MATO GROSSO, Rua Comandante Costa 2522, Cuiabá. Tel. 065/321-9121. 63 rms. MINIBAR TEL
$ **Rates:** $7–$13 room with fan; $8–$14 room with A/C; $10–$15 room with A/C and TV. AE, MC, V.
The interior of this hotel is interesting in that the rooms are off an open-air corridor, which aids in ventilation. The Mato Grosso also has a very simple restaurant, serving rooming-house quality meals at low prices. Anyone traveling the Pantanal on their own (without the benefit of a prepaid package with accommodations included) would find this an ideal place to spend an overnight in Cuiabá while in transit.

WHERE TO DINE

RESTAURANTE O REGIONALÍSSIMO, Rua 13 de Julho, at the corner of Rua Senador Metello. Tel. 322-3908.
  Cuisine: REGIONAL. **Reservations:** Not needed.
$ **Prices:** Buffet $6. No credit cards.

Open: Lunch Tues–Sun 11:30am–2:30pm; dinner Tues–Sun 7:30–11pm.
This restaurant is located in the Casa do Artesão, the city's restored colonial jail house, now a center for some of the best crafts to be found anywhere in Brazil. The state of Mato Grosso has a large Native American population, and much of the work in clay and straw comes from the hands of these artisans. The restaurant, which occupies the ground floor of the building, serves a tasty feijoada on Saturday, Mato Grosso style, including unique side dishes like *farofa de banana,* and for dessert, *doce de limão,* a compote of lime peels and sugar. The cost is about $6.

EASY EXCURSIONS

Two colonial-era towns not far from Cuiabá retain much of their old-fashioned charm. One is **Chapada de Guimarães,** the geodesic center of South America and gateway to the stunning tablelands that begin some 40 miles from the capital; the other is **Poconé,** entry point to the Transpantaneira Highway about 60 miles to the south of Cuiabá. Both places would be excellent locales for stays of indeterminate duration for those who are seeking the authenticity and quietude of small-town life in the Brazilian interior. Both are served by several country-style hotels and pensions. The main attraction around Guimarães is the rolling landscape, which is excellent for camping or hiking. From Poconé, of course, you enter the Pantanal.

There is a checkpoint at the beginning of the Transpantaneira where a guard will hand you a brochure explaining the ground rules of a visit to the preserve. You read, for example, that there is absolutely no hunting allowed. Indeed, there would be little sport in the hunt, especially for the *jacaré* (alligators), large numbers of which sunbathe in streams by the sides of the highway. The road itself is wide, and of a rough dirt surface. Every mile, or so it seems, you cross a rude bridge of planks over the endless arroyos and streams that carry the seasonal rains to the larger rivers that are also plentiful throughout the area. Already a few miles within the great marsh, you sight a dozen bird species, including the emblematic bird of the Pantanal, the *tuiuiu,* a red-collared white stork with a jet-black bill and a six-foot wingspan.

ALTA FLORESTA

Situated in the highlands of the Amazon Basin, about 475 miles from Cuiabá on the border of Mato Grosso and Pará states, is the town of Alta Floresta. The forest in this region sits on terra firma, and is said to be both lush and ancient. A new, first-class lodge with an extensive ecological program has been opened near this remote agricultural center.

The **Floresta Amazônica Hotel,** Av. Perimetral Oeste 2001 (tel. 065/521-3601; telex 65/5145), appears every bit as comfortable as the Pousada Caiman described above. The hotel offers a six-day, five-night package, which includes two overnights at the **Cristalino Jungle Lodge,** located in the 20 million-acre Cristalino Forest Reserve. Activities include hiking on jungle trails, canoe and motorboat excursions, and treetop observation of native fauna. The price per person, based on double occupancy, is $425, all meals included. To arrive at Alta Floresta, you have two options. The first is by regularly scheduled flight on TABA airlines from Cuiabá or Belém; the second is by bus from Cuiabá. The bus company is **Viação Satelite** (tel. 065/624-3156).

OTHER SUGGESTIONS FOR TOURING THE PANTANAL

Several tour operators specialize in packages to the Pantanal. See Chapter 2 for more information. Two typical tours offered by **Brazil Nuts** are:

- **The Ecological Triangle.** A five-day tour that includes three nights on a riverboat, the *Pantanal Explorer.* The cost, including overnight in Cuiabá, is $560 per person.
- **Jeep Safari.** This four-day tour drives the length of the Transpantaneira Highway, and stays in a different lodge every night along the route. Cost is $425 per person.

USEFUL WORDS & PHRASES IN BRAZILIAN PORTUGUESE

A. PRONUNCIATION GUIDE
B. VOCABULARY
C. MENU TERMS

Obviously, a mere vocabulary list at the end of a travel guide can give only limited insight into a foreign tongue, especially one as unfamiliar to most English speakers as Brazilian Portuguese. For both practical and cultural reasons, however, it is worth the traveler's while to bone up a bit on Portuguese before visiting Brazil. Few Brazilians outside the tourist orbit speak English. And even then the level of fluency is very uneven. There are times, moreover, in any foreign locale when the best way to get your point across is in *their* language rather than your own. But even more important to the success of your Brazilian adventure are the points you score by extending yourself—making an effort to communicate in the host language. Such efforts, even when only symbolic, can go a long way toward neutralizing cultural chauvinism and smoothing the way for you, especially in cases where English may be resented as much as it is spoken.

A. PRONUNCIATION GUIDE

The following notes on pronunciation are meant as a bridge—a few sturdy planks—across what may at first appear a language gap too wide to span. Both English and Portuguese writing systems use the Roman alphabet (the ABCs). But the two languages sometimes apply very different sound values to the same letters. Some of these major distinctions are described below.

VOWELS

As in the case with English and other Western languages, Portuguese uses the five vowel *symbols* provided by the alphabet to represent more than five distinct vowel *sounds*. An *o* in Portuguese can stand for two very different sounds in words that are spelled the same except for their accents. For example, *avô*, with the o sound similar to "row," means grandfather, while *avó*, with the sound of the *ou* in "cough," means grandmother. And though the words *céu* (sky, heaven) and *seu* (the pronoun "your" in its masculine singular form) are not written the same way, their *e* sounds are also pronounced differently. The *e* in *céu* is similar to that of the word "bet," as is also the case of the *e* in *café*. One of the easiest ways to pinpoint an American accent in Portuguese is when you hear someone pronounce *café* where that *e* sounds like the *ai* in "bait." *Seu*, on the other hand, *is* pronounced with the *ai* sound as in the word "bait."

Portuguese makes liberal use of **nasal vowels,** indicated either by the presence of a tilde, as in *lã* (wool) or an *m*, as in *bém* (well). (That *m* becomes an *n* when the word is pluralized, as in *bens*—worldly goods—but it remains a nasal vowel.) The proper pronunciation is a lot closer to "bangs" than to "Ben's." The way this sound is made in the mouth is similar to how we make the *ng* sound in English, as in the word "sing." In the case of the nasal vowel, however, the tongue does not make contact with the roof of the mouth, and the air from the sound escapes through the nostrils, not from between the lips. The letters **ng** will be used to indicate the approximate pronunciation of Portuguese words using nasal vowels in the vocabulary list that follows. To get the correct sound in Portuguese, however, start out as if you were going to pronounce an *ng* sound. Then tense the tongue and don't let it touch the top of your mouth. It's easy.

The **nasal diphthong** (a diphthong is a pair of vowels together) is also common in Portuguese, as in the words *pão* (bread), *cidadão* (citizen), and *não* (no). The sound is like that of "cow"—but nasalized. To practice the sound, try adding an *ng* to "cow" and you'll come close. Other common nasal diphthongs are *ãe*, as in the proper name Magalhães (Magellan's real name!), and *õe*, as in *ladrões* (thieves). The *ãe* is pronounced like the affirmation "aye" and the *õe* like the sound in "boy"—but remember that both are nasalized.

The vowel *o* when occurring at the end of a word, even when pluralized, sounds like the *oo* in "moo." Thus Rio is pronounced "*Ree*-oo," as in the vowels of "tree" and "zoo." The vowel *e* in word final position is pronounced like *ee* as in "knee." Thus *bife* (beef) is pronounced "*bee*-fee," as in the vowels of "bee" and "fee." There are two exceptions to this rule. The first is when an *o* or *e* at the end of a word receives the stress, for example in accented words like *café* or *avô*. The other is when someone is speaking with artificial formality. We do this in English too, when we pronounce "the" like "thee," rather than the way we say it in normal, unself-conscious speech, with the same sound as in the word "love."

CONSONANTS

The **c cedilla** is pronounced like a soft *s* as in the word *praça* ("*prah*-sa").

Cariocas (natives of Rio) pronounce the letters *t* and *d* that precede the vowels *e* and *i* like *ch* and *j*. The pronunciation can be illustrated with a single word, *diferente* (different), which is pronounced "jiff-eh-*rehn*-chee."

Portuguese has several ways to represent the **sh** sound, like *ch* in "Chico" (the diminutive of Francisco), which is pronounced "*She*-coo." The *sh* sound is also represented in Portuguese by the letter *x*, as in *Mexico,* pronounced "*Meh*-she-coo." In fact, practically any *s* preceded by a vowel and followed by a consonant is shush-ed in the Carioca dialect, as in *as casas* (the houses), pronounced "ahsh *cahz*-ahss."

The letter *j* in Portuguese has the same sound as the second syllable of the words "measure" or "pleasure," represented by the letters *su;* or as the *zs* in the name Zsa Zsa. This is not a sound that normally occurs in beginnings of words in English.

A **single r** in Portuguese is flapped, as in Spanish. If you say the word "fodder" fast, the double *d* is close to the Portuguese single *r*. The **double r,** or the *r* at the beginning of a word followed by a vowel, in Brazilian Portuguese is generally pronounced like our English *h*. Thus *carro* (car) is pronounced "*cah*-who," and Rio is actually pronounced "*Hee*-yoo." In some parts of Brazil, as in Portugal, the double *r* or single initial *r* is trilled, the way upper-class British pronounce the *r*.

Portuguese, like Spanish and Italian, has a **nya** sound, represented by *nh* as in *piranha*, pronounced "pee-*rahn*-ya," and a **lya** sound represented by *lh*, as in *brilhante* (brilliant), pronounced "bril-*yahn*-chee."

There are many more subtleties to Brazilian speech patterns than can be outlined in these brief introductory comments. With these hints in mind, however, you will have the key to some pronunciations that appear all the more puzzling when you compare them with the written word. After that, the best guide to pronouncing and understanding Portuguese will be your own ear.

B. VOCABULARY

Good morning	**Bom dia**	bong *gee*-ya
Good night	**Boa noite**	bwa *noy*-chee
How are you?	**Como vai?**	*coh*-moo vai
Everything ok?	**Tudo bem?**	*too*-doo bang
fine, great	**tudo bem**	*too*-doo bang
Let's get going	**Vamos embora**	*vah*-moose eng-*boh*-rah
bye	**tchau**	chow
so long	**até logo**	ah-*teh loh*-goo
What time is it?	**Que horas são?**	key *oh*-rass sowng
It's (five) o'clock	**são (cinco) horas**	sowng *seeng*-coo *oh*-rass
How much is . . . ?	**Quanto é . . . ?**	qwahn-too eh . . . ?
Where are you going?	**Onde vai?**	*own*-gee vai
Where is . . . ?	**Onde esta . . . ?**	*own*-gee eh-*stah*
the subway	**o metrô**	oo meh-*troe*
the bathroom	**o banheiro**	oo bahn-*yay*-roo
the room	**o quarto**	oo *qwahr*-too
the meal	**a comida**	ah coe-*me*-dah
I want . . .	**Quero . . .**	*care*-roo . . .
I would like . . .	**Queria . . .**	care-*ree*-ah . . .
Pardon me	**Com licença**	cong lee-*sehn*-sa
Excuse me	**Desculpe**	desh-*cul*-pee
yes	**é**	eh
no	**não**	now
I don't know	**Não sei**	now say
Do you know?	**Você sabe?**	voe-*say sah*-bee
please	**faz favor**	fayz fah-*vohr*
thank you (male)	**Obrigado**	owe-bree-*gah*-doo
thank you (female)	**Obrigada**	owe-bree-*gah*-dah
Do you have . . . ?	**Tem . . . ?**	tang . . . ?
I don't speak . . .	**Não falo . . .**	now *fah*-loo . . .
Do you speak . . . ?	**Você fala . . . ?**	voe-*say fah*-lah . . .
Portuguese	**português**	poor-too-*gays*
English	**inglês**	eeng-*glays*

MORE VOCABULARY

For the words that follow, unless otherwise noted, adjectives are shown in their masculine singular form. Since, in general, an adjective must agree with the noun it modifies in both gender and number, masculine adjectives ending in o become feminine adjectives by changing the o to a, and are pluralized by adding s to the masculine or feminine singular form. The adjectives ending in e are the same for masculine and feminine, and are pluralized by adding s.

N.B: The double oo in my phonetic transcription has the same value as the vowels in such diversely spelled English words as boo, Lew, two, true, and you. I will on occasion insert these other spellings to avoid any possible ambiguity.

the (masc. sing., plural)	**o, os**	oo, oos
the (fem. sing., plural)	**a, as**	ah, ahs
a (masc., fem.)	**um, uma**	oong, *oo*-mah
some (masc., fem.)	**uns, umas**	oongs, *oo*-mahs
good (masc., fem.)	**bon, boa**	bong, *bow*-ah
bad (masc., fem.)	**mal, mala**	mao, *mah*-lah
cheap	**barato**	bah-*rah*-too
expensive	**caro**	*cah*-roo
old	**velho**	*vehl*-yoo

new	**novo**	*no*-voo
big	**grande**	*grahn*-gee
small	**pequeno**	peh-*kay*-noo
early	**cedo**	*ceh*-doo
late	**tarde**	*tahr*-gee
hot	**quente**	*ken*-chee
cold	**frio**	*free*-you
left	**esquerda**	esh-*care*-dah
right	**direita**	gee-*ray*-tah
straight ahead	**em frente**	ang *fren*-chee
here	**aquí**	ah-*key*
there	**aí**	Ah-*ee*
over there	**alí**	ah-*lee*
yonder	**lá**	lah
today	**hoje**	O zsee (like Zsa Zsa)
yesterday	**ontem**	*ong*-tang
tomorrow	**amanhã**	ah-mahn-*yah* (nasal)
the day	**o dia**	oo *gee*-yah
the week	**a semana**	ah seh-*mahn*-ah
the weekend	**o fim de semana**	oo fing gee . . .
the year	**a ano**	oo *ah*-noo
the month	**o mês**	oo mace
Monday	**segunda-feira**	say-*goon*-dah *fay*-rah
Tuesday	**terca-feira**	*tare*-sah . . .
Wednesday	**quarta-feira**	*kwah*-tah
Thursday	**quinta-feira**	*keen*-tah
Friday	**sexta-feira**	*saysh*-tah . . .
Saturday	**sabado**	*sah*-bah-doo
Sunday	**domingo**	doe-*ming*-goo

1	**um/uma** (oong/*oo*-mah)	15	**quinze** (*keen*-zee)	60	**seissenta** (say-*sehn*-tah)
2	**dois/duas** (doysh/*doo*-ash)	16	**dezesseis** (dez-ah-*saysh*)	70	**setenta** (say-*tehn*-tah)
3	**três** (traysh)	17	**dezessete** (dez-ah-*seh*-chee)	80	**oitenta** (oy-*tenh*-tah)
4	**quatro** (*qwah*-true)	18	**dezoito** (dez-*oy*-too)	90	**noventa** (no-*venh*-tah)
5	**cinco** (*sing*-coo)	19	**dezenove** (dez-ah-*no*-vee)	100	**cem** (sang)
6	**seis** (*saysh*)	20	**vinte** (*vean*-chee)	101	**cento e um** (*senh*-too ee oong)
7	**sete** (*seh*-chee)	21	**vinte e um** (*vean*-chee-oong)		
8	**oito** (*oy*-two)	30	**trinta** (*treen*-tah)	500	**quinhenta** (keen-*yehn*-tah)
9	**nove** (*no*-vee)	40	**quarenta** (qwa-*renh*-tah)	1,000	**mil** (mil)
10	**dez** (daysh)	50	**cinquenta** (sing-*qwen*-tah)	10,000	**dez mil** (daysh mil)
11	**onze** (*own*-zee)				
12	**doze** (*doe*-zee)				
13	**treze** (*treh*-zee)				
14	**quatorze** (qwa-*tor*-zee)				

C. MENU TERMS

And now, here's a very brief guide to some of the menu terms you will probably encounter as you eat your way around Brazil.

FOOD & DRINK

a comida the food/meal
a bebida the drink

o cardápio/menu the menu
a conta the bill

a nota the receipt
mal passado rare
bem passado well done
ao ponto medium
o gelo the ice
a agua mineral the mineral water
com gas carbonated
sem gas regular

a refrigerante soda pop
a chá the tea
o café the coffee
o leite the milk
o vinho the wine
tinto red
branco white
a cerveja the beer

MEATS

carne meat
bife beef
carneiro lamb
porco pork
frango chicken
galinha chicken
costeletas chops

coelho rabbit
bode goat
peru turkey
presunto ham
linguiça sausage
vitela veal

SEAFOOD

peixe fish
frutos do mar seafood
bacalhau codfish
linguado sole
lagosta lobster
camarão shrimp

lula squid
polvo octopus
ostras oysters
siri crab
caranguejo marsh crab

SIDE DISHES, CONDIMENTS & DESSERTS

pão bread
manteiga butter
queijo cheese
sopa soup
canja chicken soup
sobremesa dessert
ovos eggs
bacon bacon
sal salt

pimenta do reino pepper
mostarda mustard
açúcar sugar
sanduiche sandwich
molho sauce
torrada toast
azeite oil
de azeitona olive oil
vinagre vinegar

VEGETABLES

batata potato
puré mashed potatoes
batatas fritas french fries
batata doce sweet potato
salada mixta mixed salad
alface lettuce
tomate tomato
alho garlic
pepino cucumber

cenoura carrot
legumes vegetables
vagens green beans
ervilhas peas
feijão preto black beans
cebola onion
azeitona olive
arroz rice
champignon mushrooms

FRUITS

limão lemon/lime
maça apple
abacaxi pineapple
melancia watermelon
melão melon
morangos strawberries
pera pear

pêssego peach
uvas grapes
cerejas cherries
figos figs
suco juice
suco de laranja orange juice

INDEX

GENERAL INFORMATION

DESTINATIONS

KEY TO ABBREVIATIONS: *B* = Budget; *E* = Expensive; *M* = Moderately priced; *R* = Reader's
recommendation; *VE* = Very Expensive; *YH* = Youth Hostel; *$* = Super-Value Choice; *** = Author's Favorite

Please Send Me the Books Checked Below

FROMMER'S COMPREHENSIVE GUIDES
(Guides listing facilities from budget to deluxe, with emphasis on the medium-priced)

	Retail Price	Code		Retail Price	Code
☐ Acapulco/Ixtapa/Taxco 1993–94	$15.00	C120	☐ Jamaica/Barbados 1993–94	$15.00	C105
☐ Alaska 1990–91	$15.00	C001	☐ Japan 1992–93	$19.00	C020
☐ Arizona 1993–94	$18.00	C101	☐ Morocco 1992–93	$18.00	C021
☐ Australia 1992–93	$18.00	C002	☐ Nepal 1992–93	$18.00	C038
☐ Austria 1993–94	$19.00	C119	☐ New England 1993	$17.00	C114
☐ Austria/Hungary 1991–92	$15.00	C003	☐ New Mexico 1993–94	$15.00	C117
☐ Belgium/Holland/ Luxembourg 1993–94	$18.00	C106	☐ New York State 1992–93	$19.00	C025
			☐ Northwest 1991–92	$17.00	C026
☐ Bermuda/Bahamas 1992–93	$17.00	C005	☐ Portugal 1992–93	$16.00	C027
			☐ Puerto Rico 1993–94	$15.00	C103
☐ Brazil, 3rd Edition	$20.00	C111	☐ Puerto Vallarta/Manzanillo/ Guadalajara 1992–93	$14.00	C028
☐ California 1993	$18.00	C112			
☐ Canada 1992–93	$18.00	C009	☐ Scandinavia 1993–94	$19.00	C118
☐ Caribbean 1993	$18.00	C102	☐ Scotland 1992–93	$16.00	C040
☐ Carolinas/Georgia 1992–93	$17.00	C034	☐ Skiing Europe 1989–90	$15.00	C030
☐ Colorado 1993–94	$16.00	C100	☐ South Pacific 1992–93	$20.00	C031
☐ Cruises 1993–94	$19.00	C107	☐ Spain 1993–94	$19.00	C115
☐ DE/MD/PA & NJ Shore 1992–93	$19.00	C012	☐ Switzerland/Liechtenstein 1992–93	$19.00	C032
☐ Egypt 1990–91	$15.00	C013	☐ Thailand 1992–93	$20.00	C033
☐ England 1993	$18.00	C109	☐ U.S.A. 1993–94	$19.00	C116
☐ Florida 1993	$18.00	C104	☐ Virgin Islands 1992–93	$13.00	C036
☐ France 1992–93	$20.00	C017	☐ Virginia 1992–93	$14.00	C037
☐ Germany 1993	$19.00	C108	☐ Yucatán 1993–94	$18.00	C110
☐ Italy 1993	$19.00	C113			

FROMMER'S $-A-DAY GUIDES
(Guides to low-cost tourist accommodations and facilities)

	Retail Price	Code		Retail Price	Code
☐ Australia on $45 1993–94	$18.00	D102	☐ Mexico on $50 1993	$19.00	D105
☐ Costa Rica/Guatemala/ Belize on $35 1993–94	$17.00	D108	☐ New York on $70 1992–93	$16.00	D016
			☐ New Zealand on $45 1993–94	$18.00	D103
☐ Eastern Europe on $25 1991–92	$17.00	D005	☐ Scotland/Wales on $50 1992–93	$18.00	D019
☐ England on $60 1993	$18.00	D107			
☐ Europe on $45 1993	$19.00	D106	☐ South America on $40 1993–94	$19.00	D109
☐ Greece on $45 1993–94	$19.00	D100			
☐ Hawaii on $75 1993	$19.00	D104	☐ Turkey on $40 1992–93	$22.00	D023
☐ India on $40 1992–93	$20.00	D010	☐ Washington, D.C. on $40 1992–93	$17.00	D024
☐ Ireland on $40 1992–93	$17.00	D011			
☐ Israel on $45 1993–94	$18.00	D101			

FROMMER'S CITY $-A-DAY GUIDES
(Pocket-size guides with an emphasis on low-cost tourist accommodations and facilities)

	Retail Price	Code		Retail Price	Code
☐ Berlin on $40 1992–93	$12.00	D002	☐ Madrid on $50 1992–93	$13.00	D014
☐ Copenhagen on $50 1992–93	$12.00	D003	☐ Paris on $45 1992–93	$12.00	D018
			☐ Stockholm on $50 1992–93	$13.00	D022
☐ London on $45 1992–93	$12.00	D013			

FROMMER'S TOURING GUIDES

(Color-illustrated guides that include walking tours,
cultural and historic sights, and practical information)

	Retail Price	Code		Retail Price	Code
☐ Amsterdam	$11.00	T001	☐ New York	$11.00	T008
☐ Barcelona	$14.00	T015	☐ Rome	$11.00	T010
☐ Brazil	$11.00	T003	☐ Scotland	$10.00	T011
☐ Florence	$ 9.00	T005	☐ Sicily	$15.00	T017
☐ Hong Kong/Singapore/	$11.00	T006	☐ Thailand	$13.00	T012
Macau			☐ Tokyo	$15.00	T016
☐ Kenya	$14.00	T018	☐ Venice	$ 9.00	T014
☐ London	$13.00	T007			

FROMMER'S FAMILY GUIDES

	Retail Price	Code		Retail Price	Code
☐ California with Kids	$17.00	F001	☐ San Francisco with Kids	$17.00	F004
☐ Los Angeles with Kids	$17.00	F002	☐ Washington, D.C. with Kids	$17.00	F005
☐ New York City with Kids	$18.00	F003			

FROMMER'S CITY GUIDES

(Pocket-size guides to sightseeing and tourist accommodations
and facilities in all price ranges)

	Retail Price	Code		Retail Price	Code
☐ Amsterdam 1993–94	$13.00	S110	☐ Miami 1993–94	$13.00	S118
☐ Athens, 9th Edition	$13.00	S114	☐ Minneapolis/St. Paul, 3rd	$13.00	S119
☐ Atlanta 1993–94	$13.00	S112	Edition		
☐ Atlantic City/Cape May 1991–92	$ 9.00	S004	☐ Montréal/Québec City 1993–94	$13.00	S125
☐ Bangkok 1992–93	$13.00	S005	☐ New Orleans 1993–94	$13.00	S103
☐ Barcelona/Majorca/ Minorca/Ibiza 1993–94	$13.00	S115	☐ New York 1993	$13.00	S120
			☐ Orlando 1993	$13.00	S101
☐ Berlin 1993–94	$13.00	S116	☐ Paris 1993–94	$13.00	S109
☐ Boston 1993–94	$13.00	S117	☐ Philadelphia 1993–94	$13.00	S113
☐ Cancún/Cozumel/Yucatán 1991–92	$ 9.00	S010	☐ Rio 1991–92	$ 9.00	S029
			☐ Rome 1993–94	$13.00	S111
☐ Chicago 1993–94	$13.00	S122	☐ Salt Lake City 1991–92	$ 9.00	S031
☐ Denver/Boulder/Colorado Springs 1990–91	$ 8.00	S012	☐ San Diego 1993–94	$13.00	S107
			☐ San Francisco 1993	$13.00	S104
☐ Dublin 1993–94	$13.00	S128	☐ Santa Fe/Taos/Albuquerque 1993–94	$13.00	S108
☐ Hawaii 1992	$12.00	S014			
☐ Hong Kong 1992–93	$12.00	S015	☐ Seattle/Portland 1992–93	$12.00	S035
☐ Honolulu/Oahu 1993	$13.00	S106	☐ St. Louis/Kansas City 1993–94	$13.00	S127
☐ Las Vegas 1993–94	$13.00	S121			
☐ Lisbon/Madrid/Costa del Sol 1991–92	$ 9.00	S017	☐ Sydney 1993–94	$13.00	S129
			☐ Tampa/St. Petersburg 1993–94	$13.00	S105
☐ London 1993	$13.00	S100			
☐ Los Angeles 1993–94	$13.00	S123	☐ Tokyo 1992–93	$13.00	S039
☐ Madrid/Costa del Sol 1993–94	$13.00	S124	☐ Toronto 1993–94	$13.00	S126
			☐ Vancouver/Victoria 1990–91	$ 8.00	S041
☐ Mexico City/Acapulco 1991–92	$ 9.00	S020	☐ Washington, D.C. 1993	$13.00	S102

Other Titles Available at Membership Prices

SPECIAL EDITIONS

	Retail Price	Code		Retail Price	Code
☐ Bed & Breakfast North America	$15.00	P002	☐ Where to Stay U.S.A.	$14.00	P015
☐ Caribbean Hideaways	$16.00	P005			
☐ Marilyn Wood's Wonderful Weekends (within a 250-mile radius of NYC)	$12.00	P017			

GAULT MILLAU'S "BEST OF" GUIDES
(The only guides that distinguish the truly superlative from the merely overrated)

	Retail Price	Code		Retail Price	Code
☐ Chicago	$16.00	G002	☐ New England	$16.00	G010
☐ Florida	$17.00	G003	☐ New Orleans	$17.00	G011
☐ France	$17.00	G004	☐ New York	$17.00	G012
☐ Germany	$18.00	G018	☐ Paris	$17.00	G013
☐ Hawaii	$17.00	G006	☐ San Francisco	$17.00	G014
☐ Hong Kong	$17.00	G007	☐ Thailand	$18.00	G019
☐ London	$17.00	G009	☐ Toronto	$17.00	G020
☐ Los Angeles	$17.00	G005	☐ Washington, D.C.	$17.00	G017

THE REAL GUIDES
(Opinionated, politically aware guides for youthful budget-minded travelers)

	Retail Price	Code		Retail Price	Code
☐ Able to Travel	$20.00	R112	☐ Kenya	$12.95	R015
☐ Amsterdam	$13.00	R100	☐ Mexico	$11.95	R016
☐ Barcelona	$13.00	R101	☐ Morocco	$14.00	R017
☐ Belgium/Holland/Luxembourg	$16.00	R031	☐ Nepal	$14.00	R018
			☐ New York	$13.00	R019
☐ Berlin	$11.95	R002	☐ Paris	$13.00	R020
☐ Brazil	$13.95	R003	☐ Peru	$12.95	R021
☐ California & the West Coast	$17.00	R121	☐ Poland	$13.95	R022
☐ Canada	$15.00	R103	☐ Portugal	$15.00	R023
☐ Czechoslovakia	$14.00	R005	☐ Prague	$15.00	R113
☐ Egypt	$19.00	R105	☐ San Francisco & the Bay Area	$11.95	R024
☐ Europe	$18.00	R122			
☐ Florida	$14.00	R006	☐ Scandinavia	$14.95	R025
☐ France	$18.00	R106	☐ Spain	$16.00	R026
☐ Germany	$18.00	R107	☐ Thailand	$17.00	R119
☐ Greece	$18.00	R108	☐ Tunisia	$17.00	R115
☐ Guatemala/Belize	$14.00	R010	☐ Turkey	$13.95	R027
☐ Hong Kong/Macau	$11.95	R011	☐ U.S.A.	$18.00	R117
☐ Hungary	$14.00	R118	☐ Venice	$11.95	R028
☐ Ireland	$17.00	R120	☐ Women Travel	$12.95	R029
☐ Italy	$13.95	R014	☐ Yugoslavia	$12.95	R030